Touchstones:
Classic Texts in the Humanities

Touchstones:
Classic Texts in the Humanities

Robert Platzner and Stephen Harris
California State University, Sacramento

Publisher	Ted Buchholz
Acquisitions Editor	Janet Wilhite
Developmental Editor	Kathryn Lang
Project Editor	Angela Williams
Manager of Production	Tad Gaither
Manager of Art and Design	Guy Jacobs
Text Design	Delgado Design, Inc.

Library of Congress Cataloging-in-Publication Data
Touchstones: classic texts in the humanities / [edited by] Robert Platzner and Stephen Harris.

p.   cm.
Includes bibliographical references.
ISBN 0-03-047504-X
1. Literature—Collections. I. Platzner, Robert Leonard.
II. Harris, Stephen L., 1937–
PN6014.T648   1990   90-39382
001.3—dc20   CIP

Cover: Honoré Daumier. *Two Collectors of Engravings.* Watercolor and ink. 18″ × 24″. Oskar Reinhart Collection "Am Römerholz," Winterthur, Switzerland.

Credits and acknowledgments appear on pages 563–564.

ISBN: 0-03-047504-X

Address for editorial correspondence: Holt, Rinehart and Winston, Inc., 301 Commerce Street, Suite 3700, Fort Worth, TX 76102

Address for orders: Holt, Rinehart and Winston, Inc., 6277 Sea Harbor Drive, Orlando, Florida 32887. 1-800-782-4479, or 1-800-433-0001 (in Florida)

PRINTED IN THE UNITED STATES OF AMERICA

1 2 3 4   069   9 8 7 6 5 4 3 2 1

Holt, Rinehart and Winston, Inc.
The Dryden Press
Saunders College Publishing

IN MEMORIUM
Glenn Edwin Harris and Joseph G. Platzner

Preface

Every anthology of readings in the Humanities represents, in microcosm, its editors' views of the current state of the literary and philosophical canon, and this volume is no exception. The ongoing debate over what students of Western civilization should read and know may never be resolved, but it has become increasingly clear that some redefinition of what is central and what is peripheral to the humanist enterprise must take place. This collection is our modest contribution to that process. We have attempted, with some deliberateness, to strike a balance between innovation and tradition, in a way that preserves the historical integrity of period concepts and styles.

Wherever possible, we have chosen texts that can be read whole, and where that was not possible, we have selected generous and representative portions of longer works in the hope that, when presented in the classroom, the original form and context of any abridgement would be restored by the instructor. Such compromises are inescapable in a volume of this size and scope. We can only hope that the virtue of compendiousness outweighs, for our readers, the vice of segmentation.

We think of this volume as serving two needs: that of a "companion" reader to existing art history or humanities survey texts, and that of an independent collection of readings in Western civilization from antiquity to the present. The chronological organization of material—complete with period subdivisions—is ideally suited to a survey course in literature. The introductory essays that preface each reading provide the beginning student with a clear and accessible view of the author, the work's major themes, and the historical context in which it should be placed. Where necessary, explanatory footnotes and interpolated narrative summaries are included as aids to comprehension.

Though formal acknowledgments are always inadequate, we thank our editor, Kathryn Lang, whose patience and belief in this project easily rivaled that of Job; Sandra Jackson, without whose nimble fingers our manuscripts might never have seen the light of day; and our colleagues at CSU Sacramento, particularly Mary Giles and Joseph Hoffman, whose encouragement and counsel made our task that much easier. We also wish to express our appreciation to the following reviewers for their generous advice and very helpful suggestions: Donald W. Andrews, Valencia Community College, Orlando, Florida; William C. Fleming, Syracuse University, New York, New York; Ellen Hofmann, Highline Community College, Seattle, Washington; Dolores LaGuardia, San Jose State/University of San Francisco, San Francisco, California; Nancy McCollum, Pikes' Peak Community College, Colorado Springs, Colorado; Sharon Rooks, Edison Community College, Ft. Myers, Florida; Katherine Wyly, Hillsboro Community College, Tampa, Florida; and Linda Zaerr, Boise State University, Boise, Idaho.

Robert Platzner and Stephen Harris
California State University

Sacramento, California
August, 1990

Table of Contents

Table of Contents

Touchstones:
Classic Texts in the Humanities

The Ancient Near East

The Epic of Gilgamesh

The so-called epic of Gilgamesh, unlike later Greek epic poetry, is really a loosely structured gathering of heroic narratives, some of which date from the early part of the second millennium (c. 2000–1600 B.C.). The central figure in nearly all of these stories is a quasi-legendary Sumerian king named Gilgamesh who ruled over the city–state of Uruk (in what is now southern Iraq) sometime during the 28th through the 26th centuries B.C. The rediscovery of these narratives more than a century ago has made it possible to discuss the emergence of the warrior–adventurer figure in ancient literature and in a much earlier context than that of the Hebrew Bible or of Greek mythology.

Two principal themes predominate in these stories: the enduring value of personal glory, and the need to resign oneself to the inevitability of death. These are not compatible views of the heroic endeavor, however, and as a consequence, *Gilgamesh* embodies two very different types of stories and worldviews rather than just one. Thus, the "heroic" Gilgamesh strives to impose his will on either Nature or the gods, and *that* Gilgamesh will not hesitate to overcome the Cedar Forest (and its supernatural guardian, Humbaba) or to insult the love goddess Ishtar to her face. The "tragic" Gilgamesh, in contrast, is himself overcome with grief at the death of his dearest friend and battle companion, Enkidu, and he attempts in vain to force or to persuade the gods to lift the curse of mortality. In neither case does the poet of Gilgamesh exhibit any illusions regarding the "afterlife," for unlike the Egyptians, the Sumerians do not appear to have developed any belief in the survival of the soul or of individual identity after death; it follows, then, that any fame that can be won through valor *must* be won in this world.

The Gilgamesh cycle also contains an account of a devastating worldwide flood, remarkably similar to the biblical flood story in circumstantial detail and in consequence. The character who recounts these events for Gilgamesh is known as Utanapishtim (often referred to as the "Sumerian Noah"); his narrative provides us with a vivid reminder of the often violent antagonism that exists between mankind and the gods in Sumerian myth.

TABLET I
■

GILGAMESH

Supreme over other kings, lordly in appearance,   *18*
he is the hero, born of Uruk, the goring wild bull.
He walks out in front, the leader,
and walks at the rear, trusted by his companions.
Mighty net, protector of his people,
raging flood-wave who destroys even walls of stone!
Offspring of Lugalbanda, Gilgamesh is strong to perfection,
son of the august cow, Rimat-Ninsun, . . . Gilgamesh is awesome to perfection.

3
■

It was he who opened the mountain passes,
who dug wells on the flank of the mountain.
It was he who crossed the ocean passes,
who dug wells on the flank of the mountain.
It was he who crossed the ocean, the vast seas, to the rising sun,
who explored the world regions, seeking life.
It was he who reached by his own sheer strength Utanapishtim, the Faraway,
who restored the sanctuaries (or: cities) that the Flood had destroyed!
. . . for teeming mankind.
Who can compare with him in kingliness?
Who can say like Gilgamesh: "I am King!"?
Whose name, from the day of his birth, was called "Gilgamesh"?
Two-thirds of him is god, one-third of him is human.   *46*
The Great Goddess [Aruru] designed (?) the model for his body,
she prepared his form . . .
. . . beautiful, handsomest of men,
. . . perfect . . .
. . .

He walks around in the enclosure of Uruk,
like a wild bull he makes himself mighty, head raised (over others).
There is no rival who can raise his weapon against him.
His fellows stand (at the alert), attentive to his (orders?),
and the men of Uruk become anxious in . . .
Gilgamesh does not leave a son to his father,
day and night he *arrogantly* (?) . . .

[The following lines are interpreted as rhetorical, perhaps spoken by the oppressed citizens
of Uruk.]

Is Gilgamesh the shepherd of Uruk-Haven,
is he the shepherd . . .
bold, eminent, knowing, and *wise?*
Gilgamesh does not leave a girl to *her mother* (?)![1]
The daughter of the warrior, the bride of the young man,   *63*
the gods kept hearing their complaints, so
the gods of the heavens implored the Lord of Uruk [Anu]:
   "You have indeed brought into being a mighty wild bull, head raised!
   There is no rival who can raise a weapon against him.
   His fellows stand (at the alert), attentive to his (orders ?),
   Gilgamesh does not leave a son to his father,
   day and night he arrogantly . . .
   Is he the shepherd of Uruk-Haven,
   is he their shepherd . . .

---

1. Or "to *her betrothed* (?)."

bold, eminent, knowing, and *wise?*
Gilgamesh does not leave a girl to *her mother* (?)!"

ENKIDU

The daughter of the warrior, the bride of the young man,
Anu listened to their complaints,
and (the gods) called out to Aruru:
  "It was you, Aruru, who created *mankind* (?),[2]
  now create a *zikru*[3] to it/him.
  Let him be equal to his (Gilgamesh's) stormy heart,
  let them be a match for each other so that Uruk may find peace!"
When Aruru heard this she created within herself the *zikru* of Anu.[3]   82
Aruru washed her hands, she pinched off some clay, and threw it into the
    wilderness.
In the wilderness (?) she created valiant Enkidu,
born of Silence, endowed with strength by Ninurta.
His whole body was shaggy with hair,
he had a full head of hair, like a woman,
his locks billowed in profusion like Ashnan.[4]
He knew neither people nor settled living,
but wore a garment like Sumukan.[5]
He ate grasses with the gazelles,
and jostled at the watering hole with the animals;
as with animals, his thirst was slaked with (mere) water.

THE TRAPPER AND THE HARLOT

A notorious trapper[6]   94
came face-to-face with him opposite the watering hole.
A first, a second, and a third day
he came face-to-face with him opposite the watering hole.
On seeing him the trapper's face went stark with fear,
and he (Enkidu?) and his animals drew back home (?).
He was rigid with fear; though stock-still
his heart pounded and his face drained of color.

---

2. Or "*Gilgamesh* (?)."
3. The Akkadian *zikru* normally means "what was ordered, commanded" or "reply, response"; neither sense really gives a clear meaning. Perhaps in these lines and VIII, 228, *zikru* may have another meaning. Whatever the sense, *zikru* is probably also a pun echoing Enkidu as the *kisru* "meteorite (?)" (of Anu) later in Tablet 1.
4. Ashnan, the goddess of grain, was portrayed with hair of billowing grain.
5. Sumukan was the god of wild animals. Enkidu was clothed in animal skins.
6. The word is commonly translated "hunter," but "trapper" seems more accurate here because the animals are captured in traps or pits, not killed by weapons. There is a play on words with the derogatory epithet *habilu* ("notorious, despicable") and a homonym which is a rare term for "trapper."

He was miserable to the core,
and his face looked like one who had made a long journey.
The trapper addressed his father saying:[7]   *104*
  "Father, a certain fellow has come from the mountains.
  He is mightiest in the land,
  his strength is as mighty as the meteorite (?) of Anu![8]
  He continually goes over the mountains,
  he continually jostles at the watering place with the animals,
  he continually plants his feet opposite the watering place.
  I was afraid, so I did not go up to him.
  He filled in the pits that I had dug,
  wrenched out my traps that I had spread,
  released from my grasp the wild animals.
  He does not let me make my rounds in the wilderness!"
The trapper's father spoke to him saying: *116*
  "My son, there lives in Uruk a certain Gilgamesh.
  There is no one stronger than he,
  he is as strong as the meteorite (?) of Anu.
  Go, set off to *Uruk,*
  tell Gilgamesh of this Man of Might.
  He will give you the harlot Shamhat, take *her with you.*
  The woman will overcome the fellow (?) as if she were strong.
  When the animals are drinking at the watering place
  have her take off her robe and expose her sex.
  When he sees her he will draw near to her,
  and his animals, who grew up in his wilderness, will be alien to him. . . ."

[The trapper informs Gilgamesh of Enkidu's existence. Gilgamesh gives him Shamhat the Harlot who, subsequently, seduces Enkidu and convinces him to return with her to Uruk and to challenge Gilgamesh.]

TABLET II
■

THE CONTEST

He (Enkidu) walked down the street of Uruk-Haven,   *87*
. . . mighty . . .

---

7. This is the first of many occurrences of the stock phrases introducing direct speech, translated variously by the formal "addressed . . . saying" or "spoke . . . saying." The phrase is used only in literature.

8. The Akkadian words *kisru sa Anu* are very difficult. Anu was the sky god, and the word *kisru* has a number of possible meanings in different contexts, including "lump of metal" and "a celestial phenomenon." Later in Tablet I, 227ff., the "*kisru* of Anu" is a heavy object that falls from the starry sky and remains intact on the ground, hence the tentative rendering "meteorite of Anu." Other proposals include "the vault of the heavens" and "concentration." See also the earlier note on *zikru.* The corresponding word in the original Old Babylonian version is damaged and is probably different, but there is no consensus on the restoration.

He blocked the way through Uruk the Sheepfold.
The land of Uruk stood around him,
the whole land assembled about him,
the populace was thronging around him,
the men were clustered about him,
and kissed his feet as if he were a little baby (?).
Suddenly a handsome young man . . .[1]   *95*
For Ishara the bed of night (?) /marriage (?) is ready,
for Gilgamesh as for a god a counterpart (?) is set up.
Enkidu blocked the entry to the marital chamber,
and would not allow Gilgamesh to be brought in.
They grappled with each other at the entry to the marital chamber,
in the street they attacked each other, the public square of the land.
The doorposts trembled and the wall shook,   *102*

[About 42 lines are missing from the Standard Version; lines 103–29 are taken from the Old Babylonian version.]

Gilgamesh bent his knees, with his other foot on the ground,
his anger abated and he turned his chest away.
After he turned his chest Enkidu said to Gilgamesh:
   "Your mother bore you ever unique (?),
   the Wild Cow of the Enclosure, Ninsun,
   your head is elevated over (other) men,
   Enlil has destined for you the kingship over the people. . . ."

[Gilgamesh and Enkidu become fast friends and undertake their first great adventure together: the conquest of the Cedar Forest and its guardian, Humbaba.]

A HERO'S CHALLENGE

[Enkidu is speaking.]

   "In order to protect the Cedar Forest   *200*
   Enlil assigned (Humbaba) as a terror to human beings—
   Humbaba's roar is a Flood, his mouth is Fire, and his breath is Death!

---

1. The Old Babylonian is fuller, but still full of obscurity.
In Uruk there were sacrifices continually,

   the men were making merry,
   a lusanu (musical instrument) was set up,
   for the man straightest (?) of feature,
   for Gilgamesh, as for a god,
   the mehru (antiphon?, counterpart?) was set up.
   For Ishara the bed was ready,
   Gilgamesh was to come together with the girls at night.

He can hear 100 leagues away any rustling (?) in his forest!
Who would go down into his forest?
Enlil assigned him as a terror to human beings,
and whoever goes down into his forest paralysis (?) will strike!"
Gilgamesh spoke to Enkidu saying:
"What you say . . ." *208*

[About 42 lines are missing here in the Standard Version; lines 228–49 are taken from the Old Babylonian.]

"Who, my Friend, can ascend to the heavens?[2]
(Only) the gods can dwell forever with Shamash.
As for human beings, their days are numbered,
and whatever they keep trying to achieve is but wind!
Now you are afraid of death—
what has become of your bold strength?
I will go in front of you,
and *your* mouth can call out: 'Go on closer, do not be afraid!'
Should I fall, I will have established my fame.
(They will say:) 'It was *Gilgamesh* who locked in battle with Humbaba the
    Terrible!"
You were born and raised in the wilderness,
a lion leaped up on you, so you have experienced it all![3]

[5 lines are fragmentary.]

I will undertake it and I will cut down the Cedar.
It is I who will establish my fame for eternity!
Come, my friend, I will go over to the forge
and have them cast the weapons in our presence!"
Holding each other by the hand they went over to the forge. *249*

[The Standard Version resumes at this point.]

The craftsmen sat and discussed with one another. *250*
    "We should fashion the axe . . .
    The hatchet should be one talent in weight . . .
    Their swords should be one talent . . .
    Their armor one talent, their armor . . ."
Gilgamesh said to the men of Uruk:
    "Listen to me, men . . .

---

2. Gilgamesh here recites proverbs on human mortality and expresses his desire to establish immortality through a great deed.
3. The sense of this line is unclear.

[5 lines are missing here.]

"You, men of Uruk, who know . . .   *262*
I want to make myself more mighty, and will go on a *distant* journey!
I will face fighting such as I have never known,
I will set out on a road I have never traveled!
Give me your blessings! . . .

[The elders of Uruk grudgingly consent to Gilgamesh's assault upon Humbaba. With the active assistance of Shamash, the Sumerian Sun god and Gilgamesh's patron, they are successful.]

TABLET V
■

THE CAPTURE OF HUMBABA

Gilgamesh spoke to Enkidu, saying: *86*
    "My Friend, Humbaba's face keeps changing![1]
    . . .
    . . ."
Enkidu spoke to Gilgamesh, saying:[2]
    "Why, my friend, are you whining so pitiably,
    hiding behind your whimpering?
    Now there, my friend, . . .
    in the coppersmith's channel, . . .
    again to blow (the bellows?) for an hour, the glowing (Metal)(?) . . . for an
        hour.
    To send the Flood, to crack the Whip.[3]
    Do not snatch your feet away, do not turn your back,
    . . . strike even harder!"   *98*

[20–25 lines are missing here.]

. . . may they be expelled.
. . . distant.
. . . head fell . . . and it/he confronted him . . .
The ground split open with the heels of their feet,
as they whirled around in circles Mt. Hermon and Lebanon split.
The white clouds darkened,

---

1. Or, is "strange, different."
2. Gilgamesh was apparently so frightened by how ferocious Humbaba's face had turned that he ran away and hid. Enkidu here tries to shore up Gilgamesh's courage in the face of Humbaba, reminding him how carefully the smiths had prepared their weapons (?) (end of Tablet III).
3. Names of mythical weapons, also mentioned in the Sumerian epic.

death rained down on them like fog.
Shamash raised up against Humbaba mighty tempests[4]—
Southwind, Northwind, Eastwind, Westwind, Whistling Wind,
Piercing Wind, Blizzard, Bad Wind, Wind of Simurru,
Demon Wind, Ice Wind, Storm, Sandstorm—
thirteen winds rose up against him and covered Humbaba's face.
He could not butt through the front, and could not scramble out the back,
so that Gilgamesh's weapons were in reach of Humbaba.
Humbaba begged for his life, saying to Gilgamesh: 134

> "You are young yet, Gilgamesh, your mother gave birth to you,
> and you are the offspring of *Rimat-Ninsun* (?) . . .
> (It was) at the word (=instigation) of Shamash, Lord of the Mountain,
> that you were roused (to this expedition).
> O scion of the heart of Uruk, King Gilgamesh!
> . . . Gilgamesh . . .
>
> . . .
>
> Gilgamesh, *let me go* (?),
> I will dwell with you *as your servant* (?).[5]
> As many trees as you command me *I will cut down for you*,
> I will guard for you myrtle wood . . .
> wood fine enough *for your palace!*"

----

4. A long Hittite fragment gives a very different version of the events preceding the sending of the winds.

> *He (Enkidu seized the axe in his hand . . .*
> *. . . but when Gilgamesh . . .*
> *then this one seized the axe . . . and felled the cedar.*
> *But when Humbaba heard the commotion he became enraged (saying:)*
> > *"Who has come and desecrated the trees,*
> > *my mountain . . . and has felled the Cedar?"*
> *Then from the sky the heavenly Shamash spoke to them (Gilgamesh and Enkidu):*
> > *"Go on in, fear not, as long as he (Humbaba) does not return. . . ."*
> *Hearing this Enkidu became angry,*
> *Enkidu and Gilgamesh entered (the forest),*
> *stirring up the anger of Humbaba in the middle of the mountain.*
> *He said to them:*
> > *"I shall carry you off and cast you down from the sky,*
> > *smash you on the* head *(?) and drive you down into the dark earth!"*
> *He carried them off but did not cast them down from the sky,*
> *on the* head *(?) he smashed them but did not drive them into the dark earth.*

[Several lines are fragmentary.]

> *He (Gilgamesh) entered the . . . of the heavenly Shamash,*
> *his tears flowing in streams, and said to heavenly Shamash:*
> > *". . . same day that in the city . . .*
> > *because he had settled again in the city . . .*
> > *So I set out for the heavenly Shamash,*
> > *have made the journey . . ."*

[The sending of the winds follows directly.]

5. The ends of the lines here are restored based on the Hittite, which reads "You will be my master, I will be your servant. I will fell for you the trees, . . . *I will build* houses *for you from it.*"

Enkidu addressed Gilgamesh, saying: *146*
    "My friend, do not listen to Humbaba,

[20 lines are missing. Apparently Humbaba sees that Gilgamesh is influenced by Enkidu, and tries to dissuade Enkidu.]

    "You understand the rules of my forest, the rules . . .   *168*
    further, you are aware of all the things 'So ordered (by Enlil)'."[6]
    I should have carried you up, and killed you at the very entrance to the
        branches of my forest.
    I should have fed your flesh to the screeching vulture.
    So now, Enkidu, clemency is up to you.
    Speak to Gilgamesh to spare (my) life!:
Enkidu addressed Gilgamesh, saying: *174*
    "My friend, Humbaba, Guardian of the Cedar Forest,
    grind up, kill, pulverize (?), and . . . him!
    Humbaba, Guardian of the Forest, grind up, kill, pulverize (?), and . . .
        him!
    Before the Preeminent God Enlil hears . . .
    and the . . . gods be filled with rage against us.
    Enlil is in Nippur, Shamash is in Sippar.
    Erect an eternal monument proclaiming . . .
    how Gilgamesh *killed* (?) Humbaba."

[Gilgamesh finally kills Humbaba, acting on Enkidu's advice. Before he dies, however, Humbaba utters a deadly curse that ultimately falls on Enkidu. They return to Uruk where Gilgamesh attracts the attention of the love goddess, Ishtar.]

TABLET VI
■

A WOMAN SCORNED

He washed out his matted hair and cleaned up his equipment (?),   *1*
shaking out his locks down over his back,
throwing off his dirty clothes and putting on clean ones.
He wrapped himself in regal garments and fastened the sash.
When Gilgamesh placed his crown on his head,
Princess Ishtar raised her eyes to the beauty of Gilgamesh.   *6*
    "Come along, Gilgamesh, be you my husband,

---

6. The sense is that Enkidu was always aware of the special protective status of Humbaba and the forest (Tablet III), and that he should bear in mind that there will surely be severe divine consequences.

to me grant your lusciousness.[1]
Be you my husband, and I will be your wife.
I will have harnessed for you a chariot of lapis lazuli and gold,
with wheels of gold and 'horns' of electrum (?).
It will be harnessed with great storming mountain mules!
Come into our house, with the fragrance of cedar.
And when you come into our house the doorpost (?) and throne dais (?)[2] will
    kiss your feet.
Bowed down beneath you will be kings, lords, and princes.
The Lullubu people[3] will bring you the produce of the mountains and
    countryside as tribute.
Your she-goats will bear triplets, your ewes twins,
your donkey under burden will overtake the mule,
your steed at the chariot will be bristling to gallop,
your ox at the yoke will have no match."
Gilgamesh addressed Princess Ishtar saying:
"What would I have to give you if I married you?
Do you need oil or garments for your body?
Do you lack anything for food or drink?
I would gladly feed you food fit for a god,
I would gladly give you wine fit for a king, . . .
may the street (?) be your home (?),
. . . may you be clothed in a garment,
and may any lusting man (?) marry!
You are an oven who . . . ice,
a half-door that keeps out neither breeze nor blast,
a palace that crushes down valiant warriors,
an elephant who devours its own covering,
pitch that blackens the hands of its bearer,
a waterskin that soaks its bearer through,
limestone that buckles out the stone wall,
a battering ram that attracts the enemy land,
a shoe that bites its owner's feet!
Where are your bridegrooms that you keep forever?   *40*
Where is your 'Little Shepherd' bird *that went up over you?*
See here now, I will recite the list of your lovers.
Of the shoulder (?) . . . his hand,
Tammuz, the lover of your earliest youth,
for him you have ordained lamentations year upon year!
You loved the colorful 'Little Shepherd' bird
and then hit him, breaking his wing, so

---

1. Literally "fruit."
2. Instead of "doorposts and throne dais" possibly "most excellent purification priests."
3. The Lullubu were a wild mountain people living in the area of modern-day western Iran. The meaning is that even the wildest, least controllable of peoples will recognize Gilgamesh's rule and bring tribute.

now he stands in the forest crying 'My Wing'!
You loved the supremely mighty lion,   49
yet you dug for him seven and again seven pits.
You loved the stallion, famed in battle,
yet you ordained for him the whip, the goad, and the lash,
ordained for him to gallop for seven and seven hours,
ordained for him drinking from muddied waters,[4]
you ordained for his mother Silili to wail continually.
You loved the Shepherd, the Master Herder,
who continually presented you with bread baked in embers,
and who daily slaughtered for you a kid.
Yet you struck him, and turned him into a wolf,
so his own shepherds now chase him
and his own dogs snap at his shins.
You loved Ishullanu, your father's date gardener,
who continually brought you baskets of dates,
and brightened your table daily.
You raised your eyes to him, and you went to him:
  'Oh my Ishullanu, let us taste of your strength,
  stretch out your hand to me, and touch our "vulva."[5]
Ishullanu said to you:
  'Me? What is it you want from me?
  Has my mother not baked, and have I not eaten
  that I should now eat food under contempt and curses
  and that alfalfa grass should be my only cover against the cold?'
As you listened to these his words
you struck him, turning him into a dwarf (?),[6]
and made him live in the middle of his (garden of) labors,
where the *mihhu* do not go up, nor the bucket of dates (?) down.
And now me! It is me you love, and you will ordain for me as for them!"

[Ishtar is furious at Gilgamesh's rejection of her advances. She obtains the Bull of Heaven from the Sky god Anu with which she hopes to destroy Gilgamesh, but with Enkidu's help, Gilgamesh manages to slay the beast.]

TABLET VII
■

A DREAM OF THE DEAD

Enkidu's innards were churning,   152
lying there so alone.

---

4. Horses put their front feet in the water when drinking, churning up mud.
5. This line probably contains a word play on *hurdatu* as "vulva" and "date palm," the latter being said (in another unrelated text) to be "like the vulva."
6. Or "frog"?

He spoke everything he felt, saying to his friend:
   "Listen, my friend, to the dream that I had last night.
   The heavens cried out and the earth replied,
   and I was standing between them.
   There appeared a man of dark visage—
   his face resembled the Anzu,[1]
   his hands were the paws of a lion,
   his nails the talons of an eagle!—
   he seized me by my hair and overpowered me.
   I struck him a blow, but he skipped about like a jump rope,
   and then he struck me and capsized me like a *raft*,
   and trampled on me like a wild bull.
   He encircled my whole body in a clamp.
     'Help me, my friend!' (I cried),   *167*
   but you did not rescue me, you were afraid and did not . . ."

[4 lines are missing here.]

   Then he . . . and turned me into a dove,
   so that my arms *were feathered* like a bird.
   Seizing me, he led me down to the House of Darkness, the dwelling of
      Irkalla,
   to the House where those who enter do not come out,
   along the road of no return,
   to the House where those who dwell do without light,
   where dirt is their drink, their food is of clay,
   where, like a bird, they wear garment of feathers,
   and light cannot be seen, they dwell in the dark,
   and upon the door and bolt lies dust.
   On entering the House of Dust,
   everywhere I looked there were royal crowns gathered in heaps,
   everywhere I listened, it was the bearers of crowns who in the past had ruled
      the land,
   but who now served Anu and Enlil cooked meats,
   served confections, and poured cool water from waterskins.
   In the House of Dust that I entered   *188*
   there sat the high priest and acolyte,
   there sat the purification priest and ecstatic,
   there sat the anointed priests of the Great Gods.
   There sat Etana, there sat Sumukan,
   there sat Ereshkigal, the Queen of the Netherworld.
   Beletseri, the Scribe of the Netherworld, knelt before her,

---

1. The lion-headed eagle of mythology.

she was holding the tablet[2] and was reading it out to her (Ereshkigal).
She raised her head and when she saw me—
    '*Who* has taken this *man?*' "   *197*

[Only the last word of a few of the next 50 lines remains; grave, Ereshkigal, ecstatic priest, flood, Egalmah. The text resumes apparently with Enkidu speaking to Gilgamesh:]

". . . *I* (?) who went through every difficulty,   *248*
remember *me and forget* (?) *not* all that I went through (with you)."

[Gilgamesh speaks:]

"My friend has had a dream that *bodes ill* (?)."
The day he had the dream . . . came to an end.

THE DEATH OF ENKIDU

Enkidu lies down a first day, a second day,   *252*
that Enkidu . . . in his bed;
a third day and fourth day, that *Enkidu . . . in his bed;*
a fifth, a sixth, and seventh, *that Enkidu . . . in his bed;*
an eighth, a ninth, a tenth, *that Enkidu . . . in his bed.*
Enkidu's illness *grew ever worse.*
The eleventh and twelfth day *his illness grew ever worse.*
Enkidu *drew up* from his bed,
and called out to Gilgamesh . . .:[3]
    "My friend hates me . . .   *261*
    (Once), while he *talked with me in Uruk*
    as I was afraid of the battle (with Humbaba), he encouraged me.
    My friend who *saved* me in battle *has now abandoned me!*
    I and *you . . .*"

[About 20 lines are missing here to the end of the tablet, telling of Enkidu's death. A passage from the Megiddo tablet may belong here.]

---

2. "The tablet" refers to the "Tablet of Destinies," inscribed with the fates of the dead.
3. Only the first half of the following lines are preserved, for which a totally different restoration and interpretation are found in A. Schott and Wolfram von Soden, *Das Gilgamesch-Epos* (Stuttgart: Philipp Reclam, 1958, rev. ed. 1982), p. 70:

        "I have been cursed, my friend, with a great curse,
        I do not die like *one who* falls in fighting,
        I was afraid of battle, so I die without peace.
        My friend, he who dies in battle is fortunate.
        But I suffer disgrace in death *(?)*."

At his noises (death rattle) *Gilgamesh* was roused . . .
Like a dove he moaned . . .
   "May he not be held, in death . . .
   O preeminent among *men* . . ."
To his friend . . .
   I will mourn him (?) . . .
   I at *his side* . . ."

[Enkidu's death—seen as divine punishment for the killing of Humbaba and the Bull of Heaven—inspires Gilgamesh to journey beyond the limits of this world and to demand immortality from the gods. He is unsuccessful in this quest, but he does meet Utanapishtim, the sole survivor (along with his family) of the Great Flood, who relates how that event took place.]

TABLET XI
■

THE STORY OF THE FLOOD[1]

Gilgamesh spoke to Utanapishtim, the Faraway: *1*
   "I have been looking at you,
   but your appearance is not strange—you are like me!
   You yourself are not different—you are like me!
   My mind was resolved to fight with you,
   (*but instead?*) my arm lies useless over you.
   Tell me, how is it that you stand in the Assembly of the Gods, and have
     found life?"
Utanapishtim spoke to Gilgamesh, saying:
   "I will reveal to you, Gilgamesh, a thing that is hidden,
   a secret of the gods I will tell you!
   Shuruppak, a city that you surely know,   *11*
   situated on the banks of the Euphrates,
   that city was very old, and there were gods inside it.
   The hearts of the Great Gods moved them to inflict the Flood.
   Their Father Anu uttered the oath (of secrecy),
   Valiant Enlil was their Adviser,
   Ninurta was their Chamberlain,
   Ennugi was their Minister of Canals.

---

1. The Flood Story told here is an adaptation or excerpt from (a version of) the flood episode in the "Myth of Atrahasis." The retelling of the Flood Story is not essential to the advancement of the Gilgamesh narrative ("secret of the gods" was already explained in Tablet X), and had not been incorporated into the Old Babylonian version. A short Flood Story exists in the Sumerian language, but it is believed to have been derived from the Akkadian-language story, and does not, therefore, derive from a more ancient Sumerian tradition. For a discussion of the literary relationships of the Mesopotamian Flood stories, see Tigay, *Evolution*, pp. 214–40.

Ea, the Clever Prince (?),[2] was under oath with them
so he repeated their talk to the reed house:

    'Reed house, reed house! Wall, wall!   *21*

    Hear, O reed house! Understand, O wall!

    O man of Shuruppak, son of Ubartutu:

    Tear down the house and build a boat!

    Abandon wealth and seek living beings!

    Spurn possessions and keep alive living beings!

    Make all living beings go up into the boat.

    The boat which you are to build,

    its dimensions must measure equal to each other:

    its length must correspond to its width.

    Roof it over like the Apsu.'

I understood and spoke to my lord, Ea:

    'My lord, thus is the command which you have uttered

    I will heed and do it.

    But what shall I answer the city, the populace, and the Elders?"

Ea spoke, commanding me, his servant:

    'You, well then, this is what you must say to them:

        "It appears that Enlil is rejecting me

        so I cannot reside in your *city* (?),

        nor set foot on Enlil's earth.

        I will go down to the Apsu to live with my lord, Ea,

        and upon you he will rain down abundance,

        a profusion of fowl, myriad (?) fishes.

        He will bring to you a harvest of wealth,

        in the morning he will let loaves of bread shower down,

        and in the evening a rain of wheat!" '

Just as dawn began to glow

the land assembled *around me*—

the carpenter carried his hatchet,

the reed worker carried his (flattening) stone,

. . . the men . . .

   . . .

The child carried the pitch,

the weak brought whatever else was needed.

On the fifth day I laid out her exterior.

It was a field in area,[3]

---

2. The word *nissiku,* translated "Clever Prince," is a word applied only to the god Ea/Enki, and its meaning is not definitely known. It seems to have connotations of cleverness or craftiness, which are pertinent to Ea's behavior in the Flood Story.

3. The boat as described is clearly a cube, not at all like ordinary Mesopotamian boats, and is probably a theological allusion to the dimensions of a ziggurat, the Mesopotamian stepped temple tower. The ziggurat was a massive solid structure with a square base and four to seven levels, the maximum height being the same as the length and width; it served as a monumental platform for a temple that stood on top.

its walls were each 10 times 12 cubits in height,
the sides of its top were of equal length, 10 times 12 cubits each.
I laid out its (interior) structure and drew a picture of it (?).   58
I provided it with six decks,
thus dividing it into seven (levels).
The inside of it I divided into nine (compartments).
I drove plugs (to keep out) water in its middle part.
I saw to the punting poles and laid in what was necessary.
Three times 3,600 (units) of raw bitumen I poured into the bitumen kiln,
three times 3,600 (units) pitch . . . into it,
there were three times 3,600 porters of casks who carried (vegetable) oil,
apart from the 3,600 (units of) oil which they consumed (?)
and two times 3,600 (units of) oil which the boatman stored away.
I butchered oxen for *the meat* (?),   69
and day upon day I slaughtered sheep.
I gave the workmen (?) ale, beer, oil, and wine, as if it were river water,
so they could make a party like the New Year's Festival.
. . . and I set my hand to the oiling (?).
The boat was finished by sunset.
The launching was very difficult.
They had to keep carrying a runway of poles front to back,
until two-thirds of it had gone into the water (?).
Whatever I had I loaded on it:
whatever silver I had I loaded on it,
whatever gold I had I loaded on it.
All the living beings that I had I loaded on it,
I had all my kith and kin go up into the boat,
all the beasts and animals of the field and the craftsmen I had go up.
Shamash had set a stated time:[4]   84
    'In the morning I will let loaves of bread shower down,
      and in the evening a rain of wheat!
      Go inside the boat, seal the entry!'
That stated time had arrived.
In the morning he let loaves of bread shower down,
and in the evening a rain of wheat.
I watched the appearance of the weather—
the weather was frightful to behold!
I went into the boat and sealed the entry.
For the caulking of the boat, to Puzuramurri, the boatman,
I gave the palace together with its contents.
Just as dawn began to glow   96
there arose from the horizon a black cloud.

---

4. Earlier, in lines 36–47, Ea, not Shamash, had given the stated time.

Adad rumbled inside of it,
before him went Shullat and Hanish,
heralds going over mountain and land.
Erragal pulled out the mooring poles,
forth went Ninurta and made the dikes overflow.
The Anunnaki lifted up the torches,
setting the land ablaze with their flare.
Stunned shock over Adad's deeds overtook the heavens,
and turned to blackness all that had been light.
The . . . land shattered like a . . . pot.
All day long the South Wind blew . . .   *108*
blowing fast, *submerging the* mountain *in water*,
overwhelming *the people* like an attack.
No one could see his fellow,
they could not recognize each other in the torrent.
The gods were frightened by the Flood,
and retreated, ascending to the heaven of Anu.
The gods were cowering like dogs, crouching by the outer wall.
Ishtar shrieked like a woman in childbirth,
the sweet-voiced Mistress of the Gods wailed:
    'The olden days have alas turned to clay,
      because I said evil things in the Assembly of the Gods!
      How could I say evil things in the Assembly of the Gods,
      ordering a catastrophe to destroy my people?!
      No sooner have I given birth to my dear people
      than they fill the sea like so many fish!"
The gods—those of the Anunnaki—were weeping with her,   *124*
the gods humbly sat weeping, sobbing with grief (?),
their lips burning, parched with thirst.
Six days and seven nights
came the wind and flood, the storm flattening the land.
When the seventh day arrived, the storm was pounding,
the flood was a war—struggling with itself like a woman writhing (in labor).
The sea calmed, fell still, the whirlwind (and) flood stopped up.
I looked around all day long—quiet had set in   *132*
and all the human beings had turned to clay!
The terrain was as flat as a roof.
I opened a vent and fresh air (daylight?) fell upon the side of my nose.
I fell to my knees and sat weeping,
tears streaming down the side of my nose.
I looked around for coastlines in the expanse of the sea,
and at twelve leagues there emerged a region (of land).
On Mt. Nimush the boat, allowing no sway.
One day and a second Mt. Nimush held the boat, allowing no sway.
A third, a fourth, Mt. Nimush held the boat, allowing no sway.
A fifth, a sixth, Mt. Nimush held the boat, allowing no sway.

When a seventh day arrived
I sent forth a dove and released it.
The dove went off, but came back to me;
no perch was visible so it circled back to me.
I sent forth a swallow and released it.
The swallow went off, but came back to me;
no perch was visible so it circled back to me.
I sent forth a raven and released it.
The raven went off, and saw the waters slither back.
It eats, it scratches, it bobs, but does not circle back to me.
Then I sent out everything in all directions and sacrificed (a sheep).   155
I offered incense in front of the mountain-ziggurat.
Seven and seven cult vessels I put in place,
and (into the fire) underneath (or: into their bowls) I poured reeds, cedar,
    and myrtle.
The gods smelled the savor,
the gods smelled the sweet savor,
and collected like flies over a (sheep) sacrifice.
Just then Beletili arrived.
She lifted up the large flies (beads)[5] which Anu had made for his enjoyment (?):
    'You gods, as surely as I shall not forget this lapis lazuli around my neck,
    may I be mindful of these days, and never forget them!
    The gods may come to the incense offering,
    but Enlil may not come to the incense offering,
    because without considering he brought about the Flood
    and consigned my people to annihilation.'
Just then Enlil arrived.   170
He saw the boat and became furious,
he was filled with rage at the Igigi gods:
    'Where did a living being escape?
    No man was to survive the annihilation!'
Ninurta spoke to Valiant Enlil, saying:
    'Who else but Ea could devise such a thing?
    It is Ea who knows every machination!'
Ea spoke to Valiant Enlil, saying: 178
    'It is *you*, O Valiant One, who is the Sage of the Gods.
    How, how could *you* bring about a Flood without consideration?
    Charge the violation to the violator,
    charge the offense to the offender,
    but be compassionate lest (mankind) be cut off,
    be patient lest *they be killed*.
    Instead of your bringing on the Flood,

---

5. A necklace with carved lapis lazuli fly beads, representing the dead offspring of the mother goddess Beletili/
Aruru.

would that a lion had appeared to diminish the people!
Instead of your bringing on the Flood,
would that famine had occurred to slay the land!
Instead of your bringing on the Flood,
would that (Pestilent) Erra had appeared to ravage the land!
It was not I who revealed the secret of the Great Gods,
I (only) made a dream appear to Atrahasis, and (thus) he heard the secret
    of the gods.
Now then! The deliberation should be about him!'
Enlil went up inside the boat   *196*
and, grasping my hand, made me go up.
He had my wife go up and kneel by my side.
He touched our forehead and, standing between us, he blessed us:
   'Previously Utanapishtim was a human being.
   But now let Utanapishtim and his wife become like us, the gods!
   Let Utanapishtim reside far away, at the Mouth of the Rivers.'
They took us far away and settled us at the Mouth of the Rivers."

The Pyramid Texts
Utterance 217

The so-called Pyramid Texts (c. 2300 B.C.) are, in fact, tomb inscriptions whose purpose was to ensure the speedy and successful resurrection of the dead Pharaoh and his acceptance into the company of the gods. These "utterances" may have served as funeral incantations, recited by priests during the Pharaoh's entombment. Along with other tomb inscriptions, the Pyramid Texts were part of an elaborate rite of passage each Pharaoh was believed to undertake on his way from this world to the next, where he would assume the identity of the resurrected Osiris, son of Re-Atum (later referred to as Re-Aton, a combined earth and sun god, and Father of the gods).

In this utterance, or funerary poem, Unas—a Pharaoh of the Fifth Dynasty—is introduced to Re-Atum as his "son," and, in turn, is brought before each of the principal deities of the Egyptian pantheon: Seth, a warrior god and brother of Osiris; Nephthys, his wife and sister; Anubis, son of Nephthys and Osiris, and chief judge of the underworld; Thoth, god of wisdom who serves Re-Atum as scribe and who serves mankind as the principal upholder of justice in the upper world; and Horus, who, as the son of Isis and Osiris, is the link between heaven and the underworld.

As the deceased Pharaoh rises from the dead to become Osiris, his successor on Earth becomes the younger Horus, thus completing the cycle of mortality and immortality that lies at the heart of the Pharaonic cult in ancient Egypt. Belief in the Pharaoh's divine nature preserved both a sense of continuity with the past and an uninterrupted communion with the gods, whose representative—in the personality of the reigning Pharaoh—would always be present among his people.

UNAS PYRAMID TEXTS
∎

UTTERANCE 217

Sarcophagus Chamber, South Wall
The king joins the sun-god[1]

Re-Atum, this Unas comes to you,
A spirit[2] indestructible
Who lays claim to the place of the four pillars!

---

1. The utterance consists of four parts in each of which the king announces his arrival in the sky to the sun-god and commands certain gods, associated with the four cardinal points, to broadcast his coming to the four sides of the universe. The symmetry of the composition is heightened by repetitions and relieved by variations.
2. The word rendered "spirit" and "spirits" is *akh* in the singular and plural forms.

Your son comes to you, this Unas comes to you,
May you cross the sky united in the dark,
May you rise in lightland, the place in which you shine!
Seth, Nephthys, go proclaim to Upper Egypt's gods
And their spirits:
"This Unas comes, a spirit indestructible,
If he wishes you to die, you will die,
If he wishes you to live, you will live!"
Re-Atum, this Unas comes to you,
A spirit indestructible
Who lays claim to the place of the four pillars!
Your son comes to you, this Unas comes to you,
May you cross the sky united in the dark,
May you rise in lightland, the place in which you shine!
Osiris, Isis, go proclaim to Lower Egypt's gods
And their spirits:
"This Unas comes, a spirit indestructible,
Like the morning star above Hapy,
Whom the water-spirits worship;
Whom he wishes to live will live,
Whom he wishes to die will die!"

Re-Atum, this Unas comes to you,
A spirit indestructible
Who lays claim to the place of the four pillars!
Your son comes to you, this Unas comes to you,
May you cross the sky united in the dark,
May you rise in lightland, the place in which you shine!
Thoth, go proclaim to the gods of the west
And their spirits:
"This Unas comes, a spirit indestructible,
Decked above the neck as Anubis,
Lord of the western height,
He will count hearts, he will claim hearts,
Whom he wishes to live will live,
Whom he wishes to die will die!"

Re-Atum, this Unas comes to you,
A spirit indestructible
Who lays claim to the place of the four pillars!
Your son comes to you, this Unas comes to you,
May you cross the sky united in the dark,
May you rise in lightland, the place in which you shine!
Horus, go proclaim to the powers of the east
And their spirits:
"This Unas comes, a spirit indestructible,

Whom he wishes to live will live,
Whom he wishes to die will die!"

Re-Atum, your son comes to you,
Unas comes to you,
Raise him to you, hold him in your arms,
He is your son, of your body, forever!

The Bible

Although a product of ancient Near Eastern culture, the Bible (c. 1000 B.C. to A.D. 140) exerts an enormous influence on contemporary Western civilization. Three world religions, Jewish, Christian, and Islamic, claim its authority for their beliefs. The Bible's strict code of ethics and concept of an Almighty Creator who demands exclusive devotion permeates almost every phase of Western life.

A collection of relatively short documents written over a period of more than a thousand years, the Bible contains two main sections. The first part is the Jewish Bible, composed largely in Hebrew and commonly known as the Old Testament. The briefer second part, the New Testament, was written in Greek by Jewish Christians between about A.D. 50 and 140.

The heart of the Jewish Bible is the covenant, a solemn agreement that Yahweh, the God of Israel, makes with his chosen people in the Sinai wilderness. Mediated through the prophet and lawgiver Moses, the Mosaic Covenant binds Israel to worship Yahweh alone and to obey all his commands (see Exodus 20). After Israel becomes a nation, Bible writers largely interpret Israel's history in terms of the covenant vow: Obedience brings prosperity and military success, whereas disobedience brings suffering and national defeat. The book of Exodus begins Israel's story with an escape from slavery in Egypt and the revelation of Yahweh's demands, the Torah, at Mount Sinai. The books of Joshua through Kings trace Israel's turbulent history from the conquest of Palestine about 1200 B.C. to the nation's destruction by Babylon six centuries later, consistently viewing historical disasters as the direct result of covenant breaking.

A general introduction to Israel's national experience, Genesis begins with the world's creation from a dark watery chaos, an echo of ancient Mesopotamian creation myths such as the Babylonian *Enuma Elish*. The anonymous writer who composed Genesis 1, however, deletes ancient mythic references to battles among many gods and emphasizes the absolute power of a single deity, Elohim [God], who creates by his word alone. In Genesis 6 through 8, Yahweh returns the world to primordial chaos, drowning all but Noah and his family. The Genesis writers draw heavily on ancient Mesopotamian traditions, paralleling many incidents from the flood story in *Gilgamesh*. The biblical theme of mercy and rebirth appears in the story of Noah's three sons and daughters-in-law who repopulate the Earth.

Not all biblical writers accepted the thesis that human suffering is the result of disobedience. The book of Job, cast in the form of a long cycle of debates between the central character and three friends who accuse him of concealed wrongdoing, explores the question of God's responsibility for evil. The prose narratives framing the poetic dialogues present a simple moral fable in which the righteous and patient Job, despite severe testing, remains loyal to Yahweh, who then rewards him materially. By contrast, the central drama shows a Job raging against Yahweh's injustice and demanding to know why an all-powerful God allows the innocent to suffer. When Yahweh at last appears to Job from a whirlwind, he does not explain his motives. Rejecting human notions of right and wrong, Yahweh points to a universe in which light and dark, good and evil, order and violence are mysteriously combined. Unlike the God of the Mosaic Covenant, the voice Job hears demands human loyalty without guaranteeing rewards for obedience.

Israel enjoyed only a brief moment of national independence and prosperity under Kings David and Solomon, followed by centuries of foreign oppression. Rome subjugated the Jewish state in 63 B.C., later ruling through an appointed local king, Herod the Great. According to 2 Samuel 7 and the prophet Isaiah, Yahweh had made an unbreakable covenant with King David that his descendants would rule Israel forever. During the Roman occupation, many Jews believed that an heir of David, a messiah, would appear and restore Israel to its former glory. The followers of Jesus of Nazareth, born near the end of Herod's reign, believed that he was that promised messiah. ("Christ" is the Greek translation of "messiah," or "anointed one.") About 50 years after the Romans executed Jesus as a political threat, later disciples wrote narratives about his life and teachings. Although many other narratives were composed, only four Gospels were viewed as authoritative by the early Christian community. The Gospel attributed to Matthew highlights the ethical teaching of Jesus, especially his reinterpretation of the Mosaic Law and his emphasis on nonviolence and forgiveness.

Although Matthew's Gospel depicts Jesus' role as Jewish messiah and reformer of the Mosaic tradition, that ascribed to John presents Jesus as a cosmic Christ. John's prologue identifies Jesus with the Word, the divine Logos or creative wisdom by which God formed the world. In John's view, the heavenly Word becomes flesh as Jesus of Nazareth, an incarnation of God's own nature. In contrast to Matthew's portrait, John's Jesus experiences no human frailties, no temptation, and no fear of death. His earthly career is a brief interval between his descent and reascension to heavenly glory. Matthew's Jesus advocates many ethical rules, whereas John's preaches only one commandment: to love.

GENESIS
■

I. THE ORIGIN OF THE WORLD AND OF MANKIND

1. The Creation and the Fall

The first account of the creation[1]

1

1/2   In the beginning God created the heavens and the earth. Now the earth was a formless void, there was darkness over the deep, and God's spirit hovered over the water.

3/4   God said, "Let there be light," and there was light. God saw that light

5   was good, and God divided light from darkness. God called light "day," and darkness he called "night." Evening came and morning came: the first day.

6   God said, "Let there be a vault[2] in the waters to divide the waters in

7   two." And so it was. God made the vault, and it divided the waters above

8   the vault from the waters under the vault. God called the vault "heaven." Evening came and morning came: the second day.

---

1. Ascribed to the "priestly" source (one of Genesis' three main authors).
2. For the ancient Semites, the "arch," or "vault" of the sky was a solid dome holding the upper waters in check.

9   God said, "Let the waters under heaven come together into a single mass,
10 and let dry land appear." And so it was. God called the dry land "earth"
and the mass of waters "seas," and God saw that it was good.

11   God said, "Let the earth produce vegetation: seed-bearing plants, and
12 fruit trees bearing fruit with their seed inside, on the earth." And so it was. The
earth produced vegetation: plants bearing seed in their several kinds, and
trees bearing fruit with their seed inside in their several kinds. God saw that
13 it was good. Evening came and morning came: the third day.

14   God said, "Let there be lights in the vault of heaven to divide day from
15 night, and let them indicate festivals, days and years. Let them be lights in
16 the vault of heaven to shine on the earth." And so it was. God made the two
great lights:[3] the greater light to govern the day, the smaller light to govern
17 the night, and the stars. God set them in the vault of heaven to shine on the
18 earth, to govern the day and the night and to divide light from darkness. God
19 saw that it was good. Evening came and morning came: the fourth day.

20   God said, "Let the waters teem with living creatures, and let birds fly above
21 the earth within the vault of heaven." And so it was. God created great sea-
serpents and every kind of living creature with which the waters teem, and
22 every kind of winged creature. God saw that it was good. God blessed them,
saying, "Be fruitful, multiply, and fill the waters of the seas; and let the birds
23 multiply upon the earth." Evening and morning came: the fifth day.

24   God said, "Let the earth produce every kind of living creature: cattle,
25 reptiles,[4] and every kind of wild beast." And so it was. God made every
kind of wild beast, every kind of cattle, and every kind of land reptile. God
saw that it was good.

26   God said, "Let us[5] make man[6] in our own image, in the likeness of
ourselves, and let them be masters of the fish of the sea, the birds of
heaven, the cattle, all the wild beasts and all the reptiles that crawl upon the
earth."

27 God created man in the image of himself,
in the image of God he created him,
male and female he created them.

28   God blessed them, saying to them, "Be fruitful, multiply, fill the earth
and conquer it. Be masters of the fish of the sea, the birds of heaven and all
29 living animals on the earth." God said, "See, I give you all the seed-bearing
plants that are upon the whole earth, and all the trees with seed-bearing
30 fruit; this shall be your food. To all wild beasts, all birds of heaven and all
living reptiles on the earth I give all the foliage of plants for food." And so it

---

3. Their names are omitted deliberately: The sun and the moon were worshiped by neighboring peoples, and here they are treated as no more than lamps to light the earth and regulate the calendar.

4. "Things which crawl," a general term for small mammals, reptiles, amphibians, and insects.

5. Perhaps the plural of majesty: the common name for God was *Elohim*, a plural form. But possibly the plural form implies a discussion between God and his heavenly court.

6. Man, *adam*, is a collective noun ("mankind"); hence the plural in "Let them be masters of. . . ."

31   was. God saw all he had made, and indeed it was very good. Evening came and morning came: the sixth day.

2

1/2   Thus heaven and earth were completed with all their array. On the seventh day God completed the work he had been doing. He rested on the

3   seventh day after all the work he had been doing. God blessed the seventh day and made it holy, because on that day he had rested after all his work of creating.

4   Such were the origins of heavens and earth when they were created.

The second account of the creation.[7] Paradise

5   At the time when Yahweh God made earth and heaven there was as yet no wild bush on the earth nor had any wild plant yet sprung up, for Yahweh God had not sent rain on the earth, nor was there any man to till

6   the soil. However, a flood was rising from the earth and watering all the

7   surface of the soil. Yahweh God fashioned man of dust from the soil. Then he breathed into his nostrils a breath of life, and thus man became a living being.

8   Yahweh God planted a garden in Eden which is in the east, and there he

9   put the man he had fashioned. Yahweh God caused to spring up from the soil every kind of tree, enticing to look at and good to eat, with the tree of life and the tree of the knowledge of good and evil in the middle of the

10   garden. A river flowed from Eden to water the garden, and from there it

11   divided to make four streams.[8] The first is named the Pishon, and this

12   encircles the whole land of Havilah where there is gold. The gold of this

13   land is pure; bdellium[9] and onyx stone are found there. The second river is

14   named the Gihon, and this encircles the whole land of Cush. The third river is named the Tigris, and this flows to the east of Ashur. The fourth river is

15   the Euphrates. Yahweh God took the man and settled him in the garden of

16   Eden to cultivate and take care of it. Then Yahweh God gave the man this

17   admonition, "You may eat indeed of all the trees in the garden. Nevertheless of the tree of the knowledge of good and evil you are not to eat, for on the day you eat of it you shall most surely die."

18   Yahweh God said, "It is not good that the man should be alone. I will

19   make him a helpmate." So from the soil Yahweh God fashioned all the wild beasts and all the birds of heaven. These he brought to the man to see what he would call them; each one was to bear the name the man would give it.

20   The man gave names to all the cattle, all the birds of heaven and all the

21   wild beasts. But no helpmate suitable for man was found for him. So Yahweh God made the man fall into a deep sleep. And while he slept, he took one of

---

7. From the "Yahwistic" source (the primary author of Israel's early history, who uses the divine name Yahweh).
8. Verses 10 through 14 are intended to fix the locality of Eden. However, the rivers Pishon and Gihon are unknown, and the two "lands" named are probably not the regions designated elsewhere by the same names.
9. An aromatic resin.

22	his ribs and enclosed it in flesh. Yahweh God built the rib he had taken
23	from the man into a woman, and brought her to the man. The man exclaimed:

> "This at last is bone from my bones,
> and flesh from my flesh!
> This is to be called woman[10]
> for this was taken from man."

24	This is why a man leaves his father and mother and joins himself to his wife, and they become one body.
25	Now both of them were naked, the man and his wife, but they felt no shame in front of each other.

The Fall

3

1	The serpent was the most subtle of all the wild beasts that Yahweh God had made. It asked the woman, "Did God really say you were not to eat from
2	any of the trees in the garden?" The woman answered the serpent, "We may
3	eat the fruit of the trees in the garden. But of the fruit of the tree in the middle of the garden God said, 'You must not eat it, nor touch it, under
4	pain of death.' " Then the serpent said to the woman, "No, You will not die!
5	God knows in fact that on the day you eat it your eyes will be opened and
6	you will be like gods, knowing good and evil." The woman saw that the tree was good to eat and pleasing to the eye, and that it was desirable for the knowledge that it could give. So she took some of its fruit and ate it. She
7	gave some also to her husband who was with her, and he ate it. Then the eyes of both of them were opened and they realised that they were naked. So they sewed fig-leaves together to make themselves loin-cloths.
8	The man and his wife heard the sound of Yahweh God walking in the garden in the cool of the day, and they hid from Yahweh God among the
9	trees of the garden. But Yahweh God called to the man. "Where are you?" he
10	asked. "I heard the sound of you in the garden," he replied, "I was afraid
11	because I was naked, so I hid." "Who told you that you were naked?" he
12	asked. "Have you been eating of the tree I forbade you to eat?" The man replied, "It was the woman you put with me; she gave me the fruit, and I ate
13	it." Then Yahweh God asked the woman, "What is this you have done?" The woman replied, "The serpent tempted me and I ate."
14	Then Yahweh God said to the serpent, "Because you have done this,

> "Be accursed beyond all cattle,
> all wild beasts.
> You shall crawl on your belly and eat dust

---

10. In Hebrew, a play on the words *ishshah* ("woman") and *ish* ("man").

every day of your life.

15 I will make you enemies of each other:
you and the woman,
your offspring and her offspring.
It will crush your head
and you will strike its heel."

16   To the woman he said:

"I will multiply your pains in childbearing,
you shall give birth to your children in pain.
Your yearning shall be for your husband,
yet he will lord it over you."

17   To the man he said, "Because you listened to the voice of your wife and
ate from the tree of which I had forbidden you to eat,

"Accursed be the soil because of you.
With suffering shall you get your food from it
every day of your life.
18 It shall yield you brambles and thistles,
and you shall eat wild plants.
19 With sweat on your brow
shall you eat your bread,
until you return to the soil,
as you were taken from it.
For dust you are
and to dust you shall return."

20 The man named his wife "Eve"[11] because she was the mother of all those
21 who live. Yahweh God made clothes out of skins for the man and his wife,
22 and they put them on. Then Yahweh God said, "See, the man has become
like one of us, with his knowledge of good and evil. He must not be allowed
to stretch his hand out next and pick from the tree of life also, and eat some
23 and live for ever." So Yahweh God expelled him from the garden of Eden, to
24 till the soil from which he had been taken. He banished the man, and in
front of the garden of Eden he posted the cherubs[12], and the flame of a
flashing sword, to guard the way to the tree of life.

2. The Flood

6

The corruption of mankind

5   Yahweh saw that the wickedness of man was great on the earth, and that
6   the thoughts in his heart fashioned nothing but wickedness all day long. Yahweh

---

11. The name "Eve," *Hawwah* is here explained by the root *haya* "to live."
12. Cherubs are winged beings, half human and half lion, that guard sacred places (1 Kings 8:6–7).

7   regretted having made man on the earth, and his heart grieved. "I will rid the earth's face of man, my own creation," Yahweh said "and of animals also, reptiles too, and the birds of heaven; for I regret having made them."

8   But Noah had found favour with Yahweh.

9   This is the story of Noah:

Noah was a good man, a man of integrity among his contemporaries, and

10   he walked with God. Noah became the father of three sons, Shem, Ham and

11/12   Japheth. The earth grew corrupt in God's sight, and filled with violence. God contemplated the earth: it was corrupt, for corrupt were the ways of all flesh on the earth.

Preparation for the flood

13   God said to Noah, "The end has come for all things of flesh; I have decided this, because the earth is full of violence of man's making, and I

14   will efface them from the earth. Make yourself an ark out of resinous wood.

15   Make it with reeds and line it with pitch inside and out. This is how to make it: the length of the ark is to be three hundred cubits, its breadth fifty cubits,

16   and its height thirty cubits. Make a roof for the ark . . . put the door of the ark high up in the side, and make a first, second and third deck.

17   "For my part I mean to bring a flood, and send the waters over the earth, to destroy all flesh on it, every living creature under heaven; everything on

18   earth shall perish. But I will establish my Covenant with you, and you must go on board the ark, yourself, your sons, your wife, and your sons' wives

19   along with you. From all living creatures, from all flesh, you must take two of each kind aboard the ark, to save their lives with yours; they must be a

20   male and a female. Of every kind of bird, of every kind of animal and of every kind of reptile on the ground, two must go with you so that their lives

21   may be saved. For your part provide yourself with eatables of all kinds, and

22   lay in a store of them, to serve as food for yourself and them." Noah did this; he did all that God had ordered him.

7

1   Yahweh said to Noah, "Go aboard the ark, you and all your household, for

2   you alone among this generation do I see as a good man in my judgment. Of all the clean animals you must take seven of each kind, both male and female;

3   of the unclean animals you must take two, a male and its female (and of the birds of heaven also, seven of each kind, both male and female), to

4   propagate their kind over the whole earth. For in seven days' time I mean to make it rain on the earth for forty days and nights, and I will rid the earth

5   of every living thing that I made." Noah did all that Yahweh ordered.

6   Noah was six hundred years old when the flood of waters appeared on the earth.

7   Noah with his sons, his wife, and his sons' wives boarded the ark to

8   escape the waters of the flood. (Of the clean animals and the animals that

9   are not clean, of the birds and all that crawls on the ground, two of each kind boarded the ark with Noah, a male and a female, according to the order

10   God gave Noah.) Seven days later the waters of the flood appeared on the earth.

11   In the six hundredth year of Noah's life, in the second month, and on the seventeenth day of that month, that very day all the springs of the great deep

12   broke through, and the sluices of heaven opened. It rained on the earth for forty days and forty nights.

13   That very day Noah and his sons Shem, Ham and Japheth boarded the

14   ark, with Noah's wife and the three wives of his sons, and with them wild beasts of every kind, cattle of every kind, reptiles of every kind that crawls

15   on the earth, birds of every kind, all that flies, everything with wings. One pair of all that is flesh and has the breath of life boarded the ark with

16   Noah; and so there went in a male and a female of every creature that is flesh, just as God had ordered him.

And Yahweh closed the door behind Noah.

The flood

17   The flood lasted forty days on the earth. The waters swelled, lifting the

18   ark until it was raised above the earth. The waters rose and swelled greatly

19   on the earth, and the ark sailed on the waters. The waters rose more and more on the earth so that all the highest mountains under the whole of

20   heaven were submerged. The waters rose fifteen cubits higher, submerging

21   the mountains. And so all things of flesh perished that moved on the earth, birds, cattle, wild beasts, everything that swarms on the earth, and every

22   man. Everything with the breath of life in its nostrils died, everything on dry

23   land. Yahweh destroyed every living thing on the face of the earth, man and animals, reptiles, and the birds of heaven. He rid the earth of them, so that

24   only Noah was left, and those with him in the ark. The waters rose on the earth for a hundred and fifty days.

The flood subsides

8

1   But God had Noah in mind, and all the wild beasts and all the cattle that were with him in the ark. God sent a wind across the earth and the waters

2   subsided. The springs of the deep and the sluices of heaven were stopped.

3   Rain ceased to fall from heaven; the waters gradually ebbed from the earth.

4   After a hundred and fifty days the waters fell, and in the seventh month, on the seventeenth day of that month, the ark came to rest on the mountains of

5   Ararat. The waters gradually fell until the tenth month when, on the first day of the tenth month, the mountain peaks appeared.

6   At the end of forty days Noah opened the porthole he had made in the ark

7   and he sent out the raven. This went off, and flew back and forth until the

8   waters dried up from the earth. Then he sent out the dove, to see whether

9   the waters were receding from the surface of the earth. The dove, finding nowhere to perch, returned to him in the ark, for there was water over the whole surface of the earth; putting out his hand he took hold of it and

10   brought it back into the ark with him. After waiting seven more days, again

11 he sent out the dove from the ark. In the evening, the dove came back to him and there it was with a new olive branch in its beak. So Noah realized
12 that the waters were receding from the earth. After waiting seven more days he sent out the dove, and now it returned to him no more.

13 It was in the six hundred and first year of Noah's life, in the first month and on the first of the month, that the water dried up from the earth. Noah lifted back the hatch of the ark and looked out. The surface of the ground was dry!

14 In the second month and on the twenty-seventh day of the month the earth was dry.

They disembark

15/16 Then God said to Noah, "Come out of the ark, you yourself, your wife,
17 your sons, and your sons' wives with you. As for all the animals with you, all things of flesh, whether birds or animals or reptiles that crawl on the earth, bring them out with you. Let them swarm on the earth; let them be fruitful
18 and multiply on the earth." So Noah went out with his sons, his wife, and his
19 sons' wives. And all the wild beasts, all the cattle, all the birds and all the reptiles that crawl on the earth went out from the ark, one kind after another.

20 Noah built an altar for Yahweh, and choosing from all the clean animals
21 and all the clean birds he offered burnt offerings on the altar. Yahweh smelled the appeasing fragrance and said to himself, "Never again will I curse the earth because of man, because his heart contrives evil from his infancy. Never again will I strike down every living thing as I have done.

22 "As long as earth lasts,
sowing and reaping,
cold and heat,
summer and winter,
day and night
shall cease no more."

The new world order

9

1 God blessed Noah and his sons, saying to them, "Be fruitful, multiply
2 and fill the earth. Be the terror and the dread of all the wild beasts and all the birds of heaven, of everything that crawls on the ground and all the fish
3 of the sea; they are handed over to you. Every living and crawling thing shall provide food for you, no less than the foliage of plants. I give you
4 everything, with this exception: you must not eat flesh with life, that is to say
5 blood, in it. I will demand an account of your life-blood. I will demand an account from every beast and from man. I will demand an account of every man's life from his fellow men.

6 "He who sheds man's blood,
shall have his blood shed by man,

for in the image of God
man was made.

7   "As for you, be fruitful, multiply, teem over the earth and be lord of it."

8/9   God spoke to Noah and his sons, "See, I establish my Covenant with you,
and with your descendants after you; also with every living creature to be

10   found with you, birds, cattle and every wild beast with you: everything that

11   came out of the ark, everything that lives on the earth. I establish my
Covenant with you: no thing of flesh shall be swept away again by the waters
of the flood. There shall be no flood to destroy the earth again."

12   God said, "Here is the sign of the Covenant I make between myself and

13   you and every living creature with you for all generations: I set my bow in

14   the clouds and it shall be a sign of the Covenant between me and the earth. When

15   I gather the clouds over the earth and the bow appears in the clouds, I will
recall the Covenant between myself and you and every living creature of
every kind. And so the waters shall never again become a flood to destroy all

16   things of flesh. When the bow is in the clouds I shall see it and call to
mind the lasting Covenant between God and every living creature of every
kind that is found on the earth."

17   God said to Noah, "This is the sign of the Covenant I have established
between myself and every living thing that is found on the earth."

EXODUS
∎

[Appearing to Moses atop Mount Sinai, Yahweh concludes a covenant with the Israelites,
whom he has just rescued from slavery in Egypt.]

III. THE COVENANT AT SINAI

A. The Covenant and the Decalogue

The Decalogue[1]

20

1/2   Then God spoke all these words. He said, "I am Yahweh your God who
brought you out of the land of Egypt, out of the house of slavery.

3   "You shall have no gods except me.

4   "You shall not make yourself a carved image or any likeness of anything

5   in heaven or on earth beneath or in the waters under the earth; you shall not
bow down to them or serve them. For I, Yahweh your God, am a jealous
God and I punish the father's fault in the sons, the grandsons, and the

---

1. This is the "priestly" version of the Ten Commandments; another version, the "Deuteronomic," is found in Dt.
5; it is the latter that has been adopted by the Church.

6 great-grandsons of those who hate me; but I show kindness to thousands of those who love me and keep my commandments.

7 "You shall not utter the name of Yahweh your God to misuse it,[2] for Yahweh will not leave unpunished the man who utters his name to misuse it.

8/9 "Remember the sabbath day and keep it holy. For six days you shall
10 labor and do all your work, but the seventh day is a sabbath for Yahweh your God. You shall do no work that day, neither you nor your son nor your daughter nor your servants, men or women, nor your animals nor the
11 stranger who lives with you. For in six days Yahweh made the heavens and the earth and the sea and all that these hold, but on the seventh day he rested; that is why Yahweh has blessed the sabbath day and made it sacred.

12 "Honor your father and your mother so that you may have a long life in the land that Yahweh your God has given to you.

13 "You shall not kill.

14 "You shall not commit adultery.

15 "You shall not steal.

16 "You shall not bear false witness against your neighbour.

17 "You shall not covet your neighbour's house. You shall not covet your neighbour's wife, or his servant, man or woman, or his ox, or his donkey, or anything that is his."

18 [3]All the people shook with fear at the peals of thunder and the lightning flashes, the sound of the trumpet, and the smoking mountain; and they kept
19 their distance. "Speak to us yourself," they said to Moses, "and we will
20 listen; but do not let God speak to us, or we shall die." Moses answered the people, "Do not be afraid; God has come to test you, so that your fear of
21 him, being always in your mind, may keep you from sinning". So the people kept their distance while Moses approached the dark cloud where God was.

THE BOOK OF JOB
■

I. PROLOGUE

Satan tests Job

1

1 There was once a man in the land of Uz[1] called Job: a sound and honest
2 man who feared God and shunned evil. Seven sons and three daughters were
3 born to him. And he owned seven thousand sheep, three thousand camels, five hundred yoke of oxen and five hundred she-donkeys, and many servants besides. This man was indeed a man of mark among all the people of the

---

2. Either in a false oath or irreverently.
3. This section probably should be read after 19:19; the Decalogue, itself, is not linked to the narrative framework.
1. Probably in the south of Edom.

4	East.[2] It was the custom of his sons to hold banquets in each other's houses, one after the other, and to send and invite their three sisters to eat and
5	drink with them. Once each series of banquets was over, Job would send for them to come and be purified, and at dawn on the following day he would offer a holocaust[3] for each of them. "Perhaps," Job would say, "my sons have sinned and in their hearts affronted God." So that was what he used to do after each series.
6	One day the Sons of God[4] came to attend on Yahweh, and among them
7	was Satan. So Yahweh said to Satan, "Where have you been?" "Around the
8	earth," he answered, "roaming about." So Yahweh asked him, "Did you notice my servant Job? There is no one like him on the earth: a sound and honest
9	man who fears God and shuns evil." "Yes," Satan said, "but Job is not God-
10	fearing for nothing, is he? Have you not put a wall round him and his house and all his domain? You have blessed all he undertakes, and his flocks
11	throng the countryside. But stretch out your hand and lay a finger on his
12	possessions: I warrant you, he will curse you to your face." "Very well," Yahweh said to Satan, "all he has is in your power. But keep your hands off his person." So Satan left the presence of Yahweh.
13	On the day when Job's sons and daughters were at their meal and
14	drinking wine at their eldest brother's house, a messenger came to Job. "Your oxen," he said, "were at the plow, with the donkeys grazing at their
15	side, when the Sabaeans[5] swept down on them and carried them off. Your
16	servants they put to the sword: I alone escaped to tell you." He had not finished speaking when another messenger arrived. "The fire of God," he said, "has fallen from the heavens and burned up all your sheep, and your
17	shepherds too: I alone escaped to tell you." He had not finished speaking when another messenger arrived. "The Chaldaeans," he said, "three bands of them, have raided your camels and made off with them. Your servants they
18	put to the sword: I alone escaped to tell you." He had not finished speaking when another messenger arrived. "Your sons and daughters," he said, "were
19	at their meal and drinking wine at their eldest brother's house, when suddenly from the wilderness a gale sprang up, and it battered all four corners of the house which fell in on the young people. They are dead: I alone escaped to tell you."
20	Job rose and tore his gown and shaved his head.[6] Then falling to the
21	ground he worshipped and said:

"Naked I came from my mother's womb,
naked I shall return.

---

2. That is, of Edomite or Arab territory to the east of Palestine.
3. A sacrificial burnt offering.
4. The angels who make up his heavenly Council.
5. Predatory nomads. So are the Chaldaeans of v. 17.
6. Mourning ritual.

Yahweh gave, Yahweh has taken back.
Blessed be the name of Yahweh!"

22   In all this misfortune Job committed no sin nor offered any insult to God.

2

1   Once again the Sons of God came to attend on Yahweh, and among them
2   was Satan. So Yahweh said to Satan, "Where have you been?" "Around the
3   earth," he answered, "roaming about." So Yahweh asked him, "Did you notice
my servant Job? There is no one like him on the earth: a sound and honest
man who fears God and shuns evil. His life continues blameless as ever; in
4   vain you provoked me to ruin him." "Skin for skin!" Satan replied. "A man will
5   give away all he has to save his life. But stretch out your hand and lay a
6   finger on his bone and flesh; I warrant you, he will curse you to your face." "Very
7   well," Yahweh said to Satan, "he is in your power. But spare his life." So Satan
left the presence of Yahweh.
He struck Job down with malignant ulcers from the sole of his foot to the
8   top of his head. Job took a piece of pot to scrape himself, and went and sat
9   in the ashpit. Then his wife said to him, "Do you now still mean to persist in
10 your blamelessness? Curse God, and die." "That is how foolish women talk,"
Job replied. "If we take happiness from God's hand, must we not take
sorrow too?" And in all this misfortune Job uttered no sinful word.
11   The news of all the disasters that had fallen on Job came to the ears of
three of his friends. Each of them set out from home—Eliphaz of Teman,
Bildad of Shuah and Zophar of Naamath[7]—and by common consent they
12 decided to go and offer him sympathy and consolation. Looking at him from
a distance, they could not recognize him; they wept aloud and tore their
13 garments and threw dust over their heads. They sat there on the ground
beside him for seven days and seven nights. To Job they spoke never a
word, so sad a sight he made.

II. THE DIALOGUE

A. First Series of Speeches

Job curses the day of his birth

3

1   In the end it was Job who broke the silence and cursed the day of his
2   birth. This is what he said:

3   May the day perish when I was born,
      and the night that told of a boy conceived.

---

7. The three towns are in Idumaean and Arab territory. Edom and "the East" were proverbially the homeland of
the sages.

4   May that day be darkness,
          may God on high have no thought for it,
          may no light shine on it.

5   May murk and deep shadow claim it for their own,
          clouds hang over it,
          eclipse swoop down on it.

6   Yes, let the dark lay hold of it,
          to the days of the year let it not be joined,
          into the reckoning of months not find its way,

7   May that night be dismal,
          no shout of joy come near it.

8   Let them curse it who curse the day.
          who are prepared to rouse Leviathan.[8]

9   Dark be the stars of its morning,
          let it wait in vain for light
          and never see the opening eyes of dawn.

10   Since it would not shut the doors of the womb on me
          to hide sorrow from my eyes.

11   Why did I not die new-born,
          not perish as I left the womb?

12   Why were there two knees to receive me,
          two breasts for me to suck?

13   Had there not been, I should now be lying in peace,
          wrapped in a restful slumber,

14   with the kings and high viziers of earth
          who build themselves vast vaults,

15   or with princes who have gold and to spare
          and houses crammed with silver.

16   Or put away like a still-born child that never came to be,
          like unborn babes that never see the light.

17   Down there,[9] bad men bustle no more,
          there the weary rest.

18   Prisoners, all left in peace,
          hear no more the shouts of the jailer.

19   Down there, high and low are all one,
          and the slave is free of his master.

20   Why give light to a man of grief?
          Why give life to those bitter of heart,

21   who long for a death that never comes,
          and hunt for it more than for a buried treasure?

---

8. The dragon of primeval chaos; he might be roused by a curse against the present order.
9. In Sheol, the underworld.

22   They would be glad to see the grave-mound
         and shout with joy if they reached the tomb.

23   Why make this gift of light to a man who does not see his way,
         whom God balks on every side?

24   My only food is sighs,
         and my groans pour out like water.

25   Whatever I fear comes true,
         whatever I dread befalls me.

26   For me, there is no calm, no peace;
         my torments banish rest.

[Job acknowledges God's strength, but questions his justice.]

9

1   Job spoke next. He said:

2   Indeed, I know it is as you say:
         how can man be in the right against God?

3   If any were so rash as to challenge him for reasons,
         one in a thousand would be more than they could answer.

4   His heart is wise, and his strength is great:
         who then can successfully defy him?

5   He moves the mountains, though they do not know it;
         he throws them down when he is angry.

6   He shakes the earth, and moves it from its place,
         making all its pillars tremble.

7   The sun, at his command, forbears to rise,
         and on the stars he sets a seal.

8   He and no other stretched out the skies,
         and trampled the Sea's tall waves.

9   The Bear, Orion too, are of his making,
         the Pleiades and the Mansions of the South.

10   His works are great, beyond all reckoning,
         his marvels, past all counting.

11   Were he to pass me, I should not see him,
         nor detect his stealthy movement.

12   Were he to snatch a prize, who could prevent him,
         or dare to say, "What are you doing?"

13   God never goes back on his anger,
         Rahab's minions still lie at his feet.[10]

14   How dare I plead my cause, then,
         or choose arguments against him?

---

10. Rahab is another name for Chaos, the first enemy conquered by God.

15	Suppose I am in the right, what use is my defense?
	For he whom I must sue is judge as well.
16	If he deigned to answer my citation,
	could I be sure that he would listen to my voice?
17	He, who for one hair crushes me,
	who, for no reason, wounds and wounds again,
18	leaving me not a moment to draw breath,
	with so much bitterness he fills me.
19	Shall I try force? Look how strong he is!
	Or go to court? But who will summon him?
20	Though I think myself right, his mouth may condemn me;
	though I count myself innocent, it may declare me a hypocrite.
21	But am I innocent after all? Not even I know that,
	and, as for my life, I find it hateful.
22	It is all one, and this I dare to say:
	innocent and guilty, he destroys all alike.
23	When a sudden deadly scourge descends,
	he laughs at the plight of the innocent.
24	When a country falls into a tyrant's hand,
	it is he who blindfolds the judges.
	Or if not he, who else?
25	My days run hurrying by,
	seeing no happiness in their flight,
26	skimming along like a reed canoe,
	or the flight of an eagle after its prey.
27	If I resolve to stifle my moans,
	change countenance, and wear a smiling face,
28	fear comes over me, at the thought of all I suffer,
	for such, I know, is not your treatment of the innocent.
29	And if I am guilty,
	why should I put myself to useless trouble?
30	No use to wash myself with snow,
	or bleach my hands pure white;
31	for you will plunge me in dung
	until my very clothes recoil from me.
32	Yes, I am man, and he is not; and so no argument,
	no suit between the two of us is possible.
33	There is no arbiter between us,
	to lay his hand on both,
34	to stay his rod from me,
	or keep away his daunting terrors.
35	Nonetheless, I shall speak, not fearing him:
	I do not see myself like that at all.

10

1   Since I have lost all taste for life,
        I will give free rein to my complaints;
        I shall let my embittered soul speak out.

2   I shall say to God, 'Do not condemn me,
        but tell me the reason for your assault.

3   Is it right for you to injure me,
        cheapening the work of your own hands
        and abetting the schemes of the wicked?

4   Have you got human eyes,
        do you see as mankind sees?

5   Is your life mortal like man's,
        do your years pass as men's days pass?

6   You, who inquire into my faults
        and investigate my sins,

7   you know very well that I am innocent,
        and that no one can rescue me from your hand.

8   Your own hands shaped me, modeled me;
        and would you now have second thoughts, and destroy me?

9   You modeled me, remember, as clay is modeled,
        and would you reduce me now to dust?

10   Did you not pour me out like milk,
        and curdle me then like cheese;

11   clothe me with skin and flesh,
        and weave me of bone and sinew?

12   And then you endowed me with life,
        watched each breath of mine with tender care.

13   Yet, after all, you were dissembling;
        biding your time, I know,

14   to mark if I should sin
        and to let no fault of mine go uncensured.

15   Woe to me, if I am guilty;
        if I am innocent, I dare not lift my head,
        so wholly abject, so drunk with pain am I.

16   And if I make a stand, like a lion you hunt me down,
        adding to the tale of your triumphs.

17   You attack, and attack me again,
        with stroke on stroke of your fury,
        relentlessly your fresh troops assail me.

18   'Why did you bring me out of the womb?
        I should have perished then, unseen by any eye,

19   a being that had never been,
        to be carried from womb to grave.

20   The days of my life are few enough:
        turn your eyes away, leave me a little joy,
21   before I go to the place of no return,
        the land of murk and deep shadow,
22   where dimness and disorder hold sway,
        and light itself is like the dead of night.'

[Job briefly considers finding justice in a future life, then rejects the concept.]

14

1   Man, born of woman,
        has a short life yet has his fill of sorrow.
2   He blossoms, and he withers, like a flower;
        fleeting as a shadow, transient.
3   And is this what you deign to turn your gaze on,
        him that you would bring before you to be judged?
4   Who can bring the clean out of the unclean?
        No man alive!
5   Since man's days are measured out,
        since his tale of months depends on you,
        since you assign him bounds he cannot pass,
6   turn your eyes from him, leave him alone,
        like a hired drudge, to finish his day.
7   There is always hope for a tree:
        when felled, it can start its life again;
        its shoots continue to sprout.
8   Its roots may be decayed in the earth,
        its stump withering in the soil,
9   but let it scent the water, and it buds,
        and puts out branches like a plant new set.
10   But man? He dies, and lifeless he remains;
        man breathes his last, and then where is he?
11   The waters of the seas may disappear,
        all the rivers may run dry or drain away;
12   but man, once in his resting place, will never rise again.
        The heavens will wear away before he wakes,
        before he rises from his sleep.

13   If only you would hide me in Sheol,
        and shelter me there until your anger is past,
14   fixing a certain day for calling me to mind—
        for once a man is dead can he come back to life?—
        day after day of my service I would wait
        for my relief to come.
15   Then you would call, and I should answer,
        you would want to see the work of your hands once more.

16   Now you count every step I take,
            but then you would cease to spy on my sins;
17   you would seal up my crime in a bag,
            and whiten my fault over.

18   But no! Soon or late the mountain falls,
            the rock moves from its place,
19   water wears away the stones,
            the cloudburst erodes the soil;
            just so do you destroy man's hope.
20   You crush him once for all, and he is gone;
            you mar him, and then you bid him go.
21   Let his sons achieve honor, he does not know of it,
            humiliation, he gives it not a thought.
22   He feels no pain for anything but his own body,
            makes no lament, save for his own life.

IV. THE SPEECHES OF YAHWEH

First Speech

Job must bow to the creator's wisdom

38

1   Then from the heart of the tempest Yahweh gave Job his answer. He said:

2   Who is this obscuring my designs
            with his empty-headed words?
3   Brace yourself like a fighter;
            now it is my turn to ask questions and yours to inform me.
4   Where were you when I laid the earth's foundations?
            Tell me, since you are so well-informed!
5   Who decided the dimensions of it, do you know?
            Or who stretched the measuring line across it?
6   What supports its pillars at their bases?
            Who laid its cornerstone
7   when all the stars of the morning were singing with joy,
            and the Sons of God in chorus were chanting praise?
8   Who pent up the sea behind closed doors
            when it leaped tumultuous out of the womb,
9   when I wrapped it in a robe of mist
            and made black clouds its swaddling bands;
10   when I marked the bounds it was not to cross
            and made it fast with a bolted gate?
11   Come thus far, I said, and no farther:
            here your proud waves shall break.

12   Have you ever in your life given orders to the morning
            or sent the dawn to its post,

43

13   telling it to grasp the earth by its edges
         and shake the wicked out of it,
14   when it changes the earth[11] to sealing clay
         and dyes it as a man dyes clothes;
15   stealing the light from wicked men[12]
         and breaking the arm raised to strike?
16   Have you journeyed all the way to the sources of the sea,
         or walked where the Abyss is deepest?
17   Have you been shown the gates of Death
         or met the janitors of Shadowland?
18   Have you an inkling of the extent of the earth?
         Tell me all about it if you have!
19   Which is the way to the home of the light,
         and where does darkness live?
20   You could then show them the way to their proper places,
         or put them on the path to where they live!
21   If you know all this, you must have been born with them,
         you must be very old by now!

22   Have you ever visited the place where the snow is kept,
         or seen where the hail is stored up,
23   which I keep for times of stress,
         for days of battle and war?
24   From which direction does the lightning fork
         when it scatters sparks over the earth?
25   Who carves a channel for the downpour,
         and hacks a way for the rolling thunder,
26   so that rain may fall on lands where no one lives,
         and the deserts void of human dwelling,
27   giving drink to the lonely wastes
         and making grass spring where everything was dry?
28   Has the rain a father?
         Who begets the dewdrops?
29   What womb brings forth the ice,
         and gives birth to the frost of heaven,
30   when the waters grow hard as stone
         and the surface of the deep congeals?

31   Can you fasten the harness of the Pleiades,
         or untie Orion's bands?
32   Can you guide the morning star season by season
         and show the Bear and its cubs which way to go?

---

11. The "clay" is red in color.
12. The light, or natural element, of the wicked, is the darkness of night.

33   Have you grasped the celestial laws?
         Could you make their writ run on the earth?

34   Can your voice carry as far as the clouds
         and make the pent-up waters do your bidding?

35   Will lightning flashes come at your command
         and answer, 'Here we are'?

36   Who gave the ibis wisdom
         and endowed the cock with foreknowledge?[13]

37   Whose skill details every cloud
         and tilts the flasks of heaven

38   until the soil cakes into a solid mass
         and clods of earth cohere together?

39   Do you find a prey for the lioness
         and satisfy the hunger of her whelps

40   when they crouch in their dens
         and lurk in their lairs?

41   Who makes provision for the raven
         when his squabs cry out to God
         and crane their necks in hunger?

Second Speech

God is master of the forces of evil

40

6   Yahweh gave Job his answer from the heart of the tempest. He said:

7   Brace yourself like a fighter,
         now it is my turn to ask questions and yours to inform me.

8   Do you really want to reverse my judgment,
         and put me in the wrong to put yourself in the right?

9   Has your arm the strength of God's,
         can your voice thunder as loud?

10   If so, assume your dignity, your state,
         robe yourself in majesty and splendor.

11   Let the spate of your anger flow free;
         humiliate the haughty at a glance!

12   Cast one look at the proud and bring them low,
         strike down the wicked where they stand.

13   Bury the lot of them in the ground,
         shut them, silent-faced, in the dungeon.

14   I myself will be the first to acknowledge
         that your own right hand can assure your triumph.

---

13. Both birds are credited with foresight; the ibis heralds the flooding of the Nile, the cock announces the dawn.

Job's final answer

42

1   This was the answer Job gave to Yahweh:

2   I know that you are all-powerful:
          what you conceive, you can perform.
3   I am the man who obscured your designs
          with my empty-headed words.
4   I have been holding forth on matters I cannot understand,
          on marvels beyond me and my knowledge. . . .
5   I knew you then only by hearsay;
          but now, having seen you with my own eyes,
6   I retract all I have said,
          and in dust and ashes I repent.

V. EPILOGUE

Yahweh rebukes the three Sages

7   When Yahweh had said all this to Job, he turned to Eliphaz of Teman.
       "I burn with anger against you and your two friends," he said, "for not
8   speaking truthfully about me as my servant Job has done. So now find seven
       bullocks and seven rams, and take them back with you to my servant Job
       and offer a holocaust for yourselves, while Job, my servant, offers prayers
       for you. I will listen to him with favor and excuse your folly in not speaking
9   of me properly as my servant Job has done." Eliphaz of Teman, Bildad of
       Shuah and Zophar of Naamath went away to do as Yahweh had ordered, and
       Yahweh listened to Job with favor.

Yahweh restores Job's fortunes

10   Yahweh restored Job's fortunes, because he had prayed for his friends.
11   More than that, Yahweh gave him double what he had before. And all his
       brothers and all his sisters and all his friends of former times came to see
       him and sat down at table with him. They showed him every sympathy, and
       comforted him for all the evils Yahweh had inflicted on him. Each of them
12   gave him a silver coin, and each a gold ring. Yahweh blessed Job's new for-
       tune even more than his first one. He came to own fourteen thousand sheep,
13   six thousand camels, a thousand yoke of oxen and a thousand she-donkeys. He
14   had seven sons and three daughters; his first daughter he called
15   "Turtledove," the second "Cassia" and the third "Mascara." Throughout the
       land there were no women as beautiful as the daughters of Job. And their
       father gave them inheritance rights like their brothers.
16   After his trials, Job lived on until he was a hundred and forty years old,
       and saw his children and his children's children up to the fourth
17   generation. Then Job died, an old man and full of days.

MATTHEW
■

The Sermon on the Mount[1]

II. THE KINGDOM OF HEAVEN PROCLAIMED

B. The Evangelical Discourse

The Beatitudes

5

1   Seeing the crowds, he [Jesus of Nazareth] went up the hill. There he sat
2   down and was joined by his disciples. Then he began to speak. This is what
he taught them:

3   "How happy are the poor in spirit;
theirs is the kingdom of heaven.
4   Happy *the gentle*:[2]
they shall have the earth for their heritage.
5   Happy those who mourn:
they shall be comforted.
6   Happy those who hunger and thirst for what is right:
they shall be satisfied.
7   Happy the merciful:
they shall have mercy shown them.
8   Happy the pure in heart:
they shall see God.
9   Happy the peacemakers:
they shall be called sons of God.
10 Happy those who are persecuted in the cause of right:
theirs is the kingdom of heaven.

11 "Happy are you when people abuse you and persecute you and speak all
12 kinds of calumny against you on my account. Rejoice and be glad, for your
reward will be great in heaven; this is how they persecuted the prophets
before you.

Salt of the earth and light of the world

13 "You are the salt of the earth. But if salt becomes tasteless, what can
make it salty again? It is good for nothing, and can only be thrown out to be
trampled underfoot by men.
14 "You are the light of the world. A city built on a hill-top cannot be

---

1. In this discourse, which occupies three chapters of this gospel, Matthew has included sayings that probably originated on other occasions (cf. their parallels in Luke).
2. Or "the lowly"; the word comes from the Greek version of Ps. 37.

15
16
hidden. No one lights a lamp to put it under a tub; they put it on the lamp-stand where it shines for everyone in the house. In the same way your light must shine in the sight of men, so that, seeing your good works, they may give the praise to your Father in heaven.

The fulfilment of the law

17
18

19
"Do not imagine that I have come to abolish the Law or the Prophets. I have come not to abolish but to complete them. I tell you solemnly, till heaven and earth disappear, not one dot, not one little stroke, shall disappear from the Law until its purpose is achieved. Therefore, the man who infringes even one of the least of these commandments and teaches others to do the same will be considered the least in the kingdom of heaven; but the man who keeps them and teaches them will be considered great in the kingdom of heaven.

The new standard higher than the old

20

21
22

23
24

25

26

27/28

29

30

31
"For I tell you, if your virtue goes no deeper than that of the scribes and Pharisees, you will never get into the kingdom of heaven.
"You have learned how it was said to our ancestors: *You must not kill;*[3] and if anyone does kill he must answer for it before the court. But I say this to you: anyone who is angry with his brother will answer for it before the court; if a man calls his brother 'Fool'[4] he will answer for it before the Sanhedrin;[5] and if a man calls him 'Renegade'[6] he will answer for it in hell fire. So then, if you are bringing your offering to the altar and there remember that your brother has something against you, leave your offering there before the altar, go and be reconciled with your brother first, and then come back and present your offering. Come to terms with your opponent in good time while you are still on the way to the court with him, or he may hand you over to the judge and the judge to the officer, and you will be thrown into prison. I tell you solemnly, you will not get out till you have paid the last penny.
"You have learned how it was said: *You must not commit adultery.*[7] But I say this to you: if a man looks at a woman lustfully, he has already committed adultery with her in his heart. If your right eye should cause you to sin, tear it out and throw it away; for it will do you less harm to lose one part of you than to have your whole body thrown into hell. And if your right hand should cause you to sin, cut it off and throw it away; for it will do you less harm to lose one part of you than to have your whole body go to hell.
"It has also been said: *Anyone who divorces his wife must give her a writ of*

---

3. Ex. 20:13.
4. Translating an Aramaic term of contempt.
5. The High Court at Jerusalem.
6. Apostasy was the most repulsive of all sins.
7. Ex. 20:14.

32	*dismissal*.[8] But I say this to you: everyone who divorces his wife, except for the case of fornication, makes her an adulteress; and anyone who marries a divorced woman commits adultery.
33 34 35 36 37	"Again, you have learned how it was said to our ancestors: *You must not break your oath, but must fulfil your oaths to the Lord*.[9] But I say this to you: do not swear at all, either by *heaven*, since that is God's throne; or by *the earth*, since that is *his footstool*; or by Jerusalem, since that is *the city of the great king*. Do not swear by your own head either, since you cannot turn a single hair white or black. All you need say is 'Yes' if you mean yes, 'No' if you mean no; anything more than this comes from the evil one.
38/39 40 42	"You have learnt how it was said: *Eye for eye and tooth for tooth*.[10] But I say this to you: offer the wicked man no resistance. On the contrary, if anyone hits you on the right cheek, offer him the other as well; if a man takes you to law and would have your tunic, let him have your cloak as well. And if anyone orders you to go one mile, go two miles with him. Give to anyone who asks, and if anyone wants to borrow, do not turn away.
43 44 45 46 47 48	"You have learnt how it was said: *You must love your neighbor* and hate your enemy.[11] But I say this to you: love your enemies and pray for those who persecute you; in this way you will be sons of your Father in heaven, for he causes his sun to rise on bad men as well as good, and his rain to fall on honest and dishonest men alike. For if you love those who love you, what right have you to claim any credit? Even the tax collectors[12] do as much, do they not? And if you save your greetings for your brothers, are you doing anything exceptional? Even the pagans do as much, do they not? You must therefore be perfect just as your heavenly Father is perfect.

Almsgiving in secret

6

1 2 3 4	"Be careful not to parade your good deeds before men to attract their notice; by doing this you will lose all reward from your Father in heaven. So when you give alms, do not have it trumpeted before you; this is what the hypocrites do in the synagogues and in the streets to win men's admiration. I tell you solemnly, they have had their reward. But when you give alms, your left hand must not know what your right is doing; your almsgiving must be secret, and your Father who sees all that is done in secret will reward you.

Prayer in secret

5	"And when you pray, do not imitate the hypocrites: they love to say their prayers standing up in the synagogues and at the street corners for people to

---

8. Dt. 24:1.
9. Ex. 20:7.
10. Ex. 21:14.
11. The quotation is from Lv. 19:18; the second part of this commandment, not in the written Law, is an Aramaic way of saying "You do not have to love your enemy."
12. They were employed by the occupying power and this earned them popular contempt.

6   see them. I tell you solemnly, they have had their reward. But when you pray, *go to your private room and, when you have shut your door, pray*[13] to your Father who is in that secret place, and your Father who sees all that is done in secret will reward you.

How to pray. The Lord's Prayer

7   "In your prayers do not babble as the pagans do, for they think that by
8   using many words they will make themselves heard. Do not be like them;
9   your Father knows what you need before you ask him. So you should pray like this:

"Our Father in heaven,
may your name be held holy,
10   your kingdom come,
your will be done,
on earth as in heaven.
11   Give us today our daily bread.
12   And forgive us our debts,
as we have forgiven those who are in debt to us.
13   And do not put us to the test,
but save us from the evil one.

14   Yes, if you forgive others their failings, your heavenly Father will forgive you
15   yours; but if you do not forgive others, your Father will not forgive your failings either.

Fasting in secret

16   "When you fast do not put on a gloomy look as the hypocrites do: they pull long faces to let men know they are fasting. I tell you solemnly, they
17   have had their reward. But when you fast, put oil on your head and wash
18   your face, so that no one will know you are fasting except your Father who sees all that is done in secret; and your Father who sees all that is done in secret will reward you.

True treasures

19   "Do not store up treasures for yourselves on earth, where moths and
20   woodworms destroy them and thieves can break in and steal. But store up treasures for yourselves in heaven, where neither moth nor woodworms
21   destroy them and thieves cannot break in and steal. For where your treasure is, there will your heart be also.

God and money

24   "No one can be the slave of two masters: he will either hate the first and love the second, or treat the first with respect and the second with scorn. You cannot be the slave both of God and of money.

---

13. Not a direct quotation but an allusion to the practice common in the Old Testament, see 2 K. 4:33.

Trust in Providence

25   "That is why I am telling you not to worry about your life and what you
are to eat, nor about your body and how you are to clothe it. Surely life

26   means more than food, and the body more than clothing! Look at the birds in
the sky. They do not sow or reap or gather into barns; yet your heavenly

27   Father feeds them. Are you not worth much more than they are? Can any of

28   you, for all his worrying, add one single cubit to his span of life? And why
worry about clothing? Think of the flowers growing in the fields; they never

29   have to work or spin; yet I assure you that not even Solomon in all his

30   regalia was robed like one of these. Now if that is how God clothes the grass
in the field which is there today and thrown into the furnace tomorrow, will

31   he not much more look after you, you men of little faith? So do not worry;
do not say, 'What are we to eat? What are we to drink? How are we to be

32   clothed?' It is the pagans who set their hearts on all these things. Your

33   heavenly Father knows you need them all. Set your hearts on his kingdom
first, and on his righteousness, and all these other things will be given you

34   as well. So do not worry about tomorrow: tomorrow will take care of itself.
Each day has enough trouble of its own.

Do not judge

7

1/2   "Do not judge, and you will not be judged; because the judgements you
give are the judgements you will get, and the amount you measure out is the

3   amount you will be given. Why do you observe the splinter in your brother's

4   eye and never notice the plank in your own? How dare you say to your
brother, 'Let me take the splinter out of your eye,' when all the time there is

5   a plank in your own? Hypocrite! Take the plank out of your own eye first,
and then you will see clearly enough to take the splinter out of your brother's
eye.

Do not profane sacred things

6   "Do not give dogs what is holy;[14] and do not throw your pearls in front of
pigs, or they may trample them and then turn on you and tear you to
pieces.

Effective prayer

7   "Ask, and it will be given to you; search, and you will find; knock, and

8   the door will be opened to you. For the one who asks always receives; the
one who searches always finds; the one who knocks will always have the door

9   opened to him. Is there a man among you who would hand his son a stone

10   when he asked for bread? Or would hand him a snake when he asked for

11   fish? If you, then, who are evil, know how to give your children what is

---

14. The meat of animals that have been offered in sacrifice in the Temple; the application is to the parading of
holy beliefs and practices in front of those who cannot understand them.

good, how much more will your Father in heaven give good things to those who ask him!

The golden rule

12   "So always treat others as you would like them to treat you; that is the meaning of the Law and the Prophets.

The two ways

13   "Enter by the narrow gate, since the road that leads to perdition is wide
14   and spacious, and many take it; but it is a narrow gate and a hard road that leads to life, and only a few find it.

False prophets

15   "Beware of false prophets[15] who come to you disguised as sheep but
16   underneath are ravenous wolves. You will be able to tell them by their fruits.
17   Can people pick grapes from thorns, or figs from thistles? In the same way, a
18   sound tree produces good fruit but a rotten tree bad fruit. A sound tree
19   cannot bear bad fruit, nor a rotten tree bear good fruit. Any tree that does
20   not produce good fruit is cut down and thrown on the fire. I repeat, you will be able to tell them by their fruits.

The true disciple

21   "It is not those who say to me, 'Lord, Lord,' who will enter the kingdom
22   of heaven, but the person who does the will of my Father in heaven. When the day[16] comes many will say to me, 'Lord, Lord, did we not prophesy in your name, cast out demons in your name, work many miracles in your
23   name?' Then I shall tell them to their faces: I have never known you; *away from me, you evil men!"*
24   "Therefore, everyone who listens to these words of mine and acts on
25   them will be like a sensible man who built his house on rock. Rain came down, floods rose, gales blew and hurled themselves against that house, and
26   it did not fall: it was founded on rock. But everyone who listens to these words of mine and does not act on them will be like a stupid man who built his house
27   on sand. Rain came down, floods rose, gales blew and struck that house, and it fell; and what a fall it had!"

The amazement of the crowds

28   Jesus had now finished what he wanted to say, and his teaching made a
29   deep impression on the people because he taught them with authority, and not like their own scribes.[17]

---

15. Lying teachers of religion.
16. The day of Judgment.
17. Doctors of the Law, who buttressed their teaching by quotation from the Scriptures and traditions.

JOHN

■

PROLOGUE

1

1   In the beginning was the Word[1]:
the Word was with God
and the Word was God.

2   He was with God in the beginning.

3   Through him all things came to be,
not one thing had its being but through him.

4   All that came to be had life in him
and that life was the light of men,

5   a light that shines in the dark,
a light that darkness could not overpower.[2]

6   A man came, sent by God.
His name was John.[3]

7   He came as a witness,
as a witness to speak for the light,
so that everyone might believe through him.

8   He was not the light,
only a witness to speak for the light.

9   The Word was the true light
that enlightens all men;
and he was coming into the world.

10   He was in the world
that had its being through him,
and the world did not know him.

11   He came to his own domain
and his own people did not accept him.

12   But to all who did accept him
he gave power to become children of God,
to all who believe in the name of him

13   who was born not out of human stock
or urge of the flesh
or will of man
but of God himself.

14   The Word was made flesh,

---

1. "Word" translates from the Greek term *Logos*, a philosophical concept denoting the divine wisdom by which the world was created.
2. Or "grasp," in the sense of "enclose" or "understand."
3. John the Baptist, pictured as Jesus' forerunner.

he lived among us,[4]
and we saw his glory,
the glory that is his as the only Son of the Father,
full of grace and truth.

15   John appears as his witness. He proclaims:
"This is the one of whom I said:
He who comes after me
ranks before me
because he existed before me."

16   Indeed, from his fullness we have, all of us, received—
yes, grace in return for grace,
17   since, though the Law was given through Moses,
grace and truth have come through Jesus Christ.
18   No one has ever seen God;
it is the only Son, who is nearest to the Father's heart,
who has made him known.

I. THE FIRST PASSOVER

A. The Opening Week

The witness of John

19   This is how John appeared as a witness. When the Jews[5] sent priests and
20   Levites from Jerusalem to ask him, "Who are you?" he not only declared, but
21   he declared quite openly, "I am not the Christ." "Well then," they asked, "are
22   you Elijah?"[6] "I am not," he said. "Are you the Prophet?"[7] He answered,
"No." So they said to him, "Who are you? We must take back an answer to
23   those who sent us. What have you to say about yourself?" So John said, "I am,
as Isaiah prophesied:
a voice that cries in the wilderness:
Make a straight way for the Lord".[8]
24/25   Now these men had been sent by the Pharisees, and they put this further
question to him, "Why are you baptizing if you are not the Christ, and not
26   Elijah, and not the prophet?" John replied, "I baptise with water; but there
27   stands among you—unknown to you—the one who is coming after me; and I

---

4. The Word (Logos) became incarnate as Jesus of Nazareth.
5. In Jn. this usually indicates the Jewish religious authorities who were hostile to Jesus; but occasionally the Jews as a whole.
6. Whose return was expected, Ml. 3:23–24.
7. The Prophet greater than Moses who was expected as Messiah, on an interpretation of Dt. 18:15.
8. Is. 40:3.

28   am not fit to undo his sandal-strap." This happened at Bethany, on the far
           side of the Jordan, where John was baptising.

29   The next day, seeing Jesus coming towards him, John said, "Look, there
30   is the lamb of God that takes away the sin of the world. This is the one I
           spoke of when I said: A man is coming after me who ranks before me

31   because he existed before me. I did not know him myself, and yet it was to
32   reveal him to Israel that I came baptizing with water." John also declared,
           "I saw the Spirit coming down on him from heaven like a dove and resting

33   on him. I did not know him myself, but he who sent me to baptize with
           water had said to me, 'The man on whom you see the Spirit come down and

34   rest is the one who is going to baptize with the Holy Spirit.' Yes, I have seen
           and I am the witness that he is the Chosen One of God."

The first disciples

35/36   On the following day as John stood there again with two of his disciples, Jesus
           passed, and John stared hard at him and said, "Look, there is the lamb of
37/38   God." Hearing this, the two disciples followed Jesus. Jesus turned round,
39   saw them following and said, "What do you want?" They answered, "Rabbi,"—
           which means Teacher—"where do you live?" "Come and see," he replied; so
           they went and saw where he lived, and stayed with him the rest of that day.
           It was about the tenth hour.[9]

40   One of these two who became followers of Jesus after hearing what John
41   had said was Andrew, the brother of Simon Peter. Early next morning,
           Andrew met his brother and said to him, "We have found the Messiah"—
42   which means the Christ—and he took Simon to Jesus. Jesus looked hard at
           him and said, "You are Simon son of John; you are to be called Cephas"—
           meaning Rock.

43   The next day, after Jesus had decided to leave for Galilee, he met Philip
44   and said, "Follow me." Philip came from the same town, Bethsaida, as
45   Andrew and Peter. Philip found Nathanael[10] and said to him, "We have
           found the one Moses wrote about in the Law, the one about whom the
46   prophets wrote: he is Jesus son of Joseph, from Nazareth." "From Nazareth?"
           said Nathanael. "Can anything good come from that place?" "Come and see,"
47   replied Philip. When Jesus saw Nathanael coming he said of him, "There is
48   an Israelite who deserves the name, incapable of deceit." "How do you know
           me?" said Nathanael. "Before Philip came to call you," said Jesus "I saw you
49   under the fig tree." Nathanael answered, "Rabbi, you are the Son of God,
50   you are the King of Israel." Jesus replied, "You believe that just because I
51   said: I saw you under the fig-tree. You will see greater things than that." And
           then he added, "I tell you most solemnly, you will see heaven laid open
           and, above the Son of Man, the angels of God ascending and descending."

---

9. 4 P.M.
10. Probably the Bartholomew of the other gospels.

The wedding at Cana

2

1 Three days later there was a wedding at Cana in Galilee. The mother of
2/3 Jesus was there, and Jesus and his disciples had also been invited. When
   they ran out of wine, since the wine provided for the wedding was all
4 finished, the mother of Jesus said to him, "They have no wine." Jesus said,
5 "Woman, why turn to me? My hour has not come yet." His mother said to
6 the servants, *"Do whatever he tells you."*[11] There were six stone water jars
   standing there, meant for the ablutions that are customary among the Jews:
7 each could hold twenty or thirty gallons. Jesus said to the servants, "Fill the
8 jars with water," and they filled them to the brim. "Draw some out now," he
9 told them, "and take it to the steward." They did this; the steward tasted the
   water, and it had turned into wine. Having no idea where it came from—
   only the servants who had drawn the water knew—the steward called the
10 bridegroom and said, "People generally serve the best wine first, and keep
   the cheaper sort till the guests have had plenty to drink; but you have kept
   the best wine till now."
11 This was the first of the signs given by Jesus: it was given at Cana in
12 Galilee. He let his glory be seen, and his disciples believed in him. After
   this he went down to Capernaum with his mother and the brothers, but they
   stayed there only a few days.

B. The Passover

The cleansing of the Temple

13/14 Just before the Jewish Passover Jesus went up to Jerusalem, and in the
   Temple he found people selling cattle and sheep and pigeons, and the money-
15 changers sitting at their counters there. Making a whip out of some cord, he
   drove them all out of the Temple, cattle and sheep as well, scattered the
16 money-changers' coins, knocked their tables over and said to the pigeon-
   sellers, "Take all this out of here and stop turning my Father's house into a
17 market." Then his disciples remembered the words of scripture: *Zeal for*
18 *your house will devour me*.[12] The Jews intervened and said, "What sign can
19 you show us to justify what you have done?" Jesus answered, "Destroy this
20 sanctuary, and in three days I will raise it up." The Jews replied, "It has
   taken forty-six years to build this sanctuary:[13] are you going to raise it up in
21/22 three days?" But he was speaking of the sanctuary that was his body, and
   when Jesus rose from the dead, his disciples remembered that he had said
   this, and they believed the scripture and the words he had said.
23 During his stay in Jerusalem for the Passover many believed in his name

---

11. Mary, unnamed in John's Gospel, echoes Pharaoh's words, giving royal authority to the Hebrew Joseph (Gen. 41:55).
12. Ps 69:9.
13. Reconstruction work on the Temple began in 19 B.C. This is, therefore, the Passover of A.D. 28.

24	when they saw the signs that he gave, but Jesus knew them all and did not
25	trust himself to them; he never needed evidence about any man; he could
	tell what a man had in him.

VI. THE FEAST OF DEDICATION

The resurrection of Lazarus

11

1	There was a man named Lazarus who lived in the village of Bethany with
2	the two sisters, Mary[14] and Martha, and he was ill.—It was the same Mary,
	the sister of the sick man Lazarus, who anointed the Lord with ointment and
3	wiped his feet with her hair. The sisters sent this message to Jesus, "Lord,
4	the man you love is ill." On receiving the message, Jesus said, "This
	sickness will end, not in death but in God's glory, and through it the Son of
	God will be glorified."
5/6	Jesus loved Martha and her sister and Lazarus, yet when he heard that
7	Lazarus was ill he stayed where he was for two more days before saying to
8	the disciples, "Let us go to Judaea." The disciples said, "Rabbi, it is not
9	long since the Jews wanted to stone you; are you going back again?" Jesus
	replied:

"Are there not twelve hours in the day?
A man can walk in the daytime without stumbling
because he has the light of this world to see by;

10	but if he walks at night he stumbles,
	because there is no light to guide him."

11	He said that and then added, "Our friend Lazarus is resting, I am going to
12	wake him." The disciples said to him, "Lord, if he is able to rest he is sure
13	to get better." The phrase Jesus used referred to the death of Lazarus,
14	but they thought that by "rest" he meant "sleep," so Jesus put it plainly,
15	"Lazarus is dead; and for your sake I am glad I was not there because now
16	you will believe. But let us go to him." Then Thomas—known as the Twin—
	said to the other disciples, "Let us go too, and die with him."
17	On arriving, Jesus found that Lazarus had been in the tomb for four days
18/19	already. Bethany is only about two miles from Jerusalem, and many Jews
20	had come to Martha and Mary to sympathize with them over their brother. When
	Martha heard that Jesus had come she went to meet him. Mary remained
21	sitting in the house. Martha said to Jesus, "If you had been here, my brother
22	would not have died, but I know that, even now, whatever you ask of God,
23/24	he will grant you." "Your brother," said Jesus to her, "will rise again." Martha

---

14. Mary, the sister of Lazarus and Martha, is not to be confused with Mary Magdalene or with the unidentified woman who performs the same service in Luke 7:37–50.

25	said, "I know he will rise again at the resurrection on the last day." Jesus said:

"I am the resurrection.
If anyone believes in me, even though he dies he will live,

| 26 | and whoever lives and believes in me |

will never die.
Do you believe this?"

27	"Yes, Lord," she said, "I believe that you are the Christ, the Son of God, the one who was to come into this world."
28	When she had said this, she went and called her sister Mary, saying in a
29	low voice, "The Master is here and wants to see you." Hearing this, Mary
30	got up quickly and went to him. Jesus had not yet come into the village; he
31	was still at the place where Martha had met him. When the Jews who were in the house sympathizing with Mary saw her get up so quickly and go out, they followed her, thinking that she was going to the tomb to weep there.
32	Mary went to Jesus, and as soon as she saw him she threw herself at his
33	feet, saying, "Lord, if you had been here, my brother would not have died." At the sight of her tears, and those of the Jews who followed her, Jesus said in
34	great distress, with a sigh that came straight from the heart, "Where have you
35/36	put him?" They said, "Lord, come and see." Jesus wept; and the Jews said,
37	"See how much he loved him!" But there were some who remarked, "He opened the eyes of the blind man, could he not have prevented this man's
38	death?" Still sighing, Jesus reached the tomb: it was a cave with a stone to
39	close the opening. Jesus said, "Take the stone away." Martha said to him,
40	"Lord, by now he will smell; this is the fourth day." Jesus replied, "Have I
41	not told you that if you believe you will see the glory of God?" So they took away the stone. Then Jesus lifted up his eyes and said:

"Father, I thank you for hearing my prayer.

| 42 | I knew indeed that you always hear me, |

but I speak
for the sake of all these who stand round me,
so that they may believe it was you who sent me."

| 43 | When he had said this, he cried in a loud voice, "Lazarus, here! Come |
| 44 | out!" The dead man came out, his feet and hands bound with bands of stuff and a cloth round his face. Jesus said to them, "Unbind him, let him go free." |

The Jewish leaders decide on the death of Jesus

45	Many of the Jews who had come to visit Mary and had seen what he did
46	believed in him, but some of them went to tell the Pharisees what Jesus had
47	done. Then the chief priests and Pharisees called a meeting. "Here is this
48	man working all these signs," they said, "and what action are we taking? If we let him go on in this way everybody will believe in him, and the Romans
49	will come and destroy the Holy Place and our nation." One of them,

50
51
Caiaphas, the high priest that year, said, "You don't seem to have grasped the situation at all; you fail to see that it is better for one man to die for the people, than for the whole nation to be destroyed." He did not speak in his own person, it was as high priest that he made this prophecy that Jesus was
52
53
54
to die for the nation—and not for the nation only, but to gather together in unity the scattered children of God. From that day they were determined to kill him. So Jesus no longer went about openly among the Jews, but left the district for a town called Ephraim, in the country bordering on the desert, and stayed there with his disciples.

[Convicted of treason, Jesus is condemned to crucifixion by the Roman governor, Pontius Pilate.]

VII. THE LAST PASSOVER

C. The Passion

Jesus before Pilate

19

1/2
Pilate then had Jesus taken away and scourged; and after this, the soldiers twisted some thorns into a crown and put it on his head, and dressed him in a purple robe.

3
They kept coming up to him and saying, "Hail, king of the Jews!"; and they slapped him in the face.

4
5
Pilate came outside again and said to them, "Look, I am going to bring him out to you to let you see that I find no case." Jesus then came out wearing the crown of thorns and the purple robe. Pilate said, "Here is the
6
man." When they saw him the chief priests and the guards shouted, "Crucify him! Crucify him!" Pilate said, "Take him yourselves and crucify
7
him: I can find no case against him." "We have a Law," the Jews replied, "and according to that Law he ought to die, because he has claimed to be the Son of God."

8/9
When Pilate heard them say this his fears increased. Re-entering the Praetorium, he said to Jesus, "Where do you come from?" But Jesus made no
10
answer. Pilate then said to him, "Are you refusing to speak to me? Surely
11
you know I have power to release you and I have power to crucify you?" "You would have no power over me," replied Jesus, "if it had not been given you from above; that is why the one who handed me over to you has the greater guilt."

Jesus is condemned to death

12
From that moment Pilate was anxious to set him free, but the Jews shouted, "If you set him free you are no friend of Caesar's; anyone who
13
makes himself king is defying Caesar." Hearing these words, Pilate had Jesus brought out, and seated himself on the chair of judgment at a place called
14
the Pavement, in Hebrew Gabbatha. It was Passover Preparation Day, about

15   the sixth hour.[15] "Here is your king," said Pilate to the Jews. "Take him away, take him away!" they said. "Crucify him!" "Do you want me to crucify your king?" said Pilate. The chief priests answered, "We have no king except

16   Caesar." So in the end Pilate handed him over to them to be crucified.

The crucifixion

17   They then took charge of Jesus, and carrying his own cross he went out of

18   the city to the place of the skull or, as it was called in Hebrew, Golgotha, where they crucified him with two others, one on either side with Jesus in the

19   middle. Pilate wrote out a notice and had it fixed to the cross; it ran: "Jesus

20   the Nazarene, King of the Jews." This notice was read by many of the Jews, because the place where Jesus was crucified was not far from the city, and

21   the writing was in Hebrew, Latin and Greek. So the Jewish chief priests said to Pilate, "You should not write 'King of the Jews,' but 'This man said: I am

22   King of the Jews.' " Pilate answered, "What I have written, I have written."

Christ's garments divided

23   When the soldiers had finished crucifying Jesus they took his clothing and divided it into four shares, one for each soldier. His undergarment was

24   seamless, woven in one piece from neck to hem; so they said to one another, "Instead of tearing it, let's throw dice to decide who is to have it." In this way the words of scripture were fulfilled:

They shared out my clothing among them.
They cast lots for my clothes.[16]

This is exactly what the soldiers did.

Jesus and his mother

25   Near the cross of Jesus stood his mother and his mother's sister, Mary

26   the wife of Clopas, and Mary of Magdala. Seeing his mother and the disciple he loved standing near her, Jesus said to his mother, "Woman, this is your

27   son." Then to the disciple he said, "This is your mother." And from that moment the disciple made a place for her in his home.

The death of Jesus

28   After this, Jesus knew that everything had now been completed, and to fulfil the scripture perfectly he said:

"I am thirsty."[17]

29   A jar full of vinegar stood there, so putting a sponge soaked in the

---

15. On Preparation Day, the Passover supper was made ready for eating after sunset. The sixth hour is midday, by which time all leaven had to be removed from the house; during the feast only unleavened bread was eaten.
16. Ps. 22:18.
17. Ps. 22:15.

30 vinegar on a hyssop stick they held it up to his mouth. After Jesus had taken the vinegar he said, "It is accomplished;" and bowing his head he gave up his spirit.

The pierced Christ

31 It was Preparation Day, and to prevent the bodies remaining on the cross during the sabbath—since that sabbath was a day of special solemnity—the
32 Jews asked Pilate to have the legs broken[18] and the bodies taken away. Consequently the soldiers came and broke the legs of the first man who had been crucified
33 with him and then of the other. When they came to Jesus, they found he was
34 already dead, and so instead of breaking his legs one of the soldiers pierced his side with a lance; and immediately there came out blood and water.
35 This is the evidence of one who saw it—trustworthy evidence, and he knows he speaks the truth—and he gives it so that you may believe
36 as well. Because all this happened to fulfil the words of scripture:

Not one bone of his will be broken;[19]

37 and again, in another place scripture says:

They will look on the one whom they have pierced.[20]

The burial

38 After this, Joseph of Arimathaea, who was a disciple of Jesus—though a secret one because he was afraid of the Jews—asked Pilate to let him remove the body of Jesus. Pilate gave permission, so they came and took it
39 away. Nicodemus came as well—the same one who had first come to Jesus at night-time—and he brought a mixture of myrrh and aloes, weighing about
40 a hundred pounds. They took the body of Jesus and wrapped it with spices
41 in linen cloths, following the Jewish burial custom. At the place where he had been crucified there was a garden, and in this garden a new tomb in
42 which no one had yet been buried. Since it was the Jewish Day of Preparation and the tomb was near at hand, they laid Jesus there.

VIII. THE DAY OF CHRIST'S RESURRECTION

The empty tomb

20

1 It was very early on the first day of the week and still dark, when Mary of Magdala came to the tomb. She saw that the stone had been moved away
2 from the tomb and came running to Simon Peter and the other disciple, the

---

18. To hasten death.
19. Two texts are here combined: Ps. 34:20 and Ex. 12:46. The allusion is both to God protecting the good man and to the ritual for preparing the Passover lamb.
20. Zc. 12:10.

one Jesus loved. "They have taken the Lord out of the tomb," she said, "and we don't know where they have put him."

3/4   So Peter set out with the other disciple to go to the tomb. They ran together, but the other disciple, running faster than Peter, reached the tomb

5 first; he bent down and saw the linen cloths lying on the ground, but did not

6 go in. Simon Peter who was following now came up, went right into the

7 tomb, saw the linen cloths on the ground, and also the cloth that had been over his head; this was not with the linen cloths but rolled up in a place by

8 itself. Then the other disciple who had reached the tomb first also went in;

9 he saw and he believed. Till this moment they had failed to understand the

10 teaching of scripture, that he must rise from the dead. The disciples then went home again.

The appearance to Mary of Magdala

11   Meanwhile Mary stayed outside near the tomb, weeping. Then, still

12 weeping, she stooped to look inside, and saw two angels in white sitting

13 where the body of Jesus had been, one at the head, the other at the feet. They said, "Woman, why are you weeping?" "They have taken my Lord away," she

14 replied, "and I don't know where they have put him." As she said this she turned around and saw Jesus standing there, though she did not recognize

15 him. Jesus said, "Woman, why are you weeping? Who are you looking for?" Supposing him to be the gardener, she said, "Sir, if you have taken him

16 away, tell me where you have put him, and I will go and remove him." Jesus said, "Mary!" She knew him then and said to him in Hebrew, "Rabbuni!"—

17 which means Master. Jesus said to her, "Do not cling to me, because I have not yet ascended to the Father. But go and find the brothers, and tell them: I

18 am ascending to my Father and your Father, to my God and your God." So Mary of Magdala went and told the disciples that she had seen the Lord and that he had said these things to her.

Appearances to the disciples

19   In the evening of that same day, the first day of the week, the doors were closed in the room where the disciples were, for fear of the Jews. Jesus came

20 and stood among them. He said to them, "Peace be with you," and showed them his hands and his side. The disciples were filled with joy when they

21 saw the Lord, and he said to them again, "Peace be with you.

"As the Father sent me,
so am I sending you."

22 After saying this he breathed on them and said:

"Receive the Holy Spirit.

23 For those whose sins you forgive,
they are forgiven;
for those whose sins you retain,
they are retained."

24 Thomas, called the Twin, who was one of the Twelve, was not with them
25 when Jesus came. When the disciples said, "We have seen the Lord," he
answered, "Unless I see the holes that the nails made in his hands and can
put my finger into the holes they made, and unless I can put my hand into
26 his side, I refuse to believe." Eight days later the disciples were in the house
again and Thomas was with them. The doors were closed, but Jesus came in
27 and stood among them. "Peace be with you," he said. Then he spoke to
Thomas, "Put your finger here; look, here are my hands. Give me your hand;
28 put it into my side. Doubt no longer but believe." Thomas replied, "My Lord
and my God!" Jesus said to him:

29 "You believe because you can see me.
Happy are those who have not seen and yet believe."

CONCLUSION

30 There were many other signs that Jesus worked and the disciples saw, but
31 they are not recorded in this book. These are recorded so that you may
believe that Jesus is the Christ, the Son of God, and that believing this you
may have life through his name.

The Hellenic World

Homer, The Iliad

Two long poems celebrating the mighty deeds of Greek heroes and their gods stand at the head of Western literature. Both the *Iliad* and the *Odyssey* are ascribed to Homer, a poet about whom nothing is known except for the unverifiable tradition that he was blind and lived on Chios, an island in the eastern Aegean Sea. Although the historian Herodotus (c. 484–428 B.C.) states that Homer lived approximately four hundred years before his time, or about 850 B.C., most scholars date the Homeric epics a century later.

Scholars believe that the *Iliad* and *Odyssey* were composed and transmitted orally and that they developed gradually over many generations. Some critics question whether Homer ever existed, arguing that he is merely a name given to schools of anonymous poets who combined ancient legendary and mythical material to compose the epic poems. The poems contain many indications that they originated orally. Approximately one third of the *Iliad's* 15,000 lines consist of conventional phrases, such as "fleet-footed Achilles" or "bright-eyed Athene," ready-made epithets that formed part of the oral poet's standard repertory. At whatever point the Homeric poems attained their present form and were written down, they established the qualities and functions of the Olympian gods and fixed standards of heroic conduct throughout the Greek world.

The *Iliad* achieves artistic unity by focusing on a few events during the tenth and last year of the Trojan war and on a single theme, the anger of Achilles and its consequences to his fellow Greeks. When Achilles refuses to make peace with his leader, Agamemnon, he initiates a series of actions that result in tragic losses, including the death of his beloved companion Patroclus. In killing the Trojan prince Hector to avenge Patroclus, Achilles knows that he hastens his own death. Fate, the inescapable power of necessity, decrees that he must die shortly thereafter. His compensation is that he earns a great warrior's immortality, undying fame.

In creating the *Iliad*, Homer perfected the epic form, a literary category that later ages have defined in terms of the Homeric achievement. A long narrative poem in majestic, deliberately archaic language celebrating the heroic actions of a military aristocracy, the Homeric epic expresses human life as a tension between humanity's almost unlimited potential and ambition on one hand and the certainty of death on the other. The Homeric gods reserve immortality and the ultimate satisfactions of power exclusively for themselves. Even heroes like Achilles cannot escape death, which the Greeks saw as terminating all of life's possibilities. This pessimistic worldview, in which death has the power to reduce all human experience to oblivion, is the context for Achilles' bold quest for heroic achievement. The personal cost of Achilles' sacrifice, made in the process of destroying an entire people, illustrates Homer's profoundly tragic view of life.

BOOK 1

Sing, goddess, the anger of Achilles, the anger which caused so many sorrows to the Greeks. It sent to Hades many souls of heroes and gave their bodies to be food of dogs and birds.

So the design of Zeus was worked out from the time when, first, Agamemnon, king of men, and great Achilles were parted in anger.

Who of the gods did this? Apollo. He sent a plague into the Greek army because Agamemnon had wronged Chryses, his priest. For the priest came to their ships with gifts to free Chryseis, his daughter, taken by the Greeks in war. In his hands were the signs that he was priest to Apollo, the Archer, and he made this prayer to all the Greeks: "The gods send that you take Troy, and come back safe to your homes—but free my dear daughter and take these gifts in exchange—for fear of the son of Zeus, Apollo the Archer!"

Then all the rest of the Greeks cried out: "Hear the priest. Take the gifts." But this did not please Agamemnon who sent Chryses roughly away, saying: "Let me not see you, old man near the hollow ships, waiting about now or coming back later. Being a priest may not keep you safe from me, if I do. Your daughter I will not free. Before that, let old age come upon her in our house, in Argos, far from her country, as she walks up and down before the loom and serves my bed. Go in peace! Do not make me angry!"

The old man went from him full of fear and in silence walked by the edge of the loud-sounding sea. When he had gone some distance he made this prayer to Apollo: "Hear me, god of the silver bow. Ruler over Chryse and Cilla and Tenedos, O Mouse-god! If ever I burned fat offerings to you give me now my desire. Let the Greeks pay through your arrows for my tears."

And Phoebus Apollo heard his prayer. He came down from the mountains of Olympus angry at heart, his bow and arrows on his shoulders shaking as he moved; and his coming was like the night. He let an arrow fly and the sound of his silver bow was fearful. First it was the mules and dogs his arrows killed and after that the men—till the fires of the dead were burning night and day.

For nine days his arrows killed. On the tenth day Achilles had the chiefs come to the meeting place—for the goddess, white-armed Hera, put this in his heart. She had sorrow for the Greeks, seeing so many of them dead. There Achilles stood and said: "Let us now hear from some priest, or from a reader of dreams (for dreams too are from Zeus), why Apollo is so angry. What have we done? What can we give him to take this plague away?"

So he said, and sat down; and then Kalchas stood before them—Kalchas, far the best of the seers who knew things past and present and to come. It was Kalchas who had guided the Greek ships to Troy by the knowledge Apollo gave him. And these were his words: "Achilles, you would have me tell why Apollo, the Archer, is angry. And I will; but take thought and swear now to help me. For what I say will anger one who rules over all the Greeks. What can such a man as I do against a king? Though he keep down his anger and wait before paying me back? Think now. Will you keep me safe?"

Then swift-footed Achilles answered: "Fear not, Kalchas, but tell what you know. For by Apollo himself, through whom you have your knowledge, no man, while I live and see the light on earth, is going to put violent hands upon you among these hollow ships—no man of all the Greeks, no, not Agamemnon himself who now says he is the greatest by far of them all."

Then Kalchas took heart and said: "It is because of Chryses—priest of Apollo—because Agamemnon wronged him and would not free Chryseis his daughter or take his gifts, that Apollo does this to us; and he will do more still. He will not stop the plague till we have given bright-eyed Chryseis freely back to her father but without gifts in exchange now, and we must send a great and holy offering to Chryse. Then it may be, the Archer will hear our prayer."

So he said and sat down and then stood up before them wide-ruling Agamemnon the King. His dark heart within him was full of anger and his eyes were like fire. "Seer of evil," he cried, "never yet did you tell of any good thing. And is this why the plague is among us? Because I would not give back this girl Chryseis? I would not; for she is better in my eyes than even my wife Clytemnestra—as beautiful, as tall, as skillful and as wise. Nonetheless, I will give her back. I would have the people safe, not dead. Only make ready for me in her place an equal prize. I will not be the only one of the Greeks to be without his prize of honor. You see how my prize is being taken from me."

At that swift-footed Achilles answered: "Great King Agamemnon, most profit-loving of men, how can the Greeks give you a prize? We have no common store. What we got from the cities we took has been divided, and we cannot now ask for it back. But do you give up this girl to her father, at Apollo's word, and we will pay you three or four times over whenever Zeus lets us take well-walled Troy."

Then Agamemnon said: "Strong you may be, godlike Achilles, but you will not trick me like this. What! Will you tell me to give my prize up, and am I to be without one while you keep yours? No! If the great-hearted Greeks will give me another prize, one pleasing to me and equal to my honor, good! But if not, then I, myself, will go and take a prize of honor— from you or from Ajax or Odysseus—and angry will he be to whom I come. But of this later. First let a black ship be made ready to put to sea and journey to Chryse with fair-faced Chryseis and the offerings. So may we be at peace with Apollo whose arrows fly so far."

Then swift-footed Achilles looked at him angrily and said: "O you without shame, how can any Greek do your will with any heart either to journey or to fight! It was not because of the Trojan spearmen that I came to this war. They never did me any wrong, never took my cattle or horses, or cut down my harvest in deep-soiled Phthia. For many things stretch between us, shadowy mountains and sounding sea. It was for you, you without shame, that we came here, to make the Trojans pay—for Menelaus and for you, you dog-face! But you think nothing now of that. You would take my prize of honor, would you, for which I fought and which the Greeks gave to me! My reward when we take a town is never as great as yours, though it is my hands which do the fighting. But now I will sail back to Phthia with my ships. It is better than going on fighting here without honor to get you more treasure and gold."

Then Agamemnon the King answered Achilles: "Run away if you will. I will not ask you to stay. I have others to honor me and, highest of all, Zeus, Lord of counsel. What if you are strong, does not that come to you from heaven? Go home now with your ships and company and lord it among your Myrmidons. What do I care for you or your anger? And know this: because Phoebus Apollo is taking away my Chryseis, I myself will come to your hut and take away your prize of honor, even fair-faced Briseis, so that you may see how much greater I am than you. Then others, in time to come, may be slower to match themselves with me."

So he said, and sorrow came upon Achilles, and his heart within him was divided between taking out his sword to kill Agamemnon and controlling his anger. While he was still in two minds about it and was putting his hand to his great sword, Athene came to him from Heaven, sent by the white-armed goddess Hera, who had love and care in her heart for Agamemnon and Achilles both. And Athene came and took Achilles by his golden hair. Now she was seen by him only and by none of the others. And Achilles turned about and knew who it was and her eyes were terribly bright. Then he said: "Why do you come here now, daughter of Zeus? Is it to see how Agamemnon pays for his pride with his life?"

Then bright-eyed Athene said: "I came from Heaven, sent by white-armed Hera who has love and care in her heart for you both. So take your hand from that sword and let him be. I tell you now that gifts three times as great will come to you through this act of his. But with words, if you will, attack him."

And swift-footed Achilles answered: "Goddess! A man must do as the two of you say, however angry he is. The gods hear those who do their will."

So Athene went back to the other gods in the house of Zeus on Olympus and Achilles turned again and let loose his anger against Agamemnon in bitter words. "You full wineskin, you; you with the face of a dog and the heart of a fawn. You never arm yourself to fight for your people. That would seem as bad as death to you! Much better, is it not, to take for yourself the prize of honor of every man who has a word to say against you? But I will say this and swear a great oath to back it. By this staff we take in our hands as we give judgment, by this staff which will never be green again or have branches or leaves, for the ax has cut them from it, by this witness to the rule of Heaven itself—there will come a time when every man of the Greeks will look long for Achilles to help him. Much help will you be to them then, for all your sorrow, as they fall before man-killing Hector. In that day you will bite on your heart in your anger because you did this wrong to the best of the Greeks."

BOOK 22

[Insulted by Agamemnon, Achilles sulks in his tent, refusing to fight and allowing the Trojans to invade the Greek camp and burn the Greek ships. Only after Hector, son of Priam and Hecuba, the king and queen of Troy, kills Patroclus does Achilles take action to avenge the death of his beloved companion.]

So throughout the city, like helpless fawns, the Trojans were wiping the sweat off them and drinking to wet their dry throats, as they rested on the fair crest of the walls, while the Greeks, with their shields on their shoulders, came toward the city. But deadly fate held Hector where he was in front of the Scaean gates.

Then Achilles turned toward Troy. Swift, as a prize-winning chariot horse running all out across the plain, so swift were Achilles' feet and knees. And the old man, Priam, was the first to see him coming. And to Priam he seemed like the star which comes out at harvest time—bright are his rays among the armies of dark night—the star men name the Dog of Orion. Brightest of all, he is but a sign of evil. Even so the bronze flashed on Achilles' breast as he ran. And the old man moaned, and took his head in his hands and cried to Hector, his son, who was standing before the gates ready to fight with Achilles: "Hector, dear son, do not wait there by yourself for Achilles. He is stronger far than you. Would that the gods loved him as I do. He would quickly enough be food for dogs and birds then. How many of my sons has he killed or sold to the islands oversea, and now I cannot see Polydorus or Lycaon among the Trojans who came back into the city! Come in, come inside the walls, my son! Save the Trojans, and have pity on me! It is not so bad for a young man's body to be seen naked, wounded by the sharp bronze—but for an old man when he is dead to be torn by dogs in full view, that is the worst thing which can come to man."

So he cried pulling at his white hair, but Hector was not to be won over. And his mother Hecuba cried to him, too. "Hector, respect me and pity me if ever I gave you the breast. Fight with Achilles from inside the walls. Do not stand there to face him. Cruel he is and if he kills you I will never have you before me on a bed to sorrow over, dear offshoot of myself, nor will your wife, but he will give you to his dogs far away from us by the Greek ships."

But Hector would not hear them as he waited there for Achilles. And deeply moved, he said to himself: "Alas, if I go inside the gates Polydamas will be the first to say that this is my doing. For he told me to bring the Trojans into the city that terrible night, when Achilles came out. But I would not hear him—how much better if I had! But now that I have brought destruction on us all, blind fool that I was, I cannot face the Trojans and their wives. Some worse man may say: 'Hector, believing too much in himself, undid us all.' They will say that. It will be far better to meet Achilles man to man and kill him and then go in; or be killed by him, in all honor, before the city. Or how would it be to put down my shield and helmet and rest my spear against the wall and go to meet unmatched Achilles and tell him we will give up Helen, and with her all the treasure Paris took from Menelaus, and give the Greeks half of all we have as well? But why do I argue with myself like this? Achilles would have no pity on me but would kill me right away as though I were a woman, if I were unarmed. This is no time for boy and girl talk with him—boy and girl talk under some rock or oak tree. Better fight at once and see on whose side Zeus will be."

As he thought so, Achilles came near in his waving helmet, with his great Pelean spear lifted; and suddenly fear moved Hector and away from the gates under the walls of Troy he ran, with swift-footed Achilles after him. Past the lookout station, and by the wind-waved fig tree away from the wall by the wagon road they went, and past the two springs which feed eddying Xanthus. One runs with warm water and a smoke goes up from it as if from a fire, the other even in summer is cold as snow or ice. And near them are the wide stone basins where the wives and daughters of the Trojans washed their clothes of old in the time of peace, before the Greeks came to Troyland. By these they ran—a good man in front but a far stronger man at his heels. And the prize they ran for was no bull's skin, or common prize for the swift-footed, but the life of horse-taming Hector.

And all the gods looked on. Then the father of gods and men said: "My heart sorrows for Hector, who has burned many thighs of oxen on the crests of Ida and in the city. Now think and take counsel, gods. Are we to save him from death or now at last kill him, a good man though he is, at Achilles' hands?"

Then the goddess, flashing-eyed Athene, said: "Father, Lord of the bright lightning and the dark cloud, what are you saying? Would you save from death a mortal man whose hour has long been fixed by fate? Do as you will, but know that we other gods are not all with you in this."

And in answer Zeus said: "Take heart, my child. I am not as serious as I seem. Do as your pleasure is and hold back no longer." And down from Olympus Athene went.

Three times round Troy Hector and Achilles ran. Whenever Hector made for the Dardanian gates to the cover of the walls, where the Trojans could help him by throwing, Achilles would head him off and turn him back toward the plain, keeping on the city side. They ran as in a dream where one man cannot escape or overtake another. And how could Hector have escaped so far, if Apollo, for the last time, had not kept up his strength and made swift his knees? And Achilles signed to the other Greeks not to throw their spears at Hector.

Three times round Troy they went, but when they came the fourth time to the springs, Zeus lifted up his golden balance and Hector's fate went down; and Phoebus Apollo left him.

Then Athene came to Achilles and said: "Stand and take breath while I go and make Hector fight with you man to man." And Achilles did so, resting on his great spear. And Athene went to Hector, putting on the form and voice of Deïphobus, his brother.

"Dear brother," she said, "now let us two meet Achilles' attack together." And Hector answered: "Deïphobus, you were always dearest to me of my brothers, but now I honor you in my heart even more. You, only, have had the courage to come out here to help me while the others stay inside."

And bright-eyed Athene said: "Truly, my brother, they did all they could, with their prayers, to keep me back—so much they fear Achilles—but now let us fight."

With such words Athene tricked him; and Hector, coming near to Achilles, said: "I will run from you no longer, Achilles, but kill you now or be killed. And let this be our agreement before all the gods as witnesses: if Zeus lets me outlive you and take your life, I will give your body back to the Greeks, after taking your armor. And you will do the same."

But with an angry look Achilles answered: "Talk not to me of agreements, Hector. Between lions and men there is no swearing of oaths. How can wolves and sheep be of one mind? They must hate one another all through. No more of this, but fight your best. For now Pallas Athene will overcome you by my spear. Now you must pay for all my sorrows for my friends you have killed."

He lifted his far-shadowing spear as he spoke and threw. Hector watched its coming and bent low so that it went over him and fixed itself in the earth. But Athene took it out and gave it back to Achilles without Hector's seeing her. And Hector cried: "So you did not know from Zeus the hour of my death, O godlike Achilles! Did you think your false tongue would make me afraid? Now escape my spear if you can."

And he lifted his far-shadowing spear and threw it and hit Achilles' shield, but the shield turned it back. And Hector saw and cried to Deïphobus loudly for a long spear. But there was no man there. Then Hector knew all in his heart and said: "Alas! Now they have brought me to my death. I thought Deïphobus was with me, but he is inside the walls and that was Athene who tricked me. Now death is very near me and there is no way of escape. This from of old was the pleasure of Zeus and his son, Apollo, who helped me before, but now my fate has come upon me. At least let me die fighting, to be honored by later men who hear of this."

And he took his sharp sword that hung by his side, a great sword and strong, and sprang on Achilles like an eagle which falls from a cloud on some lamb or hare. But Achilles ran upon him, his heart raging, his breast covered by his shield and the gold feathers on his four-horned helmet waving. As a star comes out among the stars of night, the star of evening, the most beautiful of the stars of heaven, even so came the light from the bronze of his spear as he lifted it in his right hand looking for the place most open for the blow. Now Hector's body was covered with bronze armor, the beautiful armor he had taken from great Patroclus when he killed him; but there was an opening where the collarbones come into the neck; and there, as he came on, Achilles let drive with his spear and straight through the neck went the point. But the bronze-weighted spear did not cut the windpipe, so that Hector still had his voice. Then as he fell in the dust, Achilles gloried over him: "You thought, Hector, you would be safe when you took that armor from Patroclus. Little you thought, you fool, of me, far away among my ships. But now, stronger far, I have come from them and loosed your knees. The Greeks will give him his funeral but throw you to the dogs and birds."

Then Hector, as the breath went from him, prayed: "By your life and knees and parents take the bronze and gold and all the gifts my father and mother will offer you and send my body back so that the Trojans and the Trojans' wives may give me to the fire after my death."

But with an angry look Achilles answered: "Pray me not, dog, by knees or parents. O that I could make myself cut up your flesh and eat it raw myself, for what you have done. There is no man living who can keep the dogs from your head, Hector—no, not though they paid me your weight in gold."

And dying Hector answered: "I know you for what you are, and knew it before; the heart in your breast is of iron. See that I do not bring the anger of the gods down upon you on the day when Paris and Apollo kill you, strong though you are, at the Scaean gate."

He ended and death overtook him and his spirit went from him down to the house of Hades, crying out sadly against its fate. And after his death Achilles said to him: "Lie dead there; I am ready for my own death whenever Zeus and the other immortals send it."

He pulled his spear out and put it aside and took the armor from Hector's body. And the other Greeks ran up to wonder at Hector's beauty. And all who came near wounded him with their spears. And one would say looking at another: "Hector is softer now to handle than when he burned the ships with fire." And when Achilles had taken off the armor, he stood and said to the Greeks: "Let us see what the Trojans are minded to do now that the gods have let us overcome this man who has done us more damage than all the rest together. But what am I thinking of? Patroclus still waits at the ships for his funeral. How can I forget him while I live on and my knees are quick! Even if in the house of Hades dead men forget their friends, even there I will not forget him. But come, sons of the Greeks, let us go back to the ships singing our song of glory and taking this man with us. For we have won great glory. We have killed highborn Hector to whom the Trojans throughout their city prayed as to a god."

And he cut the backs of Hector's heels and put cords of leather through and tied them to his chariot. He lifted in the armor and got in and touched the horses with his whip. Swiftly they started forward. The dust went up round Hector's dark hair outstretched and his head that was so beautiful before; for now Zeus had given him over to be shamefully handled in his own land where he was born.

Andromache, Hector's wife, knew nothing of these things. No one had come to tell her that her husband was still outside the gates. She was working on a great purple cloth in the innermost part of her house, threading into it flowers of many colors. And she told her fair-haired handmaids to put a great vessel, a tripod, on the fire, for a hot bath to be ready for Hector when he came back from the fighting. She did not know that far from all baths Athene had overthrown him by the hand of Achilles. Then she heard loud cries and moans from the wall and she was shaken and the needle fell from her hand. And to her handmaids she said: "Two of you, come with me and let us see what it is. It was Hecuba's voice I heard. I am afraid Achilles may have cut off Hector from the city."

So saying she went quickly out and onto the wall. There she stopped and looked, and saw him as he was dragged before the city. The swift horses were dragging him toward the Greek ships. Then dark night came down on her and she fell backward breathing out her spirit. From her head fell her headdress and the veil that golden Aphrodite had given her on the day that Hector took her as his bride from Eëtion's house after bringing bride gifts unnumbered. Her husband's sisters and his brothers' wives came round her and supported her, for she was near to death in her trouble. Then she breathed again. And she came to herself and lifted up her voice in sorrow among the women of Troy, saying: "Ah, Hector, to one fate we were born, you in Troy in the house of Priam and I in Thebe under wooded Placus in the house of Eëtion, ill-fated father of a cruel-fated child! Would that he had never begotten me. You go now into the house of Hades under earth and you leave me, in bitter sorrow, a widow in your house. And our son is a child. You can do nothing now for him, Hector, nor he for you. If he escapes from this war, still trouble and sorrow will be his, for other men will take your lands. A child is cut off from his friends on the day his father dies; his head is bent low and his face is wet with tears. In his need he goes to his father's friends; he takes one by the coat and pulls at the shirt of another. And of those who are moved with pity, one holds out a small cup to his mouth for a little; his lips he wets but his mouth is not made wet. And some child with a living father and mother pushes him away from the feast with blows saying: 'Out with you! No father of yours is at our table.' Then he goes back in tears to his mother—Astyanax, who ate only marrow and the rich fat of sheep on his father's knee; and when he had played till he was tired, he would sleep in his nurse's arms in a soft bed; but now that he has no father, evil days come on him, my poor Astyanax. The Trojans gave him that name because only you guarded their gates and their long walls. But now by the ships, far from your parents, worms will eat you when the dogs have ended. Naked you will lie, though here in your house are stores of linen, delicate, fair, made by the hands of women. But I will burn all this—no profit to you who will not lie in it—to be honor to you from the men and the women of Troy."

So she said in her sorrowing, and the women joined their cry.

Sappho, To a Bride, Parting, and Mother, I Cannot Mind My Wheel

Sappho (610–580 B.C.) is one of the few women whose writings have survived from antiquity and who can still speak to us today as passionately as she once spoke to her contemporaries. The biographical information we possess about her is scant and unreliable, but it would seem that she was the well-born wife of one Cercolas, an apparently wealthy man, with whom she lived on the island of Lesbos, off the northwest coast of Asia Minor. Along with other young women of her class, Sappho enjoyed a life of culture and leisure, which included the writing of poetry and correspondence with other poets of her time—the poet Alcaeus being the best known among them. She is known to have written several volumes of lyric poetry, but by the early Middle Ages, only a handful of those poems had survived and most of those in fragmentary form.

Sappho's poems express, often with startling directness, the most intimate feelings (of jealousy, anguish, and desire) for the women of her intellectual circle. Apparently, the homoerotic content of some of the nonextant poems was even more obvious than in those that have survived, attesting to a fairly widespread acceptance, throughout the Hellenic world, of bisexual and homosexual behavior. Sappho's evocation of the passions, however, is sufficiently moving to transcend questions of gender identity and sexual orientation. She apparently delighted in tracing the shifting patterns of relationships with friends or members of her own family with a spontaneity that invites the reader to share the poet's changing moods and perceptions.

Her power as a poet derives, however, not only from her emotional candor and intensity, but also from her extraordinary ability to analyze and distance herself from the very feelings she is describing. There is a curiosity at work in these poems that compares favorably with the exploration of the human psyche carried on several generations later by the leading dramatists of the fifth century.

TO A BRIDE

Blest beyond earth's bliss, with heaven I deem him
  Blest, the man that in thy presence near thee
Face to face may sit, and while thou speakest,
  Listening may hear thee,

And thy sweet-voiced laughter:—In my bosom
  The rapt heart so troubleth, wildly stirred:
Let me see thee, but a glimpse—and straightway
  Utterance of word

Fails me; no voice comes; my tongue is palsied;
　　Thrilling fire through all my flesh hath run;
Mine eyes cannot see, mine ears make dinning
　　Noises that stun;

The sweat streameth down,—my whole frame seized with
　　Shivering,—and wan paleness o'er me spread,
Greener than the grass; I seem with faintness
　　Almost as dead.

[2, tr. Walter Headlam]

PARTING
■

　　Truly I want to die.
Such was her weeping when she said Good-bye.

　　These words she said to me:
　　"What sad calamity!
Sappho, I leave you most unwillingly."

　　To her I made reply:
　　"Go with good heart, but try
Not to forget our love in days gone by.

　　Else let me call to mind,
　　If your heart proves unkind,
The soft delightful ways you leave behind.

　　Many a coronet
　　Of rose and violet,
Crocus and dill upon your brow you set:

　　Many a necklace too
　　Round your soft throat you threw,
Woven with me from buds of ravishing hue,

　　And often balm you spread
　　Of myrrh upon my head,
And royal ointment on my hair you shed."

[96, tr. C.M. Bowra]

MOTHER, I CANNOT MIND MY WHEEL
■

Sweet mother, let the weaving be,
　My hand is faint to move.
Frail Aphrodite masters me;
　I long for my young love.

[114, tr. T.F. Higham]

Sophocles, Oedipus Rex

The most popular dramatist of Athens' Golden Age, Sophocles (c. 496–406 B.C.) wrote approximately 123 plays, of which only seven survive. In his most famous work, *Oedipus Rex*, (c. 428 B.C.), Sophocles presents a devastating conflict between human ambition and divine retribution that parallels the experience of his own time. Having grown up amid a generation of heroes who had defeated the Persian armies at Marathon and Salamis, Sophocles knew men who had literally changed the course of world history. He observed his native Athens, which had led the Greeks to victory against superior forces, grow rich and domineering. He also witnessed Athenian imperialism lead to a long and exhausting war with Sparta, a harshly militaristic state that jealously opposed Athens' political power.

Produced a few years after the war between Athens and Sparta began, the play *Oedipus Rex* presents a Greek city–state in crisis, threatened with destruction because its leader unknowingly has defied the gods. Like the heroes of Marathon, Oedipus had once saved his city, but he now is the source of a plague devouring its citizens. The hero finds himself in an impossible situation because of his actions, both past and present. As a youth, he fled his supposed family in Corinth to escape the Delphic prophecy that he is doomed to kill his father and marry his mother, only to fulfill the oracle at Thebes. In Sophocles' view, Oedipus' crime is not merely his committing of murder and incest, but his overconfident attempt to control his own life, to live as if the gods' intentions can be ignored.

Sophocles highlights Oedipus' paradoxical situation through repeated use of dramatic irony, the contrast between the audience's awareness of Oedipus' situation and the ignorance of the main characters. When Oedipus vows to punish unmercifully the person guilty of Laïos' murder, he unwittingly condemns himself. When the opening chorus hails the king as one preeminent in dealing with the gods, the words are doubly ironic. Although Oedipus is a supreme example of one who is controlled by superhuman forces, he does not yet know that his entire life is an object lesson in divine manipulation. Sophocles consistently depicts Oedipus' blindness through eye and sight imagery. Teiresias, Apollo's blind prophet, sees the king's tragic position clearly, whereas Oedipus will not recognize his true predicament until he is literally blinded.

OEDIPUS REX

■

PERSONS REPRESENTED:

OEDIPUS	IOCASTE
A PRIEST	MESSENGER
CREON	SHEPHERD OF LAÏOS
TEIRESIAS	SECOND MESSENGER

CHORUS OF THEBAN ELDERS

The Scene. *Before the palace of Oedipus, King of Thebes.*
A central door and two lateral doors open onto a platform which runs the length of the façade. On the platform, right and left, are altars; and three steps lead down into the 'orchestra', or chorus-ground. At the beginning of the action these steps are crowded by suppliants who have brought branches and chaplets of olive leaves and who lie in various attitudes of despair. OEDIPUS *enters.*

PROLOGUE

OEDIPUS: My children, generations of the living
In the line of Kadmos, nursed at his ancient hearth:
Why have you strewn yourselves before these altars
In supplication, with your boughs and garlands?
The breath of incense rises from the city
With a sound of prayer and lamentation.

                                        Children,
I would not have you speak through messengers,
And therefore I have come myself to hear you—
I, Oedipus, who bear the famous name.

                                        [To a PRIEST:

You, there, since you are eldest in the company,
Speak for them all, tell me what preys upon you,
Whether you come in dread, or crave some blessing:
Tell me, and never doubt that I will help you
In every way I can; I should be heartless
Were I not moved to find you suppliant here.

PRIEST: Great Oedipus, O powerful King of Thebes!
You see how all the ages of our people
Cling to your altar steps: here are boys
Who can barely stand alone, and here are priests
By weight of age, as I am a priest of God,
And young men chosen from those yet unmarried;
As for the others, all that multitude,
They wait with olive chaplets in the squares,
At the two shrines of Pallas, and where Apollo
Speaks in the glowing embers.

                                Your own eyes
Must tell you: Thebes is in her extremity
And can not lift her head from the surge of death.
A rust consumes the buds and fruits of the earth;
The herds are sick; children die unborn,
And labour is vain. The god of plague and pyre
Raids like detestable lightning through the city,
And all the house of Kadmos is laid waste,
All emptied, and all darkened: Death alone
Battens upon the misery of Thebes.

You are not one of the immortal gods, we know;
Yet we have come to you to make our prayer
As to the man of all men best in adversity
And wisest in the ways of God. You saved us
From the Sphinx, that flinty singer, and the tribute
We paid to her so long; yet you were never
Better informed than we, nor could we teach you:
It was some god breathed in you to set us free.

Therefore, O mighty King, we turn to you:
Find us our safety, find us a remedy,
Whether by counsel of the gods or men.
A king of wisdom tested in the past
Can act in a time of troubles, and act well.
Noblest of men, restore
Life to your city! Think how all men call you
Liberator for your triumph long ago;
Ah, when your years of kingship are remembered,
Let them not say *We rose, but later fell*—
Keep the State from going down in the storm!
Once, years ago, with happy augury,
You brought us fortune; be the same again!
No man questions your power to rule the land:
But rule over men, not over a dead city!
Ships are only hulls, citadels are nothing,
When no life moves in the empty passageways.

OEDIPUS: Poor children! You may be sure I know
All that you longed for in your coming here.
I know that you are deathly sick; and yet,
Sick as you are, not one is as sick as I.
Each of you suffers in himself alone
His anguish, not another's; but my spirit
Groans for the city, for myself, for you.

I was not sleeping, you are not waking me.
No, I have been in tears for a long while
And in my restless thought walked many ways.
In all my search, I found one helpful course,
And that I have taken: I have sent Creon,
Son of Menoikeus, brother of the Queen,
To Delphi, Apollo's place of revelation,
To learn there, if he can,
What act or pledge of mine may save the city.
I have counted the days, and now, this very day,
I am troubled, for he has overstayed his time.

What is he doing? He has been gone too long.
Yet whenever he comes back, I should do ill
To scant whatever hint the god may give.

PRIEST: It is a timely promise. At this instant
They tell me Creon is here.

OEDIPUS: O Lord Apollo!
May his news be fair as his face is radiant!

PRIEST: It could not be otherwise: he is crowned with bay,
The chaplet is thick with berries.

OEDIPUS: We shall soon know;
He is near enough to hear us now.

[Enter CREON

                    O Prince:
Brother: son of Menoikeus:
What answer do you bring us from the god?

CREON: It is favourable. I can tell you, great afflictions
Will turn out well, if they are taken well.

OEDIPUS: What was the oracle? These vague words
Leave me still hanging between hope and fear.

CREON: Is it your pleasure to hear me with all these
Gathered around us? I am prepared to speak,
But should we not go in?

OEDIPUS: Let them all hear it.
It is for them I suffer, more than for myself.

CREON: Then I will tell you what I heard at Delphi.

In plain words
The god commands us to expel from the land of Thebes
An old defilement that it seems we shelter.
It is a deathly thing, beyond expiation.
We must not let it feed upon us longer.

OEDIPUS: What defilement? How shall we rid ourselves of it?

CREON: By exile or death, blood for blood. It was
Murder that brought the plague-wind on the city.

OEDIPUS: Murder of whom? Surely the god has named him?

CREON: My lord: long ago Laïos was our king,
Before you came to govern us.

OEDIPUS: I know;
I learned of him from others; I never saw him.

CREON: He was murdered; and Apollo commands us now
To take revenge upon whoever killed him.

OEDIPUS: Upon whom? Where are they? Where shall we find a clue
To solve the crime, after so many years?

CREON: Here in this land.
                          If we make enquiry,
We may touch things that otherwise escape us.

OEDIPUS: Tell me: Was Laïos murdered in his house,
Or in the fields, or in some foreign country?

CREON: He said he planned to make a pilgrimage.
He did not come home again.

OEDIPUS: And was there no one,
No witness, no companion, to tell what happened?

CREON: They were all killed but one, and he got away
So frightened that he could remember one thing only.

OEDIPUS: What was that one thing? One may be the key
To everything, if we resolve to use it.

CREON: He said that a band of highwaymen attacked them,
Outnumbered them, and overwhelmed the King.

OEDIPUS: Strange, that a highwayman should be so daring—
Unless some faction here bribed him to do it.

CREON: We thought of that. But after Laïos' death
New troubles arose and we had no avenger.

OEDIPUS: What troubles could prevent your hunting down the killers?

CREON: The riddling Sphinx's song
Made us deaf to all mysteries but her own.

OEDIPUS: Then once more I must bring what is dark to light.
It is most fitting that Apollo shows,
As you do, this compunction for the dead.
You shall see how I stand by you, as I should,
To avenge the city and the city's god,
And not as though it were for some distant friend,
But for my own sake, to be rid of evil.
Whoever killed King Laïos might—who knows?—
Decide at any moment to kill me as well.
By avenging the murdered king I protect myself.

Come, then, my children: leave the altar steps,
Lift up your olive boughs!

> One of you go
And summon the people of Kadmos to gather here.
I will do all that I can; you may tell them that.

[Exit a **PAGE**

So, with the help of God,
We shall be saved—or else indeed we are lost.

PRIEST: Let us rise, children. It was for this we came,
And now the King has promised it himself.
Phoibos has sent us an oracle; may he descend
Himself to save us and drive out the plague.

[Exeunt **OEDIPUS** *and* **CREON** *into the palace by the central door. The* **PRIEST** *and the* **SUPPLIANTS** *disperse R. and L. After a short pause the* **CHORUS** *enters the orchestra.*

PÁRODOS

[STROPHE I

CHORUS: What is the god singing in his profound
Delphi of gold and shadow?
What oracle for Thebes, the sunwhipped city?

Fear unjoints me, the roots of my heart tremble.

Now I remember, O Healer, your power, and wonder:
Will you send doom like a sudden cloud, or weave it
Like nightfall of the past?

Ah no: be merciful, issue of holy sound:
Dearest to our expectancy: be tender!

[ANTISTROPHE I

Let me pray to Athenê, the immortal daughter of Zeus,
and to Artemis her sister
Who keeps her famous throne in the market ring,

And to Apollo, bowman at the far butts of heaven—

O gods, descend! Like three streams leap against
The fires of our grief, the fires of darkness;
Be swift to bring us rest!

As in the old time from the brilliant house
Of air you stepped to save us, come again!

[STROPHE 2

Now our afflictions have no end,
Now all our stricken host lies down
And no man fights off death with his mind;

The noble plowland bears no grain,
And groaning mothers can not bear—

See, how our lives like birds take wing,
Like sparks that fly when a fire soars,
To the shore of the god of evening.

[ANTISTROPHE 2

The plague burns on, it is pitiless,
Though pallid children laden with death
Lie unwept in the stony ways,

And old grey women by every path
Flock to the strand about the altars

There to strike their breasts and cry
Worship of Zeus in wailing prayers:
Be kind, God's golden child!

[STROPHE 3

There are no swords in this attack by fire,
No shields, but we are ringed with cries.

Send the besieger plunging from our homes
Into the vast sea-room of the Atlantic
Or into the waves that foam eastward of Thrace—

For the day ravages what the night spares—

Destroy our enemy, lord of the thunder!
Let him be riven by lightning from heaven!

[ANTISTROPHE 3

Phoibos Apollo, stretch the sun's bowstring,
That golden cord, until it sing for us,
Flashing arrows in heaven!
        Artemis, Huntress,
Race with flaring lights upon our mountains!

O scarlet god, O golden-banded brow,
O Theban Bacchos in a storm of Maenads,

[Enter OEDIPUS, *C.*

Whirl upon Death, that all the Undying hate!
Come with blinding cressets, come in joy!

SCENE I

OEDIPUS: Is this your prayer? It may be answered. Come,
Listen to me, act as the crisis demands,
And you shall have relief from all these evils.

Until now I was a stranger to this tale,
As I had been a stranger to the crime.
Could I track down the murderer without a clue?
But now, friends,
As one who became a citizen after the murder,
I make this proclamation to all Thebans:

If any man knows by whose hand Laïos, son of Labdakos,
Met his death, I direct that man to tell me everything,
No matter what he fears for having so long withheld it.
Let it stand as promised that no further trouble
Will come to him, but he may leave the land in safety.

Moreover: If anyone knows the murderer to be foreign,
Let him not keep silent: he shall have his reward from me.
However, if he does conceal it; if any man
Fearing for his friend or for himself disobeys this edict,
Hear what I propose to do:

I solemnly forbid the people of this country,
Where power and throne are mine, ever to receive that man
Or speak to him, no matter who he is, or let him
Join in sacrifice, lustration, or in prayer.
I decree that he be driven from every house,
Being, as he is, corruption itself to us: the Delphic
Voice of Zeus has pronounced this revelation.
Thus I associate myself with the oracle
And take the side of the murdered king.

As for the criminal, I pray to God—
Whether it be a lurking thief, or one of a number—
I pray that that man's life be consumed in evil and wretchedness.
And as for me, this curse applies no less
If it should turn out that the culprit is my guest here,

85
▪

Sharing my hearth.
You have heard the penalty.

I lay it on you now to attend to this
For my sake, for Apollo's, for the sick
Sterile city that heaven has abandoned.
Suppose the oracle had given you no command:
Should this defilement go uncleansed for ever?
You should have found the murderer: your king,
A noble king, had been destroyed!
Now I,
Having the power that he held before me,
Having his bed, begetting children there
Upon his wife, as he would have, had he lived—
Their son would have been my children's brother,
If Laïos had had luck in fatherhood!
(But surely ill luck rushed upon his reign)—
I say I take the son's part, just as though
I were his son, to press the fight for him
And see it won! I'll find the hand that brought
Death to Labdakos' and Polydoros' child,
Heir of Kadmos' and Agenor's line.
And as for those who fail me,
May the gods deny them the fruit of the earth,
Fruit of the womb, and may they rot utterly!
Let them be wretched as we are wretched, and worse!

For you, for loyal Thebans, and for all
Who find my actions right, I pray the favour
Of justice, and of all the immortal gods.

CHORAGOS: Since I am under oath, my lord, I swear
I did not do the murder, I can not name
The murderer. Might not the oracle
That has ordained the search tell where to find him?

OEDIPUS: An honest question. But no man in the world
Can make the gods do more than the gods will.

CHORAGOS: There is one last expedient—

OEDIPUS: Tell me what it is.
Though it seem slight, you must not hold it back.

CHORAGOS: A lord clairvoyant to the lord Apollo,
As we all know, is the skilled Teiresias.
One might learn much about this from him, Oedipus.

86

OEDIPUS: I am not wasting time:
Creon spoke of this, and I have sent for him—
Twice, in fact; it is strange that he is not here.

CHORAGOS: The other matter—that old report—seems useless.

OEDIPUS: Tell me. I am interested in all reports.

CHORAGOS: The King was said to have been killed by highwaymen.

OEDIPUS: I know. But we have no witnesses to that.

CHORAGOS: If the killer can feel a particle of dread,
Your curse will bring him out of hiding!

OEDIPUS: No.
The man who dared that act will fear no curse.

> *[Enter the blind seer* TEIRESIAS, *led by a* PAGE

CHORAGOS: But there is one man who may detect the criminal.
This is Teiresias, this is the holy prophet
In whom, alone of all men, truth was born.

OEDIPUS: Teiresias: seer: student of mysteries,
Of all that's taught and all that no man tells,
Secrets of Heaven and secrets of the earth:
Blind though you are, you know the city lies
Sick with plague; and from this plague, my lord,
We find that you alone can guard or save us.

Possibly you did not hear the messengers?
Apollo, when we sent to him,
Sent us back word that this great pestilence
Would lift, but only if we established clearly
The identity of those who murdered Laïos.
They must be killed or exiled.
                              Can you use
Birdflight or any art of divination
To purify yourself, and Thebes, and me
From this contagion? We are in your hands.
There is no fairer duty
Than that of helping others in distress.

TEIRESIAS: How dreadful knowledge of the truth can be
When there's no help in truth! I knew this well,
But did not act on it: else I should not have come.

OEDIPUS: What is troubling you? Why are your eyes so cold?

TEIRESIAS: Let me go home. Bear your own fate, and I'll
Bear mine. It is better so: trust what I say.

87
▪

OEDIPUS: What you say is ungracious and unhelpful
To your native country. Do not refuse to speak.

TEIRESIAS: When it comes to speech, your own is neither temperate
Nor opportune. I wish to be more prudent.

OEDIPUS: In God's name, we all beg you—

TEIRESIAS: You are all ignorant.
No; I will never tell you what I know.
Now it is my misery; then, it would be yours.

OEDIPUS: What! You do know something, and will not tell us?
You would betray us all and wreck the State?

TEIRESIAS: I do not intend to torture myself, or you.
Why persist in asking? You will not persuade me.

OEDIPUS: What a wicked old man you are! You'd try a stone's
Patience! Out with it! Have you no feeling at all?

TEIRESIAS: You call me unfeeling. If you could only see
The nature of your own feelings . . .

OEDIPUS: Why,
Who would not feel as I do? Who could endure
Your arrogance toward the city?

TEIRESIAS: What does it matter!
Whether I speak or not, it is bound to come.

OEDIPUS: Then, if 'it' is bound to come, you are bound to tell me.

TEIRESIAS: No, I will not go on. Rage as you please.

OEDIPUS: Rage? Why not!
                         And I'll tell you what I think:
You planned it, you had it done, you all but
Killed him with your own hands: if you had eyes,
I'd say the crime was yours, and yours alone.

TEIRESIAS: So? I charge you, then,
Abide by the proclamation you have made:
From this day forth
Never speak again to these men or to me;
You yourself are the pollution of this country.

OEDIPUS: You dare say that! Can you possibly think you have
Some way of going free, after such insolence?

TEIRESIAS: I have gone free. It is the truth sustains me.

OEDIPUS: Who taught you shamelessness? It was not your craft.

TEIRESIAS: You did. You made me speak. I did not want to.

OEDIPUS: Speak what? Let me hear it again more clearly.

TEIRESIAS: Was it not clear before? Are you tempting me?

OEDIPUS: I did not understand it. Say it again.

TEIRESIAS: I say that you are the murderer whom you seek.

OEDIPUS: Now twice you have spat out infamy. You'll pay for it!

TEIRESIAS: Would you care for more? Do you wish to be really angry?

OEDIPUS: Say what you will. Whatever you say is worthless.

TEIRESIAS: I say you live in hideous love with her
Who is nearest you in blood. You are blind to the evil.

OEDIPUS: It seems you can go on mouthing like this for ever.

TEIRESIAS: I can, if there is power in truth.

OEDIPUS: There is:
But not for you, not for you,
You sightless, witless, senseless, mad old man!

TEIRESIAS: You are the madman. There is no one here
Who will not curse you soon, as you curse me.

OEDIPUS: You child of endless night! You can not hurt me
Or any other man who sees the sun.

TEIRESIAS: True: it is not from me your fate will come.
That lies within Apollo's competence,
As it is his concern.

OEDIPUS: Tell me:
Are you speaking for Creon, or for yourself?

TEIRESIAS: Creon is no threat. You weave your own doom.

OEDIPUS: Wealth, power, craft of statesmanship!
Kingly position, everywhere admired!
What savage envy is stored up against these,
If Creon, whom I trusted, Creon my friend,
For this great office which the city once
Put in my hands unsought—if for this power
Creon desires in secret to destroy!

He has bought this decrepit fortune-teller, this
Collector of dirty pennies, this prophet fraud—
Why, he is no more clairvoyant than I am!
                              Tell us:

Has your mystic mummery ever approached the truth?
When that hellcat the Sphinx was performing here,
What help were you to these people?
Her magic was not for the first man who came along:
It demanded a real exorcist. Your birds—
What good were they? or the gods, for the matter of that?
But I came by,
Oedipus, the simple man, who knows nothing—
I thought it out for myself, no birds helped me!

And this is the man you think you can destroy,
That you may be close to Creon when he's king!
Well, you and your friend Creon, it seems to me,
Will suffer most. If you were not an old man,
You would have paid already for your plot.

CHORAGOS: We can not see that his words or yours
Have been spoken except in anger, Oedipus,
And of anger we have no need. How can God's will
Be accomplished best? That is what most concerns us.

TEIRESIAS: You are a king. But where argument's concerned
I am your man, as much a king as you.
I am not your servant, but Apollo's.
I have no need of Creon to speak for me.

Listen to me. You mock my blindness, do you?
But I say that you, with both your eyes, are blind:
You can not see the wretchedness of your life,
Nor in whose house you live, no, nor with whom.
Who are your father and mother? Can you tell me?
You do not even know the blind wrongs
That you have done them, on earth and in the world below.
But the double lash of your parents' curse will whip you
Out of this land some day, with only night
Upon your precious eyes.
Your cries then—where will they not be heard?
What fastness of Kithairon will not echo them?
And that bridal-descant of yours—you'll know it then,
The song they sang when you came here to Thebes
And found your misguided berthing.
All this, and more, that you can not guess at now.
Will bring you to yourself among your children.

Be angry, then. Curse Creon. Curse my words.
I tell you, no man that walks upon the earth
Shall be rooted out more horribly than you.

OEDIPUS: Am I to bear this from him?—Damnation
Take you! Out of this place! Out of my sight!

TEIRESIAS: I would not have come at all if you had not asked me.

OEDIPUS: Could I have told that you'd talk nonsense, that
You'd come here to make a fool of yourself, and of me?

TEIRESIAS: A fool? Your parents thought me sane enough.

OEDIPUS: My parents again!—Wait: who were my parents?

TEIRESIAS: This day will give you a father, and break your heart.

OEDIPUS: Your infantile riddles! Your damned abracadabra!

TEIRESIAS: You were a great man once at solving riddles.

OEDIPUS: Mock me with that if you like; you will find it true.

TEIRESIAS: It was true enough. It brought about your ruin.

OEDIPUS: But if it saved this town?

[To the **PAGE**

TEIRESIAS: Boy, give me your hand.

OEDIPUS: Yes, boy; lead him away.
                    —While you are here
We can do nothing. Go; leave us in peace.

TEIRESIAS: I will go when I have said what I have to say.
How can you hurt me? And I tell you again:
The man you have been looking for all this time,
The damned man, the murderer of Laïos,
That man is in Thebes. To your mind he is foreign-born,
But it will soon be shown that he is a Theban,
A revelation that will fail to please.
                    A blind man,
Who has his eyes now; a penniless man, who is rich now;
And he will go tapping the strange earth with his staff.
To the children with whom he lives now he will be
Brother and father—the very same; to her
Who bore him, son and husband—the very same
Who came to his father's bed, wet with his father's blood.

Enough. Go think that over.
If later you find error in what I have said,
You may say that I have no skill in prophecy.

[Exit **TEIRESIAS,** *led by his* **PAGE.** **OEDIPUS** *goes into the palace.*

91
▪

ODE I

[STROPHE 1

CHORUS: The Delphic stone of prophecies
Remembers ancient regicide
And a still bloody hand.
That killer's hour of flight has come.
He must be stronger than riderless
Coursers of untiring wind,
For the son of Zeus armed with his father's thunder
Leaps in lightning after him;
And the Furies follow him, the sad Furies.

[ANTISTROPHE 1

Holy Parnassos' peak of snow
Flashes and blinds that secret man,
That all shall hunt him down:
Though he may roam the forest shade
Like a bull gone wild from pasture
To rage through glooms of stone.
Doom comes down on him; flight will not avail him;
For the world's heart calls him desolate,
And the immortal Furies follow, for ever follow.

[STROPHE 2

But now a wilder thing is heard
From the old man skilled at hearing Fate in the wing-beat of a bird.
Bewildered as a blown bird, my soul hovers and can not find
Foothold in this debate, or any reason or rest of mind.
But no man ever brought—none can bring
Proof of strife between Thebes' royal house,
Labdakos' line, and the son of Polybos;
And never until now has any man brought word
Of Laïos' dark death staining Oedipus the King.

[ANTISTROPHE 2

Divine Zeus and Apollo hold
Perfect intelligence alone of all tales ever told;
And well though this diviner works, he works in his own night;
No man can judge that rough unknown or trust in second sight,
For wisdom changes hands among the wise.
Shall I believe my great lord criminal
At a raging word that a blind old man let fall?
I saw him, when the carrion woman faced him of old,
Prove his heroic mind! These evil words are lies.

92
■

SCENE II

[Enter **CREON**

CREON: Men of Thebes:
I am told that heavy accusations
Have been brought against me by King Oedipus.

I am not the kind of man to bear this tamely.

If in these present difficulties
He holds me accountable for any harm to him
Through anything I have said or done—why, then,
I do not value life in this dishonour.

It is not as though this rumour touched upon
Some private indiscretion. The matter is grave.
The fact is that I am being called disloyal
To the State, to my fellow citizens, to my friends.

CHORAGOS: He may have spoken in anger, not from his mind.

CREON: But did you not hear him say I was the one
Who seduced the old prophet into lying?

CHORAGOS: The thing was said; I do not know how seriously.

CREON: But you were watching him! Were his eyes steady?
Did he look like a man in his right mind?

CHORAGOS: I do not know.
I can not judge the behaviour of great men.
But here is the King himself.

[Enter **OEDIPUS**

OEDIPUS: So you dared come back.
Why? How brazen of you to come to my house,
You murderer!
                   Do you think I do not know
That you plotted to kill me, plotted to steal my throne?
Tell me, in God's name: am I coward, a fool,
That you should dream you could accomplish this?
A fool who could not see your slippery game?
A coward, not to fight back when I saw it?
You are the fool, Creon, are you not? hoping
Without support or friends to get a throne?
Thrones may be won or bought: you could do neither.

CREON: Now listen to me. You have talked; let me talk, too.
You can not judge unless you know the facts.

93
▪

OEDIPUS: You speak well: there is one fact; but I find it hard
to learn from the deadliest enemy I have.

CREON: That above all I must dispute with you.

OEDIPUS: That above all I will not hear you deny.

CREON: If you think there is anything good in being stubborn
Against all reason, then I say you are wrong.

OEDIPUS: If you think a man can sin against his own kind
And not be punished for it, I say you are mad.

CREON: I agree. But tell me: what have I done to you?

OEDIPUS: You advised me to send for that wizard, did you not?

CREON: I did. I should do it again.

OEDIPUS: Very well. Now tell me:
How long has it been since Laïos—

CREON: What of Laïos?

OEDIPUS: Since he vanished in that onset by the road?

CREON: It was long ago, a long time.

OEDIPUS: And this prophet,
Was he practising here then?

CREON: He was; and with honour, as now.

OEDIPUS: Did he speak of me at that time?

CREON: He never did;
At least, not when I was present.

OEDIPUS: But . . . the enquiry?
I suppose you held one?

CREON: We did, but we learned nothing.

OEDIPUS: Why did the prophet not speak against me then?

CREON: I do not know; and I am the kind of man
Who holds his tongue when he has no facts to go on.

OEDIPUS: There's one fact that you know, and you could tell it.

CREON: What fact is that? If I know it, you shall have it.

OEDIPUS: If he were not involved with you, he could not say
That it was I who murdered Laïos.

CREON: If he says that, you are the one that knows it!—
But now it is my turn to question you.

OEDIPUS: Put your questions. I am no murderer.

CREON: First, then: You married my sister?

OEDIPUS: I married your sister.

CREON: And you rule the kingdom equally with her?

OEDIPUS: Everything that she wants she has from me.

CREON: And I am the third, equal to both of you?

OEDIPUS: That is why I call you a bad friend.

CREON: No. Reason it out, as I have done.
Think of this first: Would any sane man prefer
Power, with all a king's anxieties,
To that same power and the grace of sleep?
Certainly not I.
I have never longed for the king's power—only his rights.
Would any wise man differ from me in this?
As matters stand, I have my way in everything
With your consent, and no responsibilities.
If I were king, I should be a slave to policy.

How could I desire a sceptre more
than what is now mine—untroubled influence?
No, I have not gone mad; I need no honours,
Except those with the perquisites I have now.
I am welcome everywhere; every man salutes me,
And those who want your favour seek my ear,
Since I know how to manage what they ask.
Should I exchange this ease for that anxiety?
Besides, no sober mind is treasonable.
I hate anarchy
And never would deal with any man who likes it.

Test what I have said. Go to the priestess
At Delphi, ask if I quoted her correctly.
And as for this other thing: if I am found
Guilty of treason with Teiresias,
Then sentence me to death! You have my word
It is a sentence I should cast my vote for—
But not without evidence!
                         You do wrong
When you take good men for bad, bad men for good.
A true friend thrown aside—why, life itself
Is not more precious!
                         In time you will know this well:

95
▪

For time, and time alone, will show the just man,
Though scoundrels are discovered in a day.

CHORAGOS: This is well said, and a prudent man would ponder it.
Judgments too quickly formed are dangerous.

OEDIPUS: But is he not quick in his duplicity?
And shall I not be quick to parry him?
Would you have me stand still, hold my peace, and let
This man win everything, through my inaction?

CREON: And you want—what is it, then? To banish me?

OEDIPUS: No, not exile. It is your death I want,
So that all the world may see what treason means.

CREON: You will persist, then? You will not believe me?

OEDIPUS: How can I believe you?

CREON: Then you are a fool.

OEDIPUS: To save myself?

CREON: In justice, think of me.

OEDIPUS: You are evil incarnate.

CREON: But suppose that you are wrong?

OEDIPUS: Still I must rule.

CREON: But not if you rule badly.

OEDIPUS: O city, city!

CREON: It is my city, too!

CHORAGOS: Now, my lords, be still. I see the Queen,
Iocastê, coming from her palace chambers;
And it is time she came, for the sake of you both.
This dreadful quarrel can be resolved through her.

[Enter IOCASTE

IOCASTE: Poor foolish men, what wicked din is this?
With Thebes sick to death, is it not shameful
That you should rake some private quarrel up?

[To OEDIPUS

Come into the house.
                    —And you, Creon, go now:
Let us have no more of this tumult over nothing.

CREON: Nothing? No, sister: what your husband plans for me
Is one of two great evils: exile or death.

OEDIPUS: He is right.

               Why, woman I have caught him squarely
Plotting against my life.

CREON: No! Let me die
Accurst if ever I have wished you harm!

IOCASTE: Ah, believe it, Oedipus!
In the name of the gods, respect this oath of his
For my sake, for the sake of these people here!

[STROPHE I

CHORAGOS: Open your mind to her, my lord. Be ruled by her, I beg you!

OEDIPUS: What would you have me do?

CHORAGOS: Respect Creon's word. He has never spoken like a fool,
And now he has sworn an oath.

OEDIPUS: You know what you ask?

CHORAGOS: I do.

OEDIPUS: Speak on, then.

CHORAGOS: A friend so sworn should not be baited so,
In blind malice, and without final proof.

OEDIPUS: You are aware, I hope, that what you say
Means death for me, or exile at the least.

[STROPHE 2

CHORAGOS: No, I swear by Helios, first in Heaven!
   May I die friendless and accurst,
The worst of deaths, if ever I meant that!
     It is the withering fields
        That hurt my sick heart:
    Must we bear all these ills,
        And now your bad blood as well?

OEDIPUS: Then let him go. And let me die, if I must,
Or be driven by him in shame from the land of Thebes,
It is your unhappiness, and not his talk,
That touches me.
           As for him—
Wherever he is, I will hate him as long as I live.

CREON: Ugly in yielding, as you were ugly in rage!
Natures like yours chiefly torment themselves.

OEDIPUS: Can you not go? Can you not leave me?

CREON: I can.
You do not know me; but the city knows me,
And in its eyes I am just, if not in yours.

                                                    [Exit CREON

[ANTISTROPHE 1

CHORAGOS: Lady Iocastê, did you not ask the King to go to his chambers?

IOCASTE: First tell me what has happened.

CHORAGOS: There was suspicion without evidence; yet it rankled
As even false charges will.

IOCASTE: On both sides?

CHORAGOS: On both.

IOCASTE: But what was said?

CHORAGOS: Oh let it rest, let it be done with!
Have we not suffered enough?

OEDIPUS: You see to what your decency has brought you:
You have made difficulties where my heart saw none.

[ANTISTROPHE 2

CHORAGOS: Oedipus, it is not once only I have told you—
    You must know I should count myself unwise
To the point of madness, should I now forsake you—
        You, under whose hand,
            In the storm of another time,
        Our dear land sailed out free.
            But now stand fast at the helm!

IOCASTE: In God's name, Oedipus, inform your wife as well:
Why are you so set in this hard anger?

OEDIPUS: I will tell you, for none of these men deserves
My confidence as you do. It is Creon's work,
His treachery, his plotting against me.

IOCASTE: Go on, if you can make this clear to me.

OEDIPUS: He charges me with the murder of Laïos.

IOCASTE: Has he some knowledge? Or does he speak from hearsay?

OEDIPUS: He would not commit himself to such a charge,
But he has brought in that damnable soothsayer
To tell his story.

IOCASTE: Set your mind at rest.
If it is a question of soothsayers, I tell you
That you will find no man whose craft gives knowledge
Of the unknowable.

    Here is my proof:

An oracle was reported to Laïos once
(I will not say from Phoibos himself, but from
His appointed ministers, at any rate)
That his doom would be death at the hands of his own son—
His son, born of his flesh and of mine!

Now, you remember the story: Laïos was killed
By marauding strangers where three highways meet;
But his child had not been three days in this world
Before the King had pierced the baby's ankles
And had him left to die on a lonely mountain.

Thus, Apollo never caused that child
To kill his father, and it was not Laïos' fate
To die at the hands of his son, as he had feared.
This is what prophets and prophecies are worth!
Have no dread of them.
            It is God himself
Who can show us what he wills, in his own way.

OEDIPUS: How strange a shadowy memory crossed my mind,
Just now while you were speaking; it chilled my heart.

IOCASTE: What do you mean? What memory do you speak of?

OEDIPUS: If I understand you, Laïos was killed
At a place where three roads meet.

IOCASTE: So it was said;
We have no later story.

OEDIPUS: Where did it happen?

IOCASTE: Phokis, it is called: at a place where the Theban Way
Divides into the roads toward Delphi and Daulia.

OEDIPUS: When?

IOCASTE: We had the news not long before you came
And proved the right to your succession here.

OEDIPUS: Ah, what net has God been weaving for me?

IOCASTE: Oedipus! Why does this trouble you?

99
▪

OEDIPUS: Do not ask me yet.
First, tell me how Laïos looked, and tell me
How old he was.

IOCASTE: He was tall, his hair just touched
With white; his form was not unlike your own.

OEDIPUS: I think that I myself may be accurst
By my own ignorant edict.

IOCASTE: You speak strangely.
It makes me tremble to look at you, my King.

OEDIPUS: I am not sure if the blind man can not see.
But I should know better if you were to tell me—

IOCASTE: Anything—though I dread to hear you ask it.

OEDIPUS: Was the King lightly escorted, or did he ride
With a large company, as a ruler should?

IOCASTE: There were five men with him in all: one was a herald;
And a single chariot, which he was driving.

OEDIPUS: Alas, that makes it plain enough!
                                        But who—
Who told you how it happened?

IOCASTE: A household servant,
The only one to escape.

OEDIPUS: And is he still
A servant of ours?

IOCASTE: No; for when he came back at last
And found you enthroned in the place of the dead king,
He came to me, touched my hand with his, and begged
That I would send him away to the frontier district
Where only the shepherds go—
As far away from the city as I could send him.
I granted his prayer; for although the man was a slave,
He had earned more than this favour at my hands.

OEDIPUS: Can he be called back quickly?

IOCASTE: Easily.
But why?

OEDIPUS: I have taken too much upon myself
Without enquiry; therefore I wish to consult him.

IOCASTE: Then he shall come.

But am I not one also
To whom you might confide these fears of yours?

OEDIPUS: That is your right; it will not be denied you,
Now least of all; for I have reached a pitch
Of wild foreboding. Is there anyone
To whom I should sooner speak?

Polybos of Corinth is my father.
My mother is a Dorian: Meropê.
I grew up chief among the men of Corinth
Until a strange thing happened—
Not worth my passion, it may be, but strange.

At a feast, a drunken man maundering in his cups
Cries out that I am not my father's son!

I contained myself that night, though I felt anger
And a sinking heart. The next day I visited
My father and mother, and questioned them. They stormed,
Calling it all the slanderous rant of a fool;
And this relieved me. Yet the suspicion
Remained always aching in my mind;
I knew there was talk; I could not rest;
And finally, saying nothing to my parents,
I went to the shrine at Delphi.

The god dismissed my question without reply;
He spoke of other things.

Some were clear,
Full of wretchedness, dreadful, unbearable:
As, that I should lie with my own mother, breed
Children from whom all men would turn their eyes;
And that I should be my father's murderer.

I heard all this, and fled. And from that day
Corinth to me was only in the stars
Descending in that quarter of the sky,
As I wandered farther and farther on my way
To a land where I should never see the evil
Sung by the oracle. And I came to this country
Where, so you say, King Laïos was killed.

101
▪

I will tell you all that happened there, my lady.

There were three highways
Coming together at a place I passed;
And there a herald came towards me, and a chariot
Drawn by horses, with a man such as you describe
Seated in it. The groom leading the horses
Forced me off the road at his lord's command;
But as this charioteer lurched over towards me
I struck him in my rage. The old man saw me
And brought his double goad down upon my head
As I came abreast.
     He was paid back, and more!
Swinging my club in this right hand I knocked him
Out of his car, and he rolled on the ground.
        I killed him.

I killed them all.
Now if that stranger and Laïos were—kin,
Where is a man more miserable than I?
More hated by the gods? Citizen and alien alike
Must never shelter me or speak to me—
I must be shunned by all.
     And I myself
Pronounced this malediction upon myself!

Think of it: I have touched you with these hands,
These hands that killed your husband. What defilement!

Am I all evil, then? It must be so,
Since I must flee from Thebes, yet never again
See my own countrymen, my own country,
For fear of joining my mother in marriage
And killing Polybos, my father.
       Ah,
If I was created so, born to this fate,
Who could deny the savagery of God?

O holy majesty of heavenly powers!
May I never see that day! Never!
Rather let me vanish from the race of men
Than know the abomination destined me!

CHORAGOS: We too, my lord, have felt dismay at this.
But there is hope: you have yet to hear the shepherd.

OEDIPUS: Indeed, I fear no other hope is left me.

102

IOCASTE: What do you hope from him when he comes?

OEDIPUS: This much:
If his account of the murder tallies with yours,
Then I am cleared.

IOCASTE: What was it that I said
Of such importance?

OEDIPUS: Why, 'marauders', you said,
Killed the King, according to this man's story.
If he maintains that still, if there were several,
Clearly the guilt is not mine: I was alone.
But if he says one man, singlehanded, did it,
Then the evidence all points to me.

IOCASTE: You may be sure that he said there were several;
And can he call back that story now? He cán not.
The whole city heard it as plainly as I.
But suppose he alters some detail of it:
He can not ever show that Laïos' death
Fulfilled the oracle: for Apollo said
My child was doomed to kill him; and my child—
Poor baby!—it was my child that died first.

No. From now on, where oracles are concerned,
I would not waste a second thought on any.

OEDIPUS: You may be right.
                    But come: let someone go
For the shepherd at once. This matter must be settled.

IOCASTE: I will send for him.
I would not wish to cross you in anything.
And surely not in this.—Let us go in.

[Exeunt into the palace

ODE II

[STROPHE I

CHORUS: Let me be reverent in the ways of right,
Lowly the paths I journey on;
Let all my words and actions keep
The laws of the pure universe
From highest Heaven handed down.
For Heaven is their bright nurse,

Those generations of the realms of light;
Ah, never of mortal kind were they begot,
Nor are they slaves of memory, lost in sleep:
Their Father is greater than Time, and ages not.

[ANTISTROPHE 1

The tyrant is a child of Pride
Who drinks from his great sickening cup
Recklessness and vanity,
Until from his high crest headlong
He plummets to the dust of hope.
That strong man is not strong.
But let no fair ambition be denied;
May God protect the wrestler for the State
In government, in comely policy,
Who will fear God, and on His ordinance wait.

[STROPHE 2

Haughtiness and the high hand of disdain
Tempt and outrage God's holy law;
And any mortal who dares hold
No immortal Power in awe
Will be caught up in a net of pain:
The price for which his levity is sold.
Let each man take due earnings, then,
And keep his hands from holy things,
And from blasphemy stand apart—
Else the crackling blast of heaven
Blows on his head, and on his desperate heart;
Though fools will honour impious men,
In their cities no tragic poet sings.

[ANTISTROPHE 2

Shall we lose faith in Delphi's obscurities,
We who have heard the world's core
Discredited, and the sacred wood
Of Zeus at Elis praised no more?
The deeds and the strange prophecies
Must make a pattern yet to be understood.
Zeus, if indeed you are lord of all,
Throned in light over night and day,
Mirror this in your endless mind:
Our masters call the oracle
Words on the wind, and the Delphic vision blind!

Their hearts no longer know Apollo,
And reverence for the gods has died away.

SCENE III

[Enter IOCASTE

IOCASTE: Princes of Thebes, it has occurred to me
To visit the altars of the gods, bearing
These branches as a suppliant, and this incense.
Our King is not himself: his noble soul
Is overwrought with fantasies of dread,
Else he would consider
The new prophecies in the light of the old.
He will listen to any voice that speaks disaster,
And my advice goes for nothing.

[She approaches the altar, R.

To you, then, Apollo,
Lycean lord, since you are nearest, I turn in prayer.

Receive these offerings, and grant us deliverance
From defilement. Our hearts are heavy with fear
When we see our leader distracted, as helpless sailors
Are terrified by the confusion of their helmsman.

[Enter MESSENGER

MESSENGER: Friends, no doubt you can direct me:
Where shall I find the house of Oedipus,
Or, better still, where is the King himself?

CHORAGOS: It is this very place, stranger; he is inside.
This is his wife and mother of his children.

MESSENGER: I wish her happiness in a happy house,
Blest in all the fulfillment of her marriage.

IOCASTE: I wish as much for you: your courtesy
Deserves a like good fortune. But now, tell me:
Why have you come? What have you to say to us?

MESSENGER: Good news, my lady, for your house and your husband.

IOCASTE: What news? Who sent you here?

MESSENGER: I am from Corinth.
The news I bring ought to mean joy for you,
Though it may be you will find some grief in it.

IOCASTE: What is it? How can it touch us in both ways?

MESSENGER: The people of Corinth, they say,
Intend to call Oedipus to be their king.

IOCASTE: But old Polybos—is he not reigning still?

MESSENGER: No. Death holds him in his sepulchre.

IOCASTE: What are you saying? Polybos is dead?

MESSENGER: If I am not telling the truth, may I die myself.

[To a MAIDSERVANT:

IOCASTE: Go in, go quickly; tell this to your master.

O riddlers of God's will, where are you now!
This was the man whom Oedipus, long ago,
Feared so, fled so, in dread of destroying him—
But it was another fate by which he died.

[Enter OEDIPUS, C.

OEDIPUS: Dearest Iocastê, why have you sent for me?

IOCASTE: Listen to what this man says, and then tell me
What has become of the solemn prophecies.

OEDIPUS: Who is this man? What is his news for me?

IOCASTE: He has come from Corinth to announce your father's death!

OEDIPUS: Is it true, stranger? Tell me in your own words.

MESSENGER: I can not say it more clearly: the King is dead.

OEDIPUS: Was it by treason? Or by an attack of illness?

MESSENGER: A little thing brings old men to their rest.

OEDIPUS: It was sickness, then?

MESSENGER: Yes, and his many years.

OEDIPUS: Ah!
Why should a man respect the Pythian hearth, or
Give heed to the birds that jangle above his head?
They prophesied that I should kill Polybos,
Kill my own father; but he is dead and buried,
And I am here—I never touched him, never,
Unless, he died of grief for my departure,
And thus, in a sense, through me. No. Polybos
Has packed the oracles off with him underground.
They are empty words.

IOCASTE: Had I not told you so?

OEDIPUS: You had; it was my faint heart that betrayed me.

IOCASTE: From now on never think of those things again.

OEDIPUS: And yet—must I not fear my mother's bed?

IOCASTE: Why should anyone in this world be afraid,
Since Fate rules us and nothing can be foreseen?
A man should live only for the present day.

Have no more fear of sleeping with your mother:
How many men, in dreams, have lain with their mothers!
No reasonable man is troubled by such things.

OEDIPUS: This is true; only—
If only my mother were not still alive!
But she is alive. I can not help my dread.

IOCASTE: Yet this news of your father's death is wonderful.

OEDIPUS: Wonderful. But I fear the living woman.

MESSENGER: Tell me, who is this woman that you fear?

OEDIPUS: It is Meropê, man; the wife of King Polybos.

MESSENGER: Meropê? Why should you be afraid of her?

OEDIPUS: An oracle of the gods, a dreadful saying.

MESSENGER: Can you tell me about it? or are you sworn to silence?

OEDIPUS: I can tell you, and I will.
Apollo said through his prophet that I was the man
Who should marry his own mother, shed his father's blood
With his own hands. And so, for all these years
I have kept clear of Corinth, and no harm has come—
Though it would have been sweet to see my parents again.

MESSENGER: And is this the fear that drove you out of Corinth?

OEDIPUS: Would you have me kill my father?

MESSENGER: As for that
You must be reassured by the news I gave you.

OEDIPUS: If you could reassure me, I would reward you.

MESSENGER: I had that in mind, I will confess: I thought
I could count on you when you returned to Corinth.

OEDIPUS: No: I will never go near my parents again.

MESSENGER: Ah, son, you still do not know what you are doing—

OEDIPUS: What do you mean? In the name of God tell me!

MESSENGER: —If these are your reasons for not going home.

OEDIPUS: I tell you, I fear the oracle may come true.

MESSENGER: And guilt may come upon you through your parents?

OEDIPUS: That is the dread that is always in my heart.

MESSENGER: Can you not see that all your fears are groundless?

OEDIPUS: How can you say that? They are my parents, surely?

MESSENGER: Polybos was not your father.

OEDIPUS: Not my father?

MESSENGER: No more your father than the man speaking to you.

OEDIPUS: But you are nothing to me!

MESSENGER: Neither was he.

OEDIPUS: Then why did he call me son?

MESSENGER: I will tell you:
Long ago he had you from my hands, as a gift.

OEDIPUS: Then how could he love me so, if I was not his?

MESSENGER: He had no children, and his heart turned to you.

OEDIPUS: What of you? Did you buy me? Did you find me by chance?

MESSENGER: I came upon you in the crooked pass of Kithairon.

OEDIPUS: And what were you doing there?

MESSENGER: Tending my flocks.

OEDIPUS: A wandering shepherd?

MESSENGER: But your saviour, son, that day.

OEDIPUS: From what did you save me?

MESSENGER: Your ankles should tell you that.

OEDIPUS: Ah, stranger, why do you speak of that childhood pain?

MESSENGER: I cut the bonds that tied your ankles together.

OEDIPUS: I have had the mark as long as I can remember.

MESSENGER: That was why you were given the name you bear.

OEDIPUS: God! Was it my father or my mother who did it?
Tell me!

MESSENGER: I do not know. The man who gave you to me
Can tell you better than I.

OEDIPUS: It was not you that found me, but another?

MESSENGER: It was another shepherd gave you to me.

OEDIPUS: Who was he? Can you tell me who he was?

MESSENGER: I think he was said to be one of Laïos' people.

OEDIPUS: You mean the Laïos who was king here years ago?

MESSENGER: Yes; King Laïos; and the man was one of his herdsmen.

OEDIPUS: Is he still alive? Can I see him?

MESSENGER: These men here
Know best about such things.

OEDIPUS: Does anyone here
Know this shepherd that he is talking about?
Have you seen him in the fields, or in the town?
If you have, tell me. It is time things were made plain.

CHORAGOS: I think the man he means is that same shepherd
You have already asked to see. Iocastê perhaps
Could tell you something.

OEDIPUS: Do you know anything
About him, Lady? Is he the man we have summoned?
Is that the man this shepherd means?

IOCASTE: Why think of him?
Forget this herdsman. Forget it all.
This talk is a waste of time.

OEDIPUS: How can you say that,
When the clues to my true birth are in my hands?

IOCASTE: For God's love, let us have no more questioning!
Is your life nothing to you?
My own is pain enough for me to bear.

OEDIPUS: You need not worry. Suppose my mother is a slave,
And born of slaves: no baseness can touch you.

IOCASTE: Listen to me, I beg you: do not do this thing!

OEDIPUS: I will not listen; the truth must be made known.

IOCASTE: Everything that I say is for your own good!

OEDIPUS: My own good
Snaps my patience, then; I want none of it.

IOCASTE: You are fatally wrong! May you never learn who you are!

OEDIPUS: Go, one of you, and bring the shepherd here.
Let us leave this woman to brag of her royal name.

IOCASTE: Ah, miserable!
That is the only word I have for you now.
That is the only word I can ever have.

[Exit into the palace

CHORAGOS: Why has she left us, Oedipus? Why has she gone
In such a passion of sorrow? I fear this silence:
Something dreadful may come of it.

OEDIPUS: Let it come!
However base my birth, I must know about it.
The Queen, like a woman, is perhaps ashamed
To think of my low origin. But I
Am a child of Luck; I can not be dishonoured.
Luck is my mother; the passing months, my brothers,
Have seen me rich and poor.
                              If this is so,
How could I wish that I were someone else?
How could I not be glad to know my birth?

ODE III

[STROPHE

CHORUS: If ever the coming time were known
To my heart's pondering,
Kithairon, now by Heaven I see the torches
At the festival of the next full moon,
And see the dance, and hear the choir sing
A grace to your gentle shade:
Mountain where Oedipus was found,
O mountain guard of a noble race!
May the god who heals us lend his aid,
And let that glory come to pass
For our king's cradling-ground.

[ANTISTROPHE

Of the nymphs that flower beyond the years,
Who bore you, royal child,
To Pan of the hills or the timberline Apollo,
Cold in delight where the upland clears,
Or Hermês for whom Kyllenê's heights are piled?
Or flushed as evening cloud,
Great Dionysos, roamer of mountains,
He—was it he who found you there,
And caught you up in his own proud
Arms from the sweet god-ravisher
Who laughed by the Muses' fountains?

SCENE IV

OEDIPUS: Sirs: though I do not know the man,
I think I see him coming, this shepherd we want:
He is old, like our friend here, and the men
Bringing him seem to be servants of my house.
But you can tell, if you have ever seen him.

[Enter SHEPHERD *escorted by servants*

CHORAGOS: I know him, he was Laïos' man. You can trust him.

OEDIPUS: Tell me first, you from Corinth: is this the shepherd
We were discussing?

MESSENGER: This is the very man.

[To SHEPHERD:

OEDIPUS: Come here. No, look at me. You must answer
Everything I ask.—You belonged to Laïos?

SHEPHERD: Yes: born his slave, brought up in his house.

OEDIPUS: Tell me: what kind of work did you do for him?

SHEPHERD: I was a shepherd of his, most of my life.

OEDIPUS: Where mainly did you go for pasturage?

SHEPHERD: Sometimes Kithairon, sometimes the hills near-by.

OEDIPUS: Do you remember ever seeing this man out there?

SHEPHERD: What would he be doing there? This man?

OEDIPUS: This man standing here. Have you ever seen him before?

SHEPHERD: No. At least, not to my recollection.

MESSENGER: And that is not strange, my lord. But I'll refresh
His memory: he must remember when we two
Spent three whole seasons together, March to September,
On Kithairon or thereabouts. He had two flocks;
I had one. Each autumn I'd drive mine home
And he would go back with his to Laïos' sheepfold.—
Is this not true, just as I have described it?

SHEPHERD: True, yes; but it was all so long ago.

MESSENGER: Well, then: do you remember, back in those days,
That you gave me a baby boy to bring up as my own?

SHEPHERD: What if I did? What are you trying to say?

MESSENGER: King Oedipus was once that little child.

SHEPHERD: Damn you, hold your tongue!

OEDIPUS: No more of that!
It is your tongue needs watching, not this man's.

SHEPHERD: My King, my Master, what is it I have done wrong?

OEDIPUS: You have not answered his question about the boy.

SHEPHERD: He does not know . . . He is only making trouble . . .

OEDIPUS: Come, speak plainly, or it will go hard with you.

SHEPHERD: In God's name, do not torture an old man!

OEDIPUS: Come here, one of you; bind his arms behind him.

SHEPHERD: Unhappy king! What more do you wish to learn?

OEDIPUS: Did you give this man the child he speaks of?

SHEPHERD: I did,
And I would to God I had died that very day.

OEDIPUS: You will die now unless you speak the truth.

SHEPHERD: Yet if I speak the truth, I am worse than dead.

OEDIPUS: Very well; since you insist upon delaying—

SHEPHERD: No! I have told you already that I gave him the boy.

OEDIPUS: Where did you get him? From your house? From somewhere else?

SHEPHERD: Not from mine, no. A man gave him to me.

OEDIPUS: Is that man here? Do you know whose slave he was?

SHEPHERD: For God's love, my King, do not ask me any more!

OEDIPUS: You are a dead man if I have to ask you again.

SHEPHERD: Then . . . Then the child was from the palace of Laïos.

OEDIPUS: A slave child? or a child of his own line?

SHEPHERD: Ah, I am on the brink of dreadful speech!

OEDIPUS: And I of dreadful hearing. Yet I must hear.

SHEPHERD: If you must be told, then . . .
They said it was Laïos' child;
But it is your wife who can tell you about that.

OEDIPUS: My wife!—Did she give it to you?

SHEPHERD: My lord, she did.

OEDIPUS: Do you know why?

SHEPHERD: I was told to get rid of it.

OEDIPUS: An unspeakable mother!

SHEPHERD: There had been prophecies . . .

OEDIPUS: Tell me.

SHEPHERD: It was said that the boy would kill his own father.

OEDIPUS: Then why did you give him over to this old man?

SHEPHERD: I pitied the baby, my King,
And I thought that this man would take him far away
To his own country.
                                He saved him—but for what a fate!
For if you are what this man says you are,
No man living is more wretched than Oedipus.

OEDIPUS: Ah God!
It was true
            All the prophecies!
                        —Now,
O Light, may I look on you for the last time!
I, Oedipus,
Oedipus, damned in his birth, in his marriage damned,
Damned in the blood he shed with his own hand!

                                [He rushes into the palace

ODE IV

[STROPHE 1

CHORUS: Alas for the seed of men.
What measure shall I give these generations
That breathe on the void and are void
And exist and do not exist?

Who bears more weight of joy
Than mass of sunlight shifting in images,
Or who shall make his thought stay on
That down time drifts away?

Your splendour is all fallen.

O naked brow of wrath and tears,
O change of Oedipus!
I who saw your days call no man blest—
Your great days like ghósts góne.

That mind was a strong bow.

[ANTISTROPHE 1

Deep, how deep you drew it then, hard archer,
At a dim fearful range,
And brought dear glory down!

You overcame the stranger—
The virgin with her hooking lion claws—
And though death sang, stood like a tower
To make pale Thebes take heart.

Fortress against our sorrow!

Divine king, giver of laws,
Majestic Oedipus!
No prince in Thebes had ever such renown,
No prince won such grace of power.

[STROPHE 2

And now of all men ever known
Most pitiful is this man's story:
His fortunes are most changed, his state
Fallen to a low slave's
Ground under bitter fate.

O Oedipus, most royal one!
The great door that expelled you to the light
Gave at night—ah, gave night to your glory:
As to the father, to the fathering son.

All understood too late.

How could that queen whom Laïos won,
The garden that he harrowed at his height,
Be silent when that act was done?

[ANTISTROPHE 2

But all eyes fail before time's eye,
All actions come to justice there.
Though never willed, though far down the deep past,
Your bed, your dread sirings,
Are brought to book at last.

Child by Laïos doomed to die,
Then doomed to lose that fortunate little death,

114

Would God you never took breath in this air
That with my wailing lips I take to cry:

For I weep the world's outcast.

Blind I was, and can not tell why;
Asleep, for you had given ease of breath;
A fool, while the false years went by.

ÉXODUS

[Enter, from the palace, SECOND MESSENGER

SECOND MESSENGER: Elders of Thebes, most honoured in this land,
What horrors are yours to see and hear, what weight
Of sorrow to be endured, if, true to your birth,
You venerate the line of Labdakos!
I think neither Istros nor Phasis, those great rivers,
Could purify this place of the corruption
It shelters now, or soon must bring to light—
Evil not done unconsciously, but willed.

The greatest griefs are those we cause ourselves,

CHORAGOS: Surely, friend, we have grief enough already;
What new sorrow do you mean?

SECOND MESSENGER: The Queen is dead.

CHORAGOS: Iocastê? Dead? But at whose hand?

SECOND MESSENGER: Her own.
The full horror of what happened you can not know,
For you did not see it; but I, who did, will tell you
As clearly as I can how she met her death.

When she had left us,
In passionate silence, passing through the court,
She ran to her apartment in the house,
Her hair clutched by the fingers of both hands.
She closed the doors behind her; then, by that bed
Where long ago the fatal son was conceived—
That son who should bring about his father's death—
We heard her call upon Laïos, dead so many years,
And heard her wail for the double fruit of her marriage,
A husband by her husband, children by her child.

Exactly how she died I do not know:
For Oedipus burst in moaning and would not let us

Keep vigil to the end: it was by him
As he stormed about the room that our eyes were caught.
From one to another of us he went, begging a sword,
Cursing the wife who was not his wife, the mother
Whose womb had carried his own children and himself.
I do not know: it was none of us aided him,
But surely one of the gods was in control!
For with a dreadful cry
He hurled his weight, as though wrenched out of himself,
At the twin doors: the bolts gave, and he rushed in.
And there we saw her hanging, her body swaying
From the cruel cord she had noosed about her neck.
A great sob broke from him, heartbreaking to hear,
As he loosed the rope and lowered her to the ground.

I would blot out from my mind what happened next!
For the King ripped from her gown the golden brooches
That were her ornament, and raised them, and plunged them down
Straight into his own eyeballs, crying, 'No more,
'No more shall you look on the misery about me,
'The horrors of my own doing! Too long you have known
'The faces of those whom I should never have seen,
'Too long been blind to those for whom I was searching!
'From this hour, go in darkness!' And as he spoke,
He struck at his eyes—not once, but many times;
And the blood spattered his beard,
Bursting from his ruined sockets like red hail.

So from the unhappiness of two this evil has sprung,
A curse on the man and woman alike. The old
Happiness of the house of Labdakos
Was happiness enough: where is it today?
It is all wailing and ruin, disgrace, death—all
The misery of mankind that has a name—
And it is wholly and for ever theirs.

CHORAGOS: Is he in agony still? Is there no rest for him?

SECOND MESSENGER: He is calling for someone to lead him to the gates
So that all the children of Kadmos may look upon
His father's murderer, his mother's—no,
I can not say it!
        And then he will leave Thebes,
Self-exiled, in order that the curse
Which he himself pronounced may depart from the house.
He is weak, and there is none to lead him,
So terrible is his suffering.

But you will see:
Look, the doors are opening; in a moment
You will see a thing that would crush a heart of stone.

[The central door is opened; OEDIPUS, *blinded, is led in*

CHORAGOS: Dreadful indeed for men to see.
Never have my own eyes
Looked on a sight so full of fear.

Oedipus!
What madness came upon you, what daemon
Leaped on your life with heavier
Punishment than a mortal man can bear?
No: I can not even
Look at you, poor ruined one.
And I would speak, question, ponder,
If I were able. No.
You make me shudder.

OEDIPUS: God. God.
Is there a sorrow greater?
Where shall I find harbour in this world?
My voice is hurled far on a dark wind.
What has God done to me?

CHORAGOS: Too terrible to think of, or to see.

[STROPHE I

OEDIPUS: O cloud of night,
Never to be turned away: night coming on,
I can not tell how: night like a shroud!

My fair winds brought me here.
                                    O God. Again
The pain of the spikes where I had sight,
The flooding pain
Of memory, never to be gouged out.

CHORAGOS: This is not strange.
You suffer it all twice over, remorse in pain,
Pain in remorse.

[ANTISTROPHE I

OEDIPUS: Ah dear friend
Are you faithful even yet, you alone?
Are you still standing near me, will you stay here,
Patient, to care for the blind?

The blind man!
Yet even blind I know who it is attends me,
By the voice's tone—
Though my new darkness hide the comforter.

CHORAGOS: Oh fearful act!
What god was it drove you to rake black
Night across your eyes?

[STROPHE 2

OEDIPUS: Apollo. Apollo. Dear
Children, the god was Apollo.
He brought my sick, sick fate upon me.
But the blinding hand was my own!
How could I bear to see
When all my sight was horror everywhere?

CHORAGOS: Everywhere; that is true.

OEDIPUS: And now what is left?
Images? Love? A greeting even,
Sweet to the senses? Is there anything?
Ah, no, friends: lead me away.
Lead me away from Thebes.
                                    Lead the great wreck
And hell of Oedipus, whom the gods hate.

CHORAGOS: Your fate is clear, you are not blind to that.
Would God you had never found it out!

[ANTISTROPHE 2

OEDIPUS: Death take the man who unbound
My feet on that hillside
And delivered me from death to life! What life?
If only I had died,
This weight of monstrous doom
Could not have dragged me and my darlings down.

CHORAGOS: I would have wished the same.

OEDIPUS: Oh never to have come here
With my father's blood upon me! Never
To have been the man they call his mother's husband!
Oh accurst! Oh child of evil,
To have entered that wretched bed—
                                    the selfsame one!
More primal than sin itself, this fell to me.

118
•

CHORAGOS: I do not know how I can answer you.
You were better dead than alive and blind.

OEDIPUS: Do not counsel me any more. This punishment
That I have laid upon myself is just.
If I had eyes,
I do not know how I could bear the sight
Of my father, when I came to the house of Death,
Or my mother: for I have sinned against them both
So vilely that I could not make my peace
By strangling my own life.
                Or do you think my children,
Born as they were born, would be sweet to my eyes?
Ah never, never! Nor this town with its high walls,
Nor the holy images of the gods.
             For I,
Thrice miserable!—Oedipus, noblest of all the line
Of Kadmos, have condemned myself to enjoy
These things no more, by my own malediction
Expelling that man whom the gods declared
To be a defilement in the house of Laïos.
After exposing the rankness of my own guilt,
How could I look men frankly in the eyes?
No, I swear it,
If I could have stifled my hearing at its source,
I would have done it and made all this body
A tight cell of misery, blank to light and sound:
So I should have been safe in a dark agony
Beyond all recollection.
           Ah Kithairon!
Why did you shelter me? When I was cast upon you,
Why did I not die? Then I should never
Have shown the world my execrable birth.

Ah Polybos! Corinth, city that I believed
The ancient seat of my ancestors: how fair
I seemed, your child! And all the while this evil
Was cancerous within me!
           For I am sick
In my daily life, sick in my origin.

O three roads, dark ravine, woodland and way
Where three roads met: you, drinking my father's blood,
My own blood, spilled by my own hand: can you remember
The unspeakable things I did there, and the things
I went on from there to do?

O marriage, marriage!
The act that engendered me, and again the act
Performed by the son in the same bed—
                                        Ah, the net
Of incest, mingling fathers, brothers, sons,
With brides, wives, mothers: the last evil
That can be known by men: no tongue can say
How evil!
            No. For the love of God, conceal me
Somewhere far from Thebes; or kill me; or hurl me
Into the sea, away from men's eyes for ever.

Come, lead me. You need not fear to touch me.
Of all men, I alone can bear this guilt.

[Enter **CREON**

CHORAGOS: We are not the ones to decide; but Creon here
May fitly judge of what you ask. He only
Is left to protect the city in your place.

OEDIPUS: Alas, how can I speak to him? What right have I
To beg his courtesy whom I have deeply wronged?

CREON: I have not come to mock you, Oedipus,
Or to reproach you, either.

[To **ATTENDANTS:**

                            —You, standing there:
If you have lost all respect for man's dignity,
At least respect the flame of Lord Helios:
Do not allow this pollution to show itself
Openly here, an affront to the earth
And Heaven's rain and the light of day. No, take him
Into the house as quickly as you can.
For it is proper
That only the close kindred see his grief.

OEDIPUS: I pray you in God's name, since your courtesy
Ignores my dark expectation, visiting
With mercy this man of all men most execrable:
Give me what I ask—for your good, not for mine.

CREON: And what is it that you would have me do?

OEDIPUS: Drive me out of this country as quickly as may be
To a place where no human voice can ever greet me.

CREON: I should have done that before now—only,
God's will had not been wholly revealed to me.

OEDIPUS: But his command is plain: the parricide
Must be destroyed. I am that evil man.

CREON: That is the sense of it, yes; but as things are,
We had best discover clearly what is to be done.

OEDIPUS: You would learn more about a man like me?

CREON: You are ready now to listen to the god.

OEDIPUS: I will listen. But it is to you
That I must turn for help. I beg you, hear me.

The woman in there—
Give her whatever funeral you think proper:
She is your sister.
                    —But let me go, Creon!
Let me purge my father's Thebes of the pollution
Of my living here, and go out to the wild hills,
To Kithairon, that has won such fame with me,
The tomb my mother and father appointed for me,
And let me die there, as they willed I should.
And yet I know
Death will not ever come to me through sickness
Or in any natural way: I have been preserved
For some unthinkable fate. But let that be.

As for my sons, you need not care for them.
They are men, they will find some way to live.
But my poor daughters, who have shared my table,
Who never before have been parted from their father—
Take care of them, Creon; do this for me.
And will you let me touch them with my hands
A last time, and let us weep together?
Be kind, my lord,
Great prince, be kind!
                    Could I but touch them,
They would be mine again, as when I had my eyes.

[Enter ANTIGONE and ISMENE, attended

Ah, God!
Is it my dearest children I hear weeping?
Has Creon pitied me and sent my daughters?

CREON: Yes, Oedipus: I knew that they were dear to you
In the old days, and know you must love them still.

OEDIPUS: May God bless you for this—and be a friendlier
Guardian to you than he has been to me!

Children, where are you?
Come quickly to my hands: they are your brother's—
Hands that have brought your father's once clear eyes
To this way of seeing—

          Ah dearest ones,
I had neither sight nor knowledge then, your father
By the woman who was the source of his own life!
And I weep for you—having no strength to see you—,
I weep for you when I think of the bitterness
That men will visit upon you all your lives.
What homes, what festivals can you attend
Without being forced to depart again in tears?
And when you come to marriageable age,
Where is the man, my daughters, who would dare
Risk the bane that lies on all my children?
Is there any evil wanting? Your father killed
His father; sowed the womb of her who bore him;
Engendered you at the fount of his own existence!

That is what they will say of you.

               Then, whom
Can you ever marry? There are no bridegrooms for you,
And your lives must wither away in sterile dreaming.

O Creon, son of Menoikeus!
You are the only father my daughters have,
Since we, their parents, are both of us gone for ever.
They are your own blood: you will not let them
Fall into beggary and loneliness;
You will keep them from the miseries that are mine!
Take pity on them; see, they are only children,
Friendless except for you. Promise me this,
Great Prince, and give me your hand in token of it.

        [CREON clasps his right hand

Children:
I could say much, if you could understand me,
But as it is, I have only this prayer for you:
Live where you can, be as happy as you can—
Happier, please God, than God has made your father!

CREON: Enough. You have wept enough. Now go within.

OEDIPUS: I must; but it is hard.

CREON: Time eases all things.

OEDIPUS: But you must promise—

CREON: Say what you desire.

OEDIPUS: Send me from Thebes!

CREON: God grant that I may!

OEDIPUS: But since God hates me . . .

CREON: No, he will grant your wish.

OEDIPUS: You promise?

CREON: I can not speak beyond my knowledge.

OEDIPUS: Then lead me in.

CREON: Come now, and leave your children.

OEDIPUS: No! Do not take them from me!

CREON: Think no longer
That you are in command here, but rather think
How, when you were, you served your own destruction.

[Exeunt into the house all but the **CHORUS;**
the **CHORAGOS** *chants directly to the audience:*

CHORAGOS: Men of Thebes: look upon Oedipus.

This is the king who solved the famous riddle
And towered up, most powerful men.
No mortal eyes but looked on him with envy,
Yet in the end ruin swept over him.

Let every man in mankind's frailty
Consider his last day; and let none
Presume on his good fortune until he find
Life, at his death, a memory without pain.

Euripides, The Bacchants

Euripides (c. 485–406 B.C.) was the youngest of the great triad of fifth-century Athenian playwrights (which included Aeschylus and Sophocles), and in many ways, he appears to be the most "modern." His characters, for example, though taken from familiar mythological sources, are often realistically portrayed, making them seem much closer to us than to the gods and heroes of Homeric poetry. Even the most glamorous of heroic personalities—Achilles, Helen, Heracles—often undergo a kind of moral deflation in Euripidean drama, whereas others (like Jason in *Medea*) are actually transformed into antiheroic figures whom no one can admire. At times, Euripides seems to *debunk* traditional stories and values, leading many historians to conclude that the underlying vision of his plays is ironic rather than tragic. For Euripides, the irrationality and self-destructiveness of human beings is as evident as the amorality and indifference of the gods: It is little wonder that Euripides' plays rarely won first prize in dramatic competitions and that his contemporaries clearly saw him as a fascinating but disturbingly cynical personality.

The Bacchants (400 B.C.), one of the last of Euripides' plays, can be understood as a complex tragedy of human presumption and divine anger. Euripides links Pentheus' refusal to acknowledge the presence and authority of Dionysus, or to permit the women of Thebes to worship him orgiastically, to Pentheus' ignorance of his own repressed sexuality and overconfidence in the powers of reason. Pentheus cannot accept the existence of irrational forces, either in nature or in the human personality; he perceives the instinctual as alien—hence, his rejection of Dionysus, whose Asian origins and followers arouse panic and fear in Pentheus' rationalistic mind.

In characteristically Euripidean fashion, Dionysus shows no pity for any of the victims of his wrath, not even Cadmus or Agave, who have worshipped him. In sharp contrast to both Aeschylean and Sophoclean deities, the gods of Euripides seldom exhibit any of the nobler feelings that human beings, at their best, are capable of—compassion, loyalty, or generosity. Unlike Plato, Euripides can find no ideal moral or metaphysical order in a universe governed by such cruel and whimsical beings.

CHARACTERS

DIONYSUS, also called Bacchus, Bromius, Evius
CHORUS, Asiatic women, devotees of Dionysus
TIRESIAS, the Theban prophet, old and blind
CADMUS, founder and formerly king of Thebes
PENTHEUS, king of Thebes, grandson of Cadmus
THE STRANGER, a missionary prophet of Dionysus
SERVANT of Pentheus
FIRST MESSENGER, herdsman from Cithaeron
SECOND MESSENGER, servant of Pentheus
AGAVE, mother of Pentheus, daughter of Cadmus
Guards, attendants, others

The Scene: *The scene represents the front of the royal palace at Thebes.*

The Bacchants was written in Macedon, where Euripides spent the last years of his life (408–406) in virtual exile. It was played in Athens after its author's death.

[Enter Dionysus.

DIONYSUS. Zeus' child has come back to the land of the Thebans. I am Dionysus whom Cadmus' daughter, Semele, bore long ago by the flaming thunderbolt's midwifery. My form I have changed from divine to human, as I come now to Dirce's streams, to the water of Ismenus. Close by the palace here I mark the monument of my mother, the thunder-blasted. The ruins of her home, I see, are smouldering still; the divine fire is still alive—Hera's undying insult to my mother. All praise to Cadmus; he has made this spot holy ground, his daughter's chapel. But it was I who wreathed it in the greenery of the clustering vine.

I come from Lydia's fields that teem with gold, and Phrygia's. I have conquered the Persians' sun-smitten steppes and the walled towns of Bactria, the wintry land of Media and Arabia the Blest. All Asia is mine, all that lies by the salt sea and possesses fair-towered cities filled with mingled Hellenes and barbarians together. This is the first city I have come to in Hellas. Everywhere else I have instituted my dances and my mysteries, that my godhead might be manifest to mortals.

First of this Hellene land I have filled Thebes with the cries of exultant women; I have fitted the fawn-skin to their bodies and have put into their hands the militant thyrsus, entwined with ivy. For my mother's own sisters—*they* at least should have known better—said that Dionysus was no son of Zeus; that Semele had given her love to some mortal; that, schooled by Cadmus, she was fathering on Zeus her own sinful passion. That was why Zeus killed her, they vaunted aloud; because she had lied about her lover. These same sisters, therefore, I have driven in mad frenzy from their homes; they are living in the mountain, out of their minds. I have made them wear the habit of my orgies. And all the womenfolk of Thebes, every woman in the city, I have driven from home distraught, to join the daughters of Cadmus; together they sit beneath the silver firs, on the open rocks. This city must learn, whether it likes it or not, that it still wants initiation into my Bacchic rites. The cause of my mother Semele I must defend by proving to mortals that I *am* a god, borne by her to Zeus.

Now Cadmus has bestowed the kingship and its rights upon his grandson Pentheus, who opposes my worship. He thrusts me away from his offerings, and in his prayers nowhere makes mention of me. Therefore I mean to reveal myself to him and to all the Thebans as a god indeed. When I have settled things here to my satisfaction I shall direct my steps to another land and manifest myself. If the city of the Thebans becomes enraged and tries to drive the bacchants from the mountain by force of arms, I shall lead my Maenads into battle against them. That is why I have assumed this mortal form, changing myself to look like a natural man.

Ho, women that have come from Tmolus, Lydia's bulwark, my own revel band! I have brought you from among barbarians to be my companions, wherever I stay, wherever I go. Raise the native music of your Phrygian homeland, the timbrels which mother Rhea and I invented. Come to this royal palace of Pentheus, sound them loud, for the whole city to come and see. I shall go to the glens of Cithaeron where the bacchants are, and there I shall join in their dances.

[Exit Dionysus before the Chorus enters bearing thyrsi and timbrels

CHORUS *[The mark at the beginning of a line indicates a change of speaker]. From the land of Asia I come, leaving sacred Tmolus behind me. In Bromius' honor I eagerly ply my pleasant task, my toil of ease, crying glory to the Bacchic god.*
—*Is any profane man in the street? Is any within? Let him withdraw. Hushed be every lip to holy silence. Ever shall I hymn Dionysus in the old, old way.*
—*Ah, blessed is he whom the gods love, who understands the secret rites of the gods, whose life is consecrated, whose very soul dances with holy joy. In the mountains he knows the bacchic thrill, the holy purifications; he observes the orgies of Cybele, the Great Mother; he brandishes the thyrsus on high, and crowns himself with ivy in the service of Dionysus.*
—*On ye bacchants, on ye bacchants; bring home Bromius the god, the son of the god, bring Dionysus from the Phrygian mountains, bring Bromius to the open squares of Hellas, spacious for dances.*
—*Him on a time his pregnant mother with painful travail brought forth, blasted from her womb by the flying thunderbolt of Zeus. In the stroke of the lightning she lost her own life, but straightway, in the very chamber where the mother lay, Cronian Zeus received him and concealed him in his thigh, fastening him in with golden buckles, hidden from Hera.*

And when the fates had formed the babe perfect, the father brought forth the bull-horned god; and he wreathed him with the coils of serpents. That is why the Maenads catch wild serpents to twine in their hair.
—*O Thebes, Semele's nurse, crown yourself with ivy, burgeon forth, burgeon forth with verdant smilax with its bright berries. Make yourself a very bacchant with branches of oak or fir. On with the fawn-skins, dapple the hems with fleecy tufts of silvery goat's hair. Riot with the fennel-stalk, but devoutly. Soon all the land will dance—he is Bromius, whoever leads the revel-band—dance off to the mountains, to the mountains where the throng of women await, driven from loom and shuttle by the frenzy of Dionysus.*
—*O chamber of the Curetes, O holy haunts of Crete, which saw the birth of Zeus! In your caves the corybants, with helmets of triple rim, contrived this my timbrel's circle of stretched hide. For our fierce bacchic revelry they blended its note with the sweet voice of the Phrygian flute, and they placed it in the hand of Mother Rhea. To its booming the bacchants would one day utter their revel-shouts. For from the divine Mother the raving satyrs appropriated it and wedded it to the dances of the biennial festivals in which Dionysus delights.*
—*My love is in the mountains. He sinks to the ground from the racing revel-band. He wears the holy habit of fawn-skins; he hunts the goat and kills it and delights in the raw flesh. He rushes to the mountains of Phrygia, of Lydia. He is Bromius, the leader of our dance. Evoe! The ground flows with milk, flows with wine, flows with the nectar of bees. Fragrant as Syrian frankincense is the fume of the pine-torch which our bacchic leader holds aloft. Its ruddy flame shoots from the end of the fennel-stalk as he runs and dances, his delicate tresses streaming in the air, as he rouses the scattered band and shouts them to their feet. "Evoe" he cries, then loudly: "On, ye bacchants, on, bright glory of Tmolus and its golden streams, hymn Dionysus to the deep booming of the timbrels; in bacchic fashion, with Phrygian cries and call, glorify the bacchic god, while the flute, sweet-toned*

126

and holy, plays happy anthems for the wild bands trooping to the mountains, to the mountains". Then indeed the bacchant maid rejoices and gambols, light-footed, like a foal by its mother's side in the pasture.

[Enter Tiresias

TIRESIAS. Who is at the gate? Call Cadmus from the house, Agenor's son, who left the Sidonian city and built the towers of this Theban town.

Go someone, tell him that Tiresias is seeking him. He knows himself why I have come. He knows the arrangement I have made, with a man even older than myself, to dress the thyrsus and put on skins of fawns and wreathe our heads with shoots of ivy.

[Enter Cadmus

CADMUS. Ah, my wise old friend!—I knew it was you the moment I heard your wise old voice. Here I am, all ready, in this livery of the god. For he is my own daughter's child [this Dionysus who has proved his godhead to men]; and we must do all we can to glorify his might. Where do we dance? Where do we plant our feet and toss our old, grey heads? Expound it to me, Tiresias, as one old man to another. Your are the expert, I shall never weary, night or day, beating the earth with the thyrsus. In my happiness I have forgotten how old I am.

TIRESIAS. Then you feel as I do. I, too, feel young again. I, too, shall attempt the dance.

CADMUS. Well then, shall we get a carriage to carry us to the mountain?

TIRESIAS. That would not be the same tribute to the god.

CADMUS. My aged arm, then, will guide your aged feet.

TIRESIAS. The god will lead us there with no trouble.

CADMUS. Shall we be the only ones in the city to dance for Bacchus?

TIRESIAS. We alone are right. The others are wrong.

CADMUS. We delay too long. Take hold of my hand.

TIRESIAS. There you are, clasp hands, link yours with mine.

CADMUS. I am a mere mortal. I do not feel superior to the gods.

TIRESIAS. We do not rationalize about the gods. We have the traditions of our fathers, old as time itself. No argument can knock *them* down, however clever the sophistry, however keen the wit. People may say that I have no shame, at *my* age, going dancing and binding my head with ivy. Let them. The god has not specified that only the young must dance or only the old. He is pleased to receive honor from all alike. He wishes to be extolled; he does not count up a person's years.

CADMUS. Since you cannot see, Tiresias, I shall speak for you. Here is Pentheus hurrying towards the house, Echion's son, to whom I gave the rule of this land. How excited he is! What news will he tell?

[Enter Pentheus

PENTHEUS. I happened to be out of the country, but a tale of strange mischief in the city here has brought me back. Our women have left home, they tell me, in sham ecstasies.

They are frisking about on the shadowy hills, honoring with dances this new-fashioned divinity, this Dionysus of theirs. In the midst of each rowdy group a brimming wine-bowl stands. Then they slink off separately to lonely corners to serve the beds of men. Of course they pretend they are priestesses, inspired priestesses; but they make more of Aphrodite than of Bacchus.

I have caught a number of them. Jailers have them safely manacled in the public prison. Those that are missing I'll chase off the mountain [—Ino and Agave, who bore me to Echion, and Autonoe, the mother of Actaeon]. I'll catch them in iron traps and put a quick stop to this immoral revelry.

They say that a stranger has arrived, a wizard, a sorcerer from Lydia, with fragrant golden curls and ruddy face and spells of love in his eyes. He spends his days and nights in the company of young women, pretending to initiate them in the bacchic mysteries. If I catch him in this house I'll stop him from beating his thyrsus and tossing his curls. I'll cut his neck from his body.

It is he that says Dionysus is a god (yet, *he* says so) and was once sewn up in the thigh of Zeus—the child that was burnt up by the flaming thunderbolt along with his mother, because she falsely named Zeus as her lover. Is it not enough to make a man hang himself in agony—this insolent effrontery, this mysterious stranger?

But look! Here's a new phenomenon. The seer Tiresias in dappled fawn-skins! And my own grandfather—how ridiculous—playing the bacchant with a fennel wand! Sir, this is not my mother's father. So old and so foolish! Please throw that ivy away. Let go that thyrsus, rid your hand of it.

This is *your* instigation, Tiresias. This is another device of yours to make money out of your bird-gazing and burnt sacrifices—introducing a *new* god to men. It is only your grey hairs that save you from sitting in chains among the bacchants for introducing these unholy rites. When the sparkle of wine finds a place at women's feasts, there is something rotten about such celebrations, I tell you.

LEADER. What blasphemy! Stranger, have you no respect for the gods, no respect for Cadmus who sowed the crop of dragon's teeth? Will the son of Echion disgrace his family?

TIRESIAS. Give a clever man a good theme to talk on, and it is easy enough to speak well. Your tongue, indeed, runs smoothly, as if you had wit, but there is no wit in what you say. The man whose strength is his impudence, whose ability is all in his tongue, makes a bad citizen—and a stupid one.

This new divinity whom you ridicule—words cannot describe how great will be his power throughout Hellas. Mankind, young man, has two chief blessings: goddess Demeter—the earth, that is; call her whichever name you will—who sustains men with solid food, and this son of Semele, who came later and matched her gift. He invented the liquid draught of the grape and introduced it to mortals. When they get their fill of the flowing grape, it stops their grief. It gives them sleep and forgetfulness of daily sorrows. There is no other medicine for trouble. The libations we pour are the god himself making *our* peace with the gods, so that through him mankind may obtain blessings.

You sneer at the story that he was stitched inside the thigh of Zeus. I will teach you the true interpretation of that. When Zeus snatched him from the thunderbolt's flame and brought the infant god to Olympus, Hera wanted to cast him out of heaven. But Zeus contrived a counter device, as a god might. He broke off a piece of the earth-enveloping sky and gave jealous Hera an *incorporeal* Dionysus. But in time mortals got the word changed and said the child had been *incorporated* in Zeus. So they made up the story that he had been stitched inside the thigh of the god.

He is a prophetic god. Those whom his spirit fills, like people possessed, have no small prophetic power. Whenever the god enters the body in full strength, he takes possession of men and makes them tell the future. He also has taken over a part of Ares' functions. A host under arms, ay already drawn up in line, is often scattered in *panic* before raising a spear. This also is a sort of madness sent by Dionysus (and his follower *Pan*). A time will come when you will see him even on Delphi's rock, bounding over the double peak of Parnassus with his pine-torches, brandishing and tossing his bacchic wand. He shall be great throughout Hellas. Listen to *me*, Pentheus. Do not presume that mere power has influence with men. Do not be wise in your own diseased imagination. Welcome the god to the land, pour libations, wreathe your head, revel.

Not even Dionysus can compel women to be chaste. For that you must look to the women's own nature [for a chastity proof against all shocks]. Even in bacchic revels the good woman, at least, will not be corrupted.

You see, *you* take pleasure when a multitude stands at your gates and the city magnifies the name of Pentheus. He, too, I judge, takes delight in being honored. I then, and Cadmus, whom you laugh at, shall crown ourselves with ivy and dance. A hoary old pair, but dance we must. I shall not be persuaded by your logic to combat gods. You are mad, most distressingly mad. No spells can cure a disease which is itself a spell.

LEADER. Old man, your words do honor to Phoebus and you are wise in honoring Bromius; he is a mighty god.

CADMUS. My boy, Tiresias has advised you well. Dwell with us, do not break with our old ways. You are flighty at the moment. Your wisdom is unwise. Even if this is no god, as you say, pretend to yourself that he is. It is a most honorable falsehood. It makes Semele seem to be the mother of a god and it will rebound to the credit of our whole family.

You are familiar with the sorry fate of Actaeon. The flesh-devouring dogs that he himself had raised tore him to pieces in the fields because he boasted that he was better at the hunt than Artemis. Don't let anything like that happen to you. Come, let me crown your head with ivy. Join us in honoring the god.

PENTHEUS. Do not lay your hand upon me. Go play the bacchant. Do not wipe off your folly on me! This teacher of your foolishness will get what he deserves. Let someone go with all speed—go to this man's seat where he examines his birds. Heave it up with crowbars, turn it upside down. Make a general havoc of the whole place. Throw his fillets to the winds and storms. That will gall him more than anything.

Let others of you scour the city and track out this foreign epicene who has brought this strange madness upon the women and is defiling our beds. If you catch him bring him here in chains to die the death he deserves—by stoning. He will live to rue his revelry in Thebes.

[Exit Pentheus

TIRESIAS. Poor wretch, how little you know what you are saying. Now you are really mad. You did go off your head once before.

Let us go, Cadmus, and entreat the god, on this man's behalf, savage though he is, and for the city's sake, to bring no evil to pass. Come, follow me with your ivy staff. Try to hold my body up, as I do yours. It would be disgraceful for two old men to fall. However, never mind. We must serve Bacchus, son of Zeus. But beware, Cadmus, lest Pentheus bring into your house his namesake Penthos—Sorrow. That is no prophecy, but plain fact. A fool speaks folly.

[The two old men totter off

CHORUS. *Holiness, Holiness, queen of Heaven, as you turn your golden wings earthwards, do you hear these words of Pentheus? Do you hear this unholy defiance of Bromius, Semele's son, the god of lovely garlands and good cheer, the prince of the Blessed Ones? This is his realm: revelry and dancing, flute-playing and laughter and the banishing of care, whether the presence of the grape brightens the banquets of the gods, or on earth the wine bowl casts the mantle of sleep around the ivy-wreathed merrymakers.*

Of unbridled lips and lawless folly the only end is disaster; but the quiet life of wisdom abides unshaken and sustains the home. For though they dwell remote in the sky, the sons of heaven regard the affairs of men. Knowledge is not wisdom. Thoughts too long make life short. If man, in his brief moment, goes after things too great for him, he may lose the joys within his reach. To my mind, that is the way of madness and perversity.

Oh that I might come to Cyprus, Aphrodite's isle, where dwell the Loves that soothe the hearts of men; to Paphos where the hundred-mouthed streams of the barbarian river bring fruits without rain. Where stands Pieria, queen of beauty, seat of the Muses, where the holy hill of Olympus stands—thither take me, Bromius, divine Bromius, leading your bacchic rout. There the Graces dwell, there dwells Desire, there it is lawful for the bacchants to celebrate their orgies.

The deity, Zeus' son, rejoices in festivals. He loves goddess Peace, who brings prosperity and cherishes youth. To rich and poor he gives in equal measure the blessed joy of wine. But he hates the man who has no taste for such things—to live a life of happy days and sweet and happy nights, in wisdom to keep his mind and heart aloof from over-busy men. Whatever the majority, the simple folk, believe and follow, that way I will accept.

[Pentheus enters and is met by a Servant, leading attendants with the Lydian Stranger, bound

SERVANT. Pentheus, here we are. We have caught the prey you sent us to catch; our expedition was not in vain. Our quarry—here he is—is a tame creature. He did not take cover or run away. No pallor of fear chased the blood from his cheek. Of his own free will he surrendered. He even smiled as he consented to be arrested and bound. He waited for me to do my duty—he even helped me. I was touched and said to him: "Stranger, not of my will do I take you, but by the orders of Pentheus who sent me".

On the other hand, those bacchants you caught and shut up in the public jail are gone. They slipped the bonds that bound them and gambolled off to the meadows, calling upon Bromius as their god. The fetters of their feet burst asunder of their own accord, and the gates were unbarred by no human hand. This man who has come to our Thebes is full of miracles. The rest is your affair.

PENTHEUS. Free this man's hands. Trapped as he is, he cannot have the speed to escape me.

Well! You are quite handsome, stranger, for women's taste—and that is what brings you to Thebes. Your hair is long—apparently you never wrestle. It flows over your cheeks, full of appeal. And your complexion is so clear, studiously so. The sun never gets at it; it is in the shade you go hunting, hunting Aphrodite with your beauty. Tell me first who you are, of what race?

THE STRANGER. There is nothing to boast of, it is easy to tell. You have doubtless heard of flowery Tmolus.

PENTHEUS. I know. The circle of its hills surrounds the city of Sardis.

THE STRANGER. I am from there, Lydia is my country.

PENTHEUS. How come you to bring these rites to Hellas?

THE STRANGER. Dionysus initiated me, Zeus' son.

PENTHEUS. Is there a Zeus over there who begets new gods?

THE STRANGER. No, he is the same Zeus who joined in wedlock here with Semele.

PENTHEUS. Was it in a dream, or face to face, that he pressed you into his service?

THE STRANGER. He saw me and I saw him. For proof he gave me sacred rites.

PENTHEUS. These orgies of yours, what form do they take?

THE STRANGER. It is unlawful for profane mortals to know them.

PENTHEUS. What profit do they afford to the votaries?

THE STRANGER. It is not right for you to hear, but they are worth knowing.

PENTHEUS. You gild the tale well, to make me curious.

THE STRANGER. The god's orgies loathe the man who practises impiety.

PENTHEUS. You say you saw the god clearly. What like was he?

THE STRANGER. What like he pleased; it was not for me to dictate.

PENTHEUS. Again you side-step nimbly, and avoid the point.

THE STRANGER. Talk wisdom to the stupid and they will think *you* foolish.

PENTHEUS. And is this the first place to which you bring your god?

THE STRANGER. All the barbarians celebrate his rites and dances.

PENTHEUS. They have far less sense than Hellenes.

THE STRANGER. In this, at least, they have more. Customs differ.

PENTHEUS. These rites—do you perform them at night or by day?

THE STRANGER. At night, for the most part; darkness gives solemnity.

ENTHEUS. It betrays women and undermines their morals.

THE STRANGER. By day, too, shameful things may be contrived.

131
▪

PENTHEUS. You ought to be punished for your vile sophistries.

THE STRANGER. And you for your coarse blasphemies against the god.

PENTHEUS. How bold our bacchant, a pretty fencer—with words!

THE STRANGER. Tell me my fate. What is the awful thing you are going to do to me?

PENTHEUS. First I will cut off your pretty curls.

THE STRANGER. I dedicate them to the god. It is for him I keep them.

PENTHEUS. Next hand over this thyrsus.

THE STRANGER. Take it from me yourself. It is Dionysus' thyrsus I carry.

PENTHEUS. And I will shut you up safe in prison.

THE STRANGER. The god himself will free me, whenever I desire.

PENTHEUS. Perhaps so, when you stand among your bacchants and call upon him.

THE STRANGER. Even now he is near and sees what I undergo.

PENTHEUS. Then where is he? He is not apparent to *my* eyes.

THE STRANGER. He is with me, but your impiety will not let you see him.

PENTHEUS. *[to guards].* Seize him. The fellow mocks me and Thebes.

THE STRANGER. I give you sober warning: do not bind me, you fools.

PENTHEUS. But I have more authority than you. I say 'Bind'.

THE STRANGER. You do not know your station. You do not realize what you are doing. You forget who you are.

PENTHEUS. I am Pentheus, Agave's son and Echion's.

THE STRANGER. An apt name to be unlucky in.

PENTHEUS. Begone! Imprison him near the palace, in the horses' stables. Let him see glooms and darkness. Dance away *there*. These women here, whom you have brought with you, your accomplices in mischief, I shall either sell off, or keep them at the loom as my slaves. That will stop their hands from this thudding and beating of hides.

THE STRANGER. I shall go. I can but fulfil my destiny. But remember: Dionysus, whom you deny, will exact full payment for this outrage. When you assault me you are putting *him* in bonds.

[Exeunt Pentheus and the Stranger, guarded

CHORUS. *Daughter of Achelous, holy Dirce, blessed maiden! Once you received Zeus' babe in your fountains, when Zeus that begot him snatched him from the undying flame and placed him in his thigh and called aloud: "Come, Dithyrambus, enter this my male womb. By this name, my Bacchus, I proclaim you to Thebes, that they may so call you." And yet, blessed Dirce, you thrust me away when I hold my begarlanded revels in your land. Why do you disown me? Why do you avoid me? The time will come, I swear by the*

132
∎

lovely clusters of Dionysus' vine, the time will come when you too shall take thought of Bromius.

[What passion, what passion.] Pentheus publishes abroad his earth-born lineage, his descent from the Dragon of old, Pentheus earth-born Echion's son. A savage monster he is; no mortal man he, but a bloody earth-born giant battling the gods. Soon he will throw chains upon me, who belong to Bromius. Already he holds my fellow-reveller within his house, hidden away in a dark prison. Do you see these things, Dionysus, son of Zeus? Do you see your prophets amid trials and tribulations? Come, king, come down Olympus, brandishing your golden thyrsus. Quell the presumption of this bloody man.

Where, I wonder, on Nysa, the lair of wild beasts, are you holding your revels, thyrsus in hand? Or are you upon the Corycian peaks? Or perhaps you are on Olympus, embowered in thick forests, where once upon a time the music of the harp of Orpheus marshalled the trees to him, marshalled the beasts of the wildwood. You are blessed, Pieria; Evius reverences you and will come to hold his revels upon you with bacchic dances. He will cross the racing stream of Axius. He will lead his whirling maenads over Lydias, father of waters, the giver of wealth and blessing to man. Loveliest of waters are his streams, they tell me, enriching a land of noble horses.

> **[There is a roar of thunder. Lightning flashes over the tomb of Semele. The earth trembles. The Chorus dashes about shrieking. Then a voice is heard**

VOICE *[within].* *Ho, hear me, hear my voice!. Ho, bacchants, Ho, bacchants!*

SOME OF CHORUS. *What cry, what cry is that? Whence came the call, the bacchic call, to summon me?*

VOICE *[within].* *Ho! Ho! Again I call. Semele's child, the son of Zeus.*

OTHERS. *Ho! ho! our lord, our lord! Come to our revel rout, O Bromius, Bromius.*

VOICE *[within].* *Shake the earth's floor, awful Earthquake.*

SOME OF CHORUS. *Aha! aha! Soon the house of Pentheus will be shaken to ruins.*

OTHERS. *Dionysus is in the palace! Adore him!*

OTHERS. *O, we adore him!*

OTHERS. *Did you mark how the stone capitals yonder on the pillars parted asunder? Bromius chants his own triumph within the halls.*

VOICE *[within].* *Kindle the thunderbolt's lurid torch. Burn, burn down, the palace of Pentheus.*

> **[Lightning blazes over the palace and the monument of Semele**

SOME OF CHORUS. *Aha! aha! Look, see Semele's holy tomb. How it blazes! It is the flame the thunder-god left there long ago, the flame of Zeus' thunderbolt. Hurl to the ground your shuddering limbs, Maenads. Our king comes, the son of Zeus, confounding utterly these halls.*

> **[Enter the stranger**

THE STRANGER. Foreign women, are you so astounded with fear that you have fallen to the ground? You have perceived, it seems, how Bacchus shook the house of Pentheus. But raise yourselves and take courage. Still your shuddering limbs.

LEADER. O brightest light of our bacchant revel, how glad I am to see you. We were alone, forsaken.

THE STRANGER. Did you despair when they led me in and were about to hurl me into Pentheus' dark dungeons?

LEADER. Despair indeed. Who was there to be my protector if any mischance were to befall you? But how did you escape from the clutches of that godless man?

THE STRANGER. With effortless ease I saved myself unaided.

LEADER. Did he not bind your hands with chains and fetters?

THE STRANGER. There too I mocked him. He thought he was binding me but he never so much as laid a finger on me. He fed on fancy. In the stable where he took me to imprison me he found a bull, and he threw his nooses around its knees and the hooves of its feet. He panted furiously and dripped sweat from his body and dug his teeth into his lips. There I was, sitting nearby at my ease and looking on. At this moment Bacchus came and shook the building and kindled a fire on his mother's tomb. Seeing the glare, Pentheus thought the place was on fire and rushed back and forth ordering the servants to bring buckets of water. Every slave was busy at the task, but they had their trouble for nothing. Then he thought I had escaped. So he suspended these labors and rushed into the house with his dark sword drawn. But Bromius, as it seems to me—I give you my conjecture—created a phantom in the court. Pentheus attacked it with a rush and stabbed at the bright ether as if he were butchering me. Besides this, Bacchus brings these other afflictions on him: the prison he razed to the ground, everything lies in ruin. Most bitterly he must rue my imprisonment. Fatigue has made him drop his sword, and he lies exhausted. A mere man, he had the effrontery to join battle with a god. I slipped quietly out of the house and have come to you. I care nothing for Pentheus.

It seems to me—a boot is clattering in the house—he will soon come to the front. What will he say after this? Let him come in all his bluster; I shall bear it easily. A modest nonchalance—that is the mark of wisdom.

[Enter Pentheus

PENTHEUS. This is an outrage. The stranger has escaped, the one that was lately bound fast with chains. Ha! Here is the man! What is this? How is it you appear in front of my house? How did you come out?

THE STRANGER. Stay your foot! Teach your anger to walk quietly.

PENTHEUS. How did you escape from your chains and get out here?

THE STRANGER. Did I not say—or did you not hear me—that someone would free me?

PENTHEUS. Who? With you it is one strange saying after another.

THE STRANGER. He who raises the clustering vine for man.

PENTHEUS. [A sorry gift—to make men forget themselves.]

134

.

THE STRANGER. What you sneer at does him honor.

PENTHEUS. I will have every gate in the walls barred.

THE STRANGER. Why? Can gods not overleap your walls?

PENTHEUS. Clever you are, very clever—but not clever enough.

THE STRANGER. In the most important thing I am clever enough. But first hear and mark the words of this man who is coming from the mountain with some message for you. I shall await your pleasure, I shall not flee.

[Enter Herdsman

HERDSMAN. Pentheus, ruler of this Theban land, I come from Cithaeron, where . . . [the bright flakes of white snow never cease].

PENTHEUS *[interrupting]*. What tidings do you bring in such haste?

HERDSMAN. I have seen the raving bacchants, who rushed barefooted from their homes in frenzy. I am here all eager to tell you and the city, king, the fearsome things they do, things surpassing wonder. Am I to speak of these events freely or abridge my story? I want you to say, O king. I am afraid of your hasty temper, so passionate, so imperious.

PENTHEUS. Speak on. You are quite safe from punishment on my part. To grow angry with just men is not right. The more awful your story about the bacchants, the greater the punishment I shall inflict upon this man who taught the women these arts.

HERDSMAN. Our herds of pasturing kine had just begun to ascend the steep to the ridge, at the hour when the sun shoots forth his rays to warm the earth. I saw three bands of women dancers; Autonoe was leader of the first choir, your mother Agave of the second, and Ino of the third. They all lay in the sleep of exhaustion. Some were reclining with their backs against branches of fir, others had flung themselves at random on the ground on leaves of oak [modestly, not, as you charge, intoxicated with the wine-bowl and the sound of the flute and hunting Cypris in the lonely forest].

Then your mother rose up in the midst of the bacchants and called upon them to bestir their limbs from sleep when she heard the lowing of the horned kine. The women then cast the heavy sleep from their eyes and sprang upright, a sight of wondrous comeliness. There were young women and old women and maids yet unmarried. First they let their hair fly loose about their shoulders and tucked up their fawnskins, those whose fastenings had become unloosed, and girt the speckled skins about them with serpents that licked their cheek. Others held gazelles in their arms, or the untamed whelps of wolves, feeding them with white milk. These were young mothers who had left their infants behind and still had their breasts swollen with milk. Then they put on ivy wreaths and crowns of oak and flowery smilax. One took her thyrsus and struck it against a rock, and there sprang from it a dewy stream of water. Another struck her fennel wand upon the ground, and the god sent up a fountain of wine for her. Those that had a desire for the white drink scraped the earth with the tips of their fingers, and had rich store of milk. From the wands of ivy there dripped sweet streams of honey. If you had been there to see, you would have approached with prayers the god whom you now revile.

We cowherds and shepherds came together to argue and debate with one another on the fearful and wonderful things they did. One fellow who was fond of loafing about town, an experienced talker, spoke out to all and sundry: "You who dwell upon the holy terraces of the mountains, do you vote that we chase Pentheus' mother, Agave, from her bacchic revels and do our king a kindness?" He seemed to us to speak well, and so we set an ambush amidst the leafy thickets and hid ourselves. At the set time they waved the thyrsus for their revelling and all together, with one voice, invoked Bacchus, Zeus' offspring Bromius. The whole mountain cried "Bacchus" with them. The animals joined in the revelry. Everywhere there was a stirring as they raced along.

Now Agave happened to come racing by me and I jumped out and made to seize her, evacuating the ambush where I was hiding. But she raised a cry: "Ah, my fleet hounds, we are being hunted by these men! But follow me, follow with your wands in your hands for weapons."

We fled and escaped a rending at the bacchants' hands. But, with naked, unarmed, hands, the women attacked the heifers that were grazing on the grass. You could see one holding wide the legs of a well-fed calf which bellowed and bellowed. Others rent heifers apart. You could see ribs or cloven hooves tossed here and there, and pieces smeared with gore hanging from the firs, dripping blood. The wanton bulls—forgotten the menace of their levelled horns—were tripped and dragged to the ground by the hands of countless young women. Quicker were their coverings of flesh torn asunder than you could close the lids of your royal eyes. Like birds they soared off the ground in their flight as they scoured the spreading plains by the streams of Asopus which grow the fine harvests of Thebes. Like an invading army they fell upon Hysiae and Erythrae, which nestle under Cithaeron's slopes, and everywhere they wrought confusion and havoc. They pillaged homes at random. Their loot they put upon their shoulders, and though it was not tied on, it held fast; nothing fell to the dark earth, neither brass nor iron. They carried fire in their curls and it did not burn them. Some of us, angered by the depradations of the bacchants, resorted to arms. And *there* was a terrible sight to see, O king. Pointed spears drew no blood, whereas the women flung wands from their hands and wounded their assailants till they turned tail and ran. Women defeating men! There was a god with them. Then they went back whence they had started, to the fountains which the god had shot up for them. They washed off the blood, while the serpents licked clean the clots from their cheeks.

This deity then, whoever he is, O king, receive into the city. In many things he is powerful. This also they say of him, I hear, that he gave mortals the wine which ends sorrow. If *he* exists not, then neither does Cypris, nor any other joy for men at all.

[LEADER.] I am fearful of speaking out freely to one who is my master, but I shall have my say: there is no god greater than Dionysus.

[Exit Herdsman

PENTHEUS. This brings it close, like a spreading fire—this bacchic menace. We are disgraced in the eyes of Hellas. There must be no delay. Go to the Electran gates; order all the hoplites and all the riders of swift horses to muster, all those who brandish targes and those whose hands twang the bow-string. We shall march against the bacchants. This is truly going too far—to be treated like this at the hands of women.

THE STRANGER. My words, no doubt, will fail to persuade you, Pentheus; but despite the wrong you have done me I advise you not to take up arms against a god. Keep calm. Bromius will not allow you to drive his bacchants from their hills of revelry.

PENTHEUS. Do not lecture me. You have escaped from bonds; keep that in mind. Or shall I call back justice upon you?

THE STRANGER. If I were you, I would sacrifice to him rather than rage and kick against the pricks—a man against a god.

PENTHEUS. I shall sacrifice indeed—these women. I shall make great and deserved slaughter in the glens of Cithaeron.

THE STRANGER. You will all be put to flight. And that will be a disgrace—when they with their bacchic wands turn back your brazen shields.

PENTHEUS. There's no dealing with this stranger we are at grips with. Both going and coming he will have his say.

THE STRANGER. Friend, it is still possible to mend the situation.

PENTHEUS. By doing what? Being a slave to my own slaves?

THE STRANGER. I shall bring the women here without using weapons.

PENTHEUS. Ah me, this is a cunning plot against me.

THE STRANGER. How a plot, if I want to *save* you by my devices?

PENTHEUS. You are in conspiracy with them, to establish your revels for all time.

THE STRANGER. In conspiracy indeed—that is true—but with the god.

PENTHEUS *[to Servants]*. Bring me my armor here. *[To the Stranger]* And *you* stop your talk!

THE STRANGER *[after thought]*. Ah! Would you like to see them in their gatherings upon the mountain?

PENTHEUS. Very much. Ay, and pay uncounted gold for the pleasure.

THE STRANGER. Why have you conceived so strong a desire?

PENTHEUS. Though it would pain me to see them drunk with wine———

THE STRANGER. Yet you would like to see them, pain and all.

PENTHEUS. Be sure I would, if I could sit quietly under the firs.

THE STRANGER. But they will track you out, even if you come unseen.

PENTHEUS. Then it shall be openly; your point is quite right.

THE STRANGER. Do we go then? Will you undertake the journey?

PENTHEUS. Lead me with all speed. I grudge you every minute.

THE STRANGER. Put upon your body clothes of fine linen.

PENTHEUS. Why so? Am I, a man, to enroll in the other sex?

THE STRANGER. They may kill you, if you are seen there as a man.

PENTHEUS. Again your point is quite right. You are something of a veteran in guile.

THE STRANGER. It was Dionysus taught me this lore.

PENTHEUS. How then shall your advice be properly carried out?

THE STRANGER. I shall come inside and dress you.

PENTHEUS. What sort of dress? A woman's? I am ashamed.

THE STRANGER. You are no longer eager to see the spectacle of maenads.

PENTHEUS. What dress will you put on my body?

THE STRANGER. I shall spread your hair out long over your head.

PENTHEUS. What is the next item in my outfit?

THE STRANGER. Robes that reach to the feet, and on your head a snood.

PENTHEUS. Is there anything else you want to add?

THE STRANGER. A thyrsus for your hand, and the dappled skin of a fawn.

PENTHEUS. I could not possibly put on a woman's dress.

THE STRANGER. Then you will have to fight the bacchants and cause bloodshed.

PENTHEUS. Right. We must first go and reconnoitre.

THE STRANGER. If you *will* seek evil ends, it is at least wise to eschew evil means.

PENTHEUS. But how can I go through the city unseen by the citizens?

THE STRANGER. We will go by deserted ways. I will lead you.

PENTHEUS. Anything is better than to have the bacchants jeer at me. Let us go inside—I shall consider what is best.

THE STRANGER. By all means. In any event, *I* am prepared.

PENTHEUS. I will come. I shall either go under arms or take your advice.

[Exit Pentheus into palace

THE STRANGER. Women, our fish is ready for the strike. He will go to the bacchants and there he will forfeit his life.

Dionysus, the task is now yours. You are not far off. Let us punish this man. First drive him from his wits, make him a little mad. If he is in his right mind, there is no chance of his ever consenting to put on a woman's dress. But if he is driven out of his mind he will put it on. After those truculent threats of his, I want him to become a laughing-stock to the Thebans as he is led through the city looking like a woman. I shall go and dress Pentheus in the apparel which he will take with him to Hades, slaughtered by his mother's hands. He shall come to know Dionysus, son of Zeus, who is every bit a god, terrible in power, but to mankind most gentle.

[Exit into palace

CHORUS. *Shall I ever again in the night-long dances plant my white foot in bacchic revelry, tossing back my head in the dewy air, like a sportive fawn rejoicing in green*

138

▪

pastures, delivered from the terror of the chase, from the watching eyes and the well-meshed nets, from the huntsman cheering on his eager, racing pack? Sorely pressed, she flies over the river-flats, swift as a storm-wind, and rejoices in the leafy shade of forest trees, in solitudes unbroken by man.

What is wisdom? What boon from the gods is fairer among men than to hold a victorious hand over the head of one's enemies? What is fair is ever dear.

Slowly, yet surely withal, the power divine advances. It chastises those mortals who honor brutality, who in mad delusion do not give glory to the gods. The gods are cunning: they lie in wait a long march of time to trap the impious. Above the established doctrines neither knowledge nor practice should seek to go. It costs but little to believe in the power and mystery of the gods, to accept what is grounded in nature and accepted by the usage of long ages.

What is wisdom? What boon from the gods is fairer among men than to hold a victorious hand over the head of one's enemies? What is fair is ever dear.

Happy is he who has escaped the tempest at sea and found harbor. Happy is he who has risen triumphant over his toils. In one way or another one man outstrips another in the race for wealth and power. And a thousand others are cherishing a thousand hopes; some result in happiness for mortals and some fail. But I call blessed the man whose life is happy day by day.

[The Stranger enters and calls upon Pentheus, whom he has been dressing, to come out

THE STRANGER. Pentheus! If you are so eager to pry into secret things, so bent on evil, come out in front of the house; let us see how you look dressed like a woman, a bacchic maenad, off to spy on your mother and her company.

[Enter Pentheus in bacchic attire; he moves and speaks as if under some strange
influence

You *do* look like one of Cadmus' daughters.

PENTHEUS. I seem to see two suns, and a double Thebes, ay, two seven-gated cities. And a bull is leading me on—you seem to be a bull, with horns growing on your head. *Were* you ever an animal? Certainly you have the look of a bull.

THE STRANGER. The god is our escort. He was hostile before, but now he has made his peace with us. Now you see as you should.

PENTHEUS. What *do* I look like? Have I not the pose of Ino? Or Agave, yes, my own mother Agave?

THE STRANGER. When I look at you I seem to see their very selves. But here's one of your tresses out of place. It is not as I fixed it, under your snood.

PENTHEUS. I must have dislodged it inside, while I was tossing my locks up and down in bacchic ecstasy.

THE STRANGER. I will arrange it again, I am your maid. Come, hold your head up.

PENTHEUS. There, you dress it. I depend on you.

THE STRANGER. Your girdle has come undone. And the tucks of your dress are all uneven at the ankles.

PENTHEUS. I think so too, at least by the right foot. The rest hangs straight enough, by the left.

THE STRANGER. I am sure you will think me your best friend when I surprise you and show you the bacchants sober.

PENTHEUS. Do I hold the thyrsus in my right hand or in this one to be more like a bacchant?

THE STRANGER. Hold it in your right hand, and advance it when you advance your right foot. I am glad your mind is changed.

PENTHEUS. Do you think I could carry the crags of Cithaeron, bacchants and all, upon my shoulders?

THE STRANGER. You could, if you wished. The mind you had before was not sound, but now you are in a proper state.

PENTHEUS. Shall we take crowbars? Or shall I tear the crags up with my hands, putting a shoulder or an arm to the peaks?

THE STRANGER. O please! Don't destroy the shrines of the Nymphs and the haunts of Pan and his pipings.

PENTHEUS. Right you are. One does not overcome women by force. I shall conceal myself in the firs.

THE STRANGER. You will get all the concealment I think you need—creeping up to spy on the maenads.

PENTHEUS. Besides, I expect they won't leave their couches in the thickets, caught like birds—and loving it.

THE STRANGER. That is the very thing you are going to watch. Perhaps you will surprise them—if you are not surprised first yourself.

PENTHEUS. Take me through the middle of Thebes. I am the only man of them that would make this venture.

THE STRANGER. You are the only one that troubles about your city, the only one. Therefore, trials await you, fitting trials. Follow me. I shall guide you in safety; another will bring you back—

PENTHEUS. Yes, my mother.

THE STRANGER. A shining example to all.

PENTHEUS. It is for that I come.

THE STRANGER. You will be carried back—

PENTHEUS. You promise me luxury.

THE STRANGER. In your mother's hands.

PENTHEUS. You will make an elegant of me.

THE STRANGER. Elegant indeed!

PENTHEUS. My enterprise will earn it.

THE STRANGER. You are a remarkable man, remarkable indeed; and it is to a remarkable experience that you are going. You will attain renown towering to heaven. Open your arms, Agave, and you her sisters, daughters of Cadmus. I bring this bold youth to a famous contest. The victor will be I, and Bromius. The rest the event will show.

[Exit with Pentheus

CHORUS. *On, swift hounds of Madness, on to where the daughters of Cadmus hold their revels. Goad them to fury against him who masquerades in woman's attire, the maniac who spies on the maenads. His mother will see him first, as he peers from behind a smooth rock or tree-stump. She will cry out to the maenads: "Who is this sleuth who has come to the mountain, come to spy on us Thebans where we revel on the mountain? Who was the mother that bore him? Not of the blood of women is this man's birth, of some lioness, some Gorgon of Libya".*

Let Justice advance in plain sight, advance sword in hand, to strike through the throat, to slaughter the godless, the lawless, the ruthless man, the earth-born son of Echion.

With ruthless temper and lawless rage he visits your orgies, Bacchus, yours and your mother's. In the madness of his heart, in the delusion of his wits, he thinks his violence can master the Invincible. But there is One ready and willing to correct his heresies— Death. To know the limits of mortality is a life without sorrow. False knowledge I do not envy; I rejoice to hunt it down. The other things, the greater things, are not abstruse. Ah, let my life flow quietly; let me seek the good, in purity and piety from morn till night, honoring the gods and eschewing all unrighteous practices.

Let Justice advance in plain sight, advance sword in hand, to strike through the throat, to slaughter the godless, the lawless, the ruthless man, the earth-born son of Echion.

Appear as a bull, as a many-headed dragon to the view, as a fiery glaring lion to the sight. Up, Bacchus, with smiling face cast your noose around the hunter of the bacchants, fallen among the deadly band of maenads.

[Enter Messenger

MESSENGER. Ah, house once prosperous throughout Hellas, house of the old man of Sidon who in the land of the Serpent sowed the dragon's earth-born crop, how I groan for you! I am just a slave, but still—[good slaves are touched by their masters' calamities.]

LEADER. What is it? Have you news to tell of the bacchants?

MESSENGER. Pentheus is dead, the son of Echion.

CHORUS. *Lord Bromius, you show yourself a mighty god!*

MESSENGER. What do you say? What was that? Do you rejoice at the misfortunes of my master, woman?

CHORUS. *An alien I am, and in barbaric strains I hail my god. No longer do I cower in fear of chains.*

MESSENGER. Do you think Thebes is so wanting in men—

CHORUS. *It is Dionysus, Dionysus and not Thebes, who has power over me.*

MESSENGER. I can understand; but it is not fair, women, to rejoice over afflictions past cure.

LEADER. *Tell me, say, what death did he die, the wicked man, the worker of wickedness?*

MESSENGER. When we had put behind us the homesteads of this Theban land and crossed over the streams of Asopus we came to the heights of Cithaeron, Pentheus and I—I was attending my master—and the stranger who headed our pilgrimage.

First, we halted in a grassy glade. We kept silence, of tread and tongue alike, in order to see without being seen. And there, across a precipitous ravine, where the pines stood dark over the waters of a stream, the maenads were sitting, their hands busy with pleasant tasks. Some of them were wreathing afresh their worn-out wands with new tresses of ivy. Others, like colts freed from the gaudy yoke, were singing lustily their bacchic antiphons. Pentheus, poor man, did not see the crowd of women, and said: "Stranger, where we stand my eyes cannot reach these bastard maenads. If I stood at the edge and climbed a tall fir, I would get a perfect view of their wild obscenities."

Then came the miracle—I saw the stranger seize the top-most branches of a soaring fir and force it down, down, down to the black earth, till it was arched like a bow, or like an arc described by the peg-and-string in drawing the circumference of a rounded wheel. So the stranger tugged at that mountain branch with his hands, and bent it down to earth: it was no mortal deed he wrought. When he had set Pentheus on the branches of the fir, he slipped his hands along the trunk, letting it straighten again; but gently, for fear the mount should throw the rider. Aloft into the lofty air rose the sturdy fir, with my master sitting on top. And now he saw the maenads—but not so well as they saw him. They had scarcely spied him on his lofty seat, when the stranger disappeared from sight, and a voice out of the sky, I guess it was Dionysus, cried aloud: "Young women, I bring the man who has cast ridicule upon you and upon me and upon our holy rites. Take vengeance on him." Even as he spoke, he caused a mysterious pillar of fire to rise from earth to heaven.

The air was hushed, hushed were the leaves of the trees in the glen—not a cry to be heard of any creature. But the bacchants had not heard the shout distinctly. They leapt to their feet and swept the scene with their eyes. And again he exhorted them. Then the daughters of Cadmus recognized the clear command of Bacchus. They shot forth, swift as a flock of doves, speeding along on eager, straining feet, his mother Agave and her sisters and all the bacchants. Through the glen, over torrents and boulders, they leapt, maddened with the inspiration of the god. When they saw my master sitting upon the fir, they first took their stand on a towering rock opposite him and began to pelt him hard with stones. Some shot branches of fir at him, others sent their wands flying through the air. But their aim was wretched and they had no success. He sat high above their eager reach, a pitiful and helpless captive. Finally they violently rived off branches of oak and set about prying up the roots of his tree with their improvised crowbars. When they failed to achieve the end of their toils Agave spoke: "Come, stand about in a circle and take hold of the trunk. We must capture the treed beast [or he will publish the secrets of the god's dances]." Then they applied countless hands to the fir and wrenched it from the ground. Down from his lofty perch, down whirling to the earth, falls Pentheus. Many and many were his moans; for he knew his hour was near. His mother attacked him— the priestess commencing the sacrifice. He flung off his head-dress, in order that poor

Agave might recognize him and not kill him. He touched her cheek and said: "I am your child, mother, Pentheus, whom you bore in Echion's house. Pity me, mother; do not, because of *my* sins, kill *your* child."

But she was foaming at the mouth and rolling distorted eyeballs, out of her right mind, possessed by Bacchus. His pleadings were of no avail. She seized the hand of his left arm and set her foot against the poor wretch's side and tore off his arm at the shoulder—not of her own strength; it was the god who made easy the work of her hands. Ino wrought havoc on the other side, rending the flesh, while Autonoe and the whole bacchic horde pressed on. All was one wild din—he groaning with the little breath that was left him, and they shrieking in triumph. One carried off an arm, another a foot, shoe and all. They stripped the flesh from his ribs with their tearing. One and all, with blood-bespattered hands, they played ball with the flesh of Pentheus.

His body lies in pieces, part under the jagged rocks, part in the green depths of the forest; no easy thing to find. His mother has his poor head. She seized it in her hands and fixed it on the top of a thyrsus. She thinks it is the head of a mountain lion that she carries through the midst of Cithaeron. She has left her sisters at the dances of the maenads and is returning within these walls gloating over her hapless prey. She is calling upon Bacchus, her "fellow-huntsman", her "comrade in the chase", her conquering hero". Bitter for her are the fruits of victory she brings him.

I shall get out of the way of this calamity before Agave comes home. It is the loveliest thing to be virtuous and god-fearing. And I imagine it is also the *wisest* course for mortals to follow.

[Exit Messenger

CHORUS. *Let us dance to the glory of Bacchus, let us shout for the calamity of Pentheus, the spawn of the ancient serpent. He took woman's attire, he took a fair shaft of fennel: the uniform of the god—of death. And a bull showed him the way to destruction. Bacchants of Thebes, glorious is the paean you have achieved, ending in wailing and tears. It is a goodly sport to fling about one's child an arm dripping with his own blood.*

LEADER. But stay. I see Pentheus' mother, Agave, rushing wild-eyed towards the house. Welcome you the revel of the bacchic god.

[Enter Agave, frenzied, blood-stained, with Pentheus' head on her thyrsus

AGAVE. Bacchants of Asia———

CHORUS. *To what will you urge me? Oh!*

AGAVE. I bring to our halls from the mountains a tendril newly cut. Happy was the hunting.

CHORUS. *I see; and I welcome you to join our revel.*

AGAVE. Without a noose I snared it—the young whelp of a savage lion. Look and see.

CHORUS. *From where in the wilds?*

AGAVE. Cithaeron———

CHORUS. *Cithaeron?*

AGAVE. —Slew him.

CHORUS. *Who was she who smote him?*

AGAVE. Mine was the first honor. "Happy Agave" they call me in the revel.

CHORUS. *And who else?*

AGAVE. Cadmus' own—

CHORUS. *Cadmus' what?*

AGAVE. His own children. They reached the prey, but after me, after me. Happy was this hunting.

CHORUS. [LACUNA]

AGAVE. Then share in the feast.

CHORUS. *What? Shall I share it? Poor woman!*

AGAVE. The whelp is yet young; the down of his cheek is just blooming beneath his crest of delicate hair.

CHORUS. *By its mane it might be a beast of the field.*

AGAVE. Bacchus, the skilful hunter, skilfully roused the maenads against this beast.

CHORUS. *Our king is a hunter.*

AGAVE. Do you praise me?

CHORUS. *I do praise you.*

AGAVE. Soon the Thebans———

CHORUS. *Yes, and your son Pentheus———*

AGAVE. Will praise his mother for catching this quarry, this lion cub.

CHORUS. *Remarkable quarry!*

AGAVE. Remarkably caught!

CHORUS. *Are you proud?*

AGAVE. Overjoyed. Greatness, manifest greatness, I have achieved in this capture.

LEADER. Show the townspeople, poor woman, your victory's booty, which you brought with you.

AGAVE. O you that dwell in this fair-towered town of the Theban land, come and see this prey, the beast which we daughters of Cadmus hunted down, not by the looped darts of the Thessalians, not with nets, but with our white arms and hands. Why then must men boast and get instruments from the armorers in vain? With our bare hands we took this animal and tore the beast's joints asunder.

Where is my old father? Let him come near. And Pentheus, my son, where is he? Let him bring a strong step-ladder and set it against the house, so that he can nail to the triglyphs this lion's head I have brought from the hunt.

[Enter Cadmus slowly with servants carrying the remains of Pentheus on a bier

CADMUS. Follow me and bring your sad burden—the corpse of Pentheus. Follow me, servants, to the house where I am taking this body. After endless wearisome searching I found it in the trackless wood, torn to pieces in the glens of Cithaeron. No two parts were in the same spot.

I had come back from among the bacchants with the old man Tiresias, and I was already within the city's walls, when some one told me of my daughter's desperate deeds. I returned again to the mountain to fetch home her child, killed by the maenads. There I saw her that once bore Actaeon to Aristaeus, Autonoe I mean, her and Ino, still frenzy-stung, poor women, in the oak forest. But Agave, they told me, was coming back here with frenzied pace. And what I heard was not untrue; for there I see her, no happy sight.

AGAVE. Father, the proudest boast is yours to make: you have begotten daughters by far the best in all the world—all your daughters, I say, but me above all. I have left my shuttle by the loom; I have gone to greater things, to hunting animals with my hands. I bring in my arms, as you see, this prize of my courage, to hang on your walls. Take it father, in your hands. Exult in my hunting and invite your friends to a feast. You are blessed, yes blessed, in the achievement I have wrought.

CADMUS. Ah grief beyond measure—I cannot look upon it. Murder it is that you have wrought with your wretched hands. A noble victim it is that you have laid low for the gods; and now you invite this Thebes and me to the feast! Ah me for these woes, yours first and then mine. What ruin the god, king Bromius, has dealt us; with justice indeed, but not mercy, though he is born of our house.

AGAVE. What a crabbed thing old age is in men, how morose of aspect! I wish my son might take after his mother's ways, and be as lucky in the chase when he goes hunting wild beasts with the young men of Thebes. But that fellow is only good for quarreling with gods. He ought to be admonished, father; and you are the one to do it. Somebody call him here into my sight, to see me in my happiness.

CADMUS. Alas, alas! If you ever realize what you have done you will grieve with a bitter grief. But if you remain to the end in your present state, your affliction will be a blessing in disguise.

AGAVE. What is there in this that is not right? What is there to grieve for?

CADMUS. Turn your eyes first to yonder sky.

AGAVE. There. Why do you tell me to look at it?

CADMUS. Is it still the same, or does it seem different to you?

AGAVE. It is brighter than before, more pellucid.

CADMUS. Is there the same unrest in your soul?

AGAVE. Unrest? I do not know. I am becoming—somehow—[sensible. The thoughts I had have gone.]

CADMUS. Can you hear? Can you answer clearly?

AGAVE. I have forgotten what we were saying, father.

CADMUS. To whose house did you come as a bride?

AGAVE. You gave me to Echion—Echion of the Dragon race, they say.

CADMUS. What child was born to your husband in your house?

AGAVE. Pentheus, to me and his father together.

CADMUS. Whose is the face you have in your arms?

AGAVE. A lion's, at least those who hunted it said so.

CADMUS. Look right at it. It is small effort to see it.

AGAVE. Ha! What do I see? What is this I bring home in my hands?

CADMUS. Gaze at it, study it more truly.

AGAVE. I see, a mighty grief. Ah, miserable am I!

CADMUS. It doesn't seem to you to resemble a lion?

AGAVE. No, it is Pentheus' head I hold, O misery!

CADMUS. Yes, bewailed by me before *you* recognized him.

AGAVE. Who killed him? How did he come into my hands?

CADMUS. Unhappy truth, how unseasonably you dawn!

AGAVE. Speak, my heart leaps in dread of what's to come.

CADMUS. You killed him, you and your sisters.

AGAVE. Where did he die? Was it at home? Somewhere outside?

CADMUS. Where the dogs once tore Actaeon to pieces.

AGAVE. Why did the unhappy creature go to Cithaeron?

CADMUS. He went to mock the god and your bacchic revels.

AGAVE. But we—how did we get out there?

CADMUS. You were mad, the whole city was in the frenzy of Bacchus.

AGAVE. Dionysus has undone us. Too late I see it.

CADMUS. Yes, for affronts put on him; you did not count him a god.

AGAVE. My son's dear body, father—where is it?

CADMUS. Here I bring it—retrieved with difficulty.

AGAVE. Is it all decently composed? *[Cadmus is silent.]* What part had my madness in Pentheus' fate?

146

.

CADMUS. He was like you—blaspheming against the god. So the god joined all of you in a single destruction, you and this unfortunate. The house is undone and I too; for I am without male children, and I have seen this shoot from your womb, poor woman, foully and horribly slain. *[To the body of Pentheus]* To you the house looked up; you were the stay of my halls, child. Son of my own daughter, you had the city in awe of you. No one that looked upon your presence dared outrage the old man; for you would exact due penalty. But now I shall be cast out of my house dishonored—I, the great Cadmus, who sowed the race of Thebans and harvested a most excellent crop. Ah, dearest of men— yes, even in death I shall count you with the dearest, my child—never more will you touch this chin of mine with your hand and call me "mother's father" and embrace me, child, and say: "Is anyone wronging you? Is anyone dishonoring you, old man? Is anyone annoying you and vexing your heart? Tell me, and I shall punish whoever does you wrong, father."

But now it is sorrow for me and misery for you, grief for your mother and for her sisters misery. If there is anyone who disdains the deities, let him look at the death of this man and believe in the gods.

LEADER. I grieve for your sorrow, Cadmus. Your grandson has his deserts, his just deserts, but grievous for you.

AGAVE. Father, you see how all is changed for me————

[A LONG LAMENT OF AGAVE, A FEW LINES OF THE CHORUS ANNOUNCING THE APPEARANCE OF DIONYSUS, AND THE BEGINNING OF THE GOD'S SPEECH ARE LOST.]

DIONYSUS. * * * You will change and become a serpent; and your wife Harmonia, Ares' daughter, whom you got to wife though you were a mortal, will take a brutish form and be changed into a snake. A chariot drawn by bullocks, Zeus' oracle says, you will drive, your wife by your side, at the head of barbarians. You will sack many cities with an unnumbered host. But when they plunder the oracle of Loxias, they will receive a sorry homecoming. But Ares shall save you and Harmonia and establish your life in the land of the blessed.

These things say I, Dionysus, born of no mortal father but of Zeus. If you had learned wisdom then, when you would not, you would have been happy now, with the son of Zeus for your ally.

CADMUS. Dionysus, we beseech you, we have sinned.

DIONYSUS. Too late you have learned to know me. When the knowledge was wanted, you had it not.

CADMUS. We realize it. But you go too far against us.

DIONYSUS. Because you outraged my divinity.

CADMUS. It ill beseems gods to imitate the passions of mortals.

DIONYSUS. My father, Zeus, ordained these things of old.

AGAVE. Alas, it is decreed, old man—the misery of banishment.

DIONYSUS. Why then do you delay when necessity constrains?

[Dionysus disappears

CADMUS. Ah child, to what a fearful pass we have all come, you and your unhappy sisters, and I the sorrowful. In my old age I go to an alien land to dwell among barbarians. And there is also the prophecy—that I must lead a mingled barbarian host against Hellas. Myself a serpent, with my wife Harmonia, Ares' child, a wild and savage serpent too, I shall lead an army of spearsmen against altars and tombs of Hellas. Cadmus the Sorrowful! My sufferings will never end. Not even when I go down the chasm of Acheron river shall I have rest.

AGAVE. Ah, father, I shall lose you, I shall live in exile.

CADMUS. Why do you fling your arms about me, poor child—a white swan embracing its old decrepit sire?

AGAVE. Where then should I turn when I am cast out of my land?

CADMUS. I do not know, child; your father is small help.

AGAVE. Farewell, my home; farewell my native city. I leave you for misery, for exile, far from home and love.

CADMUS. Go, my child, to Aristaeus (your sister's husband); he———

AGAVE. I groan for you father.

CADMUS. And I for you, child; and I weep for your sisters.

AGAVE. In dreadful wise has king Dionysus brought this confusion upon your house.

CADMUS. Dreadful was his treatment at your hands. His name was without honor in Thebes.

AGAVE. Farewell, my father.

CADMUS. Farewell, my poor child. It will not be easy—if you ever do find welfare.

AGAVE. Take me, my guides, where I shall find my unhappy sisters, my companions in exile. Let me go where foul Cithaeron may never see me, nor my eyes see Cithaeron, to some place where stands no memorial of the thyrsus! Let others be bacchants and care for these things.

CHORUS. *Many are the forms of divine intervention; many things beyond expectation do the gods fulfil. That which was expected has not been accomplished; for that which was unexpected has god found the way. Such was the end of this story.*

[Exeunt

Thucydides, The Peloponnesian War

The greatest historian of the ancient world, Thucydides (c. 460–400 B.C.) provides a brilliant account of the wars between Athens and Sparta that ended Greece's Golden Age. He is the first writer to examine critically the deep-rooted social and political issues that bring nations into conflict and to analyze war's adverse effects on human character and behavior. An Athenian general exiled from his native city for failing to relieve a beseiged stronghold, Thucydides offers a remarkably objective report of the war's underlying cause—Sparta's jealousy of Athen's growing political and economic power.

After Athens led the Greeks to victory during the two invasions by the Persian Empire (490 and 480–479 B.C.), she formed an association of Greek city–states, the Delian League, ostensibly to fend off future military attack, but in reality to satisfy imperial ambition. Sparta, conservative and isolationist, attempted to limit Athenian influence by creating a rival confederation of Peloponnesian states. War broke out in 431 B.C. and continued intermittently until 404 B.C., when Athens was defeated.

Thucydides paints Athens' fall as if the city were a character in Greek tragedy. Though noble and powerful, Athens is fatally blinded by an ambition that leads her to corrupt the very values that made her great. The inventor of democratic government, Athens also becomes the enslaver of weaker states, attempting to impose democracy on her neighbors by force. The city reaches its moral nadir when it ruthlessly destroys the tiny state of Melos, which had attempted to remain neutral.

Thucydides illustrates Athens' gradual deterioration from political liberator to tyrant in a series of speeches that participants delivered at crucial moments during the war. The most famous speaker is Pericles, leader of Athenian democracy, who vividly expresses the principles of freedom and individual achievement for which Athens supposedly fights. Thucydides' original readers probably read Pericles' Funeral Oration (431 B.C.) with regret for a vanished and ideal way of life. In the war's second year, a disastrous plague struck Athens, killing a third of the city's population including Pericles. The civilization he so eloquently describes, the most dazzlingly creative in history, did not long survive him.

PERICLES' FUNERAL ORATION
■

'I have no wish to make a long speech on subjects familiar to you all: so I shall say nothing about the warlike deeds by which we acquired our power or the battles in which we or our fathers gallantly resisted our enemies, Greek or foreign. What I want to do is, in the first place, to discuss the spirit in which we faced our trials and also our constitution and the way of life which has made us great. After that I shall speak in praise of the dead, believing that this kind of speech is not inappropriate to the present occasion, and that this whole assembly, of citizens and foreigners, may listen to it with advantage.

'Let me say that our system of government does not copy the institutions of our neighbours. It is more the case of our being a model to others, than of our imitating anyone else. Our constitution is called a democracy because power is in the hands not of a minority but of the whole people. When it is a question of settling private disputes, everyone is equal before the law; when it is a question of putting one person before another in positions of public responsibility, what counts is not membership of a particular class, but the actual ability which the man possesses. No one, so long as he has it in him to be of service to the state, is kept in political obscurity because of poverty. And, just as our political life is free and open, so is our day-to-day life in our relations with each other. We do not get into a state with our next-door neighbour if he enjoys himself in his own way, nor do we give him the kind of black looks which, though they do no real harm, still do hurt people's feelings. We are free and tolerant in our private lives; but in public affairs we keep to the law. This is because it commands our deep respect.

'We give our obedience to those whom we put in positions of authority, and we obey the laws themselves, especially those which are for the protection of the oppressed, and those unwritten laws which it is an acknowledged shame to break.

'And here is another point. When our work is over, we are in a position to enjoy all kinds of recreation for our spirits. There are various kinds of contests and sacrifices regularly throughout the year; in our own homes we find a beauty and a good taste which delight us every day and which drive away our cares. Then the greatness of our city brings it about that all the good things from all over the world flow in to us, so that to us it seems just as natural to enjoy foreign goods as our own local products.

'Then there is a great difference between us and our opponents in our attitude towards military security. Here are some examples: Our city is open to the world, and we have no periodical deportations in order to prevent people observing or finding out secrets which might be of military advantage to the enemy. This is because we rely, not on secret weapons, but on our own real courage and loyalty. There is a difference, too, in our educational systems. The Spartans, from their earliest boyhood, are submitted to the most laborious training in courage; we pass our lives without all these restrictions, and yet are just as ready to face the same danger as they are. Here is a proof of this: When the Spartans invade our land, they do not come by themselves, but bring all their allies with them; whereas we, when we launch an attack abroad, do the job by ourselves, and, though fighting on foreign soil, do not often fail to defeat opponents who are fighting for their own hearths and homes. As a matter of fact none of our enemies has ever yet been confronted with our total strength, because we have to divide our attention between our navy and the many missions on which our troops are sent on land. Yet, if our enemies engage a detachment of our forces and defeat it, they give themselves credit for having thrown back our entire army; or, if they lose, they claim that they were beaten by us in full strength. There are certain advantages, I think, in our way of meeting danger voluntarily, with an easy mind, instead of with a laborious training, with natural rather than with state-induced courage. We do not have to spend our time practising to meet sufferings which are still in the future; and when they are actually upon us we show ourselves just as brave as these others who are always in strict training. This is one point in which, I think, our city deserves to be admired. There are also others:

'Our love of what is beautiful does not lead to extravagance; our love of the things of the mind does not make us soft. We regard wealth as something to be properly used, rather than as something to boast about. As for poverty, no one need be ashamed to admit it: the real shame is in not taking practical measures to escape from it. Here each individual is interested not only in his own affairs but in the affairs of the state as well: even those who are mostly occupied with their own business are extremely well-informed on general politics—this is a peculiarity of ours: we do not say that a man who takes no interest in politics is a man who minds his own business; we say that he has no business here at all. We Athenians, in our own persons, take our decisions on policy or submit them to proper discussion: for we do not think that there is an incompatibility between words and deeds; the worst thing is to rush into action before the consequences have been properly debated. And this is another point where we differ from other people. We are capable at the same time of taking risks and of estimating them beforehand. Others are brave out of ignorance; and, when they stop to think, they begin to fear. But the man who can most truly be accounted brave is he who best knows the meaning of what is sweet in life and of what is terrible, and then goes out undeterred to meet what is to come.

'Again, in questions of general good feeling there is a great contrast between us and most other people. We make friends by doing good to others, not by receiving good from them. This makes our friendship all the more reliable, since we want to keep alive the gratitude of those who are in our debt by showing continued goodwill to them: whereas the feelings of one who owes us something lack the same enthusiasm, since he knows that, when he repays our kindness, it will be more like paying back a debt than giving something spontaneously. We are unique in this. When we do kindnesses to others, we do not do them out of any calculations of profit or loss: we do them without afterthought, relying on our free liberality. Taking everything together then, I declare that our city is an education to Greece, and I declare that in my opinion each single one of our citizens, in all the manifold aspects of life, is able to show himself the rightful lord and owner of his own person, and do this, moreover, with exceptional grace and exceptional versatility. And to show that this is no empty boasting for the present occasion, but real tangible fact, you have only to consider the power which our city possesses and which has been won by those very qualities which I have mentioned. Athens, alone of the states we know, comes to her testing time in a greatness that surpasses what was imagined of her. In her case, and in her case alone, no invading enemy is ashamed of being defeated, and no subject can complain of being governed by people unfit for their responsibilities. Mighty indeed are the marks and monuments of our empire which we have left. Future ages will wonder at us, as the present age wonders at us now. We do not need the praises of a Homer, or of anyone else whose words may delight us for the moment, but whose estimation of facts will fall short of what is really true. For our adventurous spirit has forced an entry into every sea and into every land; and everywhere we have left behind us everlasting memorials of good done to our friends or suffering inflicted on our enemies.

'This, then, is the kind of city for which these men, who could not bear the thought of losing her, nobly fought and nobly died. It is only natural that every one of us who survive them should be willing to undergo hardships in her service. And it was for this reason that I have spoken at such length about our city, because I wanted to make it clear that for us there is more at stake than there is for others who lack our advantages; also I wanted my words of praise for the dead to be set in the bright light of evidence. And now the most important of these words has been spoken. I have sung the praises of our city; but it was the courage and gallantry of these men, and of people like them, which made her splendid. Nor would you find it true in the case of many of the Greeks, as it is true of them, that no words can do more than justice to their deeds.

'To me it seems that the consummation which has overtaken these men shows us the meaning of manliness in its first revelation and in its final proof. Some of them, no doubt, had their faults; but what we ought to remember first is their gallant conduct against the enemy in defence of their native land. They have blotted out evil with good, and done more service to the commonwealth than they ever did harm in their private lives. No one of these men weakened because he wanted to go on enjoying his wealth: no one put off the awful day in the hope that he might live to escape his poverty and grow rich. More to be desired than such things, they chose to check the enemy's pride. This, to them, was a risk most glorious, and they accepted it, willing to strike down the enemy and relinquish everything else. As for success or failure, they left that in the doubtful hands of Hope, and when the reality of battle was before their faces, they put their trust in their own selves. In the fighting, they thought it more honourable to stand their ground and suffer death than to give in and save their lives. So they fled from the reproaches of men, abiding with life and limb the brunt of battle; and, in a small moment of time, the climax of their lives, a culmination of glory, not of fear, were swept away from us.

'So and such they were, these men—worthy of their city. We who remain behind may hope to be spared their fate, but must resolve to keep the same daring spirit against the foe. It is not simply a question of estimating the advantages in theory. I could tell you a long story (and you know it as well as I do) about what is to be gained by beating the enemy back. What I would prefer is that you should fix your eyes every day on the greatness of Athens as she really is, and should fall in love with her. When you realize her greatness, then reflect that what made her great was men with a spirit of adventure, men who knew their duty, men who were ashamed to fall below a certain standard. If they ever failed in an enterprise, they made up their minds that at any rate the city should not find their courage lacking to her, and they gave to her the best contribution that they could. They gave her their lives, to her and to all of us, and for their own selves they won praises that never grow old, the most splendid of sepulchres—not the sepulchre in which their bodies are laid, but where their glory remains eternal in men's minds, always there on the right occasion to stir others to speech or to action. For famous men have the whole earth as their memorial: it is not only the inscriptions on their graves in their own country that mark them out; no, in foreign lands also, not in any visible form but in people's hearts, their memory abides and grows. It is for you to try to be like them. Make up your minds that happiness depends on being free, and freedom depends on being courageous. Let there be no relaxation in face of the perils of the war. The people who have most excuse for despising death are not the wretched and unfortunate, who have no hope of doing well for themselves, but those who run the risk of a complete reversal in their lives, and who would feel the difference most intensely, if things went wrong for them. Any intelligent man would find a humiliation caused by his own slackness more painful to bear than death, when death comes to him unperceived, in battle, and in the confidence of his patriotism.

Plato, The Republic

Greek thinkers were the first to attempt to explain the universe rationally, without relying on religion or ancient mythology. Philosophy, the love of wisdom, was born about 600 B.C. in the Ionian city of Miletus. Using keen observation and logic as tools for discovering truth, philosophers investigated natural phenomena, such as planetary movement, and human behavior, particularly the standards by which we distinguish acceptable ethical conduct.

Following the lead of early philosophers like Pythagoras, who combined mathematics with mysticism, the Athenian Socrates (c. 469–399 B.C.) turned from studying science to examining human values. Although Socrates did not offer his disciples a comprehensive worldview, he created an effective method of questioning and challenging popular assumptions about life's priorities and values. He compared himself to a gadfly that stings people awake, forcing them to consider whether there are more important goals than making money or wielding political influence. After decades of strolling barefoot through Athens urging his fellow citizens to think clearly and behave justly, Socrates was charged with corrupting young men and threatening the state religion. Refusing to change his ways, he was condemned to death.

Although not present at Socrates' execution, Plato (c. 429–347 B.C.) recreates his teacher's last hours in the *Phaedo,* a dialogue that presents the philosopher calmly, even humorously, discussing the soul's probable immortality as he prepares to die. Following Pythagoras and the Orphic mystery cults, Socrates argues that death is only the separation of the mortal body from the imperishable soul. The soul originates in the invisible spirit realm, a dimension of perfect and eternal forms, the ideal patterns that give shape and coherence to this visible world of change and decay. Death frees the soul to return to its natural home.

In the *Republic,* a dialogue about the ideal human community, Plato has Socrates explain why it is so difficult for us, trapped in physical bodies, to understand the superiority of the spirit world. The famous "Allegory of the Cave" compares physical existence to imprisonment in a dark cavern, where the only light is a bonfire that casts shadows of imitation objects on the cave walls. Having lived all their lives in this shadowy prison, the people chained there naturally mistake shadows for reality. If someone were to escape and return to tell cave dwellers that he had seen the real sun, for which the bonfire is a poor substitute, and real trees and cities instead of the shadows cast by cardboard cutouts, the prisoners would think him crazy. So it is with the philosopher who catches glimpses of the eternal forms of wisdom, truth, or beauty, when he attempts to share his vision with ordinary people who confuse the material world with the real one.

The "Myth of Er," which concludes the *Republic,* reveals what the soul experiences after death. A soldier apparently killed in battle, Er leaves his body to visit the unseen realm where souls are judged, rewarded for virtue, or punished for evil deeds. He witnesses the mysterious process of reincarnation in which souls choose their next lives on earth. Some who have enjoyed a thousand years of heavenly bliss choose unwisely, whereas others, having painfully learned from their punishments, carefully select a good life. In Plato's universe, the gods are not responsible for human folly or wickedness; all souls freely assume their own destinies.

THE ALLEGORY OF THE CAVE
■

The progress of the mind from the lowest state of unenlightenment to knowledge of the Good is now illustrated by the famous parable comparing the world of appearance to an underground Cave. In Empedocles' religious poem the powers which conduct the soul to its incarnation say,'We have come under this cavern's roof.' The image was probably taken from mysteries held in caves or dark chambers representing the underworld, through which the candidates for initiation were led to the revelation of sacred objects in a blaze of light. The idea that the body is a prison-house, to which the soul is condemned for past misdeeds, is attributed by Plato to the Orphics.

One moral of the allegory is drawn from the distress caused by a too sudden passage from darkness to light. The earlier warning against plunging untrained minds into the discussion of moral problems, as the Sophists and Socrates himself had done, is reinforced by the picture of the dazed prisoner dragged out into the sunlight. Plato's ten years' course of pure mathematics is to habituate the intellect to abstract reasoning before moral ideas are called in question.

Next, said [Socrates], here is a parable to illustrate the degrees in which our nature may be enlightened or unenlightened. Imagine the condition of men living in a sort of cavernous chamber underground, with an entrance open to the light and a long passage all down the cave.[1] Here they have been from childhood, chained by the leg and also by the neck, so that they cannot move and can see only what is in front of them, because the chains will not let them turn their heads. At some distance higher up is the light of a fire burning behind them; and between the prisoners and the fire is a track[2] with a parapet built along it, like the screen at a puppet-show, which hides the performers while they show their puppets over the top.

I see, said [Glaucon, Plato's brother].

Now behind this parapet imagine persons carrying along various artificial objects, including figures of men and animals in wood or stone or other materials, which project above the parapet. Naturally, some of these persons will be talking, others silent.[3]

It is a strange picture, he said, and a strange sort of prisoners.

---

1. The *length* of the 'way in' (*eisodos*) to the chamber where the prisoners sit is an essential feature, explaining why no daylight reaches them.

2. The track crosses the passage into the cave at right angles, and is *above* the parapet built along it.

3. A modern Plato would compare his Cave to an underground cinema, where the audience watch the play of shadows thrown by the film passing before a light at their backs. The film itself is only an image of 'real' things and events in the world outside the cinema. For the film Plato has to substitute the clumsier apparatus of a procession of artificial objects carried on their heads by persons who are merely part of the machinery, providing for the movement of the objects and the sounds whose echo the prisoners hear. The parapet prevents these persons' shadows from being cast on the wall of the Cave.

Like ourselves, I replied; for in the first place prisoners so confined would have seen nothing of themselves or of one another, except the shadows thrown by the fire-light on the wall of the Cave facing them, would they?

Not if all their lives they had been prevented from moving their heads.

And they would have seen as little of the objects carried past.

Of course.

Now, if they could talk to one another, would they not suppose that their words referred only to those passing shadows which they saw?[4]

Necessarily.

And suppose their prison had an echo from the wall facing them? When one of the people crossing behind them spoke, they could only suppose that the sound came from the shadow passing before their eyes.

No doubt.

In every way, then, such prisoners would recognize as reality nothing but the shadows of those artificial objects.[5]

Inevitably.

Now consider what would happen if their release from the chains and the healing of their unwisdom should come about in this way. Suppose one of them set free and forced suddenly to stand up, turn his head, and walk with eyes lifted to the light; all these movements would be painful, and he would be too dazzled to make out the objects whose shadows he had been used to see. What do you think he would say, if someone told him that what he had formerly seen was meaningless illusion, but now, being somewhat nearer to reality and turned towards more real objects, he was getting a truer view? Suppose further that he were shown the various objects being carried by and were made to say, in reply to questions, what each of them was. Would he not be perplexed and believe the objects now shown him to be not so real as what he formerly saw?[6]

Yes, not nearly so real.

And if he were forced to look at the fire-light itself, would not his eyes ache, so that he would try to escape and turn back to the things which he would see distinctly, convinced that they really were clearer than these other objects now being shown to him?

Yes.

And suppose someone were to drag him away forcibly up the steep and rugged ascent and not let him go until he had hauled him out into the sunlight, would he not suffer pain and vexation at such treatment, and, when he had come out into the light, find his eyes so full of its radiance that he could not see a single one of the things that he was now told were real?

Certainly he would not see them all at once.

He would need, then, to grow accustomed before he could see things in that upper world.[7] At first it would be easiest to make out shadows, and then the images of men and things

---

4. Adam's text and interpretation. The prisoners, having seen nothing but shadows, cannot think their words refer to the objects carried past behind their backs. For them shadows (images) are the only realities.

5. The state of mind called *eikasia* [imagining] in the previous chapter.

6. The first effect of Socratic questioning is perplexity.

7. Here is the moral—the need of habituation by mathematical study before discussing moral ideas and ascending through them to the Form of the Good.

reflected in water, and later on the things themselves. After that, it would be easier to watch the heavenly bodies and the sky itself by night, looking at the light of the moon and stars rather than the Sun and the Sun's light in the day-time.

Yes, surely.

Last of all, he would be able to look at the Sun and contemplate its nature, not as it appears when reflected in water or any alien medium, but as it is in itself in its own domain.

No doubt.

And now he would begin to draw the conclusion that it is the Sun that produces the seasons and the course of the year and controls everything in the visible world, and moreover is in a way the cause of all that he and his companions used to see.

Clearly he would come at last to that conclusion.

Then if he called to mind his fellow prisoners and what passed for wisdom in his former dwelling-place, he would surely think himself happy in the change and be sorry for them. They may have had a practice of honouring and commending one another, with prizes for the man who had the keenest eye for the passing shadows and the best memory for the order in which they followed or accompanied one another, so that he could make a good guess as to which was going to come next.[8] Would our released prisoner be likely to covet those prizes or to envy the men exalted to honour and power in the Cave? Would he not feel like Homer's Achilles, that he would far sooner 'be on earth as a hired servant in the house of a landless man'[9] or endure anything rather than go back to his old beliefs and live in the old way?

Yes, he would prefer any fate to such a life.

Now imagine what would happen if he went down again to take his former seat in the Cave. Coming suddenly out of the sunlight, his eyes would be filled with darkness. He might be required once more to deliver his opinion on those shadows, in competition with the prisoners who had never been released, while his eyesight was still dim and unsteady; and it might take some time to become used to the darkness. They would laugh at him and say that he had gone up only to come back with his sight ruined; it was worth no one's while even to attempt the ascent. If they could lay hands on the man who was trying to set them free and lead them up, they would kill him.[10]

Yes, they would.

Every feature in this parable, my dear Glaucon, is meant to fit our earlier analysis. The prison dwelling corresponds to the region revealed to us through the sense of sight, and the fire-light within it to the power of the Sun. The ascent to see the things in the upper world you may take as standing for the upward journey of the soul into the region of the intelligible; then you will be in possession of what I surmise, since that is what you wish to be told. Heaven knows whether it is true; but this, at any rate, is how it appears to me. In the world of knowledge, the last thing to be perceived and only with great difficulty is the essential Form of Goodness. Once it is perceived, the conclusion must follow that, for all things, this is the cause of whatever is right and good; in the visible world it gives birth to light and to

---

8. The empirical politician, with no philosophic insight, but only a 'knack of remembering what usually happens' (*Gorg*. 501 A). He has *eikasia* = conjecture as to what is likely (*eikos*).

9. This verse . . . spoken by the ghost of Achilles, suggests that the Cave is comparable with Hades.

10. An allusion to the fate of Socrates.

the lord of light, while it is itself sovereign in the intelligible world and the parent of intelligence and truth. Without having had a vision of this Form no one can act with wisdom, either in his own life or in matters of state.

So far as I can understand, I share your belief.

Then you may also agree that it is no wonder if those who have reached this height are reluctant to manage the affairs of men. Their souls long to spend all their time in that upper world—naturally enough, if here once more our parable holds true. Nor, again, is it at all strange that one who comes from the contemplation of divine things to the miseries of human life should appear awkward and ridiculous when, with eyes still dazed and not yet accustomed to the darkness, he is compelled, in a law-court or elsewhere, to dispute about the shadows of justice or the images that cast those shadows, and to wrangle over the notions of what is right in the minds of men who have never beheld Justice itself.[11]

It is not at all strange.

No; a sensible man will remember that the eyes may be confused in two ways—by a change from light to darkness or from darkness to light; and he will recognize that the same thing happens to the soul. When he sees it troubled and unable to discern anything clearly, instead of laughing thoughtlessly, he will ask whether, coming from a brighter existence, its unaccustomed vision is obscured by the darkness, in which case he will think its condition enviable and its life a happy one; or whether, emerging from the depths of ignorance, it is dazzled by excess of light. If so, he will rather feel sorry for it; or, if he were inclined to laugh, that would be less ridiculous than to laugh at the soul which has come down from the light.

That is a fair statement.

If this is true, then, we must conclude that education is not what it is said to be by some, who profess to put knowledge into a soul which does not possess it, as if they could put sight into blind eyes. On the contrary, our own account signifies that the soul of every man does possess the power of learning the truth and the organ to see it with; and that, just as one might have to turn the whole body round in order that the eye should see light instead of darkness, so the entire soul must be turned away from this changing world, until its eye can bear to contemplate reality and that supreme splendour which we have called the Good. Hence there may well be an art whose aim would be to effect this very thing, the conversion of the soul, in the readiest way; not to put the power of sight into the soul's eye, which already has it, but to ensure that, instead of looking in the wrong direction, it is turned the way it ought to be.

Yes, it may well be so.

It looks, then, as though wisdom were different from those ordinary virtues, as they are called, which are not far removed from bodily qualities, in that they can be produced by habituation and exercise in a soul which has not possessed them from the first. Wisdom, it seems, is certainly the virtue of some diviner faculty, which never loses its power, though its use for good or harm depends on the direction towards which it is turned. You must have noticed in dishonest men with a reputation for sagacity the shrewd glance of a narrow intelligence piercing the objects to which it is directed. There is nothing wrong with their

---

11. In the *Gorgias* 486 A, Callicles, forecasting the trial of Socrates, taunts him with the philosopher's inability to defend himself in a court.

power of vision, but it has been forced into the service of evil, so that the keener its sight, the more harm it works.

Quite true.

And yet if the growth of a nature like this had been pruned from earliest childhood, cleared of those clinging overgrowths which come of gluttony and all luxurious pleasure and, like leaden weights charged with affinity to this mortal world, hang upon the soul, bending its vision downwards; if, freed from these, the soul were turned round towards true reality, then this same power in these very men would see the truth as keenly as the objects it is turned to now.

Yes, very likely.

Is it not also likely, or indeed certain after what has been said, that a state can never be properly governed either by the uneducated who know nothing of truth or by men who are allowed to spend all their days in the pursuit of culture? The ignorant have no single mark before their eyes at which they must aim in all the conduct of their own lives and of affairs of state; and the others will not engage in action if they can help it, dreaming that, while still alive, they have been translated to the Islands of the Blest.

Quite true.

It is for us, then, as founders of a commonwealth, to bring compulsion to bear on the noblest natures. They must be made to climb the ascent to the vision of Goodness, which we called the highest object of knowledge; and, when they have looked upon it long enough, they must not be allowed, as they now are, to remain on the heights, refusing to come down again to the prisoners or to take any part in their labours and rewards, however much or little these may be worth.

Shall we not be doing them an injustice, if we force on them a worse life than they might have?

You have forgotten again, my friend, that the law is not concerned to make any one class specially happy, but to ensure the welfare of the commonwealth as a whole. By persuasion or constraint it will unite the citizens in harmony, making them share whatever benefits each class can contribute to the common good; and its purpose in forming men of that spirit was not that each should be left to go his own way, but that they should be instrumental in binding the community into one.

True, I had forgotten.

You will see, then, Glaucon, that there will be no real injustice in compelling our philosophers to watch over and care for the other citizens. We can fairly tell them that their compeers in other states may quite reasonably refuse to collaborate: there they have sprung up, like a self-sown plant, in despite of their country's institutions; no one has fostered their growth, and they cannot be expected to show gratitude for a care they have never received. 'But,' we shall say, 'it is not so with you. We have brought you into existence for your country's sake as well as for your own, to be like leaders and king-bees in a hive; you have been better and more thoroughly educated than those others and hence you are more capable of playing your part both as men of thought and as men of action. You must go down, then, each in his turn, to live with the rest and let your eyes grow accustomed to the darkness. You will then see a thousand times better than those who live there always; you will recognize every image for what it is and know what it represents, because you have seen justice, beauty, and goodness in their reality; and so you and we shall find life in our commonwealth no mere dream, as it is in most existing states, where men live fighting one another about shadows and quarrelling for power, as if that were a great prize; whereas in truth government can be at its best and free from dissension only where the destined rulers are least desirous of holding office.'

THE REWARDS OF JUSTICE AFTER DEATH.
THE MYTH OF ER
▪

Several other dialogues (Gorgias, Phaedo, Phaedrus) *describe the fate of the soul before birth and after death in the poetical imagery of myth, since no certain knowledge is attainable, but Plato believed that the indestructible soul must reap the consequences of its deeds, good or bad. Unlike Dante, he leaves the scenery and topography of the other world fluid and vague. Probably some details are borrowed from dramatic representations or* tableaux vivants *shown to initiates in Orphic and other Mysteries.*[1] *Features common to Plato's myths and to Empedocles' religious poem, Pindar's* Dirges, *Orphic amulets found in graves, and Virgil's sixth* Aeneid, *point to a common source, which may have been an Orphic apocalypse, a Descent of Orpheus to Hades. They include the divine origin of the soul; its fall to be incarnated in a cycle of births as a penalty for former sins; the guardian genius; the judgement after death; the torments of the unjust and the happiness of the just in the millennial intervals between incarnations; the hope of final deliverance for the purified; and certain topographical features: the Meadow (probably adapted from the Homeric Meadow of Asphodel); the two Ways to right and left; the waters of Lethe (or of Unmindfulness . . .) and of Memory.*

Such then, I [Socrates] went on, are the prizes, rewards, and gifts that the just man may expect at the hands of gods and men in his life-time, in addition to those other blessings which come simply from being just.

Yes, the rewards are splendid and sure.

These, however, are as nothing, in number or in greatness, when compared with the recompense awaiting the just and the unjust after death. This must now be told, in order that each may be paid in full what the argument shows to be his due.

Go on; there are not many things I would sooner hear about.

My story will not be like Odysseus' tale to Alcinous;[2] but its hero was a valiant man, Er, the son of Armenius, a native of Pamphylia, who was killed in battle. When the dead were taken up for burial ten days later, his body alone was found undecayed. They carried him

---

1. Gilbert Murray, 'The Conception of Another Life,' *Edin. Rev.*, 1914, reprinted in *Stoic, Christian and Humanist*, 1940. A learned and sober account of Orphism will be found in W. K. C. Guthrie's *Orpheus and Greek Religion*, 1935. Dieterich's *Nekyia* contains a study of the eschatological myths. [Greek mystery religions commonly involved an initiation into the secrets of the afterlife. See Walter Burkert, *Ancient Mystery Cults*, Harvard University Press, 1987.]

2. Odysseus' recital of his adventures to Alcinous, King of Phaeacia, fills four books of the *Odyssey*, including Odysseus' voyage to the realm of the dead, which Plato would reject as a misleading picture of the after-life. It became proverbial for a long story.

home, and two days afterwards were going to bury him, when he came to life again as he lay on the funeral pyre. He then told what he had seen in the other world.

He said that, when the soul had left his body, he journeyed with many others until they came to a marvellous place, where there were two openings side by side in the earth, and opposite them two others in the sky above. Between them sat Judges,[3] who, after each sentence given, bade the just take the way to the right upwards through the sky, first binding on them in front tokens signifying the judgement passed upon them. The unjust were commanded to take the downward road to the left, and these bore evidence of all their deeds fastened on their backs. When Er himself drew near, they told him that he was to carry tidings of the other world to mankind, and he must now listen and observe all that went on in that place. Accordingly he saw the souls which had been judged departing by one of the openings in the sky and one of those in the earth; while at the other two openings souls were coming up out of the earth travel-stained and dusty, or down from the sky clean and bright. Each company, as if they had come on a long journey, seemed glad to turn aside into the Meadow, where they encamped like pilgrims at a festival. Greetings passed between acquaintances, and as either party questioned the other of what had befallen them, some wept as they sorrowfully recounted all that they had seen and suffered on their journey under the earth, which had lasted a thousand years;[4] while others spoke of the joys of heaven and sights of inconceivable beauty. There was much, Glaucon, that would take too long to tell; but the sum, he said, was this. For every wrong done to any man sinners had in due course paid the penalty ten times over, that is to say, once in each hundred years, such being the span of human life, in order that the punishment for every offence might be tenfold. Thus, all who have been guilty of bringing many to death or slavery by betraying their country or their comrades in arms, or have taken part in any other iniquity, suffer tenfold torments for each crime; while deeds of kindness and a just and sinless life are rewarded in the same measure. Concerning infants who die at birth or live but a short time he had more to say, not worthy of mention.[5]

The wages earned by honouring the gods and parents, or by dishonouring them and by doing murder, were even greater. He was standing by when one spirit asked another, 'Where is Ardiaeus the Great?' This Ardiaeus had been despot in some city of Pamphylia just a thousand years before, and, among many other wicked deeds, he was said to have killed his old father and his elder brother. The answer was: 'He has not come back hither, nor will he ever come. This was one of the terrible sights we saw. When our sufferings were ended and we were near the mouth, ready to pass upwards, suddenly we saw Ardiaeus and others with him. Most of them were despots, but there were some private persons who had been great sinners. They thought that at last they were going to mount upwards, but the mouth would not admit them; it bellowed whenever one whose wickedness was incurable or who had not paid the penalty in full tried to go up.[6] Then certain fierce and fiery-looking men, who stood

---

3. In the myth of the Judgement of the Dead in the *Gorgias*, 523 E, Minos, Rhadamanthys, and Aeacus give judgement 'in the Meadow at the parting of the two ways, one to the Islands of the Blest, the other to Tartarus.'

4. This figure, probably taken from some Orphic or Pythagorean source, is repeated by Virgil, *Aeneid* vi. 748.

5. This suggests that a limbo for infants was a feature of the Orphic apocalypse. It appears in *Aeneid* vi. 426 ff., discussed by Cumont, *After-Life in Roman Paganism*, 128 ff.

6. So in Virgil, *Georgic* iv. 493, a roar is heard when Orpheus, returning from Hades with Eurydice, looks back, and Eurydice vanishes.

by and knew what the sound meant, seized some and carried them away; but Ardiaeus and others they bound hand and foot and neck and flinging them down flayed them. They dragged them along the wayside, carding their flesh like wool with thorns and telling all who passed by why this was done to them and that they were being taken to be cast into Tartarus. We had gone through many terrors of every sort, but none so great as the fear each man felt lest the sound should come as he went up; and when it was not heard, his joy was great.' Such were the judgements and penalties, and the blessings received were in corresponding measure.

Now when each company had spent seven days in the Meadow, on the eighth they had to rise up and journey on. And on the fourth day afterwards they came to a place whence they could see a straight shaft of light, like a pillar, stretching from above throughout heaven and earth, more like the rainbow than anything else, but brighter and purer. To this they came after a day's journey, and there, at the middle of the light, they saw stretching from heaven the extremities of its chains; for this light binds the heavens, holding together all the revolving firmament, like the undergirths of a ship of war[7]. . . .

The Spindle turned on the knees of Necessity. Upon each of its circles stood a Siren, who was carried round with its movement, uttering a single sound on one note, so that all the eight made up the concords of a single scale.[8] Round about, at equal distances, were seated, each on a throne, the three daughters of Necessity, the Fates, robed in white with garlands on their heads, Lachesis, Clotho, and Atropos, chanting to the Sirens' music, Lachesis of things past, Clotho of the present, and Atropos of things to come. And from time to time Clotho lays her right hand on the outer rim of the Spindle and helps to turn it, while Atropos turns the inner circles likewise with her left, and Lachesis with either hand takes hold of inner and outer alternately.

The souls, as soon as they came, were required to go before Lachesis. An Interpreter first marshalled them in order; and then, having taken from the lap of Lachesis a number of lots and samples of lives, he mounted on a high platform and said:

'The word of Lachesis, maiden daughter of Necessity. Souls of a day, here shall begin a new round of earthly life, to end in death. No guardian spirit will cast lots for you,[9] but you shall choose your own destiny. Let him to whom the first lot falls choose first a life to which he will be bound of necessity. But Virtue owns no master: as a man honours or dishonours

---

7. Undergirths were ropes or braces used, either as fixtures or as temporary expedients, to strengthen a ship's hull, Acts xxvii. 17: 'they used helps, undergirding the ship.' It is disputed whether the bond holding the universe together is simply the straight axial shaft or a circular band of light, suggested by the Milky Way, girdling the heaven of Fixed Stars.

8. Aristotle, *de caelo* ii. 9: 'It seems to some thinkers [Pythagoreans] that bodies so great must inevitably produce a sound by their movement: even bodies on the earth do so . . . and as for the sun and the moon, and the stars, so many in number and enormous in size, all moving at a tremendous speed, it is incredible that they should fail to produce a noise of surpassing loudness. Taking this as their hypothesis, and also that the speeds of the stars, judged by their distances, are in the ratios of the musical consonances, they affirm that the sound of the stars as they revolve is concordant. To meet the difficulty that none of us is aware of this sound, they account for it by saying that the sound is with us right from birth and has thus no contrasting silence to show it up; for voice and silence are perceived by contrast with each other, and so all mankind is undergoing an experience like that of a coppersmith, who becomes by long habit indifferent to the din around him' (trans. W. K. C. Guthrie). Aristotle refutes this theory.

9. The idea that the *daemon* (guardian spirit, genius, personified destiny) has an individual allotted to it as its portion appears in Lysias, *Epitaphius* 78, Theocritus iv. 40, and Plato's *Phaedo* (myth) 107 D.

her, so shall he have more of her or less. The blame is his who chooses; Heaven is blameless.'[10]

With these words the Interpreter scattered the lots among them all. Each took up the lot which fell at his feet and showed what number he had drawn; only Er himself was forbidden to take one. Then the Interpreter laid on the ground before them the sample lives, many more than the persons there. They were of every sort: lives of all living creatures, as well as of all conditions of men. Among them were lives of despots, some continuing in power to the end, others ruined in mid course and ending in poverty, exile, or beggary. There were lives of men renowned for beauty of form and for strength and prowess, or for distinguished birth and ancestry; also lives of unknown men; and of women likewise. All these qualities were variously combined with one another and with wealth or poverty, health or sickness, or intermediate conditions; but in none of these lives was there anything to determine the condition of the soul, because the soul must needs change its character according as it chooses one life or another.

Here, it seems, my dear Glaucon, a man's whole fortunes are at stake. On this account each one of us should lay aside all other learning, to study only how he may discover one who can give him the knowledge enabling him to distinguish the good life from the evil, and always and everywhere to choose the best within his reach, taking into account all these qualities we have mentioned and how, separately or in combination, they affect the goodness of life. Thus he will seek to understand what is the effect, for good or evil, of beauty combined with wealth or with poverty and with this or that condition of the soul, or of any combination of high or low birth, public or private station, strength or weakness, quickness of wit or slowness, and any other qualities of mind, native or acquired; until, as the outcome of all these calculations, he is able to choose between the worse and the better life with reference to the constitution of the soul, calling a life worse or better according as it leads to the soul becoming more unjust or more just. All else he will leave out of account; for, as we have seen, this is the supreme choice for a man, both while he lives and after death. Accordingly, when he goes into the house of death he should hold this faith like adamant, that there too he may not be dazzled by wealth and such-like evils, or fling himself into the life of a despot or other evil-doer, to work irremediable harm and suffer yet worse things himself, but may know how to choose always the middle course that avoids both extremes, not only in this life, so far as he may, but in every future existence; for there lies the greatest happiness for man.

To return to the report of the messenger from the other world. The Interpreter then said: 'Even for the last comer, if he choose with discretion, there is left in store a life with which, if he will live strenuously, he may be content and not unhappy. Let not the first be heedless in his choice, nor the last be disheartened.'

After these words, he who had drawn the first lot at once seized upon the most absolute despotism he could find. In his thoughtless greed he was not careful to examine the life he chose at every point, and he did not see the many evils it contained and that he was fated to devour his own children; but when he had time to look more closely, he began to beat his breast and bewail his choice, forgetting the warning proclaimed by the Interpreter; for he

10. These last words 'became a kind of rallying-cry among the champions of the freedom of the will in the early Christian era' (Adam). They are inscribed on a bust of Plato of the first century B.C. found at Tibur.

laid the blame on fortune, the decrees of the gods, anything rather than himself. He was one of those who had come down from heaven, having spent his former life in a well-ordered commonwealth and become virtuous from habit without pursuing wisdom. It might indeed be said that not the least part of those who were caught in this way were of the company which had come from heaven, because they were not disciplined by suffering; whereas most of those who had come up out of the earth, having suffered themselves and seen others suffer, were not hasty in making their choice. For this reason, and also because of the chance of the lot, most of the souls changed from a good life to an evil, or from an evil life to a good. Yet, if upon every return to earthly life a man seeks wisdom with his whole heart, and if the lot so fall that he is not among the last to choose, then this report gives good hope that he will not only be happy here, but will journey to the other world and back again hither, not by the rough road underground, but by the smooth path through the heavens.

It was indeed, said Er, a sight worth seeing, how the souls severally chose their lives— a sight to move pity and laughter and astonishment; for the choice was mostly governed by the habits of their former life. He saw one soul choosing the life of a swan; this had once been the soul of Orpheus, which so hated all womankind because of his death at their hands that it would not consent to be born of woman.[11] And he saw the soul of Thamyras[12] take the life of a nightingale, and a swan choose to be changed into a man, and other musical creatures do the same. The soul which drew the twentieth lot took a lion's life; this had been Ajax, the son of Telamon, who shrank from being born as a man, remembering the judgement concerning the arms of Achilles.[13] After him came the soul of Agamemnon,[14] who also hated mankind because of his sufferings and took in exchange the life of an eagle. Atalanta's[15] soul drew a lot about half-way through. She took the life of an athlete, which she could not pass over when she saw the great honours he would win. After her he saw the soul of Epeius,[16] son of Panopeus, passing into the form of a craftswoman; and far off, among the last, the buffoon Thersites' soul clothing itself in the body of an ape. It so happened that the last choice of all fell to the soul of Odysseus, whose ambition was so abated by memory of his former labours that he went about for a long time looking for a life of quiet obscurity. When at last he found it lying somewhere neglected by all the rest, he chose it gladly, saying that he would have done the same if his lot had come first. Other souls in like manner passed from beasts into men and into one another, the unjust changing into the wild creatures, the just into the tame, in every sort of combination.

Now when all the souls had chosen their lives, they went in the order of their lots to Lachesis; and she gave each into the charge of the guardian genius he had chosen, to escort him through life and fulfil his choice. The genius led the soul first to Clotho, under her hand as it turned the whirling Spindle, thus ratifying the portion which the man had chosen when

---

11. Orpheus was torn in pieces by the Maenads, the women-worshippers of Dionysus.
12. Another singer, who was deprived of sight and of the gift of song for challenging the Muses to a contest.
13. After Achilles' death a contest between Ajax and Odysseus for his arms ended in the defeat and suicide of Ajax. The first mention is in *Odyssey* xi. 543, where the soul of Ajax, summoned from Hades, will not speak to Odysseus.
14. The conqueror of Troy, murdered by his wife Clytemnestra on his return home.
15. Atalanta's suitors had to race with her for her hand and were killed if defeated. Milanion won by dropping three golden apples given him by Aphrodite, which Atalanta paused to pick up.
16. Maker of the wooden horse in which the Greek chieftains entered Troy.

his lot was cast. And, after touching her, he led it next to the spinning of Atropos, thus making the thread of destiny irreversible. Thence, without looking back, he passed under the throne of Necessity. And when he and all the rest had passed beyond the throne, they journeyed together to the Plain of Lethe through terrible stifling heat; for the plain is bare of trees and of all plants that grow on the earth. When evening came, they encamped beside the River of Unmindfulness, whose water no vessel can hold. All are required to drink a certain measure of this water, and some have not the wisdom to save them from drinking more. Every man as he drinks forgets everything. When they had fallen asleep, at midnight there was thunder and an earthquake, and in a moment they were carried up, this way and that, to their birth, like shooting stars. Er himself was not allowed to drink of the water. How and by what means he came back to the body he knew not; but suddenly he opened his eyes and found himself lying on the funeral pyre at dawn.

And so, Glaucon, the tale was saved from perishing; and if we will listen, it may save us, and all will be well when we cross the river of Lethe. Also we shall not defile our souls; but, if you will believe with me that the soul is immortal and able to endure all good and ill, we shall keep always to the upward way and in all things pursue justice with the help of wisdom. Then we shall be at peace with Heaven and with ourselves, both during our sojourn here and when, like victors in the Games collecting gifts from their friends, we receive the prize of justice; and so, not here only, but in the journey of a thousand years of which I have told you, we shall fare well.

Hellenistic and Roman Civilization

Epicurus, To Herodotus

Epicurus (341–270 B.C.) was born just a few years after the death of Plato, but no two philosophers could be more unlike. As a thoroughgoing materialist, Epicurus—like Democritus who lived a hundred years before him—believed that the universe consisted solely of particles of matter in motion. Everything we perceive, including the human soul, is made up of these particles or "atoms," and since these atoms have always existed, there is no need to posit a divine being or a theory of creation to explain their existence. The principles of motion and of chance are quite sufficient, Epicurus held, to account for the formation of the world as we know it.

The ultimate goal of Epicurus' teaching was not, however, simply that of providing his disciples with an adequate account of physical laws; what he hoped to do, finally, was to affect the disposition of the individual soul in a universe where, even if the gods *did* exist, no rewards or punishments would follow after death. Epicurus repeatedly reminds his pupils (the "Herodotus" of this letter being one of those) that they have nothing to fear from either the gods or the afterlife, because death represents nothing more than the dispersion of the body's atoms out into the universe.

By emphasizing the subjective and material aspects of the perceptual process, Epicurus shifts the focus of both moral and political philosophy away from discussions of the immortal soul and the ideal republic to the condition of the individual moral agent within an anonymous environment, where the greatest good is not justice or peace for the many but *ataraxia* (or inner tranquility) for the one. The political outlook that Epicurean philosophy presupposes is that of Greece *after* Alexander the Great (356–323 B.C.), when the sheer magnitude of Alexander's conquests, and of the empire he left behind him, served only to dwarf the average citizen of such a state and to inspire a turning inward. What matters in life, Epicurus taught, is sensation and the refinement of emotion in the search for tranquillity, not participation in the active, adversarial world of the polis.

TO HERODOTUS

For those who are unable, Herodotus, to work in detail through all that I have written about nature, or to peruse the larger books which I have composed, I have already prepared at sufficient length an epitome of the whole system, that they may keep adequately in mind at least the most general principles in each department, in order that as occasion arises they may be able to assist themselves on the most important points, in so far as they undertake the study of nature.

. . . First of all, that nothing is created out of that which does not exist: for if it were, everything would be created out of everything with no need of seeds. And again, if that which disappears were destroyed into that which did not exist, all things would have perished, since that into which they were dissolved would not exist. Furthermore, the universe always was such as it is now, and always will be the same. For there is nothing into which it changes: for outside the universe there is nothing which could come into it and bring about the change.

Moreover, the universe is bodies and space: for that bodies exist, sense itself witnesses in the experience of all men, and in accordance with the evidence of sense we must of necessity judge of the imperceptible by reasoning, as I have already said. And if there were not that which we term void and place and intangible existence, bodies would have nowhere to exist and nothing through which to move. And besides these two nothing can even be thought of either by conception or on the analogy of things conceivable such as could be grasped as whole existences and not spoken of as the accidents or properties of such existences. Furthermore, among bodies some are compounds, and others those of which compounds are formed. And these latter are indivisible and unalterable (if, that is, all things are not to be destroyed into the non-existent, but something permanent is to remain behind at the dissolution of compounds): they are completely solid in nature, and can by no means be dissolved in any part. So it must needs be that the first-beginnings are indivisible corporeal existences.

Moreover, the universe is boundless. For that which is bounded has an extreme point: and the extreme point is seen against something else. So that as it has no extreme point, it has no limit; and as it has no limit, it must be boundless both in the number of the bodies and in the extent of the void. For if on the one hand the void were boundless, and the bodies limited in number, the bodies could not stay anywhere, but would be carried about and scattered through the infinite void, not having other bodies to support them and keep them in place by means of collisions. But if, on the other hand, the void were limited, the infinite bodies would not have room wherein to take their place.

Besides this the indivisible and solid bodies, out of which too the compounds are created and into which they are dissolved, have an incomprehensible number of varieties in shape: for it is not possible that such great varieties of things should arise from the same atomic shapes, if they are limited in number. And so in each shape the atoms are quite infinite in number, but their differences of shape are not quite infinite, but only incomprehensible in number.

And the atoms move continuously for all time, some of them falling straight down, others swerving, and others recoiling from their collisions. And of the latter, some are borne on, separating to a long distance from one another, while others again recoil and recoil, whenever they chance to be checked by the interlacing with others, or else shut in by atoms interlaced around them. For on the one hand the nature of the void which separates each atom by itself brings this about, as it is not able to afford resistance, and on the other hand the hardness which belongs to the atoms makes them recoil after collision to as great a distance as the interlacing permits separation after the collision. And these motions have no beginning, since the atoms and the void are the cause.

These brief sayings, if all these points are borne in mind, afford a sufficient outline for our understanding of the nature of existing things.

Furthermore, there are infinite worlds both like and unlike this world of ours. For the atoms being infinite in number, as was proved already, are borne on far out into space. For those atoms, which are of such nature that a world could be created out of them or made by them, have not been used up either on one world or on a limited number of worlds, nor again on all the worlds which are alike, or on those which are different from these. So that there nowhere exists an obstacle to the infinite number of the worlds. . . .

Every image which we obtain by an act of apprehension on the part of the mind or of the sense-organs, whether of shape or of properties, this image is the shape or the properties of the concrete object, and is produced by the constant repetition of the image or the impression it has left. Now falsehood and error always lie in the addition of opinion with regard to what is waiting to be confirmed or not contradicted, and then is not confirmed or is contradicted. For the similarity between the things which exist, which we call real and the images received as a likeness of things and produced either in sleep or through some other acts of apprehension on the part of the mind or the other instruments of judgment, could never be, unless there were some effluences of this nature actually brought into contact with our senses. And error would not exist unless another kind of movement too were produced inside ourselves, closely linked to the apprehension of images, but differing from it; and it is owing to this, supposing it is not confirmed, or is contradicted, that falsehood arises; but if it is confirmed or not contradicted, it is true. Therefore, we must do our best to keep this doctrine in mind, in order that on the one hand the standards of judgment dependent on the clear visions may not be undermined, and on the other error may not be as firmly established as truth and so throw all into confusion. . . .

Next, referring always to the sensations and the feelings, for in this way you will obtain the most trustworthy ground of belief, you must consider that the soul is a body of fine particles distributed throughout the whole structure, and most resembling wind with a certain admixture of heat, and in some respects like to one of these and in some to the other. There is also the part which is many degrees more advanced even than these in fineness of composition, and for this reason is more capable of feeling in harmony with the rest of the structure as well. Now all this is made manifest by the activities of the soul and the feelings and the readiness of its movements and its processes of thought and by what we lose at the moment of death. Further, you must grasp that the soul possesses the chief cause of sensation: yet it could not have acquired sensation, unless it were in some way enclosed by the rest of the structure. And this in its turn having afforded the soul this cause of sensation acquires itself too a share in this contingent capacity from the soul. Yet it does not acquire all the capacities which the soul possesses: and therefore when the soul is released from the body, the body no longer has sensation. For it never possessed this power in itself, but used to afford opportunity for it to another existence, brought into being at the same time with itself: and this existence, owing to the power now consummated within itself as a result of motion, used spontaneously to produce for itself the capacity of sensation and then to communicate it to the body as well, in virtue of its contact and correspondence of movement, as I have already said. Therefore, so long as the soul remains in the body, even though some other part of the body be lost, it will never lose sensation; nay more, whatever portions of the soul may perish too, when that which enclosed it is removed either in whole or in part, if the soul continues to exist at all, it will retain sensation. On the other hand the rest of the structure, though it continues to exist either as a whole or in part, does not retain sensation, if it has once lost that sum of atoms, however small it be, which together goes to produce the nature of the soul. Moreover, if the whole structure is dissolved, the soul is dispersed and no longer has the same powers nor performs its movements, so that it does not possess sensation either. For it is impossible to imagine it with sensation, if it is not in this organism and cannot effect these movements, when what encloses and surrounds it is no longer the same as the surroundings in which it now exists and performs these movements. . . .

Furthermore, the motions of the heavenly bodies and their turnings and eclipses and risings and settings, and kindred phenomena to these, must not be thought to be due to any being who controls and ordains or has ordained them and at the same time enjoys perfect bliss together with immortality (for trouble and care and anger and kindness are not consistent with a life of blessedness, but these things come to pass where there is weakness and fear and dependence on neighbours). Nor again must we believe that they, which are but fire agglomerated in a mass, possess blessedness, and voluntarily take upon themselves these movements. But we must preserve their full majestic significance in all expressions which we apply to such conceptions, in order that there may not arise out of them opinions contrary to this notion of majesty. Otherwise this very contradiction will cause the greatest disturbance in men's souls. Therefore we must believe that it is due to the original inclusion of matter in such agglomerations during the birth-process of the world that this law of regular succession is also brought about. . . .

And besides all these matters in general we must grasp this point, that the principal disturbance in the minds of men arises because they think that these celestial bodies are blessed and immortal, and yet have wills and actions and motives inconsistent, with these attributes; and because they are always expecting or imagining some everlasting misery, such as is depicted in legends, or even fear the loss of feeling in death as though it would concern them themselves; and, again, because they are brought to this pass not by reasoned opinion, but rather by some irrational presentiment, and therefore, as they do not know the limits of pain, they suffer a disturbance equally great or even more extensive than if they had reached this belief by opinion. But peace of mind is being delivered from all this, and having a constant memory of the general and most essential principles.

Wherefore we must pay attention to internal feelings and to external sensations in general and in particular, according as the subject is general and in particular, and to every immediate intuition in accordance with each of the standards of judgment. For if we pay attention to these, we shall rightly trace the causes whence arose our mental disturbance and fear, and by learning the true causes of celestial phenomena and all other occurrences that come to pass from time to time, we shall free ourselves from all which produces the utmost fear in other men.

Marcus Aurelius, The Meditations

The origins of Stoicism can be traced to the teachings of Zeno (334–262 B.C.), who, according to tradition, taught his pupils under the *stoa* or porches of the Athenian agora. Like the followers of Epicurus, Zeno's contemporary, the Stoics sought to achieve both a clearer vision of reality and a condition of spiritual self-sufficiency in the diverse cosmopolitan world of Hellenistic culture. By adopting a consistently materialistic view of the universe, the Stoics found that they could explain not only the processes of nature, but even the activities of the human soul, which they regarded as a refined material substance endowed with the divine "spark" of reason.

What distinguished the Stoics from the Epicureans, however, was their understanding of how the universe was governed and how a morally responsible individual ought to behave. At the heart of Stoic teaching was the belief that all matter was permeated by a divine "fire" or energy, which later Stoics referred to as the *Logos* or the principle of heavenly reason. In such a universe, where "god" is everywhere, nothing happens by chance. The course of nature, as well as the course of every individual human life, is the result of a rational and universal plan, called "Fate" or "Providence," from which nothing has been left out. To resist this cosmic determinism is futile, the Stoics believed; the only reasonable option was to submit gracefully to one's destiny, playing one's "part" with as much dignity and self-control as possible. To achieve maximum self-control—a state of mind the Stoics termed "apathy"—one must ultimately cultivate a profound indifference to either pleasure or pain, for only then could reason hope to triumph over passion.

Marcus Aurelius [Antoninus], emperor of Rome from A.D. 121 to 180, provides one of the best examples of late Stoic writing and thought. His *Meditations* (which he entitled, simply, "To Himself") were never intended for publication and represent a philosophical diary kept over a period of many years. Despite its lack of organization Marcus' *Meditations* contain nearly all of the major concepts of Stoic philosophy, expressed with a spareness of language and emotion that perfectly embodies the austere Stoic ideal of self-detachment and inner tranquility.

THE MEDITATIONS
■

SECTION II

5. Every moment think steadily as a Roman and a man to do what you have in hand with perfect and simple dignity and feeling of affection, and freedom, and justice; and to give yourself relief from all other thoughts. And you will give yourself relief, if you do every act of your life as if it were the last, laying aside all carelessness and passionate aversion from the commands of reason, and all hypocrisy, and self-love, and discontent with the portion which has been given to you. You see how few the things are, which if a man lays hold of, he is able to live a life which flows in quiet, and is like the existence of the gods; for the gods on their part will require nothing more from him who observes these things.

7. Do the things external which fall upon you distract you? Give yourself time to learn something new and good, and cease to be whirled around. But then you must also avoid being carried about the other way. For those too are triflers who have wearied themselves in life by their activity, and yet have no object to which to direct every movement, and, in a word, all their thoughts.

11. Since it is possible that you may depart from life this very moment, regulate every act and thought accordingly. But to go away from among men, if there are gods, is not a thing to be afraid of, for the gods will not involve you in evil; but if indeed they do not exist, or if they have no concern about human affairs, what is it to me to live in a universe devoid of gods or devoid of providence? But in truth they do exist, and they do care for human things, and they have put all the means in man's power to enable him not to fall into real evils. And as to the rest, if there was anything evil, they would have provided for this also, that it should be altogether in a man's power not to fall into it.

SECTION III

6. If you find in human life anything better than justice, truth, temperance, fortitude, and in a word, anything better than your own mind's self-satisfaction in the things which it enables you to do according to right reason, and in the condition that is assigned to you without your own choice; if, I say, you see anything better than this, turn to it with all your soul, and enjoy that which you have found to be the best. But if nothing appears to be better than the deity which is planted in you, which has subjected to itself all your appetites, and carefully examines all the impressions, and, as Socrates said, has detached itself from the persuasions of sense, and has submitted itself to the gods, and cares for mankind; if you find everything else smaller and of less value than this, give place to nothing else, for if you once diverge and incline to it, you will no longer without distraction be able to give the preference to that good thing which is your proper possession and your own; for it is not right that anything of any other kind, such as praise from the many, or power, or enjoyment of pleasure, should come into competition with that which is rationally and practically good. All these things, even though they may seem to adapt themselves in a small degree, obtain the superiority all at once, and carry us away. But do you, I say, simply and freely choose the better, and hold to it.

But that which is useful is the better.

Well then, if it is useful to you as a rational being, keep to it; but if it is only useful to you as an animal, say so, and maintain your judgment without arrogance: only take care that you make the inquiry by a sure method.

. . . But perhaps you are dissatisfied with that which is assigned to you out of the universe.

Recall this alternative: either there is providence or fortuitous atoms; or remember the arguments by which it has been proved that the world is a kind of political community.

But perhaps corporeal things will still fasten upon you.

Consider then further that the mind does not mingle with the breath, whether moving gently or violently, when it has once drawn itself apart and discovered its own power, and think also of all that you have heard and assented to about pain and pleasure.

But perhaps the desire of the thing called fame will torment you.

See how soon everything is forgotten, and look at the chaos of infinite time on each side of the present, and the emptiness of applause, and the changeableness and want of judgment in those who pretend to give praise, and the narrowness of the space within which it is circumscribed. For the whole earth is a point, and how small a nook in it is this your dwelling, and how few are there in it, and what kind of people are they who will praise you.

This then remains: Remember to retire into this little territory of your own, and above all do not distract or strain yourself, but be free, and look at things as a man, as a human being, as a citizen, as a mortal.

SECTION IV

24. If you would be tranquil, occupy yourself with few things, says the philosopher. But consider if it would not be better to say, "Do what is necessary," and whatever the reason of the animal which is naturally social requires, and as it requires. For this brings not only the tranquility which comes from doing well, but also that which comes from doing few things. For the greatest part of what we say and do being unnecessary, if a man takes this away, he will have more leisure and less uneasiness. Accordingly on every occasion a man should ask himself, "Is this one of the unnecessary things?" Now a man should take away not only unnecessary acts, but also unnecessary thoughts, for thus superfluous acts will not follow after.

25. Try how the life of the good man suits you, the life of him who is satisfied with his portion out of the whole, and satisfied with his own just acts and benevolent disposition.

26. Have you seen those things? Look also at these. Do not disturb yourself. Make yourself all simplicity. Does anyone do wrong? It is to himself that he does the wrong. Has anything happened to you? Well, out of the universe from the beginning everything which happens has been apportioned and spun out to you. In a word, your life is short. You must turn the present to profit by the aid of reason and justice. Be sober in your relaxation.

43. Time is like a river made up of the events which happen, and a violent stream; for as soon as a thing has been seen, it is carried away, and another comes in its place, and this will be carried away too.

44. Everything which happens is as familiar and well known as the rose to spring and the fruit in summer; for such is disease, and death, and calumny, and treachery, and whatever else delights fools or vexes them.

45. In the series of things those which follow are always aptly fitted to those which have gone before; for this series is not like a mere enumeration of disjointed things, which has only a necessary sequence, but it is a rational connection: and as all existing things are arranged together harmoniously, so the things which come into existence exhibit no mere succession, but a certain wonderful relationship.

46. Always remember the saying of Heraclitus, that the death of earth is to become water, and the death of water is to become air, and the death of air is to become fire, and reversely. And think too of him who forgets where the way leads, and that men quarrel with that with which they are most constantly in communion, the reason which governs the universe; and the things which they daily meet with seem to them strange: and consider that we ought not to act and speak as if we were asleep, for even in sleep we seem to act and speak; and that we ought not, like children who learn from their parents, simply to act and speak as we have been taught.

47. If any god told you that you shall die tomorrow, or certainly on the day after tomorrow, you would not care much whether it was on the third day or on the morrow, unless you were

in the highest degree mean-spirited—for how small is the difference?—so think it no great thing to die after as many years as you can name rather than tomorrow.

48. Think continually how many physicians are dead after often contracting their eyebrows over the sick; and how many astrologers after predicting, with great pretensions, the deaths of others; and how many philosophers after endless discourses on death or immortality; how many heroes after killing thousands; and how many tyrants who have used their power over men's lives with terrible insolence as if they were immortal; and how many cities are entirely dead, so to speak, Helice and Pompeii and Herculanum, and others innumerable. Add to the reckoning all whom you have known, one after another. One man after burying another has been laid out dead, and another buries him; and all this in a short time. To conclude, always observe how ephemeral and worthless human things are, and what was yesterday a little mucus, tomorrow will be a mummy or ashes. Pass then through this little space of time conformably to nature, and end your journey in content, just as an olive falls off when it is ripe, blessing nature who produced it, and thanking the tree on which it grew.

49. Be like the promontory against which the waves continually break, but it stands firm and tames the fury of the water around it.

Unhappy am I, because this has happened to me—Not so, but happy am I, though this has happened to me, because I continue free from pain, neither crushed by the present nor fearing the future. For such a thing as this might have happened to every man; but every man would not have continued free from pain on such an occasion. Why then is that rather a misfortune than this a good fortune? And do you in all cases call that a man's misfortune, which is not a deviation from man's nature? And does a thing seem to you to be a deviation from man's nature, when it is not contrary to the will of man's nature? Well, you know the will of nature. Will this which has happened prevent you from being just, magnanimous, temperate, prudent, secure against inconsiderate opinions and falsehood; will it prevent you from having modesty, freedom, and everything else, by the presence of which man's nature obtains all that is its own? Remember too on every occasion which leads you to vexation to apply this principle: not that this is a misfortune, but that to bear it nobly is good fortune.

50. It is a vulgar, but still a useful help toward contempt of death, to pass in review those who have tenaciously stuck to life. What more then have they gained than those who have died early? Certainly they lie in their tombs somewhere at last, Cadicianus, Fabius, Julianus, Lepidus, or anyone else like them, who have carried out many to be buried, and then were carried out themselves. Altogether the interval is small, and consider with how much trouble, and in company with what sort of people and in what a feeble body this interval is laboriously passed. Do not then consider life a thing of any value. For look to the immensity of time behind you, and to the time which is before you, another boundless space. In this infinity then what is the difference between him who lives three days and him who lives three generations?

Virgil, The Aeneid

Virgil's masterpiece, the *Aeneid* (30–19 B.C.), celebrates the triumph of Roman rule over most of the civilized world. An epic poem written in conscious imitation of Homer's *Iliad* and *Odyssey*, the *Aeneid* narrates the adventures of the Trojan prince Aeneas, whom many believed to be an ancestor of the Roman people. The first part of the poem, modeled on Odysseus' wanderings, is a narration of Aeneas' flight from Greek-captured Troy, his shipwreck on the north African coast, his love affair with Dido, queen of Carthage, and his descent into the Underworld. The second half of the epic depicts Aeneas in war, as he and his Trojan followers struggle to establish a new home in Italy. Virgil's purpose is both patriotic and artistic: his poem presents Aeneas as chosen by the gods to found a royal line that will eventually create the Roman Empire. Virgil (70–19 B.C.) also paints for his Roman audience a heroic past worthy of comparison with the older Greek mythology. Combining several ancient traditions, Virgil makes Aeneas the ancestor of the twin brothers Romulus and Remus, the legendary founders of Rome.

In Book VI, Aeneas descends into Hades to consult the spirit of his dead father, Anchises. Guided by Apollo's prophetess, the Sibyl, Aeneas finally understands that his personal losses and sufferings are part of a divine plan to establish the future empire of Rome. The gods grant him a vision of Rome's ultimate power and splendor, culminating in the glorious reign of Augustus (30 B.C.–A.D. 14), the emperor reigning in Virgil's day.

Virgil provides a detailed geography of the next world, which souls enter by crossing the River Styx in Charon's boat. Wicked souls suffer fiery torment in an iron citadel, whereas famous heroes revel in an earthlike paradise. Anchises, who enjoys a blissful afterlife, explains to his son that souls are purified in Hades and then reincarnated in new bodies to serve the gods' will. Strengthened by this revelation of divine purpose, Aeneas is now ready to undertake his predestined conquest of Latium in Italy, unselfishly devoting his life to a future he will not live to see.

BOOK I

THE LANDING NEAR CARTHAGE

Arms and the man I sing, the first who came,
Compelled by fate, an exile out of Troy,
To Italy and the Lavinian coast,
Much buffeted on land and on the deep
By violence of the gods, through that long rage,
That lasting hate, of Juno's. And he suffered
Much, also, in war, till he should build his town
And bring his gods to Latium, whence, in time,
The Latin race, the Alban fathers, rose
And the great walls of everlasting Rome.

Help me, O Muse, recall the reasons: why,
Why did the queen of heaven drive a man
So known for goodness, for devotion, through
So many toils and perils? Was there slight,
Affront, or outrage? Is vindictiveness
An attribute of the celestial mind?

There was an ancient city, Carthage, once
Founded by Tyrians, facing Italy
And Tiber's mouth, far-off, a wealthy town,
War-loving, and aggressive; and Juno held
Even her precious Samos in less regard.
Here were her arms, her chariot, and here,
Should fate at all permit, the goddess burned
To found the empire of the world forever.
But, she had heard, a Trojan race would come,
Some day, to overthrow the Tyrian towers,
A race would come, imperious people, proud
In war, with wide dominion, bringing doom
For Libya. Fate willed it so. And Juno
Feared, and remembered: there was the old war
She fought at Troy for her dear Greeks; her mind
Still fed on hurt and anger; deep in her heart
Paris' decision rankled, and the wrong
Offered her slighted beauty; and the hatred
Of the whole race; and Ganymede's honors—
All that was fuel to fire; she tossed and harried
All over the seas, wherever she could, those Trojans
Who had survived the Greeks and fierce Achilles,
And so they wandered over many an ocean,
Through many a year, fate-hounded. Such a struggle
It was to found the race of Rome! . . .

[Guided by the Sibyl, Aeneas descends into Hades to explore the mysteries of the afterlife and experiences a symbolic death and rebirth.]

BOOK VI

THE LOWER WORLD

. . . Vague forms in lonely darkness, they were going
Through void and shadow, through the empty realm
Like people in a forest, when the moonlight
Shifts with a baleful glimmer, and shadow covers
The sky, and all the colors turn to blackness.
At the first threshold, on the jaws of Orcus,
Grief and avenging Cares have set their couches,
And pale Diseases dwell, and sad Old Age,
Fear, evil-counselling Hunger, wretched Need,

Forms terrible to see, and Death and Toil,
And Death's own brother, Sleep, and evil Joys,
Fantasies of the mind, and deadly War,
The Furies' iron chambers, Discord, raving,
Her snaky hair entwined in bloody bands.
An elm-tree loomed there, shadowy and huge,
The aged boughs outspread, beneath whose leaves,
Men say, the false dreams cling, thousands on thousands.
And there are monsters in the dooryard, Centaurs,
Scyllas, of double shape, the beast of Lerna,
Hissing most horribly, Briareus,
The hundred-handed giant, A Chimaera
Whose armament is fire, Harpies, and Gorgons,
A triple-bodied giant. In sudden panic
Aeneas drew his sword, the edge held forward,
Ready to rush and flail, however blindly,
Save that his wise companion warned him, saying
They had no substance, they were only phantoms
Flitting about, illusions without body.

From here, the road turns off to Acheron,
River of Hell; here, thick with muddy whirling,
Cocytus boils with sand. Charon is here,
The guardian of these mingling waters, Charon,
Uncouth and filthy, on whose chin the hair
Is a tangled mat, whose eyes protrude, are burning,
Whose dirty cloak is knotted at the shoulder.
He poles a boat, tends to the sail, unaided,
Ferrying bodies in his rust-hued vessel.
Old, but a god's senility is awful
In its raw greenness. To the bank come thronging
Mothers and men, bodies of great-souled heroes,
Their life-time over, boys, unwedded maidens,
Young men whose fathers saw their pyres burning,
Thick as the forest leaves that fall in autumn
With early frost, thick as the birds to landfall
From over the seas, when the chill of the year compels
    them
To sunlight. There they stand, a host, imploring
To be taken over first. Their hands, in longing,
Reach out for the farther shore. But the gloomy boatman
Makes choice among them, taking some, and keeping
Others far back from the stream's edge. Aeneas,
Wondering, asks the Sibyl, "Why the crowding?
What are the spirits seeking? What distinction
Brings some across the livid stream, while others

177
▪

Stay on the farther bank?" She answers, briefly:
"Son of Anchises, this is the awful river,
The Styx, by which the gods take oath; the boatman
Charon; those he takes with him are the buried,
Those he rejects, whose luck is out, the graveless.
It is not permitted him to take them over
The dreadful banks and hoarse-resounding waters
Till earth is cast upon their bones. They haunt
These shores a hundred restless years of waiting
Before they end postponement of the crossing."
Aeneas paused, in thoughtful mood, with pity
Over their lot's unevenness . . .

                And they went on,
Nearing the river, and from the stream the boatman
Beheld them cross the silent forest, nearer,
Turning their footsteps toward the bank. He challenged:—
"Whoever you are, O man in armor, coming
In this direction, halt where you are, and tell me
The reason why you come. This is the region
Of shadows, and of Sleep and drowsy Night;
I am not allowed to carry living bodies
In the Stygian boat; and I must say I was sorry
I ever accepted Hercules and Theseus
And Pirithous, and rowed them over the lake,
Though they were sons of gods and great in courage.
One of them dared to drag the guard of Hell,
Enchained, from Pluto's throne, shaking in terror,
The others to snatch our queen from Pluto's chamber."
The Sibyl answered briefly: "No such cunning
Is plotted here; our weapons bring no danger.
Be undisturbed: the hell-hound in his cavern
May bark forever, to keep the bloodless shadows
Frightened away from trespass; Proserpine,
Untouched, in pureness guard her uncle's threshold.
Trojan Aeneas, a man renowned for goodness,
Renowned for nerve in battle, is descending
To the lowest shades; he comes to find his father.
If such devotion has no meaning to you,
Look on this branch at least, and recognize it!"
And with the word she drew from under her mantle
The golden bough; his swollen wrath subsided.
No more was said; he saw the bough, and marvelled
At the holy gift, so long unseen; came sculling
The dark-blue boat to the shore, and drove the spirits,
Lining the thwarts, ashore, and cleared the gangway,
And took Aeneas aboard; as that big man

Stepped in, the leaky skiff groaned under the weight,
And the strained seams let in the muddy water,
But they made the crossing safely, seer and soldier,
To the far margin, colorless and shapeless,
Grey sedge and dark-brown ooze. They heard the baying
Of Cerberus, that great hound, in his cavern crouching,
Making the shore resound, as all three throats
Belled horribly; and serpents rose and bristled
Along the triple neck. The priestess threw him
A sop with honey and drugged meal; he opened
The ravenous throat, gulped, and subsided, filling
The den with his huge bulk. Aeneas, crossing,
Passed on beyond the bank of the dread river
Whence none return. . . .

    They came to happy places, the joyful dwelling,
The lovely greenery of the groves of the blessèd.
Here ampler air invests the fields with light,
Rose-colored, with familiar stars and sun.
Some grapple on the grassy wrestling-ground
In exercise and sport, and some are dancing.
And others singing; in his trailing robe
Orpheus strums the lyre; the seven clear notes
Accompany the dance, the song. And heroes
Are there, great-souled, born in the happier years,
Ilus, Assaracus; the city's founder,
Prince Dardanus. Far off, Aeneas wonders,
Seeing the phantom arms, the chariots,
The spears fixed in the ground, the chargers browsing,
Unharnessed, over the plain. Whatever, living,
The men delighted in, whatever pleasure
Was theirs in horse and chariot, still holds them
Here under the world. To right and left, they banquet
In the green meadows, and a joyful chorus
Rises through groves of laurel, whence the river
Runs to the upper world. The band of heroes
Dwell here, all those whose mortal wounds were suffered
In fighting for the fatherland; and poets,
The good, the pure, the worthy of Apollo;
Those who discovered truth and made life nobler;
Those who served others—all, with snowy fillets
Blinding their temples, throng the lovely valley.
And these the Sibyl questioned, most of all
Musaeus, for he towered above the center
Of that great throng:—"O happy souls, O poet,
Where does Anchises dwell? For him we come here,

For him we have traversed Erebus' great rivers."
And he replied:—"It is all our home, the shady
Groves, and the streaming meadows, and the softness
Along the river-banks. No fixed abode
Is ours at all; but if it is your pleasure,
Cross over the ridge with me; I will guide you there
By easy going." And so Musaeus led them
And from the summit showed them fields, all shining,
And they went on over and down.

    Deep in a valley of green, father Anchises
Was watching, with deep earnestness, the spirits
Whose destiny was light, and counting them over,
All of his race to come, his dear descendants,
Their fates and fortunes and their works and ways,
And as he saw Aeneas coming toward him
Over the meadow, his hands reached out with yearning,
He was moved to tears, and called:—"At last, my son,—
Have you really come, at last? and the long road nothing
To a son who loves his father? Do I, truly,
See you, and hear your voice? I was thinking so,
I was hoping so, I was counting off the days,
And I was right about it. O my son!
What a long journey, over land and water,
Yours must have been! What buffeting of danger!
I feared, so much, the Libyan realm would hurt you."
And his son answered:—"It was your spirit, father,
Your sorrowful shade, so often met, that led me
To find these portals. The ships ride safe at anchor,
Safe in the Tuscan sea. Embrace me, father;
Let hand join hand in love; do not forsake me."
And as he spoke, the tears streamed down. Three times
He reached out toward him, and three times the image
Fled like the breath of the wind or a dream on wings.

    He saw, in a far valley, a separate grove
Where the woods stir and rustle, and a river,
The Lethe, gliding past the peaceful places,
And tribes of people thronging, hovering over,
Innumerable as the bees in summer
Working the bright-hued flowers, and the shining
Of the white lilies, murmuring and humming.
Aeneas, filled with wonder, asks the reason
For what he does not know, who are the people
In such a host, and to what river coming?
Anchises answers:—"These are spirits, ready

Once more for life; they drink of Lethe's water
The soothing potion of forgetfulness.
I have longed, for long, to show them to you, name them,
Our children's children; Italy discovered,
So much the greater happiness, my son."
"But, O my father, is it thinkable
That souls would leave this blessedness, be willing
A second time to bear the sluggish body,
Trade Paradise for earth? Alas poor wretches,
Why such a mad desire for light?" Anchises
Gives detailed answer: "First, my son, a spirit
Sustains all matter, heaven and earth and ocean,
The moon, the stars; mind quickens mass, and moves it.
Hence comes the race of man, of beast, of wingèd
Creatures of air, of the strange shapes which ocean
Bears down below his mottled marble surface.
All these are blessed with energy from heaven;
The seed of life is a spark of fire, but the body
A clod of earth, a clog, a mortal burden.
Hence humans fear, desire, grieve, and are joyful,
And even when life is over, all the evil
Ingrained so long, the adulterated mixture,
The plagues and pestilences of the body
Remain, persist. So there must be a cleansing,
By penalty, by punishment, by fire,
By sweep of wind, by water's absolution,
Before the guilt is gone. Each of us suffers
His own peculiar ghost. But the day comes
When we are sent through wide Elysium,
The Fields of the Blessed, a few of us, to linger
Until the turn of time, the wheel of ages,
Wears off the taint, and leaves the core of spirit
Pure sense, pure flame. A thousand years pass over
And the god calls the countless host to Lethe
Where memory is annulled, and souls are willing
Once more to enter into mortal bodies."

  The discourse ended; the father drew his son
And his companion toward the hum, the center
Of the full host; they came to rising ground
Where all the long array was visible,
Anchises watching, noting, every comer.
"Glory to come, my son, illustrious spirits
Of Dardan lineage, Italian offspring,
Heirs of our name, begetters of our future!
These I will name for you and tell our fortunes:

181
▪

First, leaning on a headless spear, and standing
Nearest the light, that youth, the first to rise
To the world above, is Silvius; his name
Is Alban; in his veins Italian blood
Will run with Trojan; he will be the son
Of your late age; Lavinia will bear him,
A king and sire of kings; from him our race
Will rule in Alba Longa. . . .
The son of a god, Augustus Caesar, founder
Of a new age of gold, in lands where Saturn
Ruled long ago; he will extend his empire
Beyond the Indies, beyond the normal measure
Of years and constellations, where high Atlas
Turns on his shoulders the star-studded world.
Maeotia and the Caspian seas are trembling
As heaven's oracles predict his coming,
And all the seven mouths of Nile are troubled.
Not even Hercules, in all his travels,
Covered so much of the world. . . ."

Early Christian Thought

St. Augustine, The Confessions of St. Augustine

Only a few churchmen have had a greater influence on the history of Christian thought than St. Augustine (A.D. 354–430), and very few writers in any century have left a deeper impression on the literature of their age. Many of the key doctrines of medieval Christian faith—the Trinity, original sin, divine grace, to name just a few—assumed the form they did because of Augustine's preeminence and continuing influence on later generations. As bishop of Hippo (Augustine was a native of North Africa), he was able to affect the intellectual life of the Church directly and at one of the really crucial junctures in its history, that period in which the Roman Empire began to collapse under the weight of repeated barbarian invasions.

As he tells us in his *Confessions* (c. 399), Augustine was born to a pagan father and a Christian mother, and that dual, conflicting heritage—and the deeper sense of spiritual duality he found within his own nature—became one of the central insights around which he attempted to wrap the events of his life. In fact, for Augustine, the meaning and purpose of his life became clear only after his conversion to Christianity, and it followed, therefore, that all of his life experiences would have to be reevaluated in the light of that one crucial event. The *Confessions* are really religious meditations, then, rather than merely autobiographical anecdotes, and the story that Augustine has to tell is the story of his alienation from and ultimate reconciliation to the Christian God.

The dramatic turning point in Augustine's account of his intellectual and spiritual development occurs at the very end of Book Eight, where we find him in despair over the irresoluteness of the moral will and over the "uncleanness" of the human body. Suddenly, Augustine hears a child say the words "take and read," and convinced that he has heard the voice of God speaking through this child, Augustine turns to Paul's epistle to the Romans, where he finds in Paul's vision of Christ's redemptive love the only answer to his spiritual dilemma.

BOOK ONE
■

VII

O God hear me! Woe unto men for their sins! When man cries thus, You have mercy upon him, for You made man but not the sin in him. Who shall remind me of the sins of my infancy: *for in Thy sight there is none pure from sin, not even the infant whose life is but a day upon the earth*. But who is to inform me? Perhaps this or that tiny child in whom I can see what I no longer remember of myself [If he is to teach me] what then were my sins at that age? That I wailed too fiercely for the breast? For if today I were to make as gluttonously and as clamorously, not of course for my mother's breasts, but for the food I now eat, I should be ridiculed and quite properly condemned. This means that what I did then was in fact reprehensible, although, since I could not understand words of blame, neither custom nor commonsense allowed me to be blamed. As we grow older we root out such ways and cast them from us: [which means that we hold them to be bad]—for no man engaged in removing evil would knowingly cast out what is good. Surely it was not good, even for that time of life, to scream for things that would have been thoroughly bad for me; to fly into hot rage because older persons—and free, not slaves—were not obedient to me; to strike out as hard as I could, with sheer will to hurt, at my parents and other sensible folk for not yielding to demands which could only have been granted at my peril. Thus the innocence of children is in the helplessness of their bodies rather than any quality in their minds. I have myself seen a small baby jealous; it was too young to speak, but it was livid with anger as it watched another infant at the breast.

There is nothing unusual in this. Mothers and nurses will tell you that they have their own way of curing these fits of jealousy. But at any rate it is an odd kind of innocence when a baby cannot bear that another—in great need, since upon that one food his very life depends—should share the milk that flows in such abundance. These childish tempers are borne with lightly, not because they are not faults, or only small faults; but because they will pass with the years. This is clearly so: for though we bear with them now, the same things would not be tolerated in an older person.

You, O Lord my God, gave me in my infancy life and a body; and You supplied the body with senses, fitted it with limbs, gave it shape and proportion, and for its general well-being and security implanted in it all the instincts of a living being. And You, Lord, doer of all these things, command me to praise You in them, *to confess unto Thee and sing to Thy name, O most high;* because You are God, omnipotent and good, even if You had done these things alone: for none other can do them save You, the One, who are the exemplar of all things, the All-Beautiful, who form and set in order all things by Your law.

Thus, Lord, I do not remember living this age of my infancy; I must take the word of others about it and can only conjecture how I spent it—even if with a fair amount of certainty—from watching others now in the same stage. I am loth, indeed to count it as part of the life I live in this world. For it is buried in the darkness of the forgotten as completely as the period earlier still that I spent in my mother's womb. But if *I was conceived in iniquity, and in sin my mother nourished me in the womb,* then where, my god, where, O Lord, where or when was I, Your servant, innocent? But I pass now from that time. For what concern have I now with a time of which I can recall no trace?

VIII

From infancy I came to boyhood, or rather it came to me, taking the place of infancy. Yet infancy did not go: for where was it to go to? Simply it was no longer there. For now I was not an infant, without speech, but a boy, speaking. This I remember; and I have since discovered by observation how I learned to speak. I did not learn by elders teaching me words in any systematic way, as I was soon after taught to read and write. But of my own motion, using the mind which You, my God, gave me, I strove with cries and various sounds and much moving of my limbs to utter the feeling of my heart—all this in order to get my own way. Now I did not always manage to express the right meanings to the right people. So I began to reflect. [I observed that] my elders would make some particular sound, and as they made it would point at or move towards some particular thing: and from this I came to realize that the thing was called by the sound they made when they wished to draw my attention to it. That they intended this was clear from the motions of their body, by a kind of natural language common to all races which consists in facial expressions, glances of the eye, gestures, and the tones by which the voice expresses the mind's state—for example whether things are to be sought, kept, thrown away, or avoided. So, as I heard the same words again and again properly used in different phrases, I came gradually to grasp what things they signified; and forcing my mouth to the same sounds, I began to use them to express my own wishes. Thus I learnt to convey what I meant to those about me; and so took another long step along the stormy way of human life in society, while I was still subject to the authority of my parents and at the beck and call of my elders.

IX

O God, my God, what emptiness and mockeries did I now experience: for it was impressed upon me as right and proper in a boy to obey those who taught me, that I might get on in the world and excel in the handling of words to gain honor among men and deceitful riches. I, poor wretch, could not see the use of the things I was sent to school to learn; but if I proved idle in learning, I was soundly beaten. For this procedure seemed wise to our ancestors: and many, passing the same way in days past, had built a sorrowful road by which we too must go, with multiplication of grief and toil upon the sons of Adam.

Yet, Lord, I observed men praying to You: and I learnt to do likewise, thinking of You (to the best of my understanding) as some great being who, though unseen, could hear and help me. As a boy I fell into the way of calling upon You, my Help and my Refuge; and in those prayers I broke the strings of my tongue—praying to You, small as I was but with no small energy, that I might not be beaten at school. And when You did not hear me *(not as giving me over to folly)*, my elders and even my parents, who certainly wished me no harm, treated my stripes as a huge joke, which they were very far from being to me. Surely, Lord, there is no one so steeled in mind or cleaving to You so close—or even so insensitive, for that might have the same effect—as to make light of the racks and hooks and other torture instruments (from which in all lands men pray so fervently to be saved) while truly loving those who are in such bitter fear of them. Yet my parents seemed to be amused at the torments inflicted upon me as a boy by my masters, though I was no less afraid of my punishments or zealous in my prayers to You for deliverance. But in spite of my terrors I still did wrong, by writing or reading or studying less than my set tasks. It was not, Lord, that I lacked mind or memory, for You had given me as much of these as my age required; but the one thing I revelled in was play; and for this I was punished by men who after all were doing exactly the same things themselves. But the idling of men is called business; the idling of boys, though exactly like, is punished by those same men: and no one pities either boys or men. Perhaps an unbiased observer would hold that I was rightly punished as a boy for playing with a ball: because this hindered my progress in studies—studies which would give me the opportunity as a man to play at things more degraded. And what difference was there between me and the master who flogged me? For if on some trifling point he had the worst of the argument with some fellow-master, he was more torn with angry vanity than I when I was beaten in a game of ball.

X

Yet in acting against the commands of my parents and schoolmasters, I did wrong, O Lord my god, Creator and Ruler of all things, but of sin not Creator but Ruler only: for I might later have made good use of those lessons that they wanted me to learn, whatever may have been their motive in wanting it. I disobeyed, not because I had chosen better, but through sheer love of play: I loved the vanity of victory, and I loved too to have my ears tickled with the fictions of the theatre which set them to itching ever more burningly: and in my eyes a similar curiosity burned increasingly for the games and shows of my elders. Yet those who put on such shows are held in high esteem. And most people would be delighted to have their sons grow up to give similar shows in their turn—and meanwhile fully concur in the beatings those same sons get if these shows hinder study: for study is the way to the prosperity necessary for giving them! Look down in mercy, Lord, upon such things; and set us free who now beseech Thee: and not only us, but those also who have never besought Thee—that they may turn to Thee and be made free.

BOOK TWO
■

III

Everyone of course praised my father because, although his means did not allow it, he had somehow provided the wherewithal for his son to travel so far for the sake of his studies. Many a very much richer citizen did no such thing for his children. Yet this same father never bothered about how I was growing towards You or how chaste or unchaste I might be, so long as I grew in eloquence, however much I might lack of Your cultivation O God, who are the one true and good Lord of your field, my heart.

But during that sixteenth year between Madaura and Carthage, owing to the narrowness of the family fortunes I did not go to school, but lived idly at home with my parents. The briars of unclean lusts grew so that they towered over my head, and there was no hand to root them out. On the contrary my father saw me one day in the public baths, now obviously growing towards manhood and showing the turbulent signs of adolescence. The effect upon him was that he already began to look forward to grandchildren, and went home in happy excitement to tell my mother. He rejoiced, indeed, through that intoxication in which the world forgets You its Creator and loves what You have created instead of You, the intoxication of the invisible wine of a will perverted and turned towards baseness. But in my mother's breast You had already laid the foundation of Your temple and begun Your holy habitation: whereas my father was still only a catechumen, and a new catechumen at that. So that she was stricken with a holy fear. And though I was not as yet baptised, she was in terror of my walking in the crooked ways of those who walk with their backs towards You and not their faces.

I have dared to say that You were silent, my God, when I went afar from You. But was it truly so? Whose but Yours were the words You dinned into my ears through the voice of my mother, Your faithful servant? Not that at that time any of it sank into my heart to make me do it. I still remember her anxiety and how earnestly she urged upon me not to sin with women, above all not with any man's wife. All this sounded to me womanish and I should have blushed to obey. Yet it was from You, though I did not know it and thought that You were silent and she speaking: whereas You were speaking to me through her, and in ignoring her I was ignoring You: I, her son, the son of Your handmaid, Your servant. But I realised none of this and went headlong on my course, so blinded that I was ashamed among the other youths that my viciousness was less than theirs; I heard them boasting of their exploits, and the viler the exploits the louder the boasting; and I set about the same exploits not only for the pleasure of the act but for the pleasure of boasting.

Nothing is utterly condemnable save vice: yet I grew in vice through desire of praise; and when I lacked opportunity to equal others in vice, I invented things I had not done, lest I might be held cowardly for being innocent, or contemptible for being chaste. With the basest companions I walked the streets of Babylon [the city of this World as opposed to the city of God] and wallowed in its filth as if it had been a bed of spices and precious ointments. To make me cleave closer to that city's very center, the invisible Enemy trod me down and seduced me, for I was easy to seduce. My mother had by now fled out of the center of Babylon, but she still lingered in its outskirts. She had urged me to chastity but she did not follow up what my father had told her of me: and though she saw my sexual passions as most evil now and full of peril for the future, she did not consider that if they could not be pared down to the quick, they had better be brought under control within the bounds of married love. She did not want me married because she feared that a wife might be a hindrance to my prospects—not those hopes of the world to come which my mother had in You, O God, but my prospects as a student. Both my parents were unduly set upon the success of my studies, my father because he had practically no thought of You and only vain ambition for me, my mother because she thought that the usual course of studies would be not only no hindrance to my coming to You but an actual help. Recalling the past as well as I can, that is how I read my parents' characters. Anyhow, I was left to do pretty well as I liked, and go after pleasure not only beyond the limit of reasonable discipline but to sheer dissoluteness in many kinds of evil. And in all this, O God, a mist hung between my eyes and the brightness of Your truth: *and mine iniquity had come forth as it were from fatness.*

IV

Your law, O Lord, punishes theft; and this law is so written in the hearts of men that not even the breaking of it blots it out: for no thief bears calmly being stolen from—not even if he is rich and the other steals through want. Yet I chose to steal, and not because want drove me to it—unless a want of justice and contempt for it and an excess of iniquity. For I stole things which I already had in plenty and of better quality. Nor had I any desire to enjoy the things I stole, but only the stealing of them and the sin. There was a pear tree near our vineyard, heavy with fruit, but fruit that was not particularly tempting either to look at or to taste. A group of young blackguards, and I among them, went out to knock down the pears and carry them off late one night, for it was our bad habit to carry on our games in the streets till very late. We carried off an immense load of pears, not to eat—for we barely tasted them before throwing them to the hogs. Our only pleasure in doing it was that it was forbidden. Such was my heart, O God, such was my heart: yet in the depth of the abyss You had pity on it. Let that heart now tell You what it sought when I was thus evil for no object, having no cause for wrongdoing save my wrongness. The malice of the act was base and I loved it—that is to say I loved my own undoing, I loved the evil in me—not the thing for which I did the evil, simply the evil: my soul was depraved, and hurled itself down from security in You into utter destruction, seeking no profit from wickedness but only to be wicked.

VI

What was it then that in my wretched folly I loved in You, O theft of mine, deed wrought in that dark night when I was sixteen? For you were not lovely: you were a theft. Or are you anything at all, that I should talk with you? The pears that we stole were beautiful for they were created by Thee, Thou most Beautiful of all Creator of all, Thou good God, my Sovereign and true Good. The pears were beautiful but it was not pears that my empty soul desired. For I had any number of better pears of my own, and plucked those only that I might steal. For once I had gathered them I threw them away, tasting only my own sin and savouring that with delight; for if I took so much as a bite of any one of those pears, it was the sin that sweetened it. And now, Lord my god, I ask what was it that attracted me in that theft, for there was no beauty in it to attract. I do not mean that it lacked the beauty that there is in justice and prudence, or in the mind of man or his senses and vegetative life: or even so much as the beauty and glory of the stars in the heavens, or of earth and sea with their oncoming of new life to replace the generations that pass. It had not even that false show of shadow of beauty by which sin tempts us. . . .

So once again what did I enjoy in that theft of mine? Of what excellence of my Lord was I making perverse and vicious imitation? Perhaps it was the thrill of acting against Your law—at least in appearance, since I had no power to do so in fact, the delight a prisoner might have in making some small gesture of liberty—getting a deceptive sense of omnipotence from doing something forbidden without immediate punishment. I was that slave, who fled from his Lord and pursued his Lord's shadow. O rottenness, O monstrousness of life and abyss of death! Could you find pleasure only in what was forbidden, and only because it was forbidden?

BOOK SEVEN
■

III

But though I said and firmly held that the Lord God was incorruptible and unalterable and in no way changeable, the true God who made not only our souls but our bodies also, and not only our souls and bodies, but all things whatsoever, as yet I did not see, clear and unravelled, what was the cause of Evil. Whatever that cause might be, I saw that no explanation would do which would force me to believe the immutable God mutable; for if I did that I should have been the very thing I was trying to find [namely a cause of evil]. From now it was with no anxiety that I sought it, for I was sure that what the Manichees said was not true. With all my heart I rejected them, because I saw that while they inquired as to the source of evil, they were full of evil themselves, in that they preferred rather to hold that Your substance suffered evil than that their own substance committed it.

So I set myself to examine an idea I had heard—namely that our free-will is the cause of our doing evil, and Your just judgment the cause of our suffering evil. I could not clearly discern this. I endeavoured to draw the eye of my mind from the pit, but I was again plunged into it; and as often as I tried, so often was I plunged back. But it raised me a little towards Your light that I now was as much aware that I had a will as that I had life. And when I willed to do or not do anything, I was quite certain that it was myself and no other who willed, and I came to see that the cause of my sin lay there.

But what I did unwillingly, it still seemed to me that I rather suffered than did, and I judged it to be not my fault but my punishment: though as I held You most just, I was quite ready to admit that I was being justly punished.

But I asked further: "Who made me? Was it not my God, who is not only Good but Goodness itself? What root reason is there for my willing evil and failing to will good, which would make it just for me to be punished? Who was it that set and ingrafted in me this root of bitterness, since I was wholly made by my most loving God? If the devil is the author, where does the devil come from? And if by his own perverse will he was turned from a good angel into a devil, what was the origin in him of the perverse will by which he became a devil, since by the all-good Creator he was made wholly angel?" By such thoughts I was cast down again and almost stifled; yet I was not brought down so far as the hell of that error, where no man confesses unto You, the error which holds rather that You suffer evil than that man does it.

V

I sought for the origin of evil, but I sought in an evil manner, and failed to see the evil that there was in my manner of enquiry. I ranged before the eyes of my mind the whole creation, both what we are able to see—earth and sea and air and stars and trees and mortal creatures; and what we cannot see—like the firmament of the Heaven above, and all its angels and spiritual powers: though even these I imagined as if they were bodies disposed each in its own place. And I made one great mass of God's Creation, distinguished according to the kinds of bodies in it, whether they really were bodies, or only such bodies as I imagined spirits to be. I made it huge, not as huge as it is, which I had no means of knowing, but as huge as might be necessary, though in every direction finite. And I saw You, Lord, in every part containing and penetrating it, Yourself altogether infinite: as if Your Being were a sea, infinite and immeasurable everywhere, though still only a sea: and within it there were some mighty but not infinite sponge, and that sponge filled in every part with the immeasurable sea. Thus I conceived Your Creation as finite, and filled utterly by Yourself, and You were Infinite. And I said: "Here is God, and here is what God has created; and God is good, mightily and incomparably better than all these; but of His goodness He created them good: and see how He contains and fills them.

"When then is evil, and what is its source, and how has it crept into the Creation? What is its root, what is its seed? Can it be that it is wholly without being? But why should we fear and be on guard against what is not? Or if our fear of it is groundless, then our very fear is itself an evil thing. For by it the heart is driven and tormented for no cause; and that evil is all the worse, if there is nothing to fear yet we do fear. Thus either there is evil which we fear, or the fact that we fear is evil.

"Whence then is evil, since God who is good made all things good? It was the greater and supreme Good who made these lesser goods, but Creator and Creation are alike good.

Whence then comes evil? Was there perhaps some evil matter of which He made this creation, matter which He formed and ordered, while yet leaving in it some element which He did not convert into good? But why? Could He who was omnipotent be unable to change matter wholly so that no evil might remain in it? Indeed why did He choose to make anything of it and not rather by the same omnipotence cause it wholly not to be? Could it possibly have existed against His will? And if it had so existed from eternity, why did He allow it so long to continue through the infinite spaces of time past, and then after so long a while choose to make something of it? If He did suddenly decide to act, surely the Omnipotent should rather have caused it to cease to be, that He Himself, the true and supreme and infinite Good, alone should be. Or, since it was not good that He who was good should frame and create something not good, could He not have taken away and reduced to nothing that matter which was evil, and provided good matter of which to create something good without the aid of matter which He had not created."

Such thoughts I revolved in my unhappy heart, which was further burdened and gnawed at by the fear that I should die without having found the truth. But at least the faith of Your Christ, Our Lord and Saviour, taught by the Catholic Church, stood firm in my heart, though on many points I was still uncertain and swerving from the norm of doctrine. Yet my mind did not forsake it, but drank of it more deeply with every day that passed.

BOOK EIGHT
∎

XI

Thus I was sick at heart and in torment, accusing myself with a new intensity of bitterness, twisting and turning in my chain in the hope that it might be utterly broken, for what held me was so small a thing! But it still held me. And You stood in the secret places of my soul, O Lord, in the harshness of Your mercy redoubling the scourges of fear and shame lest I should give way again and that small slight tie which remained should not be broken but should grow again to full strength and bind me closer even than before. For I kept saying within myself: "Let it be now, let it be now," and by the mere words I had begun to move towards the resolution. I almost made it, yet I did not quite make it. But I did not fall back into my original state, but as it were stood near to get my breath. And I tried again and I was almost there, and now I could all but touch it and hold it: yet I was not quite there, I did not touch it or hold it. I still shrank from dying unto death and living unto life. The lower condition which had grown habitual was more powerful than the better condition which I had not tried. The nearer the point of time came in which I was to become different, the more it struck me with horror; but it did not force me utterly back nor turn me utterly away, but held me there between the two.

Those trifles of all trifles, and vanities of vanities, my one-time mistresses, held me back, plucking at my garment of flesh and murmuring softly: "Are You sending us away?" And "From this moment shall we not be with You, now or forever?" And "From this moment shall this or that not be allowed You, now or forever?" What were they suggesting to me in the phrase I have written "this or that," what were they suggesting to me, O my God? Do You in Your mercy keep from the soul of Your servant the vileness and uncleanness they were suggesting. And now I began to hear them not half so loud; they no longer stood against me face to face, but were softly muttering behind my back and, as I tried to depart, plucking stealthily at me to make me look behind. Yet even that was enough, so hesitating was I, to keep me from snatching myself free, from shaking them off and leaping upwards on the way I was called: for the strong force of habit said to me: "Do you think you can live without them?"

But by this time its voice was growing fainter. In the direction towards which I had turned my face and was quivering in fear of going. I could see the austere beauty of Continence, serene and indeed joyous but not evilly, honourably soliciting me to come to her and not linger, stretching forth loving hands to receive and embrace me, hands full of multitudes of good examples. With her I saw such hosts of young men and maidens, a multitude of youth and of every age, gray widows and women grown old in virginity, and in them all Continence herself, not barren but the fruitful mother of children, her joys, by You, Lord, her Spouse. And she smiled upon me and her smile gave courage as if she were saying: "Can you not do what these men have done, what these women have done? Or could men or women have done such in themselves, and not in the Lord their God? The Lord their God gave me to them. Why do you stand upon yourself and so not stand at all? Cast yourself upon Him and be not afraid; He will not draw away and let you fall. Cast yourself without fear, He will receive you and heal you."

Yet I was still ashamed, for I could still hear the murmuring of those vanities, and I still hung hesitant. And again it was as if she said: "Stop your ears against your unclean members, that they may be mortified. They tell you of delights, but not of such delights as the law of the Lord your God tells." This was the controversy raging in my heart, a controversy about myself against myself. And Alypius stayed by my side and awaited in silence the issue of such agitation as he had never seen in me.

XII

When my most searching scrutiny had drawn up all my vileness from the secret depths of my soul and heaped it in my heart's sight, a mighty storm arose in me, bringing a mighty rain of tears. That I might give way to my tears and lamentations, I rose from Alypius: for it struck me that solitude was more suited to the business of weeping. I went far enough from him to prevent his presence from being an embarrassment to me. So I felt, and he realized it. I suppose I had something and the sound of my voice was heavy with tears. I arose, but he remained where we had been sitting, still in utter amazement. I flung myself down somehow under a certain fig tree and no longer tried to check my tears, which poured forth from my eyes in a flood, *an acceptable sacrifice to Thee*. And much I said not in these words but to this effect: "*And Thou, O Lord, how long? How long, Lord, wilt Thou be angry forever? Remember not our former iniquities*." For I felt that I was still bound by them. And I continued my miserable complaining: "How long, how long shall I go on saying tomorrow and again tomorrow? Why not now, why not have an end to my uncleanness this very hour?"

Such things I said, weeping in the most bitter sorrow of my heart. And suddenly I heard a voice from some nearby house, a boy's voice or a girl's voice, I do not know: but it was a sort of sing-song, repeated again and again, "Take and read, take and read." I ceased weeping and immediately began to search my mind most carefully as to whether children were accustomed to chant these words in any kind of game, and I could not remember that

I had ever heard any such thing. Damming back the flood of my tears I arose, interpreting the incident as quite certainly a divine command to open my book of Scripture and read the passage at which I should open. For it was part of what I had been told about Antony, that from the Gospel which he happened to be reading he had felt that he was being admonished as though what he read was spoken directly to himself: *Go, sell what thou hast and give to the poor and thou shalt have treasure in heaven; and come follow Me.* By this experience he had been in that instant converted to You. So I was moved to return to the place where Alypius was sitting, for I had put down the Apostle's book there when I arose. I snatched it up, opened it and in silence read the passage upon which my eyes first fell: *Not in rioting and drunkenness, not in chambering and impurities, not in contention and envy, but put ye on the Lord Jesus Christ and make not provision for the flesh in its concupiscences. [Romans xiii,13.]* I had no wish to read further, and no need. For in that instant, with the very ending of the sentence, it was as though a light of utter confidence shone in all my heart, and all the darkness of uncertainty vanished away. Then leaving my finger in the place or marking it by some other sign, I closed the book and in complete calm told the whole thing to Alypius and he similarly told me what had been going on in himself, of which I knew nothing. He asked to see what I had read. I showed him, and he looked further than I had read. I had not known what followed. And this is what followed: *"Now him that is weak in faith, take unto you."* He applied this to himself and told me so. And he was confirmed by this message, and with no troubled wavering gave himself to God's good-will and purpose—a purpose indeed most suited to his character, for in these matters he had been immeasurably better than I.

Then we went in to my mother and told her, to her great joy. We related how it had come about: she was filled with triumphant exultation, and praised You who are mighty beyond what we ask or conceive: for she saw that You had given her more than with all her pitiful weeping she had ever asked. For You converted me to Yourself so that I no longer sought a wife nor any of this world's promises, but stood upon that same rule of faith in which You had shown me to her so many years before. Thus You changed her mourning into joy, a joy far richer than she had thought to wish, a joy much dearer and purer than she had thought to find in grandchildren of my flesh.

The Rule of St. Benedict

St. Benedict of Nursia (c. 480–547) was one of the principal architects of the monastic system in the West. In Benedict himself—who sought refuge from the world in a cave not far from Rome before establishing his own monastic community—we can see the transition from the singular piety of the hermit to the collective spiritual discipline of the great monastic orders. And with fitting irony, the year in which Benedict founded the monastery that bears his name at Monte Cassino (A.D. 529) was also the year in which Justinian abolished the pagan philosophical schools of Athens.

Benedict's *Rule* was remarkable in its own time for preserving both a sense of community and a measure of respect for the rights of the individual monk. Benedict is particularly emphatic on the obligations of the Abbot, who, as spiritual head of the monastery, must temper authority with understanding, and create an environment suitable for study and prayer. Animating the whole of Benedict's *Rule*, however, is the belief that both monk and Abbot have been summoned by God to model the ideal Christian life, albeit out of the world and its secular concerns, and that the virtues each is expected to embody are those from which the kingdom of God will be made.

PROLOGUE

■

Hearken, my son, to the precepts of the master and incline the ear of thy heart; freely accept and faithfully fulfil the instructions of a loving father, that by the labour of obedience thou mayest return to him from whom thou has strayed by the sloth of disobedience. To thee are my words now addressed, whosoever thou mayest be that renouncing thine own will to fight for the true King, Christ, dost take up the strong and glorious weapons of obedience.

And first of all, whatever good work thou undertakest, ask him with most instant prayer to perfect it, so that he who has deigned to count us among his sons may never be provoked by our evil conduct. For we must always so serve him with the gifts which he has given us, that he may never as an angry father disinherit his children, nor yet as a dread lord be driven by our sins to cast into everlasting punishment the wicked servants who would not follow him to glory.

Up with us then at last, for the Scripture arouseth us, saying: *Now is the hour for us to rise from sleep.* Let us open our eyes to the divine light, and let us hear with attentive ears the warning that the divine voice crieth daily to us: *Today if ye will hear his voice, harden not your hearts.* And again: *He that hath ears to hear, let him hear what the Spirit saith to the churches.* And what doth he say? *Come, ye children, hearken unto me: I will teach you the fear of the Lord. Run while ye have the light of life, lest the darkness of death overtake you.*

Let us, therefore, gird our loins with faith and the performance of good works, and following the guidance of the Gospel walk in his paths, so that we may merit to see him who has called us unto his kingdom. And, if we wish to dwell in the tabernacle of his kingdom, except we run thither with good deeds we shall not arrive. But let us ask the Lord with the prophet: *Lord, who shall dwell in thy tabernacle, or who shall rest upon thy holy hill?* Then, brethren, let us hear the Lord answering and showing us the way to that tabernacle and saying: *He that walketh without blemish and doth that which is right; he that speaketh truth in his heart, who hath used no deceit in his tongue, nor done evil to his neighbour, nor believed ill of his neighbour.* He that taketh the evil spirit that tempteth him, and casteth him and his temptation from the sight of his heart, and bringeth him to naught; who graspeth his evil suggestions as they arise and dasheth them to pieces on the rock that is Christ. Such men as these, fearing the Lord, are not puffed up on account of their good works, but judging that they can do no good of themselves and that all cometh from God, they magnify the Lord's work in them, using the word of the prophet: *Not unto us, O Lord, not unto us, but unto thy name give the glory.* So the apostle Paul imputed nothing of his preaching to himself, but said: *By the grace of God I am what I am.* And again he saith: *He that glorieth, let him glory in the Lord.*

So, brethren, we have asked the Lord about the dwellers in his tabernacle and have heard what is the duty of him who would dwell therein; it remains for us to fulfil this duty. Therefore our hearts and bodies must be made ready to fight under the holy obedience of his commands; and let us ask God that he be pleased, where our nature is powerless, to give us the help of his grace. And if we would escape the pains of hell and reach eternal life, then must we—while there is still time, while we are in this body and can fulfil all these things by the light of this life—hasten to do now what may profit us for eternity.

Therefore must we establish a school of the Lord's service; in founding which we hope to ordain nothing that is harsh or burdensome. But if, for good reason, for the amendment of evil habit or the preservation of charity, there be some strictness of discipline, do not be at once dismayed and run away from the way of salvation, of which the entrance must needs be narrow. But, as we progress in our monastic life and in faith, our hearts shall be enlarged, and we shall run with unspeakable sweetness of love in the way of God's commandments; so that, never abandoning his rule but persevering in his teaching in the monastery until death, we shall share by patience in the sufferings of Christ, that we may deserve to be partakers also of his kingdom. Amen.
END OF PROLOGUE

CHAPTER 2

■

WHAT KIND OF MAN THE ABBOT SHOULD BE

An abbot who is worthy to rule a monastery should always remember what he is called and realize in his actions the name of a superior. For he is believed to be the representative of Christ in the monastery, and for that reason is called by a name of his, according to the words of the Apostle: *Ye have received the spirit of the adoption of sons, whereby we cry Abba, Father.* Therefore the abbot ought not to teach, or ordain, or command anything which is against the law of the Lord; on the contrary, his commands and teaching should be infused into the minds of his disciples like the leaven of divine justice. Let the abbot remember always that at the dread Judgement of God there will be an examination of both these matters, of his teaching and of the obedience of his disciples. And let the abbot realize that the shepherd will have to answer for any lack of profit which the Father of the family may discover in his sheep. On the other hand, if the shepherd have spent all diligence on an unruly and disobedient flock and devoted his utmost care to the amending of its vicious ways, then he will be acquitted at the Judgement and may say to the Lord with the prophet: *I have not hid thy justice within my heart: I have declared thy truth and thy salvation; but they have despised and rejected me*. And so at the last, for these sheep disobedient to his care, let death itself bring its penalty.

Therefore, when anyone has received the name of abbot, he ought to rule his disciples with a twofold teaching, displaying all goodness and holiness by deeds and by words, but by deeds rather than by words. To intelligent disciples let him expound the Lord's commandments in words; but to those of harder hearts and ruder minds let him show forth the divine precepts by his example. And whatever he has taught his disciples to be contrary to God's law, let him show by his example that it is not to be done, lest while preaching to others he should himself become a castaway, and lest God should some day say to him in his sin: *Why dost thou repeat my commandments by rote, and boast of my covenant with thee? For thou hast hated to amend thy life and hast cast my words behind thee*. And again: *Thou sawest the speck of dust in thy brother's eye and didst not see the beam in thy own*.

Let him not make any distinction of persons in the monastery. Let him not love one more than another, unless he find him better in good works and obedience. Let not a freeborn monk be put before one that was a slave, unless there be some other reasonable ground for it. But if the abbot, for just reason, think fit so to do, let him fix anyone's order as he will; otherwise let them keep their due places; because, whether slaves or freemen, we are all one in Christ, and have to serve alike in the army of the same Lord. *For there is no respect of persons with God*. In this regard only are we distinguished in his sight, if we be found better than others in good works and humility. Therefore let the abbot show an equal love to all, and let the same discipline be imposed on all in accordance with their deserts.

For the abbot in his teaching ought always to observe the rule of the apostle, wherein he says: *Reprove, persuade, rebuke*. He must adapt himself to circumstances, now using severity and now persuasion, displaying the rigour of a master or the loving kindness of a father. That is to say, that he must sternly rebuke the undisciplined and restless; but the obedient, meek, and patient, these he should exhort to advance in virtue. As for the negligent and rebellious, we warn him to reprimand and punish them. And let him not shut his eyes to the faults of offenders; but as soon as they begin to appear, let him, as he can, cut them out by the roots, mindful of the fate of Heli, the priest of Silo. Those of gentle disposition and good understanding should be punished, for the first and second time, by verbal admonition; but bold, hard, proud, and disobedient characters should be checked at the very beginning of their ill-doing by the rod and corporal punishment, according to the text: *The fool is not corrected with words*; and again: *Beat thy son with the rod and thou shalt deliver his soul from death*.

The abbot should always remember what he is and what he is called, and should know that to whom more is committed, from him more is required. Let him realize also how difficult and arduous a task he has undertaken, of ruling souls and adapting himself to many dispositions. One he must humour, another rebuke, another persuade, according to each one's disposition and understanding, and thus adapt and accommodate himself to all in such a way, that he may not only suffer no loss in the sheep committed to him, but may even rejoice in the increase of a good flock.

Above all let him not have greater solicitude for fleeting, earthly, and perishable things, and so overlook or undervalue the salvation of the souls committed to him; but let him always remember that he has undertaken the government of souls and will have to give an account of them. And if he be tempted to complain of lack of means, let him remember the words: *Seek ye first the kingdom of God and his approval, and all these things shall be yours without the asking.* And again: *Those that fear him never go wanting.* And let him know that he who has undertaken the government of souls, must prepare himself to render an account of them. And whatever number of brethren he knows he has under his care, let him regard it as certain that he will have to give the Lord an account of all these souls on the Day of Judgement, and certainly of his own soul also. And thus, fearing always the examination which the shepherd will have to face for the sheep entrusted to him, and anxious regarding the account which will have to be given for others, he is made solicitous for his own sake also; and while by his admonitions helping others to amend, he himself is cleansed of his faults.

CHAPTER 4

THE TOOLS OF GOOD WORKS

In the first place, to love the Lord God with all one's heart, all one's soul, and all one's strength.

Then, one's neighbour as oneself.
Then not to kill.
Not to commit adultery.
Not to steal.
Not to covet.
Not to bear false witness.
To honour all men.
Not to do to another what one would not have done to oneself.
To deny oneself, in order to follow Christ.
To chastise the body.
Not to seek soft living.
To love fasting.
To relieve the poor.
To clothe the naked.
To visit the sick.
To bury the dead.
To help the afflicted.
To console the sorrowing.
To avoid worldly conduct.
To prefer nothing to the love of Christ.

Not to yield to anger.

Not to nurse a grudge.

Not to hold guile in one's heart.

Not to make a feigned peace.

Not to forsake charity.

Not to swear, lest perchance one forswear oneself.

To utter truth from heart and mouth.

Not to render evil for evil.

To do no wrong to anyone, and to bear patiently wrongs done to oneself.

To pray for one's enemies in the love of Christ.

To make peace with one's adversary before sundown.

And never to despair of God's mercy.

Behold these are the tools of the spiritual craft. If we employ them unceasingly day and night, and on the Day of Judgement render account of them, then we shall receive from the Lord in return that reward which he himself has promised: *Eye hath not seen nor ear heard, what God hath prepared for those that love him*. Now the workshop, wherein we shall diligently execute all these tasks, is the enclosure of the monastery and stability in the community.

The Medieval Period

The Song of Roland

The Song of Roland was probably composed early in the eleventh century, and although we are not certain who the author of this poem was, the historical incidents on which the poem is based are well established. In the year 778, as the French King Charlemagne ("Charles the Great," in English) was withdrawing his army from northern Spain after laying siege unsuccessfully to the Muslim-held town of Saragossa, his rearguard was wiped out by a raiding party of Basque fighters. Listed among the dead was "Roland, duke of the Marches of Brittany"; that was all the ninth-century historian Eginhardt had to say about the hero of this poem. Folklore and medieval literary imagination did the rest.

Narratives like *The Song of Roland* were known in the Middle Ages as *chansons de geste:* literally, "songs of deeds." The "deeds" in question were deeds of valor and military conquest through which the protagonist displayed not only his prowess, but also the heroic ideals of the aristocratic warrior class to which he belonged. The highest virtue of that class—apart from personal courage—was *fealty*, or loyalty to one's king or liege lord. Roland's determination to fight to the death rather than flee or surrender to Charlemagne's enemies is motivated by just that ideal of conduct.

Yet, for all his dauntless courage and the almost superhuman powers he displays in battle, Roland is not without certain flaws of character, the most serious of which is pride. Rather than summon Charlemagne and the rest of the French army to his aid, Roland refuses his friend Oliver's request that he sound the battle horn until it is too late. And like the tragic heroes of classical drama, Roland realizes the magnitude of his mistake only after an irreversible and disastrous chain of events has been set in motion. It is at that moment that Roland rises above his *hubris* and becomes something more than an obstinate and self-destructive warrior.

It is worth noting that the world of *The Song of Roland* is a man's world, in which women play, at best, only a secondary role. This is perhaps inevitable in a poem in which the principal action takes place on a battlefield, but it stands in sharp contrast to later works of medieval literature where devotion to the lady and the practice of courtly love give women a central part in the sagas of knighthood and adventure.

1.

Charles the King, our Emperor, the Great,
has been in Spain for seven full years,
has conquered the high land down to the sea.
There is no castle that stands against him now,
no wall, no citadel left to break down—   5
except Saragossa, high on a mountain.
King Marsilion holds it, who does not love God,

who serves Mahumet and prays to Apollin.
He cannot save himself: his ruin will find him there. AOI.[1]

2.

King Marsilion was in Saragossa.   *10*
He has gone forth into a grove, beneath its shade,
and he lies down on a block of blue marble,
twenty thousand men, and more, all around him.
He calls aloud to his dukes and his counts:
"Listen, my lords, to the troubles we have.   *15*
The Emperor Charles of the sweet land of France
has come into this country to destroy us.
I have no army able to give him battle,
I do not have the force to break his force.
Now act like my wise men: give me counsel,   *20*
save me, save me from death, save me from shame!"
No pagan there has one word to say to him
except Blancandrin, of the castle of Valfunde.

3.

One of the wisest pagans was Blancandrin,
brave and loyal, a great mounted warrior,   *25*
a useful man, the man to aid his lord;
said to the King: "Do not give way to panic.
Do this: send Charles, that wild, terrible man
tokens of loyal service and great friendship:
you will give him bears and lions and dogs,   *30*
seven hundred camels, a thousand molted hawks,
four hundred mules weighed down with gold and silver,
and fifty carts, to cart it all away:
he'll have good wages for his men who fight for pay.
Say he's made war long enough in this land: *35*
let him go home, to France, to Aix,[2] at last—
come Michaelmas[3] you will follow him there,
say you will take their faith, become a Christian,
and be his man with honor, with all you have.
If he wants hostages, why, you'll send them,   *40*
ten, or twenty, to give him security.

---

[1]AOI: these three mysterious letters appear at certain moments throughout the text, 180 times in all. No one has ever adequately explained them, though every reader feels their effect.
[2]Aix: Aachen (Aix-la-Chapelle), capital of Charlemagne's empire.
[3]Michaelmas: either September 29 or October 16.

Let us send him the sons our wives have borne.
I'll send my son with all the others named to die.
It is better that they should lose their heads
than that we, Lord, should lose our dignity   45
and our honors—and be turned into beggars!: AOI.

6.

Marsilion brought his council to an end,
said to his men: "Lords, you will go on now,
and remember: olive branches in your hands;   80
and in my name tell Charlemagne the King
for his god's sake to have pity on me—
he will not see a month from this day pass
before I come with a thousand faithful;
say I will take that Christian religion   85
and be his man in love and loyalty.
If he wants hostages, why he'll have them."
Said Blancandrin: "Now you will get good terms." AOI

9.

Blancandrin spoke, he was the first to speak,
said to the King: "Greetings, and God save you,
that glorious God whom we all must adore.
Here is the word of the great king Marsilion: 125
he has looked into this law of salvation,
wants to give you a great part of his wealth,
bears and lions and hunting dogs on chains,
seven hundred camels, a thousand molted hawks,
four hundred mules packed tight with gold and silver, 130
and fifty carts, to cart it all away;
and there will be so many fine gold bezants,
you'll have good wages for the men in your pay.
You have stayed long—long enough!—in this land,
it is time to go home, to France, to Aix.   135
My master swears he will follow you there."
The Emperor holds out his hands toward God,
bows down his head, begins to meditate. AOI.

10.

The Emperor held his head bowed down;
never was he too hasty with his words: 140
his custom is to speak in his good time.
When his head rises, how fierce the look of him;

he said to them: "You have spoken quite well.
King Marsilion is my great enemy.
Now all these words, that you have spoken here—   *145*
how far can I trust them? How can I be sure?"
The Saracen: "He wants to give you hostages.
How many will you want? ten? fifteen? twenty?
I'll put my son with the others named to die.
You will get some, I think, still better born.   *150*
When you are at home in your high royal palace,
at the great feast of Saint Michael-in-Peril,
the lord who nurtures me will follow you,
and in those baths—the baths God made for you—
my lord will come and want to be made Christian."   *155*
King Charles replies: "He may yet save his soul." AOI

[Charles summons his barons to council and asks for their response to Marsilion's offer.
Count Roland warns Charles not to believe the Saracen king, while Roland's stepfather,
Ganelon, urges Charles to accept the offer of peace and then heaps scorn on Roland for
suggesting otherwise, thus precipitating a bitter quarrel between them. Duke Naimon seconds
Ganelon's pleas for peace, Charles accepts his advice, and at Roland's suggestion Ganelon
is chosen to appear before Marsilion as Charles' representative. At Marsilion's court Ganelon
decides to betray the French cause and plots with Blancandrin to ambush Roland.]

55.

King Charlemagne laid waste the land of Spain,
stormed its castles, ravaged its citadels.
The King declares his war is at an end.   *705*
The Emperor rides toward the land of sweet France.
Roland the Count affixed the gonfanon,
raised it toward heaven on the height of a hill;
the men of France make camp across that country.
Pagans are riding up through these great valleys,   *710*
their hauberks on, their tunics of double mail,
their helms laced on, their swords fixed on their belts,
shields on their necks, lances trimmed with their banners.
In a forest high in the hills they gathered:
four hundred thousand men waiting for dawn.   *715*
God, the pity of it! the French do not know! AOI

57.

And after that he dreamed another vision: *725*
he was in France, in his chapel at Aix,

a cruel wild boar was biting his right arm;
saw coming at him—from the Ardennes—a leopard,
it attacked him, fell wildly on his body.
And a swift hound running down from the hall   *730*
came galloping, bounding over to Charles,
tore the right ear off that first beast, the boar,
turns, in fury, to fight against the leopard.
And the French say: It is a mighty battle,
but cannot tell which one of them will win.   *735*
Charlemagne sleeps, his dream does not wake him. AOI.

58.

The day goes by, and the bright dawn arises.
Throughout that host. . . .
The Emperor rides forth with such fierce pride.
"Barons, my lords," said the Emperor Charles   *740*
"look at those passes, at those narrow defiles—
pick me a man to command the rear-guard."
Ganelon answers: "Roland, here, my stepson.
You have no baron as great and brave as Roland."
When he hears that, the King stares at him in fury;   *745*
and said to him: "You are the living devil,
a mad dog—the murderous rage in you!
And who will precede me, in the vanguard?"
Ganelon answers, "Why, Ogier of Denmark,
you have no baron who could lead it so well."   *750*

60.

When Roland hears he will lead the rear-guard,
he spoke in great fury to his stepfather:
"Hah! you nobody, you base-born little fellow,
and did you think the glove would fall from my hands
as the staff fell from yours before King Charles?" AOI.   *765*

63.

The Emperor calls forth Roland the Count:
"My lord, my dear nephew, of course you know
I will give you half my men, they are yours.   *785*
Let them serve you, it is your salvation."
"None of that!" said the Count. "May God strike me
if I discredit the history of my line.
I'll keep twenty thousand Franks—they are good men.

Go your way through the passes, you will be safe.   *790*
You must not fear any man while I live."

[In spite of a dream warning, Charles prepares to lead his army across the Pyrenees and
back to France, leaving Roland and the twelve peers to guard the mountain passes at
Roncevaux. No sooner has Charles departed, than the warriors at Marsilion's court boast of
their intention to kill Roland and his comrades-at-arms.]

79.

They arm themselves in Saracen hauberks,
all but a few are lined with triple mail;   *995*
they lace on their good helms of Saragossa,
gird on their swords, the steel forged in Vienne;
they have rich shields, spears of Valencia,
and gonfanons of white and blue and red.
They leave the mules and riding horses now,   *1000*
mount their war horses and ride in close array.
The day was fair, the sun was shining bright,
all their armor was aflame with the light;
a thousand trumpets blow: that was to make it finer.
That made a great noise, and the men of France heard.   *1005*
Said Oliver: "Companion, I believe
we may yet have a battle with the pagans."
Roland replies: "Now may God grant us that.
We know our duty: to stand here for our King.
A man must bear some hardships for his lord,   *1010*
stand everything, the great heat, the great cold,
lose the hide and hair on him for his good lord.
Now let each man make sure to strike hard here:
let them not sing a bad song about us!
Pagans are wrong and Christians are right!   *1015*
They'll make no bad example of me this day!" AOI.

80.

Oliver climbs to the top of a hill,
looks to his right, across a grassy vale,
sees the pagan army on its way there;
and called down to Roland, his companion: *1020*
"That way, toward Spain: the uproar I see coming!
All their hauberks, all blazing, helmets like flames!
It will be a bitter thing for our French.
Ganelon knew, that criminal, that traitor,
when he marked us out before the Emperor."   *1025*

"Be still, Oliver," Roland the Count replies.
"He is my stepfather—my stepfather.
I won't have you speak one word against him."

83.

Said Oliver: "The pagan force is great;
from what I see, our French here are too few.   *1050*
Roland, my companion, sound your horn then,
Charles will hear it, the army will come back."
Roland replies: "I'd be a fool to do it.
I would lose my good name all through sweet France.
I will strike with Durendal,   *1055*
the blade will be bloody to the gold from striking!
These pagan traitors came to these passes doomed!
I promise you, they are marked men, they'll die." AOI.

[Oliver pleads with Roland three times to sound the oliphant and to summon Charles to their
aid. Roland proudly refuses.]

92.

Said Oliver: "I will waste no more words.   *1170*
You did not think it right to sound your olifant,
there'll be no Charles coming to your aid now.
He knows nothing, brave man, he's done no wrong;
those men down there—they have no blame in this.
Well, then, ride now, and ride with all your might!   *1175*
Lords, you brave men, stand your ground, hold the field!
Make up your minds. I beg you in God's name,
to strike some blows, take them and give them back!
Here we must not forget Charlemagne's war cry."
And with that word the men of France cried out.   *1180*
A man who heard that shout: Munjoie! Munjoie!
would always remember what manhood is.
Then they ride, God! look at their pride and spirit!
and they spur hard, to ride with all their speed,
come on to strike—what else would these men do?   *1185*
The Saracens kept coming, never fearing them.
Franks and pagans, here they are, at each other.

110.

The battle is fearful and full of grief.
Oliver and Roland strike like good men,
the Archbishop, more than a thousand blows,

209
■

and the Twelve Peers do not hang back, they strike!   *1415*
the French fight side by side, all as one man.
The pagans die by hundreds, by thousands:
whoever does not flee finds no refuge from death,
like it or not, there he ends all his days.
And there the men of France lose their greatest arms;   *1420*
they will not see their fathers, their kin again,
or Charlemagne, who looks for them in the passes.
Tremendous torment now comes forth in France,
a mighty whirlwind, tempests of wind and thunder,
rains and hailstones, great and immeasurable,   *1425*
bolts of lightning hurtling and hurtling down:
it is, in truth, a trembling of the earth.
From Saint Michael-in-Peril to the Saints,
from Besancon to the port of Wissant,
there is no house whose veil of walls does not crumble.   *1430*
A great darkness at noon falls on the land,
there is no light but when the heavens crack.
No man sees this who is not terrified,
and many say: "The Last Day! Judgment Day!
The end! The end of the world is upon us!"   *1435*
They do not know, they do not speak the truth:
it is the worldwide grief for the death of Roland.

[In spite of their heroism, Roland, Oliver, Archbishop Turpin, and the twelve peers are hopelessly outnumbered by their Saracen enemies, and the tide of battle begins to turn against them.]

128.

Count Roland sees the great loss of his men,
calls on his companion, on Oliver:
"Lord, Companion, in God's name, what would you do?
All these good men you see stretched on the ground.
We can mourn for sweet France, fair land of France!   *1695*
a desert now, stripped of such great vassals.
Oh King, and friend, if only you were here!
Oliver, Brother, how shall we manage it?
What shall we do to get word to the King?"
Said Oliver: "I don't see any way.   *1700*
I would rather die now than hear us shamed." AOI.

129.

And Roland said: "I'll sound the olifant,
Charles will hear it, drawing through the passes,

I promise you, the Franks will return at once."
Said Oliver: "That would be a great disgrace, 1705
a dishonor and reproach to all your kin,
the shame of it would last them all their lives.
When I urged it, you would not hear of it;
you will not do it now with my consent.
It is not acting bravely to sound it now— 1710
look at your arms, they are covered with blood."
The Count replies: "I've fought here like a lord." AOI

131.

And Roland said: "Why are you angry at me?"
Oliver answers: "Companion, it is your doing.
I will tell you what makes a vassal good.
          It is judgment, it is never madness;
restraint is worth more than the raw nerve of a fool. 1725
Frenchmen are dead because of your wildness.
And what service will Charles ever have from us?
If you had trusted, my lord would be here,
we would have fought this battle through to the end,
Marsilion would be dead, or our prisoner. 1730
Roland, your prowess—had we never seen it!
          And now, dear friend, we've seen the last of it.
No more aid from us now for Charlemagne,
a man without equal till Judgment Day,
you will die here, and your death will shame France.
We kept faith, you and I, we were companions; 1735
          and everything we were will end today.
We part before evening, and it will be hard." AOI.

132.

Turpin the Archbishop hears their bitter words,
digs hard into his horse with golden spurs
and rides to them; begins to set them right:
"You, Lord Roland, and you, Lord Oliver, 1740
I beg you in God's name do not quarrel.
To sound the horn could not help us now, true,
but still it is far better that you do it:
let the King come, he can avenge us then—
these men of Spain must not go home exulting! 1745
Our French will come, they'll get down on their feet,
and find us here—we'll be dead, cut to pieces.
They will lift us into coffins on the backs of mules,
and weep for us, in rage and pain and grief,

and bury us in the courts of churches;   *1750*
and we will not be eaten by wolves or pigs or dogs."
Roland replies, "Lord, you have spoken well." AOI.

133.

Roland has put the olifant to his mouth,
he sets it well, sounds it with all his strength.
The hills are high, and that voice ranges far,   *1755*
they heard it echo thirty great leagues away.
King Charles heard it, and all his faithful men.
And the King says: "Our men are in a battle."
And Ganelon disputed him and said:
"Had someone else said that, I'd call him liar!: AOI.   *1760*

134.

And now the mighty effort of Roland the Count:
he sounds his olifant; his pain is great,
and from his mouth the bright blood comes leaping out,
and the temple bursts in his forehead.
That horn, in Roland's hands, has a mighty voice: *1765*
King Charles hears it drawing through the passes.
Naimon heard it, the Franks listen to it.
And the King said: "I hear Count Roland's horn;
he'd never sound it unless he had a battle."
Says Ganelon: "Now no more talk of battles!   *1770*
You are old now, your hair is white as snow,
the things you say make you sound like a child.
You know Roland and that wild pride of his—
what a wonder God has suffered it so long!
Remember? he took Noples without your command: *1775*
the Saracens rode out, to break the siege;
they fought with him, the great vassal Roland.
Afterwards he used the streams to wash the blood
from the meadows: so that nothing would show.
He blasts his horn all day to catch a rabbit,   *1780*
he's strutting now before his peers and bragging—
who under heaven would dare meet him on the field?
So now: ride on! Why do you keep on stopping?
The Land of Fathers lies far ahead of us." AOI

135.

The blood leaping from Count Roland's mouth,   *1785*
the temple broken with effort in his forehead,

212
∎

he sounds his horn in great travail and pain.
King Charles heard it, and his French listen hard.
And the King said: "That horn has a long breath!"
Naimon answers: "It is a baron's breath.   *1790*
There is battle there, I know there is.
He betrayed him! and now asks you to fail him!
Put on your armor! Lord, shout your battle cry,
and save the noble barons of your house!
You hear Roland's call. He is in trouble."   *1795*

[King Charles orders his men to seize Ganelon—whom he now suspects of treachery—and rides with his army to Roland's rescue, fearing he may be too late.]

140.

Roland looks up on the mountains and slopes,
sees the French dead, so many good men fallen,
and weeps for them, as a great warrior weeps:
"Barons, my lords, may God give you his grace,
may he grant Paradise to all your souls,   *1855*
make them lie down among the holy flowers.
I never saw better vassals than you.
All the years you've served me, and all the times,
the mighty lands you conquered for Charles our King!
The Emperor raised you for this terrible hour!   *1860*
Land of France, how sweet you are, native land,
laid waste this day, ravaged, made a desert.
Barons of France, I see you die for me,
and I, your lord—cannot protect you.
May God come to your aid, that God who never failed.   *1865*
Oliver, brother, now I will not fail you.
I will die here—of grief, if no man kills me.
Lord, Companion, let us return and fight."

141.

Roland returned to his place on the field,
strikes—a brave man keeping faith—with Durendal,   *1870*
struck through Faldrun de Pui, cut him to pieces,
and twenty-four of the men they valued most;
no man will ever want his vengeance more!
As when the deer turns tail before the dogs,
so the pagans flee before Roland the Count.   *1875*
Said the Archbishop: "You! Roland! What a fighter!
Now that's what every knight must have in him
who carries arms and rides on a fine horse:

he must be strong, a savage, when he's in battle;
for otherwise, what's he worth? Not four cents!   *1880*
Let that four-cent man be a monk in some minster,
and he can pray all day long for our sins."
Roland replies: "Attack, do not spare them!"
And with that word the Franks began again.
There was a heavy loss of Christian men.   *1885*

145.

The Saracens, when they saw these few French,   *1940*
looked at each other, took courage, and presumed,
telling themselves: "The Emperor is wrong!"
The Algalife rides a great sorrel horse,
digs into it with his spurs of fine gold,
strikes Oliver, from behind, in the back,   *1945*
shattered the white hauberk upon his flesh,
drove his spear through the middle of his chest;
and speaks to him: "Now you feel you've been struck!
Your great Charles doomed you when he left you in this pass.
That man wronged us, he must not boast of it.   *1950*
I've avenged all our dead in you alone!

146.

Oliver feels: he has been struck to death;
grips Halteclere, that steel blade shining, strikes
on the gold-dressed pointed helm of the Algalife,
sends jewels and flowers crackling down to the earth,   *1955*
into the head, into the little teeth;
draws up his flashing sword, casts him down, dead,
and then he says: "Pagan, a curse on you!
If only I could say Charles has lost nothing—
but no woman, no lady you ever knew   *1960*
will hear you boast, in the land you came from,
that you could take one thing worth a cent from me,
or do me harm, or do any man harm";
then cries out to Roland to come to his aid. AOI.

149.

Here is Roland, lords, fainted on his horse,
and Oliver the Count, wounded to death: *1990*
he has lost so much blood, his eyes are darkened—
he cannot see, near or far, well enough
to recognize a friend or enemy:

struck when he came upon his companion,
strikes on his helm, adorned with gems in gold,   *1995*
cuts down straight through, from the point to the nasal,
but never harmed him, he never touched his head.
Under this blow, Count Roland looked at him;
and gently, softly now, he asks of him:
"Lord, Companion, do you mean to do this?   *2000*
It is Roland, who always loved you greatly.
You never declared that we were enemies."
Said Oliver: "Now I hear it is you—
I don't see you, may the Lord God see you.
Was it you that I struck? Forgive me then."   *2005*
Roland replies: "I am not harmed, not harmed,
I forgive you, Friend, here and before God."
And with that word, each bowed to the other.
And this is the love, lords, in which they parted.

150.

Oliver feels: death pressing hard on him;   *2010*
his two eyes turn, roll up into his head,
all hearing is lost now, all sight is gone;
gets down on foot, stretches out on the ground,
cries out now and again: *mea culpa!*
his two hands joined, raised aloft toward heaven,   *2015*
he prays to God: grant him His Paradise;
and blesses Charles, and the sweet land of France,
his companion, Roland, above all men.
The heart fails him, his helmet falls away,
the great body settles upon the earth.   *2020*
The Count is dead, he stands with us no longer.
Roland, brave man, weeps for him, mourns for him,
you will not hear a man of greater sorrow.

[Roland swoons from grief and loss of blood, but in spite of his weakened condition, he
rallies to aid Archbishop Turpin.]

156.

Roland the Count fights well and with great skill,
but he is hot, his body soaked with sweat;   *2100*
has a great wound in his head, and much pain,
his temple broken because he blew the horn.
But he must know whether King Charles will come;
draws out the olifant, sounds it, so feebly.
The Emperor drew to a halt, listened.   *2105*

"Seigneurs," he said, "it goes badly for us—
My nephew Roland falls from our ranks today.
I hear it in the horn's voice: he hasn't long.
Let every man who wants to be with Roland
ride fast! Sound trumpets! Every trumpet in this host!"   2110
Sixty thousand, on these words, sound, so high
the mountains sound, and the valleys resound.
The pagans hear: it is no joke to them;
cry to each other: "We're getting Charles on us!"

158.

Roland the Count, when he sees them coming,
how strong and fierce and alert he becomes!   2125
He will not yield to them, not while he lives.
He rides the horse they call Veillantif, spurs,
digs into it with his spurs of fine gold,
and rushes at them all where they are thickest,
the Archbishop—that Turpin!—at his side.   2130
Said one man to the other: "Go at it, friend.
The horns we heard were the horns of the French,
King Charles is coming back with all his strength."

165.

The Archbishop, when he saw Roland faint,
felt such pain then as he had never felt;
stretched out his hand and grasped the olifant.
At Rencesvals there is a running stream: 2225
he will go there and fetch some water for Roland;
and turns that way, with small steps, staggering;
he is too weak, he cannot go ahead,
he has no strength: all the blood he has lost.
In less time than a man takes to cross a little field   2230
that great heart fails, he falls forward, falls down;
and Turpin's death comes crushing down on him.

168.

Now Roland feels that death is very near.
His brain comes spilling out through his two ears: 2260
prays to God for his peers: let them be called;
and for himself, to the angel Gabriel;
took the oliphant: there must be no reproach!
took Durendal his sword in his other hand,
and farther than a crossbow's farthest shot   2265

he walks toward Spain, into a fallow land
and climbs a hill: there beneath two fine trees
stand four great blocks of stone, all are of marble;
and he fell back, to earth, on the green grass,
has fainted there, for death is very near.   *2270*

169.

High are the hills, and high, high are the trees;
there stand four blocks of stone, gleaming of marble.
Count Roland falls fainting on the green grass,
and is watched, all this time, by a Saracen:
who has feigned death and lies now with the others,   *2275*
has smeared blood on his face and on his body;
and quickly now gets to his feet and runs—
a handsome man, strong, brave, and so crazed with pride
that he does something mad and dies for it:
laid hands on Roland, and on the arms of Roland,   *2280*
and cried: "Conquered! Charles's nephew conquered!
I'll carry this sword home to Arabia!"
As he draws it, the Count begins to come round.

170.

Now Roland feels: *someone taking his sword!*
opened his eyes, and had one word for him: *2285*
"I don't know you, you aren't one of our";
grasps that olifant that he will never lose,
strikes on the helm beset with gems in gold,
shatters the steel, and the head, and the bones,
sent his two eyes flying out of his head,   *2290*
dumped him over stretched out at his feet dead;
and said: "You nobody! how could you dare
lay hands on me—rightly or wrongly: how?
Who'll hear of this and not call you a fool?
Ah! the bell-mouth of the olifant is smashed,   *2295*
the crystal and the gold fallen away."

171.

Now Roland the Count feels: his sight is gone;
gets on his feet, draws on his final strength,
the color on his face lost now for good.
Before him stands a rock; and on that dark rock   *2300*
in rage and bitterness he strikes ten blows;
the steel blade grates, it will not break, it stands unmarked.

"Ah!" said the Count, "Blessed Mary, your help!
Ah Durendal, good sword, your unlucky day,
for I am lost and cannot keep you in my care.   2305
The battles I have won, fighting with you,
the mighty lands that holding you I conquered,
that Charles rules now, our King, whose beard is white!
Now you fall to another: it must not be
    a man who'd run before another man!
For a long while a good vassal held you: 2310
there'll never be the like in France's holy land."

173.

Roland the Count strikes down on a dark rock,
and the rock breaks, breaks more than I can tell,
and the blade grates, but Durendal will not break,   2340
the sword leaped up, rebounded toward the sky.
The Count, when he sees that sword will not be broken,
softly, in his own presence, speaks the lament:
"Ah Durendal, beautiful, and most sacred,
the holy relics in this golden pommel!   2345
Saint Peter's tooth and blood of Saint Basile,
a lock of hair of my lord Saint Denis,
and a fragment of blessed Mary's robe:
your power must not fall to the pagans,
you must be served by Christian warriors.   2350
May no coward ever come to hold you!
It was with you I conquered those great lands
that Charles has in his keeping, whose beard is white,
the Emperor's lands, that make him rich and strong."

174.

Now Roland feels: death coming over him,   2355
death descending from his temples to his heart.
He came running underneath a pine tree
and there stretched out, face down, on the green grass,
lays beneath him his sword and the olifant.
He turned his head toward the Saracen hosts,   2360
and this is why: with all his heart he wants
King Charles the Great and all his men to say,
he died, that noble Count, a conqueror;
makes confession, beats his breast often, so feebly,
offers his glove, for all his sins, to God. AOI.   2365

218
▪

175.

Now Roland feels that his time has run out;
he lies on a steep hill, his face toward Spain;
and with one of his hands he beat his breast:
"Almighty God, *mea culpa* in thy sight,
forgive my sins, both the great and the small,　　　　　　　2370
sins I committed from the hour I was born
until this day, in which I lie struck down."
And then he held his right glove out to God.
Angels descend from heaven and stand by him. AOI.

176.

Count Roland lay stretched out beneath a pine;　　　　　　2375
he turned his face toward the land of Spain,
began to remember many things now:
how many lands, brave man, he had conquered;
and he remembered: sweet France, the men of his line,
remembered Charles, his lord, who fostered him:　　　　　2380
cannot keep, remembering, from weeping, sighing;
but would not be unmindful of himself:
he confesses his sins, prays God for mercy:
"Loyal Father, you who never failed us,
who resurrected Saint Lazarus from the dead,　　　　　　2385
and saved your servant Daniel from the lions:
now save the soul of me from every peril
for the sins I committed while I still lived."
Then he held out his right glove to his Lord:
Saint Gabriel took the glove from his hand.　　　　　　　2390
He held his head bowed down upon his arm,
he is gone, his two hands joined, to his end.
Then God sent him his angel Cherubin
and Saint Michael, angel of the sea's Peril;
and with these two there came Saint Gabriel:　　　　　　2395
they bear Count Roland's soul to Paradise.

[Charles arrives at Roncevaux only to discover the bodies of Roland, his comrades, and hundreds of Saracen warriors. With divine assistance, French forces overcome their Saracen foes, but the final victory comes only when Charlemagne has defeated the Saracen champion, Baligant, Emir of Babylon, in hand-to-hand combat.]

Marie de France, Chaitivel

The "lais" of Marie de France are short poems whose characters and incidents reflect the literary interests of the French aristocracy during the twelfth and thirteenth centuries. Because of their brevity, each of these lais focuses on one heightened incident—usually a romantic crisis—in the lives of the knights and ladies who populate her fictional world. Through her analysis of conflicting emotions and loyalties, Marie attempts to represent the ideal sexual morality of her time and class. Medieval historians have termed this morality *fine amor* or "courtly love." Underlying the variations of this concept we find one basic notion that Marie and her aristocratic audience eagerly accepted: Passionate love is by its very nature adulterous and therefore potentially tragic.

In a society where nearly all marriages among the nobility were arranged, it is not difficult to see why secular writers of romantic fiction (and their readers) thought it next to impossible that any husband and wife could experience the pangs and the pleasures of true love; after all, it was reasoned, how could any married couple long passionately (and hopelessly) for one another, or why would they endure the exquisite suffering of jealous, parted lovers when no one could oppose their union? Love thrives, courtly writers believed, on difficulty and pain, and in her tales, Marie wrote of lovers who experienced both.

Just *who* Marie de France really was remains something of a mystery today. Several candidates have been proposed—all of them women of high birth and considerable education—but no consensus has emerged among medievalists on her identity. One thing is clear, however. She was the first woman in the Middle Ages to write publicly in the vernacular (in this case, Old French) and to become one of the best-read authors of her time. Along with her contemporary, Chretien de Troyes, she was instrumental in transforming the self-image of the medieval knight (from mere warrior to warrior–courtier) by introducing into the code of chivalry ideas of courtesy, devotion, and self-sacrifice on behalf of one's lady love. Thus, it is the women in Marie's stories, rather than the men who serve them, who seem to be at the spiritual and emotional center of medieval life, redefining the purposes of adventure and warfare for their lovers.

CHAITIVEL

■

In the city of Nantes in Brittany there dwelt a lady distinguished by her beauty, education and good breeding. There existed no knight in the region with any merit at all who, having once seen her, would not have fallen in love with her and wooed her. It was not possible for her to love them all, but neither did she wish to repulse them. It would be less dangerous for a man to court every lady in an entire land than for a lady to remove a single besotted lover from her skirts, for he will immediately attempt to strike back. She satisfied the desires of each lover at the behest of good will. Yet, even if a lady has no wish to listen to their pleas, she should not speak insultingly to her suitors: rather should she honour and cherish them, serve them appropriately and be grateful to them. The lady whose story I wish to relate was courted constantly because of her beauty and worth and was the object of their attentions night and day.

There lived in Brittany four men whose names I do not know. They were not very old, but were exceedingly handsome, brave and valiant knights, generous, courtly and liberal. They were held in very high esteem and were amongst the region's noblemen. The four of them loved the lady and strove to perform brave deeds. Each man did his utmost to win her and have her love, taking great pains to woo her for himself. Each one of them would have thought himself capable of outdoing the others. The lady, who possessed great intelligence, gave careful thought to which of them was more worthy of her love. They all had such great merit that she was unable to choose the best, yet she did not wish to lose all three in order to retain just one. To each she displayed a friendly mien; she gave them love tokens and sent her messengers to them. Each was unaware of the other's success, but she could not distinguish between them in any way. Each one thought he could gain the upper hand by the quality of his service and his entreaties. When knights assembled, each one, if he could, would lead all the rest in performing brave deeds in order to please the lady. They all regarded her as their beloved, wore her love token, a ring, sleeve or pennant, and used her name as a rallying cry. She loved and retained all four, until one year, after Easter, a tournament was proclaimed before the city of Nantes. To meet the four lovers, men came from other regions: French, Norman and Flemish knights, those from Brabant, Boulogne and Anjou and from the immediate neighbourhood. They were all glad to come and had been lodged there a good while. On the eve of the tournament fierce fighting broke out. The four lovers left the city, fully armed: their knights followed them, but the main burden of the combat rested on these four. Their opponents, recognizing them by their ensigns and shields, sent knights to oppose them, two from Flanders and two from Hainault, ready and equipped for combat. To a man they were keen to join battle. The lovers saw them approach, but had no thought of flight. Lance lowered and at full speed, each one picked out his opponent. The blows were so vehement that the four adversaries were unhorsed. The lovers did not trouble to seize the horses, but left them riderless. They took up position against the fallen combatants whose knights came to their aid; a great melée ensued as their men tried to rescue them and swords struck many a blow. From a tower the lady could see clearly her knights and their men. She witnessed her lovers giving a good account of themselves and did not know which merited her esteem the most.

The tournament began. The ranks increased and swelled and many battles were joined that day before the city gates. Her four lovers performed so well that by nightfall, when it was time to leave the field, they had carried off all the honours. Very foolishly they strayed far from their followers and for this they paid the price. For three of them were killed and the fourth was injured and wounded in the thigh in such a way that the lance passed right through his body. They were hit by a lateral attack and all four were unhorsed. Those who had mortally wounded them threw their shields to the ground, grief-stricken on their account, as they had not intended to kill them. A great outcry and clamour arose; such sorrow had never before been heard. The inhabitants of the city came out on to the field with no fear of the other fighters. In their grief over the knights a full two thousand men unfastened their visors and tore at their hair and beards, united in their sorrow. Each knight was placed on his shield and carried into the city to the lady who had loved them. As soon as she discovered what had happened, she fell to the ground in a swoon. When she revived, she lamented each one by name. 'Alas,' she said, 'whatever shall I do? I shall never again be happy! I loved these four knights and desired each one for his own sake. There was a great deal of good in them all and they loved me above everything. Because they were so handsome, brave, worthy and generous, I made them compete for my love, not wishing to lose them all to have just one. I do not know which of them to mourn the most, but I can no longer disguise or hide my feelings. One of them I now see wounded and three are dead. There remains no comfort for me in this world, so I shall bury the dead, and if the injured knight can be healed, I shall gladly take care of him and provide him with a good doctor.' She had him carried into her chamber and then arranged for the other to be laid out for burial, lovingly, nobly and lavishly arrayed. She gave a large offering and substantial gift to a rich abbey where they were buried. May God have mercy on them! She had summoned learned doctors and the knight lying wounded in her chamber was placed in their charge until he was cured. She visited him often and comforted him very well. But she mourned the others and was grief-stricken at what had befallen them.

One summer's day, after dinner, the lady was conversing with the knight. She was reminded of her great sorrow and deep in thought bowed her face and head. He looked at her, realizing she was lost in thought, and spoke kindly to her: 'My lady, you are in distress. What are you thinking about? Tell me. Put aside your grief and be comforted.' 'My friend,' she replied, 'I was thinking, and recalling your companions. Never will a lady of my lineage, however beautiful, worthy or wise, love four such men at once and in a single day lose them all, except for you alone who were wounded. You came dangerously close to death, so because of my great love for you all, I want my grief to be remembered. I shall compose a lay about the four of you and entitle it *The Four Sorrows*.' When he heard these words, the knight replied quickly: 'My lady, compose the new lay, but call it *The Unhappy One*. I shall explain why it should have this title. The others have long since ended their days and used up their span of life. What great anguish they suffered on account of the love they bore for you! But I who have escaped alive, bewildered and forlorn, constantly see the woman I love more than anything on earth, coming and going; she speaks to me morning and evening, yet I cannot experience the joy of a kiss or an embrace or of any pleasure other than conversation. You cause me to suffer a hundred such ills and death would be preferable for me. Therefore the lay will be named after me and called *The Unhappy One*. Anyone who calls it *The Four Sorrows* will be changing its true name.' 'Upon my word,' she replied, 'I am agreeable to this: let us now call it *The Unhappy One*.'

Thus was the lay begun, and later completed and performed. Some of those who put it into circulation call it *The Four Sorrows*. Each name is appropriate and supported by the subject matter. It is commonly known as *The Unhappy One*. Here it ends, for there is no more. I have heard no more, know no more and shall relate no more to you.

Dante Alighieri, The Divine Comedy

Dante Alighieri's *Divine Comedy* is the supreme literary expression of medieval European civilization. The poem, which narrates Dante's visionary journey through Hell, Purgatory, and Heaven, describes the entire universe, encompassing nearly all that was then known of science, philosophy, theology, and human psychology. Most of the poem was written after 1302 when Dante (1265–1321) was exiled from his native city, Florence, Italy, on a false charge of embezzlement. Because it begins in suffering but ends in joy, Dante called his work a comedy: Later generations added the adjective "divine."

Transcending the older categories of epic and drama, the poem is an allegorical quest in which characters and events are symbols of unseen realities. In Dante's elaborate allegory, Hell, Purgatory, and Heaven are not only literal places the narrator visits during Easter week of the year 1300, but also states of mind, conditions of the soul, and images of sin, repentance, and salvation. Virgil, who guides Dante through the Inferno and to the gates of Paradise atop Mount Purgatory, is both the ghost of a dead Latin poet and an embodiment of human reason. Beatrice, whose intervention in heaven makes possible Dante's odyssey through the afterlife, is both a young woman Dante loved and a symbol of divine compassion. When Dante, purified by suffering, reaches a state of sinlessness represented by his entrance into the Garden of Eden, Beatrice replaces Virgil as Dante's guide and escorts him to Heaven. Reason can bring men to a knowledge of error (Hell) and a desire for spiritual cleansing (Purgatory), but only divine grace can reveal the splendors of Heaven.

Dante's worldview is based on Ptolemaic astronomy, endorsed by the Roman Catholic Church, which held that the Earth is the center of the universe. The sun, moon, planets, and stars rotate around the Earth, their respective orbits tracing a series of nine concentric circles around our globe. An inversion of the solar system, Hell is a funnel-shaped hole extending into the center of the Earth and containing nine concentric terraces or levels. Because each successive level of the Inferno is a step farther removed from God and closer to the Devil, who inhabits Earth's hollow core, Dante finds that the sins are worse and their punishment more severe as he descends into the pit. Organized to illustrate a scheme of retributive justice, the Inferno is divided into three general areas of mortal sin: Incontinence or self-indulgence, Violence, and Fraud. The fraudulent include those who betrayed friends and masters, such as Brutus, Cassius, and Judas, each of whom is savagely chewed in one of Satan's three mouths.

Virgil and Dante emerge from Hell in the southern hemisphere, opposite the side of the Earth on which they entered it. Entirely surrounded by water, the Mount of Purgatory rises in nine levels toward Heaven. While souls in Hell suffer eternally without hope, those in Purgatory rejoice in their pain, which cleanses them of sin and prepares them for Heaven. Reaching Purgatory's summit, Virgil disappears, replaced by Beatrice who leads Dante upward through the nine orbits of planets and stars encircling the Earth.

Dante's emphasis on nine and other multiples of three reflects his devotion to the triune nature of God. According to the dogma of the Holy Trinity, God is One but manifests himself in three aspects: Father, Son, and Holy Spirit. Dante honors the Trinity by dividing his poem into three parts and further subdividing the three realms of Hell, Purgatory, and

Heaven into nine sections, a square of three. He describes each realm in 33 cantos, a double symbol of the Trinity, and adds an introductory canto to produce a total of 100, which is both the symbol of perfection and a multiple of God's unity. Dante invented a new verse form for his poem, the *terza rima*, which contains three lines in each stanza, in which the first and third lines rhyme. In Dante's highly structured cosmos, nothing is without significance.

THE DIVINE COMEDY

INFERNO

■

CANTO I

The Dark Wood of Error

Midway in his allotted threescore years and ten, Dante comes to himself with a start and realizes that he has strayed from the True Way into the Dark Wood of Error (Worldliness). As soon as he has realized his loss, Dante lifts his eyes and sees the first light of the sunrise (the Sun is the Symbol of Divine illumination) lighting the shoulders of a little hill (The Mount of Joy). It is the Easter Season, the time of resurrection, and the sun is in its equinoctial rebirth. This juxtaposition of joyous symbols fills Dante with hope and he sets out at once to climb directly up the Mount of Joy, but almost immediately his way is blocked by the Three Beasts of Worldliness: THE LEOPARD OF MALICE AND FRAUD, THE LION OF VIOLENCE AND AMBITION, and THE SHE-WOLF OF INCONTINENCE. These beasts, and especially the She-Wolf, drive him back despairing into the darkness of error. But just as all seems lost, a figure appears to him. It is the shade of VIRGIL, Dante's symbol of HUMAN REASON.

Virgil explains that he has been sent to lead Dante from error. There can, however, be no direct ascent past the beasts: the man who would escape them must go a longer and harder way. First he must descend through Hell (The Recognition of Sin), then he must ascend through Purgatory (The Renunciation of Sin), and only then may he reach the pinnacle of joy and come to the Light of God. Virgil offers to guide Dante, but only as far as Human Reason can go. Another guide (BEATRICE, symbol of DIVINE LOVE) must take over for the final ascent, for Human Reason is self-limited. Dante submits himself joyously to Virgil's guidance and they move off.

Midway IN OUR LIFE'S JOURNEY, I WENT ASTRAY
   from the straight road and woke to find myself
   alone in a dark wood. How shall I say

what wood that was! I never saw so drear,
   so rank, so arduous a wilderness!
   Its very memory gives a shape to fear.

Death could scarce be more bitter than that place!
  But since it came to good, I will recount
  all that I found revealed there by God's grace.

How I came to it I cannot rightly say,
  so drugged and loose with sleep had I become
  when I first wandered there from the True Way.

But at the far end of that valley of evil
  whose maze had sapped my very heart with fear!
  I found myself before a little hill   *(15)*

and lifted up my eyes. Its shoulders glowed
  already with the sweet rays of that planet
  whose virtue leads men straight on every road,

and the shining strengthened me against the fright
  whose agony had wracked the lake of my heart
  through all the terrors of that piteous night.

Just as a swimmer, who with his last breath
  flounders ashore from perilous seas, might turn
  to memorize the wide water of his death—

so did I turn, my soul still fugitive
  from death's surviving image, to stare down
  that pass that none had ever left alive.

And there I lay to rest from my heart's race
  till calm and breath returned to me. Then rose
  and pushed up that dead slope at such a pace   *(30)*

each footfall rose above the last. And lo!
  almost at the beginning of the rise
  I faced a spotted Leopard, all tremor and flow

and gaudy pelt. And it would not pass, but stood
  so blocking my every turn that time and again
  I was on the verge of turning back to the wood.

This fell at the first widening of the dawn
  as the sun was climbing Aries with those stars
  that rode with him to light the new creation.

Thus the holy hour and the sweet season
    of commemoration did much to arm my fear
    of that bright murderous beast with their good omen.

Yet not so much but what I shook with dread
    at sight of a great Lion that broke upon me
    raging with hunger, its enormous head   *(45)*

held high as if to strike a mortal terror
    into the very air. And down his track,
    a She-Wolf drove upon me, a starved horror

ravening and wasted beyond all belief.
    She seemed a rack for avarice, gaunt and craving.
    Oh many the souls she has brought to endless grief!

She brought such heaviness upon my spirit
    at sight of her savagery and desperation
    I died from every hope of that high summit.

And like a miser—eager in acquisition
    but desperate in self-reproach when Fortune's wheel
    turns to the hour of his loss—all tears and attrition

I wavered back; and still the beast pursued,
    forcing herself against me bit by bit
    till I slid back into the sunless wood.   *(60)*

And as I fell to my soul's ruin, a presence
    gathered before me on the discolored air,
    the figure of one who seemed hoarse from long silence.

At sight of him in that friendless waste I cried:
    "Have pity on me, whatever thing you are,
    whether shade or living man." And it replied:

"Not man, though man I once was, and my blood
    was Lombard, both my parents Mantuan.
    I was born, though late, *sub Julio,* and bred

in Rome under Augustus in the noon
    of the false and lying gods. I was a poet
    and sang of old Anchises' noble son

who came to Rome after the burning of Troy.
    But you—why do *you* return to these distresses
    instead of climbing that shining Mount of Joy   *(75)*

which is the seat and first cause of man's bliss?"
    "And are you then that Virgil and that fountain
    of purest speech?" My voice grew tremulous:

"Glory and light of poets! now may that zeal
    and love's apprenticeship that I poured out
    on your heroic verses serve me well!

For you are my true master and first author,
    the sole maker from whom I drew the breath
    of that sweet style whose measures have brought me honor.

See there, immortal sage, the beast I flee.
    For my soul's salvation, I beg you, guard me from her,
    for she has struck a mortal tremor through me."

And he replied, seeing my soul in tears:
    "He must go by another way who would escape
    this wilderness, for that mad beast that fleers   *(90)*

before you there, suffers no man to pass.
    She tracks down all, kills all, and knows no glut,
    but, feeding, she grows hungrier than she was.

She mates with any beast, and will mate with more
    before the Greyhound comes to hunt her down.
    He will not feed on lands nor loot, but honor

and love and wisdom will make straight his way.
    He will rise between Feltro and Feltro, and in him
    shall be the resurrection and new day

of that sad Italy for which Nisus died,
    and Turnus, and Euryalus, and the maid Camilla.
    He shall hunt her through every nation of sick pride

till she is driven back forever to Hell
    whence Envy first released her on the world.
    Therefore, for you own good, I think it well   *(105)*

you follow me and I will be your guide
    and lead you forth through an eternal place.
    There you shall see the ancient spirits tried

in endless pain, and hear their lamentation
    as each bemoans the second death of souls.
    Next you shall see upon a burning mountain

souls in fire and yet content in fire,
    knowing that whensoever it may be
    they yet will mount into the blessed choir.

To which, if it is still your wish to climb,
    a worthier spirit shall be sent to guide you.
    With her shall I leave you, for the King of Time,

who reigns on high, forbids me to come there
    since, living, I rebelled against his law.
    He rules the waters and the land and air
                                                    (120)

and there holds court, his city and his throne.
    Oh blessed are they he chooses!" And I to him:
    "Poet, by that God to you unknown,

lead me this way. Beyond this present ill
    and worse to dread, lead me to Peter's gate
    and be my guide through the sad halls of Hell."

And he then: "Follow." And he moved ahead
in silence, and I followed where he led.

NOTES

1. *midway in our life's journey:* The Biblical life span is three-score years and ten. The action opens in Dante's thirty-fifth year, i.e., 1300 A.D.

17. *that planet:* The sun. Ptolemaic astronomers considered it a planet. It is also symbolic of God as He who lights man's way.

31. *each footfall rose above the last:* The literal rendering would be: "So that the fixed foot was ever the lower." "Fixed" has often been translated "right" and an ingenious reasoning can support that reading, but a simpler explanation offers itself and seems more competent: Dante is saying that he climbed with such zeal and haste that every footfall carried him above the last despite the steepness of the climb. At a slow pace, on the other hand, the rear foot might be brought up only as far as the forward foot. This device of selecting a minute but exactly-centered detail to convey the whole of a larger action is one of the central characteristics of Dante's style.

THE THREE BEASTS: These three beasts undoubtedly are taken from Jeremiah v, 6. Many additional and incidental interpretations have been advanced for them, but the central interpretation must remain as noted. They foreshadow the three divisions of Hell (incontinence, violence, and fraud) which Virgil explains at length in Canto Xl, 16–111. I am not at all sure but what the She-Wolf is better interpreted as Fraud and the Leopard as Incontinence. Good arguments can be offered either way.

38–9. *Aries . . . that rode with him to light the new creation:* The medieval tradition had it that the sun was in Aries at the time of the Creation. The significance of the astronomical and religious conjunction is an important part of Dante's intended allegory. It is just before dawn of Good Friday 1300 A.D. when he awakens in the Dark Wood. Thus his new life begins under Aries, the sign of creation, at dawn (rebirth) and in the Easter season (resurrection). Moreover the moon is full and the sun is in the equinox, conditions that did not fall together on any Friday of 1300. Dante is obviously constructing poetically the perfect Easter as a symbol of his new awakening.

69. *sub Julio:* In the reign of Julius Caesar.

95. *The Greyhound . . . Feltro and Feltro:* Almost certainly refers to Can Grande della Scala (1290–1329), great Italian leader born in Verona, which lies between the towns of Feltre and Montefeltro.

100–101. *Nisus, Turnus, Euryalus, Camilla:* All were killed in the war between the Trojans and the Latians when, according to legend, Aeneas led the survivors of Troy into Italy. Nisus and Euryalus (*Aeneid* IX) were Trojan comrades-in-arms who died together. Camilla (*Aeneid* XI) was the daughter of the Latian king and one of the warrior women. She was killed in a horse charge against the Trojans after displaying great gallantry. Turnus (*Aeneid* XII) was killed by Aeneas in a duel.

110. *the second death:* Damnation. "This is the second death, even the lake of fire." (*Revelation* xx, 14)

118. *forbids me to come there since, living, etc.:* Salvation is only through Christ in Dante's theology. Virgil lived and died before the establishment of Christ's teachings in Rome, and cannot therefore enter Heaven.

125. *Peter's gate:* The gate of Purgatory. (See *Purgatorio* IX, 76 ff.) The gate is guarded by an angel with a gleaming sword. The angel is Peter's vicar (Peter, the first Pope, symbolized all Popes; i.e., Christ's vicar on earth) and is entrusted with the two great keys.

Some commentators argue that this is the gate of Paradise, but Dante mentions no gate beyond this one in his ascent to Heaven. It should be remembered, too, that those who pass the gate of Purgatory have effectively entered Heaven.

The three great gates that figure in the entire journey are: the gate of Hell (Canto III, 1–11), the gate of Dis (Canto VIII, 79–113, and Canto IX, 86–87); and the gate of Purgatory, as above.

CANTO II

The Descent

It is evening of the first day (Friday). Dante is following Virgil and finds himself tired and despairing. How can he be worthy of such a vision as Virgil has described? He hesitates and seems about to abandon his first purpose.

To comfort him Virgil explains how Beatrice descended to him in Limbo and told him of her concern for Dante. It is she, the symbol of Divine Love, who sends Virgil to lead Dante from error. She has come into Hell itself on this errand, for Dante cannot come to Divine Love unaided; Reason must lead him. Moreover Beatrice has been sent with the prayers of the Virgin Mary (COMPASSION), and of Saint Lucia (DIVINE LIGHT). Rachel (THE CONTEMPLATIVE LIFE) also figures in the heavenly scene which Virgil recounts.

Virgil explains all this and reproaches Dante: how can he hesitate longer when such heavenly powers are concerned for him, and Virgil himself has promised to lead him safely?

Dante understands at once that such forces cannot fail him, and his spirits rise in joyous anticipation.

The light was departing. The brown air drew down
   all the earth's creatures, calling them to rest
   from their day-roving, as I, one man alone,

prepared myself to face the double war
   of the journey and the pity, which memory
   shall here set down, nor hesitate, nor err.

O Muses! O High Genius! Be my aid!
   O Memory, recorder of the vision,
   here shall your true nobility be displayed!

Thus I began: "Poet, you who must guide me,
   before you trust me to that arduous passage,
   look to me and look through me—can I be worthy?

You sang how the father of Sylvius, while still
   in corruptible flesh won to that other world,
   crossing with mortal sense the immortal sill.   *(15)*

But if the Adversary of all Evil
   weighing his consequence and who and what
   should issue from him, treated him so well—

that cannot seem unfitting to thinking men,
   since he was chosen father of Mother Rome
   and of her Empire by God's will and token.

Both, to speak strictly, were founded and foreknown
   as the established Seat of Holiness
   for the successors of Great Peter's throne.

In that quest, which your verses celebrate,
    he learned those mysteries from which arose
    his victory and Rome's apostolate.

There later came the chosen vessel, Paul,
    bearing the confirmation of that Faith
    which is the one true door to life eternal.   *(30)*

But I—how should I dare? By whose permission?
    I am not Aeneas. *I* am not Paul.
    Who could believe me worthy of the vision?

How, then, may I presume to this high quest
    and not fear my own brashness? You are wise
    and will grasp what my poor words can but suggest."

As one who unwills what he wills, will stay
    strong purposes with feeble second thoughts
    until he spells all his first zeal away—

so I hung back and balked on that dim coast
    till thinking had worn out my enterprise,
    so stout at starting and so early lost.

"I understand from your words and the look in your eyes,"
    that shadow of magnificence answered me,
    "your soul is sunken in that cowardice   *(45)*

that bears down many men, turning their course
    and resolution by imagined perils,
    as his own shadow turns the frightened horse.

To free you of this dread I will tell you all
    of why I came to you and what I heard
    when first I pitied you. I was a soul

among the souls of Limbo, when a Lady
    so blessed and so beautiful, I prayed her
    to order and command my will, called to me.

Her eyes were kindled from the lamps of Heaven.
    Her voice reached through me, tender, sweet, and low.
    An angel's voice, a music of its own:

'O gracious Mantuan whose melodies
    live in earth's memory and shall live on
    till the last motion ceases in the skies,   *(60)*

my dearest friend, and fortune's foe, has strayed
    onto a friendless shore and stands beset
    by such distresses that he turns afraid

from the True Way, and news of him in Heaven
    rumors my dread he is already lost.
    I come, afraid that I am too-late risen.

Fly to him and with your high counsel, pity,
    and with whatever need be for his good
    and soul's salvation, help him, and solace me.

It is I, Beatrice, who send you to him.
    I come from the blessed height for which I yearn.
    Love called me here. When amid Seraphim

I stand again before my Lord, your praises
    shall sound in Heaven.' She paused, and I began:
    'O Lady of that only grace that raises   *(75)*

feeble mankind within its mortal cycle
    above all other works God's will has placed
    within the heaven of the smallest circle;

so welcome is your command that to my sense,
    were it already fulfilled, it would yet seem tardy.
    I understand, and am all obedience.

But tell me how you dare to venture thus
    so far from the wide heaven of your joy
    to which your thoughts yearn back from this abyss.'

'Since what you ask,' she answered me, 'probes near
    the root of all, I will say briefly only
    how I have come through Hell's pit without fear.

Know then, O waiting and compassionate soul,
    that is to fear which has the power to harm
    and nothing else is fearful even in Hell.   *(90)*

I am so made by God's all-seeing mercy
    your anguish does not touch me, and the flame
    of this great burning has no power upon me.

There is a Lady in Heaven so concerned
    for him I send you to, that for her sake
    the strict decree is broken. She has turned

and called Lucia to her wish and mercy
    saying: 'Thy faithful one is sorely pressed;
    in his distresses I commend him to thee.'

Lucia, that soul of light and foe of all
    cruelty, rose and came to me at once
    where I was sitting with the ancient Rachel,

saying to me: 'Beatrice, true praise of God,
    why dost thou not help him who loved thee so
    that for thy sake he left the vulgar crowd?   *(105)*

Dost thou not hear his cries? Canst thou not see
    the death he wrestles with beside that river
    no ocean can surpass for rage and fury?

No soul of earth was ever as rapt to seek
    its good or flee its injury as I was—
    when I had heard my sweet Lucia speak—

to descend from Heaven and my blessed seat
    to you, laying my trust in that high speech
    that honors you and all who honor it.'

She spoke and turned away to hide a tear
    that, shining, urged me faster. So I came
    and freed you from the beast that drove you there,

blocking the near way to the Heavenly Height.
    And now what ails you? Why do you lag? Why
    this heartsick hesitation and pale fright   *(120)*

when three such blessed Ladies lean from Heaven
    in their concern for you and my own pledge
    of the great good that waits you has been given?"

As flowerlets drooped and puckered in the night
    turn up to the returning sun and spread
    their petals wide on his new warmth and light—

just so my wilted spirits rose again
    and such a heat of zeal surged through my veins
    that I was born anew. Thus I began:

"Blesséd be that Lady of infinite pity,
    and blesséd be thy taxed and courteous spirit
    that came so promptly on the word she gave thee.

Thy words have moved my heart to its first purpose.
    My Guide! My Lord! My Master! Now lead on:
    one will shall serve the two of us in this."   *(135)*

He turned when I had spoken, and at his back
I entered on that hard and perilous track.

NOTES

13–30. AENEAS AND THE FOUNDING OF ROME.

    Here is a fair example of the way in which Dante absorbed pagan themes into his Catholicism.

    According to Virgil, Aeneas is the son of mortal Anchises and of Venus. Venus, in her son's interest, secures a prophecy and a promise from Jove to the effect that Aeneas is to found a royal line that shall rule the world. After the burning of Troy, Aeneas is directed by various signs to sail for the Latian lands (Italy) where his destiny awaits him. After many misadventures, he is compelled (like Dante) to descend to the underworld of the dead. There he finds his father's shade, and there he is shown the shades of the great kings that are to stem from him. (*Aeneid* VI, 921 ff.) Among them are Romulus, Julius Caesar, and Augustus Caesar. The full glory of the Roman Empire is also foreshadowed to him.

    Dante, however, continues the Virgilian theme and includes in the predestination not only the Roman Empire but the Holy Roman Empire and its Church. Thus what Virgil presented as an arrangement of Jove, a concession to the son of Venus, becomes part of the divine scheme of the Catholic God, and Aeneas is cast as a direct forerunner of Peter and Paul.

13. *father of Sylvius:* Aeneas.

51–52. *I was a soul among the souls in Limbo:* See Canto IV, lines 31–45, where Virgil explains his state in Hell.

78. *the heaven of the smallest circle:* The moon. "Heaven" here is used in its astronomical sense. All within that circle is the earth. According to the Ptolemaic system the earth was the center of creation and was surrounded by nine heavenly spheres (nine heavens) concentrically placed around it. The moon was the first of these, and therefore the smallest. A cross section of this universe could be represented by drawing nine concentric circles (at

varying distances about the earth as a center). Going outward from the center these circles would indicate, in order, the spheres of

> The Moon
> Mercury
> Venus
> The Sun
> Mars
> Jupiter
> Saturn
> The Fixed Stars
> The Primum Mobile

Beyond the Primum Mobile lies the Empyrean.

97. *Lucia:* (Loo-TCHEE-yah) Allegorically she represents Divine Light. Her name in Italian inevitably suggests "luce" (light), and she is the patron saint of eyesight. By a process quite common in medieval religion, the special powers attributed to Lucia seem to have been suggested by her name rather than her history. (In France, by a similar process, St. Clair is the patroness of sight.)

102. *Rachel:* Represents the Contemplative Life.

A note on "thee" and "thou": except for the quotations from the souls in Heaven and for Dante's fervent declamation to Virgil, I have insisted on "you" as the preferable pronoun form. I have used "thee" and "thou" in these cases with the idea that they might help to indicate the extraordinary elevation of the speakers and of the persons addressed.

CANTO III

The Vestibule of Hell

The Opportunists

The Poets pass the Gate of Hell and are immediately assailed by cries of anguish. Dante sees the first of the souls in torment. They are THE OPPORTUNISTS, those souls who in life were neither for good nor evil but only for themselves. Mixed with them are those outcasts who took no sides in the Rebellion of the Angels. They are neither in Hell nor out of it. Eternally unclassified, they race round and round pursuing a wavering banner that runs forever before them through the dirty air; and as they run they are pursued by swarms of wasps and hornets, who sting them and produce a constant flow of blood and putrid matter which trickles down the bodies of the sinners and is feasted upon by loathsome worms and maggots who coat the ground.

The law of Dante's Hell is the law of symbolic retribution. As they sinned so are they punished. They took no sides, therefore they are given no place. As they pursued the ever-shifting illusion of their own advantage, changing their courses with every changing wind, so they pursue eternally an elusive, ever-shifting banner. As their sin was a darkness, so they move in darkness. As their own guilty conscience pursued them, so they are pursued by swarms of wasps and hornets. And as their actions were a moral filth, so they run eternally through the filth of worms and maggots which they themselves feed.

Dante recognizes several, among them POPE CELESTINE V, but without delaying to speak to any of these souls, the Poets move on ACHERON, the first of the rivers of Hell. Here the newly-arrived souls of the damned gather and wait for monstrous CHARON to ferry them over to punishment. Charon recognizes Dante as a living man and angrily refuses him passage. Virgil forces Charon to serve them, but Dante swoons with terror, and does not reawaken until he is on the other side.

I AM THE WAY INTO THE CITY OF WOE.
I AM THE WAY TO A FORSAKEN PEOPLE.
I AM THE WAY INTO ETERNAL SORROW.

SACRED JUSTICE MOVED MY ARCHITECT.
I WAS RAISED HERE BY DIVINE OMNIPOTENCE,
PRIMORDIAL LOVE AND ULTIMATE INTELLECT.

ONLY THOSE ELEMENTS TIME CANNOT WEAR
WERE MADE BEFORE ME, AND BEYOND TIME I STAND.
ABANDON ALL HOPE YE WHO ENTER HERE.

These mysteries I read cut into stone
    above a gate. And turning I said: "Master,
    what is the meaning of this harsh inscription?"

And he then as initiate to novice:
    "Here must you put by all division of spirit
    and gather your soul against all cowardice.   *(15)*

This is the place I told you to expect.
    Here you shall pass among the fallen people,
    souls who have lost the good of intellect."

So saying, he put forth his hand to me,
    and with a gentle and encouraging smile
    he led me through the gate of mystery.

Here sighs and cries and wails coiled and recoiled
    on the starless air, spilling my soul to tears.
    A confusion of tongues and monstrous accents toiled

in pain and anger. Voices hoarse and shrill
    and sounds of blows, all intermingled, raised
    tumult and pandemonium that still

whirls on the air forever dirty with it
    as if a whirlwind sucked at sand. And I,
    holding my head in horror, cried: "Sweet Spirit,   *(30)*

what souls are these who run through this black haze?"
    And he to me: "These are the nearly soulless
    whose lives concluded neither blame nor praise.

They are mixed here with that despicable corps
    of angels who were neither for God nor Satan,
    but only for themselves. The High Creator

scourged them from Heaven for its perfect beauty,
    and Hell will not receive them since the wicked
    might feel some glory over them." And I:

"Master, what gnaws at them so hideously
    their lamentation stuns the very air?"
    "They have no hope of death," he answered me,

"and in their blind and unattaining state
    their miserable lives have sunk so low
    that they must envy every other fate.   *(45)*

No word of them survives their living season.
    Mercy and Justice deny them even a name.
    Let us not speak of them: look, and pass on."

I saw a banner there upon the mist.
    Circling and circling, it seemed to scorn all pause.
    So it ran on, and still behind it pressed

a never-ending rout of souls in pain.
    I had not thought death had undone so many
    as passed before me in that mournful train.

And some I knew among them; last of all
    I recognized the shadow of that soul
    who, in his cowardice, made the Great Denial.

At once I understood for certain: these
    were of that retrograde and faithless crew
    hateful to God and to His enemies.   *(60)*

These wretches never born and never dead
    ran naked in a swarm of wasps and hornets
    that goaded them the more the more they fled,

and made their faces stream with bloody gouts
    of pus and tears that dribbled to their feet
    to be swallowed there by loathsome worms and maggots.

Then looking onward I made out a throng
    assembled on the beach of a wide river,
    whereupon I turned to him: "Master, I long

to know what souls these are, and what strange usage
    makes them as eager to cross as they seem to be
    in this infected light." At which the Sage:

"All this shall be made known to you when we stand
    on the joyless beach of Acheron." And I
    cast down my eyes, sensing a reprimand   *(75)*

in what he said, and so walked at his side
    in silence and ashamed until we came
    through the dead cavern to that sunless tide.

There, steering toward us in an ancient ferry
    came an old man with a white bush of hair,
    bellowing: "Woe to you depraved souls! Bury

here and forever all hope of Paradise:
    I come to lead you to the other shore,
    into eternal dark, into fire and ice.

And you who are living yet, I say begone
    from these who are dead." But when he saw me stand
    against his violence he began again:

"By other windings and by other steerage
    shall you cross to that other shore. Not here! Not here!
    A lighter craft than mine must give you passage."   *(90)*

And my Guide to him: "Charon, bite back your spleen:
    this has been willed where what is willed must be,
    and is not yours to ask what it may mean."

The steersman of that marsh of ruined souls,
    who wore a wheel of flame around each eye,
    stifled the rage that shook his woolly jowls.

But those unmanned and naked spirits there
  turned pale with fear and their teeth began to chatter
  at sound of his crude bellow. In despair

they blasphemed God, their parents, their time on earth,
  the race of Adam, and the day and the hour
  and the place and the seed and the womb that gave them birth.

But all together they drew to that grim shore
  where all must come who lose the fear of God.
  Weeping and cursing they come for evermore,   *(105)*

and demon Charon with eyes like burning coals
  herds them in, and with a whistling oar
  flails on the stragglers to his wake of souls.

As leaves in autumn loosen and stream down
  until the branch stands bare above its tatters
  spread on the rustling ground, so one by one

the evil seed of Adam in its Fall
  cast themselves, at his signal, from the shore
  and streamed away like birds who hear their call.

So they are gone over that shadowy water,
  and always before they reach the other shore
  a new noise stirs on this, and new throngs gather.

"My son," the courteous Master said to me,
  "all who die in the shadow of God's wrath
  converge to this from every clime and country.   *(120)*

And all pass over eagerly, for here
  Divine Justice transforms and spurs them so
  their dread turns wish: they yearn for what they fear.

No soul in Grace comes ever to this crossing;
  therefore if Charon rages at your presence
  you will understand the reason for his cursing."

When he had spoken, all the twilight country
  shook so violently, the terror of it
  bathes me with sweat even in memory:

the tear-soaked ground gave out a sigh of wind
    that spewed itself in flame on a red sky,
    and all my shattered senses left me. Blind,

like one whom sleep comes over in a swoon,
I stumbled into darkness and went down.

NOTES

7–8. *Only those elements time cannot wear:* The Angels, the Empyrean, and the First Matter are the elements time cannot wear, for they will last to all time. Man, however, in his mortal state, is not eternal. The Gate of Hell, therefore, was created before man. The theological point is worth attention. The doctrine of Original Sin is, of course, one familiar to many creeds. Here, however, it would seem that the preparation for damnation predates Original Sin. True, in one interpretation, Hell was created for the punishment of the Rebellious Angels and not for man. Had man not sinned, he would never have known Hell. But on the other hand, Dante's God was one who knew all, and knew therefore that man would indeed sin. The theological problem is an extremely delicate one.

    It is significant, however, that having sinned, man lives out his days on the rind of Hell, and that damnation is forever below his feet. This central concept of man's sinfulness, and, opposed to it, the doctrine of Christ's ever-abounding mercy, are central to all of Dante's theology. Only as man surrenders himself to Divine Love may he hope for salvation, and salvation is open to all who will surrender themselves.

8. *and to all time I stand:* So odious is sin to God that there can be no end to its just punishment.

9. *Abandon all hope ye who enter here:* The admonition, of course, is to the damned and not to those who come on Heaven-sent errands. The Harrowing of Hell (see Canto IV, note to 1.53) provided the only exemption from this decree, and that only through the direct intercession of Christ.

57. *who, in his cowardice, made the Great Denial:* This is almost certainly intended to be Celestine V, who became Pope in 1294. He was a man of saintly life, but allowed himself to be convinced by a priest named Benedetto that his soul was in danger since no man could live in the world without being damned. In fear for his soul he withdrew from all worldly affairs and renounced the papacy. Benedetto promptly assumed the mantle himself and became Boniface VIII, a Pope who became for Dante a symbol of all the worst corruptions of the church. Dante also blamed Boniface and his intrigues for many of the evils that befell Florence. We shall learn in Canto XIX that the fires of Hell are waiting for Boniface in the pit of the Simoniacs, and we shall be given further evidence of his corruption in Canto XXVII. Celestine's great guilt is that his cowardice (in selfish terror for his own welfare) served as the door through which so much evil entered the church.

80. *an old man:* Charon. He is the ferryman of dead souls across the Acheron in all classical mythology.

88–90. *By other windings:* Charon recognizes Dante not only as a living man but as a soul in grace, and knows, therefore, that the Infernal Ferry was not intended for him. He is probably referring to the fact that souls destined for Purgatory and Heaven assemble not at his ferry point, but on the banks of the Tiber, from which they are transported by an Angel.

100. *they blasphemed God:* The souls of the damned are not permitted to repent, for repentance is a divine grace.

123. *they yearn for what they fear:* Hell (allegorically Sin) is what the souls of the damned really wish for. Hell is their actual and deliberate choice, for divine grace is denied to none who wish for it in their hearts. The damned must, in fact, deliberately harden their hearts to God in order to become damned. Christ's grace is sufficient to save all who wish for it.

133–34. DANTE'S SWOON: This device (repeated at the end of Canto V) serves a double purpose. The first is technical: Dante uses it to cover a transition. We are never told how he crossed Acheron, for that would involve certain narrative matters he can better deal with when he crosses Styx in Canto VII. The second is to provide a point of departure for a theme that is carried through the entire descent: the theme of Dante's emotional reaction to Hell. These two swoons early in the descent show him most susceptible to the grief about him. As he descends, pity leaves him, and he even goes so far as to add to the torments of one sinner. The allegory is clear: we must harden ourselves against every sympathy for sin.

CANTO IV

Circle One: Limbo

The Virtuous Pagans

Dante wakes to find himself across Acheron. The Poets are now on the brink of Hell itself, which Dante conceives as a great funnel-shaped cave lying below the northern hemisphere with its bottom point at the earth's center. Around this great circular depression runs a series of ledges, each of which Dante calls a CIRCLE. Each circle is assigned to the punishment of one category of sin.

As soon as Dante's strength returns, the Poets begin to cross the FIRST CIRCLE. Here they find the VIRTUOUS PAGANS. They were born without the light of Christ's revelation, and, therefore, they cannot come into the light of God, but they are not tormented. Their only pain is that they have no hope.

Ahead of them Dante sights a great dome of light, and a voice trumpets through the darkness welcoming Virgil back, for this is his eternal place in Hell. Immediately the great Poets of all time appear—HOMER, HORACE, OVID, and LUCAN. They greet Virgil, and they make Dante a sixth in their company.

With them Dante enters the Citadel of Human Reason and sees before his eyes the Master Souls of Pagan Antiquity gathered on a green, and illuminated by the radiance of Human Reason. This is the highest state man can achieve without God, and the glory of it dazzles Dante, but he knows also that it is nothing compared to the glory of God.

A monstrous clap of thunder broke apart
   the swoon that stuffed my head; like one awakened
   by violent hands, I leaped up with a start.

And having risen; rested and renewed,
 I studied out the landmarks of the gloom
 to find my bearings there as best I could.

And I found I stood on the very brink of the valley
 called the Dolorous Abyss, the desolate chasm
 where rolls the thunder of Hell's eternal cry,

so depthless-deep and nebulous and dim
 that stare as I might into its frightful pit
 it gave me back no feature and no bottom.

Death-pale, the Poet spoke: "Now let us go
 into the blind world waiting here below us.
 I will lead the way and you shall follow."   *(15)*

And I, sick with alarm at his new pallor,
 cried out, "How can I go this way when you
 who are my strength in doubt turn pale with terror?"

And he: "The pain of these below us here,
 drains the color from my face for pity,
 and leaves this pallor you mistake for fear.

Now let us go, for a long road awaits us."
 So he entered and so he led me in
 to the first circle and ledge of the abyss.

No tortured wailing rose to greet us here
 but sounds of sighing rose from every side,
 sending a tremor through the timeless air,

a grief breathed out of untormented sadness,
 the passive state of those who dwelled apart,
 men, women, children—a dim and endless congress.   *(30)*

And the Master said to me: "You do not question
 what souls these are that suffer here before you?
 I wish you to know before you travel on

that these were sinless. And still their merits fail,
 for they lacked Baptism's grace, which is the door
 of the true faith *you* were born to. Their birth fell

before the age of the Christian mysteries,
    and so they did not worship God's Trinity
    in fullest duty. I am one of these.

For such defects are we lost, though spared the fire
    and suffering Hell in one affliction only:
    that without hope we live on in desire."

I thought how many worthy souls there were
    suspended in that Limbo, and a weight
    closed on my heart for what the noblest suffer.   *(45)*

"Instruct me, Master and most noble Sir,"
    I prayed him then, "better to understand
    the perfect creed that conquers every error:

has any, by his own or another's merit,
    gone ever from this place to blessedness?"
    He sensed my inner question and answered it:

"I was still new to this estate of tears
    when a Mighty One descended here among us,
    crowned with the sign of His victorious years.

He took from us the shade of our first parent,
    of Abel, his pure son, of ancient Noah,
    of Moses, the bringer of law, the obedient.

Father Abraham, David the King,
    Israel with his father and his children,
    Rachel, the holy vessel of His blessing,   *(60)*

and many more He chose for elevation
    among the elect. And before these, you must know,
    no human soul had ever won salvation."

We had not paused as he spoke, but held our road
    and passed meanwhile beyond a press of souls
    crowded about like trees in a thick wood.

And we had not traveled far from where I woke
    when I made out a radiance before us
    that struck away a hemisphere of dark.

We were still some distance back in the long night,
    yet near enough that I half-saw, half-sensed,
    what quality of souls lived in that light.

"O ornament of wisdom and of art,
    what souls are these whose merit lights their way
    even in Hell. What joy sets them apart?"   *(75)*

And he to me: "The signature of honor
    they left on earth is recognized in Heaven
    and wins them ease in Hell out of God's favor."

And as he spoke a voice rang on the air:
    "Honor the Prince of Poets; the soul and glory
    that went from us returns. He is here! He is here!"

The cry ceased and the echo passed from hearing;
    I saw four mighty presences come toward us
    with neither joy nor sorrow in their bearing.

"Note well," my Master said as they came on,
    "that soul that leads the rest with sword in hand
    as if he were their captain and champion.

It is Homer, singing master of the earth.
    Next after him is Horace, the satirist,
    Ovid is third, and Lucan is the fourth.   *(90)*

Since all of these have part in the high name
    the voice proclaimed, calling me Prince of Poets,
    the honor that they do me honors them."

So I saw gathered at the edge of light
    the masters of that highest school whose song
    outsoars all others like an eagle's flight.

And after they had talked together a while,
    they turned and welcomed me most graciously,
    at which I saw my approving Master smile.

And they honored me far beyond courtesy,
    for they included me in their own number,
    making me sixth in that high company.

So we moved toward the light, and as we passed
    we spoke of things as well omitted here
    as it was sweet to touch on there. At last   *(105)*

we reached the base of a great Citadel
    circled by seven towering battlements
    and by a sweet brook flowing round them all.

This we passed over as if it were firm ground.
    Through seven gates I entered with those sages
    and came to a green meadow blooming round.

There with a solemn and majestic poise
    stood many people gathered in the light,
    speaking infrequently and with muted voice.

Past that enameled green we six withdrew
    into a luminous and open height
    from which each soul among them stood in view.

And there directly before me on the green
    the master souls of time were shown to me.
    I glory in the glory I have seen!   *(120)*

Electra stood in a great company
    among whom I saw Hector and Aeneas
    and Caesar in armor with his falcon's eye.

I saw Camilla, and the Queen Amazon
    across the field. I saw the Latian King
    seated there with his daughter by his throne.

And the good Brutus who overthrew the Tarquin:
    Lucrezia, Julia, Marcia, and Cornelia;
    and, by himself apart, the Saladin.

And raising my eyes a little I saw on high
    Aristotle, the master of those who know,
    ringed by the great souls of philosophy.

All wait upon him for their honor and his.
    I saw Socrates and Plato at his side
    before all others there. Democritus   *(135)*

who ascribes the world to chance, Diogenes,
    and with him there Thales, Anaxagoras,
    Zeno, Heraclitus, Empedocles.

And I saw the wise collector and analyst—
    Dioscorides I mean. I saw Orpheus there,
    Tully, Linus, Seneca the moralist,

Euclid the geometer, and Ptolemy,
    Hippocrates, Galen, Avicenna,
    and Averhoës of the Great Commentary.

I cannot count so much nobility;
    my longer theme pursues me so that often
    the word falls short of the reality.   *(150)*

The company of six is reduced by four.
    My Master leads me by another road
    out of that serenity to the roar

and trembling air of Hell. I pass from light
into the kingdom of eternal night.

NOTES

13 ff. *death-pale:* Virgil is most likely affected here by the return to his own place in Hell. "The pain of these below" then (line 19) would be the pain of his own group in Limbo (the Virtuous Pagans) rather than the total of Hell's suffering.

31 ff. *You do not question:* A master touch of characterization. Virgil's *amour propre* is a bit piqued at Dante's lack of curiosity about the position in Hell of Virgil's own kind. And it may possibly be, by allegorical extension, that Human Reason must urge the soul to question the place of reason. The allegorical point is conjectural, but such conjecture is certainly one of the effects inherent in the use of allegory; when well used, the central symbols of the allegory continue indefinitely to suggest new interpretations and shades of meaning.

53. *a Mighty One:* Christ. His name is never directly uttered in Hell.

53. *descended here:* The legend of the Harrowing of Hell is Apocryphal. It is based on I *Peter* iii, 19: "He went and preached unto the spirits in prison." The legend is that Christ in the glory of His resurrection descended into Limbo and took with Him to Heaven the first human souls to be saved. The event would, accordingly, have occurred in 33 or 34 A.D. Virgil died in 19 B.C.

102. *making me sixth in that high company:* Merit and self-awareness of merit may well be a higher thing than modesty. An additional point Dante may well have had in mind, however, is the fact that he saw himself as one pledged to continue in his own times the classic tradition represented by these poets.

103–105. These lines amount to a stylistic note. It is good style (*'l tacere è bello* where *bello* equals "good style") to omit this discussion, since it would digress from the subject and, moreover, his point is already made. Every great narrator tends to tell his story from climax to climax. There are times on the other hand when Dante delights in digression.

106. A GREAT CITADEL. The most likely allegory is that the Citadel represents philosophy (that is, human reason without the light of God) surrounded by seven walls which represent the seven liberal arts, or the seven sciences, or the seven virtues. Note that Human Reason makes a light of its own, but that it is a light in darkness and forever separated from the glory of God's light. The *sweet brook flowing* round them all has been interpreted in many ways. Clearly fundamental, however, is the fact that it divides those in the Citadel (those who wish to know) from those in the outer darkness.

109. *as if it were firm ground:* Since Dante still has his body, and since all others in Hell are incorporeal shades, there is a recurring narrative problem in the *Inferno* (and through the rest of the *Commedia*): how does flesh act in contact with spirit? In the *Purgatorio* Dante attempts to embrace the spirit of Casella and his arms pass through him as if he were empty air. In the Third Circle, below (Canto VI, 34–36), Dante steps on some of the spirits lying in the slush and his foot passes right through them. (The original lines offer several possible readings of which I have preferred this one.) And at other times Virgil, also a spirit, picks Dante up and carries him bodily.

It is clear, too, that Dante means the spirits of Hell to be weightless. When Virgil steps into Phlegyas' bark (Canto VIII) it does not settle into the water, but it does when Dante's living body steps aboard. There is no narrative reason why Dante should not sink into the waters of this stream and Dante follows no fixed rule in dealing with such phenomena, often suiting the physical action to the allegorical need. Here, the moat probably symbolizes some requirement (The Will to Know) which he and the other poets meet without difficulty.

THE INHABITANTS OF THE CITADEL. They fall into three main groups:

1. *The heroes and heroines:* All of these it must be noted were associated with the Trojans and their Roman descendants. (See note on AENEAS AND THE FOUNDING OF ROME, Canto II.) The Electra Dante mentions here is not the sister of Orestes (see Euripides' *Electra*) but the daughter of Atlas and the mother of Dardanus, the founder of Troy.

2. *The philosophers:* Most of this group is made up of philosophers whose teachings were, at least in part, acceptable to church scholarship. Democritus, however, "who ascribed the world to chance," would clearly be an exception. The group is best interpreted, therefore, as representing the highest achievements of Human Reason unaided by Divine Love. *Plato and Aristotle:* Through a considerable part of the Middle Ages Plato was held to be the fountainhead of all scholarship, but in Dante's time practically all learning was based on Aristotelian theory as interpreted through the many commentaries. *Linus:* the Italian is "Lino" and for it some commentators read "Livio" (Livy).

3. *The naturalists:* They are less well known today. In Dante's time their place in scholarship more or less corresponded to the role of the theoretician and historian of science in our universities. *Avicenna* (his major work was in the eleventh century) and *Avverhoës* (twelfth century) were Arabian philosophers and physicians especially famous in Dante's time for their commentaries on Aristotle. *Great Commentary:* has the force of a title, i.e., The Great Commentary as distinguished from many lesser commentaries.

The Saladin: This is the famous Saladin who was defeated by Richard the Lion-Heart, and whose great qualities as a ruler became a legend in medieval Europe.

CANTO V

Circle Two

The Carnal

The Poets leave Limbo and enter the SECOND CIRCLE. Here begin the torments of Hell proper, and here, blocking the way, sits MINOS, the dread and semi-bestial judge of the damned who assigns to each soul its eternal torment. He orders the Poets back; but Virgil silences him as he earlier silenced Charon, and the Poets move on.

They find themselves on a dark ledge swept by a great whirlwind, which spins within it the souls of the CARNAL, those who betrayed reason to their appetites. Their sin was to abandon themselves to the tempest of their passions: so they are swept forever in the tempest of Hell, forever denied the light of reason and of God. Virgil identifies many among them. SEMIRAMIS is there, and DIDO, CLEOPATRA, HELEN, ACHILLES, PARIS, and TRISTAN. Dante sees PAOLO and FRANCESCA swept together, and in the name of love he calls to them to tell their sad story. They pause from their eternal flight to come to him, and Francesca tells their history while Paolo weeps at her side. Dante is so stricken by compassion at their tragic tale that he swoons once again.

So we went down to the second ledge alone;
 a smaller circle of so much greater pain
 a voice of the damned rose in a bestial moan.

There Minos sits, grinning, grotesque, and hale,
 He examines each lost soul as it arrives
 and delivers his verdict with his coiling tail.

That is to say, when the ill-fated soul
 appears before him it confesses all,
 and that grim sorter of the dark and foul

decides which place in Hell shall be its end,
 then wraps his twitching tail about himself
 one coil for each degree it must descend.

The soul descends and others take its place:
 each crowds in its turn to judgment, each confesses,
 each hears its doom and falls away through space.   *(15)*

"O you who come into this camp of woe,"
 cried Minos when he saw me turn away
 without awaiting his judgment, "watch where you go

once you have entered here, and to whom you turn!
 Do not be misled by that wide and easy passage!"
 And my Guide to him: "That is not your concern;

it is fate to enter every door.
    This has been willed where what is willed must be,
    and is not yours to question. Say no more."

Now the choir of anguish, like a wound,
    strikes through the tortured air. Now I have come
    to Hell's full lamentation, sound beyond sound.

I came to a place stripped bare of every light
    and roaring on the naked dark like seas
    wracked by a war of winds. Their hellish flight   *(30)*

of storm and counterstorm through time foregone,
    sweeps the souls of the damned before its charge.
    Whirling and battering it drives them on,

and when they pass the ruined gap of Hell
    through which we had come, their shrieks begin anew.
    There they blaspheme the power of God eternal.

And this, I learned, was the never ending flight
    of those who sinned in the flesh, the carnal and lusty
    who betrayed reason to their appetite.

As the wings of wintering starlings bear them on
    in their great wheeling flights, just so the blast
    wherries these evil souls through time foregone.

Here, there, up, down, they whirl and, whirling, strain
    with never a hope of hope to comfort them,
    not of release, but even of less pain.   *(45)*

As cranes go over sounding their harsh cry,
    leaving the long streak of their flight in air,
    so come these spirits, wailing as they fly.

And watching their shadows lashed by wind, I cried:
    "Master, what souls are these the very air
    lashes with its black whips from side to side?"

"The first of these whose history you would know,"
    he answered me, "was Empress of many tongues.
    Mad sensuality corrupted her so

that to hide the guilt of her debauchery
    she licensed all depravity alike,
    and lust and law were one in her decree.

She is Semiramis of whom the tale is told
    how she married Ninus and succeeded him
    to the throne of that wide land the Sultans hold.   *(60)*

The other is Dido; faithless to the ashes
    of Sichaeus, she killed herself for love.
    The next whom the eternal tempest lashes

is sense-drugged Cleopatra. See Helen there,
    from whom such ill arose. And great Achilles,
    who fought at last with love in the house of prayer.

And Paris. And Tristan." As they whirled above
    he pointed out more than a thousand shades
    of those torn from the mortal life by love.

I stood there while my Teacher one by one
    named the great knights and ladies of dim time;
    and I was swept by pity and confusion.

At last I spoke: "Poet, I should be glad
    to speak a word with those two swept together
    so lightly on the wind and still so sad."   *(75)*

And he to me: "Watch them. When next they pass,
    call to them in the name of love that drives
    and damns them here. In that name they will pause."

Thus, as soon as the wind in its wild course
    brought them around, I called: "O wearied souls!
    if none forbid it, pause and speak to us."

As mating doves that love calls to their nest
    glide through the air with motionless raised wings,
    borne by the sweet desire that fills each breast—

Just so those spirits turned on the torn sky
    from the band where Dido whirls across the air;
    such was the power of pity in my cry.

"O living creature, gracious, kind, and good,
  going this pilgrimage through the sick night,
  visiting us who stained the earth with blood, *(90)*

were the King of Time our friend, we would pray His peace
  on you who have pitied us. As long as the wind
  will let us pause, ask of us what you please.

The town where I was born lies by the shore
  where the Po descends into its ocean rest
  with its attendant streams in one long murmur.

Love, which in gentlest hearts will soonest bloom
  seized my lover with passion for that sweet body
  from which I was torn unshriven to my doom.

Love, which permits no loved one not to love,
  took me so strongly with delight in him
  that we are one in Hell, as we were above.

Love led us to one death. In the depths of Hell
  Caïna waits for him who took our lives."
  This was the piteous tale they stopped to tell. *(105)*

And when I had heard those world-offended lovers
  I bowed my head. At last the Poet spoke:
  ""What painful thoughts are these your lowered brow covers?"

When at length I answered, I began: "Alas!
  What sweetest thoughts, what green and young desire
  led these two lovers to this sorry pass."

Then turning to those spirits once again,
  I said: "Francesca, what you suffer here
  melts me to tears of pity and of pain.

But tell me: in the time of your sweet sighs
  by what appearances found love the way
  to lure you to his perilous paradise?"

And she: "The double grief of a lost bliss
  is to recall its happy hour in pain.
  Your Guide and Teacher knows the truth of this. *(120)*

But if there is indeed a soul in Hell
    to ask of the beginning of our love
    out of his pity, I will weep and tell:

On a day for dalliance we read the rhyme
    of Lancelot, how love had mastered him.
    We were alone with innocence and dim time.

Pause after pause that high old story drew
    our eyes together while we blushed and paled;
    but it was one soft passage overthrew

our caution and our hearts. For when we read
    how her fond smile was kissed by such a lover,
    he who is one with me alive and dead

breathed on my lips the tremor of his kiss.
    That book, and he who wrote it, was a pander.
    That day we read no further." As she said this,   *(135)*

the other spirit, who stood by her, wept
    so piteously, I felt my senses reel
    and faint away with anguish. I was swept

by such a swoon as death is, and I fell,
as a corpse might fall, to the dead floor of Hell.

NOTES

2. *a smaller circle:* The pit of Hell tapers like a funnel. The circles of ledges accordingly grow smaller as they descend.

4. *Minos:* Like all the monsters Dante assigns to the various offices of Hell, Minos is drawn from classical mythology. He was the son of Europa and of Zeus who descended to her in the form of a bull. Minos became a mythological king of Crete, so famous for his wisdom and justice that after death his soul was made judge of the dead. Virgil presents him fulfilling the same office at Aeneas' descent to the underworld. Dante, however, transforms him into an irate and hideous monster with a tail. The transformation may have been suggested by the form Zeus assumed for the rape of Europa—the monster is certainly bullish enough here—but the obvious purpose of the brutalization is to present a figure symbolic of the guilty conscience of the wretches who come before it to make their confessions. Dante freely reshapes his materials to his own purposes.

8. *it confesses all:* Just as the souls appeared eager to cross Acheron, so they are eager to confess even while they dread. Dante is once again making the point that sinners elect their Hell by an act of their own will.

27. *Hell's full lamentation:* It is with the second circle that the real tortures of Hell begin.

34. *the ruined gap of Hell:* See note to Canto II, 53. At the time of the Harrowing of Hell a great earthquake shook the underworld shattering rocks and cliffs. Ruins resulting from the same shock are noted in Canto XII, 34, and Canto XXI, 112 ff. At the beginning of Canto XXIV, the Poets leave the *bolgia* of the Hypocrites by climbing the ruined slabs of a bridge that was shattered by this earthquake.

THE SINNERS OF THE SECOND CIRCLE (THE CARNAL): Here begin the punishments for the various sins of Incontinence (the sins of the She-Wolf). In the second circle are punished those who sinned by excess of sexual passion. Since this is the most natural sin and the sin most nearly associated with love, its punishment is the lightest of all to be found in Hell proper. The Carnal are whirled and buffeted endlessly through the murky air (symbolic of the beclouding of their reason by passion) by a great gale (symbolic of their lust).

53. *Empress of many tongues:* Semiramis, a legendary queen of Assyria who assumed full power at the death of her husband, Ninus.

61. *Dido:* Queen and founder of Carthage. She had vowed to remain faithful to her husband, Sichaeus, but she fell in love with Aeneas. When Aeneas abandoned her she stabbed herself on a funeral pyre she had had prepared.

According to Dante's own system of punishments, she should be in the Seventh Circle (Canto XIII) with the suicides. The only clue Dante gives to the tempering of her punishment is his statement that "she killed herself for love." Dante always seems readiest to forgive in that name.

65. *Achilles:* He is placed among this company because of his passion for Polyxena, the daughter of Priam. For love of her, he agreed to desert the Greeks and to join the Trojans, but when he went to the temple for the wedding (according to the legend Dante has followed) he was killed by Paris.

74. *those two swept together:* Paolo and Francesca (PAH-oe-loe: Frahn-CHAY-ska).

Dante's treatment of these two lovers is certainly the tenderest and most sympathetic accorded any of the sinners in Hell, and legends immediately began to grow about this pair.

The facts are these. In 1275 Giovanni Malatesta (Djoe-VAH-nee Mahl-ah-TEH-stah) of Rimini, called Giovanni the Lame, a somewhat deformed but brave and powerful warrior, made a political marriage with Francesca, daughter of Guido da Polenta of Ravenna. Francesca came to Rimini and there an amour grew between her and Giovanni's younger brother Paolo. Despite the fact that Paolo had married in 1269 and had become the father of two daughters by 1275, his affair with Francesca continued for many years. It was sometime between 1283 and 1286 that Giovanni surprised them in Francesca's bedroom and killed both of them.

Around these facts the legend has grown that Paolo was sent by Giovanni as his proxy to the marriage, that Francesca thought he was her real bridegroom and accordingly gave him her heart irrevocably at first sight. The legend obviously increases the pathos, but nothing in Dante gives it support.

102. *that we are one in Hell, as we were above:* At many points of *The Inferno* Dante makes clear the principle that the souls of the damned are locked so blindly into their own guilt that none can feel sympathy for another, or find any pleasure in the presence of another. The temptation of many readers is to interpret this line romantically: *i.e.,* that the love of

Paolo and Francesca survives Hell itself. The more Dantean interpretation, however, is that they add to one another's anguish (a) as mutual reminders of their sin, and (b) as insubstantial shades of the bodies for which they once felt such great passion.

104. *Caïna waits for him:* Giovanni Malatesta was still alive at the writing. His fate is already decided, however, and upon his death, his soul will fall to Caïna, the first ring of the last circle (Canto XXXII), where lie those who performed acts of treachery against their kin.

124–5. *the rhyme of Lancelot:* The story exists in many forms. The details Dante makes use of are from an Old French version.

126. *dim time:* The original simply reads "We were alone, suspecting nothing." "Dim time" is rhyme-forced, but not wholly outside the legitimate implications of the original, I hope. The old courtly romance may well be thought of as happening in the dim ancient days. The apology, of course, comes after the fact: one does the possible then argues for justification, and there probably is none.

134. *that book, and he who wrote it, was a pander:* "Galeotto," the Italian word for "pander," is also the Italian rendering of the name of Gallehault, who in the French Romance Dante refers to here, urged Lancelot and Guinevere on to love.

CANTO XXXIII

Circle Nine: Cocytus

Compound Fraud

Round Two: Antenora

The Treacherous to Country

Round Three: Ptolomea

The Treacherous to Guests and Hosts

In reply to Dante's exhortation, the sinner who is gnawing his companion's head looks up, wipes his bloody mouth on his victims' hair, and tells his harrowing story. He is COUNT UGOLINO and the wretch he gnaws is ARCHBISHOP RUGGIERI. Both are in Antenora for treason. In life they had once plotted together. Then Ruggieri betrayed his fellow-plotter and caused his death, by starvation, along with his four "sons." In the most pathetic and dramatic passage of the Inferno, *Ugolino details how their prison was sealed and how his "sons" dropped dead before him one by one, weeping for food. His terrible tale serves only to renew his grief and hatred, and he has hardly finished it before he begins to gnaw Ruggieri again with renewed fury. In the immutable Law of Hell, the killer-by-starvation becomes the food of his victim.*

The Poets leave Ugolino and enter PTOLOMEA, so named for the Ptolomaeus of Macca-bees, who murdered his father-in-law at a banquet. Here are punished those who were TREACHEROUS AGAINST THE TIES OF HOSPITALITY. They lie with only half their faces above the ice and their tears freeze in their eye sockets, sealing them with little crystal visors. Thus even the comfort of tears is denied them. Here Dante finds FRIAR ALBERIGO and BRANCA D'ORIA, and discovers the terrible power of Ptolomea: so great is its sin that the souls of the guilty fall to its torments even before they die, leaving their bodies still on earth, inhabited by Demons.

The sinner raised his mouth from his grim repast
    and wiped it on the hair of the bloody head
    whose nape he had all but eaten away. At last

he began to speak: "You ask me to renew
    a grief so desperate that the very thought
    of speaking of it tears my heart in two.

But if my words may be a seed that bears
    the fruit of infamy for him I gnaw,
    I shall weep, but tell my story through my tears.

Who you may be, and by what powers you reach
    into this underworld, I cannot guess,
    but you seem to me a Florentine by your speech.

I was Count Ugolino, I must explain;
    this reverend grace is the Archbishop Ruggieri:
    now I will tell you why I gnaw his brain.   *(15)*

That I, who trusted him, had to undergo
    imprisonment and death through his treachery,
    you will know already. What you cannot know—

that is, the lingering inhumanity
    of the death I suffered—you shall hear in full:
    then judge for yourself if he has injured me.

A narrow window in that coop of stone
    now called the Tower of Hunger for my sake
    (within which others yet must pace alone)

had shown me several waning moons already
    between its bars, when I slept the evil sleep
    in which the veil of the future parted for me.

This beast appeared as master of a hunt
    chasing the wolf and his whelps across the mountain
    that hides Lucca from Pisa. Out in front   *(30)*

of the starved and shrewd and avid pack he had placed
    Gualandi and Sismondi and Lanfranchi
    to point his prey. The father and sons had raced

a brief course only when they failed of breath
    and seemed to weaken; then I thought I saw
    their flanks ripped open by the hounds' fierce teeth.

Before the dawn, the dream still in my head,
    I woke and heard my sons, who were there with me,
    cry from their troubled sleep, asking for bread.

You are cruelty itself if you can keep
    your tears back at the thought of what foreboding
    stirred in my heart; and if you do not weep,

at what are you used to weeping?—The hour when food
    used to be brought, drew near. They were now awake,
    and each was anxious from his dream's dark mood.   *(45)*

And from the base of that horrible tower I heard
    the sound of hammers nailing up the gates:
    I stared at my sons' faces without a word.

I did not weep: I had turned stone inside.
    They wept. 'What ails you, Father, you look so strange,'
    my little Anselm, youngest of them, cried.

But I did not speak a word nor shed a tear:
    not all that day nor all that endless night,
    until I saw another sun appear.

When a tiny ray leaked into that dark prison
    and I saw staring back from their four faces
    the terror and the wasting of my own,

I bit my hands in helpless grief. And they,
    thinking I chewed myself for hunger, rose
    suddenly together. I heard them say: *(60)*

'Father, it would give us much less pain
    if you ate us: it was you who put upon us
    this sorry flesh; now strip it off again.'

I calmed myself to spare them. Ah! hard earth,
    why did you not yawn open? All that day
    and the next we sat in silence. On the fourth,

Gaddo, the eldest, fell before me and cried,
    stretched at my feet upon that prison floor:
    'Father, why don't you help me?' There he died.

And just as you see me, I saw them fall
    one by one on the fifth day and the sixth.
    Then, already blind, I began to crawl

from body to body shaking them frantically.
    Two days I called their names, and they were dead.
    Then fasting overcame my grief and me."   (75)

His eyes narrowed to slits when he was done,
    and he seized the skull again between his teeth
    grinding it as a mastiff grinds a bone.

Ah, Pisa! foulest blemish on the land
    where "si" sounds sweet and clear, since those nearby you
    are slow to blast the ground on which you stand,

may Caprara and Gorgona drift from place
    and dam the flooding Arno at its mouth
    until it drowns the last of your foul race!

For if to Ugolino falls the censure
    for having betrayed your castles, you for your part
    should not have put his sons to such a torture:

you modern Thebes! those tender lives you spilt—
    Brigata, Uguccione, and the others
    I mentioned earlier—were too young for guilt!   (90)

We passed on further, where the frozen mine
    entombs another crew in greater pain;
    these wraiths are not bent over, but lie supine.

Their very weeping closes up their eyes;
    and the grief that finds no outlet for its tears
    turns inward to increase their agonies:

for the first tears that they shed knot instantly
    in their eye-sockets, and as they freeze they form
    a crystal visor above the cavity.

And despite the fact that standing in that place
 I had become as numb as any callus,
 and all sensation had faded from my face,

somehow I felt a wind begin to blow,
 whereat I said: "Master, what stirs this wind?
 Is not all heat extinguished here below?"   *(105)*

And the Master said to me: "Soon you will be
 where your own eyes will see the source and cause
 and give you their own answer to the mystery."

And one of those locked in that icy mall
 cried out to us as we passed: "O souls so cruel
 that you are sent to the last post of all,

relieve me for a little from the pain
 of this hard veil; let my heart weep a while
 before the weeping freeze my eyes again."

And I to him: "If you would have my service,
 tell me your name; then if I do not help you
 may I descend to the last rim of the ice."

"I am Friar Alberigo," he answered therefore,
 "the same who called for the fruits from the bad garden.
 Here I am given dates for figs full store."   *(120)*

"What! Are you dead already?" I said to him.
 And he then: "How my body stands in the world
 I do not know. So privileged is this rim

of Ptolomea, that often souls fall to it
 before dark Atropos has cut their thread.
 And that you may more willingly free my spirit

of this glaze of frozen tears that shrouds my face,
 I will tell you this: when a soul betrays as I did,
 it falls from flesh, and a demon takes its place,

ruling the body till its time is spent.
 The ruined soul rains down into this cistern.
 So, I believe, there is still evident

in the world above, all that is fair and mortal
   of this black shade who winters here behind me.
   If you have only recently crossed the portal   *(135)*

from that sweet world, you surely must have known
   his body: Branca D'Oria is its name,
   and many years have passed since he rained down."

"I think you are trying to take me in," I said,
   "Ser Branca D'Oria is a living man;
   he eats, he drinks, he fills his clothes and his bed."

"Michel Zanche had not yet reached the ditch
   of the Black Talons," the frozen wraith replied,
   "there where the sinners thicken in hot pitch,

when this one left his body to a devil,
   as did his nephew and second in treachery,
   and plumbed like lead through space to this dead level.

But now reach out your hand, and let me cry."
   And I did not keep the promise I had made,
   for to be rude to him was courtesy.

Ah, men of Genoa! souls of little worth,
   corrupted from all custom of righteousness,
   why have you not been driven from the earth?

For there beside the blackest soul of all
   Romagna's evil plain, lies one of yours
   bathing his filthy soul in the eternal

glacier of Cocytus for his foul crime,
while he seems yet alive in world and time!

NOTES

1–90. *Ugolino and Ruggieri:* (Oog-oh-LEE-noe: Roo-DJAIR-ee) Ugolino, Count of Donor-
atico and a member of the Guelph family della Gherardesca. He and his nephew, Nino de'
Visconti, led the two Guelph factions of Pisa. In 1288 Ugolino intrigued with Archbishop
Ruggieri degli Ubaldini, leader of the Ghibellines, to get rid of Visconti and to take over
the command of all the Pisan Guelphs. The plan worked, but in the consequent weakening
of the Guelphs, Ruggieri saw his chance and betrayed Ugolino, throwing him into prison
with his sons and his grandsons. In the following year the prison was sealed up and they

were left to starve to death. The law of retribution is clearly evident: in life Ruggieri sinned against Ugolino by denying him food; in Hell he himself becomes food for his victim.

18. *you will know already:* News of Ugolino's imprisonment and death would certainly have reached Florence, *what you cannot know:* No living man could know what happened after Ugolino and his sons were sealed in the prison and abandoned.

22. *coop:* Dante uses the word *muda,* in Italian signifying a stone tower in which falcons were kept in the dark to moult. From the time of Ugolino's death it became known as The Tower of Hunger.

25. *several waning moons:* Ugolino was jailed late in 1288. He was sealed in to starve early in 1289.

28. *This beast:* Ruggieri.

29–30. *the mountain that hides Lucca from Pisa:* These two cities would be in view of one another were it not for Monte San Giuliano.

32. *Gualandi and Sismondi and Lanfranchi:* (Gwah-LAHN-dee . . . Lahn-FRAHN-kee) Three Pisan nobles, Ghibellines and friends of the Archbishop.

51–71. UGOLINO'S "SONS": Actually two of the boys were grandsons and all were considerably older than one would gather from Dante's account. Anselm, the younger grandson, was fifteen. The others were really young men and were certainly old enough for guilt despite Dante's charge in line 90.

75. *Then fasting overcame my grief and me:* i.e., He died. Some interpret the line to mean that Ugolino's hunger drove him to cannibalism. Ugolino's present occupation in Hell would certainly support that interpretation but the fact is that cannibalism is the one major sin Dante does not assign a place to in Hell. So monstrous would it have seemed to him that he must certainly have established a special punishment for it. Certainly he could hardly have relegated it to an ambiguity. Moreover, it would be a sin of bestiality rather than of fraud, and as such it would be punished in the Seventh Circle.

79–80. *the land where "sì" sounds sweet and clear:* Italy.

82. *Caprara and Gorgona:* These two islands near the mouth of the Arno were Pisan possessions in 1300.

86. *betrayed your castles:* In 1284, Ugolino gave up certain castles to Lucca and Florence. He was at war with Genoa at the time and it is quite likely that he ceded the castles to buy the neutrality of these two cities, for they were technically allied with Genoa. Dante, however, must certainly consider the action as treasonable, for otherwise Ugolino would be in Caïna for his treachery to Visconti.

88. *you modern Thebes:* Thebes, as a number of the foregoing notes will already have made clear, was the site of some of the most hideous crimes of antiquity.

91. *we passed on further:* Marks the passage into Ptolomea.

105. *is not all heat extinguished:* Dante believed (rather accurately, by chance) that all winds resulted from "exhalations of heat." Cocytus, however, is conceived as wholly devoid of heat, a metaphysical absolute zero. The source of the wind, as we discover in the next Canto, is Satan himself.

117. *may I descend to the last rim of the ice:* Dante is not taking any chances; he has to go on to the last rim in any case. The sinner, however, believes him to be another damned soul and would interpret the oath quite otherwise than as Dante meant it.

118. *Friar Alberigo:* (Ahl-beh-REE-ghoe) Of the Manfredi of Faenza. He was another Jovial Friar. In 1284 his brother Manfred struck him in the course of an argument. Alberigo

pretended to let it pass, but in 1285 he invited Manfred and his son to a banquet and had them murdered. The signal to the assassins was the words: "Bring in the Fruit." "Friar Alberigo's bad fruit," became a proverbial saying.

125. *Atropos:* The Fate who cuts the thread of life.

137. *Branca d'Oria:* (DAW-ree-yah) A Genoese Ghibelline. His sin is identical in kind to that of Friar Alberigo. In 1275 he invited his father-in-law, Michel Zanche (see Canto XXII), to a banquet and had him and his companions cut to pieces. He was assisted in the butchery by his nephew.

CANTO XXXIV

Ninth Circle: Cocytus

Compound Fraud

Round Four: Judecca

The Treacherous to Their Masters

The Center

Satan

"On march the banners of the King," Virgil begins as the Poets face the last depth. He is quoting a medieval hymn, and to it he adds the distortion and perversion of all that lies about him. "On march the banners of the King—of Hell." And there before them, in an infernal parody of Godhead, they see Satan in the distance, his great wings beating like a windmill. It is their beating that is the source of the icy wind of Cocytus, the exhalation of all evil.

All about him in the ice are strewn the sinners of the last round, JUDECCA, named for Judas Iscariot. These are the TREACHEROUS TO THEIR MASTERS. They lie completely sealed in the ice, twisted and distorted into every conceivable posture. It is impossible to speak to them, and the Poets move on to observe Satan.

He is fixed into the ice at the center to which flow all the rivers of guilt; and as he beats his great wings as if to escape, their icy wind only freezes him more surely into the polluted ice. In a grotesque parody of the Trinity, he has three faces, each a different color, and in each mouth he clamps a sinner whom he rips eternally with his teeth. JUDAS ISCARIOT is in the central mouth: BRUTUS and CASSIUS in the mouths on either side.

Having seen all, the Poets now climb through the center, grappling hand over hand down the hairy flank of Satan himself—a last supremely symbolic action—and at last, when they have passed the center of all gravity, they emerge from Hell. A long climb from the earth's center to the Mount of Purgatory awaits them, and they push on without rest, ascending along the sides of the river Lethe, till they emerge once more to see the stars of Heaven, just before dawn on Easter Sunday.

"On march the banners of the King of Hell,"
    my Master said. "Toward us. Look straight ahead:
    can you make him out at the core of the frozen shell?"

Like a whirling windmill seen afar at twilight,
    or when a mist has risen from the ground—
    just such an engine rose upon my sight

stirring up such a wild and bitter wind
    I cowered for shelter at my Master's back,
    there being no other windbreak I could find.

I stood now where the souls of the last class
    (with fear my verses tell it) were covered wholly;
    they shone below the ice like straws in glass.

Some lie stretched out; others are fixed in place
    upright, some on their heads, some on their soles;
    another, like a bow, bends foot to face.   *(15)*

When we had gone so far across the ice
    that it pleased my Guide to show me the foul creature
    which once had worn the grace of Paradise,

he made me stop, and, stepping aside, he said:
    "Now see the face of Dis! This is the place
    where you must arm your soul against all dread."

Do not ask, Reader, how my blood ran cold
    and my voice choked up with fear. I cannot write it:
    this is a terror that cannot be told.

I did not die, and yet I lost life's breath:
    imagine for yourself what I became,
    deprived at once of both my life and death.

The Emperor of the Universe of Pain
    jutted his upper chest above the ice;
    and I am closer in size to the great mountain   *(30)*

the Titans make around the central pit,
    than they to his arms. Now, starting from this part,
    imagine the whole that corresponds to it!

If he was once as beautiful as now
    he is hideous, and still turned on his Maker,
    well may he be the source of every woe!

With what a sense of awe I saw his head
    towering above me! for it had three faces:
    one was in front, and it was fiery red;

the other two, as weirdly wonderful,
    merged with it from the middle of each shoulder
    to the point where all converged at the top of the skull;

the right was something between white and bile;
    the left was about the color that one finds
    on those who live along the banks of the Nile.   *(45)*

Under each head two wings rose terribly,
    their span proportioned to so gross a bird:
    I never saw such sails upon the sea.

They were not feathers—their texture and their form
    were like a bat's wings—and he beat them so
    that three winds blew from him in one great storm:

it is these winds that freeze all Cocytus.
    He wept from his six eyes, and down three chins
    the tears ran mixed with bloody froth and pus.

In every mouth he worked a broken sinner
    between his rake-like teeth. Thus he kept three
    in eternal pain at his eternal dinner.

For the one in front the biting seemed to play
    no part at all compared to the ripping: at times
    the whole skin of his back was flayed away.   *(60)*

"That soul that suffers most," explained my Guide,
    "is Judas Iscariot, he who kicks his legs
    on the fiery chin and has his head inside.

Of the other two, who have their heads thrust forward,
    the one who dangles down from the black face
    is Brutus: note how he writhes without a word.

And there, with the huge and sinewy arms, is the soul
    of Cassius.—But the night is coming on
    and we must go, for we have seen the whole."

Then, as he bade, I clasped his neck, and he,
    watching for a moment when the wings
    were opened wide, reached over dexterously

and seized the shaggy coat of the king demon;
    then grappling matted hair and frozen crusts
    from one tuft to another, clambered down. *(75)*

When we had reached the joint where the great thigh
    merges into the swelling of the haunch,
    my Guide and Master, straining terrible,

turned his head to where his feet had been
    and began to grip the hair as if he were climbing;
    so that I thought we moved toward Hell again.

"Hold fast!" my Guide said, and his breath came shrill
    with labor and exhaustion. "There is no way
    but by such stairs to rise above such evil."

At last he climbed out through an opening
    in the central rock, and he seated me on the rim;
    then joined me with a nimble backward spring.

I looked up, thinking to see Lucifer
    as I had left him, and I saw instead
    his legs projecting high into the air. *(90)*

Now let all those whose dull minds are still vexed
    by failure to understand what point it was
    I had passed through, judge if I was perplexed.

"Get up. Up on your feet," my Master said.
    "The sun already mounts to middle tierce,
    and a long road and hard climbing lie ahead."

It was no hall of state we had found there,
    but a natural animal pit hollowed from rock
    with a broken floor and a close and sunless air.

"Before I tear myself from the Abyss,"
    I said when I had risen, "O my Master,
    explain to me my error in all this:

where is the ice? and Lucifer—how has he
    been turned from top to bottom: and how can the sun
    have gone from night to day so suddenly?"   *(105)*

And he to me: "You imagine you are still
    on the other side of the center where I grasped
    the shaggy flank of the Great Worm of Evil

which bores through the world—you *were* while I climbed down,
    but when I turned myself about, you passed
    the point to which all gravities are drawn.

You are under the other hemisphere where you stand;
    the sky above us is the half opposed
    to that which canopies the great dry land.

Under the mid-point of that other sky
    the Man who was born sinless and who lived
    beyond all blemish, came to suffer and die.

You have your feet upon a little sphere
    which forms the other face of the Judecca.
    There it is evening when it is morning here.   *(120)*

And this gross Fiend and Image of all Evil
    who made a stairway for us with his hide
    is pinched and prisoned in the ice-pack still.

On this side he plunged down from heaven's height,
    and the land that spread here once hid in the sea
    and fled North to our hemisphere for fright;

and it may be that moved by that same fear,
    the one peak that still rises on this side
    fled upward leaving this great cavern here.

Down there, beginning at the further bound
    of Beelzebub's dim tomb, there is a space
    not known by sight, but only by the sound

of a little stream descending through the hollow
    it has eroded from the massive stone
    in its endlessly entwining lazy flow."   *(135)*

My Guide and I crossed over and I began
    to mount that little known and lightless road
    to ascend into the shining world again.

He first, I second, without thought of rest
    we climbed the dark until we reached the point
    where a round opening brought in sight the blest

and beauteous shining of the Heavenly cars.
And we walked out once more beneath the Stars.

NOTES

1. *On march the banners of the King:* The hymn (*Vexilla regis prodeunt*) was written in the sixth century by Venantius Fortunatus, Bishop of Poitiers. The original celebrates the Holy Cross, and is part of the service for Good Friday to be sung at the moment of uncovering the cross.

17. *the foul creature:* Satan.

38. *three faces:* Numerous interpretations of these three faces exist. What is essential to all explanation is that they be seen as perversions of the qualities of the Trinity.

54. *bloody froth and pus:* The gore of the sinners he chews which is mixed with his slaver.

62. *Judas:* Note how closely his punishment is patterned on that of the Simoniacs (Canto XIX).

67. *huge and sinewy arms:* The Cassius who betrayed Caesar was more generally described in terms of Shakespeare's "lean and hungry look." Another Cassius is described by Cicero (*Catiline* III) as huge and sinewy. Dante probably confused the two.

68. *the night is coming on:* It is now Saturday evening.

82. *his breath came shrill:* CF. Canto XXIII, 85, where the fact that Dante breathes indicates to the Hypocrites that he is alive. Virgil's breathing is certainly a contradiction.

95. *middle tierce:* In the canonical day tierce is the period from about six to nine A.M. Middle tierce, therefore, is seven-thirty. In going through the center point, they have gone from night to day. They have moved ahead twelve hours.

128. *the one peak:* The Mount of Purgatory.

129. *this great cavern:* The natural animal pit of line 98. It is also "Beelzebub's dim tomb," line 131.

133. *a little stream:* Lethe. In classical mythology, the river of forgetfulness, from which souls drank before being born. In Dante's symbolism it flows down from Purgatory, where it has washed away the memory of sin from the souls who are undergoing purification. That memory it delivers to Hell, which draws all sin to itself.

143. *Stars:* As part of his total symbolism Dante ends each of the three divisions of the *Commedia* with this word. Every conclusion of the upward soul is toward the stars, God's shining symbols of hope and virtue. It is just before dawn of Easter Sunday that the Poets emerge—a further symbolism.

THE PARADISO

■

CANTO XXXII

The Empyrean

St. Bernard
The Virgin Mary
The Thrones of the Blessed

HIS EYES FIXED BLISSFULLY on the vision of the Virgin Mary, Bernard recites the orders of the Mystic Rose, identifying the thrones of the most blessed.

MARY'S THRONE is on the topmost tier of the Heavenly Stadium. Directly across from it rises the THRONE OF JOHN THE BAPTIST. From her throne to the central arena (The Yellow of the Rose) descends a LINE OF HEBREW WOMEN. These two radii form a diameter that divides the stadium. On one side are throned THOSE WHO BELIEVE IN CHRIST TO COME; on the other, THOSE WHO BELIEVED IN CHRIST DESCENDED. The lower half of the Rose contains, on one side, the PRE-CHRISTIAN CHILDREN SAVED BY LOVE, and on the other, the CHRISTIAN CHILDREN SAVED BY BAPTISM.

Through all these explanations, Bernard has kept his eyes fixed in adoration upon the Virgin. Having finished his preliminary instruction of Dante, Bernard now calls on him to join in a PRAYER TO THE VIRGIN.

Still rapt in contemplation, the sainted seer
   assumed the vacant office of instruction,
   beginning with these words I still can hear: *3*

"The wound that Mary healed with balm so sweet
   was first dealt and then deepened by that being
   who sits in such great beauty at her feet.   *6*

Below her, in the circle sanctified
   by the third rank of loves, Rachel is throned
   with Beatrice, as you see, there at her side.   *9*

Sarah and Rebecca and Judith and she
   who was the great-grandmother of the singer
   who for his sins cried, 'Lord, have mercy on me!'—   *12*

as I go down the great ranks tier by tier,
   naming them for you in descending order,
   petal by petal, you shall see them clear.   *15*

And down from the seventh, continuing from those
   in the first six tiers, a line of Hebrew women
   forms a part in the tresses of the rose.   *18*

Arranged to form a wall thus, they divide
    all ranks according to the view of Christ
    that marked the faith of those on either side.   *21*

On this side, where the flower is in full bloom
    to its last petal, are arranged all those
    whose faith was founded upon Christ to Come;   *24*

on that, where the half circles show the unblended
    gaps of empty seats, are seated those
    whose living faith was fixed on Christ Descended.   *27*

And as, on this side, the resplendent throne
    of Heaven's Lady, with the thrones below it,
    establishes the line of that division;   *30*

so, facing hers, does the throned blessedness
    of the Great John who, ever holy, bore
    the desert, martyrdom, and Hell's distress;   *33*

and under him, forming that line are found
    Francis, Benedict, Augustine, and others
    descending to this center round by round.   *36*

Now marvel at all-foreseeing profundity:
    this garden shall be complete when the two aspects
    of the one faith have filled it equally.   *39*

And know that below that tier that cuts the two
    dividing walls at their centerpoint, no being
    has won his seat of glory by his own virtue,   *42*

but by another's, under strict condition;
    for all of these were spirits loosed from flesh
    before they had matured to true volition.   *45*

You can yourself make out their infant graces:
    you need no more than listen to their treble
    and look attentively into their faces.   *48*

You do not speak now: many doubts confound you.
    Therefore, to set you free I shall untie
    the cords in which your subtle thoughts have bound you.   *51*

Infinite order rules in this domain.
    Mere accidence can no more enter in
    than hunger can, or thirst, or grief, or pain.   *54*

All you see here is fixed by the decree
    of the eternal law, and is so made
    that the ring goes on the finger perfectly.   *57*

These, it follows, who had so short a pause
    in the lower life are not ranked higher or lower
    among themselves without sufficient cause.   *60*

The king in whom this realm abides unchanging
    in so much love and bliss that none dares will
    increase of joy, creating and arranging   *63*

the minds of all in the glad Paradise
    of His own sight, grants them degrees of grace
    as He sees fit. Here let the effect suffice.   *66*

Holy Scripture clearly and expressly
    notes this effect upon those twins who fought
    while still within their mother. So we see   *69*

how the Supreme light fittingly makes fair
    its aureole by granting them their graces
    according to the color of their hair.   *72*

Thus through no merit of their works and days
    they are assigned their varying degrees
    by variance only in original grace.   *75*

In the first centuries of man's creation
    their innocence and the true faith of their parents
    was all they needed to achieve salvation.   *78*

When the first age of man had run its course,
    then circumcision was required of males,
    to give their innocent wings sufficient force.   *81*

But when the age of grace came to mankind
    then, unless perfectly baptized in Christ,
    such innocents went down among the blind.   *84*

Look now on her who most resembles Christ,
   for only the great glory of her shining
   can purify your eyes to look on Christ."   *87*

I saw such joy rain down upon that face—
   borne to it by those blest Intelligences
   created thus to span those heights of space—   *90*

that through all else on the long road I trod
   nothing had held my soul so fixed in awe,
   nor shown me such resemblances to God.   *93*

The self-same Love that to her first descended
   singing *"Ave Maria, gratia plena"*
   stood before her with its wings extended.   *96*

Thus rang the holy chant to Heaven's Queen
   and all the blessed court joined in the song,
   and singing, every face grew more serene.   *99*

"O holy Father, who endures for me
   the loss of being far from the sweet place
   where fate has raised your throne eternally,   *102*

who is that angel who with such desire
   gazes into the eyes of our sweet Queen,
   so rapt in love he seems to be afire?"   *105*

Thus did I seek instruction from that Great One
   who drew the beauty of his light from Mary
   as the morning star draws beauty from the sun.   *108*

And he: "As much as angel or soul can know
   of exultation, gallantry, and poise
   there is in him; and we would have it so,   *111*

for it was he who brought the victory
   to Mary when the Son of God had willed
   to bear the weight of human misery.   *114*

But let your eyes go where my words point out
   among this court, and note the mighty peers
   of the empire of the just and the devout.   *117*

Those two whose bliss it is to sit so close
    to the radiance of the Empress of All Joy
    are the two eternal roots of this our rose: *120*

The one just to the left of her blessedness
    is the father whose unruly appetite
    left man the taste for so much bitterness;   *123*

and on her right, that ancient one you see
    is the father of Holy Church to whom Christ gave
    the twin keys to this flower of timeless beauty.   *126*

And that one who in his prophetic sight
    foretold the evil days of the Sweet Bride
    won by the spear and nails, sits on his right.   *129*

While by the other father and first man
    sits the great leader to whom manna fell
    to feed an ingrate and rebellious clan.   *132*

Across the circle from Peter, behold Anna.
    She feels such bliss in looking at her daughter
    she does not move her eyes to sing 'Hosanna!'   *135*

And opposite the father of us all
    sits Lucy, who first urged your lady to you
    when you were blindly bent toward your own fall.   *138*

But the time allowed for this dream vision flies.
    As a tailor must cut the gown from what cloth is given,
    just so must we move on, turning our eyes   *141*

to the Primal Love, that as your powers advance
    with looking toward him, you may penetrate
    as deep as may be through His radiance.   *144*

But lest you should fall backward when you flare
    your mortal wings, intending to mount higher,
    remember grace must be acquired through prayer.   *147*

Therefore I will pray that blessed one
    who has the power to aid you in your need.
    See that you follow me with such devotion   *150*

your heart adheres to every word I say."
And with those words the saint began to pray.

NOTES

1–3. *Still rapt in contemplation:* Of the Virgin. His eyes have not left her. Nor do they turn again to Dante. Following his own preachment in XXXI, 112–117, he keeps his eyes on high. The text permits the assumption that Bernard turns his eyes from the Virgin to look at the various parts of the Mystic Rose as he identifies them, later, for Dante. Certainly, however, Bernard could identify every detail of the Rose without having to look at it, and every quality of Dante's mind and style would be better honored by thinking of Bernard as staring adoringly on the Virgin throughout. *the vacant office of instruction:* Formerly held by Beatrice. *I still can hear:* A rhyme-forced addition, not in Dante's text.

4–6. Mary, Mother of God, sits in the uppermost tier. At her feet in the second tier sits Eve, Mother of Man. *the wound:* Original sin. *balm so sweet:* Jesus. *opened:* The first fault, Eve's disobedience. *driven deeper:* Her seduction of Adam, thus spreading sin to all mankind. *in such great beauty:* Eve, having been created directly by God, was perfect in her beauty.

8–9. *Rachel . . . Beatrice at her side:* See *Inferno*, II, 102: "Where I was sitting with the ancient Rachel." Rachel, the younger wife of Jacob, symbolizes the contemplative life, as her sister Leah, also Jacob's wife, symbolizes the active life. In relation to Bernard she may be taken allegorically to be Contemplation and he to be the Contemplative Soul.

10–12. *Sarah:* Wife of Abraham. *Hebrews*, XI, 11–14, cites her as the mother (by miraculous fertility in her old age) of the Jews who foresaw Christ's coming and believed in him. *Rebecca:* Wife of Isaac. *Judith:* She killed Holofernes and freed the Jews. *and she:* Ruth, great-grandmother of David. *that singer:* David. *who for his sins:* His lust for Bathsheba, wife of Uriah. In order to marry Bathsheba, David sent Uriah to his death in the first line of battle. David's lament is in *Psalm L*.

Thus, the first descending rank, down tier by tier from Mary, is made up of Hebrew women, mothers of the children of God.

18. *part . . . tresses:* As if the rose were a head of hair and that vertical row of Hebrew women formed a part in it. In the next line the part becomes a wall.

22. *in full bloom:* That half of the rose-stadium that holds the pre-Christian believers would naturally be completely filled. On the other side there are thrones waiting for those who have yet to win salvation through Christ Descended. Dante, in fact, is laboring to earn one of them for himself. The Day of Judgment will be upon mankind when the last throne is filled, for Heaven will then be complete.

32–33. *the Great John:* The Baptist. He denounced Herod Antipos and was beheaded two years before the Crucifixion. He had to wait in Limbo for two years, therefore, till Christ came for him at the Resurrection. For the Harrowing of Hell, see *Inferno*, IV, 53, note.

40. ff. *below that tier:* The lower half of the rose-stadium contains the blessed infants, the souls of those who died before they had achieved the true volition of reason and faith. They could not, therefore, win salvation by their own merit, *but by another's, under strict condition:* The necessary qualification for election is belief in Christ. These souls were too young at death to have formed their faith. Salvation is granted them not directly through belief in Christ but through the faith and prayers of their parents, relatives, and others of the faithful who interceded for them.

49. *many doubts:* The infants are ranked in tiers that indicate degrees of heavenly merit. But if they were saved through no merit of their own, how can one be more worthy than the other? Such is Dante's doubt, which Bernard goes on to set at rest by telling him, in essence, that God knows what He is doing.

58–59. These . . . who had so short a pause: The infants paused only briefly in the mortal life.

62. dares: I have no explanation of Dante's word choice here. "Not to dare" cannot fail to suggest intimidation. But in Paradise there can be no daring: every soul is in bliss exactly to the degree it is capable of bliss, and its capacity keeps increasing as it looks upon God. To dare (*ausare*, or in modern Italian, *osare*) must be taken as an impurity from the mortal vocabulary (in the sense of "even to think of") and not strictly of the heavenly tongue.

66. the effect: The cause is buried in God's mind. The effect must speak for itself.

67–72. The reference here is to Jacob and Esau. According to *Genesis*, XXV, 21 ff., they were at odds while still in their mother's womb. (Cf. the legend of Polyneices and Eteocles, twin sons of Oedipus and Jocasta.) Dante follows St. Paul (*Romans*, IX, 11–13) in interpreting the division between Jacob and Esau as a working of God's unfathomable will. "Even as it is written, Jacob I loved, but Esau I hated." Man can note the will of God in such matters ("the effect") but cannot plumb its causes, *according to the color of their hair:* For what may seem to be superficial reasons. Esau (*Genesis*, XXV, 25) was red-headed.

81. sufficient force: To mount to Heaven.

84. among the blind: Among the souls of Hell. Such infants were assigned to Limbo.

85. on her who most resembles Christ: The Virgin Mary.

88–99. THE GLORY OF THE VIRGIN. As Bernard directs, Dante fixes his attention on Mary and beholds her blazing in a splendor that rains down upon her in a host of angel beings. These fly from God to the Rose and back again like bees between the hive and the flower, with the difference that these bees bring the rain of light to the flower and are themselves the glorious rain.

88. that face: Mary's.

94. the same Love: The archangel Gabriel, the Angel of the Annunciation. Dante seems to conceive of Gabriel suspended in air before her, repeating the blissful chant of the Annunciation as he had first hymned it in Nazareth.

112. the victory: (Dante says "the palm.") Of God's election. Some commentators gloss it as Mary's triumph over all other Jewish women, all of whom would have been eager to bear the promised Messiah; and possibly so, but to be chosen by God would be triumph enough itself, and any thought of outshining the ladies of the neighborhood would be trivial by comparison.

118–126. Those two: Adam and St. Peter. Adam as Father of Mankind, Peter as Father of the Church. Note that Peter has the place of honor on the right.

127. that one: St John the Evangelist. His *Apocalypse* was received as the prophetic book in which the entire history of the Church is foretold. He sits on Peter's right.

131. that leader: Moses. As the second great figure of the Old Testament he sits to the left of Adam.

133–135. Anna: Ste. Anna, Ste. Anne, mother of the Virgin. Her position directly across the circle from Peter's puts her to the right of John the Baptist. *does not move her eyes to sing 'Hosanna!':* Like all the other heavenly beings, she constantly sings the praise of God. All others, naturally enough, look up as they sing. She, however, is so filled with bliss by the sight of Mary that she does not turn her eyes from her blessed daughter. She praises God while looking at Mary. This detail can be interpreted in many ways, but all of them, of course, must center on the special position of Mary in Catholic doctrine and feeling.

136–138. Lucy: See *Inferno*, II, 97–100. It was she who first sent Beatrice to rescue Dante from the Dark Wood of Error. She sits opposite Adam. She would, accordingly, be to the left of John the Baptist.

139–141. The time granted for Dante's vision is limited. As a tailor must cut the gown from what cloth he is given, so Dante must get on with it, making what he can of his experience in the time allotted him.

142–144. In the act of looking at God man is given the power to see Him. Such is the gift of grace, and to the extent that grace is given, a man may see more or less deeply into God's glory.

148. *that blessed one:* Mary.

CANTO XXXIII

The Empyrean

St. Bernard
Prayer to the Virgin
The Vision of God

ST. BERNARD offers a lofty PRAYER TO THE VIRGIN, asking her to intercede in Dante's behalf, and in answer Dante feels his soul swell with new power and grow calm in rapture as his eyes are permitted the DIRECT VISION OF GOD.

There can be no measure of how long the vision endures. It passes, and Dante is once more mortal and fallible. Raised by God's presence, he had looked into the Mystery and had begun to understand its power and majesty. Returned to himself, there is no power in him capable of speaking the truth of what he saw. Yet the impress of the truth is stamped upon his soul, which he now knows will return to be one with God's Love.

"Virgin Mother, daughter of thy son;
   humble beyond all creatures and more exalted;
   predestined turning point of God's intention;   *3*

thy merit so ennobled human nature
   that its divine Creator did not scorn
   to make Himself the creature of His creature.   *6*

The Love that was rekindled in Thy womb
   sends forth the warmth of the eternal peace
   within whose ray this flower has come to bloom.   *9*

Here, to us, thou art the noon and scope
   of Love revealed; and among mortal men,
   the living fountain of eternal hope.   *12*

Lady, thou art so near God's reckonings
   that who seeks grace and does not first seek thee
   would have his wish fly upward without wings.   *15*

Not only does thy sweet benignity
    flow out to all who beg, but oftentimes
    thy charity arrives before the plea.   *18*

In thee is pity, in thee munificence,
    in thee the tenderest heart, in thee unites
    all that creation knows of excellence!   *21*

Now comes this man who from the final pit
    of the universe up to this height has seen,
    one by one, the three lives of the spirit.   *24*

He prays to thee in fervent supplication
    for grace and strength, that he may raise his eyes
    to the all-healing final revelation.   *27*

And I, who never more desired to see
    the vision myself than I do that he may see It,
    add my own prayer, and pray that it may be   *30*

enough to move you to dispel the trace
    of every mortal shadow by the prayers
    and let him see revealed the Sum of Grace.   *33*

I pray thee further, all-persuading Queen,
    keep whole the natural bent of his affections
    and of his powers after his eyes have seen.   *36*

Protect him from the stirrings of man's clay;
    see how Beatrice and the blessed host
    clasp reverent hands to join me as I pray."   *39*

The eyes that God reveres and loves the best
    glowed on the speaker, making clear the joy
    with which true prayer is heard by the most blest.   *42*

Those eyes turned then to the Eternal Ray,
    through which, we must indeed believe, the eyes
    of others do not find such ready way.   *45*

And I, who neared the goal of all my nature,
    felt my soul, at the climax of its yearning,
    suddenly, as it ought, grow calm with rapture.   *48*

Bernard then, smiling sweetly, gestured to me
   to look up, but I had already become
   within myself all he would have me be.   *51*

Little by little as my vision grew
   it penetrated further through the aura
   of the high lamp which in Itself is true.   *54*

What then I saw is more than tongue can say.
   Our human speech is dark before the vision.
   The ravished memory swoons and falls away.   *57*

As one who sees in dreams and wakes to find
   the emotional impression of his vision
   still powerful while its parts fade from his mind—   *60*

just such am I, having lost nearly all
   the vision itself, while in my heart I feel
   the sweetness of it yet distill and fall.   *63*

So, in the sun, the footprints fade from snow.
   On the wild wind that bore the tumbling leaves
   the Sybil's oracles were scattered so.   *66*

O Light Supreme who doth Thyself withdraw
   so far above man's mortal understanding,
   lend me again some glimpse of what I saw;   *69*

make Thou my tongue so eloquent it may
   of all Thy glory speak a single clue
   to those who follow me in the world's day;   *72*

for by returning to my memory
   somewhat, and somewhat sounding in these verses,
   Thou shalt show man more of Thy victory.   *75*

So dazzling was the splendor of that Ray,
   that I must certainly have lost my senses
   had I, but for an instant, turned away.   *78*

And so it was, as I recall, I could
   the better bear to look, until at last
   my vision made one with the Eternal Good.   *81*

Oh grace abounding that had made me fit
   to fix my eyes on the eternal light
   until my vision was consumed in it!   *84*

I saw within Its depth how It conceives
   all things in a single volume bound by Love,
   of which the universe is the scattered leaves;   *87*

substance, accident, and their relation
   so fused that all I say could do no more
   than yield a glimpse of that bright revelation.   *90*

I think I saw the universal form
   that binds these things, for as I speak these words
   I feel my joy swell and my spirits warm.   *93*

Twenty-five centuries since Neptune saw
   the Argo's keel have not moved all mankind,
   recalling that adventure, to such awe   *96*

as I felt in an instant. My tranced being
   stared fixed and motionless upon that vision,
   ever more fervent to see in the act of seeing.   *99*

Experiencing that Radiance, the spirit
   is so indrawn it is impossible
   even to think of ever turning from It.   *102*

For the good which is the will's ultimate object
   is all subsumed in It; and, being removed,
   all is defective which in It is perfect.   *105*

Now in my recollection of the rest
   I have less power to speak than any infant
   wetting its tongue yet at its mother's breast;   *108*

and not because that Living Radiance bore
   more than one semblance, for It is unchanging
   and is forever as it was before;   *111*

rather, as I grew worthier to see,
   the more I looked, the more unchanging semblance
   appeared to change with every change in me.   *114*

Within the depthless deep and clear existence
   of that abyss of light three circles shown—
   three in color, one in circumference: *117*

the second from the first, rainbow from rainbow;
   the third, and exhalation of pure fire
   equally breathed forth by the other two.   *120*

But oh how much my words miss my conception,
   which is itself so far from what I saw
   that to call it feeble would be rank deception!   *123*

O Light Eternal fixed in Itself alone,
   by Itself alone understood, which from Itself
   loves and glows, self-knowing and self-known;   *126*

the second aureole which shone forth in Thee,
   conceived as a reflection of the first—
   or which appeared so to my scrutiny—   *129*

seemed in Itself of Its own coloration
   to be painted with man's image. I fixed my eyes
   on that alone in rapturous contemplation.   *132*

Like a geometer wholly dedicated
   to squaring the circle, but who cannot find,
   think as he may, the principle indicated—   *135*

so did I study the supernal face.
   I yearned to know just how our image merges
   into that circle, and how it there finds place;   *138*

but mine were not the wings for such a flight.
   Yet, as I wished, the truth I wished for came
   cleaving my mind in a great flash of light.   *141*

Here my powers rest from their high fantasy,
   but already I could feel my being turned—
   instinct and intellect balanced equally   *144*

as in a wheel whose motion nothing jars—
by the Love that moves the Sun and the other stars.

NOTES

1–39. ST. BERNARD'S PRAYER TO THE VIRGIN MARY. No reader who has come this far will need a lengthy gloss of Bernard's prayer. It can certainly be taken as a summarizing statement of the special place of Mary in Catholic faith. For the rest only a few turns of phrase need underlining. 3. *predestined turning point of God's intention:* All-foreseeing God built his whole scheme for mankind with Mary as its pivot, for through her He would become man. 7. *The Love that was rekindled in thy womb:* God. In a sense he withdrew from man when Adam and Eve sinned. In Mary He returned and Himself became man. 35. *keep whole the natural bent of his affections:* Bernard is asking Mary to protect Dante lest the intensity of the vision overpower his faculties. 37. *Protect him from the stirrings of man's clay:* Protect him from the stirrings of base human impulse, especially from pride, for Dante is about to receive a grace never before granted to any man and the thought of such glory might well move a mere mortal to an hybris that would turn glory to sinfullness.

40. *the eyes:* Of Mary.

50. *but I had already become:* i.e., "But I had already fixed my entire attention upon the vision of God." But if so, how could Dante have seen Bernard's smile and gesture? Eager students like to believe they catch Dante in a contradiction here. Let them bear in mind that Dante is looking directly at God, as do the souls of Heaven, who thereby acquire—insofar as they are able to contain it—God's own knowledge. As a first stirring of that heavenly power, therefore, Dante is sharing God's knowledge of St. Bernard.

54. *which in Itself is true:* The light of God is the one light whose source is Itself. All others are a reflection of this.

65–66. *tumbling leaves . . . oracles:* The Cumean Sybil (Virgil describes her in *Aeneid*, III, 441 ff.) wrote her oracles on leaves, one letter to a leaf, then sent her message scattering on the wind. Presumably, the truth was all contained in that strew, could one only gather all the leaves and put the letters in the right order.

76–81. How can a light be so dazzling that the beholder would swoon if he looked away for an instant? Would it not be, rather, in looking at, not away from, the overpowering vision that the viewer's senses would be overcome? So it would be on earth. But now Dante, with the help of all heaven's prayers, is in the presence of God and strengthened by all he sees. It is by being so strengthened that he can see yet more. So the passage becomes a parable of grace. Stylistically it once more illustrates Dante's genius: even at this height of concept, the poet can still summon and invent new perceptions, subtlety exfoliating from subtlety.

The simultaneous metaphoric statement, of course, is that no man can lose his good in the vision of God, but only in looking away from it.

85–87. The idea here is Platonic: the essence of all things (form) exists in the mind of God. All other things exist as exempla.

88. *substance:* Matter, all that exists in itself. *accident:* All that exists as a phase of matter.

92. *these things:* Substance and accident.

109–114. In the presence of God the soul grows ever more capable of perceiving God. Thus, the worthy soul's experience of God is a constant expansion of awareness. God appears to change as He is better seen. Being perfect, He is changeless within himself, for any change would be away from perfection.

130–144. The central metaphor of the entire *Comedy* is the image of God and the final triumphant inGodding of the elected soul returning to its Maker. On the mystery of that image, the metaphoric symphony of the *Comedy* comes to rest.

In the second aspect of Trinal-unity, in the circle reflected from the first, Dante thinks he sees the image of mankind woven into the very substance and coloration of God. He turns the entire attention of his soul to that mystery, as a geometer might seek to shut out every other thought and dedicate himself to squaring the circle. In *Il Convivio*, II, 14, Dante asserted that the circle could not be squared, but that impossibility had not yet been firmly demonstrated in Dante's time and mathematicians still worked at the problem. Note, however, that Dante assumes the impossibility of squaring the circle as a weak mortal example of mortal impossibility. How much more impossible, he implies, to resolve the mystery of God, study as man will.

The mystery remains beyond Dante's mortal power. Yet, there in Heaven, in a moment of grace, God revealed the truth to him in a flash of light—revealed it, that is, to the God-enlarged power of Dante's emparadised soul. On Dante's return to the mortal life, the details of that revelation vanished from his mind but the force of the revelation survives in its power on Dante's feelings.

So ends the vision of the *Comedy*, and yet the vision endures, for ever since that revelation, Dante tells us, he feels his soul turning ever as one with the perfect motion of God's love.

Geoffrey Chaucer, The Canterbury Tales

Geoffrey Chaucer (c. 1340–1400) is widely regarded as the greatest English poet of the Middle Ages. Like Dante, Chaucer possesses a breadth of vision, depth of psychological insight, and powers of poetic expression and observation that few poets in any age can lay claim to. Unlike Dante, however, Chaucer's most successful poems—and particularly his masterpiece, *The Canterbury Tales* (begun about 1386)—are often both comic and ironic in language and perspective. Chaucer's imagination turned toward this world rather than the next, and his many vivid characterizations reflect his varied life experiences as a soldier, courtier, diplomat, and political office holder.

The original "plan" of *The Canterbury Tales*, which we catch a glimpse of in the "General Prologue," required a vast narrative framework (similar to Boccaccio's *Decameron*) of no less than 116 tales, or four tales apiece told by 29 pilgrims on their way to the shrine of the twelfth-century English martyr, St. Thomas à Becket. Chaucer completed only 24 of them.

Viewed collectively, the tales and the "General Prologue" offer a remarkable cross-section view of late medieval society, ranging from the knight, at the top of the social hierarchy, to the plowman, at the bottom. Each of these figures represents a class or an occupational group, however individualized these portraits may seem. The wife of Bath, for example, whose moral and sexual attitudes and personal character traits reflect not only Chaucer's view of one woman's struggle for dominance within marriage (and more generally, within a patriarchal society), also represents a traditional antifeminist perception of woman's supposed lasciviousness, which medieval churchmen cited as the cause of mankind's downfall. Chaucer expresses such views and at the same time subverts them by allowing the wife of Bath to speak for herself—both directly, in the "Prologue" to her tale, and indirectly through the tale itself. She elicits our sympathy for the very things medieval men objected to in women (self-assertiveness, aggressive sexuality, and guile), traits they reserved for themselves. By endowing the wife with a typically masculine bluntness and complacency about the battle between the sexes, Chaucer inverts (and challenges) the customary perspective, setting up the distinctive dramatic irony informing these tales.

GENERAL PROLOGUE

■

HERE BEGINS THE BOOK OF THE TALES OF CANTERBURY: When April with its gentle showers has pierced the March drought to the root and bathed every plant in the moisture which will hasten the flowering; when Zephyrus with his sweet breath has stirred the new shoots in every wood and field, and the young sun has run its half-course in the Ram, and small birds sing melodiously, so touched in their hearts by Nature that they sleep all night with open eyes—then folks long to go on pilgrimages, and palmers to visit foreign shores and distant shrines, known in various lands; and especially from every shire's end of England they travel to Canterbury, to seek the holy blessed martyr who helped them when they were sick.

One day in that season when I stopped at the Tabard in Southwark, ready to go on my pilgrimage to Canterbury with a truly devout heart, it happened that a group of twenty-nine people came into that inn in the evening. They were people of various ranks who had come together by chance, and they were all pilgrims who planned to ride to Canterbury. The rooms and stables were large enough for each of us to be well lodged, and, shortly after the sun had gone down, I had talked with each of these pilgrims and had soon made myself one of their group. We made our plans to get up early in order to start our trip, which I am going to tell you about. But, nevertheless, while I have time and space, before I go farther in this account, it seems reasonable to tell you all about each of the pilgrims, as they appeared to me; who they were, and of what rank, and also what sort of clothes they wore. And I shall begin with a Knight.

There was among us a brave KNIGHT who had loved chivalry, truth, and honor, generosity and courtesy, from the time of his first horseback rides. He had performed admirably in his lord's wars, during which he had traveled as widely as any man, in both Christendom and heathen countries, and he had always been cited for his bravery. He had been at Alexandria when it was conquered, and had sat at the head of the table many times in Prussia, above all the foreign knights. He had fought successfully in Lithuania and in Russia more frequently than any other Christian knight of similar rank. Also he had been in Granada at the siege of Algeciras, and had fought in Benmarin. He had been at Ayas and Attalia when they were won, and had taken part in many an armed expedition in the Mediterranean. He had fought in fifteen large battles, in addition to the three times he had defended our faith in lists in Algeria, and each time he had killed his opponent. This same brave Knight had once been with the lord of Palathia to fight against another heathen in Turkey, and he had always been given valuable loot. But though he was brave, he was prudent, and as meek in his conduct as a maid. He had never yet in all his life spoken discourteously to anybody. He was a true and perfect gentle Knight. But let me tell you of his clothing and equipment: his horses were good, but he was not gaily dressed. He wore a thick cotton coat, which was all stained by his breastplates, for he had just returned from his travels and had set out at once on his pilgrimage.

With him there was his son, a young SQUIRE, a lover and a lusty bachelor, with hair as curly as if it had been set. He was about twenty years old, I would say, and he was of average height, remarkable agile, and very strong. He had already been on cavalry raids in Flanders, in Artois, and in Picardy, where he had borne himself well for one so young, in an effort to win favor with his lady. His clothes were as covered as a meadow with white and red flowers. All day he sang or played the flute; in fact, he was as joyful as the month of May. His cloak was short, with long, wide sleeves, and he sat his horse well and rode excellently. He could compose the words and music for songs, joust and also dance, and draw and write very well. So ardently did he love that he slept no more at night than a nightingale. He was courteous, humble, and helpful, and carved at the table for his father.

The Knight had brought along only one servant, for he wished to travel that way, and the YEOMAN was dressed in a green coat and hood. He carefully carried a sheaf of bright, keen peacock arrows attached to his belt, and a strong bow in his hand. He knew very well how to care for his equipment, and the feathers on his arrows never drooped. His hair was cut short, and his complexion was brown. He understood all the tricks of woodcraft. He wore a bright leather wristguard, and carried a sword and a small shield on one side, and a fine ornamented dagger, as sharp as the point of a spear, on the other. A Christopher hung on his breast, and he had a hunter's horn with a green cord. In my opinion he was a real forester.

There was also a Nun, a PRIORESS, whose smile was very quiet and simple. Her harshest curse was "by St. Loy," and she was named Madam Eglantine. She sang the divine service very well, with excellent nasal intonation, and spoke French fluently and carefully with the accent of the school at Stratford-Bow, for the French of Paris was unknown to her. Her table manners were admirable: she allowed no crumb to fall from her lips, nor did she wet her fingers deeply in her sauce; she knew exactly how to carry the food to her mouth and made sure that no drops spilled upon her breast. She was very much interested in etiquette. So carefully did she wipe her lips that no trace of grease could be seen in her cup when she had drunk from it. She reached for her food very daintily, and truly she was very merry, with a pleasant disposition and an amiable manner. She took pains to imitate court behavior, to be dignified in bearing, and to be considered worthy of respect. But to tell you of her tender feelings: she was so kind and so full of pity that she would weep if she saw a dead or bleeding mouse caught in a trap. She had several small dogs which she fed with roasted meat or milk and fine bread; if one of her dogs died, or if someone beat it with a stick, she cried bitterly. Indeed, with her everything was tenderness and a soft heart. Her wimple was very neatly pleated, her nose shapely, her eyes blue, and her mouth very small, soft, and red. But, truly, she had a fair forehead; it was almost a hand's-breadth wide, I swear, for, to tell the truth, she was not particularly small. I noticed that her cloak was very well made. On her arm she wore a coral rosary with large green beads for the Paternosters, from which hung a brightly shining golden brooch. And on this brooch was first inscribed a capital *A*, surmounted by a crown, and after that *Amor vincit omnia*. This Prioress had another NUN, who was her chaplain, and three priests with her.

There was a MONK, an outstanding one, whose job it was to supervise the monastery's estates, and who loved hunting. He was a manly person, quite capable of serving as abbot. He had many excellent horses in his stable, and when he rode you could hear his bridle jingling in the whistling wind as clearly and also as loudly as the chapel bell at the subordinate monastery where this lord was prior. Because the rule of St. Maurus or of St. Benedict was old and somewhat stringent, this monk let old-fashioned things go and followed newfangled ideas. He didn't give a plucked hen for that text which says that hunters are not holy, and that a monk who is irresponsible is like a fish out of water—that is to say, a monk out of his cell. For he thought that text not worth an oyster; and I said his reasoning was good. Why should he study and drive himself crazy, always poring over a book in his cloister, or work and slave with his hands as St. Augustine orders? How shall that serve the world? Let Augustine have his labor for himself! Therefore this monk was a true hunter: he had greyhounds as swift as birds in flight; his greatest pleasure, for which he would spare no cost, was to ride and hunt the hare. I saw his sleeves edged at the wrist with fur, and that the finest in the land; and he had a very rare pin made of gold, with a love knot in the larger end, to fasten his hood under his chin. His head was bald and shone like glass, as did his face also, as if he had been oiled. He was a fine, fat lord, and in good shape. His protruding eyes rolled in his head and gleamed like coals under a pot. His boots were supple, and his horse richly equipped. Now surely he was a fair prelate; he was not pale as a tormented ghost. Of all roasts he loved a fat swan best. His horse was as brown as a berry.

There was a wanton, merry FRIAR, a licensed beggar and a very gay man. No member of all four orders knew so much of gossip and flattering talk. He had found husbands for many young women at his own expense. A noble representative he was of his order. Among the franklins all over his district, and also among the respectable women in the towns, he was well liked and intimate, for he had, as he said himself, more power of confession than a parish priest, since he was licensed by his order. He heard confession very agreeably, and his absolution was pleasant. When he thought he would get a good present, he was an easy man in giving penance. For to give a present to a poor order is a sign that a man is well shriven. He even boasted that he knew that a man who contributed was repentant, for there are many men with hearts so stern that they cannot weep, even when they are contrite. Therefore, instead of weeping and praying, people could give silver to the poor friars. His cloak was always stuffed full of knives and pins to be given to pretty women. And, certainly, he had a pleasant voice: he could sing and play the fiddle excellently. At ballad-singing he won the prize hands down. His neck was as white as the lily, but he was as strong as a champion wrestler. He knew the taverns well in every town, and cared more for every innkeeper and barmaid than for a leper or a beggar; it was not fitting, as far as he could see, for such an important man to be acquainted with lepers. It is not honest, and it will not advance a man, to deal with such poor folks; rather, he should deal with the rich and with the food-merchants. And, above everything, wherever there was a chance for profit, this Friar was courteous and humbly helpful. There was no man anywhere more capable at this work. He was the best beggar in his order, and paid a certain sum for his grant so that none of his brethren came into his district. And even if a widow did not own a shoe, his greeting was so pleasant that before he left he would have got a coin. The money which he picked up on the sly amounted to more than his regular income. And he could frolic just like a puppy. During court meetings he could be of great help, for then he was not like a cloisterer with a coat as threadbare as a poor scholar's but like a master or a pope. His short coat was of double worsted, as neat as if it were freshly pressed. He intentionally lisped a bit in his joking, in order to make his English roll sweetly from his tongue, and when he played the harp after singing, his eyes twinkled in his head just like the stars on a frosty night. This worthy licensed beggar was named Hubert.

There was a MERCHANT with a forked beard, dressed in clothes of varied colors and sitting proudly on his horse; he wore a beaver hat from Flanders, and his boots were neatly fastened. He spoke his opinions very pompously, talking always about the increase in his profits. He wished the sea were kept open at all costs between Middelburg and Orwell, and was expert in selling money on the exchange. This responsible man kept his wits about him: so closemouthed was he about his dealings in bargaining and in borrowing and lending that no one knew when he was in debt. Nevertheless, he was really a worthy man; but, to tell the truth, I don't know what he was called.

There was also a CLERIC from Oxford, who had long ago applied himself to the study of logic. His horse was as thin as a rake, and he himself, I assure you, was by no means fat, but looked hollow and solemn. His overcoat was threadbare, for as yet he had found no benefice, and he was not worldly enough to hold a secular position. For he would rather have twenty books of Aristotle and his philosophy bound in red or black at the head of his bed than rich clothes, or a fiddle, or a gay psaltery. But though he was a philosopher, he still had but little gold in his chest, for he spent all he could get out of his friends on books and on schooling, and prayed earnestly for the souls of those who gave him money with which to go to school. He was most concerned and occupied with studying. He spoke not one word more than was necessary, and that which he did say was correct and modest, brief and to the point, and filled with worth-while meaning. His talk centered on moral themes, and gladly would he learn and gladly teach.

A LAWYER, careful and wise, a most excellent man long practiced in legal discourse, was also there. He was discreet and well thought of—at least he seemed so, his words were so wise. Many times he had served as justice at assizes, appointed by letters from the King and also in the regular way. He had earned many large fees and presents of clothes as a result of his skill and his wide reputation. There was nowhere so able a buyer of land: he always sought unentailed ownership, and his papers were never invalidated. No man was so busy as he, and yet he seemed busier than he was. He had all the cases and decisions which had occurred since the time of King William at the tip of his tongue. He could compose and draw up a legal paper so that no one could complain about his phrasing, and he could recite every statute by heart. He rode unostentatiously in a coat of mixed color, with a silk belt on which there were small bars—I shall tell no more about his dress.

A FRANKLIN was with the Lawyer. His beard was as white as a daisy, and he was sanguine by nature. Dearly did he love his bread dipped in wine in the morning. He had the habit of living for pleasure, for he was a true son of Epicurus, who held that pure pleasure was truly perfect bliss. He was a substantial landowner, St. Julian in his part of the country. Always his bread and ale were of the best, and nobody had a better cellar. His house was never without baked fish and meat in such quantity that it snowed food and drink, the choicest that you could imagine. His menus changed in accordance with the various seasons of the year. Many a fat bird was in his coop, and many a bream and pike in his fishpond. Woe to his cook unless the sauce were pungent and sharp and all the equipment in order. All day long his table stood ready laid in the hall. He was lord and sire of the sessions and had frequently served as member of parliament from his shire. A short dagger and a pouch of silk hung from his milk-white belt. He had served as administrator and as auditor for his shire. Nowhere was there such a worthy sub-vassal.

A HABERDASHER and a CARPENTER, a WEAVER, a DYER, and a TAPESTRY-MAKER were with us, all clothed in the uniform of a great and important guild. Their equipment was all freshly and newly decorated: their knives were mounted with silver, not with brass; their belts and pouches were in every respect well and cleanly made. Indeed, each of them seemed suited to sit on a dais in the guildhall as burgess. Each, because of his wisdom, was able to serve as alderman. For they owned sufficient goods and money, as even their wives had to agree, or else they certainly would be blameworthy. It is a very fine thing to be called "Madam," to go in first to evening services, and to have a train carried like royalty.

These guildsmen had a COOK with them for the trip to boil chickens with the bones and with the flavoring powder and the spice. He could easily recognize a draught of London ale, and could roast and boil, broil, fry, make stew, and bake good pies. But it was a shame, I thought, that he had a large sore on his shin. For he could make blancmange with the best.

There was a SAILOR who lived far in the west; for all I know he was from Dartmouth. He rode upon a nag as best he could, in a coarse gown which came to his knees. Under his arm he had a dagger which hung down on a cord about his neck. The hot summer sun had tanned him heavily, and certainly he was a good fellow. Often while the wine-merchant, he had tapped the wine casks he brought from Bordeaux. He gave no heed to scruples. When he fought and had the upper hand, he made his prisoners walk the plank. But in his business—the correct reckoning of tides and streams; the handling of the ship's controls; the knowledge of the harbors, the moon, and the compass—there was none so good from Hull to Carthage. He was bold and wise in any undertaking. His beard had been shaken by many a tempest. He knew the condition of all the anchorages from Gotland Isle to Cape Finisterre, and every creek in Spain and Brittany. His ship was called the "Magdalen."

With us there was a PHYSICIAN; in all the world there was not another like him for talk of medicines and of surgery, for he was trained in astrology. He skillfully and carefully observed his patient through the astrological hours, and was quite able to place the waxen images of his patient so that a fortunate planet was ascendant. He knew the cause of every disease—whether hot, cold, moist, or dry—and how it developed, and of what humour. Indeed, he was the perfect practitioner: the cause and root of the disease determined, at once he gave the sick man his remedy. He had his apothecaries quite ready to send him drugs and sirups, for each of them worked to the other's profit—their friendship was not newly begun. This Physician knew well ancient Aesculapius and Dioscorides, and also Rufus, Hippocrates, Haly and Galen, Serapion, Rhazes, Avicenna, Averroes, Damascenus and Constantine, Bernard, Gatesden, and Gilbertine. His diet was moderate—not too much, but that little nourishing and digestible. But little time did he devote to the study of the Bible. He was dressed in red and blue cloth lined with taffeta and with silk; and yet he was not quick to spend his money. He held on to that which he gained during a plague. For, in medicine, gold is healthful in drinks; therefore, he especially loved gold.

There was a good WIFE from near Bath, but she was somewhat deaf, which was a shame. She had such skill in clothmaking that she surpassed the weavers of Ypres and Ghent. In all her parish there was no woman who could go before her to the offertory; and if someone did, the Wife of Bath was certainly so angry that she lost all charitable feeling. Her kerchiefs were of fine texture; those she wore upon her head on Sunday weighed, I swear, ten pounds. Her fine scarlet hose were carefully tied, and her shoes were uncracked and new. Her face was bold and fair and red. All of her life she had been an estimable woman: she had had five husbands, not to mention other company in her youth—but of that we need not speak now. And three times she had been to Jerusalem; she had crossed many a foreign river; she had been to Rome, to Bologna, to St. James' shrine in Galicia, and to Cologne. About journeying through the country she knew a great deal. To tell the truth she was gap-toothed. She sat her gentle horse easily, and wore a fine headdress with a hat as broad as a buckler or a shield, a riding skirt about her large hips, and a pair of sharp spurs on her heels. She knew how to laugh and joke in company, and all the remedies of love, for her skill was great in that old game.

There was a good man of the church, a poor parish PRIEST, but rich in holy thoughts and works. He was also a learned man, a cleric, who wished to preach Christ's gospel truly and to teach his parishioners devoutly. He was benign, wonderfully diligent, and extremely patient in adversity, as he had proved many times. He did not at all like to have anyone excommunicated for non-payment of tithes; rather, he would give, without doubt, a portion of the offering and also of his salary to his poor parishioners. He needed little to fill his own needs. His parish was wide and the houses far apart, but he never failed, rain or shine, sick or well, to visit the farthest in his parish, be he rich or poor, traveling on foot with a staff in his hand. To his congregation he gave this noble example: first he practiced good deeds, and afterward he preached them. He took this idea from the gospels and added to it another: if gold rust, what shall iron do? For if a priest whom we trust is not worthy, it is no wonder that an ignorant man sins. And it is a shame, if a priest only realizes it, to see a wicked priest and a godly congregation. Surely a parson should set an example by his godliness as to how his parishioners should live. This Priest did not hire out his benefice and leave his people in difficulties while he ran off to St. Paul's in London to look for an endowment singing masses for the dead, or to be retained by a guild. He stayed at home and guarded his parish well so that evil did not corrupt it. He was a pastor and not a mercenary. And yet, though he himself was holy and virtuous, he was not contemptuous of sinners, nor overbearing and proud in his talk; rather, he was discreet and kind in his teaching. His business was to draw folk to heaven by fairness and by setting a good example. But if any sinner, whether of high or low birth, was obstinate, this Parson would at once rebuke him for it sharply. I don't believe there is a better priest anywhere. He cared nothing for pomp and reverence, nor did he affect an overly nice conscience; he taught the lore of Christ and His twelve Apostles, but first he followed it himself.

With him there was a PLOWMAN, his brother, who had hauled many a load of manure. He was a good and true laborer, living in peace and perfect charity. With all his heart, he loved God best at all times, whether it profited him or not, and next he loved his neighbor as himself. He would thresh and also ditch and dig, free of charge, for the sake of Christ, to help a poor neighbor, if it were at all possible. He paid his tithes promptly and honestly, both by working himself and with his goods. Dressed in a laborer's coat, he rode upon a mare.

There were also a Reeve, a Miller, a Summoner, and a Pardoner, a Manciple, and myself—there were no more.

The MILLER was a very husky fellow, tremendous in bone and in brawn which he used well to get the best of all comers; in wrestling he always won the prize. He was stocky, broad, and thickset. There was no door which he could not pull off its hinges or break by ramming it with his head. His beard was as red as any sow or fox, and as broad as a spade. At the right on top of his nose he had a wart, from which there grew a tuft of hairs red as the bristles of a sow's ears, and his nostrils were wide and black. A sword and a shield hung at his side. His mouth was as huge as a large furnace, and he was a jokester and a ribald clown, most of whose jests were of sin and scurrility. He knew quite well how to steal grain and charge thrice over, but yet he really remained reasonably honest. The coat he wore was white and the hood blue. He could play the bagpipe well and led us out of town to its music.

There was a friendly MANCIPLE of an Inn of Court whom other stewards might well imitate in order to buy provisions wisely. For no matter whether he bought for cash or on credit, he always watched his purchases so closely that he was constantly solvent and even ahead. Now isn't that a fine gift from God, that such an uneducated man can outwit a whole heap of learned men? He had more than thirty masters, who were expert and deep in legal matters; a full dozen of them were capable of serving as steward of the moneys and the lands of any lord in England, and of making that lord live within his own income and honorably out of debt (unless he were crazy), or just as sparingly as he wished. And these lawyers could take care of any emergency that occurred in the administration of a shire; and yet this Manciple made fools of them all.

The REEVE was a slender, choleric man. His beard was shaved as close as possible, and his hair was cut round by his ears and clipped short in front like a priest's. His legs were as long and lean as sticks, completely lacking calves. He knew fully how to keep a granary and a bin; there was no accountant who could get the best of him. From the drought and from the rainfall he could tell the expected yield of his seed and grain. His lord's sheep, cattle, dairy, swine, horses, equipment, and poultry were wholly under this Reeve's care, and his word had been accepted on the accounting ever since his lord was twenty years old. There was no one who could find him in arrears. There was no bailiff, no sheepherder, nor any other laborer, whose petty tricks and stealings were not known to the Reeve; they were as afraid of him as of death. His house was well placed upon a heath and shadowed by green trees. He was better able to buy than was his lord. He had privately accumulated considerable money, for he knew very well how to please his lord subtly, to give and lend him money from the lord's own stock and therefore to receive thanks, plus a coat and hood. As a youth he had learned a good trade: he was a very fine woodworker, a carpenter. This Reeve rode upon a large, fine dappled-gray horse called Scot. He wore a long blue topcoat, and carried a rusty sword by his side. This Reeve that I am telling about was from Norfolk, near a town called Bawdswell. His coat was tucked up like a friar's, and he always rode last in our procession.

There was a SUMMONER with us there who had a fiery-red babyish face, for he was leprous and had close-set eyes. He was as passionate and lecherous as a sparrow, and had black scabby brows and a scraggly beard. Children were frightened by his face. There was no quicksilver, litharge, or brimstone, borax, white lead, or any oil of tartar, or ointment which would rid him of his white pimples or of the bumps on his face. He really loved garlic, onions, and also leeks, and to drink strong wine, red as blood, after which he would speak and shout like a madman. Then, when he had drunk his fill of the wine, he would speak no word but Latin; he knew a few phrases, two or three, that he had learned out of some church paper—that is not unusual, for he heard Latin all day; and you know very well how a jay bird can say "Wat" as well as the Pope. But if anyone attempted to discuss other learned matter with the Summoner, it was at once evident that he had spent all of his philosophy; he would always cry: "The question is what is the law?" He was a friendly and a kind rascal; you couldn't find a better fellow. For a quart of wine, he would allow a good fellow to have his mistress for a year, and excuse him fully. And he could pull the same trick quite expertly on someone else. If he came across a good companion, he would teach him to have no fear of the archdeacon's excommunication, unless that man's soul was in his purse; for the punishment was sure to be in his purse, since, as the Summoner said, "The purse is the archdeacon's Hell." But I know very well that he certainly lied; every guilty man ought to be afraid of excommunication, which will as surely kill the soul as absolution will save it, and a man should also beware of a *Significavit*. This Summoner controlled all the young people of the diocese in his own way, and he knew their secrets and was their favorite adviser. He had placed a bouquet on his head, large enough to decorate an alehouse signpost. He had made himself a shield of a cake.

With him there rode an amiable PARDONER from Rouncivalle, his friend and colleague, who had just come from the court at Rome. Loudly he sang, "Come hither, Love, to me!": The Summoner, singing bass, harmonized with him; never was there a trumpet with half so loud a tone. This Pardoner had hair of a waxy yellow, but it hung as smoothly as strands of flax, and he wore what hair he had gathered into small bunches on top but then thinly spread out over his shoulders. But for sport he did not wear his hood, for it was tied up in his bag. He affected to ride all in the new fashion, uncovered except for his little cap. He had eyes which glared like those of a hare. A religious talisman was sewn to his cap. He carried his bag, stuffed full of pardons hot from Rome, before him in his lap. His voice was small and goatlike. He had no beard, and never would have; his face was as smooth as if freshly shaven. I believe he was a eunuch. But in his business, there was not another such pardoner from Berwyck to Ware. For in his bag he had a pillowcase which he said had served as the veil of Our Lady; he claimed to have a piece of the sail with which St. Peter went to sea until Jesus Christ caught him. He had a metal cross embedded with stones, and also he had pig's bones in a jar. And with these same relics, when he found a poor parson living out in the country, he made more money in one day than the parson made in two months. And thus, with feigned flattery and tricks, he made monkeys of the parson and the people. But, finally, to tell the truth, he was in church a noble ecclesiastic. He could read a lesson or a parable very effectively, but best of all he could sing the offertory; for he knew very well that, when that service was over, he must sweeten his tongue and preach to make money as best he could. Therefore, he sang merrily and loud.

Now I have told you very briefly about the rank, the dress, and the number of these pilgrims, and also why this group was assembled in Southwark at this good inn called the Tabard, close to the Bell. But the time has come to tell you what we did that same night we arrived at the inn, and afterwards I shall tell you about our trip and all the rest of our pilgrimage. But, first, I beg you in your kindness not to consider me vulgar because I speak plainly in this account and give you the statements and the actions of these pilgrims, or if I repeat their exact words. For you know just as well as I that whosoever repeats a tale must include every word as nearly as he possibly can, if it is in the story, no matter how crude and low; otherwise, he tells an untrue tale, or makes up things, or finds new words. He cannot spare even his brother's feelings; he must say one word just as well as any other. Christ himself spoke quite crudely in Holy Writ, and you know very well that there is no vulgarity in that. Even Plato says, to those who can read him, that the words must be cousin to the deeds. Also I ask you to forgive me for not arranging the people in my tale by their rank as they should be. My wit is short, as you can well imagine.

Our HOST made each of us very comfortable and soon sat us down to supper. He served us with the best food; the wine was strong, and we were glad to drink. Our Host was a seemly man, fit to serve as major-domo of a banquet hall. He was a large man with protruding eyes—no more impressive burgess is to be found in Cheapside—frank in his speech, wise, and well schooled, and nothing lacking in manliness. Also, he was a very merry man, and after supper began to play and told many jokes, among other things, after we had paid our bills. Then he said: "Now, ladies and gentlemen, truly you are heartily welcome here, for by my troth, if I do not lie, all this year I haven't seen so gay a group together in this inn as now. I would like to make you happy if I knew the way; in fact, I just now thought of a way to please you, and it shall cost you nothing.

"You are going to Canterbury—God speed you, and may the blessed martyr give you your reward! And I know very well that as you go along the road you plan to tell tales and to play, for truly, there's no fun or pleasure in riding along as dumb as a stone. Therefore, I shall make you a proposition, as I said before, and do you a favor. And if you are unanimously agreed to stand by my judgment and to do as I shall suggest, tomorrow when you ride along the road, by the soul of my dead father, if you don't have fun I'll give you my head! Hold up your hands without more talk."

It didn't take us long to reach a decision. We didn't think the matter worth much careful discussion, and we voted his way without debate. Then we told him to explain his plan as he wished.

"Ladies and gentlemen," he said, "now listen carefully; but, I beg you, don't be contemptuous. Here is the point, to be brief and plain: that each of you, to make our trip seem short, shall tell two tales of old adventures on the way to Canterbury—I mean it that way—and two more coming home. And the one of you who tells the best tales of all, that is to say, those greatest in moral teaching and in entertainment value, shall have a supper at the expense of all of us here in this inn, right by this column, when we come back from Canterbury. And, to make your trip more enjoyable, I will ride with you myself, at my own expense, and be your guide; and whoever will not accept my judgment along the way will have to bear the full expense of the trip for everybody. Now, if you agree to this plan, say so at once, without any more talk, and I shall immediately get myself ready."

We agreed, and gladly gave our oaths to obey; then we asked him also to agree to serve as our manager, and to judge and report our tales, and to arrange for a supper at a set price. Also, we agreed to be ruled in all things as he saw fit. Thus unanimously we accepted his suggestion, and at once the wine was fetched. We drank, and everyone went to bed without further loitering.

The next morning, when the day began to dawn, our Host got up, roused us, and gathered us all together in a bunch. Then we rode the short distance to the Well of St. Thomas, where the Host halted his horse and said:

"Ladies and gentlemen, listen, if you please; you remember your agreement, and I remind you of it. Now let's see who shall tell the first story. Just as surely as I hope always to drink wine and ale, whoever rebels against my judgment shall stand the whole expense of this trip. Now draw straws, before we go farther; whoever draws the shortest shall be first. Sir Knight," he said, "my master and my lord, now draw a straw, for that is my wish. Come near, my lady Prioress," he said, "and you, Sir Cleric, don't be bashful or think too hard. Fall to, everyone!"

We all immediately drew straws, and, to make a long story short, either by luck, or chance, or fortune, the truth is that the draw fell to the Knight, for which everyone was content and glad; and in accordance with our promise and agreement, as you have heard, he must tell his tale. What need is there to say more?

When this good man saw the situation, since he was wise and willingly held to his promise, he said: "Well, since I must start the game, I welcome the decision, in the name of God! Now, let's ride on, and listen to what I say."

After those words we rode ahead on our way, and he at once very cheerfully began his tale, and spoke in the following manner.

THE WIFE OF BATH

■

HERE BEGINS THE TALE OF THE WIFE OF BATH: In the old days of King Arthur, of whom the Britons speak with such respect, all this land was filled with the supernatural. The fairy queen with her jolly band danced often in many a green meadow. At least, I have read that this was the old belief; the time of which I speak was many hundred years ago. But now one can no longer see the elves, for all kinds of holy friars, as thick as dust in a sunbeam, with their great charity and prayers seek out every land and river, blessing halls,

■

chambers, kitchens, bedrooms, cities, towns, castles, high towers, villages, dairies, barns, stables—this is why there are no fairies. For where an elf once walked there now walks a friar, mornings and afternoons, saying his prayers as he begs through his district. Nowadays women can safely travel past every bush and tree; there is no other evil spirit abroad but the friar, and he can only do us physical dishonor.

It happened that King Arthur had in his court a lusty squire who one day rode along the river where he saw a girl walking ahead of him, alone as she was born, and, despite her resistance, he ravished her. This misdeed caused such an outcry and such protest was made to King Arthur that the knight was condemned to death by a court of law. He would have lost his head—perhaps this was the law then—had not the Queen and other ladies begged so hard for mercy that the King granted him his life and gave him to the Queen to decide as she wished whether he would live or die.

The Queen heartily thanked the King, and then one day when she found the opportunity she spoke to the knight: "Your situation is still such that your life is not safe. I will grant you your life if you can tell me what it is that women desire most. Take care, now, and save your neck from the ax! And if you cannot give the answer now, I will give you leave to travel for a year and a day to seek and learn a satisfactory answer to my question. But before you go, I must have your pledge that you will return."

The knight was sad and sighed deeply, but what could he do? He was not able to do as he liked. At last he decided to go away and to return at the end of a year with whatever answer God might provide. He took his leave and went on his way.

He sought out every house and place in which he hoped he might have the luck to learn what it is that women love most. But he could in no way manage to find two creatures who were in agreement on this subject. Some said women loved riches best; some said honor; some said gaiety; some said finery; some said love-making and to be frequently widows and wives. Some said that our hearts are most comforted when we are flattered and pleased. I won't deny that those folk are very near the truth. A man can best win us by flattery; we are all caught by constant attentions and consideration. Some others said that we love our freedom best, and to do just as we please, so that no man will scold us for our faults, but rather say that we are wise and in no way foolish. Actually, there is no one of us that will not kick if anybody scratches us on a sore spot. Let a man try it, and he'll find that true; for no matter how evil we are inside, we wish to be thought wise and pure. Some said that we take great delight in being considered stable and discreet, steadfast in purpose, not giving away secrets told to us. But that answer is not worth a rake-handle. By God, we women can keep no secret; witness Midas—do you want to hear the story?

Ovid, among other details, mentions that Midas had two ass's ears growing on his head under his long hair, and that he was able to hide this defect cunningly from the sight of everyone except his wife; no one else knew of it. He loved her deeply and also trusted her, and he begged her to tell no one of his disfigurement. She swore that she would not tell for all the world; she would not be so low or wicked as to bring a bad name upon her own husband, nor, by telling, to bring shame upon herself. Nevertheless, she thought that she would die from keeping a secret so long. The desire to tell pained her heart so sorely that she thought the words would burst from her. Since she dared tell no one, she ran down to a nearby marsh—her heart seemed on fire until she got there—and, like a heron sputtering in the mud, she put her mouth to the water and said, "Don't betray me, water, with your sound; I'll tell you and no other: my husband has two long ass's ears! Now it is out, and my heart is whole. Truly, I could keep the secret no longer." You see by this that, though we women can keep a secret for a while, it must come out; we can hide nothing. If you want to know the rest of that story, read Ovid and learn it from him.

When this knight, who is the subject of my tale, saw that he could not learn what women love most, his spirit was sad within him. But home he went; he could not linger, for the day had arrived when he had to return. On his way he happened to ride, greatly troubled, by the side of a forest, where he saw more than twenty-four ladies dancing. He went eagerly toward the dancers, in the hope of learning something useful. But before he reached them the dancers vanished, he could not tell where. He saw nobody except a woman sitting on the grass—an uglier creature no one can imagine. This old woman rose to meet the knight and said: "Sir Knight, there is no path this way. Tell me truly what you seek. Perhaps I can help you; old folks know many things."

"Dear mother," he said, "I am really as good as dead, unless I can say what it is that women most desire. If you can inform me, I shall pay you well."

"Take my hand and swear," she said, "that you will do the next thing I ask of you if it is in your power, and before nightfall I will tell you the answer."

"You have my word," said the knight. "I consent."

"Then I can truly say that your life is saved," she said, "for I will stake my life that the Queen will agree with my answer. Let's see the proudest wearer of kerchief or headdress dare to disagree with what I shall teach you. Come, let us go, without more talk." Then she whispered a message into his ear and bade him be happy and not worry.

When they arrived at the court, the knight said that he had kept to the day that he had promised, and that he was ready with the answer. Many high-born wives and maidens, and many wise widows had assembled there, and the Queen herself sat as judge to hear his answer. Then the knight was told to appear. Silence was ordered, and the knight was instructed to tell the audience what thing mortal women love best. The knight did not stand like a dumb beast, but at once answered the question in a manly voice so that all the court heard: "My liege lady," he said, "in general, women wish to have complete control over both their husbands and love-affairs, and to be masters of their men. That is your greatest desire, though you kill me for saying so. Do what you will with me; I'm at your disposal."

In all the court there was not one wife or maid or widow who denied what he had said; all agreed that he deserved to live.

At that decision the old woman whom the knight had seen sitting on the grass jumped up and cried, "Mercy, my sovereign lady Queen! Before you go, do me justice. I taught this answer to the knight, and in return he swore to me that he would do the first thing I asked him if it lay in his power. Before this court, then, Sir Knight, I ask you to take me as your bride, for you know well that I've saved your life. If I lie, say no, upon your honor."

The knight answered, "Alas, woe is me! I know very well that that was my promise. For the love of God, ask something else! Take all my money, and let my body go."

"No," she replied, "in that case I'd curse us both. Not for all the metal and ore that lies on this earth or is buried under it would I give up being your beloved wife, though I'm old and ugly and poor."

"My beloved?" he exclaimed, "rather my damnation! Alas, that anyone of my birth should be so foully shamed!" But all was in vain; the conclusion was that he was forced to marry her and to take his old wife to bed with him.

Now some people will perhaps say that I did not take the trouble to tell you about all the gaiety and finery which was to be seen at the wedding feast that day. I will answer them briefly: there was no joy nor any feast at all; there was nothing but sadness and much sorrow. The knight married her secretly in the morning and then hid himself like an owl all day, so troubled was he by the ugliness of his wife.

The knight's thoughts were very miserable when he took his wife to bed; he tossed and turned back and forth. His old wife lay there with a steady smile, and said: "Bless me, dear husband; does every knight treat his wife as you do? Is this the law of King Arthur's court? Is every one of his knights so standoffish? I'm your own love and also your bride, the one who saved your life, and truly I've done you no wrong. Why do you treat me so on the first night? You act like a man who has lost his mind. What have I done? For the love of God, tell me and I will amend it if I can."

"Amend it!" replied the knight. "Alas, no, no! It will never be amended. You are so ugly, so old, and of such low birth, it's little wonder that I toss and turn. I wish to God my heart would burst!"

"Is this the cause of your discontent?" she asked.

"Yes, of course," he answered, "and no wonder."

"Now, sir," she said, "I could change all this, if I wanted to, within three days, if you conducted yourself properly toward me. But you say that nobility of character is inherent in riches; that you wealthy folk are therefore gentlemen. Such arrogance is not worth a hen. See who is most quietly and unostentatiously virtuous and most diligent in doing whatever kind deeds he can; take him as the greatest gentleman. Christ wishes us to claim our nobility of character from Him and not from our forefathers because of their wealth. Though they left us all their possessions and we claim therefore to be of a noble family, they cannot bequeath to any of us any part of the virtuous way of life which made them gentlemen, and which served as an example for us to follow.

"Dante, the wise poet of Florence, could speak well about this subject. His story runs something like this: 'Man rarely rises by his own little efforts, for God in His goodness wishes us to derive our nobility of character from Him.' We can receive only temporal things from our ancestors, things which hurt and harm man.

"Everyone knows as well as I that if nobility of character were the natural, exclusive inheritance of a particular family, the members of that family could never cease to be truly noble, because it would be impossible for them to do evil and to have faults.

"Take a torch and carry it into the darkest house between here and the Caucasus; shut the door and go away. The torch will still blaze and burn as brightly as if twenty thousand men watched it. It will carry out its natural function, I'll stake my life, until it burns out. You can clearly see from this that nobility is not connected with wealth, for people do not always act from natural causes as the torch does. God knows, one finds often enough a lord's son doing wicked and shameful deeds. The man who wishes to be considered gentlemanly because he is born of virtuous ancestors, and yet will not act virtuously as did his ancestors, is not a gentleman, even though he is a duke or an earl. For wicked deeds make a scoundrel. Nobility of character is not just the reputation of your ancestors, resulting from their noble deeds, for that is no part of you. Your nobility of character comes from God alone; from Him comes all our true distinction; it was not left to us along with our position.

"Look how noble Tullus Hostilius was, who rose, as Valerius relates, from poverty to high rank. Read Seneca and also Boethius; there you'll find it plainly stated that there is no doubt that the man is noble who does noble deeds. Therefore, dear husband, I conclude as follows: though my ancestors were lowly, God can, as I hope He will, grant me the grace to live virtuously. When I begin to live in that fashion and to give up sin, then I am a gentlewoman.

"You also scorned my poverty, but God in whom we trust chose to live His whole life in poverty. And surely every man, maid, or wife knows that Jesus, the King of Heaven, would not choose an evil way of living. Contented poverty is an honest thing, certainly; Seneca and other writers say that. I consider the man who is satisfied with his poverty rich, even though he does not own so much as a shirt. The covetous man is poor, for he desires more than he can have. But he who has nothing and covets nothing is rich, although you look down on him. True poverty sings happily. Juvenal speaks gaily of poverty: 'The poor man as he goes along the road can sing and play in front of thieves.' Poverty is a harsh virtue, but I believe it makes for industry. It also adds wisdom, if it is borne patiently. These things are true of poverty, even though it seems a wretched state no one should wish to be in. When a man is depressed, by poverty he often comes to know his God and also himself. It seems to me that poverty is an eyeglass through which one may see his true friends. Therefore, since I do not trouble you, don't complain any more about my poverty.

"Now, sir, you reproached me for my age. Surely, even if there were no authority for it in any book, you honorable gentlefolk agree that one must be courteous to an old man and call him father, in order to considered well-mannered. I think, also, that I could find support for that statement among the writers. Since you find me old and ugly, don't be afraid that I'll make you a cuckold, for ugliness and age, I'll warrant, are fine guardians of chastity. Nevertheless, since I know your pleasure, I'll satisfy your physical desire.

"Choose one of these two things," she said, "to have me ugly and old until I die, but a true and humble wife who will never displease you as long as I live; or to have me young and lovely and take your chances on the traffic there will be in and out of your house, or quite possibly elsewhere, on account of me. Take your choice; whichever you want."

The knight thought hard and sighed deeply. At last he replied, "My lady, my love, my dear wife, I put myself under your wise control. You yourself choose whichever you think will be more agreeable and honorable for both of us. I don't care which; whatever you like suits me."

"Then am I now your master," she asked, "since I can decide and do as I wish?"

"Certainly, wife," he said, "I think that will be best."

"Kiss me," she commanded, "we are no longer at odds, for by my troth, I will be both things to you; that is to say, both lovely and faithful. I pray God that I may die insane unless I am as loyal as ever any wife since the world began. And if by tomorrow morning I am not as beautiful as any lady, empress, or queen between the east and the west, you may kill me or not as you wish. Lift up the curtain and see for yourself."

When the knight saw that she was truly beautiful and young, he joyfully clasped her in his arms, his heart filled with happiness. He kissed her a thousand times over, and she obeyed him in everything which might give him happiness or pleasure.

Thus they lived all their lives in perfect joy. May Jesus Christ send us husbands meek, young, and lusty abed, and the luck to outlast them. And I also pray Jesus to hasten the death of those who will not be ruled by their wives. And may God soon send a severe pestilence to old and stingy husbands! HERE ENDS THE WIFE OF BATH'S TALE.

The Renaissance

Pico della Mirandola, Oration on the Dignity of Man

A leading scholar of the Italian Renaissance, Pico della Mirandola (1463–1494) enthusiastically championed the revival of classical learning, particularly its emphasis on the unique value of the individual. His *Oration on the Dignity of Man* (1486) echoes Sophocles' famous dictum that of all the world's marvels, none is more wonderful than the human being. Combining Greco–Roman philosophy and Jewish mysticism, Pico was an influential proponent of Christian humanism, the school of thought that places primary importance on man's reason, creativity, and centrality in the universe. Christian thinkers of the Middle Ages agreed that man reflects the divine image and is lord of creation, but Pico adds that man's potential greatness is nearly infinite. Humanity is not only the pinnacle of earthly creation, but human beings also have the capacity to become one with God.

ORATION ON THE DIGNITY OF MAN

∎

I have read in the records of the Arabians, reverend Fathers, that Abdala the Saracen,[1] when questioned as to what on this stage of the world, as it were, could be seen most worthy of wonder, replied: "There is nothing to be seen more wonderful than man." In agreement with this opinion is the saying of Hermes Trismegistus: "A great miracle, Asclepius, is man."[2] But when I weighed the reason for these maxims, the many grounds for the excellence of human nature reported by many men failed to satisfy me—that man is the intermediary between creatures, the intimate of the gods, the king of the lower beings, by the acuteness of his senses, by the discernment of his reason, and by the light of his intelligence the interpreter of nature, the interval between fixed eternity and fleeting time, and (as the Persians say) the bond, nay, rather, the marriage song of the world, on David's testimony but little lower than the angels.[3] Admittedly great though these reasons be, they are not the principal grounds, that is, those which may rightfully claim for themselves the privilege of the highest admiration. For why should we not admire more the angels themselves and the blessed choirs of heaven? At last it seems to me I have come to understand why man is the most fortunate of creatures and consequently worthy of all admiration and what precisely is that rank which is his lot in the universal chain of Being—a rank to be envied not only by brutes but even by the stars and by minds beyond this world. It is a matter past faith and a wondrous one. Why should it not be? For it is on this very account that man is rightly called and judged a great miracle and a wonderful creature indeed.

2. But hear, Fathers, exactly what this rank is and, as friendly auditors, conformably to

---

1. [Abdala, that is, Abd Allah, probably the cousin of Mohammed.]
2. [Frag. 623 (Marx).]
3. [Ps. 8:5.]

your kindness, do me this favor. God the Father, the supreme Architect, had already built this cosmic home we behold, the most sacred temple of His godhead, by the laws of His mysterious wisdom. The region above the heavens He had adorned with Intelligences, the heavenly spheres He had quickened with eternal souls, and the excrementary and filthy parts of the lower world He had filled with a multitude of animals of every kind. But, when the work was finished, the Craftsman kept wishing that there were someone to ponder the plan of so great a work, to love its beauty, and to wonder at its vastness. Therefore, when everything was done (as Moses and Timaeus bear witness), He finally took thought concerning the creation of man. But there was not among His archetypes that from which He could fashion a new offspring, nor was there in His treasure-houses anything which He might bestow on His new son as an inheritance, nor was there in the seats of all the world a place where the latter might sit to contemplate the universe. All was now complete; all things had been assigned to the highest, the middle, and the lowest orders.[4] But in its final creation it was not the part of the Father's power to fail as though exhausted. It was not the part of His wisdom to waver in a needful matter through poverty of counsel. It was not the part of His kindly love that he who was to praise God's divine generosity in regard to others should be compelled to condemn it in regard to himself.

3. At last the best of artisans ordained that that creature to whom He had been able to give nothing proper to himself should have joint possession of whatever had been peculiar to each of the different kinds of being. He therefore took man as a creature of indeterminate nature and, assigning him a place in the middle of the world, addressed him thus: "Neither a fixed abode nor a form that is thine alone nor any function peculiar to thyself have we given thee, Adam, to the end that according to thy longing and according to thy judgment thou mayest have and possess what abode, what form, and what functions thou thyself shalt desire. The nature of all other beings is limited and constrained within the bounds of laws prescribed by Us. Thou, constrained by no limits, in accordance with thine own free will, in whose hand We have placed thee, shalt ordain for thyself the limits of thy nature. We have set thee at the world's center that thou mayest from thence more easily observe whatever is in the world. We have made thee neither of heaven nor of earth, neither mortal nor immortal, so that with freedom of choice and with honor, as though the maker and molder of thyself, thou mayest fashion thyself in whatever shape thou shalt prefer. Thou shalt have the power to degenerate into the lower forms of life, which are brutish. Thou shalt have the power, out of thy soul's judgment, to be reborn into the higher forms, which are divine."

4. O supreme generosity of God the Father, O highest and most marvelous felicity of man! To him it is granted to have whatever he chooses, to be whatever he wills. Beasts as soon as they are born (so says Lucilius) bring with them from their mother's womb all they will ever possess. Spiritual beings, either from the beginning or soon thereafter, become what they are to be for ever and ever. On man when he came into life the Father conferred the seeds of all kinds and the germs of every way of life. Whatever seeds each man cultivates will grow to maturity and bear in him their own fruit. If they be vegetative, he will be like a plant. If sensitive, he will become brutish. If rational, he will grow into a heavenly being. If intellectual, he will be an angel and the son of God. And if, happy in the lot of no created

---

4. [Cf. Plato *Protagoras* 321 *c* ff.]

thing, he withdraws into the center of his own unity, his spirit, made one with God, in the solitary darkness of God, who is set above all things, shall surpass them all. Who would not admire this our chameleon? Or who could more greatly admire aught else whatever? It is man who Asclepius of Athens, arguing from his mutability of character and from his self-transforming nature, on just grounds says was symbolized by Proteus in the mysteries. Hence those metamorphoses renowned among the Hebrews and the Pythagoreans.

Machiavelli, The Prince

No writer of the Italian Renaissance enjoyed a more sinister reputation than Niccolo Machiavelli (1469–1527). Centuries after his death, his name remains a byword for political cynicism and treachery. The source of his notoriety was *The Prince* (1514), a work of political commentary and theory into which he poured all the insight and passion of a lifetime spent in the practice of diplomacy. His apparent purpose in writing *The Prince* was to arouse the interest and enlist the support of the Medicis, one of Italy's most powerful aristocratic houses (to whom Machiavelli dedicated this book), in the cause of Italian unification. Far from being a disillusioned cynic, Machiavelli was an ardent patriot who longed for the day when foreign rulers and their armies would be driven from Italy forever and when its constantly warring city–states would unite around a single banner or charismatic personality.

At times, *The Prince* reads like a how-to manual of political science. Instead of describing an ideal ruler, as earlier medieval writers might have done, Machiavelli recounts in grim detail how some of his more ruthless contemporaries—like Cesare Borgia, the illegitimate son of Pope Alexander VI—seized power and maintained themselves in office through violence and cunning. Machiavelli's fascination with the amoral, yet successful, political personalities of his day, and his almost clinical detachment in describing their most brutal deeds, earned him the unsavory reputation he continues to bear today.

Whenever possible, Machiavelli cites a Roman author or an event from Roman history to illustrate or confirm his own observations. Like his fellow humanists, Machiavelli respected the ancients and assumed that what was true in the first century was certain to be true in the sixteenth. For all his admiration of antiquity, the final test of any policy or belief was the test of *experience*. To be valid, political ideas had to work, or more precisely, they had to ensure a greater measure of social and political order than either the Church or the State had managed to achieve in Machiavelli's lifetime. Behind Machiavelli's pragmatism, one finds a certain moral desperation and a determination to end the chaos of Italian politics by the only practical means at his society's disposal.

THE PRINCE
∎

XV. The things for which men, and especially princes, are praised or blamed

It now remains for us to see how a prince should govern his conduct towards his subjects or his friends. I know that this has often been written about before, and so I hope it will not be thought presumptuous for me to do so, as, especially in discussing this subject, I draw up an original set of rules. But since my intention is to say something that will prove of practical use to the inquirer, I have thought it proper to represent things as they are in real truth, rather than as they are imagined. Many have dreamed up republics and principalities which have never in truth been known to exist; the gulf between how one should live and how one does live is so wide that a man who neglects what is actually done for what should

300
∎

be done learns the way to self-destruction rather than self-preservation. The fact is that a man who wants to act virtuously in every way necessarily comes to grief among so many who are not virtuous. Therefore if a prince wants to maintain his rule he must learn how not to be virtuous, and to make use of this or not according to need.

So leaving aside imaginary things, and referring only to those which truly exist, I say that whenever men are discussed (and especially princes, who are more exposed to view), they are noted for various qualities which earn them either praise or condemnation. Some, for example, are held to be generous, and others miserly (I use the Tuscan word rather than the word avaricious: we call a man who is mean with what he possesses, miserly, and a man who wants to plunder others, avaricious).* Some are held to be benefactors, others are called grasping; some cruel, some compassionate; one man faithless, another faithful; one man effeminate and cowardly, another fierce and courageous; one man courteous, another proud; one man lascivious, another pure; one guileless, another crafty; one stubborn, another flexible; one grave, another frivolous; one religious, another sceptical; and so forth. I know everyone will agree that it would be most laudable if a prince possessed all the qualities deemed to be good among those I have enumerated. But human nature being what it is, princes cannot possess those qualities, or rather they cannot always exhibit them. So a prince should be so prudent that he knows how to escape the evil reputation attached to those vices which could lose him his state, and how to avoid those vices which are not so dangerous, if he possibly can; but, if he cannot, he need not worry so much about the latter. And then, he must not flinch from being blamed for vices which are necessary for safeguarding the state. This is because, taking everything into account, he will find that some of the things that appear to be virtues will, if he practises them, ruin him, and some of the things that appear to be wicked will bring him security and prosperity.

XVI. Generosity and parsimony

So, starting with the first of the qualities I enumerated above, I say it would be splendid if one had a reputation for generosity; nonetheless if your actions are influenced by the desire for such a reputation you will come to grief. This is because if your generosity is good and sincere it may pass unnoticed and it will not save you from being reproached for its opposite. If you want to acquire a reputation for generosity, therefore, you have to be ostentatiously lavish; and a prince acting in that fashion will soon squander all his resources, only to be forced in the end, if he wants to maintain his reputation, to lay excessive burdens on the people, to impose extortionate taxes, and to do everything else he can to raise money. This will start to make his subjects hate him, and, since he will have impoverished himself, he will be generally despised. As a result, because of this generosity of his, having injured many and rewarded few, he will be vulnerable to the first minor setback, and the first real danger he encounters will bring him to grief. When he realizes this and tries to retrace his path he will immediately be reputed a miser.

So as a prince cannot practise the virtue of generosity in such a way that he is noted for it, except to his cost, he should if he is prudent not mind being called a miser. In time he will be recognized as being essentially a generous man, seeing that because of his parsimony

---

*The two words Machiavelli uses are misero and avaro.

his existing revenues are enough for him, he can defend himself against an aggressor, and he can embark on enterprises without burdening the people. So he proves himself generous to all those from whom he takes nothing, and they are innumerable, and miserly towards all those to whom he gives nothing, and they are few. In our own times great things have been accomplished only by those who have been held miserly, and the others have met disaster. Pope Julius II made use of a reputation for generosity to win the papacy, but subsequently he made no effort to maintain this reputation, because he wanted to be able to finance his wars. The present king of France has been able to wage so many wars without taxing his subjects excessively only because his long-standing parsimony enabled him to meet the additional expenses involved. Were the present king of Spain renowned for his generosity he would not have started and successfully concluded so many enterprises.

So if a prince does not have to rob his subjects, if he can defend himself, if he is not plunged into poverty and shame, if he is not forced to become rapacious, he ought not to worry about being called a miser. Miserliness is one of those vices which sustain his rule. Someone may object: Caesar came to power by virtue of his generosity, and many others, because they practised and were known for their generosity, have risen to the very highest positions. My answer to this is as follows. Either you are already a prince, or you are on the way to becoming one. In the first case, your generosity will be to your cost; in the second, it is certainly necessary to have a reputation for generosity. Caesar was one of those who wanted to establish his own rule over Rome; but if, after he had established it, he had remained alive and not moderated his expenditure he would have fallen from power.

Again, someone may retort: there have been many princes who have won great successes with their armies, and who have had the reputation of being extremely generous. My reply to this is: the prince gives away what is his own or his subjects', or else what belongs to others. In the first case he should be frugal; in the second, he should indulge his generosity to the full. The prince who campaigns with his armies, who lives by pillaging, sacking, and extortion, disposes of what belongs to aliens; and he must be open-handed, otherwise the soldiers would refuse to follow him. And you can be more liberal with what does not belong to you or your subjects, as Caesar, Cyrus, and Alexander were. Giving away what belongs to strangers in no way affects your standing at home; rather it increases it. You hurt yourself only when you give away what is your own. There is nothing so self-defeating as generosity: in the act of practising it, you lose the ability to do so, and you become either poor and despised or, seeking to escape poverty, rapacious and hated. A prince should try to avoid, above all else, being despised and hated; and generosity results in your being both. Therefore it is wiser to incur the reputation of being a miser, which invites ignominy but not hatred, than to be forced by seeking a name for generosity to incur a reputation for rapacity, which brings you hatred as well as ignominy.

XVII. Cruelty and compassion; and whether it is better to be loved than feared, or the reverse

Taking others of the qualities I enumerated above, I say that a prince should want to have a reputation for compassion rather than for cruelty: nonetheless, he should be careful that he does not make bad use of compassion. Cesare Borgia was accounted cruel; nevertheless, this cruelty of his reformed the Romagna, brought it unity, and restored order and obedience. On reflection, it will be seen that there was more compassion in Cesare than in the Florentine people, who, to escape being called cruel allowed Pistoia to be devastated.* So a prince should not worry if he incurs reproach for his cruelty so long as he keeps his subjects united and loyal. By making an example or two he will prove more compassionate than those who being too compassionate, allow disorders which lead to murder and rapine. These nearly always harm the whole community, whereas executions ordered by a prince only affect individuals. A new prince, of all rulers, finds it impossible to avoid a reputation for cruelty, because of the abundant dangers inherent in a newly won state. Vergil, through the mouth of Dido says: *Res dura, et regni novitas me talia co gunt Moliri, et late fines custode tueri*.**

Nonetheless, a prince should be slow to take action, and should watch that he does not come to be afraid of his own shadow; his behaviour should be tempered by humanity and prudence so that over-confidence does not make him rash or excessive distrust make him unbearable.

From this arises the following question: whether it is better to be loved than feared, or the reverse. The answer is that one would like to be both the one and the other; but because it is difficult to combine them, it is far better to be feared than loved if you cannot be both. One can make this generalization about men: they are ungrateful, fickle, liars, and deceivers, they shun danger and are greedy for profit; while you treat them well, they are yours. They would shed their blood for you, risk their property, their lives, their children, so long, as I said above, as danger is remote; but when you are in danger they turn against you. Any prince who has come to depend entirely on promises and has taken no other precautions ensures his own ruin; friendship which is bought with money and not with greatness and nobility of mind is paid for, but it does not last and it yields nothing. Men worry less about doing an injury to one who makes himself loved than to one who makes himself feared. The bond of love is one which men, wretched creatures that they are, break when it is to their advantage to do so; but fear is strengthened by a dread of punishment which is always effective.

The prince should nonetheless make himself feared in such a way that, if he is not loved, at least he escapes being hated. For fear is quite compatible with an absence of hatred; and the prince can always avoid hatred if he abstains from the property of his subjects and citizens and from their women. If, even so, it proves necessary to execute someone, this should be done only when there is proper justification and manifest reason for it. But above all a prince should abstain from the property of others; because men sooner forget the death of their father than the loss of their patrimony. It is always possible to find pretexts for confiscating someone's property; and a prince who starts to live by rapine always finds pretexts for seizing what belongs to others. On the other hand, pretexts for executing someone are harder to find and they are less easily sustained. However, when a prince is campaigning with his soldiers and is in command of a large army then he need not worry about having a reputation for cruelty; because, without such a reputation, he can never keep his army united and disciplined. Among the admirable achievements of Hannibal is included this: that although he led a huge army, made up of countless different races, on foreign campaigns,

---

*Pistoia was a subject-city of Florence, which forcibly restored order there when conflict broke out between two rival factions in 1501–2. Machiavelli was concerned with this business at first hand.
**'Harsh necessity, and the newness of my kingdom, force me to do such things and to guard my frontiers everywhere.' Aeneid i, 563.

there was never any dissension, either among the troops themselves or against their leader, whether things were going well or badly. For this, his inhuman cruelty was wholly responsible. It was this, along with his countless other qualities, which made him feared and respected by his soldiers. If it had not been for his cruelty, his other qualities would not have been enough. The historians, having given little thought to this, on the one hand admire what Hannibal achieved and on the other condemn what made his achievements possible.

That his other qualities would not have been enough by themselves can be proved by looking at Scipio, a man unique in his own time and through all recorded history. His armies mutinied against him in Spain, and the only reason for this was his excessive leniency, which allowed his soldiers more licence than was good for military discipline. Fabius Maximus reproached him for this in the Senate and called him a corrupter of the Roman legions. Again, when the Locri were plundered by one of Scipio's officers, he neither gave them satisfaction nor punished his officer's insubordination; and this was all because of his having too lenient a nature. By way of excuse for him some senators argued that many men were better at not making mistakes themselves than at correcting them in others. But in time Scipio's lenient nature would have spoilt his fame and glory had he continued to indulge it during his command; when he lived under orders from the Senate, however, this fatal characteristic of his was not only concealed but even brought him glory.

So, on this question of being loved or feared, I conclude that since some men love as they please but fear when the prince pleases, a wise prince should rely on what he controls, not on what he cannot control. He should only endeavour, as I said, to escape being hated.

XVIII. *How princes should honour their word*

Everyone realizes how praiseworthy it is for a prince to honour his word and to be straightforward rather than crafty in his dealings; nonetheless contemporary experience shows that princes who have achieved great things have been those who have given their word lightly, who have known how to trick men with their cunning, and who, in the end, have overcome those abiding by honest principles.

You should understand, therefore, that there are two ways of fighting: by law or by force. The first way is natural to men, and the second to beasts. But as the first way often proves inadequate one must needs have recourse to the second. So a prince must understand how to make a nice use of the beast and the man. The ancient writers taught princes about this by an allegory, when they described how Achilles and many other princes of the ancient world were sent to be brought up by Chiron, the centaur, so that he might train them his way. All the allegory means, in making the teacher half beast and half man, is that a prince must know how to act according to the nature of both, and that he cannot survive otherwise.

So, as a prince is forced to know how to act like a beast, he should learn from the fox and the lion: because the lion is defenceless against traps and a fox is defenceless against wolves. Therefore one must be a fox in order to recognize traps, and a lion to frighten off wolves. Those who simply act like lions are stupid. So it follows that a prudent ruler cannot, and should not, honour his word when it places him at a disadvantage and when the reasons for which he made his promise no longer exist. If all men were good, this precept would not be good; but because men are wretched creatures who would not keep their word to you, you need not keep your word to them. And a prince will never lack good excuses to colour his bad faith. One could give innumerable modern instances of this, showing how many pacts and promises have been made null and void by the bad faith of princes: those who have known best how to imitate the fox have come off best. But one must know how to colour one's actions and to be a great liar and deceiver. Men are so simple, and so much creatures of circumstance, that the deceiver will always find someone ready to be deceived.

There is one fresh example I do not want to omit. Alexander VI was always, and he thought only of, deceiving people; and he always found victims for his deceptions. There never was a man capable of such convincing asseverations, or so ready to swear to the truth of something, who would honour his word less. Nonetheless his deceptions always had the result he intended, because he was a past master in the art.

A prince, therefore, need not necessarily have all the good qualities I mentioned above, but he should certainly appear to have them. I would even go so far as to say that if he has these qualities and always behaves accordingly he will find them ruinous; if he only appears to have them they will render him service. He should appear to be compassionate, faithful to his word, guileless, and devout. And indeed he should be so. But his disposition should be such that, if he needs to be the opposite, he knows how. You must realize this: that a prince, and especially a new prince, cannot observe all those things which give men a reputation for virtue, because in order to maintain his state he is often forced to act in defiance of good faith, of charity, of kindness, of religion. And so he should have a flexible disposition, varying as fortune and circumstances dictate. As I said above, he should not deviate from what is good, if that is possible, but he should know how to do evil, if that is necessary.

Castiglione, The Book of the Courtier

At the opposite end of the political and literary spectrum from Machiavelli's *The Prince* is Baldassare Castiglione's *The Book of the Courtier* (1528), which is a gracefully written tribute to Renaissance idealism and to the ideal of the "universal man." Castiglione (1428–1529) had served as soldier and diplomat for many years before attempting to write this book. He was able to draw on his own experiences at the court of Guidobaldo Da Montefeltro, Duke of Urbino, in his account of court etiquette. Written in the form of a pseudo-Platonic dialogue, *The Courtier* introduces us to some remarkable, real-life personalities whom Castiglione had met at the ducal court, noblemen like Pietro Bembo (a secretary to Pope Leo X, and later a Cardinal) and Giuliano De' Medici (of the famous Medici family). Castiglione sets Pietro, Giuliano, and their friends, in four successive evenings in March of 1507, to talking and debating over topics ranging from the nature of love and true friendship to the status of women in a male-dominated society, but the focus of nearly all of these conversations is the concept of the perfect courtier.

As Castiglione admitted, his ideal courtier was no less imaginary than Plato's philosopher-king. He was a composite of every conceivable virtue an aristocratic audience is likely to admire. Castiglione insists that his courtier possess not only physical courage and martial prowess—the essential skills of any warrior—but also personal beauty and humility, a wide knowledge and appreciation of the arts, and an instinctive sense of decorum and self-composure. Most important, the courtier must possess fortitude and moral insight if he is to understand the nature of the soul and its longing to ascend beyond this imperfect world of material things and impure desires. For Castiglione, the Renaissance knight becomes a virtual mystic, following the precepts of a newly revived Neoplatonist philosophy in his quest for spiritual perfection, ultimately rising (as Pietro Bembo imagines it) from the love of earthly beauty to the love of God.

THE BOOK OF THE COURTIER
■

Bembo [explained]: 'I say, therefore, that as defined by the philosophers of the ancient world Love is simply a certain longing to possess beauty; and since this longing can only be of things that are known already, knowledge must always of necessity precede desire, which by its nature wishes for what is good, but of itself is blind and so cannot perceive what is good. So Nature has ruled that every appetitive faculty, or desire, be accompanied by a cognitive faculty or power of understanding. Now in the human soul there are three faculties by which we understand or perceive things: namely, the senses, rational thought and intellect. Thus the senses desire things through sensual appetite or the kind of appetite which we share with the animals; reason desires things through rational choice, which is, strictly speaking, proper to man; and intellect, which links man to the angels, desires things through pure will. It follows that the sensual appetite desires only those things that are perceptible by the senses, whereas man's will finds its satisfaction in the contemplation of spiritual things that can be apprehended by intellect. And then man, who is rational by his very nature and is placed between the two extremes of brute matter and pure spirit, can choose to follow the senses or to aspire to the intellect, and so can direct his appetites or desires now in the one direction, now in the other. In either of these two ways, therefore, he can long for beauty, which is the quality possessed by all natural or artificial things that are composed in the good proportion and due measure that befit their nature.

'However, I shall speak of the kind of beauty I now have in mind, which is that seen in the human body and especially the face and which prompts the ardent desire we call love; and we shall argue that this beauty is an influx of the divine goodness which, like the light of the sun, is shed over all created things but especially displays itself in all its beauty when it discovers and informs a countenance which is well proportioned and composed of a certain joyous harmony of various colours enhanced by light and shadow and by symmetry and clear definition. This goodness adorns and illumines with wonderful splendour and grace the object in which it shines, like a sunbeam striking a lovely vase of polished gold set with precious gems. And thus it attracts to itself the gaze of others, and entering through their eyes it impresses itself upon the human passion and desire. Thus the mind is seized by desire for the beauty which it recognizes as good, and, if it allows itself to be guided by what its senses tell it, it falls into the gravest errors and judges that the body is the chief cause of the beauty which it enshrines, and so to enjoy that beauty it must necessarily achieve with it as intimate a union as possible. But this is untrue; and anyone who thinks to enjoy that beauty by possessing the body is deceiving himself and is moved not by true knowledge, arrived at by rational choice, but by a false opinion derived from the desire of the senses. So the pleasure that follows is also necessarily false and deceptive. Consequently, all those lovers who satisfy their impure desires with the women they love meet with one of two evils: either as soon as they achieve the end they desire they experience satiety and distaste and even begin to hate what they love, as if their desire repented of its error and recognized the way it had been deceived by the false judgement of the senses, which had made it believe that evil was good; or else they are still troubled by the same avidity and desire, since they have not in fact attained the end they were seeking. Admittedly, confused by their short-sighted view of things, they imagine that they are experiencing pleasure, just as sometimes a sick man dreams that he is drinking from a clear fountain. Nevertheless, they enjoy neither rest nor satisfaction, and these are precisely what they would enjoy as the natural consequences of desiring and then possessing what is good. On the contrary, deceived by the resemblance they see, they soon experience unbridled desire once more and in the same agitation as before they again find themselves with a raging and unquenchable thirst for what they hope to possess utterly. Lovers of this kind, therefore, are always most unhappy; for either they never attain their desires, and this causes them great misery, or if they do attain them they find themselves in terrible distress, and their wretchedness is even greater. For both at the beginning and during the course of this love of theirs they never know other than anguish, torment, sorrow, exertion and distress; and so lovers, it is supposed, must always be characterized by paleness and dejection, continuous sighings and weepings, mournfulness and lamentations, silences and the desire for death.

'We see, therefore, that the senses are the chief cause of this desolation of the spirit; and they are at their full strength in youth, when they are stimulated by the urges of the flesh which sap a man's powers of reason in exact proportion to their own vigor and so easily persuade the soul to yield to desire. For since it is sunk in an earthly prison and deprived of spiritual contemplation, the soul cannot of itself clearly perceive the truth when it is carrying out its duties of governing the body. So in order to understand things properly it must appeal to the senses for its first notions. In consequence it believes whatever they tell it and respects and trusts them, especially when they are so vigorous that they almost compel it; and because the senses are deceptive they fill the soul with errors and mistaken ideas. As a result, young men are invariably absorbed by this sensual kind of love and wholly rebellious against reason, and so they make themselves unworthy of enjoying the blessings and advantages that love gives to its true devotees; and the only pleasures they experience in love are the same as those enjoyed by unreasoning animals, though the distress they suffer is far more terrible than theirs. Therefore on this premise, which I insist is the absolute truth, I argue that lovers who are more mature in age experience the contrary; for in their case the soul is no longer weighed down by the body and their natural ardour has begun to cool, and so if they are inflamed by beauty and their desire for it is guided by rational choice, they are not deceived and they possess completely the beauty they love. Consequently its possession brings them nothing but good, since beauty is goodness and so the true love of beauty is good and holy and always benefits those in whose souls the bridle of reason restrains the iniquity of the senses; and this is something the old can do far more easily than the young.

'So it is not unreasonable to argue also that the old can love blamelessly and more happily than the young, accepting that by old we do not mean those who are senile or whose bodily organs have grown so feeble that the soul cannot perform its operations through them, but men whose intellectual powers are still in their prime. I must also add this: namely, that in my opinion although sensual love is bad at every age, yet in the young it may be excused and perhaps in some sense even permitted. For although it brings them afflictions, dangers, exertions and all the unhappiness we have mentioned, yet there are many who perform worthy acts in order to win the favour of the women whom they love, and though these acts are not directed to a good end they are good in themselves. And so from all that bitterness they extract a little sweetness, and the adversities they endure finally teach them the error of their ways. So just as I think those young people who subdue their desires and love in a rational manner are truly heroic, I excuse those who allow themselves to be overcome by the sensual love to which human weakness inclines them, provided that they then display gentleness, courtesy, worthiness and all the other qualities these gentlemen mentioned, and that when they are no longer young they abandon it completely and leave sensual desire behind them, as the lowest rung of the ladder by which we can ascend to true love. But no blame is too severe for those who when they are old still allow the fires of passion to burn in their cold hearts and make strong reason obey their feeble senses; for they deserve the endless shame of being numbered like idiots among the animals which lack reason, because the thoughts and ways of sensual love are wholly unbecoming to men of mature years. . . .'

All were listening very attentively to what Bembo was saying; and then, after a moment's pause, he added:

'Since you have made me begin to teach the courtier who is no longer young about love that is truly happy, I want to lead him a little further still. For to stop at this point is very dangerous, because, as we have said several times already, the soul is strongly inclined towards the senses; and although reason may choose well in its operation and recognize that beauty does not arise from the body, and therefore act as a check to impure desires, yet the constant contemplation of physical beauty often perverts true judgement. And even if no other evil resulted from this, absence from the person one loves causes much suffering. This is because when beauty is physically present, its influx into the lover's soul brings him intense pleasure, and by warming his heart it arouses and melts certain hidden and congealed powers which the warmth of love nourishes and causes to flow and well up round his heart and send through his eyes those spirits or most subtle vapours, composed of the purest and brightest part of the blood, to receive the image of her beauty and embellish it with a thousand varied adornments. In consequence, the soul is filled with wonder and delight; it is frightened and yet it rejoices; as if dazed, it experiences along with its pleasure the fear and reverence invariably inspired by sacred things, and it believes it has entered into its Paradise.

'Therefore the lover who is intent only on physical beauty loses all this good and happiness as soon as the woman he loves by her absence leaves his eyes deprived of their splendor and, consequently, his soul widowed of its good. For, since her beauty is far away, there is no influx of affection to warm his heart as it did when she was there, and so the openings of his body become arid and dry; yet the memory of her beauty still stirs the powers of his soul a little, so that they seek to pour those spirits forth. Although their paths are blocked and there is no exit for them, they still strive to depart, and thus tormented and enclosed they begin to prick the soul and cause it to suffer bitterly, as children do when the teeth begin to grow through their tender gums. This causes the tears, the sighs, the anguish and the torments of lovers, because the soul is in constant pain and turmoil and almost raging in fury until its cherished beauty appears once more; and then suddenly it is calmed and breathes again, and wholly absorbed it draws strength from the delicious food before it and wishes never to part from such a ravishing vision. Therefore, to escape the torment caused by the absence and to enjoy beauty without suffering, with the help of reason the courtier should turn his desire completely away from the body to beauty alone. He should contemplate beauty as far as he is able in its own simplicity and purity, create it in his imagination as an abstraction distinct from any material form, and thus make it lovely and dear to his soul, and enjoy it there always, day and night and in every time and place, without fear of ever losing it; and he will always remember that the body is something altogether distinct from beauty, whose perfection it diminishes rather than enhances. In this way the courtier of ours who is no longer young will put himself out of reach of the anguish and distress invariably experienced by the young in the form of jealousy, suspicion, disdain, anger, despair and a certain tempestuous fury that occasionally leads them so much astray that some not only beat the women they love but take their own lives. He will do no injury to the husband, father, brothers or family of the lady he loves; he will cause her no shame; he will not be forced sometimes to drag his eyes away and curb his tongue for fear of revealing his desires to others; or to endure suffering when they part or during her absence. For he will always carry the treasure that is so precious to him safe in his heart; and by the power of his imagination he will also make her beauty far more lovely than it is in reality.

'However, among all these blessings the lover will find one that is far greater still, if he will determine to make use of this love as a step by which to climb to another that is far more sublime; and this will be possible if he continually reflects how narrowly he is confined by always limiting himself to the contemplation of a single body. And so in order to escape from this confinement, he will gradually add so many adornments to his idea of beauty that, by uniting all possible forms of beauty in his mind, he will form a universal concept and so reduce all the many varieties to the unity of that single beauty which sheds itself over human nature as a whole. And thus he will come to contemplate not the particular beauty of a single woman but the universal beauty which adorns all human bodies: and then, dazzled by this greater light, he will not concern himself with the lesser; burning with a more perfect flame, he will feel little esteem for what he formerly prized so greatly. Now this stage of love, although so noble that few attain it, still cannot be called perfect. For the human imagination is a corporeal faculty and acquires knowledge only through the data supplied to it by the senses, and so it is not wholly purged of the darkness of material things. Thus although it may consider this universal beauty in the abstract and simply in itself, yet it perceives it not at all clearly nor within a certain ambiguity because of the affinities that the images it forms have with the body itself; and so those who reach this stage of love are like fledglings which on their feeble wings can lift themselves a little in flight but dare not stray far from the nest or trust themselves to the winds and the open sky.

'Therefore when our courtier has arrived at this stage, even though he can be called most happy in comparison with those lovers who are still sunk in the miseries of sensual love, I wish him not to be satisfied but to move boldly onwards along the sublime path of love and follow his guide towards the goal of true happiness. So instead of directing his thoughts to the outward world, as those must do who wish to consider bodily beauty, let him turn within himself to contemplate what he sees with the eyes of the mind, which begin to be penetrating and clear-sighted once those of the body have lost the flower of their delight; and in this manner, having shed all evil, purged by the study of true philosophy, directed towards the life of the spirit, and practised in the things of the intellect, the soul turns to contemplate its own substance, and as if awakened from deepest sleep it opens the eyes which all men possess but few use and perceives in itself a ray of that light which is the true image of the angelic beauty that has been transmitted to it, and of which in turn it transmits a faint impression to the body. Thus, when it has become blind to earthly things, the soul opens its eyes wide to those of heaven; and sometimes when the faculties of the body are totally absorbed by assiduous contemplation, or bound to sleep, no longer hindered by their influence the soul tastes a certain hidden savour of the true angelic beauty, and ravished by the loveliness of that light it begins to burn and to pursue the beauty it sees so avidly that it seems almost drunk and beside itself in its desire to unite with it. For the soul then believes that it has discovered the traces of God, in the contemplation of which it seeks its final repose and bliss. And so, consumed in this most joyous flame, it ascends to its noblest part, which is the intellect; and there no more overshadowed by the dark night of earthly things, it glimpses the divine beauty itself. Even so, it does not yet enjoy this perfectly, since it contemplates it only in its own particular intellect, which cannot comprehend universal beauty in all its immensity. And so, not even satisfied with bestowing this blessing, love gives the soul greater happiness still. For just as from the particular beauty of a single body it guides the soul to the universal beauty of all bodies, so, in the last stage of perfection, it guides the soul from the particular intellect to the universal intellect. And from there, aflame with the sacred fire of true divine love, the soul flies to unite itself with the angelic nature, and it not only abandons the senses but no longer has need of reason itself. For, transformed into an angel, it understands all intelligible things and without any veil or cloud it gazes on the wide sea of pure divine beauty, which it receives into itself to enjoy the supreme happiness the senses cannot comprehend.'

William Shakespeare, The Tempest

England's most celebrated playwright, William Shakespeare (1564–1616) excelled in tragedy and comedy, creating profoundly serious dramas, such as *Hamlet, Macbeth,* and *King Lear,* as well as light-hearted romps, such as *A Midsummer Night's Dream* and *The Merry Wives of Windsor.* One of his last and most imaginative works, *The Tempest* (c. 1611) skillfully combines tragic and comic elements to create one of the most delightful romances ever written for the stage.

Prospero, the main character, is a magician, a master of illusion and enchantment. With his young daughter, Miranda, he lives on a desert island that the witch Sycorax, now dead, had placed under a spell. Prospero controls two strange creatures, the brutish and treacherous Caliban, Sycorax's son, and the boyish spirit Ariel, whom he liberates from a pine tree in which Sycorax had imprisoned him. Representing two different aspects of human nature, bestial appetite and undisciplined will, Caliban and Ariel reluctantly submit to Prospero's rational authority.

After Prospero raises a storm to destroy their passing ship, his brother Antonio, Prince Ferdinand, and the King of Naples are marooned on the island. We learn that Prospero is the rightful Duke of Milan whom Antonio, aided by the King of Naples, had driven from his throne and left adrift at sea in a small boat, which eventually carried him and Miranda to their enchanted island. After many years, fate at last brings Prospero's enemies into his power. Shakespeare uses this fantastic situation to explore the character of a political leader who, like Prospero, must deal with his associates' treacherous ambition. The ruler, weighing questions of justice and mercy, must decide whether his enemies deserve punishment or clemency. Miranda, who can remember seeing no other human beings except her father, marvels at the physical splendor of her shipwrecked visitors. Prospero, experienced in others' perfidy, is not so easily beguiled. His daughter's growing love for the noble Ferdinand, son of the Neapolitan king, foreshadows Prospero's decision and the peaceful reconciliation that ends the play.

Although *The Tempest* may lack dramatic conflict, it contains some of Shakespeare's finest poetry. In Act IV, Prospero creates a gloriously imaginative world, complete with castles and temples, that delights onlookers before he banishes the mirage. Preparing to reenter the real world of governmental responsibility in Milan, he then breaks his scepter, renouncing his magical powers. Some commentators have interpreted this passage as Shakespeare's personal farewell to his theatrical art, but more significantly it reflects his awareness of the painful choice between private dream and public duty.

THE TEMPEST

■

DRAMATIS PERSONAE

ALONSO, King of Naples.
SEBASTIAN, his brother.

PROSPERO, the right Duke of Milan.
ANTONIO, his brother, the usurping
    Duke of Milan.

FERDINAND, son to the King of Naples.
GONZALO, an honest old Counsellor.
ADRIAN,
FRANCISCO, } Lords.
CALIBAN, a savage and deformed Slave.
TRINCULO, a jester.
STEPHANO, a drunken Butler.
MASTER of a Ship.
BOATSWAIN.

MARINERS.
MIRANDA, daughter to Prospero.
ARIEL, an airy Spirit.
IRIS,
CERES,
JUNO, } presented by Spirits
NYMPHS,
REAPERS,
Other Spirits attending on Prospero

SCENE   *A ship at Sea: an island.*

ACT I.

Scene I.   *On a ship at sea: a tempestuous noise of thunder and lightning heard.*
                                Enter a Ship-Master and a Boatswain.

MAST. Boatswain!

BOATS. Here, master: what cheer?

MAST. Good, speak to the mariners: fall to't, yarely,
or we run ourselves aground: bestir, bestir.

                                                [Exit.
                                Enter Mariners.

BOATS. Heigh, my hearts! Cheerly, cheerly, my
hearts! yare, yare! Take in the topsail! Tend to the
master's whistle. Blow till thou burst thy wind, if
room enough!
        *Enter ALONSO, SEBASTIAN, ANTONIO, FERDINAND, GONZALO, and
                                        others.*

ALON. Good boatswain, have care. Where's the master? Play the men.   *11*

BOATS. I pray now, keep below.

ANT. Where is the master, boatswain?

BOATS. Do you not hear him? You mar our labour:
keep your cabins: you do assist the storm.

GON. Nay, good, be patient.

BOATS. When the sea is. Hence! What cares these
roarers for the name of king? To cabin: silence!
trouble us not.

GON. Good, yet remember whom thou hast aboard.

BOATS. None that I more love than myself. You are a
counsellor; if you can command these elements to

silence, and work the peace of the present, we will not
hand a rope more; use your authority; if you cannot,
give thanks you have lived so long, and make yourself
ready in your cabin for the mischance of the hour, if
it so hap. Cheerly, good hearts! Out of our way, I
say.

[Exit.   29

GON. I have great comfort from this fellow: methinks he hath no drowning mark upon him; his
complexion is perfect gallows. Stand fast, good Fate,
to his hanging: make the rope of his destiny our cable,
for our own doth little advantage. If he be not born
to be hanged, our case is miserable.

36

[Exeunt.
Re-enter Boatswain.

BOATS. Down with the topmast! yare! lower, lower!
Bring her to try with main-course. *[A cry within.]* A
plague upon this howling! they are louder than the
weather or our office.

Re-enter SEBASTIAN, ANTONIO, and GONZALO.

Yet again! what do you here? Shall we give o'er and
drown? Have you a mind to sink?

SEB. A pox o' your throat, you bawling, blas-
phemous, incharitable dog!

BOATS. Work you then.

ANT. Hang, cur! hang, you whoreson, insolent
noisemaker! We are less afraid to be drowned than
thou art.

GON. I'll warrant him for drowning; though the
ship were no stronger than a nutshell and as leaky as
an unstanched wench.

51

BOATS. Lay her a-hold, a-hold! set her two courses off to
sea again; lay her off.

Enter Mariners wet.

MARINERS. All lost! to prayers, to prayers! all lost!

BOATS. What, must our mouths be cold?

GON. The king and prince at prayers! let's assist them,
For our case is as theirs.

SEB.   I'm out of patience.

ANT. We are merely cheated of our lives by drunkards:
This wide-chapp'd rascal—would thou mightst lie drowning
The washing of ten tides!

GON.   He'll be hang'd yet,   *61*
Though every drop of water swear against it
And gape at widest to glut him.
[*A confused noise within:* 'Mercy on us!'—
'We split, we split!'— 'Farewell my wife and children!'—
'Farewell, brother!'—'We split, we split, we split!']

ANT. Let 's all sink with the king.

SEB. Let 's take leave of him.

[Exeunt Ant. and Seb.

GON. Now would I give a thousand furlongs of sea
for an acre of barren ground, long heath, brown furze,
any thing. The wills above be done! but I would fain
die a dry death.

[Exeunt.

SCENE II.   *The island. Before PROSPERO'S cell.*

Enter PROSPERO and MIRANDA.

MIR. If by your art, my dearest father, you have
Put the wild waters in this roar, allay them.
The sky, it seems, would pour down stinking pitch,
But that the sea, mounting to the welkin's cheek,
Dashes the fire out. O, I have suffer'd
With those that I saw suffer: a brave vessel,
Who had, no doubt, some noble creature in her,
Dash'd all to pieces. O, the cry did knock
Against my very heart. Poor souls, they perish'd.
Had I been any god of power, I would   *10*
Have sunk the sea within the earth or ere
It should the good ship so have swallow'd and
The fraughting souls within her.

PROS.   Be collected:
No more amazement: tell your piteous heart
There's no harm done.

    MIR.   O, woe the day!

PROS.   No harm.
I have done nothing but in care of thee,
Of thee, my dear one, thee, my daughter, who
Art ignorant of what thou art, nought knowing
Of whence I am, nor that I am more better

Than Prospero, master of a full poor cell,   *20*
    And thy no greater father.

  MIR.   More to know
Did never meddle with my thoughts.

  PROS.   'Tis time
I should inform thee farther. Lend thy hand,
And pluck my magic garment from me. So:

                                [Lays down his mantle.

Lie there, my art. Wipe thou thine eyes; have comfort.
The direful spectacle of the wreck, which touch'd
The very virtue of compassion in thee,
I have with such provision in mine art
So safely ordered that there is no soul—
No, not so much perdition as an hair
Betid to any creature in the vessel   *30*
Which thou heard'st cry, which thou saw'st sink. Sit down;
For thou must now know farther.

  MIR.   You have often
Begun to tell me what I am, but stopp'd
And left me to a bootless inquisition,
Concluding 'Stay: not yet.'

  PROS.   The hour's now come;
The very minute bids thee ope thine ear;
Obey and be attentive. Canst thou remember
A time before we came unto this cell?
I do not think thou canst, for then thou wast not   *40*
Out three years old.

  MIR.   Certainly, sir, I can.

  PROS. By what? by any other house or person?
Of any thing the image tell me that
Hath kept with thy remembrance.

  MIR.   'Tis far off
And rather like a dream than an assurance
That my remembrance warrants. Had I not
Four or five women once that tended me?

  PROS. Thou hadst, and more, Miranda. But how is it
That this lives in thy mind? What seest thou else
In the dark backward and abysm of time?   *50*
If thou remember'st aught ere thou camest here,
How thou camest here thou mayst.

  MIR.   But that I do not.

PROS. Twelve year since, Miranda, twelve year since,
Thy father was the Duke of Milan and
A prince of power.

MIR.　　　　Sir, are not you my father?

PROS. Thy mother was a piece of virtue, and
She said thou wast my daughter; and thy father
Was Duke of Milan; and thou his only heir
And princess no worse issued.

MIR.　　　　O the heavens!
What foul play had we, that we came from thence?　　　　60
Or blessed was't we did?

PROS.　　　　Both, both, my girl:
By foul play, as thou say'st, were we heaved thence,
But blessedly holp hither.

MIR.　　　　O, my heart bleeds
To think o' the teen that I have turn'd you to,
Which is from my remembrance! Please you, farther.

PROS. My brother and thy uncle, call'd Antonio—
I pray thee, mark me—that a brother should
Be so perfidious!—he whom next thyself
Of all the world I loved and to him put
The manage of my state; as at that time　　　　70
Through all the signories it was the first
And Prospero the prime duke, being so reputed
In dignity, and for the liberal arts
Without a parallel; those being all my study,
The government I cast upon my brother
And to my state grew stranger, being transported
And rapt in secret studies. Thy false uncle—
Dost thou attend me?

MIR.　　　　Sir, most heedfully.

PROS. Being once perfected how to grant suits,
How to deny them, who to advance and who　　　　80
To trash for over-topping, new created
The creatures that were mine, I say, or changed 'em,
Or else new form'd 'em; having both the key
Of officer and office, set all hearts i' the state
To what tune pleased his ear; that now he was
The ivy which had hid my princely trunk,
And suck'd my verdure out on 't. Thou attend'st not.

MIR. O, good sir, I do.

PROS. I pray thee, mark me.
I, thus neglecting worldly ends, all dedicated
To closeness and the bettering of my mind   90
With that which, but by being so retired,
O'er-prized all popular rate, in my false brother
Awaked an evil nature; and my trust,
Like a good parent, did beget of him
A falsehood in its contrary as great
As my trust was; which had indeed no limit,
A confidence sans bound. He being thus lorded,
Not only with what my revenue yielded,
But what my power might else exact, like one
Who having into truth, by telling of it,   100
Made such a sinner of his memory,
To credit his own lie, he did believe
He was indeed the duke; out o' the substitution,
And executing the outward face of royalty,
With all prerogative: hence his ambition growing—
Dost thou hear?

MIR. Your tale, sir, would cure deafness.

PROS. To have no screen between this part he play'd
And him he play'd it for, he needs will be
Absolute Milan. Me, poor man, my library
Was dukedom large enough: of temporal royalties   110
He thinks me now incapable; confederates—
So dry he was for sway—wi' the King of Naples
To give him annual tribute, do him homage,
Subject his coronet to his crown and bend
The dukedom yet unbow'd—alas, poor Milan!—
To most ignoble stooping.

MIR. O the heavens!

PROS. Mark his condition and the event; then tell me
If this be a brother.

MIR. I should sin
To think but nobly of my grandmother:
Good wombs have borne bad sons.

PROS. Now the condition.   120
This King of Naples, being an enemy
To me inveterate, hearkens my brother's suit;
Which was, that he, in lieu o' the premises
Of homage and I know not how much tribute,
Should presently extirpate me and mine

Out of the dukedom and confer fair Milan
With all the honours on my brother: whereon,
A treacherous army levied, one midnight
Fated to the purpose did Antonio open
The gates of Milan, and, i' the dead of darkness,   130
The ministers for the purpose hurried thence
Me and thy crying self.

MIR.   Alack, for pity!
I, not remembering how I cried out then,
Will cry it o'er again: it is a hint
That wrings mine eyes to 't.

PROS.   Hear a little further
And then I'll bring thee to the present business
Which now 's upon 's; without the which this story
Were most impertinent.

MIR.   Wherefore did they not
That hour destroy us?

PROS.   Well demanded, wench:
My tale provokes that question. Dear, they durst not,   140
So dear the love my people bore me, nor set
A mark so bloody on the business, but
With colours fairer painted their foul ends.
In few, they hurried us aboard a bark,
Bore us some leagues to sea; where they prepared
A rotten carcass of a boat, not rigg'd,
Nor tackle, sail, nor mast; the very rats
Instinctively have quit it: there they hoist us,
To cry to the sea that roar'd to us, to sigh
To the winds whose pity, sighing back again,   150
Did us but loving wrong.

MIR.   Alack, what trouble
Was I then to you!

PROS.   O, a cherubin
Thou wast that did preserve me. Thou didst smile,
Infused with a fortitude from heaven,
When I have deck'd the sea with drops full salt,
Under my burthen groan'd; which raised in me
An undergoing stomach, to bear up
Against what should ensue.

MIR.   How came we ashore?

PROS. By Providence divine.
Some food we had and some fresh water that   160

A noble Neapolitan, Gonzalo,
Out of his charity, who being then appointed
Master of this design, did give us, with
Rich garments, linens, stuffs and necessaries,
Which since have steaded much; so, of his gentleness,
Knowing I loved my books, he furnish'd me
From mine own library with volumes that
I prize above my dukedom.

MIR.   Would I might
But ever see that man!

PROS.   Now I arise:

[Resumes his mantle.   170

Sit still, and hear the last of our sea-sorrow.
Here in this island we arrived; and here
Have I, thy schoolmaster, made thee more profit
Than other princesses can that have more time
For vainer hours and tutors not so careful.

MIR. Heavens thank you for 't! And now, I pray you, sir,
For still 'tis beating in my mind, your reason
For raising this sea-storm?

PROS.   Know thus far forth.
By accident most strange, bountiful Fortune,
Now my dear lady, hath mine enemies
Brought to this shore; and by my prescience   180
I find my zenith doth depend upon
A most auspicious star, whose influence
If now I court not but omit, my fortunes
Will ever after droop. Here cease more questions:
Thou art inclined to sleep; 'tis a good dulness,
And give it way: I know thou canst not choose.

[Miranda sleeps.

Come away, servant, come. I am ready now.
Approach, my Ariel, come.

Enter ARIEL.

ARI. All hail, great master! grave sir, hail! I come
To answer thy best pleasure; be 't to fly,   190
To swim, to dive into the fire, to ride
On the curl'd clouds, to thy strong bidding task
Ariel and all his quality.

PROS.   Hast thou, spirit,
Perform'd to point the tempest that I bade thee?

ARI. To every article.
I boarded the king's ship; now on the beak,
Now in the waist, the deck, in every cabin,
I flamed amazement: sometime I'ld divide,
And burn in many places; on the topmast,
The yards and bowsprit, would I flame distinctly,   200
Then meet and join. Jove's lightnings, the precursors
O' the dreadful thunder-claps, more momentary
And sight-outrunning were not; the fire and cracks
Of sulphurous roaring the most mighty Neptune
Seem to besiege and make his bold waves tremble,
Yea, his dread trident shake.

PROS.   My brave spirit!
Who was so firm, so constant, that this coil
Would not infect his reason?

ARI.   Not a soul
But felt a fever of the mad and play'd
Some tricks of desperation. All but mariners   210
Plunged in the foaming brine and quit the vessel,
Then all afire with me: the king's son, Ferdinand,
With hair up-staring,—then like reeds, not hair,—
Was the first man that leap'd; cried, 'Hell is empty,
And all the devils are here.'

PROS.   Why, that's my spirit!
But was not this nigh shore?

ARI.   Close by, my master.

PROS.   But are they, Ariel, safe?

ARI.   Not a hair perish'd;
On their sustaining garments not a blemish,
But fresher than before: and, as thou badest me,
In troops I have dispersed them 'bout the isle.   220
The king's son have I landed by himself;
Whom I left cooling of the air with sighs
In an odd angle of the isle and sitting,
His arms in this sad knot.

PROS.   Of the king's ship
The mariners say how thou hast disposed
And all the rest o' the fleet.

ARI.   Safely in harbour
Is the king's ship; in the deep nook, where once
Thou call'dst me up at midnight to fetch dew
From the still-vexed Bermoothes, there she's hid:

The mariners all under hatches stow'd;   *230*
Who, with a charm join'd to their suffer'd labour,
I have left asleep: and for the rest o' the fleet
Which I dispersed, they all have met again
And are upon the Mediterranean flote
Bound sadly home for Naples,
Supposing that they saw the king's ship wreck'd
And his great person perish.

PROS.   Ariel, thy charge
Exactly is perform'd: but there's more work.
What is the time o' the day?

ARI.   Past the mid season.

PROS. At least two glasses. The time 'twixt six and now   *240*
Must by us both be spent most preciously.

ARI. Is there more toil? Since thou dost give me pains,
Let me remember thee what thou hast promised,
Which is not yet perform'd me.

PROS.   How now? moody?
What is 't thou canst demand?

ARI.   My liberty.

PROS.   Before the time be out? no more!

ARI.   I prithee,
Remember I have done thee worthy service;
Told thee no lies, made thee no mistakings, served
Without or grudge or grumblings: thou didst promise
To bate me a full year.

PROS.   Dost thou forget   *250*
From what a torment I did free thee?

ARI.   No.

PROS. Thou dost, and think'st it much to tread the ooze
Of the salt deep,
To run upon the sharp wind of the north,
To do me business in the veins o' the earth
When it is baked with frost.

ARI.   I do not, sir.

321
▪

PROS. Thou liest, malignant thing! Hast thou forgot
The foul witch Sycorax, who with age and envy
Was grown into a hoop? hast thou forgot her?

ARI. No, sir.

PROS.   Thou hast. Where was she born? speak; tell me.   *260*

ARI. Sir, in Argier.

PROS.   O, was she so? I must
Once in a month recount what thou hast been,
Which thou forget'st. This damn'd witch Sycorax,
For mischiefs manifold and sorceries terrible
To enter human hearing, from Argier,
Thou know'st, was banish'd: for one thing she did
They would not take her life. Is not this true?

ARI. Ay, sir.

PROS. This blue-eyed hag was hither brought with child
And here was left by the sailors. Thou, my slave,   *270*
As thou report'st thyself, wast then her servant;
And, for thou wast a spirit too delicate
To act her earthy and abhorr'd commands,
Refusing her grand hests, she did confine thee,
By help of her more potent ministers
And in her most unmitigable rage,
Into a cloven pine; within which rift
Imprison'd thou didst painfully remain
A dozen years; within which space she died
And left thee there; where thou did'st vent thy groans   *280*
As fast as mill-wheels strike. Then was this island—
Save for the son that she did litter here,
A freckled whelp hag-born—not honour'd with
A human shape.

ARI.   Yes, Caliban her son.

PROS. Dull thing, I say so; he, that Caliban
Whom now I keep in service. Thou best know'st
What torment I did find thee in; thy groans
Did make wolves howl and penetrate the breasts
Of ever angry bears: it was a torment
To lay upon the damn'd, which Sycorax   *290*
Could not again undo: it was mine art,
When I arrived and heard thee, that made gape
The pine and let thee out.

ARI.   I thank thee, master.

PROS. If thou more murmur'st, I will rend an oak
And peg thee in his knotty entrails till
Thou hast howl'd away twelve winters.

ARI.   Pardon, master;
I will be correspondent to command
And do my spiriting gently.

PROS.   Do so, and after two days
I will discharge thee.

ARI.   That's my noble master!
What shall I do? say what; what shall I do?   *300*

PROS. Go make thyself like a nymph o' the sea: be subject
To no sight but thine and mine, invisible
To every eyeball else. Go take this shape
And hither come in 't: go, hence with diligence!

                                        [Exit Ariel.

Awake, dear heart, awake! thou hast slept well;
Awake!

MIR.   The strangeness of your story put
Heaviness in me.

PROS.   Shake it off. Come on;
We'll visit Caliban my slave, who never
Yields us kind answer.

MIR.   'Tis a villain, sir,
I do not love to look on.

PROS.   But, as 'tis,   *310*
We cannot miss him: he does make our fire,
Fetch in our wood and serves in offices
That profit us. What, ho! slave! Caliban!
Thou earth, thou! speak.

CAL.   *[Within]* There's wood enough within.

PROS. Come forth, I say! there's other business for thee:
Come, thou tortoise! when?
                        Re-enter ARIEL like a water-nymph.

Fine apparition! My quaint Ariel,
Hark in thine ear.

ARI.   My lord, it shall be done.
                                        [Exit.

PROS. Thou poisonous slave, got by the devil himself
Upon thy wicked dam, come forth!   *320*

Enter CALIBAN.

CAL. As wicked dew as e'er my mother brush'd
With raven's feather from unwholesome fen
Drop on you both! a south-west blow on ye
And blister you all o'er!

PROS. For this, be sure, to-night thou shalt have cramps,
Side-stitches that shall pen thy breath up; urchins
Shall, for that vast of night that they may work,
All exercise on thee; thou shalt be pinch'd
As thick as honeycomb, each pinch more stinging
Than bees that made 'em.

CAL.   I must eat my dinner.   *330*
This island's mine, by Sycorax my mother,
Which thou takest from me. When thou camest first,
Thou strokedst me and madest much of me, wouldst give me
Water with berries in 't, and teach me how
To name the bigger light, and how the less,
That burn by day and night: and then I loved thee
And show'd thee all the qualities o' the isle,
The fresh springs, brine-pits, barren place and fertile:
Cursed be I that did so! All the charms
Of Sycorax, toads, beetles, bats, light on you!   *340*
For I am all the subjects that you have,
Which first was mine own king: and here you sty me
In this hard rock, whiles you do keep from me
The rest o' the island.

PROS.   Thou most lying slave,
Whom stripes may move, not kindness! I have used thee,
Filth as thou art, with human care, and lodged thee
In mine own cell, till thou didst seek to violate
The honour of my child.

CAL. O ho, O ho! would 't had been done!
Thou didst prevent me; I had peopled else   *350*
This isle with Calibans.

PROS.   Abhorred slave,
Which any print of goodness wilt not take,
Being capable of all ill! I pitied thee,
Took pains to make thee speak, taught thee each hour
One thing or other: when thou didst not, savage,
Know thine own meaning, but wouldst gabble like
A thing most brutish, I endow'd thy purposes
With words that made them known. But thy vile race,

Though thou didst learn, had that in 't which good natures
Could not abide to be with; therefore wast thou   *360*
Deservedly confined into this rock,
Who hadst deserved more than a prison.

CAL. You taught me language; and my profit on 't
Is, I know how to curse. The red plague rid you
For learning me your language!

PROS.   Hag-seed, hence!
Fetch us in fuel; and be quick, thou 'rt best,
To answer other business. Shrug'st thou, malice?
If thou neglect'st or dost unwillingly
What I command, I'll rack thee with old cramps,
Fill all thy bones with aches, make thee roar   *370*
That beasts shall tremble at thy din.

CAL.   No, pray thee.
[Aside] I must obey: his art is of such power,
It would control my dam's god, Setebos,
And make a vassal of him.

PROS.   So, slave; hence!

> *[Exit Caliban.*
> *Re-enter ARIEL, invisible, playing and singing;*
> *FERDINAND following.*
> *ARIEL'S song.*

Come unto these yellow sands,
    And then take hands:
Courtsied when you have and kiss'd
    The wild waves whist,
Foot it featly here and there;   *380*
    And, sweet sprites, the burthen bear.
Burthen [dispersedly]. Hark, hark!
    Bow-wow.
The watch-dogs bark:
    Bow-wow.

ARI. Hark, hark! I hear
    The strain of strutting chanticleer
    Cry, Cock-a-diddle-dow.

FER. Where should this music be? i' the air or the earth?
It sounds no more: and, sure, it waits upon
Some god o' the island. Sitting on a bank,
Weeping again the king my father's wreck,   *390*
This music crept by me upon the waters,
Allaying both their fury and my passion

With its sweet air: thence I have follow'd it,
Or it hath drawn me rather. But 'tis gone.
No, it begins again.

ARIEL *sings*.

    Full fathom five thy father lies;
        Of his bones are coral made;
    Those are pearls that were his eyes:
        Nothing of him that doth fade
    But doth suffer a sea-change   *400*
    Into something rich and strange.
    Sea-nymphs hourly ring his knell:

Burthen. Ding-dong.

ARI. Hark! now I hear them,—Ding-dong, bell.

FER. The ditty does remember my drown'd father.
This is no mortal business, nor no sound
That the earth owes. I hear it now above me.

PROS. The fringed curtains of thine eye advance
And say what thou seest yond.

MIR.   What is 't? a spirit?
Lord, how it looks about! Believe me, sir,   *410*
It carries a brave form. But 'tis a spirit.

PROS. No, wench; it eats and sleeps and hath such senses
As we have, such. This gallant which thou seest
Was in the wreck; and, but he's something stain'd
With grief that 's beauty's canker, thou mightst call him
A goodly person: he hath lost his fellows
And strays about to find 'em.

MIR.   I might call him
A thing divine, for nothing natural
I ever saw so noble.

PROS.   *[Aside]* It goes on, I see
As my soul prompts it. Spirit, fine spirit! I'll free thee   *420*
Within two days for this.

FER.   Most sure, the goddess
On whom these airs attend! Vouchsafe my prayer
May know if you remain upon this island;
And that you will some good instruction give
How I may bear me here: my prime request,
Which I do last pronounce, is, O you wonder!
If you be maid or no?

MIR.   No wonder, sir;
But certainly a maid.

FER.   My language! heavens!
I am the best of them that speak this speech,
Were I but where 'tis spoken.

PROS.   How? the best?   *430*
What wert thou, if the King of Naples heard thee?

FER. A single thing, as I am now, that wonders
To hear thee speak of Naples. He does hear me;
And that he does I weep: myself am Naples,
Who with mine eyes, never since at ebb, beheld
The king my father wreck'd

MIR.   Alack, for mercy!

FER. Yes, faith, and all his lords; the Duke of Milan
And his brave son being twain.

PROS.   *[Aside]* The Duke of Milan
And his more braver daughter could control thee,
If now 'twere fit to do 't. At the first sight   *440*
They have changed eyes. Delicate Ariel,
I'll set thee free for this. *[To Fer.]* A word, good sir;
I fear you have done yourself some wrong: a word.

MIR. Why speaks my father so ungently? This
Is the third man that e'er I saw, the first
That e'er I sigh'd for: pity move my father
To be inclined my way!

FER.   O, if a virgin,
And your affection not gone forth, I'll make you
The queen of Naples.

PROS.   Soft sir! one word more.
[Aside] They are both in either's powers; but this swift business   *450*
I must uneasy make, lest too light winning
Make the prize light. *[To Fer.]* One word more; I charge thee
That thou attend me: thou dost here usurp
The name thou owest not; and hast put thyself
Upon this island as a spy, to win it
From me, the lord on 't.

FER.   No, as I am a man.

MIR. There's nothing ill can dwell in such a temple:
If the ill spirit have so fair a house,
Good things will strive to dwell with 't.

PROS.   Follow me.   460
Speak not you for him; he 's a traitor. Come;
I'll manacle thy neck and feet together:
Sea-water shalt thou drink; thy food shall be
The fresh-brook mussels, wither'd roots and husks
Wherein the acorn cradled. Follow.

FER.   No;
I will resist such entertainment till
Mine enemy has more power.

[Draws, and is charmed from moving.

MIR.   O dear father,
Make not too rash a trial of him, for
He 's gentle and not fearful.

PROS.   What? I say,
My foot my tutor? Put thy sword up, traitor;
Who makest a show but darest not strike, thy conscience   470
Is so possess'd with guilt: come from thy ward,
For I can here disarm thee with this stick
And make thy weapon drop.

MIR.   Beseech you, father.

PROS. Hence! hang not on my garments.

MIR.   Sir, have pity;
I'll be his surety.

PROS.   Silence! one word more
Shall make me chide thee, if not hate thee. What!
An advocate for an impostor! hush!
Thou think'st there is no more such shapes as he,
Having seen but him and Caliban: foolish wench!
To the most of men this is a Caliban   480
And they to him are angels.

MIR.   My affections
Are then most humble; I have no ambition
To see a goodlier man.

PROS.   Come on; obey:
Thy nerves are in their infancy again
And have no vigour in them.

FER.   So thy are;
My spirits as in a dream, are all bound up.
My father's loss, the weakness which I feel,
The wreck of all my friends, nor this man's threats,
To whom I am subdued, are but light to me,

Might I but through my prison once a day   *490*
Behold this maid: all corners else o' the earth
Let liberty make use of; space enough
Have I in such a prison.

PROS.   *[Aside]* It works. *[To Fer.]* Come on.
Thou hast done well, fine Ariel! *[To Fer.]* Follow me.
[To Ari.] Hark what thou else shalt do me.

MIR.   Be of comfort;
My father's of a better nature, sir,
Than he appears by speech: this is unwonted
Which now came from him.

PROS.   Thou shalt be as free
As mountain winds: but then exactly do
All points of my command.

ARI.   To the syllable.   *500*

PROS. Come, follow. Speak not for him.

                                        [Exeunt.

NOTES

ACT I. SCENE I. 1. **Boatswain,** under-officer in a ship, having to do with sails and rigging and the supervision of the crew at work. 3. **Good,** probably, good friend. 3–4. **fall . . . yarely,** set to work nimbly. 8. **Tend,** attend. 11. **Play the men.** New Cambridge editors define as "pipe all hands." 19. **cares,** described as a singular verb used with a plural subject on account of haste; also as an old northern plural of the verb in *s*. **roarers,** waves or winds, or both; allusion to *roarer* meaning "bully," "blusterer." 24–25. **work . . . present,** calm the storm. 25. **hand,** handle. 32. **complexion . . . gallows,** appearance shows he was born to be hanged. 35. **doth little advantage,** is of little benefit. 38. **Bring . . . course,** sail her close to the wind by means of the mainsail. 40. **they . . . office,** the passengers make more noise than the winds or than we do at work. 49. **warrant him for drowning,** guarantee that he will never be drowned. 52. **a-hold,** close to the wind. 53. **courses,** probably, sails; i.e., they would set her foresail as well as her mainsail. 56. **must . . . cold,** let us heat up our mouths with liquor. 59. **merely,** absolutely, entirely. 60. **wide-chapp'd,** with mouth wide open. 60–61. **lie . . . tides.** Pirates were hanged on the shore and left until three tides had come in. 63. **glut,** swallow. 64. **split,** i.e., on the rocks. 69. **long heath,** defined as "open barren ground"; also as "heather." 70. **furze,** broom, or gorse (a prickly shrub); F: *firrs,* taken to mean "firs" (New Cambridge).
SCENE II. 3. **stinking pitch,** suggestion of heat. 4. **But that,** were is not that. 13. **fraughting,** forming the cargo. 14. **amazement,** astonishment, bewilderment. **piteous,** pitiful. 20. **full,** very, exceedingly. 22. **meddle,** mingle. 24. **So,** used with a gesture, meaning "good," "very well." 28. **provision,** foresight. 29. **no soul,** i.e., lost; many emendations. 30. **perdition,** loss. 35. **bootless inquisition,** profitless inquiry. 45–46, **assurance . . . warrants,** certainty that my memory guarantees. 56. **piece,** masterpiece.

59. **issued,** born. 64. **teen . . . to,** trouble I have brought you into. 65. **from,** i.e., has no place in. 71. **signories,** states of northern Italy. 73. **liberal arts,** allusion to the learned studies of the Middle Ages. 76. **state,** position as ruler. 77. **secret studies,** magic, the occult. 79. **perfected,** informed completely. 81. **trash,** check a hound by tying a weight to its neck. **over-topping,** running too far ahead of the pack. 83. **key,** tool for tuning stringed instruments, with suggestion of the usual meaning. 90. **closeness,** retirement, seclusion. 91–92. **but . . . rate,** except that it was done in retirement, (would have) surpassed in value all popular estimate. 93. **Awaked.** *I* in line 89 is the subject. 95. **in its contrary,** of an opposite kind. 97. **lorded,** raised to lordship. 100–102. **Who . . . lie,** a difficult passage; the meaning is: He had lied so long that he believed his own lies. New Cambridge editors read *minted* for *into,* interpreting the passage as a figure from coining of baser metals, so that *telling* means "counting," *substitution* means "the substituting of baser metals for gold," and *executing . . . royalty* means "stamping the coins." 109. **Absolute Milan,** actual duke of Milan. 110. **royalties,** prerogatives and rights of a sovereign. 111. **confederates,** conspires. 112. **dry,** thirsty. 123. **in . . . premises,** in return for the stipulations. 134. **hint,** occasion. 138. **impertinent,** irrelevant. 139. **wench,** used as a term of affectionate address. 144. **few,** few words. 146. **boat, F:** *butt,* which should be retained with the meaning "tub" (for boat). 151. **loving wrong,** figure of speech called oxymoron, in which, to emphasize a contrast, contradictory terms are associated; the *wrong* done by sea and winds was wrought by seeming sympathy. 152. **cherubin,** plural used as singular; applied to an angelic woman. 155. **deck'd.** New Cambridge editors read *eked,* increased. 156. **which,** i.e., the smile. 157. **undergoing stomach,** courage to undergo. 181. **zenith,** height of fortune; astrological term. 185. **dulness,** drowsiness. 187. **Come away,** come. 192. **task,** make demands upon. 194. **point,** i.e., to the smallest detail. 196. **beak,** prow. 197. **waist,** midship. **deck,** poopdeck at the stern. 200. **distinctly,** separately. 202. **momentary,** instantaneous. 209. **fever of the mad,** i.e., such as madmen feel. Some editors follow Dryden in reading *mind.* 213. **up-staring,** standing on end. 218. **sustaining garments,** probably, garments that sustained them in the sea. 223. **angle,** corner. 227. **nook,** bay. 228. **fetch dew,** for some incantation. 229. **Bermoothes,** Bermudas; a possible reference to *A Discovery of the Bermudas* (1609), one of the sources of the play. 234. **flote,** sea, or possibly, flotilla, i.e., making for the Mediterranean flotilla (New Cambridge). 240. **glasses,** i.e., hourglasses. 243. **remember,** remind. 248. **mistakings,** errors. 250. **bate . . . year,** remit me a year of service. Ariel, as a spirit, longs for freedom; as a spirit, he is also incapable of affection or gratitude as entertained by human beings. 261. **Argier,** Algiers. 266. **one thing she did,** allusion not explained; taken by New Cambridge editors as evidence of a cut in the play. Lamb suggested that Shakespeare was thinking of the witch who saved Algiers from Charles V in 1541 by raising a storm that dispersed his fleet. 269. **blue-eyed,** usually interpreted as referring to dark circles under the eyes. Staunton suggested *blear-eyed.* 274. **hests,** commands. 283. **freckled,** spotted. 297. **correspondent,** responsive, submissive. 311. **miss,** do without. 321. **wicked,** mischievous, harmful. 323. **southwest,** i.e., wind (bringing disease). 326. **urchins,** hedgehogs; here, suggesting goblins. 327. **vast,** long hours. 328. **exercise,** practice, work. 334. **berries.** Strachey's *Repertory,* one of the sources, says that the Bermudas were full of thickets of "goodly Cedar . . . the Berries whereof, our men seething, straining and letting stand some three or foure daies, made a kind of pleasant drinke." 338. **brine-pits,** salt springs. 342. **sty,** put in sty. 346. **human,** humane. 351–362. **Abhorred . . . prison.** F assigns this speech to Miranda. This

may be correct, since Prospero seems to break in suddenly in line 365. 357–358. **endow'd
. . . known,** enabled you to make known what was going on in your mind. 358. **race,**
natural disposition. 364. **red plague,** bubonic plague. **rid,** destroy, with play on *red*. 365.
Hag-seed, hag's offspring. 370. **aches,** pronounced "aitches." 373. **Setebos,** mentioned
in Eden's *History of Travel* (1577) as a deity, or devil, of the Patagonians. 376–378. **Come
. . . kiss'd** three motions before the dance—take hands, curtsy, kiss (New Cambridge).
379. **whist,** silent. 380. **featly,** neatly. 381. **burthen,** refrain. 405. **remember,** commemo-
rate. 415. **canker,** cankerworm (feeding on buds and leaves). 419. **It goes on,** my charm
works. 423. **remain,** dwell. 429. **best,** i.e., in birth. 432. **single,** solitary, with a suggestion
of feebleness. 439. **control,** confute. 441. **changed eyes,** exchanged amorous glances,
with suggestion of the eye as the origin of the passion of love. 443. **done . . . wrong,** are
mistaken. 451. **uneasy,** difficult. 451,452. **light, light,** easy, cheap. 465. **entertainment,**
treatment. 468. **gentle,** well-born, high-spirited. **not fearful,** not dangerous (because
incapable of treachery). 469. **foot,** subordinate. Miranda (the foot) presumes to instruct
Prospero (the head). 471. **come . . . ward.** New Cambridge editors read comma after *come*,
with the meaning, "Come, off thy guard." 484. **nerves,** sinews. 491–492. **all . . . of,** those
who are free may have all the rest of the world.

ACT II.

SCENE I.   *Another part of the island.*
Enter ALONSO, SEBASTIAN, ANTONIO, GONZALO,
ADRIAN, FRANCISCO, and others.

GON. Beseech you, sir, be merry; you have cause,
So have we all, of joy; for our escape
Is much beyond our loss. Our hint of woe
Is common; every day some sailor's wife,
The masters of some merchant and the merchant
Have just our theme of woe; but for the miracle,
I mean our preservation, few in millions
Can speak like us: then wisely, good sir, weigh
Our sorrow with our comfort.

ALON.   Prithee, peace.

SEB. He receives comfort like cold porridge.   *10*

ANT. The visitor will not give him o'er so.

SEB. Look, he 's winding up the watch of his wit; by
and by it will strike.

GON. Sir,—

SEB. One: tell.

GON. When every grief is entertain'd that 's offer'd,
Comes to the entertainer—

SEB. A dollar.

GON. Dolour comes to him, indeed: you have spoken truer than you purposed. *20*

SEB. You have taken it wiselier than I meant you should.

GON. Therefore, my lord,—

ANT. Fie, what a spendthrift is he of his tongue!

ALON. I prithee, spare.

GON. Well, I have done: but yet,—

SEB. He will be talking.

ANT. Which, of he or Adrian, for a good wager, first begins to crow?

SEB. The old cock. *30*

ANT. The cockerel.

SEB. Done. The wager?

ANT. A laughter.

SEB. A match!

ADR. Though this island seem to be desert,—

SEB. Ha, ha, ha! So, you're paid.

ADR. Uninhabitable and almost inaccessible,—

SEB. Yet,—

ADR. Yet,—

ANT. He could not miss 't. *40*

ADR. It must needs be of subtle, tender and delicate temperance.

ANT. Temperance was a delicate wench.

SEB. Ay, and a subtle; as he most learnedly delivered.

ADR. The air breathes upon us here most sweetly.

SEB. As if it had lungs and rotten ones.

ANT. Or as 'twere perfumed by a fen.

GON. Here is every thing advantageous to life.

ANT. True; save means to live. *50*

SEB. Of that there 's none, or little.

GON. How lush and lusty the grass looks! how green!

ANT. The ground indeed is tawny.

SEB. With an eye of green in 't.

ANT. He misses not much.

SEB. No; he doth but mistake the truth totally.

GON. But the rarity of it is,—which is indeed almost
beyond credit,—

SEB. As many vouched rarities are.   60

GON. That our garments, being, as they were,
drenched in the sea, hold notwithstanding their freshness
and glosses, being rather new-dyed than stained
with salt water.

ANT. If but one of his pockets could speak, would it
not say he lies?

SEB. Ay, or very falsely pocket up his report.

GON. Methinks our garments are now as fresh as
when we put them on first in Afric, at the marriage
of the king's fair daughter Claribel to the King of
Tunis.   71

SEB. 'Twas a sweet marriage, and we prosper well in
our return.

ADR. Tunis was never graced before with such a
paragon to their queen.

GON. Not since widow Dido's time.

ANT. Widow! a pox o' that! How came that widow
in? widow Dido!

SEB. What if he had said 'widower Aeneas' too? Good
Lord, how you take it!   80

ADR. 'Widow Dido' said you? you make me study
of that: she was of Carthage, not of Tunis.

GON. This Tunis, sir, was Carthage.

ADR. Carthage?

GON. I assure you, Carthage.   85

SEB. His word is more than the miraculous harp; he
hath raised the wall and houses too.

ANT. What impossible matter will he make easy next?

SEB. I think he will carry this island home in his
pocket and give it his son for an apple.   *91*

ANT. And, sowing the kernels of it in the sea, bring
forth more islands.

GON. Ay.

ANT. Why, in good time.

GON. Sir, we were talking that our garments seem
now as fresh as when we were at Tunis at the marriage
of your daughter, who is now queen.

ANT. And the rarest that e'er came there.

SEB. Bate, I beseech you, widow Dido.   *100*

ANT. O, widow Dido! ay, widow Dido.

GON. Is not, sir, my doublet as fresh as the first day I wore it? I mean, in a
sort.

ANT. That sort was well fished for.

GON. When I wore it at your daughter's marriage?

ALON. You cram these words into mine ears against
The stomach of my sense. Would I had never
Married my daughter there! for, coming thence,
My son is lost and, in my rate, she too,
Who is so far from Italy removed   *110*
I ne'er again shall see her, O thou mine heir
Of Naples and of Milan, what strange fish
Hath made his meal on thee?

FRAN.   Sir, he may live:
I saw him beat the surges under him,
And ride upon their backs; he trod the water,
Whose enmity he flung aside, and breasted
The surge most swoln that met him; his bold head
'Bove the contentious waves he kept, and oar'd
Himself with his good arms in lusty stroke
To the shore, that o'er his wave-worn basis bow'd,   *120*
As stooping to relieve him: I not doubt
He came alive to land.

ALON.   No, no, he's gone.

334
∎

SEB. Sir, you may thank yourself for this great loss,
That would not bless our Europe with your daughter,
But rather loose her to an African;
Where she at least is banish'd from your eye,
Who hath cause to wet the grief on 't.

ALON.   Prithee, peace.

SEB. You were kneel'd to and importuned otherwise
By all of us, and the fair soul herself
Weigh'd between loathness and obedience, at   *130*
Which end o' the beam should bow. We have lost
        your son,
I fear, for ever: Milan and Naples have
Moe widows in them of this business' making
Than we bring men to comfort them:
The fault 's your own.

ALON.   So is the dear'st o' the loss.

GON. My lord Sebastian,
The truth you speak doth lack some gentleness
And time to speak it in: you rub the sore,
When you should bring the plaster.

SEB.   Very well.

ANT. And most chirurgeonly.   *140*

GON. It is foul weather in us all, good sir,
When you are cloudy.

SEB.   Foul weather?

ANT.   Very foul.

GON. Had I plantation of this isle, my lord,—

ANT. He 'ld sow 't with nettle-seed.

SEB.   Or docks, or mallows.

GON. And were the king on 't, what would I do?

SEB. 'Scape being drunk for want of wine.

GON. I' the commonwealth I would by contraries
Execute all things; for no kind of traffic
Would I admit; no name of magistrate;
Letters should not be known; riches, poverty,   *150*
And use of service, none; contract, succession,
Bourn, bound of land, tilth, vineyard, none;
No use of metal, corn, or wine, or oil;

335
▪

No occupation; all men idle, all;
And women too, but innocent and pure;
No sovereignty;—

SEB.   Yet he would be king on 't.

ANT. The latter end of his commonwealth forgets the
beginning.

GON. All things in common nature should produce
Without sweat or endeavour: treason, felony,
Sword, pike, knife, gun, or need of any engine,
Would I not have; but nature should bring forth,
Of it own kind, all foison, all abundance,
To feed my innocent people.

                  160

SEB. No marrying 'mong his subjects?

ANT. None, man; all idle: whores and knaves.

GON. I would with such perfection govern, sir,
To excel the golden age.

SEB.   God save his majesty!

ANT. Long live Gonzalo!

GON.   And,—do you mark me, sir?

ALON. Prithee, no more: thou dost talk nothing to me.

                  171

GON. I do well believe your highness; and did it to
minister occasion to these gentlemen, who are of such
sensible and nimble lungs that they always use to
laugh at nothing.

ANT. 'Twas you we laughed at.

GON. Who in this kind of merry fooling am nothing
to you: so you may continue and laugh at nothing
still.

ANT. What a blow was there given!

                  180

SEB. An it had not fallen flat-long.

GON. You are gentlemen of brave mettle: you would
lift the moon out of her sphere, if she would continue
in it five weeks without changing.

      Enter ARIEL, invisible, playing solemn music.

SEB. We would so, and then go a bat-fowling.

ANT. Nay, good my lord, be not angry.

GON. No, I warrant you; I will not adventure my
discretion so weakly. Will you laugh me asleep, for I
am very heavy?

ANT. Go sleep, and hear us.   *190*

> [*All sleep except Alon., Seb., and Ant.*

ALON. What, all so soon asleep! I wish mine eyes
Would, with themselves, shut up my thoughts: I find
They are inclined to do so.

SEB.   Please you, sir,
Do not omit the heavy offer of it:
It seldom visits sorrow; when it doth,
It is a comforter.

ANT.   We two, my lord,
Will guard your person while you take your rest,
And watch your safety.

ALON.   Thank you, Wondrous heavy.

> [*Alonso sleeps. Exit Ariel.*

SEB. What a strange drowsiness possesses them!

ANT. It is the quality o' the climate.

SEB.   Why   *200*
Doth it not then our eyelids sink? I find not
Myself disposed to sleep.

ANT.   Nor I; my spirits are nimble.
They fell together all, as by consent;
They dropp'd, as by a thunder-stroke. What might,
Worthy Sebastian? O, what might?—No more:—
And yet methinks I see it in thy face,
What thou shouldst be: the occasion speaks thee, and
My strong imagination sees a crown
Dropping upon thy head.

SEB.   What, art thou waking?

ANT. Do you not hear me speak?

SEB.   I do; and surely   *210*
It is a sleepy language and thou speak'st
Out of thy sleep. What is it thou didst say?
This is a strange repose, to be asleep
With eyes wide open; standing, speaking, moving,
And yet so fast asleep.

ANT.   Noble Sebastian
Thou let'st thy fortune sleep—die, rather; wink'st
Whiles thou art waking.

SEB.   Thou dost snore distinctly;
There's meaning in thy snores.

ANT. I am more serious than my custom: you
Must be so too, if heed me; which to do   *220*
Trebles thee o'er.

SEB.   Well, I am standing water.

ANT. I'll teach you how to flow.

SEB.   Do so: to ebb
Hereditary sloth instructs me.

ANT.   O,
If you but knew how you the purpose cherish
Whiles thus you mock it! how, in stripping it,
You more invest it! Ebbing men, indeed,
Most often do so near the bottom run
By their own fear or sloth.

SEB.   Prithee, say on:
The setting of thine eye and cheek proclaim
A matter from thee, and a birth indeed   *230*
Which throes thee much to yield.

ANT.   Thus, sir:
Although this lord of weak remembrance, this,
Who shall be of as little memory
When he is earth'd, hath here almost persuaded,—
For he's a spirit of persuasion, only
Professes to persuade,—the king his son 's alive,
'Tis as impossible that he 's undrown'd
As he that sleeps here swims.

SEB.   I have no hope
That he 's undrown'd.

ANT.   O, out of that 'no hope'
What great hope have you! no hope that way is   *240*
Another way so high a hope that even
Ambition cannot pierce a wink beyond,
But doubt discovery there. Will you grant with me
That Ferdinand is drown'd?

SEB.   He 's gone.

ANT.   Then, tell me,
Who's the next heir of Naples?

SEB.   Claribel.

ANT. She that is queen of Tunis; she that dwells
Ten leagues beyond man's life; she that from Naples
Can have no note, unless the sun were post—
The man i' the moon 's too slow—till new-born chins
Be rough and razorable; she that—from whom?   *250*
We all were sea-swallow'd, though some cast again,
And by that destiny to perform an act
Whereof what 's past is prologue, what to come
In yours and my discharge.

SEB.   What stuff is this! how say you?
'Tis true, my brother's daughter 's queen of Tunis;
So is she heir of Naples; 'twixt which regions
There is some space.

ANT.   A space whose every cubit
Seems to cry out, 'How shall that Claribel
Measure us back to Naples? Keep in Tunis,
And let Sebastian wake.' Say, this were death   *260*
That now hath seized them; why, they were no worse
Than now they are. There be that can rule Naples
As well as he that sleeps; lords that can prate
As amply and unnecessarily
As this Gonzalo; I myself could make
A chough of as deep chat. O, that you bore
The mind that I do! what a sleep were this
For your advancement! Do you understand me?

SEB. Methinks I do.

ANT.   And how does your content
Tender your own good fortune?

SEB.   I remember   *270*
You did supplant your brother Prospero.

ANT.   True:
And look how well my garments sit upon me;
Much feater than before: my brother's servants
Were then my fellows; now they are my men.

SEB. But, for your conscience?

ANT. Ay, sir; where lies that? if 'twere a kibe,
'Twould put me to my slipper: but I feel not
This deity in my bosom: twenty consciences,
That stand 'twixt me and Milan, candied be they
And melt ere they molest! Here lies your brother,   *280*

No better than the earth he lies upon,
If he were that which now he 's like, that 's dead;
Whom I, with this obedient steel, three inches of it,
Can lay to bed for ever; whiles you, doing thus,
To the perpetual wink for aye might put
This ancient morsel, this Sir Prudence, who
Should not upbraid our course. For all the rest,
They'll take suggestion as a cat laps milk;
They'll tell the clock to any business that
We say befits the hour.

SEB.   Thy case, dear friend,   *290*
Shall be my precedent; as thou got'st Milan,
I'll come by Naples. Draw thy sword: one stroke
Shall free thee from the tribute which thou payest;
And I the king shall love thee.

ANT.   Draw together;
And when I rear my hand, do you the like,
To fall it on Gonzalo.

SEB.   O, but one word.

[They talk apart.
Re-enter ARIEL, invisible.

ARI. My master through his art foresees the danger
That you, his friend, are in; and sends me forth—
For else his project dies—to keep them living.

[Sings in Gonzalo's ear.

While you here do snoring lie,   *300*
   Open-eyed conspiracy
      His time doth take.
If of life you keep a care,
Shake off slumber, and beware:
   Awake, awake!

ANT. Then let us both be sudden.

GON.   Now, good angels
Preserve the king.

[They wake.

ALON. Why, how now? ho, awake! Why are you drawn?
Wherefore this ghastly looking?

GON.   What 's the matter?

SEB. Whiles we stood here securing your repose,   *310*
Even now, we heard a hollow burst of bellowing
Like bulls, or rather lions: did 't not wake you?
It struck mine ear most terribly.

ALON. I heard nothing.

ANT. O, 'twas a din to fright a monster's ear,
To make an earthquake! sure, it was the roar
Of a whole herd of lions.

ALON. Heard you this, Gonzalo?

GON. Upon mine honour, sir, I heard a humming,
And that a strange one too, which did awake me:
I shaked you, sir, and cried: as mine eyes open'd,
I saw their weapons drawn: there was a noise,   320
That 's verily. 'Tis best we stand upon our guard,
Or that we quit this place: let 's draw our weapons.

ALON. Lead off this ground; and let 's make further search
For my poor son.

GON. Heavens keep him from these beasts!
For he is, sure, i' the island.

ALON. Lead away.

ARI. Prospero my lord shall know what I have done:
So, king, go safely on to seek thy son.

[Exeunt.

SCENE II.   *Another part of the island.*
**Enter CALIBAN with a burden of wood. A noise of
thunder heard.**

CAL. All the infections that the sun sucks up
From bogs, fens, flats, on Prosper fall and make him
By inch-meal a disease! His spirits hear me
And yet I needs must curse. But they'll nor pinch,
Fright me with urchin-shows, pitch me i' the mire,
Nor lead me, like a firebrand, in the dark
Out of my way, unless he bid 'em; but
For every trifle are they set upon me;
Sometime like apes that mow and chatter at me
And after bite me, then like hedgehogs which   10
Lie tumbling in my barefoot way and mount
Their pricks at my footfall; sometime am I
All wound with adders who with cloven tongues
Do hiss me into madness.

Enter TRINCULO.

Lo, now, lo!
Here comes a spirit of his, and to torment me
For bringing wood in slowly. I'll fall flat;
Perchance he will not mind me.   17

TRIN. Here 's neither bush nor shrub, to bear off any weather at all, and another storm brewing; I hear it sing i' the wind: yond same black cloud, yond huge one, looks like a foul bombard that would shed his liquor. If it should thunder as it did before, I know not where to hide my head: yond same cloud cannot choose but fall by pailfuls. What have we here? a man or a fish? dead or alive? A fish: he smells like a fish; a very ancient and fish-like smell; a kind of not of the newest Poor-John. A strange fish! Were I in England now, as once I was, and had but this fish painted, not a holiday fool there but would give a piece of silver: there would this monster make a man; any strange beast there makes a man: when they will not give a doit to relieve a lame beggar, they will lay out ten to see a dead Indian. Legged like a man! and his fins like arms! Warm o' my troth! I do now let loose my opinion; hold it no longer: this is no fish, but an islander, that hath lately suffered by a thunderbolt. *[Thunder.]* Alas, the storm is come again! my best way is to creep under his gaberdine; there is no other shelter hereabout: misery acquaints a man with strange bed-fellows. I will here shroud till the dregs of the storm be past.

Enter STEPHANO, singing: a bottle in his hand.

STE. I shall no more to sea, to sea,   44
            Here shall I die ashore—
This is a very scurvy tune to sing at a man's funeral:
well, here's my comfort.   *[Drinks.*

[Sings.]

    The master, the swabber, the boatswain and I,
        The gunner and his mate
Loved Mall, Meg and Marian and Margery,   50
        But none of us cared for Kate;
        For she had a tongue with a tang,
        Would cry to a sailor, Go hang!
She loved not the savour of tar nor of pitch,
Yet a tailor might scratch her where'er she did itch:
        Then to sea, boys, and let her go hang!

This is a scurvy tune too: but here's my comfort

[Drinks.

CAL. Do not torment me: Oh!   58

STE. What 's the matter? Have we devils here? Do
you put tricks upon 's with savages and men of Ind,
ha? I have not 'scaped drowning to be afeard now of
your four legs; for it hath been said, As proper a man
as ever went on four legs cannot make him give
ground; and it shall be said so again while Stephano
breathes at nostrils.

CAL. The spirit torments me; Oh!   66

STE. This is some monster of the isle with four legs,
who hath got, as I take it, an ague. Where the devil
should he learn our language? I will give him some

relief, if it be but for that. If I can recover him and
keep him tame and get to Naples with him, he 's a
present for any emperor that ever trod on neat's-leather.   73

CAL. Do not torment me, prithee; I'll bring my
wood home faster.

STE. He 's in his fit now and does not talk after the
wisest. He shall taste of my bottle: if he have never
drunk wine afore, it will go near to remove his fit. If I
can recover him and keep him tame, I will not take
too much for him; he shall pay for him that hath him,
and that soundly.

CAL. Thou dost me yet but little hurt; thou wilt anon, I know it by thy
trembling: now Prosper works
upon thee.   84

STE. Come on your ways; open your mouth; here is
that which will give language to you, cat: open your
mouth; this will shake your shaking, I can tell you,
and that soundly: you cannot tell who 's your friend:
open your chaps again.   89

TRIN. I should know that voice: it should be—but
he is drowned; and these are devils: O defend me!

STE. Four legs and two voices: a most delicate
monster! His forward voice now is to speak well of his
friend; his backward voice is to utter foul speeches
and to detract. If all the wine in my bottle will recover
him, I will help his ague. Come. Amen! I will
pour some in thy other mouth.

TRIN. Stephano!   100

STE. Doth thy other mouth call me? Mercy, mercy!
This is a devil, and no monster: I will leave him; I
have no long spoon.

TRIN. Stephano! If thou beest Stephano, touch me
and speak to me; for I am Trinculo—be not afeard—
thy good friend Trinculo.

STE. If thou beest Trinculo, come forth: I'll pull
thee by the lesser legs: if any be Trinculo's legs, these
are they. Thou art very Trinculo indeed! How camest
thou to be the siege of this moon-calf? can he vent
Trinculos?   111

TRIN. I took him to be killed with a thunder-stroke.
But art thou not drowned, Stephano? I hope now
thou art not drowned. Is the storm overblown? I hid
me under the dead moon-calf's gaberdine for fear of
the storm. And art thou living, Stephano? O Stephano,
two Neapolitans 'scaped!

STE. Prithee, do not turn me about; my stomach is
not constant.

CAL. *[Aside]* These be fine things, an if they be not sprites.
That's a brave god and bears celestial liquor.   122
   I will kneel to him.

STE. How didst thou 'scape? How camest thou
hither? swear by this bottle how thou camest hither.
I escaped upon a butt of sack which the sailors
heaved o'erboard, by this bottle! which I made of the
bark of a tree with mine own hands since I was cast
ashore.

CAL. I'll swear upon that bottle to be thy true
subject; for the liquor is not earthly.   130

STE. Here; swear then how thou escapedst.

TRIN. Swum ashore, man, like a duck: I can swim
like a duck, I'll be sworn.

STE. Here, kiss the book. Though thou canst swim
like a duck, thou art made like a goose.

TRIN. O Stephano, hast any more of this?

STE. The whole butt, man: my cellar is in a rock by
the sea-side where my wine is hid. How now, moon-
calf! how does thine ague?   139

CAL. Hast thou not dropp'd from heaven?

STE. Out o' the moon, I do assure thee: I was the
man i' the moon when time was.

CAL. I have seen thee in her and I do adore thee:
My mistress show'd me thee and thy dog and thy bush.

STE. Come, swear to that; kiss the book: I will
furnish it anon with new contents: swear.

TRIN. By this good light, this is a very shallow
monster! I afeard of him! A very weak monster! The
man i' the moon! A most poor credulous monster!
Well drawn, monster, in good sooth!   151

CAL. I'll show thee every fertile inch o' th' island;
And I will kiss thy foot: I prithee, be my god.

TRIN. By this light, a most perfidious and drunken
monster! when 's god 's asleep, he'll rob his bottle.

CAL. I will kiss thy foot; I'll swear myself thy subject.

STE. Come on then; down, and swear.

TRIN. I shall laugh myself to death at this puppy-
headed monster. A most scurvy monster! I could find
in my heart to beat him,—

STE. Come, kiss.   *161*

TRIN. But that poor monster 's in drink: an
abominable monster!

CAL. I'll show thee the best springs; I'll pluck thee berries;
I'll fish for thee and get thee wood enough.
A plague upon the tyrant that I serve!
I'll bear him no more sticks, but follow thee,
Thou wondrous man.

TRIN. A most ridiculous monster, to make a wonder
of a poor drunkard!   *170*

CAL. I prithee, let me bring thee where crabs grow;
And I with my long nails will dig thee pig-nuts;
Show thee a jay's nest and instruct thee how
To snare the nimble marmoset; I'll bring thee
To clustering filberts and sometimes I'll get thee
Young scamels from the rock. Wilt thou go with me?

STE. I prithee now, lead the way without any more
talking. Trinculo, the king and all our company else
being drowned, we will inherit here: here; bear my
bottle: fellow Trinculo, we'll fill him by and by again.

CAL. *[Sings drunkenly]*
Farewell, master; farewell, farewell!   *182*

TRIN. A howling monster; a drunken monster!

CAL. No more dams I'll make for fish;
   Nor fetch in firing
   At requiring;
Nor scrape trencher, nor wash dish:
   'Ban, 'Ban, Cacaliban
   Has a new master: get a new man.
Freedom, hey-day! hey-day!, freedom! freedom, heyday, freedom!   *191*

STE. O brave monster! Lead the way.

[*Exeunt.*

NOTES

ACT II. SCENE I. 5. **merchant, merchant,** merchant vessel, merchant. 11. **visitor,** one taking nourishment to the sick. 18. **dollar,** widely circulated coin, the German *Thaler* and the Spanish *piece of eight*. 33. **laughter,** sitting of eggs. When Adrian (the *cockerel*) begins to speak (l. 35), Sebastian loses the bet and pays with a *laugh* (Ha, ha, ha! l. 36) for a *laughter*. 34. **A match,** a bargain; agreed. 40. **He . . . miss 't,** i.e., even if it is uninhabitable and inaccessible, he could not refrain from talking about it. 42. **temperance,** temperature. 43. **Temperance,** a Puritan name for women, thought also to refer to Temperance, a character in Chapman's *May Day* (1611). 54. **tawny,** dull brown. 55. **eye,** tinge. 63. **glosses** New Cambridge: *gloss*. 65. **pockets.** Some editors suppose that reference is made to mud in the pockets. There is, at any rate, some peculiarity in Gonzalo's appearance; cf. line 30. 76. **widow Dido,** queen of Carthage deserted by Aeneas; possible topical reference to Chapman's *Widow's Tears,* or some other play. 86. **miraculous harp,** allusion to Amphion's harp with which he raised the walls of Thebes. 95. **in good time,** vague expression of agreement or approbation. 104. **sort,** lucky catch after much angling; probable suggestion of the age of the garment, with a play on *sort* in line 103. 113–122. **Sir . . . land,** Francisco's only speech. New Cambridge editors think the speech belongs to Gonzalo, and see in its assignment to Francisco a relic of an older version. 120. **basis,** foot, base. 125. **loose,** so F; Globe: *lose*. 127. **Who,** which (eye). 129–131. **the fair . . . bow,** the fair soul herself was poised uncertain between unwillingness and obedience as to which end of the scale should sink. 140. **chirurgeonly,** like a skilled surgeon. 143. **plantation,** colonization; subsequent play on the literal meaning. 147–156. **I' the . . . sovereignty.** This passage on man in his primitive state is based on Montaigne, *Essays*, I, xxx, and derived from Florio's translation (1603). 150. **Letters,** learning. 151. **use of service,** custom of employing servants. **succession,** holding of property by right of inheritance. 152. **Bourn,** boundaries. **bound of land,** landmarks. **tilth,** tillage of soil. 161. **engine,** instrument of warfare. 163. **it,** its. **foison,** plenty. 168. **God.** Omitted in F in deference to the statute forbidding profanity on the stage. 174. **nimble,** easily excited. 181. **flat-long,** with the flat of the sword. 182. **mettle,** temper, nature. 183. **lift . . . sphere.** As a planet in the old astronomy, the moon had a crystal sphere in which she moved. Gonzalo means that they would lift the moon out of her sphere if she remained steady in it. 185. **bat-fowling,** hunting birds at night with lantern and stick: also, gulling a simpleton. Gonzalo is the simpleton (or fowl), and Sebastian will use the moon as his lantern. 187. **adventure,** risk. 190. **Go . . . us,** let our laughing send you to sleep, or, go to sleep and hear us laugh at you. 194. **omit,** neglect. **heavy,** drowsy. 203. **consent,** agreement as to a course of action. 207. **speaks,** calls upon, proclaims (thee) king. 217. **distinctly,** with separate and individual sounds. 221. **Trebles.** New Cambridge editors read *Troubles* in view of *standing water*. Onions defines as "makes thee three times as great." **standing water,** water which neither flows nor ebbs. 224. **purpose,** i.e., of being king. 225. **stripping it,** stripping off all pretense, revealing it. 226. **Ebbing men,** men whose fortunes ebb, leaving them stranded. 229. **setting,** set expression. 230. **matter,** matter of importance. 231. **throes,** pains. 232. **this lord,** Gonzalo. **remem-**

brance, power of remembering. 234. **earth'd,** buried. 236. **Professes to persuade,** he was a privy councilor. 240. **that way,** i.e., in regard to Ferdinand's being saved. 242–243. **Ambition . . . there,** ambition itself cannot see any further than that hope (of the crown) without doubting the reality of the objects it sees. Furness, following Nicholson's conjecture of *dout* (extinguish) for *doubt,* interprets, "when ambition pierces to its furthest wink there discovery ceases, and the crown is found." 247. **Ten . . . life,** it would take more than a lifetime to get there. 248. **note,** intimation. 250. **she . . . whom,** broken and difficult construction. **from whom?** Probably, from whom will she learn? 251. **cast,** were disgorged, with pun on *casting* (of parts for a play). 254. **discharge,** performance, i.e., to get done. 259. **Measure us,** find (her) way. 259–260. **Keep . . . wake,** let her stay in Tunis, and let Sebastian wake (to his good fortune). 265–266. **I . . . chat,** I could teach a jackdaw to talk as wisely. 269. **content,** desire, contentment. 270. **Tender,** provide for. 273. **feater,** more becomingly. 276. **kibe,** sore on the heel. 279. **candied,** frozen, congealed. 302. **time,** opportunity. 306. **sudden,** swift in action. 317. **humming,** i.e., Ariel's song.

SCENE II. 3. **inch-meal,** little by little. 9. **mow,** make faces. 19. **bear off,** keep off. 22. **foul bombard,** dirty leathern bottle. 29. **Poor-John,** salted hake, type of poor fare. **fish.** Malone cites a license issued by the Master of the Revels (1632) "to shew a strange fish for half a yeare." 33. **make a man,** i.e., make his fortune. 40. **gaberdine,** cloak, loose upper garment. 43. **shroud,** take shelter. **dregs,** last remains. 61. **Ind,** India, or vaguely, the East. 71. **recover,** restore. 73. **neat's-leather,** leather from the skin of an animal of the ox kind. 80. **take too much,** ironical, meaning: He will take as much as he can get. 83. **trembling,** suggestion of demonic possession. 87. **cat . . . mouth,** allusion to the proverb, "Good liquor will make a cat speak." 103. **long spoon,** allusion to the proverb, "He that sups with the devil has need of a long spoon." 111. **moon-calf,** monster, abortion (supposed to be caused by the influence of the moon). 120. **not constant,** unsteady. 126. **butt of sack,** barrel of Canary wine. 134. **kiss the book.** He gives him the bottle instead of the Bible on which to make his oath. 142. **when time was,** once upon a time. 144. **dog . . . bush.** See *A Midsummer-Night's Dream,* V, i, 136. 150. **Well drawn.** Caliban takes a good draft of the wine. 172. **pig-nuts,** roundish tubers of *bunium flexuosum;* earth-chestnuts. 174. **marmoset,** small monkey. 176. **scamels,** not explained. Keightley conjectured *seamels* (seagulls), Theobald: *stannels* (kestrels); New Cambridge editors call attention to the fact that "seamews" occurs in Strachey's letter. 179. **inherit,** take possession. 187. **trencher,** trenchers, collectively (Onions).

ACT III

SCENE I.   *Before PROSPERO'S cell.*

Enter FERDINAND, bearing a log.

FER. There be some sports are painful, and their labour
Delight in them sets off: some kinds of baseness
Are nobly undergone and most poor matters
Point to rich ends. This my mean task
Would be as heavy to me as odious, but
The mistress which I serve quickens what's dead
And makes my labours pleasures; O, she is
Ten times more gentle than her father's crabbed,

And he 's composed of harshness. I must remove
Some thousands of these logs and pile them up, 10
Upon a sore injunction: my sweet mistress
Weeps when she sees me work, and says, such baseness
Had never like executor. I forget:
But these sweet thoughts do even refresh my labours,
Most busy lest, when I do it.

> *Enter MIRANDA; and PROSPERO at a distance, unseen.*

MIR.   Alas, now, pray you,
Work not so hard: I would the lightning had
Burnt up those logs that you are enjoin'd to pile!
Pray, set it down and rest you: when this burns,
'Twill weep for having wearied you. My father
Is hard at study; pray now, rest yourself; 20
He's safe for these three hours.

FER.   O most dear mistress,
The sun will set before I shall discharge
What I must strive to do.

MIR.   If you'll sit down,
I'll bear your logs the while: pray, give me that;
I'll carry it to the pile.

FER.   No, precious creature;
I had rather crack my sinews, break my back,
Than you should such dishonour undergo,
While I sit lazy by.

MIR.   It would become me
As well as it does you: and I should do it
With much more ease; for my good will is to it, 30
And yours it is against.

PROS.   Poor worm, thou art infected!
This visitation shows it.

MIR.   You look wearily.

FER. No, noble mistress; 'tis fresh morning with me
When you are by at night. I do beseech you—
Chiefly that I might set it in my prayers—
What is your name?

MIR.   Miranda.—O my father,
I have broke your hest to say so!

FER.   Admired Miranda!
Indeed the top of admiration! worth
What's dearest to the world! Full many a lady
I have eyed with best regard and many a time 40

The harmony of their tongues hath into bondage
Brought my too diligent ear: for several virtues
Have I liked several women; never any
With so full soul, but some defect in her
Did quarrel with the noblest grace she owed
And put it to the foil: but you, O you,
So perfect and so peerless, are created
Of every creature's best!

MIR.   I do not know
One of my sex; no woman's face remember,
Save, from my glass, mine own; nor have I seen   *50*
More that I may call men than you, good friend,
And my dear father: how features are abroad,
I am skilless of; but, by my modesty,
The jewel in my dower, I would not wish
Any companion in the world but you,
Nor can imagination form a shape,
Besides yourself, to like of. But I prattle
Something too wildly and my father's precepts
I therein do forget.

FER.   I am in my condition
A prince, Miranda; I do think, a king;   *60*
I would, not so!—and would no more endure
This wooden slavery than to suffer
The flesh-fly blow my mouth. Hear my soul speak:
The very instant that I saw you, did
My heart fly to your service; there resides,
To make me slave to it; and for your sake
Am I this patient log-man.

MIR.   Do you love me?

FER. O heaven, O earth, bear witness to this sound
And crown what I profess with kind event
If I speak true! if hollowly, invert   *70*
What best is boded me to mischief! I
Beyond all limit of what else i' the world
Do love, prize, honour you.

MIR.   I am a fool
To weep at what I am glad of.

PROS.   Fair encounter
Of two most rare affections! Heavens rain grace
On that which breeds between 'em!

FER.   Wherefore weep you?

MIR. At mine unworthiness that dare not offer
What I desire to give, and much less take
What I shall die to want. But this is trifling;
And all the more it seeks to hide itself,   *80*
The bigger bulk it shows. Hence, bashful cunning!
And prompt me, plain and holy innocence!
I am your wife, if you will marry me;
If not, I'll die your maid: to be your fellow
You may deny me; but I'll be your servant,
Whether you will or no.

FER.   My mistress, dearest;
And I thus humble ever.

MIR.   My husband, then?

FER. Ay, with a heart as willing
As bondage e'er of freedom: here's my hand.

MIR. And mine, with my heart in 't: and now
      farewell   *90*
Till half an hour hence.

FER.   A thousand thousand!

                                        [Exeunt Fer. and Mir. severally.

PROS. So glad of this as they I cannot be,
Who are surprised withal; but my rejoicing
At nothing can be more. I'll to my book,
For yet ere supper-time must I perform
Much business appertaining.   *[Exit.*

SCENE II.   *Another part of the island.*

                          Enter CALIBAN, STEPHANO, and TRINCULO.

STE. Tell not me; when the butt is out, we will drink
water; not a drop before: therefore bear up, and
board 'em. Servant-monster, drink to me.

TRIN. Servant-monster! the folly of this island! They
say there's but five upon this isle: we are three of
them; if th' other two be brained like us, the state
totters.

STE. Drink, servant-monster, when I bid thee: thy
eyes are almost set in thy head.   *10*

TRIN. Where should they be set else? he were a
brave monster indeed, if they were set in his tail.

STE. My man-monster hath drown'd his tongue in
sack: for my part, the sea cannot drown me; I swam,

ere I could recover the shore, five and thirty leagues off and on. By this light, thou shalt be my lieutenant, monster, or my standard.   20

TRIN. Your lieutenant, if you list; he's no standard.

STE. We'll not run, Monsieur Monster.

TRIN. Nor go neither; but you'll lie like dogs and yet say nothing neither.

STE. Moon-calf speak once in thy life, if thou beest a good moon-calf.

CAL. How does thy honour? Let me lick thy shoe. I'll not serve him; he is not valiant.   27

TRIN. Thou liest, most ignorant monster: I am in case to justle a constable. Why, thou deboshed fish, thou, was there ever man a coward that hath drunk so much sack as I to-day? Wilt thou tell a monstrous lie, being but half a fish and half a monster?

CAL. Lo, how he mocks me! wilt thou let him, my lord?

TRIN. 'Lord' quoth he. That a monster should be such a natural!   37

CAL. Lo, lo, again! bite him to death, I prithee.

STE. Trinculo, keep a good tongue in your head· if you prove a mutineer,—the next tree! The poor monster's my subject and he shall not suffer indignity.

CAL. I thank my noble lord. Wilt thou be pleased to hearken once again to the suit I made to thee?

STE. Marry, will I: kneel and repeat it; I will stand, and so shall Trinculo.

[Enter ARIEL, invisible.

CAL. As I told thee before, I am subject to a tyrant, a sorcerer, that by his cunning hath cheated me of the island.   50

ARI. Thou liest.

CAL. Thou liest, thou jesting monkey, thou: I would my valiant master would destroy thee! I do not lie.

STE. Trinculo, if you trouble him any more in 's tale, by this hand, I will supplant some of your teeth.

TRIN. Why, I said nothing.

STE. Mum, then, and no more. Proceed.

CAL. I say, by sorcery he got this isle;   60
From me he got it. If thy greatness will
Revenge it on him,—for I know thou darest,
But this thing dare no,—

STE. That's most certain.

CAL. Thou shalt be lord of it and I'll serve thee.

STE. How now shall this be compassed?
Canst thou bring me to the party?

CAL. Yea, yea, my lord: I'll yield him thee asleep,
Where thou mayst knock a nail into his head.

ARI. Thou liest, thou canst not.   70

CAL. What a pied ninny's this! Thou scurvy patch!
I do beseech thy greatness, give him blows
And take his bottle from him: when that 's gone
He shall drink nought but brine; for I'll not show him
Where the quick freshes are.

STE. Trinculo, run into no further danger: interrupt
the monster one word further, and, by this hand, I'll turn my
mercy out o' doors and make a stock-fish
of thee.

TRIN. Why, what did I? I did nothing. I'll go
farther off.   81

STE. Didst thou not say he lied?

ARI. Thou liest.

STE. Do I so? take thou that. *[Beats Trin.]* As you
like this, give me the lie another time.

TRIN. I did not give the lie. Out o' your wits and
hearing too? A pox o' your bottle! this can sack and
drinking do. A murrain on your monster, and the
devil take your fingers!

CAL. Ha, ha, ha!   90

STE. Now, forward with your tale. Prithee, stand
farther off.

CAL. Beat him enough: after a little time
I'll beat him too.

STE.   Stand farther. Come, proceed.

CAL. Why, as I told thee, 'tis a custom with him,
I' th' afternoon to sleep: there thou mayst brain him,
Having first seized his books, or with a log
Batter his skull, or paunch him with a stake,
Or cut his wezand with thy knife. Remember
First to possess his books; for without them   *100*
He 's but a sot, as I am, nor hath not
One spirit to command: they all do hate him
As rootedly as I. Burn but his books.
He has brave utensils,—for so he calls them,—
Which, when he has a house, he'll deck withal.
And that most deeply to consider is
The beauty of his daughter; he himself
Calls her a nonpareil: I never saw a woman,
But only Sycorax my dam and she;
But she as far surpasseth Sycorax   *110*
    As great'st does least.

STE.   Is it so brave a lass?

CAL. Ay, lord; she will become thy bed, I warrant.
And bring thee forth brave brood.

STE. Monster, I will kill this man: his daughter and I will
be king and queen,—save our graces!—and
Trinculo, and thyself shall be viceroys. Dost thou like
the plot, Trinculo?

TRIN. Excellent.

STE. Give me thy hand: I am sorry I beat thee; but,
while thou livest, keep a good tongue in thy head.   *121*

CAL. Within this half hour will he be asleep:
Wilt thou destroy him then?

STE.   Ay, on mine honour.

ARI. This will I tell my master.

CAL. Thou makest me merry; I am full of pleasure:
Let us be jocund: will you troll the catch
You taught me but while-ere?

STE. At thy request, monster, I will do reason, any
reason. Come on, Trinculo, let us sing.

                                        [*Sings.*

Flout 'em and scout 'em;   *130*
And scout 'em and flout 'em;
    Thought is free.

CAL. That 's not the tune.

[Ariel plays the tune on a tabor and pipe.

STE. What is this same?

TRIN. This is the tune of our catch, played by the
picture of Nobody.

STE. If thou beest a man, show thyself in thy likeness:
if thou beest a devil, take 't as thou list.

TRIN. O, forgive me my sins!

STE. He that dies pays all debts: I defy thee. Mercy
upon us!   *141*

CAL. Art thou afeard?

STE. No, monster, not I.

CAL. Be not afeard; the isle is full of noises,
Sounds and sweet airs, that give delight and hurt not.
Sometimes a thousand twangling instruments
Will hum about mine ears, and sometime voices
That, if I then had waked after long sleep,
Will make me sleep again: and then, in dreaming,
The clouds methought would open and show riches   *150*
Ready to drop upon me, that, when I waked,
I cried to dream again.

STE. This will prove a brave kingdom to me, where
I shall have my music for nothing.

CAL. When Prospero is destroyed.

STE. That shall be by and by: I remember the story.

TRIN. The sound is going away; let's follow it, and
after do our work.

STE. Lead, monster; we'll follow. I would I could
see this taborer; he lays it on.   *160*

TRIN. Wilt come? I'll follow, Stephano.

[Exeunt.

SCENE III.   *Another part of the island.*

**Enter ALONSO, SEBASTIAN, ANTONIO, GONZALO,
ADRIAN, FRANCISCO, and others.**

GON. By 'r lakin, I can go no further, sir;
My old bones ache: here 's a maze trod indeed
Through forth-rights and meanders! By your patience,
I needs must rest me.

ALON.   Old lord, I cannot blame thee,
Who am myself attach'd with weariness,
To the dulling of my spirits: sit down, and rest.
Even here I will put off my hope and keep it
No longer for my flatterer: he is drown'd
Whom thus we stray to find, and the sea mocks
Our frustrate search on land. Well, let him go.   10

ANT. *[Aside to Seb.]* I am right glad that he's so out
    of hope.
Do not, for one repulse, forego the purpose
That you resolved to effect.

SEB.   *[Aside to Ant.]* The next advantage
Will we take throughly.

ANT.   *[Aside to Seb.]* Let it be to-night;
For, now they are oppress'd with travel, they
Will not, nor cannot, use such vigilance
As when they are fresh.

SEB. *[Aside to Ant.]* I say, to-night: now more.

                                    [Solemn and strange music.

ALON. What harmony is this? My good friends, hark!

GON. Marvellous sweet music!

            *Enter PROSPERO above, invisible. Enter several strange
            Shapes, bringing in a banquet; they dance about it with
            gentle actions of salutation; and, inviting the King, &c.
                                    to eat, they depart.*

ALON. Give us kind keepers, heavens! What were these?   20

SEB. A living drollery. Now I will believe
That there are unicorns, that in Arabia
There is one tree, the phoenix' throne, one phoenix
At this hour reigning there.

ANT.   I'll believe both;
And what does else want credit, come to me,
And I'll be sworn 'tis true: travellers ne'er did lie,
Though fools at home condemn 'em.

GON.   If in Naples
I should report this now, would they believe me?
If I should say, I saw such islanders—
For, certes, these are people of the island—   30
Who, though they are of monstrous shape, yet, note,
Their manners are more gentle-kind than of

Our human generation you shall find
Many, nay, almost any.

PROS. *[Aside]* Honest lord,
Thou hast said well; for some of you there present
Are worse than devils.

ALON.   I cannot too much muse
Such shapes, such gesture and such sound, expressing,
Although they want the use of tongue, a kind
Of excellent dumb discourse.

PROS.   *[Aside]* Praise in departing.

FRAN. They vanish'd strangely.

SEB.   No matter, since   40
They have left their viands behind; for we have stomachs.
Will 't please you taste of what is here?

ALON.   Not I.

GON. Faith, sir, you need not fear. When we were boys,
Who would believe that there were mountaineers
Dew-lapp'd like bulls, whose throats had hanging at 'em
Wallets of flesh? or that there were such men
Whose heads stood in their breasts? which now we find
Each putter-out of five for one will bring us
Good warrant of.

ALON.   I will stand to and feed,
Although my last: no matter, since I feel   50
The best is past. Brother, my lord the duke,
Stand to and do as we.

> *Thunder and lightning. Enter ARIEL,*
> *like a harpy; claps his wings upon the table;*
> *and, with a quaint device, the banquet vanishes.*

ARI. You are three men of sin, whom Destiny,
That hath to instrument this lower world
And what is in 't, the never-surfeited sea
Hath caused to belch up you; and on this island
Where man doth not inhabit; you 'mongst men
Being most unfit to live. I have made you mad;
And even with such-like valour men hang and drown
Their proper selves.

> *[Alon., Seb. &c. draw their swords.*

          You fools! I and my fellows   60
Are ministers of Fate: the elements,
Of whom your swords are temper'd, may as well

Wound the loud winds, or with bemock'd-at stabs
Kill the still-closing waters, as diminish
One dowle that 's in my plume: my fellow-ministers
Are like invulnerable. If you could hurt,
Your swords are now too massy for your strengths
And will not be uplifted. But remember—
For that 's my business to you—that you three
From Milan did supplant good Prospero; 70
Exposed unto the sea, which hath requit it,
Him and his innocent child: for which foul deed
The powers, delaying, not forgetting, have
Incensed the seas and shores, yea, all the creatures,
Against your peace. Thee of thy son, Alonso,
They have bereft; and do pronounce by me
Lingering perdition, worse than any death
Can be at once, shall step by step attend
You and your ways; whose wraths to guard you from—
Which here, in this most desolate isle, else falls 80
Upon your heads—is nothing but heart-sorrow
And a clear life ensuing.

*He vanishes in thunder; then, to soft music, enter the Shapes again, and dance,
with mocks and mows, and carrying out the table.*

PROS. Bravely the figure of this harpy hast thou
Perform'd, my Ariel; a grace it had, devouring:
Of my instruction hast thou nothing bated
In what thou hadst to say: so, with good life
And observation strange, my meaner ministers
Their several kinds have done. My high charms work
And these mine enemies are all knit up
In their distractions; they now are in my power; 90
And in these fits I leave them, while I visit
Young Ferdinand, whom they suppose is drown'd
And his and mine loved darling. *[Exit above.*

GON. I' the name of something holy, sir, why stand you
In this strange stare?

ALON.   O, it is monstrous, monstrous!
Methought the billows spoke and told me of it;
The winds did sing it to me, and the thunder,
That deep and dreadful organ-pipe, pronounced
The name of Prosper: it did bass my trespass.
Therefore my son i' the ooze is bedded, and 100
I'll seek him deeper than e'er plummet sounded
And with him there lie mudded. *[Exit.*

SEB.   But one fiend at a time,
I'll fight their legions o'er.

ANT.   I'll be thy second.   *[Exeunt Seb. and Ant.*

GON. All three of them are desperate: their great guilt,
Like poison given to work a great time after,
Now 'gins to bite the spirits. I do beseech you
That are of suppler joints, follow them swiftly
And hinder them from what this ecstasy
May now provoke them to.

ADR.   Follow, I pray you.

                                                              [Exeunt.

NOTES

ACT III. SCENE I. 11. **sore,** grievous, severe. 15. **Most . . . lest,** unexplained; Spedding suggests *Most busiest when idlest;* New Cambridge editors suggest *busy-idlest,* employed in trifles. 46. **put . . . foil,** disgraced it; a wrestling phrase. 53. **skilless,** ignorant. 70. **hollowly,** insincerely, falsely.
SCENE II. 3. **bear up,** put the helm up so as to bring the ship into the wind. **board 'em,** climb aboard; both phrases refer to drinking. 10. **thy eyes . . . head,** current description of drunkenness meaning that the eyes are fixed in a stare, or dimmed by drink. 19. **standard,** standard-bearer. 20. **standard,** something that stands up. 29. **case,** condition. 30. **deboshed,** debauched. 37. **natural,** idiot. 71. **pied ninny,** fool in motley. **patch,** common word for *fool.* 75. **quick freshes,** running springs. 79. **stock-fish,** dried cod beaten before boiling. 88. **murrain,** plague. 99. **wezand,** windpipe. 101. **sot,** fool. 108. **nonpareil,** one having no equal. 126. **troll the catch,** sing the song. 127. **while-ere,** a while since. 130. **scout,** deride (Onions). New Cambridge editors emend, *cout* (befool). 133. *Stage Direction:* **tabor,** small drum. 136. **picture of Nobody,** an unexplained topical allusion. New Cambridge editors suggest a reference to the sign of "Nobody" used by John Trundle, bookseller and printer.
SCENE III. 1. **By 'r lakin,** by our Lady. 3. **forth-rights and meanders,** paths straight and crooked. 20. **keepers,** guardian angels. 21. **drollery,** puppet show. 30. **certes,** certainly. 39. **Praise in departing,** proverbial expression meaning, "Praise comes at the end." Yale editor interprets as "Save your praise until the end of the performance." 45. **Dew-lapp'd,** having a dewlap, or fold of skin hanging from the neck, as cattle; often supposed to refer to people afflicted with goiter. 48. **putter-out . . . one,** one who invests money, or gambles on the risks of travel on the condition that, if he returns safely, he is to receive five times the amount deposited. 52. Stage Direction: **harpy,** a fabulous monster with a woman's face and vulture's body supposed to be a minister of divine vengeance. **quaint device,** ingenious stage contrivance; perhaps harpies seemed to swallow the food. 54. **to,** as. 65. **dowle,** soft, fine feather. **plume,** plumage (?) (Onions). 66. **like,** likewise, similarly. 71. **requit,** requited, avenged. 82. **clear,** unspotted, innocent. 84. **devouring.** New Cambridge editors conjecture *devoiring* (serving, waiting at table). 86. **so . . . life,** with faithful reproduction. 87. **observation strange,** rare attention to detail. 99. **bass my trespass,** proclaimed my trespass like a bass note in music. 106. **bite the spirits,** i.e., conscience troubles them.

ACT IV

SCENE I.   *Before PROSPERO'S cell.*
                    Enter PROSPERO, FERDINAND, and MIRANDA.

PROS. If I have too austerely punish'd you,
Your compensation makes amends, for I
Have given you here a thrid of mine own life,
Or that for which I live; who once again
I tender to thy hand: all thy vexations
Were but my trials of thy love, and thou
Hast strangely stood the test: here, afore Heaven,
I ratify this my rich gift. O Ferdinand,
Do not smile at me that I boast her off,
For thou shalt find she will outstrip all praise   10
And make it halt behind her.

FER.   I do believe it
Against an oracle.

PROS. Then, as my gift and thine own acquisition
Worthily purchased, take my daughter: but
If thou dost break her virgin-knot before
All sanctimonious ceremonies may
With full and holy rite be minister'd
No sweet aspersion shall the heavens let fall
To make this contract grow; but barren hate,
Sour-eyed disdain and discord shall bestrew   20
The union of your bed with weeds so loathly
That you shall hate it both: therefore take heed,
As Hymen's lamps shall light you.

FER.   As I hope
For quiet days, fair issue and long life,
With such love as 'tis now, the murkiest den,
The most opportune place, the strong'st suggestion
Our worser genius can, shall never melt
Mine honour into lust, to take away
The edge of that day's celebration
When I shall think, or Phoebus' steeds are founder'd   30
Or Night kept chain'd below.

PROS.   Fairly spoke.
Sit then and talk with her; she is thine own.
What, Ariel! my industrious servant, Ariel!

Enter ARIEL.

ARI. What would my potent master? here I am.

PROS. Thou and thy meaner fellows your last service
Did worthily perform; and I must use you
In such another trick. Go bring the rabble,
O'er whom I give thee power, here to this place:
Incite them to quick motion; for I must

Bestow upon the eyes of this young couple   40
Some vanity of mine art: it is my promise,
And they expect it from me.

ARI.   Presently?

PROS. Ay, with a twink.

ARI. Before you can say 'come' and 'go,'
        And breathe twice and cry 'so, so,'
        Each one, tripping on his toe,
        Will be here with mop and mow.
        Do you love me, master? no?

PROS. Dearly, my delicate Ariel. Do not approach
Till thou dost hear me call.

ARI.   Well, I conceive.   50

                                                                        [Exit.

PROS. Look thou be true; do not give dalliance
Too much the rein: the strongest oaths are straw
To the fire i' the blood: be more abstemious,
Or else, good night your vow!

FER.   I warrant you, sir;
The white cold virgin snow upon my heart
Abates the ardour of my liver.

PROS.   Well.
Now come, my Ariel! bring a corollary,
Rather than want a spirit: appear, and pertly!
No tongue! all eyes! be silent.

                                                        [Soft music.
                                                        Enter IRIS.

IRIS. Ceres, most bounteous lady, thy rich leas   60
Of wheat, rye, barley, vetches, oats and pease;
Thy turfy mountains, where live nibbling sheep,
And flat meads thatch'd with stover, them to keep;
Thy banks with pioned and twilled brims,
Which spongy April at thy hest betrims,
To make cold nymphs chaste crowns; and thy broom-groves,
Whose shadow the dismissed bachelor loves,
Being lass-lorn; thy pole-clipt vineyard;
And thy sea-marge, sterile and rocky-hard,
Where thou thyself dost air;—the queen o' the sky,   70
Whose watery arch and messenger am I,
Bids thee leave these, and with her sovereign grace,
Here on this grass-plot, in this very place,
To come and sport: her peacocks fly amain:
Approach, rich Ceres, her to entertain.

Enter CERES.

CER. Hail, many-colour'd messenger, that ne'er
Dost disobey the wife of Jupiter;
Who with thy saffron wings upon my flowers
Diffusest honey-drops, refreshing showers,
And with each end of thy blue bow dost crown   80
My bosky acres and my unshrubb'd down,
Rich scarf to my proud earth; why hath thy queen
Summon'd me hither, to this short-grass'd green?

IRIS. A contract of true love to celebrate;
and some donation freely to estate
On the blest lovers.

CER.   Tell me, heavenly bow,
If Venus or her son, as thou dost know,
Do now attend the queen? Since they did plot
The means that dusky Dis my daughter got,
Her and her blind boy's scandal'd company   90
I have forsworn.

IRIS.   Of her society
Be not afraid: I met her deity
Cutting the clouds towards Paphos and her son
Dove-drawn with her. Here thought they to have done
Some wanton charm upon this man and maid,
Whose vows are, that no bed-right shall be paid
Till Hymen's torch be lighted: but in vain;
Mars's hot minion is return'd again;
Her waspish-headed son has broke his arrows,
Swears he will shoot no more but play with sparrows   100
And be a boy right out.

CER.   High'st queen of state,
Great Juno, comes; I know her by her gait.

Enter JUNO.

JUNO. How does my bounteous sister? Go with me
To bless this twain, that they may prosperous be
And honour'd in their issue.

[They sing:

JUNO.

Honour, riches, marriage-blessing,
Long continuance, and increasing,
Hourly joys be still upon you!
Juno sings her blessings on you.

CER.

Earth's increase, foison plenty,   *110*
Barns and garners never empty,
Vines with clustering bunches growing,
Plants with goodly burthen bowing;

Spring come to you at the farthest
In the very end of harvest!
Scarcity and want shall shun you;
Ceres' blessing so is on you.

FER. This is a most majestic vision, and
Harmonious charmingly. May I be bold
To think these spirits?

PROS.   Spirits, which by mine art   *120*
I have from their confines call'd to enact
My present fancies.

FER.   Let me live here ever;
So rare a wonder'd father and a wife
Makes this place Paradise.
                    [Juno and Ceres whisper, and send Iris on employment.
PROS.   Sweet, now, silence!
Juno and Ceres whisper seriously;
There's something else to do: hush, and be mute,
Or else our spell is marr'd.

IRIS. You nymphs, call'd Naiads, of the windring brooks,
With your sedged crowns and ever-harmless looks,
Leave your crisp channels and on this green land   *130*
Answer your summons; Juno does command:
Come, temperate nymphs, and help to celebrate
A contract of true love; be not too late.

                              Enter certain Nymphs.

You sunburnt sicklemen, of August weary,
Come hither from the furrow and be merry:
Make holiday; your rye-straw hats put on
And these fresh nymphs encounter every one
In country footing.
                    *Enter certain Reapers, properly habited: they join with the
                         Nymphs in a graceful dance; towards the end whereof
                    PROSPERO starts suddenly, and speaks; after which, to a
                         strange, hollow, and confused noise, they heavily vanish.*

PROS. *[Aside]* I had forgot that foul conspiracy
Of the beast Caliban and his confederates   *140*

Against my life: the minute of their plot
Is almost come. *[To the Spirits.]* Well done! avoid; no more!

FER. This is strange: your father's in some passion
That works him strongly.

MIR.   Never till this day
Saw I him touch'd with anger so distemper'd.

PROS. You do look, my son, in a moved sort,
As if you were dismay'd: be cheerful, sir.
Our revels now are ended. These our actors,
As I foretold you, were all spirits and
Are melted into air, into thin air: *150*
And, like the baseless fabric of this vision,
The cloud-capp'd towers, the gorgeous palaces,
The solemn temples, the great globe itself,
Yea, all which it inherit, shall dissolve
And, like this insubstantial pageant faded,
Leave not a rack behind. We are such stuff
As dreams are made on, and our little life
Is rounded with a sleep. Sir, I am vex'd;
Bear with my weakness; my old brain is troubled:
Be not disturb'd with my infirmity: *160*
If you be pleased, retire into my cell
And there repose: a turn or two I'll walk,
To still my beating mind.

FER. MIR.   We wish your peace.

                                              [Exeunt.

                                    Enter ARIEL.

PROS. Come with a thought. I thank thee, Ariel: come.

ARI. Thy thoughts I cleave to. What 's thy pleasure?

PROS.   Spirit,
We must prepare to meet with Caliban.

ARI. Ay, my commander; when I presented Ceres,
I thought to have told thee of it, but I fear'd
Lest I might anger thee.

PROS. Say again, where didst thou leave these varlets?   *170*

ARI. I told you, sir, they were red-hot with drinking;
So full of valour that they smote the air
For breathing in their faces; beat the ground
For kissing of their feet; yet always bending
Towards their project. Then I beat my tabor;
At which, like unback'd colts, they prick'd their ears,

363
▪

Advanced their eyelids, lifted up their noses
As they smelt music: so I charm'd their ears
That calf-like they my lowing follow'd through
Tooth'd briers, sharp furzes, pricking goss and thorns,   *180*
Which enter'd their frail shins: at last I left them
I' the filthy-mantled pool beyond your cell,
There dancing up to the chins, that the foul lake
O'erstunk their feet.

PROS.   This was well done, my bird.
Thy shape invisible retain thou still:
The trumpery in my house, go bring it hither,
For stale to catch these thieves.

ARI.   I go, I go.

                                     [Exit.

PROS. A devil, a born devil, on whose nature
Nurture can never stick; on whom my pains,
Humanely taken, all, all lost, quite lost;   *190*
And as with age his body uglier grows,
So his mind cankers. I will plague them all,
Even to roaring.

                Re-enter ARIEL, loaden with glistering apparel, &c.

         Come, hang them on this line.

           PROSPERO and ARIEL remain, invisible. Enter CALIBAN,
                          STEPHANO, and TRINCULO, all wet.

CAL. Pray you, tread softly, that the blind mole may not
Hear a foot fall: we now are near his cell.

STE. Monster, your fairy, which you say is a harmless
fairy, has done little better than played the Jack with
us.

TRIN. Monster, I do smell all horse-piss; at which
my nose is in great indignation.   *200*

STE. So is mine. Do you hear, monster? If I should
take a displeasure against you, look you,—

TRIN. Thou wert but a lost monster.

CAL. Good my lord, give me thy favour still.
Be patient, for the prize I'll bring thee to
Shall hoodwink this mischance: therefore speak softly.
All 's hush'd as midnight yet.

TRIN. Ay, but to lose our bottles in the pool,—   *208*

STE. There is not only disgrace and dishonour in
that, monster, but an infinite loss.

TRIN. That 's more to me than my wetting: yet this
is your harmless fairy, monster.

STE. I will fetch off my bottle, though I be o'er ears
for my labour.

CAL. Prithee, my king, be quiet. See'st thou here,
This is the mouth o' the cell: no noise, and enter.
Do that good mischief which may make this island
Thine own for ever, and I, thy Caliban,
For aye thy foot-licker.

STE. Give me thy hand. I do begin to have bloody
thoughts.   *220*

TRIN. O king Stephano! O peer! O worthy Stephano!
look what a wardrobe here is for thee!

CAL. Let it alone, thou fool; it is but trash.

TRIN. O, ho, monster! we know what belongs to a
frippery. O king Stephano!

STE. Put off that gown, Trinculo; by this hand, I'll
have that gown.

TRIN. Thy grace shall have it.

CAL. The dropsy down this fool! what do you mean   *230*
To dote thus on such luggage? Let's alone
And do the murder first: if he awake,
From toe to crown he'll fill our skins with pinches,
Make us strange stuff.

STE. Be you quiet, monster. Mistress line, is not this
my jerkin? Now is the jerkin under the line: now,
jerkin, you are like to lose your hair and prove a bald
jerkin.

TRIN. Do, do: we steal by line and level, an 't like
your grace.   *240*

STE. I thank thee for that jest; here 's a garment
for 't: wit shall not go unrewarded while I am king of
this country. 'Steal by line and level' is an excellent
pass of pate; there 's another garment for 't.

TRIN. Monster, come, put some lime upon your
fingers, and away with the rest.

CAL. I will have none on 't: we shall lose our time,
And all be turn'd to barnacles, or to apes
With foreheads villanous low.   *250*

STE. Monster, lay to your fingers: help to bear this
away where my hogshead of wine is, or I'll turn you
out of my kingdom: go to, carry this.

TRIN. And this.

STE. Ay, and this.

A noise of hunters heard. Enter divers Spirits, in shape of
dogs and hounds, and hunt them about, PROSPERO and
ARIEL setting them on.

PROS. Hey, Mountain, hey!

ARI. Silver! there it goes, Silver!

PROS. Fury, Fury! there, Tyrant, there! hark! hark!

[Cal., Ste., and Trin. are driven out.

Go charge my goblins that they grind their joints
With dry convulsions, shorten up their sinews   *260*
With aged cramps, and more pinch-spotted make them
Than pard or cat o' mountain.

ARI.   Hark, they roar!

PROS. Let them be hunted soundly. At this hour
Lie at my mercy all mine enemies:
Shortly shall all my labours end, and thou
Shalt have the air at freedom: for a little
Follow, and do me service.

[Exeunt.

NOTES

ACT IV. SCENE I. 3. **thrid,** defined as "thread," "narrative"; F: *third,* which is correct—
the other thirds were Prospero himself and his wife. 7. **strangely,** extraordinarily. 16.
sanctimonious, sacred. 18. **aspersion,** dew, shower. 23. **Hymen's.** Hymen was the Greek
and Roman god of marriage. 27. **genius,** evil genius, or evil attendant spirit. 30. **founder'd,**
broken down, made lame. 37. **rabble,** band, i.e., the *meaner fellows* of line 35. 41. **vanity,**
illusion. 47. **mop and mow,** grimace and made faces. 56. **liver,** as the seat of the passions.
57. **corollary,** supernumerary. 58. **pertly,** briskly. 60–138. **Ceres . . . footing.** This is
the most perfect example of the masque in Shakespeare. His authorship of it has, however,
sometimes been called in question. It is a masque in honor of betrothal. For another example
of a masque in honor of betrothal see the end of *A Midsummer-Night's Dream*. 63. **stover,**
fodder for cattle. 64. **pioned and twilled,** unexplained; excavated (?) or trenched (?)
(Onions), ridged (New Cambridge), grown over with peonies and lilies (Hanmer). 66. **broom-
groves,** groves of broom (?) 68. **pole-clipt,** hedged in with poles. 71. **watery arch,**
rainbow. 74. **amain,** with full force or speed. 81. **bosky,** covered with shrubs. **unshrubb'd
down,** shrubless upland. 89. **Dis . . . got.** Pluto, god of the infernal regions, carried off
Persephone, daughter of Ceres, to be his bride in Hades. 90. **scandal'd,** brought into

disrepute; New Cambridge editors suggest *sandal'd*. 93. **Paphos,** a town in the island of Cyprus, sacred to Venus. 98. **Mars's . . . minion,** Venus, the beloved of Mars. 99. **waspish-headed,** fiery, hot-headed (?). 110. **foison plenty,** plentiful harvest. 123. **won-der'd,** wonder-performing. 128. **windring,** wandering (?) or winding (?) 130. **crisp,** curled, rippled. 132. **temperate,** chaste. 138. **country footing,** country-dancing. 142. **avoid,** depart, withdraw. 144. **works,** affects. 145. **distemper'd,** vexed. 146. **sort,** state, condi-tion. 156. **rack,** mass of cloud driven before the wind in the upper air (Onions). 164. **with a thought,** on the instant. 176. **unback'd,** unbroken, unridden. 180. **goss,** gorse, a prickly shrub. 182. **filthy-mantled,** covered with vegetable coating, slimy. 184. **feet,** New Cambridge conjectures: *sweat*. **bird,** used as a term of endearment. 187. **stale,** decoy. 193. **line,** probably, lime tree. 198. **played the Jack,** done a mean trick. *Jack* has a double meaning, "knave" and "will-o'-the-wisp." 206. **hoodwink,** cover up; hawking term. 221. **king Stephano,** allusion to the old ballad beginning, "King Stephen was a worthy peer." 226. **frippery,** place where cast-off clothes are sold. 231. **luggage,** impedimenta, heavy stuff to be carried. 236. **jerkin,** jacket made of leather. 237. **under the line,** under the lime tree, with punning allusion, probably, to the equinoctial line. 238. **lose your hair.** The jerkin will lose all its hair when Stephano wears it. 239. **by line and level,** i.e., by means of instruments, or, methodically, like dishonest carpenters and masons. 244. **pass of pate,** folly of wit. 246. **lime,** birdlime. 249. **barnacles,** barnacle geese, formerly supposed to be hatched from seashells attached to trees and to fall thence into the water; possibly, the ordinary meaning is intended. 260. **convulsions,** cramps. 262. **pard,** panther or leopard. **cat o' mountain,** wildcat.

ACT V.

SCENE I.   *Before PROSPERO'S cell.*
Enter PROSPERO in his magic robes, and ARIEL.

PROS. Now does my project gather to a head:
My charms crack not; my spirits obey; and time
Goes upright with his carriage. How 's the day?

ARI. On the sixth hour; at which time, my lord,
You said our work should cease.

PROS.   I did say so,
When first I raised the tempest. Say, my spirit,
How fares the king and 's followers?

ARI.   Confined together
In the same fashion as you gave in charge,
Just as you left them; all prisoners, sir,
In the line-grove which weather-fends your cell;   *10*
They cannot budge till your release. The king,
His brother and yours, abide all three distracted
And the remainder mourning over them,
Brimful of sorrow and dismay; but chiefly
Him that you term'd, sir, 'The good old lord, Gonzalo;'

His tears run down his beard, like winter's drops
From eaves of reeds. Your charm so strongly works 'em
That if you now beheld them, your affections
Would become tender.

PROS. Dost thou think so, spirit?

ARI. Mine would, sir, were I human.

PROS.   And mine shall.   *20*
  Hast thou, which art but air, a touch, a feeling
Of their afflictions, and shall not myself,
One of their kind, that relish all as sharply,
Passion as they, be kindlier moved than thou art?
Though with their high wrongs I am struck to the quick,
Yet with my nobler reason 'gainst my fury
Do I take part: the rarer action is
In virtue than in vengeance: they being penitent,
The sole drift of my purpose doth extend
Not a frown further. Go release them, Ariel: *30*
My charms I'll break, their senses I'll restore,
And they shall be themselves.

ARI.   I'll fetch them, sir.

                [Exit.

PROS. Ye elves of hills, brooks, standing lakes and groves,
And ye that on the sands with printless foot
Do chase the ebbing Neptune and do fly him
When he comes back; you demi-puppets that
By moonshine do the green sour ringlets make,
Whereof the ewe not bites, and you whose pastime
Is to make midnight mushrooms, that rejoice
To hear the solemn curfew; by whose aid,   *40*
Weak masters though ye be, I have bedimm'd
The noontide sun, call'd forth the mutinous winds,
And 'twixt the green sea and the azured vault
Set roaring war: to the dread rattling thunder
Have I given fire and rifted Jove's stout oak
With his own bolt; the strong-based promontory
Have I made shake and by the spurs pluck'd up
The pine and cedar: graves at my command
Have waked their sleepers, oped, and let 'em forth
By my so potent art. But this rough magic   *50*
I here abjure, and, when I have required
Some heavenly music, which even now I do,
To work mine end upon their senses that
This airy charm is for, I'll break my staff,
Bury it certain fathoms in the earth,

And deeper than did ever plummet sound
I'll drown my book.

[Solemn music.
Re-enter ARIEL before: then ALONSO, with a frantic gesture, attended by
GONZALO; SEBASTIAN and ANTONIO in like manner, attended by ADRIAN
and FRANCISCO: they all enter the circle which PROSPERO had made, and
there stand charmed; which PROSPERO observing, speaks:

A solemn air and the best comforter
To an unsettled fancy cure thy brains,
Now useless, boil'd within thy skull! There stand,   60
For you are spell-stopp'd.
Holy Gonzalo, honourable man,
Mine eyes, even sociable to the show of thine,
Fall fellowly drops. The charm dissolves apace,
And as the morning steals upon the night,
Melting the darkness, so their rising senses
Begin to chase the ignorant fumes that mantle
Their clearer reason. O good Gonzalo,
My true preserver, and a loyal sir
To him thou follow'st! I will pay thy graces   70
Home both in word and deed. Most cruelly
Didst thou, Alonso, use me and my daughter:
Thy brother was a furtherer in the act.
Thou art pinch'd for 't now, Sebastian. Flesh and blood,
You, brother mine, that entertain'd ambition,
Expell'd remorse and nature; who, with Sebastian,
Whose inward pinches therefore are most strong,
Would here have kill'd your king; I do forgive thee,
Unnatural though thou art. Their understanding
Begins to swell, and the approaching tide   80
Will shortly fill the reasonable shore
That now lies foul and muddy. Not one of them
That yet looks on me, or would know me: Ariel,
Fetch me the hat and rapier in my cell:
I will discase me, and myself present
As I was sometime Milan: quickly, spirit;
Thou shalt ere long be free.

ARIEL sings and helps to attire him.

Where the bee sucks, there suck I:
In a cowslip's bell I lie;
There I couch when owls do cry.   90
On the bat's back I do fly
After summer merrily.
Merrily, merrily shall I live now
Under the blossom that hangs on the bough.

PROS. Why, that 's my dainty Ariel! I shall miss thee;
But yet thou shalt have freedom: so, so, so.
To the king's ship, invisible as thou art:
There shalt thou find the mariners asleep
Under the hatches; the master and the boatswain
Being awake, enforce them to this place,   *100*
And presently, I prithee.

ARI. I drink the air before me, and return
Or ere your pulse twice beat.

[Exit.

GON. All torment, trouble, wonder and amazement
Inhabits here: some heavenly power guide us
Out of this fearful country!

PROS.   Behold, sir king,
The wronged Duke of Milan, Prospero:
For more assurance that a living prince
Does now speak to thee, I embrace thy body;
And to thee and thy company I bid   *110*
A hearty welcome.

ALON.   Whether thou be'st he or no,
Or some enchanted trifle to abuse me,
As late I have been, I not know: thy pulse
Beats as of flesh and blood; and, since I saw thee,
The affliction of my mind amends, with which,
I fear, a madness held me: this must crave,
An if this be at all, a most strange story.
Thy dukedom I resign and do entreat
Thou pardon me my wrongs. But how should Prospero
Be living and be here?

PROS.   First, noble friend,   *120*
Let me embrace thine age, whose honour cannot
Be measured or confined.

GON.   Whether this be
Or be not, I'll not swear.

PROS.   You do yet taste
Some subtilties o' the isle, that will not let you
Believe things certain. Welcome, my friends all!
[Aside to Seb. and Ant.] But you, my brace of lords, were I so minded,
I here could pluck his highness' frown upon you
And justify you traitors: at this time
I will tell no tales.

SEB.   *[Aside]* The devil speaks in him.

370
■

PROS.   No.
For you, most wicked sir, whom to call brother   *130*
Would even infect my mouth, I do forgive
Thy rankest fault; all of them; and require
My dukedom of thee, which perforce, I know,
Thou must restore.

ALON.   If thou be'st Prospero,
Give us particulars of thy preservation;
How thou hast met us here, who three hours since
Were wreck'd upon this shore; where I have lost—
How sharp the point of this remembrance is!—
My dear son Ferdinand.

PROS.   I am woe for 't, sir.

ALON. Irreparable is the loss, and patience   *140*
Says it is past her cure.

PROS.   I rather think
You have not sought her help, of whose soft grace
For the like loss I have her sovereign aid
And rest myself content.

ALON.   You the like loss!

PROS. As great to me as late; and, supportable
To make the dear loss, have I means much weaker
Than you may call to comfort you, for I
Have lost my daughter.

ALON.   A daughter?
O heavens, that they were living both in Naples,
The king and queen there! that they were, I wish   *150*
Myself were mudded in that oozy bed
Where my son lies. When did you lose your daughter?

PROS. In this last tempest. I perceive, these lords
At this encounter do so much admire
That they devour their reason and scarce think
Their eyes do offices of truth, their words
Are natural breath: but, howso'er you have
Been justled from your senses, know for certain
That I am Prospero and that very duke
Which was thrust forth of Milan, who most strangely   *160*
Upon this shore, where you were wreck'd, was landed,
To be the lord on 't. No more yet of this;
For 'tis a chronicle of day by day,
Not a relation for a breakfast nor
Befitting this first meeting. Welcome, sir;

This cell 's my court: here have I few attendants
And subjects none abroad: pray you, look in.
My dukedom since you have given me again,
I will requite you with as good a thing;
At least bring forth a wonder, to content ye   *170*
As much as me my dukedom.

Here PROSPERO discovers FERDINAND and MIRANDA,
playing at chess.

MIR. Sweet lord, you play me false.

FER.   No, my dear'st love,
I would not for the world.

MIR. Yes, for a score of kingdoms you should wrangle,
And I would call it fair play.

ALON.   If this prove
A vision of the Island, one dear son
Shall I twice lose.

SEB.   A most high miracle!

FER. Though the seas threaten, they are merciful;
I have cursed them without cause.

[Kneels.

ALON.   Now all the blessings
Of a glad father compass thee about!   *180*
Arise, and say how thou camest here.

MIR.   O, wonder!
How many goodly creatures are there here!
How beauteous mankind is! O brave new world,
That has such people in 't!

PROS.   'Tis new to thee.

ALON. What is this maid with whom thou wast at play?
Your eld'st acquaintance cannot be three hours:
Is she the goddess that hath sever'd us,
And brought us thus together?

FER.   Sir, she is mortal;
But by immortal Providence she 's mine:
I chose her when I could not ask my father   *190*
For his advice, nor thought I had one. She
Is daughter to this famous Duke of Milan,
Of whom so often I have heard renown,
But never saw before; of whom I have

Received a second life; and second father
This lady makes him to me.

ALON.   I am hers:
But, O, how oddly will it sound that I
Must ask my child forgiveness!

PROS.   There, sir, stop:
Let us not burthen our remembrance with
A heaviness that 's gone.

GON.   I have inly wept   *200*
Or should have spoke ere this. Look down, you gods,
And on this couple drop a blessed crown!
For it is you that have chalk'd forth the way
Which brought us hither.

ALON.   I say, Amen, Gonzalo!

GON. Was Milan thrust from Milan, that his issue
Should become kings of Naples? O, rejoice
Beyond a common joy, and set it down
With gold on lasting pillars: In one voyage
Did Claribel her husband find at Tunis
And Ferdinand, her brother, found a wife   *210*
Where he himself was lost, Prospero his dukedom
In a poor isle and all of us ourselves
When no man was his own.

ALON.   *[To Fer. and Mir.]* Give me your hands:
Let grief and sorrow still embrace his heart
That doth not wish you joy!

GON.   Be it so! Amen!
                    Re-enter ARIEL, with the Master and Boatswain amazedly
                                                            following.

O, look, sir, look, sir! here is more of us:
I prophesied, if a gallows were on land,
This fellow could not drown. Now, blasphemy,
That swear'st grace o'erboard, not an oath on shore?
Hast thou no mouth by land? What is the news?   *220*

BOATS. The best news is, that we have safely found
Our king and company; the next, our ship—
Which, but three glasses since, we gave out split—
Is tight and yare and bravely rigg'd as when
We first put out to sea.

ARI.   *[Aside to Pros.]* Sir, all this service
Have I done since I went.

PROS.   *[Aside to Ari.]* My tricksy spirit!

ALON. These are not natural events; they strengthen
From strange to stranger. Say, how came you hither?

BOATS. If I did think, sir, I were well awake,
I 'ld strive to tell you. We were dead of sleep,   *230*
And—how we know not—all clapp'd under hatches;
Where but even now with strange and several noises
Of roaring, shrieking, howling, jingling chains,
And moe diversity of sounds, all horrible,
We were awaked; straightway, at liberty;
Where we, in all her trim, freshly beheld
Our royal, good and gallant ship, our master
Capering to eye her: on a trice, so please you,
Even in a dream, were we divided from them
And were brought moping hither.

ARI.   *[Aside to Pros.]* Was 't well done?   *240*

PROS.   *[Aside to Ari.]* Bravely, my diligence. Thou shalt be free.

ALON. This is as strange a maze as e'er men trod;
And there is in this business more than nature
Was ever conduct of: some oracle
Must rectify our knowledge.

PROS.   Sir, my liege,
Do not infest your mind with beating on
The strangeness of this business; at pick'd leisure
Which shall be shortly, single I'll resolve you,
Which to you shall seem probable, of every
These happen'd accidents; till when, be cheerful   *250*
And think of each thing well. *[Aside to Ari.]* Come
    hither, spirit:
Set Caliban and his companions free;
Untie the spell. *[Exit Ariel.]* How fares my gracious
    sir?
There are yet missing of your company
Some few odd lads that you remember not.
        Re-enter ARIEL, driving in CALIBAN, STEPHANO and
                TRINCULO, in their stolen apparel.

STE. Every man shift for all the rest, and let no man
take care for himself; for all is but fortune. Coragio,
bully-monster, coragio!

TRIN. If these be true spies which I wear in my
head, here 's a goodly sight.   *260*

374
■

CAL. O Setebos, these be brave spirits indeed!
How fine my master is! I am afraid
He will chastise me.

SEB.　　　　Ha, ha!
What things are these, my lord Antonio?
Will money buy 'em?

ANT.　　　　Very like; one of them
Is a plain fish, and, no doubt, marketable.

PROS. Mark but the badges of these men, my lords,
Then say if they be true. This mis-shapen knave,
His mother was a witch, and one so strong
That could control the moon, make flows and ebbs,　　　*270*
And deal in her command without her power.
These three have robb'd me; and this demi-devil—
For he 's a bastard one—had plotted with them
To take my life. Two of these fellows you
Must know and own; this thing of darkness I
Acknowledge mine.

CAL.　　　　I shall be pinch'd to death.

ALON. Is not this Stephano, my drunken butler?

SEB. He is drunk now: where had he wine?

ALON. And Trinculo is reeling ripe: where should they
Find this grand liquor that hath gilded 'em?　　　*280*
How camest thou in this pickle?

TRIN. I have been in such a pickle since I saw you
last that, I fear me, will never out of my bones: I shall
not fear fly-blowing.

SEB. Why, how now, Stephano!

STE. O, touch me not; I am not Stephano, but a
cramp.

PROS. You 'ld be king o' the isle, sirrah?

STE. I should have been a sore one then.

ALON. This is a strange thing as e'er I look'd on.

[Pointing to Caliban.

PROS. He is as disproportion'd in his manners　　　*290*
As in his shape. Go, sirrah, to my cell;
Take with you your companions; as you look
To have my pardon, trim it handsomely.

CAL. Ay, that I will; and I'll be wise hereafter
And seek for grace. What a thrice-double ass
Was I, to take this drunkard for a god
And worship this dull fool!

PROS.　　　　Go to; away!

ALON. Hence, and bestow your luggage where you found it.

SEB. Or stole it, rather.

　　　　　　　　　　　　　[Exeunt Cal., Ste., and Trin.

PROS. Sir, I invite your highness and your train　　　　　　*300*
To my poor cell, where you shall take your rest
For this one night; which, part of it, I'll waste
With such discourse as, I not doubt, shall make it
Go quick away; the story of my life
And the particular accidents gone by
Since I came to this isle: and in the morn
I'll bring you to your ship and so to Naples,
Where I have hope to see the nuptial
Of these our dear-beloved solemnized;
And thence retire me to my Milan, where　　　　　　*310*
Every third thought shall be my grave.

ALON.　　　　I long
To hear the story of your life, which must
Take the ear strangely.

PROS.　　　　I'll deliver all;
And promise you calm seas, auspicious gales
And sail so expeditious that shall catch
Your royal fleet far off. *[Aside to Ari.]* My Ariel, chick,
That is thy charge: then to the elements
Be free, and fare thou well! Please you, draw near.

　　　　　　　　　　　　　　　　[Exeunt.

EPILOGUE

　　　　　　　　　　　　　　　Spoken by Prospero

Now my charms are all o'erthrown,
And what strength I have 's mine own,
Which is most faint: now, 'tis true,
I must be here confined by you,
Or sent to Naples. Let me not,
Since I have my dukedom got
And pardon'd the deceiver, dwell
In this bare island by your spell;
But release me from my bands

With the help of your good hands: *10*
Gentle breath of yours my sails
Must fill, or else my project fails,
Which was to please. Now I want
Spirits to enforce, art to enchant,
And my ending is despair,
Unless I be relieved by prayer,
Which pierces so that it assaults
Mercy itself and frees all faults.
As you from crimes would pardon'd be,
Let your indulgence set me free.   *20*

NOTES

ACT V. SCENE I. 2. **crack,** figure not entirely clear; possibly, since his project gathers "to a head," the reference is to an ulcer; "the breaking of magic bands" has been suggested. He may merely mean that his charms do not fail. 3. **carriage,** burden. **How's the day?** What time is it? 10. **line-grove,** grove of lime trees. **weather-fends,** protects from the weather. 17. **eaves of reeds,** thatch. 23. **all,** quite. 27. **rarer,** nobler. 35–57. **Ye . . . book.** This famous passage is an embellished paraphrase of Golding's translation of Ovid's *Metamorphoses*, vii, 197–219. Critics have often seen in Prospero's farewell to magic an analogue to Shakespeare's farewell to the stage. *The Tempest* is the next to his last complete play. After writing it he probably retired to Stratford. 36. **demi-puppets,** elves and fairies; literally, puppets of half-size. 37. **green sour ringlets,** fairy rings, circles of grass produced by fungus within the soil. 44–45. **to . . . fire,** the dread rattling thunderbolt I have discharged. 60. **boil'd,** made hot with humors. 63. **sociable,** sympathetic. **show,** appearance. 67. **ignorant fumes.** The fumes which rose up into the brain to produce sleep brought with them unconsciousness. 85. **disease,** undress. 90. **couch,** to lie down as on a couch, or, more probably, lie hidden. 96. **so, so, so,** that will do very well. 112. **trifle,** trick of magic. 124. **subtilties,** illusions. 128. **justify you,** prove you to be. 139. **woe,** sorry. 145. **late,** i.e., as great to me as it is recent. 155. **devour,** render null, destroy. 174. **score,** double meaning: game or wager in which the score is reckoned by kingdoms, and also twenty kingdoms. **wrangle,** meaning (1) contend in a game or wager, and (2) argue or contend in words. 186. **eld'st,** earliest. 193 **renown,** report. 213. **own,** i.e., master of his senses. 224. **yare,** ready. 244. **conduct,** guide, leader. 246. **infest,** harass, disturb. 247. **pick'd,** chosen. 248. **single,** i.e., when we are along together. F. has no comma after *shortly*, in which reading *single* means "unbroken," "absolute." 258. **Coragio,** courage. **bully-monster,** gallant monster. 267. **badges,** emblems of cloth or silver worn on the arms of retainers. 271. **deal . . . power,** wield the moon's power, either without her authority, or beyond her influence. The line is ambiguous. 280. **gilded,** flushed, made drunk. 305. **accidents,** occurrences, events.
EPILOGUE. 10. **hands,** applause.

The Counter Reformation/ Baroque

John Donne, The Flea, The Canonization, Holy Sonnet 10

Of all the English lyric poets of the late Renaissance, John Donne (1572–1631) is probably the most popular and certainly the most appealing to modern tastes. His poems reflect both the complexity of his mind and the mercurial qualities of his temperament and with a directness that is often startling. Donne was trained as a lawyer, and many of his best poems possess an ingenuity and toughmindedness that one often associates with legal argumentation. Nevertheless, it was as a preacher that Donne made his mark on contemporary audiences, and it is easy to find, even in what appear to be his most "secular" poems, an undercurrent of religious concern, though often expressed in the most ironic language.

Donne's career took many curious turns, and by any standard, Donne himself would be considered something of a paradox. Although born into a largely Catholic family—his brother was imprisoned for harboring a priest—Donne finally made his way into the Anglican church, taking orders in 1615, and ultimately rose to the prestigious position of Dean of St. Paul's in London. His earlier years, however, were spent in pursuit of a military and diplomatic career, and just when it seemed likely that preferment at the court of James I was at hand, Donne threw away all chance of personal advancement by eloping with the niece of his employer and aristocratic patron—to the astonishment of friends who thought Donne a complete cynic on the question of love and marriage. He was a man of wide learning and remarkably inquisitive intellect, perhaps even something of a skeptic, yet in his religious writings, he repeatedly asks for an experience of faith that would force him to relinquish all doubts and submit helplessly to God's grace.

Donne's "wit," that is, his ability to combine seemingly discordant images and feelings, and his flair for the demonstrative and the dialectical, are the very qualities that made him stand out in his own time. And as much as any poet of his age, Donne was acutely aware of how profoundly new discoveries in science (which his contemporaries referred to as the "new philosophy") had altered the mental landscape of the seventeenth century. We can see, in Donne's poetry, just how the perceived relationship between the human world and the physical world (or between the "microcosm" of mankind and the "macrocosm" of a divinely governed universe) is beginning to break down, and we can sense the philosophical tension between belief and disbelief in even his most light-hearted verses.

THE FLEA

Mark but this flea, and mark in this
How little that which thou deny'st me is;
   It suck'd me first, and now sucks thee,
And in this flea our two bloods mingled be.
   Thou know'st that this cannot be said

A sin, nor shame, nor loss of maidenhead,
    Yet this enjoys before it woo,
And pamper'd, swells with one blood made of two,
And this, alas, is more than we would do.

    O stay, three lives in one flea spare,
Where we almost, yea more than married are.
      This flea is you and I, and this
Our marriage bed and marriage temple is;
      Though parents grudge, and you, we're met
And cloister'd in these living walls of jet.
      Though use make you apt to kill me,
Let not to that, self-murder added be,
And sacrilege: three sins in killing three.

      Cruel and sudden, hast thou since
Purpled thy nail in blood of innocence?
      Wherein could this flea guilty be,
Except in that drop which it suck'd from thee?
      Yet thou triumph'st, and say'st that thou
Find'st not thyself nor me the weaker now.
      'Tis true. Then learn how false fears be:
Just so much honor, when thou yield'st to me,
Will waste, as this flea's death took life from thee.

THE CANONIZATION
■

For God's sake hold your tongue and let me love!
    Or chide my palsy or my gout,
My five gray hairs or ruin'd fortune flout;
With wealth your state, your mind with arts improve,
    Take you a course, get you a place,
    Observe His Honor or His Grace,
Or the King's real or his stamped face
    Contemplate; what you will, approve,
    So you will let me love.

Alas, alas, who's injur'd by my love?
    What merchant's ships have my sighs drown'd?
Who says my tears have overflow'd his ground?
When did my colds a forward spring remove?
    When did the heats which my veins fill
    Add one more to the plaguy bill?
Soldiers find wars, and lawyers find out still

Litigious men which quarrels move,
Though she and I do love.

Call us what you will, we are made such by love.
Call her one, me another fly,
We're tapers too, and at our own cost die;
And we in us find th' eagle and the dove.
The phoenix riddle hath more wit,
By us; we two, being one, are it.
So to one neutral thing both sexes fit;
We die and rise the same, and prove
Mysterious by this love.

We can die by it, if not live by love,
And if unfit for tombs and hearse
Our legend be, it will be fit for verse;
And if no piece of chronicle we prove,
We'll build in sonnets pretty rooms
(As well a well-wrought urn becomes
The greatest ashes, as half-acre tombs),
And by these hymns all shall approve
Us canoniz'd for love,

And thus invoke us: "You whom reverend love
Made one another's hermitage,
You to whom love was peace, that now is rage,
Who did the whole world's soul extract, and drove
Into the glasses of your eyes
(So made such mirrors and such spies
That they did all to you epitomize)
Countries, towns, courts: beg from above
A pattern of your love!"

HOLY SONNET 10
[BATTER MY HEART]
■

Batter my heart, three-person'd God, for You
As yet but knock, breathe, shine, and seek to mend.
That I may rise and stand, o'erthrow me and bend
Your force to break, blow, burn, and make me new.
I, like an usurp'd town, to another due,
Labor to admit You, but O, to no end!
Reason, your viceroy in me, me should defend,
But is captiv'd, and proves weak or untrue.

Yet dearly I love you and would be loved fain,
But am betroth'd unto Your enemy.
Divorce me, untie, or break that knot again,
Take me to You, imprison me, for I
Except You enthrall me, never shall be free,
Nor ever chaste except You ravish me.

Molière (Jean-Baptiste Poquelin), The Would-Be Gentleman

France's most brilliant comic playwright, Molière (1622–1673) developed his theatrical skills while touring provincial towns with a small company of actors. Returning to Paris, his birthplace, Molière attracted the patronage of King Louis XIV, who supported the writer during the intense controversies his plays aroused. After scoring popular successes with *The Ridiculous Literary Ladies* (1659) and *School for Wives* (1662), Molière was violently criticized for *Tartuffe* (1664), a play exposing religious hypocrisy. *Tartuffe* generated such adverse public reaction that the King was persuaded to forbid its performance for five years, a period when Molière's detractors repeatedly attacked him for trying to discredit religion. Undeterred, Molière then produced *Don Juan* (1665), which further outraged his critics.

Despite unremitting accusations that Molière's plays were immoral, Louis XIV granted the playwright a pension and established his troupe as special "Players to the King." Molière continued to write, produce, and act in new comedies for the royal court and Parisian audiences to the end of his life. He died while acting the role of Argan in his last play, *The Imaginary Invalid* (1673).

A critical thinker as well as a comic genius, Molière ridiculed the fads and social pretentions of his day. His characters are more than targets for satire, they display a vital individuality that makes them as relevant today as they were when first created. In *The Would-Be Gentlemen* (1670), a work that combines ballet, orchestral music, and farce, Molière turned an amused and satirical eye on a social phenomenon of his day— the newly rich businessman who aspires to imitate the manners and culture of the hereditary aristocracy. While the social climber, Mr. Jourdain, blunders hilariously, the other characters perform an elaborate mating ritual that culminates in a festival of dance and song.

CHARACTERS IN THE PLAY

MONSIEUR JOURDAIN, bourgeois
MADAME JOURDAIN, his wife
LUCILE, his daughter
CLEONTE, in love with Lucile
DORIMENE, a marquise
DORANTE, a count
NICOLE, servant of Monsieur Jourdain
COVIELLE, manservant of Cléonte
A MUSIC MASTER
THE MUSIC MASTER'S PUPIL

A DANCING MASTER
A FENCING MASTER
A PHILOSOPHY MASTER
A MERCHANT TAILOR
A JOURNEYMAN TAILOR
TWO LACKEYS, several SINGERS,
  INSTRUMENTALISTS, DANCERS,
  COOKS, TAILOR'S APPRENTICES,
  and other characters in the ballets.

The scene is in Paris, in Monsieur Jourdain's house.

ACT ONE

After the overture, the curtain rises. The MUSIC MASTER'S PUPIL is working at a table. He may rise, strike some notes on a harpsichord, and return to his composition. He hums his tune, trying both the men's and women's parts.

                 Enter the MUSIC MASTER, *three* SINGERS, *and two* VIOLINISTS.

MUSIC MASTER *(to his musicians)*: All right, come in here, and take a rest until he comes.

          (*Enter from the opposite side the* DANCING MASTER *and four* DANCERS.)

DANCING MASTER *(to his dancers)*: Come in this way.

MUSIC MASTER *(to* PUPIL*)*: All done?

PUPIL: Yes.

MUSIC MASTER: Let me see it a minute. *(Inspects composition)* That will do nicely.

DANCING MASTER: Is it something new?

MUSIC MASTER: Yes; it's the music for a serenade I've had him working on here, while we're waiting for our man to get up.

DANCING MASTER: May I take a look?

MUSIC MASTER: You will hear it, with the words, when he comes. He won't be long.

DANCING MASTER: We're certainly occupied now, both of us.

MUSIC MASTER: That's right. We've both found the man we've been looking for. This Monsieur Jourdain is a very nice property, with his visions of nobility and gallantry. In the interests of your art of dance and mine of music, we could well wish there were many more like him.

DANCING MASTER: Well, not exactly like him. I could wish he had more appreciation of the things we do for him.

MUSIC MASTER: It's true he doesn't know much about them. But he pays well; and that's what our arts need more than anything else right now.

DANCING MASTER: Well, personally, I admit I enjoy a little recognition. Applause really stimulates me. And I find it an actual torture to perform for idiots, and to bear their uncouth comments on our creations. There is genuine pleasure, confess it, in working for people who can recognize the fine points of our art, and reward us for our work with heart-warming approval. Yes, the best payment we can receive is to see our work appreciated, and welcomed with the applause which does us honor. There is no better return for all our labor and fatigue; and enlightened praise gives exquisite delight.

MUSIC MASTER: I agree; I enjoy such praise as much as you do. Certainly nothing gratifies us like that kind of applause. But you can't live on applause; praise alone won't pay the rent. We need something a bit more solid; the best hand people can give us is a hand with cash in it. True enough, our man has no cultivation; he gets everything all wrong, and he is sure to applaud the wrong thing; but his money purifies his bad taste. His fat purse is full of critical insight; his approval is convertible into cash; and this ignorant commoner is a lot more useful to us, as you are well aware, than that noble amateur of the arts who introduced us to him.

DANCING MASTER: There is some truth in what you're saying. But I think you dwell on money a little too much. Material advantage is so base a thing that a man of character should never show any concern for it.

MUSIC MASTER: Still, you seem to accept the money our man hands you.

DANCING MASTER: By all means; but I don't make my happiness depend upon it; and I could wish that with all his wealth he had some tincture of good taste.

MUSIC MASTER: Naturally I should like that too. That's what we're both laboring to bring about, as best we can. But at any rate, he is helping us to get a reputation; he will underwrite the things that others will applaud for him.

DANCING MASTER: Here he is now.

Enter **MONSIEUR JOURDAIN** *and two* **LACKEYS. MONSIEUR JOURDAIN** *wears a gorgeous striped dressing gown, lined with green and orange.*

M. JOURDAIN: Well, sirs, how's things? You're going to show me your little thingamajig?

DANCING MASTER: What? What little thingamajig?

M. JOURDAIN: Why, the—what d'you call it? Your prologue or dialogue of song and dance.

DANCING MASTER: Ha, ha!

MUSIC MASTER: We are quite ready, sir.

M. JOURDAIN: I've held you up a little. But the fact is I'm dressing today in court style; and my tailor sent me some silk stockings I thought I'd never get on.

MUSIC MASTER: We are here only to await your leisure.

M. JOURDAIN: I'll ask you both not to leave until they've brought my coat, so you can see it.

DANCING MASTER: Whatever you wish.

M. JOURDAIN: You'll see me turned out properly from head to foot.

MUSIC MASTER: We don't doubt it.

M. JOURDAIN: I've just had this dressing gown made.

DANCING MASTER: It is very handsome.

M. JOURDAIN: My tailor told me that people of quality are like this in the morning.

MUSIC MASTER: It looks very well on you.

M. JOURDAIN: Lackeys! Hey, my two lackeys!

FIRST LACKEY: What do you wish, sir?

M. JOURDAIN: Nothing. I just wanted to see if you hear me all right. *(To the two* **MASTERS)** What do you think of my servants' liveries?

DANCING MASTER: Magnificent.

M. JOURDAIN *(opens his dressing gown, displaying tight red velvet breeches and a short green velvet jacket):* And here's a little sports costume to do my exercises in, in the morning.

DANCING MASTER: Very smart.

M. JOURDAIN: Lackey!

FIRST LACKEY: Yes sir!

M. JOURDAIN: Other lackey!

SECOND LACKEY: Yes sir?

M. JOURDAIN: Here, hold my gown. *(He removes his gown)* How do you like me this way?

DANCING MASTER: Splendid. It couldn't be more perfect.

M. JOURDAIN: Now let's have your little business.

MUSIC MASTER: First, I should like to have you hear a composition which this young man here has just done for the serenade you ordered. He is one of my pupils; he is very gifted for this sort of thing.

M. JOURDAIN: Yes; but you shouldn't have had it done by a pupil. You aren't too good to do the job yourself.

MUSIC MASTER: Don't let the word "pupil" put you off, sir. Such pupils as this know as much as the greatest masters; and the melody is as lovely as it can be. Just listen.

M. JOURDAIN: Give me my dressing gown so I can listen better . . . Wait a minute, I think it will be better without the dressing gown . . . No, give it back to me. It'll be better that way.

A WOMAN SINGER:
Ah, grievous is my woe, I languish night and day
Since thy imperious eye has brought me 'neath thy sway;
If thus thou deal'st, my fair, with one who loves thee so,
Ah, what must be the fate of one who is thy foe?

M. JOURDAIN: That song seems to me rather dismal. It puts you to sleep. I wish you could brighten it up a little here and there.

MUSIC MASTER: It is necessary, sir, that the music fit the words.

M. JOURDAIN: I learned a very pretty one a little while ago. Wait a minute . . . now . . . how did it go?

DANCING MASTER: Really, I don't know.

M. JOURDAIN: Something about a sheep.

DANCING MASTER: A Sheep?

M. JOURDAIN: Yes. Aha! *(He sings)*

I thought my dear Jeannette
Was just a little lamb;
I thought my dear Jeannette
Was sweet as currant jam.
Oh, dear, oh, dear, oh, dear!
I must have made a bungle!
She's crueler, it's clear,
Than a tiger in the jungle!

Isn't that pretty?

MUSIC MASTER: Extremely pretty.

DANCING MASTER. And you sing it well.

M. JOURDAIN: And yet I never studied music!

MUSIC MASTER: You ought to learn music, sir, as you are learning the dance. The two arts have a very close connection.

DANCING MASTER: And they open a man's mind to things of beauty.

M. JOURDAIN: Do people of quality study music too?

MUSIC MASTER: Oh, yes, sir.

M. JOURDAIN: Well, then, I'll study it. But I don't know how I'll find the time; for not to mention the fencing master who's giving me lessons, I have hired a philosophy professor; he's to begin this morning.

MUSIC MASTER: Philosophy is very fine; but music, sir, music—

DANCING MASTER: Music and the dance; music and the dance, that's all you really need.

MUSIC MASTER: There is nothing so useful in a state as music.

DANCING MASTER: There is nothing so necessary to men as the dance.

MUSIC MASTER: Without music—the state can hardly persist.

DANCING MASTER: Without the dance, a man is totally helpless.

MUSIC MASTER: All the disorders and wars in the world come about because men haven't learned music.

DANCING MASTER: All men's misfortunes, and the appalling disasters of history, the blunders of statesmen and the errors of great generals, they have all occurred for lack of knowledge of dancing.

M. JOURDAIN: How is that?

MUSIC MASTER: Doesn't war come from discords among men?

M. JOURDAIN: That's true.

MUSIC MASTER: And if everybody should learn music, wouldn't that be a way to harmonize everything, and to bring universal peace to the world?

M. JOURDAIN: You're right.

DANCING MASTER: When a man has made some blunder, whether in his family affairs, or in government, or in generalship, don't we always say: "So-and-so has made a false step in such a matter"?

M. JOURDAIN: Yes, we say that.

DANCING MASTER: And taking a false step, can that result from anything else than not knowing how to dance?

M. JOURDAIN: That's true. You're both in the right!

DANCING MASTER: It's just to show you the excellence and utility of dancing and music.

M. JOURDAIN: I understand that now.

MUSIC MASTER: Do you want to see our productions?

M. JOURDAIN: Yes.

MUSIC MASTER: I have already told you, this is a little effort of mine to delineate the various emotions that music can express.

M. JOURDAIN: Very good.

MUSIC MASTER: *(to the singers).* Step forward please. *(to MONSIEUR JOURDAIN)* You must imagine that they are dressed as shepherds.

M. JOURDAIN: Why are they always shepherds? All I ever see around is shepherds.

MUSIC MASTER: When one wants to make people speak in music, one must always put them in a pastoral setting. That's what we call verisimilitude. Singing has always been the specialty of shepherds and shepherdesses. It is hardly natural, in a dramatic dialogue, that princes or commoners should sing their emotions.

M. JOURDAIN: All right, all right. Let's hear it.

WOMAN SINGER:

A heart that tyrant love's dictation captures
    Is filled with turbulence incessantly.
They say that languishing and sighs are raptures,
    But still our dearest boon is liberty!

FIRST MALE SINGER:

Nought is so sweet as tender ardors thronging
    To make twin hearts blend in a lover's kiss.

There is no happiness without love's longing;
    Take love from life, you cancel all its bliss.

SECOND MALE SINGER:
It would be sweet to enter love's domain,
    If one could find in love true steadfastness;
But oh, alas! Oh, cruelty and pain!
    How can one find a faithful shepherdess?
The sex is fickle and inconstant; hence
    One must renounce for aye love's blandishments!

SECOND MALE SINGER:

Dear love is revealed—

WOMAN SINGER:

How delightful to yield—

SECOND MALE SINGER:

But love is a cheat!

FIRST MALE SINGER:

My darling, my sweet!

WOMAN SINGER *(to* **SECOND MALE SINGER***):*

Dear love, I adjure you—

SECOND MALE SINGER:

I cannot endure you!

FIRST MALE SINGER *(to* **SECOND MALE SINGER***):*

Ah, learn to love, forget your peevishness!

WOMAN SINGER:

And I shall gladly tell you where you'll see
    A faithful shepherdess!

SECOND MALE SINGER:

Where to discover such a prodigy?

WOMAN SINGER *(to* **SECOND MALE SINGER***):*

Just in defense of womankind,
I offer here my heart to you!

SECOND MALE SINGER:

Sweet shepherdess, and shall I find
    That it will be forever true?

WOMAN SINGER:
Let us essay, and make a test
Which of us two can love the best!

SECOND MALE SINGER:
And may the one accursed be
Who first shall fail in constancy!

THE THREE SINGERS:
The power that kindles deathless fires
    Now let us all pay tribute to!
How sweet it is when love inspires
    Two hearts that ever shall be true!

M. JOURDAIN: Is that all?

MUSIC MASTER: Yes.

M. JOURDAIN: A neat job. Very neat. There were some remarks in it that weren't bad.

DANCING MASTER: Now, as my part of the performance, here is a little effort to display the most beautiful postures and evolutions with which a dance may be varied.

M. JOURDAIN: More shepherds?

DANCING MASTER: They are anything you please.
> (*Four* DANCERS *execute various steps and evolutions at the* DANCING MASTER'S *order. This is the first Interlude, marking the division of the play into acts.*)

ACT TWO

The action is continuous. After the Interlude, the dancers retire, leaving MONSIEUR JOURDAIN, *the* MUSIC MASTER, *the* DANCING MASTER, *and the two* LACKEYS.

M. JOURDAIN: No nonsense about that! Those boys cut some fine capers.

MUSIC MASTER: When the dance is combined with the music, it will be much more effective. You will find very gallant the little ballet we have organized for you.

M. JOURDAIN: Have it ready soon, anyhow. The person I've ordered all this for is to do me the honor of coming to dinner today.

DANCING MASTER: It's all ready.

MUSIC MASTER: Incidentally, sir, you should go farther. A person like you, doing things in a big way, and with a taste for the finer things of life, should have a musicale at home every Wednesday or Thursday.

M. JOURDAIN: Do people of quality have that?

MUSIC MASTER: Yes, sir.

M. JOURDAIN: I'll have it, then. It will be nice, will it?

MUSIC MASTER: Certainly. You will need three voices: a soprano, a counter-tenor, and a basso; they will be accompanied by a bass viol, a theorbo or archlute, and a harpsichord for the sustained bass, with two violins to play the refrains.

M. JOURDAIN: You ought to put in an accordion too. The accordion is an instrument I like; it's harmonious.

MUSIC MASTER: Just let us arrange things.

M. JOURDAIN: Anyway, don't forget to send me some singers by and by, to sing at the dinner.

MUSIC MASTER: You will have everything you need.

M. JOURDAIN: And especially, be sure the ballet is nice.

MUSIC MASTER: You will be pleased, especially with certain minuets you will see.

M. JOURDAIN: The minuet! That's my dance! You should see me dance the minuet! Come on, dancing master!

DANCING MASTER: A hat for the gentleman, please! *(MONSIEUR JOURDAIN seizes a lackey's hat, claps it on over his nightcap, removing it to make the sweeping bows required by the dance; the DANCING MASTER sings the music, and also his instructions)* La, la, la; La, la, la, la, la, la. La, la, la, repeat. La, la, la; La, la. Keep in tune—if you please. La, la, la, la. Right leg stiff, la, la, la. Don't move shoulders—quite so much. La, la, la, la, la; La, la, la, la, la. Both your arms—are they crippled? La, la, la, la, la. Lift your head—turn toe out. La, la, la. Stand up straight.

M. JOURDAIN *(with an intonation between "I'm done in!" and "How's that?")*: Uh!

MUSIC MASTER: Splendid! Splendid!

M. JOURDAIN: This reminds me. Teach me how to make a bow to salute a marquise. I'm going to need it soon.

DANCING MASTER: A bow to salute a marquise?

M. JOURDAIN: Yes. A marquise named Doriméme.

DANCING MASTER: Give me your hand.

M. JOURDAIN: No, you do it alone. I'll get the idea.

DANCING MASTER: If you want to make a very respectful salute, you must first make a bow stepping backward, then advance toward the lady with three forward bows, and at the last you bow down to the level of her knees.

M. JOURDAIN: Show me . . . Good.

(Enter a LACKEY.)

LACKEY: Monsieur, here is your fencing master who's come.

M. JOURDAIN: Tell him to come in and give me my lesson. *(Exit LACKEY)* I want you two to watch how I do it.

(Enter FENCING MASTER. He salutes and hands MONSIEUR JOURDAIN a foil.)

FENCING MASTER: Now, sir; first make your bow . . . Body straight . . . Weight a little more on the left thigh. Legs not so wide apart. Feet on the same line. Your wrist in line with your forward hip. The point of your weapon on the level of your shoulder. The arm not quite so straight out. The left hand at the level of the eye. Left shoulder drawn back a little more. Head up. Put on a confident look . . . Advance . . . Keep the body tense. Engage my foil in quart, and carry through . . . One, two . . . Recover . . . Thrust again, keeping feet in same position . . . Backward jump . . . When you make your thrust, sir, the sword should start before the foot, and you must keep your body protected . . . One, two . . . Now, touch my sword in tierce, and carry through . . . Advance . . . Thrust from that position. One, two . . . Recover . . . Thrust . . . Backward jump . . . On guard, sir, on guard! *(Penetrating* **MONSIEUR JOURDAIN'**s *guard, he pinks his breast.)*

M. JOURDAIN: Uh?

MUSIC MASTER: You're doing marvelously.

FENCING MASTER: As I have already told you, the whole secret of swordplay consists in two things: to give; and not to receive. And as I proved the other day, with demonstrative logic, it is impossible for you to receive, if you know how to divert your enemy's weapon from the line of your body; and that depends only on a simple twist of the wrist, either inward or outward.

M. JOURDAIN: So a person who may not be very brave can be sure of killing his man, and not getting killed?

FENCING MASTER: Exactly! Didn't you see the demonstration?

M. JOURDAIN: Yes.

FENCING MASTER: Thus we can see how highly we swordsmen should be esteemed in a state, and how far the science of fencing is superior to the useless branches of knowledge, like dancing, music, and—

DANCING MASTER: Wait a minute, swordsman; please speak of the dance with respect.

MUSIC MASTER: And learn, I beg of you, to treat music with proper consideration.

FENCING MASTER: You're a funny pair, trying to compare your subjects with mine!

MUSIC MASTER: Look at the great man, will you?

DANCING MASTER: He's a comic sight, with his padded chest protector!

FENCING MASTER: My little dancing master, I'll show you some new steps. And you, my little musician, I'll make you sing—but small!

DANCING MASTER: My good blacksmith, I'll teach you your trade!

M. JOURDAIN *(to the* **DANCING MASTER***):* Are you crazy, to pick a fight with him, who knows all about tierce and quart, and can kill a man by demonstrative logic?

DANCING MASTER: Little I care for his demonstrative logic, and his tierce and quart.

M. JOURDAIN: Take it easy, I tell you.

FENCING MASTER *(to* **DANCING MASTER***)*: What, you impertinent puppy!

M. JOURDAIN: Now, now, fencing master.

DANCING MASTER: What you big cart horse!

M. JOURDAIN: Now, now, dancing master.

FENCING MASTER: If I let myself go—

M. JOURDAIN: Easy, easy there!

DANCING MASTER: If I lay a finger on you—

M. JOURDAIN: Gently, gently!

FENCING MASTER: I'll beat you to a pulp!

M. JOURDAIN: Please!

DANCING MASTER: I'll trim you down to size!

M. JOURDAIN: I beg and pray you!

MUSIC MASTER: We'll teach him how to talk!

M. JOURDAIN: Dear God! Stop, stop! *(Enter* **PHILOSOPHY MASTER***)* Hello, Monsieur Philosopher, you arrive in the nick of time with your philosophy. Come and make peace among these people.

PHILOSOPHY MASTER: What is it? What is the matter, good sirs?

M. JOURDAIN: They have got angry about the standing of their professions, to the point of calling each other names and starting to fight.

PHILOSOPHY MASTER: Dear, dear! My friends, should you let yourselves get so excited? Haven't you read the learned treatise Seneca composed upon anger? Is anything more base and shameful than that passion, which turns man into a wild beast? Should not reason be the mistress of all our actions?

DANCING MASTER: Why, sir, he goes and insults us both, sneering at my trade, the dance; and at music, which is *his* profession!

PHILOSOPHY MASTER: A wise man is superior to any insult he may hear. The proper reply one should make to all affronts is moderation and patience.

FENCING MASTER: They have both had the audacity to compare their professions to mine.

PHILOSOPHY MASTER: Should such a thing move you? Men should not dispute about vainglory and precedence; what truly distinguishes men one from another is wisdom and virtue.

DANCING MASTER: I am simply telling him that dancing is a science which can hardly be sufficiently honored.

MUSIC MASTER: And I was saying that music is a science revered throughout history.

FENCING MASTER: And I was pointing out that the science of arms is the most beautiful and necessary of all sciences.

PHILOSOPHY MASTER: And what, then, is the place of philosophy? I find all three of you very impudent, to speak before me with this arrogance, and to give brazenly the name of science to things which one should not even honor with the title of craft, and which can be grouped only under the denomination of wretched trades of gladiator, minstrel, and posturer!

FENCING MASTER: Get out, you pig of a philosopher!

MUSIC MASTER: Get out, you half-wit highbrow!

DANCING MASTER: Get out, you crackpot professor!

PHILOSOPHY MASTER: What, you yokels!
(He throws himself upon them; the other three unite to beat him.)
M. JOURDAIN: Philosopher, sir!

PHILOSOPHY MASTER: The insolent scoundrels! The rascals!

M. JOURDAIN: Philosopher, sir!

FENCING MASTER: Devil take the swine!

M. JOURDAIN: Dear sirs!

PHILOSOPHY MASTER: Impudent rogues!

M. JOURDAIN: Philosopher, sir!

DANCING MASTER: To hell with the jackass!

M. JOURDAIN: My friends!

PHILOSOPHY MASTER: Blackguards!

M. JOURDAIN: Philosopher, sir!

MUSIC MASTER: Damn him and his insolence!

M. JOURDAIN: My dear sirs!

PHILOSOPHY MASTER: Villains! Beggars! Traitors! Impostors!

M. JOURDAIN: Philosopher, sir! Dear sirs! Philosopher, sir! My friends! Philosopher, sir! *(Exit the four* MASTERS, *fighting)* Oh, fight all you like. There's nothing I can do about it, and I won't get my dressing gown dirty trying to separate you. I'd be crazy to get into that mess; I might get a nasty bang.

(Enter PHILOSOPHY MASTER, *tidying his clothing.)*
PHILOSOPHY MASTER: And now let's have our lesson.

M. JOURDAIN: Ah, sir, I'm sorry for the blows you've received.

PHILOSOPHY MASTER: That's nothing. A philosopher knows how to take things as they come; and I am going to compose a satire against them, in the style of Juvenal, which will settle their hash. We'll drop the matter. What do you want to learn?

M. JOURDAIN: Everything I can, for I am crazy to be a scholar. It makes me furious that my father and mother didn't make me study all the branches of knowledge when I was young.

PHILOSOPHY MASTER: That is a very laudable sentiment. *Nam sine doctrina vita est quasi mortis imago.* You understand that; you know Latin, of course.

M. JOURDAIN: Yes; but let's pretend I don't know it. Explain to me what that means.

PHILOSOPHY MASTER: That means: "Without knowledge, life is almost an image of death."

M. JOURDAIN: That Latin is right.

PHILOSOPHY MASTER: Don't you have some basic elements, some beginnings in the fields of study?

M. JOURDAIN: Oh, yes; I know how to read and write.

PHILOSOPHY MASTER: Now where would you like to begin? Would you like to have me teach you logic?

M. JOURDAIN: Just what is that logic?

PHILOSOPHY MASTER: Logic teaches the three operations of the mind.

M. JOURDAIN: What are these three operations of the mind?

PHILOSOPHY MASTER: The first, the second, and the third. The first is true conception by means of the universals. The second is true judgment by means of categories; and the third, the true drawing of logical consequences by means of the figures Barbara, Celarent, Darii, Ferio, Baralipton, and so forth.

M. JOURDAIN: Those words sound kind of repulsive. I don't like that logic. Let's learn something prettier.

PHILOSOPHY MASTER: Would you like to learn ethics?

M. JOURDAIN: Ethics?

PHILOSOPHY MASTER: Yes.

M. JOURDAIN: What do they do?

PHILOSOPHY MASTER: Ethics treats of the nature of happiness, teaches men to moderate their passions, and—

M. JOURDAIN: No, none of that. I have a devilish excitable nature; no ethics for me. When I want to get mad, I want to get good and mad.

PHILOSOPHY MASTER: Would you like to learn physics?

M. JOURDAIN: Why not leave them to the doctors?

PHILOSOPHY MASTER: Physics is the science which explains the principles of the natural world and the properties of matter. It treats the nature of the elements, of the metals, of minerals, stones, plants, and animals, and teaches us the causes of meteors, rainbows, shooting stars, comets, lightning, thunder and thunderbolts, rain, snow, hail, winds and whirlwinds.

M. JOURDAIN: There's too much rowdydow in that; too much rumpus and ruckus.

PHILOSOPHY MASTER: Well, then, what do you want me to teach you?

M. JOURDAIN: Teach me spelling.

PHILOSOPHY MASTER: Gladly.

M. JOURDAIN: And afterwards, you can teach me the almanac, so I'll know when there's a moon and when there isn't.

PHILOSOPHY MASTER: Very well. To follow your idea and to treat this subject from a philosophical point of view, one must proceed according to the natural order of things, by an exact understanding of the nature of the letters, and of the different manner of pronouncing them. I shall first inform you that the letters are divided into vowels, from the Latin meaning "vocal," so called because they express the voiced sounds; and into consonants, meaning "with-sounding," so called because they "sound with" the vowels, and merely mark the various articulation of the voiced sounds. There are five vowels, or voiced sounds: A,E,I,O,U.

M. JOURDAIN: I understand all that.

PHILOSOPHY MASTER: The vowel A, pronounced *ah*, is formed by opening the mouth wide: *Ah*.

M. JOURDAIN: *Ah, Ah*. Yes, yes.

PHILOSOPHY MASTER: The vowel E, pronounced *euh*, is formed by bringing the lower jaw closer to the upper jaw: *Euh. Ah, euh*.

M. JOURDAIN: *Ah, euh; ah, euh*. Bless my soul, yes! Oh, how beautiful that is!

PHILOSOPHY MASTER: The vowel I, pronounced *Ee*, is made by bringing the jaws still closer together, and by widening the mouth, or extending its corners toward the ears: *Ee. Ah, euh, ee*.

M. JOURDAIN: *Ah, euh, ee, ee, ee*. That's true! Hurrah for science!

PHILOSOPHY MASTER: The vowel O is formed by opening the jaws again, and by bringing the corners of the mouth closer together: *Oh*.

M. JOURDAIN: *Oh, oh*. Nothing could be truer! *Ah, euh, ee, oh, ee, oh*. That's wonderful! *Ee, oh, ee, oh!*[1]

---

1. [Traditionally, the actor here imitates an ass braying.—Trans.]

PHILOSOPHY MASTER: The opening of the mouth makes, as it happens, a small circle which represents an *O*.

M. JOURDAIN: *Oh, oh, oh.* You're right: *oh.* Oh, what a fine thing it is to know something!

PHILOSOPHY MASTER: The vowel U[2] is formed by bringing the teeth close together, without their quite touching, and by thrusting out the lips, thus making a small aperture: *U*.

M. JOURDAIN: *U, u.* It couldn't be truer! *U!*

PHILOSOPHY MASTER: The lips are extended as if you are pouting; hence it comes that if you want to make this sound at someone, expressing contempt, all you say to him is *U*.[3]

M. JOURDAIN: *U, u.* That's right! Oh, why didn't I study sooner, to learn all that?

PHILOSOPHY MASTER: To-morrow we shall take up the other letters, the consonants.

M. JOURDAIN: Are they as remarkable as these vowels?

PHILOSOPHY MASTER: Certainly. The consonant D, for example, is pronounced by touching the tip of the tongue to the hard palate, just above teeth: *Da*.

M. JOURDAIN: *Da! Da!* Yes. Oh, how wonderful, wonderful!

PHILOSOPHY MASTER: The F is pronounced by applying the upper teeth to the lower lip: *Fa*.

M. JOURDAIN: *Fa, Fa.* It's the truth! Oh, Father and Mother, how I blame you!

PHILOSOPHY MASTER: And the R, by placing the tip of the tongue against the upper palate, so that it is brushed by the air, forcefully expelled, and yields to it, and returns constantly to the same position, making a kind of vibration: Rra.

M. JOURDAIN: *R, r, ra; R, rr, rrra.* That's right! Oh, what a clever man you are! And how much time I've lost! *Rrrra.*

PHILOSOPHY MASTER: I shall explain to you all these important facts in detail.

M. JOURDAIN: Please do. And by the way, I must take you into my confidence. I am in love with a person of very high rank, and I should like to have your help in writing something in a little note I want to drop at her feet.

PHILOSOPHY MASTER: I shall be delighted.

M. JOURDAIN: It will be in the gallant style, yes?

PHILOSOPHY MASTER: Certainly. Is it poetry you want to write her?

M. JOURDAIN: No, no; no poetry.

---

2. [The French U, like a German ü.—Trans.]
3. [The sound is used by the French for booing.—Trans.]

PHILOSOPHY MASTER: You want only prose?

M. JOURDAIN: No. I don't want either poetry or prose.

PHILOSOPHY MASTER: Well, it has to be either one or the other.

M. JOURDAIN: Why?

PHILOSOPHY MASTER: For the reason, sir, that we have no means of expression other than prose and poetry.

M. JOURDAIN: There's nothing but prose or poetry?

PHILOSOPHY MASTER: Quite so, sir. All that is not prose is poetry; and all that is not poetry is prose.

M. JOURDAIN: And when a man talks, what's that?

PHILOSOPHY MASTER: Prose.

M. JOURDAIN: What? When I say: "Nicole, bring me my slippers and give me my nightcap," that's prose?

PHILOSOPHY MASTER: Yes, sir.

M. JOURDAIN: Well, I'll be hanged! For more than forty years I've been talking prose without any idea of it; I'm very much obliged to you for telling me that. So, I'd like to put in a letter: "Beautiful Marquise, your lovely eyes make me die of love." But I'd like to have it put in the gallant style; neatly turned, you know.

PHILOSOPHY MASTER: Put it, then, that the rays of her eyes reduce your heart to ashes; that for her sake you suffer night and day the tortures of—

M. JOURDAIN: No, no, no. I don't want that at all. I just want what I told you: "Beautiful Marquise, your lovely eyes make me die of love."

PHILOSOPHY MASTER: Well, you ought to stretch it out a little.

M. JOURDAIN: No, I tell you. I just want only those words in the letter; but elegantly put, properly arranged. So I'm asking you to tell me, out of curiosity, the different ways you could write them.

PHILOSOPHY MASTER: Well, firstly, you could put them the way you said: "Beautiful Marquise, your lovely eyes make me die of love." Or else: "Of love, beautiful Marquise, your beautiful eyes make me die." Or else: "Your eyes, lovely, of love, Marquise beautiful, make die me." Or else: "Die, beautiful Marquise, of love your lovely eyes me make." Or else: "Me your lovely eyes of love make die, beautiful Marquise."

M. JOURDAIN: But of all those ways, which one is the best?

PHILOSOPHY MASTER: The one you said: "Beautiful Marquise, your lovely eyes make me die of love."

M. JOURDAIN: And nevertheless I have never studied; I did that straight off! I thank you with all my heart; please come again tomorrow early.

PHILOSOPHY MASTER: I won't fail to.

(Exit PHILOSOPHY MASTER.)

M. JOURDAIN *(to his LACKEYS):* Look here, hasn't my new suit come yet?

SECOND LACKEY: No, sir.

M. JOURDAIN: That damned tailor makes me wait until a day when I have so much to do! He makes me furious. May the quartan fever take that hangbird tailor! To the devil with the tailor! May the galloping plague seize the tailor! If I had him here now, that infernal tailor, that dog of a tailor, that pig of a tailor, I'd . . . *(Enter MERCHANT TAILOR and his APPRENTICE, carrying M. JOURDAIN's suit)* Oh here you are! I was on the point of getting angry with you.

(The TAILOR has come in, followed by his APPRENTICE carrying the suit.)

MERCHANT TAILOR: I couldn't come sooner; I have had twenty journeymen working on your coat.

M. JOURDAIN: The silk stockings you sent me were so tight that I had a terrible time getting them on, and already there are a couple of stitches broken.

MERCHANT TAILOR: They will get looser.

M. JOURDAIN: Yes, if all the stitches break. And what's more, you made me some shoes which hurt frightfully.

MERCHANT TAILOR: Not at all, sir.

M. JOURDAIN: What do you mean, not at all?

MERCHANT TAILOR: They don't hurt you.

M. JOURDAIN: I tell you they do hurt me!

MERCHANT TAILOR: You just imagine it.

M. JOURDAIN: I imagine it because I feel it. What kind of talk is that?

MERCHANT TAILOR: Now look, here is the finest coat in all the court, the most harmoniously matched. It is a great achievement to have invented a formal coat which is not black. I defy the most eminent tailors to equal it in a dozen tries.

M. JOURDAIN: What's this? You've got the flowers upside down.

MERCHANT TAILOR: You didn't tell me you wanted them right side up.

M. JOURDAIN: Did I have to tell you that?

MERCHANT TAILOR: Yes, indeed. All the people of quality wear them this way.

M. JOURDAIN: People of quality wear the flowers upside down?

MERCHANT TAILOR: Yes, sir.

M. JOURDAIN: Oh, well, it's all right then.

MERCHANT TAILOR: If you prefer, I'll turn them right side up.

M. JOURDAIN: No, no.

MERCHANT TAILOR: You have only to say so.

M. JOURDAIN: No, I tell you. You did all right . . . Do you think the costume will look well on me?

MERCHANT TAILOR: What a question! I defy any artist to paint a finer ensemble. I have a workman who, for assembling a wide trouser, is the greatest genius on earth; and another who, for confecting a doublet, is the hero of our age.

M. JOURDAIN: The peruke and the plumes, are they all right?

MERCHANT TAILOR: Perfect.

M. JOURDAIN (*noticing the* **TAILOR's** *coat*): Ah, master tailor, there is some material from the last coat you made me! I recognize it perfectly.

MERCHANT TAILOR: The fact is, the material seemed to me so beautiful that I made a coat for myself from it.

M. JOURDAIN: Yes, but you shouldn't have made it with my material.

TAILOR: Do you want to try on your coat?

M. JOURDAIN: Yes; give it to me.

MERCHANT TAILOR: Wait a moment! That's not the way to do it. I have brought some men to dress you to music; that kind of costume has to be put on with ceremony. Hola! Come in, you men. (*Enter four* **JOURNEYMEN TAILORS**) Put this coat on the gentleman, in the way you do for persons of quality.
　　　(*Two* **TAILORS** *remove* **MONSIEUR JOURDAIN's** *breeches, two others remove his jacket. They try on his new coat.* **MONSIEUR JOURDAIN** *promenades among them for their inspection. All takes place to the music of the entire orchestra.*)

A TAILOR: Gentleman, sir, will you give a little tip to the workmen?

M. JOURDAIN: What did you call me?

TAILOR: Gentleman, sir.

M. JOURDAIN: Gentleman, sir! That's what comes from dressing like a person of quality. If you go around always dressed as a commoner, no one will say to you: "Gentleman, sir!" Here; that's for "gentleman, sir."

TAILOR: Monsignor, we are very much obliged to you.

M. JOURDAIN: Monsignor! Oh, oh, Monsignor! Wait a bit, my friend; "Monsignor" deserves a little something. Here; that's a present from Monsignor.

TAILOR: Monsignor, we shall all drink to the health of Your Grace.

M. JOURDAIN: Your Grace! Oh, oh, oh! Wait; don't go away. "Your Grace" —to me! Faith, if he goes as far as Royal Highness he'll have my whole purse! . . . Here; that's for My Grace.

TAILOR: Monsignor, we thank you very humbly for your generosity.

M. JOURDAIN: A good thing he stopped there. I was going to give him the whole business.

(The four **JOURNEYMEN TAILORS** *express their joy in a dance, which forms the second* **INTERLUDE.***)*

ACT THREE

The MERCHANT TAILOR *and his assistants exit, leaving* MONSIEUR JOURDAIN *and his two* LACKEYS *on the stage.*

M. JOURDAIN: Follow me, while I take a little walk to show my new suit around town. And especially, both of you be sure to walk directly behind me, so that everybody can see that you belong to me.

LACKEYS: Yes, sir.

M. JOURDAIN: Get Nicole for me. I want to give her some orders. No, don't move. Here she is now. *(Enter* **NICOLE***)* Nicole!

NICOLE: Yes what is it?

M. JOURDAIN: Listen to me.

NICOLE: He, he, he, he!

M. JOURDAIN: What is there to laugh at?

NICOLE: He, he, he, he, he, he!

M. JOURDAIN: What does the rascal mean?

NICOLE: He, he, he! How funny you look! He, he, he!

M. JOURDAIN: What's the matter?

NICOLE: Oh, oh, good Lord! He, he, he, he, he!

M. JOURDAIN: You scamp! Are you trying to make fun of me?

NICOLE: Oh, no, sir. I'd hate to do that. He, he, he, he, he, he!

M. JOURDAIN: I'll land one on your nose, if you laugh any more.

NICOLE: Monsieur, I can't help it. He, he, he, he, he, he!

M. JOURDAIN: You won't stop?

NICOLE: Monsieur, I beg your pardon. But you look so funny, I can't keep from laughing. He, he, he!

M. JOURDAIN: I never saw such impudence.

NICOLE: You're so comical like that. He, he!

M. JOURDAIN: I'm going to—

NICOLE: I beg you to excuse me. He, he, he, he!

M. JOURDAIN: Look here, if you laugh once more, I swear I'll apply to your cheek the biggest slap that has ever been slapped.

NICOLE: It's all over, sir. I won't laugh any more.

M. JOURDAIN: Make sure you don't. Now, I want you to clean up, in preparation for—

NICOLE: He, he!

M. JOURDAIN: To clean up properly—

NICOLE: He, he!

M. JOURDAIN: What, again!

NICOLE: Look here, sir, I'd rather have you beat me and let me laugh myself out. That will do me more good. He, he, he, he, he!

M. JOURDAIN: You'll drive me crazy!

NICOLE: Please, monsieur, I beg you to let me laugh. He, he, he!

M. JOURDAIN: If I catch you—

NICOLE: Monsieu-eur, I'll blow-ow-ow up, if I don't laugh. He, he, he!

M. JOURDAIN: Has anyone ever seen such a hussy! She comes and laughs insolently in my face, instead of obeying my orders!

NICOLE: What do you want me to do, sir?

M. JOURDAIN: I want you, you rogue, to see to getting the house ready for the company that is due to come soon.

NICOLE: Well, my sakes, I've lost all fancy to laugh. Your company always makes such a mess around here that the mere mention of it is enough to put me out of humor.

M. JOURDAIN: So, for your convenience, I ought to shut my door to everybody?

NICOLE: At least, you ought to shut it to certain people.

(Enter MADAME JOURDAIN.)

MME. JOURDAIN: Aha, here's something new! Tell me, my good husband, what's this getup of yours? Are you crazy, to go and rig yourself out that way? Do you want people to mock you everywhere?

M. JOURDAIN: My good wife, only the fools, male and female, will mock me.

MME. JOURDAIN: Well, they haven't waited for this occasion to start. Your behavior has been making everybody laugh for quite some time.

M. JOURDAIN: Everybody! What do you mean by everybody, if you please?

404

.

MME. JOURDAIN: I mean everybody who knows what's what, and who has got more sense than you. For my part, I am scandalized by the kind of life you are leading. I vow I don't recognize our own house. You'd say it was carnival time here every day; and to make sure of it, from early morning on there's nothing but a great row of fiddlers and singers, enough to disturb the whole neighborhood.

NICOLE: Madame is quite right. I can never keep the house clean any more, with all that gang of people you bring in here. They've got big feet which go and hunt for mud in every quarter of the city, in order to bring it back here. And poor Françoise is worn almost to a shadow, scrubbing the floors that your fine folks dirty up regularly every day.

M. JOURDAIN: Now, now, Nicole, you've got to be quite a speech-maker for a peasant servant girl.

MME. JOURDAIN: Nicole is quite right; she's got more sense than you. I'd like to know what you think you're doing with a dancing teacher, at your age.

NICOLE: And with a great big bully of a fighter, who stamps so he shakes the whole house, and loosens up all the tiles on the parlor floor.

M. JOURDAIN: Shut up, servant; and shut up, wife.

MME. JOURDAIN: You want to learn how to dance, for when you won't be able to walk?

NICOLE: You want to kill somebody?

M. JOURDAIN: Shut up, I tell you! You are both ignorant fools; you don't know the prerogatives of all that.

MME. JOURDAIN: You ought to think rather of marrying off your daughter. She's of an age to have a husband now.

M. JOURDAIN: I'll think of marrying my daughter when a proper match for her appears. But I also want to think of learning the finer things of life.

NICOLE: I've also heard, madame, that to top it off he took on a philosophy teacher today.

M. JOURDAIN: Quite right. I want to sharpen my wits, and be able to discuss things among intelligent people.

MME. JOURDAIN: One of these days you'll be going to school to get yourself whipped, at your age.

M. JOURDAIN: Why not? I wish to heaven I could be whipped now, in front of everybody, if I could know what one learns in school.

NICOLE: Yes, my faith! Much good that would do you!

M. JOURDAIN: It would indeed.

MME. JOURDAIN: A lot of use that would be for running your house.

M. JOURDAIN: You're right, it would. You both talk like simpletons, and I'm ashamed of your ignorance. *(To* **MADAME JOURDAIN***)* For example, do you know what you're saying now?

MME. JOURDAIN: Yes, I know that what I am saying is very well said, and you ought to think of changing your way of life.

M. JOURDAIN: I'm not talking of that. I ask you, what are the words that you are saying now?

MME. JOURDAIN: They are very sensible words, and that's what your conduct is not.

M. JOURDAIN: I'm not talking of that, I tell you. I ask you; what I'm speaking to you, what I'm saying to you now, what is it?

MME. JOURDAIN: Stuff and nonsense.

M. JOURDAIN: No, no, not at all. What we are both saying, the language we are talking now?

MME. JOURDAIN: Well?

M. JOURDAIN: What is that called?

MME. JOURDAIN: That is called whatever you've a mind to call it.

M. JOURDAIN: It is called prose, ignorant woman!

MME. JOURDAIN: Prose?

M. JOURDAIN: Yes, prose! Everything which is prose is not poetry; and everything which is not poetry is not prose. Ha, that's what comes of studying! *(To* **NICOLE***)* And you, do you know what you have to do to make an U?

NICOLE: How's that?

M. JOURDAIN: Yes. What do you do when you make a U?

NICOLE: What?

M. JOURDAIN: Say U, for example.

NICOLE: All right, U.

M. JOURDAIN: Now what are you doing?

NICOLE: I'm saying U.

M. JOURDAIN: Yes, but when you say U, what are you doing?

NICOLE: I'm doing what you tell me.

M. JOURDAIN: Oh, what a dreadful thing it is to have to deal with idiots! You thrust your lips outward, and you bring the upper jaw down close to the lower jaw: U. You see, U. I pout: U.

NICOLE: Yes, that's right pretty.

MME. JOURDAIN: Wonderful!

M. JOURDAIN: It's quite different, if you'd seen O, and Da, da, and Fa, fa.

MME. JOURDAIN: What's all this rubbish?

NICOLE: What does all this cure you of?

M. JOURDAIN: It makes me sick to see such ignorant women.

MME. JOURDAIN: You ought to kick all those fellows out, with their moonshine.

NICOLE: And especially that big gawk of a fencing master, who fills the whole house with dust.

M. JOURDAIN: Yes, that fencing master worries you a lot. I'll show you how stupid you are, right away. *(He has a* **LACKEY** *bring him the foils, takes one, and hands one to* **NICOLE***)* Take this. Logical demonstration, the line of the body. When you thrust in quart, this is all you have to do. And when you thrust in tierce, that's what you do. In this way, you can never get killed. Isn't it fine, to be assured of the result, when you're fighting with someone? There now, just make a thrust, to try it out.

NICOLE: All right. *(She makes several lunges, pricking* **MONSIEUR JOURDAIN***.)*

M. JOURDAIN: Hold on! Hey, easy there! The devil take the wench!

NICOLE: You told me to thrust.

M. JOURDAIN: Yes, but you thrust in tierce before thrusting in quart; and you wouldn't wait for me to parry.

MME. JOURDAIN: You're crazy, my poor husband, with your fancy ideas. It's all happened since you took into your head to hang around with the nobility.

M. JOURDAIN: When I hang around with the nobility, I show my good judgment. It's a lot finer thing than to hang around with your bourgeoisie.

MME. JOURDAIN: Really now! There's a lot to be gained by associating with your nobles! You've done some nice business with that Monsieur le Comte you're so fascinated with.

M. JOURDAIN: Quiet! Think what you're saying. Are you aware, wife, that when you mention him, you don't know who he really is? He is a person of greater importance than you think, a lord who is highly considered at court. He speaks to the King just the way I am speaking to you. Isn't it a very honorable thing for people to see a person of such quality come to my house so often, calling me his dear friend, and treating me as if I were his equal? He has done me some kindnesses you would never guess; and in front of everybody he shows me such special regards that I am embarrassed myself.

MME. JOURDAIN: Yes, he does you kindnesses, and he shows you special regards; but he borrows your money.

M. JOURDAIN: Well, isn't it an honor for me to lend money to a man of that rank? And can I do any less for a lord who calls me his dear friend?

MME. JOURDAIN: And this lord, what does he do for you?

M. JOURDAIN: He does things that would astonish people, if they were known.

MME. JOURDAIN: What things, for instance?

M. JOURDAIN: Enough; I won't explain. Let it suffice that if I have lent him money, he will repay me well, and that soon.

MME. JOURDAIN: Yes; you can expect it any minute.

M. JOURDAIN: Certainly; didn't he tell me so?

MME. JOURDAIN: Yes, yes; he won't fail to do nothing of the sort.

M. JOURDAIN: He gave me his word as a gentleman.

MME. JOURDAIN: Nonsense!

M. JOURDAIN: You are very obstinate, wife. I tell you he'll keep his word. I'm sure of it.

MME. JOURDAIN: And I tell you he won't; and all the attentions he shows you are just to take you in.

M. JOURDAIN: Shut up; here he is.

MME. JOURDAIN: That's the last straw. Perhaps he's coming to get another loan from you. The sight of him takes away my appetite.

M. JOURDAIN: Shut up, I tell you.

(Enter **DORANTE.***)*

DORANTE: My dear friend Monsieur Jourdain, and how are you?

M. JOURDAIN: Very well, sir, at your humble service.

DORANTE: And Madame Jourdain here, how is she doing?

MME. JOURDAIN: Madame Jourdain is doing the best she can.

DORANTE: Well, well, Monsieur Jourdain! How elegantly you're gotten up!

M. JOURDAIN: Well, you see.

DORANTE: You look very brave in that suit; we have no young sprigs at court better turned out than you are.

M. JOURDAIN: He, he!

MME. JOURDAIN *(aside):* He scratches him where he itches.

DORANTE: Turn around. It's really stylish.

MME. JOURDAIN *(aside):* Yes, as silly behind as in front.

DORANTE: 'Pon my word, Monsieur Jourdain, I have been extraordinarily anxious to see you. I have a higher opinion of you than of absolutely anyone else. I was talking about you this very morning in the King's bedchamber.

M. JOURDAIN: You do me too much honor, sir. *(To* **MADAME JOURDAIN***)* In the King's bedchamber!

DORANTE: Come, come; put on your hat.

M. JOURDAIN: Monsieur, I know the respect I owe you.

DORANTE: Good Lord, put it on! Let's have no ceremony between us, please.

M. JOURDAIN: Monsieur . . .

DORANTE: Cover, I tell you, Monsieur Jourdain; you are my friend.

M. JOURDAIN: Monsieur, I am your humble servant.

DORANTE: I won't cover, if you don't.

M. JOURDAIN *(covering):* I'd rather be unmannerly than troublesome.

DORANTE: I am your debtor, as you know.

MME. JOURDAIN *(aside):* Yes, we know it only too well.

DORANTE: You have generously lent me money on several occasions, and you have obliged me with the best grace in the world, most assuredly.

M. JOURDAIN: You're joking, sir.

DORANTE: But I make a point of repaying all loans, and recognizing the kindnesses that are done me.

M. JOURDAIN: I don't doubt it, sir.

DORANTE: I want to clean matters up between us. I've come so we can go over our accounts together.

M. JOURDAIN *(to* **MADAME JOURDAIN***):* See how unjust you were!

DORANTE: I am the kind of fellow who likes to pay off his debts as soon as possible.

M. JOURDAIN *(to* **MADAME JOURDAIN***):* I told you so!

DORANTE: Let's see how much I owe you?

M. JOURDAIN *(to* **MADAME JOURDAIN***):* You and your ridiculous suspicions!

DORANTE: Do you remember exactly how much you lent me?

M. JOURDAIN: I think so. I made a little memorandum. Here it is. On one occasion, given to you, two hundred louis.

DORANTE: That's right.

M. JOURDAIN: Another time, a hundred twenty.

DORANTE: Yes.

M. JOURDAIN: And another time, a hundred and forty.

DORANTE: You're right.

M. JOURDAIN: These three items add up to four hundred and sixty louis, which makes five thousand and sixty francs.

DORANTE: The accounting is excellent. Five thousand and sixty francs.

M. JOURDAIN: One thousand eight hundred and thirty-two francs to your feather supplier.

DORANTE: Exactly.

M. JOURDAIN: Two thousand seven hundred and eighty francs to your tailor.

DORANTE: True enough.

M. JOURDAIN: Four thousand three hundred seventy-nine francs twelve sous and eight farthings to your haberdasher.

DORANTE: Excellent. Twelve sous eight farthings. Very exact accounting.

M. JOURDAIN: Add one thousand seven hundred forty-eight francs seven sous and four farthings to your saddler.

DORANTE: That's all correct. How much does it come to?

M. JOURDAIN: Sum total, fifteen thousand eight hundred francs.

DORANTE: The sum total is quite correct: fifteen thousand eight hundred francs. Now add two hundred pistoles you can give me now; that will make exactly eighteen thousand francs, which I will pay you at the earliest possible moment.

MME. JOURDAIN *(to* **MONSIEUR JOURDAIN***):* Well, didn't I guess it?

M. JOURDAIN *(to* **MADAME JOURDAIN***):* Silence!

DORANTE: Would it be inconvenient for you to give me that amount?

M. JOURDAIN: No, no.

MME. JOURDAIN *(to* **MONSIEUR JOURDAIN***):* That fellow is milking you like a cow.

M. JOURDAIN *(to* **MADAME JOURDAIN***):* Shut up!

DORANTE: If it's inconvenient, I can get it somewhere else.

M. JOURDAIN: No, indeed.

MME. JOURDAIN *(to* **MONSIEUR JOURDAIN***):* He won't be satisfied until he's ruined you.

M. JOURDAIN *(to* **MADAME JOURDAIN***):* Shut up, I tell you!

DORANTE: If it embarrasses you, you have only to say so.

M. JOURDAIN: Not at all, sir.

MME. JOURDAIN *(to* **MONSIEUR JOURDAIN***):* He's nothing but a crook.

M. JOURDAIN *(to* **MADAME JOURDAIN***):* Will you shut up?

MME. JOURDAIN (*to* **MONSIEUR JOURDAIN**): He'll suck you dry, down to your last penny.

M. JOURDAIN (*to* **MADAME JOURDAIN**): I tell you to shut your mouth!

DORANTE: There are plenty of people who would be delighted to lend it to me; but since you're my best friend, I thought I would be doing you an injury if I asked anyone else.

M. JOURDAIN: You do me too much honor, my dear sir. I'll go and fetch what you want.

MME. JOURDAIN (*to* **MONSIEUR JOURDAIN**): What! You're going to give it to him?

M. JOURDAIN (*to* **MADAME JOURDAIN**): What can I do? Do you expect me to refuse a man of such rank, who talked of me this very morning in the King's bedchamber?

MME. JOURDAIN (*to* **MONSIEUR JOURDAIN**): Go on, you're just an easy mark!

(Exit MONSIEUR JOURDAIN.)

DORANTE: You seem cast down about something. What is the matter, Madame Jourdain?

MME. JOURDAIN: I've cut my eyeteeth; I wasn't born yesterday.

DORANTE: And your charming daughter, I don't see her. Where is she?

MME. JOURDAIN: My charming daughter is all right where she is.

DORANTE: How is she getting along?

MME. JOURDAIN: She is getting along on her two legs.

DORANTE: Wouldn't you like to bring her some day to see the command performance of the ballet and comedy before the King?

MME. JOURDAIN: Oh, yes, we certainly need a good laugh; a good laugh is certainly what we need.

DORANTE: I think, Madame Jourdain, you must have had many admirers in your youth; you must have been so pretty and of such a charming humor.

MME. JOURDAIN: Good land, sir, is Madame Jourdain doddering already? She's got one foot in the grave, maybe?

DORANTE: 'Pon my soul, Madame Jourdain, I ask your pardon. I didn't realize you're still young; I'm so unobservant. I beg you to excuse my impoliteness.

(Enter MONSIEUR JOURDAIN.)

M. JOURDAIN: Here are two hundred louis exactly.

DORANTE: I assure you, Monsieur Jourdain, that I am very much at your service; I am most eager to do you some good turn at court.

M. JOURDAIN: I am very deeply obliged to you.

DORANTE: If Madame Jourdain wants to see the performance before His Majesty, I shall get the best seats in the house for her.

MME. JOURDAIN: Madame Jourdain kisses your hands with gratitude.

DORANTE *(aside to* MONSIEUR JOURDAIN*):* As I told you in my note, our lovely Marquise will come here soon for the ballet and the refreshments. I have finally persuaded her to accept the party you want to give her.

M. JOURDAIN *(aside to* DORANTE*):* Let us move little further off, for good reason.

DORANTE: I haven't seen you for a week, and I haven't given you any news of the diamond ring you asked me to present to her in your name. But the fact is I had all sorts of trouble in overcoming her scruples, and it's only today she made up her mind to accept it.

M. JOURDAIN: How did she find it?

DORANTE: Marvelous! And unless I'm much mistaken, the beauty of the diamond will work wonders for you.

M. JOURDAIN: Would to God it were so!

MME JOURDAIN *(to* NICOLE*):* When he once gets with that Count, he can't leave him.

DORANTE *(to* MONSIEUR JOURDAIN*):* I played up to her properly the value of the present and the greatness of your love.

M. JOURDAIN: Your kindness overwhelms me, sir. I am embarrassed beyond words to see a person of your rank lower himself to do what you are doing for me.

DORANTE: Are you joking? Between friends, does one worry about scruples of that sort? Wouldn't you do the same thing for me, if the occasion should arise?

M. JOURDAIN: Oh, assuredly; with the utmost willingness.

MME. JOURDAIN *(to* NICOLE*):* I can't abide seeing that fellow around.

DORANTE: Personally, I stick at nothing when it's a question of serving a friend. And when you confided to me your passion for my friend, the charming Marquise, you saw that I immediately offered to aid your love.

M. JOURDAIN: That's true. I am confounded by your kindnesses.

MME. JOURDAIN *(to* NICOLE*):* Won't he ever go away?

NICOLE: They just like each other's company.

DORANTE: You have take the right course to touch her heart. Women love above all things to have people spend money on them; and your frequent serenades, and the continual offerings of flowers, and the superb fireworks on the lake, and the diamond ring she received in your name, and the party you are preparing for her—that sort of thing speaks far better in favor of your love than all the words you might utter to her in person.

M. JOURDAIN: There are no expenditures I wouldn't make, if they would help me find the way to touch her heart. A lady of quality has ravishing charms for me; I would pay any price for the honor of her love.

412
.

MME. JOURDAIN *(to* **NICOLE***):* What can they be argufying so much about? Sneak over and see if you can't pick up something.

DORANTE: Very soon you will enjoy at your ease the pleasure of seeing her; and your eyes will have plenty of time to satisfy their longing.

M. JOURDAIN: To get free, I have arranged that my wife shall go and dine with her sister, and she'll spend the whole afternoon there.

DORANTE: That's very prudent. Your wife might have made trouble. I have given all the directions to the caterer, in your name; and I've done everything necessary for the ballet. I worked out the scheme for it myself; if the execution comes up to my idea, I am sure it will be found—

M. JOURDAIN *(perceiving that* **NICOLE** *is listening, gives her a box on the ear):* What's this, saucebox! *(To* **DORANTE***)* Please, let's get out of here.

(Exit **MONSIEUR JOURDAIN** *and* **DORANTE.***)*

NICOLE: My stars, madame, curiosity cost me something. But I think there's more here than meets the eye. They're talking about some affair they don't want you to know about.

MME. JOURDAIN: Well, Nicole, this isn't the first time I've had suspicions about my husband. Unless I am very much mistaken, he's setting his cap at someone, and I'm trying to find out who it is. But let's think about my daughter a moment. You know how Cléonte loves her. He's a man I like, and I want to help his suit, and give Lucile to him, if I can.

NICOLE: Really, madame, I am just delighted to know you feel that way; for if you like the master, I like the manservant just as much, and it would make me very happy if our marriage could take place in the shadow of theirs.

MME. JOURDAIN: Go and give him a message from me. Tell him to come and see me soon, and we'll go together to my husband and ask my daughter's hand.

NICOLE: I'll do so right away, madame, and very gladly. I couldn't do a pleasanter errand. *(Exit* **MADAME JOURDAIN***)* I think I'm going to make some people very happy. *(Enter* **CLEONTE** *and* **COVIELLE***)* Ah, here you are, by a lucky chance! I bring you good news. I've come—

CLEONTE: Withdraw, perfidious creature! Don't try to distract me with your treacherous words!

NICOLE: So that's the way you take—

CLEONTE: Withdraw, I tell you! And go straightway and tell your faithless mistress that she will never befool the too confiding Cléonte!

NICOLE: What kind of a fit is this? My dear Covielle, do tell me what this means.

COVIELLE: Your dear Covielle! You scoundrel! Quick, out of my sight, villain! Leave me in peace!

NICOLE: What! You too—

413

▪

COVIELLE: Out of my sight, I tell you! Never speak to me again!

NICOLE *(aside):* Ouch! What's biting them both? I'd better go right away and tell my mistress of this fine to-do.

(Exit NICOLE.*)*

CLEONTE: What! To treat in such a way a lover, the most faithful and ardent of all lovers!

COVIELLE: It's appalling, how they treat us both.

CLEONTE: I display for a certain person all the ardor and affection conceivable. I love only her in all the world; I have her alone in my thought; she has all my devotion, all my desires, all my joy; I speak only of her, I think only of her, I dream only of her, I breathe only for her, my heart exists only for her; and here is the fit reward for so much love! I pass two days without seeing her, which are to me two frightful centuries; I meet her by chance; and at the sight my heart is utterly transported, my joy manifests itself upon my countenance. Ravished with delight, I fly to her; and the faithless one turns her face from me, and passes grimly by, as if she had never seen me in her life!

COVIELLE: I say—exactly the same thing.

CLEONTE: Has anything, Covielle, ever matched the perfidy of the ingrate Lucile?

COVIELLE: Or that, sir, of the hussy Nicole?

CLEONTE: After so many devout sacrifices, sighs, and vows that I have offered to her charms!

COVIELLE: After so many attentions, services, and helping hands I have extended to her in her kitchen.

CLEONTE: So many tears I have shed at her knees!

COVIELLE: So many buckets of water I have pulled up out of the well for her!

CLEONTE: So much ardor I have evidenced, in cherishing her more than my own self!

COVIELLE: So much heat I have endured in turning the spit for her!

CLEONTE: She flees me with contempt!

COVIELLE: She turns her back on me with an uppity air!

CLEONTE: It is perfidy deserving the utmost chastisement.

COVIELLE: It is treason deserving a thousand slaps in the face.

CLEONTE: Never, I beg you, take it into your head to speak in her defense.

COVIELLE: I, sir? Heaven forbid!

CLEONTE: Don't try to excuse the action of the faithless one.

COVIELLE: Don't be afraid, I won't.

CLEONTE: No. For you see, all your efforts to defend her will avail nothing.

COVIELLE: Defend her? Who could have that idea?

CLEONTE: I want to keep my resentment fresh, and break off all relations with her.

COVIELLE: I give my consent.

CLEONTE: That Monsieur le Comte who goes to her house dazzles her perhaps; and I can see that she may let herself be allured by rank and quality. But, for my own honor, I must forestall the public revelation of her inconstancy. I can see her moving in the direction of a change of heart, and I want to keep step with her, and not let her have all the credit for quitting me.

COVIELLE: That's very well said. I share in all your feelings.

CLEONTE: Come to the aid of my rancor, and support my resolution against any lingering remains of love that might speak in her favor. Tell me, please, all the evil you can about her; paint me a portrait of her person which will make her despicable to me; and to complete my disillusionment, point out all the defects you can see in her.

COVIELLE: What, in her, sir? She's a fine poser, an affected show-off, for you to fall in love with! She seems very ordinary to me; you could find a hundred girls worthier of you. In the first place, her eyes are too small.

CLEONTE: That's true; her eyes are small. But they are full of fire, very brilliant and sparkling, and unusually touching.

COVIELLE: She has a big mouth.

CLEONTE: Perhaps. But one sees in it graces that are not in ordinary mouths. That mouth, when one looks at it, inspires desires. It is the most attractive and amorous mouth on earth.

COVIELLE: For her figure, it isn't a tall one.

CLEONTE: No; but it's dainty and flexible.

COVIELLE: She affects a kind of carefree speech and behavior.

CLEONTE: True; but she does so gracefully, and her manners are engaging; she has a certain charm which insinuates itself into the heart.

COVIELLE: As for wit—

CLEONTE: Ah, that she has, Covielle, the keenest and most delicate.

COVIELLE: Her conversation—

CLEONTE: Her conversation is delightful.

COVIELLE: She is always serious.

CLEONTE: Well, do you want broad gaiety, everlasting outbursts of glee? Is there anything more tiresome than those women who are always laughing at everything?

COVIELLE: But finally, she's as capricious as anybody alive.

CLEONTE: Yes, she's capricious, I agree. But that suits a beauty. We can bear anything from a beauty.

COVIELLE: Since that's the way of it, I can see that you want to love her forever.

CLEONTE: I? I'd rather die. I am going to hate her as much as I have loved her.

COVIELLE: And how will you do that, if you find her so perfect?

CLEONTE: That is exactly how my revenge is going to be so sensational, and how I'm going to show so clearly the resolution of my heart, in hating and leaving her, beautiful, attractive, and lovable as she is . . . But here she is.

(Enter LUCILE with NICOLE.)

NICOLE *(to LUCILE):* As for me, I was quite scandalized.

LUCILE: The only explanation, Nicole, is what I was telling you . . . But there he is.

CLEONTE *(to COVIELLE):* I won't even speak to her.

COVIELLE: I'll do just like you.

LUCILE: What is it, Cléonte? What is the matter?

NICOLE: What's got into you, Covielle?

LUCILE: Why this distress of mind?

NICOLE: Why are you so sulky?

LUCILE: Are you dumb, Cléonte?

NICOLE: Has the cat got your tongue, Covielle?

CLEONTE *(to COVIELLE):* What an outrageous way to act!

COVIELLE: Just a couple of Judases!

LUCILE *(to CLEONTE):* I see that our recent encounter has troubled you.

CLEONTE *(to COVIELLE):* Aha! She realizes what she has done.

NICOLE *(to COVIELLE):* Our greeting this morning has got your goat.

COVIELLE *(to CLEONTE):* They've guessed where the shoe pinches.

LUCILE: Isn't it true, Cléonte, that that is the cause of your ill humor?

CLEONTE: Yes, perfidious one, it is, since I must speak. And I have this information for you: that you won't laugh off your infidelity as you expect, that I intend to be the first to break with you, and that you won't have the satisfaction of dismissing me. No doubt I shall have trouble in conquering my love for you. That will cause me some pain; I shall suffer for a time. But I shall overmaster it, and I'll sooner pierce my own heart than be so weak as to return to you.

COVIELLE: With me, ditto.

LUCILE: That's a lot of fuss about nothing, Cléonte. I want to tell you why I avoided your greeting this morning.

CLEONTE *(turning his back):* No, I don't want to hear a word.

NICOLE *(to* COVIELLE, *who turns his back):* I want to tell you the reason we went by so quick.

COVIELLE: I won't listen.

LUCILE: Know then, that this morning—

CLEONTE: No, I tell you.

NICOLE: Here are the facts—

COVIELLE: No, traitor.

LUCILE: Listen—

CLEONTE: There's no use talking.

NICOLE: Let me tell you—

COVIELLE: I'm deaf.

LUCILE: Cléonte!

CLEONTE: No.

NICOLE: Covielle!

COVIELLE: I won't!

LUCILE: But stop—

CLEONTE: Rubbish!

NICOLE: Listen to me!

COVIELLE: Fiddlededee!

LUCILE: Just a moment!

CLEONTE: Not at all!

NICOLE: Be patient.

COVIELLE: Applesauce!

LUCILE: Just two words—

CLEONTE: No, it's all over.

NICOLE: Just one word—

COVIELLE: I'll have no truck with you.

LUCILE: Well, since you won't listen to me, think what you please, and do what you please.

(LUCILE and NICOLE, who have been following CLEONTE and COVIELLE about the stage, cease their pursuit. The business is reversed, the men interceding with the girls.)

NICOLE: Since that's the way you behave, take it any way you like.

CLEONTE *(to LUCILE):* You might as well tell me why you greeted me so coldly.

LUCILE: I don't feel like telling you now.

COVIELLE: Go on, tell us the story.

NICOLE: I don't want to any more.

CLEONTE: Tell me—

LUCILE: No, I won't say a thing.

COVIELLE: Go ahead; speak up.

NICOLE: Not a word.

CLEONTE: Please!

LUCILE: No, I tell you.

COVIELLE: Oh, be nice—

NICOLE: Nothing doing.

CLEONTE: I beg you—

LUCILE: Let me alone.

COVIELLE: I beseech you—

NICOLE: Get out!

CLEONTE: Lucile!

LUCILE: No.

COVIELLE: Nicole!

NICOLE: Not on your life.

CLEONTE: In heaven's name!

LUCILE: I don't want to.

COVIELLE: Speak to me!

NICOLE: I won't.

CLEONTE: Explain my doubts away!

LUCILE: I'll do nothing of the sort.

COVIELLE: Cure my ailing mind!

NICOLE: I don't feel like it.

CLEONTE: Well, since you care so little about relieving my suffering and justifying yourself for the unworthy way you have treated my devotion, you see me, ingrate, for the last time. I am going far away to die of grief and love.

COVIELLE: And I'll be right behind you.

(COVIELLE *and* CLEONTE *start for the exit.*)

LUCILE: Cléonte!

NICOLE: Covielle!

CLEONTE: Eh?

COVIELLE: What is it?

LUCILE: Where are you going?

CLEONTE: Where I told you.

COVIELLE: We're going to die!

LUCILE: *You* are going to die, Cléonte?

CLEONTE: Yes, cruel beauty, since that is what you wish.

LUCILE: You mean I wish you to die?

CLEONTE: Yes you wish it.

LUCILE: Who told you so?

CLEONTE: Don't you wish my death, if you refuse to clear up my suspicions?

LUCILE: Is that my fault? If you had been willing to listen to me, wouldn't I have told you that the occurrence this morning, which, you're complaining about, was caused by the presence of my old aunt, who is convinced that the mere approach of a man dishonors a girl? She lectures us perpetually on this theme, and she pictures all men to us as devils we must flee from.

NICOLE: That's the secret of the whole business.

CLEONTE: You aren't deceiving me, Lucile?

COVIELLE: You aren't trying to bamboozle me?

LUCILE: It's absolutely true.

NICOLE: That's just the way things happened.

COVIELLE *(to* CLEONTE*):* Do we surrender to that?

CLEONTE: Ah, Lucile, how a word from your lips can appease my heart's tumult! How readily one lets oneself be convinced by a loved one!

COVIELLE: How easily a man is hooked by those confounded creatures!

(Enter MADAME JOURDAIN.)

MME. JOURDAIN: I am very glad to see you, Cléonte; you are here at just the right moment. My husband is coming; so take this chance to ask him for Lucile's hand.

CLEONTE: Ah, madame, how sweet are these words! How they flatter my desires! Could I receive a more delightful order? A more precious favor? *(Enter MONSIEUR JOURDAIN)* Sir, I did not wish to get any intermediary to make to you a request I have been long meditating. This request touches me so closely that I have chosen to undertake it myself. Without further preamble, I shall tell you that the honor of being your son-in-law would be a glorious favor which I beg you to bestow upon me.

M. JOURDAIN: Before giving you an answer, sir, I ask you to tell me if you are a gentleman.

CLEONTE: Sir, most people do not hesitate long at such a question. The word is easily spoken. People assume the appellation without scruple, and common usage today seems to authorize its theft. But as for me, I freely grant, I have somewhat more delicate feelings on the subject. I think that any imposture is unworthy of a decent man, and I think it is mean and base to conceal the state to which it has pleased God to call us, and to adorn oneself in the world's eye with a stolen title, and to try to pass oneself off for what one is not. Certainly, I am the son of a line which has held honorable offices. In the army I acquired the merit of six years of service; and I am possessed of sufficient wealth to sustain a very respectable position in society. But with all that, I am unwilling to give myself a name which others, in my place, would feel justified in assuming; and I will tell you frankly that I am not a gentleman.

M. JOURDAIN: Shake hands, sir; my daughter is not for you.

CLEONTE: What?

M. JOURDAIN: You are not a gentleman; you won't have my daughter.

MME. JOURDAIN *(to MONSIEUR JOURDAIN)*: What do you mean, with this gentleman business? Are we descended from the rib of Saint Louis?

M. JOURDAIN: Shut up, wife. I see what you're driving at.

MME. JOURDAIN: Were our ancestors anything but good bourgeois?

M. JOURDAIN: Slander!

MME. JOURDAIN: Wasn't your father a merchant, just like mine?

M. JOURDAIN: Drat the woman! She never misses a chance! If your father was a merchant, so much the worse for him; but as for my father, it's only the ignorant who say so. All I have to tell you is that I want a son-in-law who's a gentleman.

MME. JOURDAIN: What your daughter needs is a husband who suits her, and she'd much better have an honorable man who is rich and handsome than some ugly gentleman without a penny.

NICOLE: That's right. There's the son of the gentleman in our village, he's the biggest booby and ninny ever seen.

M. JOURDAIN: Shut up, saucebox. You're always sticking your oar in the conversation. I have enough property for my daughter; all I need is honor; and I want to make her a marquise.

MME. JOURDAIN: Marquise?

M. JOURDAIN: Yes, marquise.

MME. JOURDAIN: Alas, God forbid!

M. JOURDAIN: It's something I've made up my mind to.

MME. JOURDAIN: As for me, it's something I'll never consent to. Alliances with people above our own rank are always likely to have very unpleasant results. I don't want to have my son-in-law able to reproach my daughter for her parents, and I don't want her children to be ashamed to call me their grandma. If she should happen to come and visit me in her grand lady's carriage, and if by mistake she should fail to salute some one of the neighbors, you can imagine how they'd talk. "Take a look at that fine Madame la Marquise showing off," they'd say. "She's the daughter of Monsieur Jourdain, and when she was little, she was only too glad to play at being a fine lady. She wasn't always so high and mighty as she is now, and both her grandfathers sold dry goods besides the Porte Saint Innocent. They both piled up money for their children, and now perhaps they're paying dear for it in the next world; you don't get so rich by being honest." Well, I don't want that kind of talk to go on; and in short, I want a man who will feel under obligation to my daughter, and I want to be able to say to him: "Sit down there, my boy, and eat dinner with us."

M. JOURDAIN: Those views reveal a mean and petty mind, that wants to remain forever in its base condition. Don't answer back to me again. My daughter will be a marquise in spite of everyone; and if you get me angry, I'll make her a duchess.

(Exit MONSIEUR JOURDAIN.)

MME. JOURDAIN: Cléonte, don't lose courage yet. Lucile, come with me; and tell your father straight out that if you can't have him, you won't marry anybody.

(Exit MADAME JOURDAIN, LUCILE, and NICOLE.)

COVIELLE: You've got yourself into a nice mess with your high principles.

CLEONTE: Well, what can I do? I have serious scruples on that point, that can't be overcome by the example others set us.

COVIELLE: It's foolish to take your scruples seriously with a man like that. Don't you see he's crazy? Would it have cost you anything to fall in with his fancies?

CLEONTE: No doubt you're right. But I didn't think one had to give proofs of nobility to be the son-in-law of Monsieur Jourdain.

COVIELLE: Ha, ha, ha!

CLEONTE: What are you laughing at?

COVIELLE: At an idea I had to take the fellow in, and get you what you want.

CLEONTE: How's that?

COVIELLE: It's rather funny.

CLEONTE: What is it, then?

COVIELLE: There's been a comic performance recently which would fit in perfectly here. I could work the troupe into a practical joke we could play on our joker. It would be rather on the burlesque side, perhaps; but with him you can go to any lengths; you don't have to be too fussy. He could act his own part in it perfectly; he'd play up to all the farce. I can get the actors, and they have the costumes all ready. Just let me manage it.

CLEONTE: But tell me—

COVIELLE: I'll tell you everything. But he's coming back; let's get out.

(Exit COVIELLE and CLEONTE. Enter MONSIEUR JOURDAIN.)

M. JOURDAIN: What the devil! The only thing they have to reproach me for is my noble friends; and as for me, I think there's nothing so splendid as to associate with noble lords. They have the monopoly of honor and civility. I'd gladly give two fingers off my hand, to have been born a count or a marquis.

(Enter a LACKEY.)

LACKEY: Monsieur, here is Monsieur le Comte, and a lady on his arm.

M. JOURDAIN: Oh, good God! I have some orders to give. Tell them I'll be here right away.

(Exit MONSIEUR JOURDAIN. Enter DORIMENE and DORANTE.)

LACKEY: The master has just gone and said he'd be here right away.

DORANTE: Very well.

(Exit LACKEY.)

DORIMENE: I don't know, Dorante; it seems to me rather peculiar, to let you bring me into a house where I don't know anyone.

DORANTE: Well, my dear lady, what place can my love find to entertain you properly, since, to avoid gossip, you won't let me use either your house or mine?

DORIMENE: Yes, but you don't say that I am becoming involved every day, by accepting such excessive evidences of your devotion. I do my best to refuse, but you wear down my resistance; and you show a polite obstinacy which makes me yield gently to anything you like. The frequent visits began it; and then the impassioned declarations; and they brought along the serenades and the parties; and then came the presents. I made opposition to everything; but you don't let yourself be discouraged, and step by step you are breaking down my resolutions. Really, I can no longer be quite sure of myself; and I think that in the end you will drag me into marriage, in spite of my reluctance.

DORANTE: My word, madame, you ought to be already in that happy state. You are a widow; you have no obligations to anyone but yourself. I am independent; and I love you more than my life. What obstacle is there to your making me immediately the happiest of men?

DORIMENE: Good heavens, Dorante, for a happy married life many qualities are necessary in both parties; and the most reasonable pair of people alive often have much trouble in forming a quite satisfactory union.

DORANTE: You are absurd, my dear, in imagining so many difficulties. From one unfortunate experience you should not draw conclusions about all the others.

DORIMENE: Anyway, I keep coming back to the same point. I am disturbed by the expenditures I see you making for me, and for two reasons: one, that they obligate me more than I like; and two, that I am sure—if you will forgive me—that you aren't making them without embarrassment; and I don't want that.

DORANTE: Ah, madam, they are mere trifles! It is not by such means—

DORIMENE: I know what I am saying. Among other things, the diamond you forced me to accept is of such value—

DORANTE: Oh, madam, please! Don't rate so highly something my love regards as all unworthy of you! And permit— But here comes the master of the house.

> *(Enter* **MONSIEUR JOURDAIN.** *He makes two sweeping bows, stepping forward. He finds himself close to* **DORIMENE.***)*

M. JOURDAIN: Stand back a little, madame.

DORIMENE: What?

M. JOURDAIN: One step back, please.

DORIMENE: What for?

M. JOURDAIN: Back up a little, for the third.

DORANTE: Madame, Monsieur Jourdain knows his etiquette.

M. JOURDAIN: Madame, it is a very great distinction to me to find myself so fortunate as to be so happy as to have the happiness that you have had the kindness to grant me the grace of doing me the honor of honoring me with the favor of your presence; and if I had also the merit of meriting a merit like yours, and if heaven . . . envious of my bliss . . . had granted me . . . the privilege of finding myself worthy . . . of the . . .

DORANTE: Monsieur Jourdain, that is enough. Madame does not care for high compliments, and she knows that you are an intelligent man. *(Aside to* **DORIMENE***)* He is a good bourgeois, and rather ridiculous in his behavior, as you see.

DORIMENE *(aside to* **DORANTE***):* That's not hard to recognize.

DORANTE: Madame, this is the best of my friends.

M. JOURDAIN: You do me too much honor.

DORANTE: A man of the world, absolutely.

DORIMENE: I have much esteem for him.

M. JOURDAIN: I have done nothing as yet, madame, to deserve such kindness.

DORANTE *(aside to* **MONSIEUR JOURDAIN***):* Be sure, anyway, you don't mention the diamond ring you've given her.

M. JOURDAIN *(aside to* **DORANTE***):* Couldn't I even ask her how she likes it?

DORANTE *(aside to* **MONSIEUR JOURDAIN***):* Not by any means. That would be horribly vulgar. As a man of the world, you must act as if you hadn't made the present at all. *(To* **DORIMENE***)* Madame, Monsieur Jourdain says he is overjoyed to see you in his house.

DORIMENE: He honors me deeply.

M. JOURDAIN *(aside to* **DORANTE***):* How much obliged I am to you for speaking to her in such a way!

DORANTE *(aside to* **MONSIEUR JOURDAIN***):* I had a dreadful time getting her to come here.

M. JOURDAIN *(aside to* **DORANTE***):* I don't know how to thank you.

DORANTE: He says, madame, that he thinks you are the most beautiful person on earth.

DORIMENE: It is very kind of him.

M. JOURDAIN: Madame, the kindness is all on your side, and . . .

(Enter a **LACKEY.***)*

DORANTE: Let's think about dinner.

LACKEY: Everything is ready, sir.

DORANTE: Then let's sit down; and send in the musicians.

Six cooks enter dancing. They bring in a table covered with various dishes. This makes the third INTERLUDE.*)*

ACT FOUR

After the Interlude, DORIMENE, DORANTE, MONSIEUR JOURDAIN, *two* MALE SINGERS, *and a* WOMAN SINGER, *and several* LACKEYS *remain on the stage.*

DORIMENE: Why, Dorante! What a magnificent repast!

M. JOURDAIN: You are joking, madame. I wish it were more worthy of being offered to you.

(DORIMENE, DORANTE, MONSIEUR JOURDAIN *and the* **SINGERS** *sit at table.)*

DORANTE: Monsieur Jourdain is quite right, madame, in speaking in that way, and he puts me under a deep obligation by doing so well the honors of his house. I agree with him that the repast is unworthy of you. As it was I who ordered it, and as I have not the finesse of some of our friends on this subject, you will not find here a culinary symphony, and you will perhaps notice some gastronomic incongruities, some solecisms of good taste. If Damis had had a hand in it, the rules would be strictly observed; you would recognize a mingling of elegance and erudition. He would not fail to call your attention to the dishes he would serve; he would make you applaud his high capacity in the science of cookery. He would mention the rolls, cooked golden-brown on the hearth's edge with a uniform crust, crumbling delicately under the tooth; the wine with a velvet bouquet, somewhat young and saucy, but not to the point of impudence; a breast of lamb pinked with parsley; a loin of riverside veal from Normandy, no longer than that, white, dainty, like almond paste on the tongue; partridges prepared with a special spice and mushroom sauce; and for his crowning triumph, a young fat turkey flanked by squabs, crested with white onions blended with chicory, swimming in a pearl bouillon. But for my part, I must admit my ignorance; and as Monsieur Jourdain has very well said, I could wish that the repast was more worthy of being offered you.

DORIMENE: I reply to this compliment by devouring the dinner as I do.

M. JOURDAIN: Oh, what beautiful hands!

DORIMENE: The hands are ordinary hands, Monsieur Jourdain; but you notice the diamond, which is indeed beautiful.

M. JOURDAIN: I, madame? God forbid that I should mention it. That would not be the action of a man of the world. The diamond is nothing much.

DORIMENE: You are hard to please.

M. JOURDAIN: You are too kind—

DORANTE (*with a cautionary gesture to* **MONSIEUR JOURDAIN**): Come, some wine for Monsieur Jourdain, and for our musical guests, who will give us the pleasure of singing us a drinking song.

DORIMENE: There's no better seasoning for good cheer than to combine it with music. I am being magnificently regaled here.

M. JOURDAIN: Madame, it is not—

DORANTE: Monsieur Jourdain, let us lend an ear to the musicians; their songs will express our feelings better than we could in words.
(*The* **SINGERS** *take glasses in hand, and sing two drinking songs, accompanied by the orchestra.*)

DUET

Phyllis, a drop of wine, to make the moment pass!
How daintily your hand holds the delightful glass!
Ah, Phyllis, you and wine, you lend each other arms,
For wine and love together increase each other's charms.
So you and wine and I, come let us vow to be
    A constant trinity.
The wine that wets your lip itself doth beautify;
And yet your lovely lip is lovelier thereby.
The lips, they bid me drink; the wine, it bids me kiss!
Ah, what intoxication can ever equal this!
So you and wine and I, come let us vow to be
    A constant trinity.

DUET

Drink, my comrades, drink;
    The hour's propitious.
Let your glasses clink;

The wine's delicious.
Too swift our steps we bend
    To the dark shore,
Where love is at an end,
    And we drink no more.
The scholars can't agree
    Where lives the soul;
By our philosophy
    It's in the bowl.
Not glory, wealth, nor wit
    Chase care away;
But wine doth still permit
    Man to be gay.

CHORUS
Come wine for all, my lads; and never cease to pour,
    And pour and pour again, while men can ask for more!

DORIMENE: That couldn't be better sung. It was really lovely.

M. JOURDAIN: I can see something even lovelier around here.

DORIMENE: Oho! Monsieur Jourdain is more gallant than I thought.

DORANTE: Why, madame, what do you take Monsieur Jourdain for?

M. JOURDAIN: I wish she would take me for something I could suggest.

DORIMENE: You're still at it?

DORANTE *(to DORIMENE):* You don't know him.

M. JOURDAIN: She can know me better whenever she likes.

DORIMENE: Oh, I give up!

DORANTE: He always has an answer ready. But you haven't noticed, madame, that Monsieur Jourdain eats all the bits that your spoon has touched in the serving dish.

DORIMENE: Monsieur Jourdain is a man who ravishes me.

M. JOURDAIN: If I could ravish your heart, I would be—

                              (Enter MADAME JOURDAIN.)

MME. JOURDAIN: Aha! I find some fine company here, and I can see that I wasn't expected. So, it's for this pretty business, my good husband, that you were so anxious to send me off to dine with my sister? I've just seen a kind of a theatre downstairs; and here I see a kind of a wedding feast. So that's how you spend your money? And that's the way you put on a big party for ladies in my absence, and you give them music and a play, while you send me to Jericho?

DORANTE: What do you mean, Madame Jourdain? You must have hallucinations, to get it into your head that your husband is spending his own money, and that he's the one who is giving the party for Madame. Let me inform you that I'm footing the bill. He is merely lending me his house; you ought to be more careful about what you say.

M. JOURDAIN: Yes, insolence! It's Monsieur le Comte who is giving all this to Madame, who is a lady of quality. He does me the honor to borrow my house, and to ask me to join him.

MME. JOURDAIN: Stuff and nonsense! I know what I know.

DORANTE: Madame Jourdain, you need some new spectacles.

MME. JOURDAIN: I don't need any spectacles at all, monsieur; I can see all right without them. I've known what's up for quite some time now; I'm not such a fool. It's a very cheap business for you, a great lord, to encourage my husband's follies the way you're doing. And you, madame, for a great lady, it's neither pretty nor decent for you to bring trouble into a family, and to allow my husband to be in love with you.

DORIMENE: What is the meaning of all this? Dorante, you're unpardonable, to expose me to the delusions of this fantastic creature. *(She starts to leave.)*

DORANTE *(following DORIMENE):* Madame, look here! Madame, where are you running off to?

(Exit DORIMENE.)

M. JOURDAIN: Madame! . . . Monsieur le Comte, make my apologies to her, and try to bring her back.

(Exit DORANTE.)

(To MADAME JOURDAIN) Impudence! These are nice tricks of yours! You come and insult me before everybody, and you drive people of quality out of the house!

MME. JOURDAIN: I don't care a straw for their quality.

M. JOURDAIN: You cursed troublemaker, I don't know why I don't crack your skull with the leftovers of the dinner you ruined!

(The LACKEYS carry out the table and dishes.)

MME. JOURDAIN: I don't care a pin. I'm defending my rights; and every woman will be on my side. *(She starts for the door.)*

M. JOURDAIN: You do well to escape my anger. *(Exit MADAME JOURDAIN)* What a time she picked to interrupt! I was just in the mood to say some very neat things. I never felt myself so bubbling over with inspiration . . . But what's all this?

(Enter COVIELLE, wearing an Oriental costume and a long beard.)

COVIELLE: Monsieur, I don't know if I have the honor of being known to you.

M. JOURDAIN: No, sir.

COVIELLE: I last saw you when you weren't any bigger than that. *(Holds his hand a foot from the floor.)*

M. JOURDAIN: Me?

COVIELLE: Yes, you were the prettiest child ever seen, and all the ladies would take you in their arms to kiss you.

M. JOURDAIN: To kiss me!

COVIELLE: Yes. I was a great friend of your late honorable father.

M. JOURDAIN: My late honorable father?

COVIELLE: Yes. He was a very worthy gentleman.

M. JOURDAIN: What did you say?

COVIELLE: I said he was a very worthy gentleman.

M. JOURDAIN: My father?

COVIELLE: Yes.

M. JOURDAIN: You knew him well?

COVIELLE: Certainly.

M. JOURDAIN: And you knew him to be a gentleman?

COVIELLE: Of course.

M. JOURDAIN: The world is certainly a funny place!

COVIELLE: How is that?

M. JOURDAIN: There are some stupid people who try to tell me he was a merchant.

COVIELLE: He, a merchant? It's pure slander; he never was anything of the sort. The fact is, he was very obliging, very helpful by nature. And as he was a remarkable judge of woolens, he used to go here and there and pick them out, and have them brought to his house; and then he would give them to his friends —for money.

M. JOURDAIN: I'm delighted to know you, and to have your testimony that my father was a gentleman.

COVIELLE: I will testify to the fact before everyone.

M. JOURDAIN: That's very kind. And what brings you here?

COVIELLE: Since the time when I knew your late honorable father, that worthy gentleman, I have been roving the wide world.

M. JOURDAIN: The wide world!

COVIELLE: Yes.

M. JOURDAIN: That must be quite a trip.

COVIELLE: It is certainly. I returned from my far journeys only four days ago; and because of my interest in everything that concerns you, I have come to announce to you some excellent news.

M. JOURDAIN: What's that?

COVIELLE: You know that the son of the Grand Turk is here?

M. JOURDAIN: Me? No.

COVIELLE: Really! He has come with a magnificent retinue. Everyone goes to see him; and he was received in this country as a noble lord of great importance.

M. JOURDAIN: Bless me! I didn't know that.

COVIELLE: And what concerns you, to your great advantage, is that he has fallen in love with your daughter.

M. JOURDAIN: The son of the Grand Turk?

COVIELLE: Yes, and he wants to be your son-in-law.

M. JOURDAIN: My son-in-law. The son of the Grand Turk?

COVIELLE: The son of the Grand Turk wants to be your son-in-law. I went to call on him; and as I understand his language perfectly, he said to me, after discussing various matters: "Accaim croc soler ouch alla moustaph gidelum amanahem varahini oussere carbulath?"[4] That is, "Have you by chance seen a beautiful girl, the daughter of Monsieur Jourdain, a Parisian gentleman?"

M. JOURDAIN: The son of the Grand Turk said that about me?

COVIELLE: Yes. When I replied that I had a particular acquaintance with you, and that I had chanced to see your daughter, he said: "Ah! marababa sahem!" That means, "Oh how much I love her!"

M. JOURDAIN: "Marababa sahem" means "Oh, how much I love her?"

COVIELLE: Yes.

M. JOURDAIN: Bless my soul, I'm glad you told me, for personally I would never have imagined that "marababa sahem" could mean "Oh how much I love her." Turkish is certainly a wonderful language.

COVIELLE: More wonderful than you would think. Do you know what "cacaracamouchen" means?

M. JOURDAIN: "Cacaracamouchen"? No.

COVIELLE: It means "my darling."

M. JOURDAIN: "Cacaracamouchen" means "my darling"?

COVIELLE: Yes.

M. JOURDAIN: That's really marvelous. "Cacaracamouchen; my darling." Can you imagine? You amaze me.

---

4. [Molière's Turkish is a mingling of genuine Turkish, Arabic, and Hebrew with mere gibberish.—Trans.]

COVIELLE: In short, to fulfill the purpose of my embassy, he wants to ask the hand of your daughter in marriage. And to have a father-in-law of a rank suitable for him, he wants to make you a mamamouchi, which is a certain high dignity of his own country.

M. JOURDAIN: A mamamouchi?

COVIELLE: Yes, a mamamouchi. That is to say, in our language, a paladin. The paladins, they were those old-time—well, in short, paladins. There is nothing nobler than that anywhere. You will be the equal of the greatest lords on earth.

M. JOURDAIN: The son of the Grand Turk honors me very profoundly. I beg you to take me to his presence so that I can express my thanks.

COVIELLE: It's unnecessary. He's coming here.

M. JOURDAIN: He's coming here?

COVIELLE: Yes. And he's bringing everything needful for the ceremony of your ennoblement.

M. JOURDAIN: He certainly works fast.

COVIELLE: His love is such that he can bear no delay.

M. JOURDAIN: There's just one awkward thing. My daughter is very stubborn, and she's gone and set her mind on a certain Cléonte, and she swears she won't marry anyone else but him.

COVIELLE: She will change her views when she sees the son of the Grand Turk. And also—a very remarkable fact—the son of the Grand Turk has a striking resemblance to Cléonte; I had him pointed out to me. Her love for the one may easily shift to the other; and . . . But I think I hear him coming. Indeed, here he is.

> *(Enter* CLEONTE *in Turkish costume, with three* PAGES *carrying his train.)*

CLEONTE: Ambousahim oqui boraf, Jordina salamalequi!

COVIELLE *(to* MONSIEUR JOURDAIN*):* That is, "Monsieur Jourdain, may your heart be all year long like a rosebush in bloom!" That is a courteous expression in those countries.

M. JOURDAIN: I am the very humble servant of his Turkish Highness.

COVIELLE: Carigar camboto oustin moraf.

CLEONTE: Oustin yoc catamalequi basum base alla moran!

COVIELLE: He says: "May Heaven give you the strength of lions and the prudence of serpents!"

M. JOURDAIN: His Turkish Highness does me too much honor, and I wish him every kind of prosperity.

COVIELLE: Ossa binamin sadoc babally oracaf ouram.

CLEONTE: Bel-men.

COVIELLE: He says you must go with him right away to make preparations for the ceremony, and afterwards you'll see your daughter and conclude the marriage.

M. JOURDAIN: All that in two words?

COVIELLE: Yes, the Turkish language is like that. It says a great deal in very few words. You go where he wants you to, quickly.

(Exit MONSIEUR JOURDAIN, CLEONTE, *and* PAGES.*)*

COVIELLE: Ha, ha, ha! That was a good one! What a dupe he is! He couldn't play his part better if he'd learned it by heart! Ha, ha, ha! *(Enter* DORANTE*)* I beg you, sir, to help us out in a little performance we're staging.

DORANTE: Ha, ha! Covielle, I would never have recognized you! What kind of getup is this?

COVIELLE: Well, take a look. Ha, ha!

DORANTE: What are you laughing at?

COVIELLE: At something, sir, which deserves a laugh.

DORANTE: How's that?

COVIELLE: You'd never guess, sir, the trick we're playing on Monsieur Jourdain, to induce him to give his daughter to my master.

DORANTE: I can't guess the trick, but I can guess that it is pretty sure to work, since you are organizing it.

COVIELLE: Evidently, sir, you are a judge of character.

DORANTE: Tell me the story.

COVIELLE: Be so kind as to come to one side, and give room to what I see coming in. You will see a part of the story, and I will tell you the rest.

(The Turkish ceremony of the ennobling of MONSIEUR JOURDAIN, *performed with music and dance, forms the fourth Interlude.*

Six DANCING TURKS *enter gravely, two by two, to the full orchestra. They carry three long carpets, with which they make various evolutions, and finally raise them high. The* TURKISH MUSICIANS *and other instrumentalists pass beneath. Four* DERVISHES, *accompanying the* MUFTI, *or legal-religious dignitary, close the procession.*

The TURKS *spread the carpets on the ground and kneel upon them. The* MUFTI, *standing in the middle, makes an invocation with contortions and grimaces, turning up his face, and wiggling his hands outward from his head, like wings. The* TURKS *bow forward, touching their foreheads to the floor, singing "Ali"; they resume the kneeling position, singing "Allah." They continue thus to the end of the invocation; then they all stand, singing "Allah akbar."*

Then the DERVISHES *bring before the* MUFTI MONSIEUR JOURDAIN, *dressed in Turkish costume, clean-shaven, without turban or sword. The* MUFTI *sings in solemn tones.)*

MUFTI:
Se ti sabir,
Ti respondir;

Se non sabir,
Tazir, tazir.

Mi star muphty;
Ti qui star ti?
Non intendir:
Tazir, tazir.[5]

(Two DERVISHES lead out MONSIEUR JOURDAIN. The MUFTI questions the TURKS as to the candidate's religion.)

MUFTI: Dice, Turque, qui star quista?
Anabatista, anabatista?[6]

TURKS: Ioc.[7]

MUFTI: Zwinglista?[8]

TURKS: Ioc.

MUFTI: Coffita?[9]

TURKS: Ioc.

MUFTI: Hussita? Morista? Fronista?[10]

TURKS: Ioc. Ioc. Ioc.

MUFTI: Ioc, Ioc, Ioc!
Star pagana?

TURKS: Ioc.

MUFTI: Luterana?

TURKS: Ioc.

MUFTI: Puritana?

TURKS: Ioc.

MUFTI: Bramina? Moffina? Zurina?[11]

TURKS: Ioc. Ioc. Ioc.

---

5. ["If you know, answer; if you don't know, keep still, keep still. I am a mufti; you, who are you? You don't understand: keep still, keep still." Most of the language of the Turkish ceremony is *lingua franca*, once used for commercial and diplomatic purposes around the Mediterranean, still known to sailors and harbor men. It is a blend mostly of French, Spanish, Italian, and Arabic. All grammatical forms are simplified; verbs have only the infinitive form. (A sort of Basic Romance.) Any Frenchman, or Spaniard or Italian, could understand the Mufti well enough.—Trans.]
6. ["Tell me, Turks, what is this man? An Anabaptist?"—Trans.]
7. ["No." An authentic Turkish word.—Trans.]
8. [Follower of Zwingli, Protestant reformer.—Trans.]
9. [Member of the Coptic Church.—Trans.]
10. [A Hussite, follower of Bohemian reformer John Huss. The meaning of the other two words is obscure.—Trans.]
11. [Brahmin; "Moffina" and "Zurina" are apparently invented words.—Trans.]

MUFTI: Ioc. Ioc. Ioc.
Mahametana? Mahametana?

TURKS: Hey valla! Hey valla!¹²

MUFTI: Como chamara? Como chamara?¹³

TURKS: Giourdina, Giourdina.

MUFTI: Giourdina! *(He leaps high, and peers in all directions)* Giourdina? Giourdina? Giourdina?

TURKS: Giourdina! Giourdina! Giourdina!

MUFTI:

Mahameta per Giourdina
Mi pregar sera e matina;
Voler far un paladina
De Giourdina, de Giourdina.
Dar turbanta e dar scarcina
Con galera e brigantina
Per deffender Palestina.
Mahameta per Giourdina
Mi pregar sera e mattina.¹⁴

(Questioning the TURKS)

Star bon Turca Giourdina?
Star bon Turca Giourdina?

TURKS:
Hey valla, hey valla!
Hey valla, hey valla!

MUFTI *(dancing):*
Hu la ba ba la chou ba la ba ba la da!

(The MUFTI exits; the TURKS dance and sing.)

TURKS:
Hu la ba ba la chou ba la ba ba la da!

(The MUFTI returns, wearing an enormous ceremonial turban, adorned with four or five rows of blazing candles. Two DERVISHES accompany him, wearing pointed hats, also adorned with lighted candles. They solemnly bear the Koran. The two other DERVISHES conduct MONSIEUR JOURDAIN, who is terrified by the ceremony. They make him kneel down with his back to the MUFTI: then they make him bend forward till his hands rest on the floor. They put the Koran on his back, which serves as a reading desk for the MUFTI. The MUFTI makes a burlesque invocation, scowling and opening and shutting

---

12. ["Yes, by Allah!" (Arabic.)—Trans.]
13. ["What is his name?"—Trans.]
14. ["I pray to Mahomet for Jourdain night and morning. I want to make a paladin of Jourdain, of Jourdain. Give a turban and a scimitar, with a galley and a brigantine, to defend Palestine. I pray to Mahomet for Jourdain night and morning."—Trans.]

his mouth without uttering a word. Then he speaks vehemently, now muttering, now shouting with terrifying passion, slapping his sides as if to force out his words, occasionally striking the Koran, turning its leaves briskly. He finally raises his hands and exclaims loudly: "Hou!"[15] During this invocation, the TURKS sing, "Hou, hou, hou!" bending forward three times, then straightening up, singing, "Hou, hou, hou!" They continue doing so throughout the MUFTI's invocation. After the invocation, the DERVISHES remove the Koran from MONSIEUR JOURDAIN's back. He exclaims, "Ouf!" with relief. The DERVISHES raise him to his feet.)

MUFTI *(to MONSIEUR JOURDAIN)*::
Ti non star furba?[16]

TURKS: No, no, no.

MUFTI: Non star forfanta?[17]

TURKS: No, no, no.

MUFTI *(to the TURKS)*:
Donar turbanta, donar turbanta.[18]

> *(Exit the MUFTI. The TURKS repeat the MUFTI's words, and with song and dance present the turban to MONSIEUR JOURDAIN. The MUFTI re-enters with a scimitar, which he presents to MONSIEUR JOURDAIN.)*

MUFTI: Ti star nobile, non star fabola.
Pigliar schiabola.[19]

(Exit the MUFTI. The TURKS draw their scimitars and repeat the MUFTI's words. Six of them dance around MONSIEUR JOURDAIN, feigning to strike him with their weapons. The MUFTI returns.)

MUFTI: Dara, dara bastonara, bastonara, bastonara.[20]

> *(Exit the MUFTI. The TURKS repeat his words, beating MONSIEUR JOURDAIN to music. Re-enter the MUFTI.)*

MUFTI: Non tener honta;
Questa star l'ultima affronta.[21]

> *(The TURKS repeat the MUFTI's words. The MUFTI, leaning on the DERVISHES, makes another invocation, to the full orchestra. Evidently fatigued by the ceremony, he is respectfully supported by the DERVISHES. The TURKS, leaping, dancing, and singing around the MUFTI, conduct him offstage to the sound of Turkish musical instruments.)*

ACT FIVE

After the Interlude, all retire except MONSIEUR JOURDAIN. *Enter* MADAME JOURDAIN.

---

15. [*He*, or *God*, in Arabic.—Trans.]
16. ["You aren't an evildoer?"—Trans.]
17. ["You aren't a rascal?"—Trans.]
18. ["Give the turban."—Trans.]

19. ["You're a noble, it's no lie. Take this sword."—Trans.]

20. ["Give him a beating."—Trans.]

21. ["Feel no shame; this is the last affront."—Trans.]

MME. JOURDAIN: Lord have mercy on us! What's all this? What a figure of fun! You're dressing up for Hallowe'en at this time of year? Tell me, what's going on? Who rigged you up that way?

M. JOURDAIN: Insolent creature, to talk that way to a mamamouchi!

MME. JOURDAIN: How's that?

M. JOURDAIN: Yes, now you've got to show me some respect. I've just been made a mamamouchi.

MME. JOURDAIN: What do you mean with your mamamouchi?

M. JOURDAIN: Mamamouchi, I tell you I'm a mamamouchi!

MME. JOURDAIN: What kind of creature is that?

M. JOURDAIN: Mamamouchi! That is, in our language, a paladin.

MME. JOURDAIN: Aballadin'! You're going to go around aballadin', at your age?

M. JOURDAIN: Such ignorance! I said a paladin. That's a dignity that just has been conferred upon me, with due ceremony.

MME. JOURDAIN: What kind of ceremony?

M. JOURDAIN: Mahameta per Giourdina!

MME. JOURDAIN: What does that mean?

M. JOURDAIN: Giourdina, that is, Jourdain.

MME. JOURDAIN: Well, what of it, Jourdain?

M. JOURDAIN: Voler far un paladina de Giourdina.

MME. JOURDAIN: What?

M. JOURDAIN: Dar turbanta con galera.

MME. JOURDAIN: What sense is there in that?

M. JOURDAIN: Per deffender palestina.

MME. JOURDAIN: What are you trying to say?

M. JOURDAIN: Dara dara bastonara.

MME. JOURDAIN: What's all that gibberish?

M. JOURDAIN: Non tener honta; questa star l'ultima affronta.

MME. JOURDAIN: What's the idea, anyway?

M. JOURDAIN *(singing and dancing):* Hou la ba ba chou ba la ba ba la da.

MME. JOURDAIN: Alas, dear God! My husband has gone crazy!

M. JOURDAIN: Silence, insolent woman! Show proper respect to a noble mamamouchi.

(Exit MONSIEUR JOURDAIN.)

MME. JOURDAIN: How has he gone and lost his wits? I must keep him from going out. Oh, dear, oh, dear, this is the last straw! There's nothing but trouble everywhere!

(Exit MADAME JOURDAIN. After a moment, enter DORANTE and DORIMENE.)

DORANTE: Yes, madame, you will see a very amusing sight. I don't think you will ever find a crazier man than he is. And besides, madame, we must try to aid Cléonte's love affair, and fall in with his masquerade. He's a very decent fellow, who deserves our interest and help.

DORIMENE: I think very highly of him; he merits good fortune in his enterprise.

DORANTE: Besides, we have a ballet due us. We shouldn't let it be wasted. And I want to see if my scheme for the performance works out well.

DORIMENE: I've just seen some of the preparations; they are magnificent. And I must tell you, Dorante, that I simply cannot allow this sort of thing. I must put a stop to your lavishness; and to check your mad spending of money on me, I have decided to marry you very soon. That's the best solution; with marriage, all the extravagances stop.

DORANTE: Ah, madame, is it possible that you have made so welcome a resolution in my favor?

DORIMENE: It's only to prevent you from ruining yourself. Otherwise, I can see that soon you wouldn't have a penny.

DORANTE: What an obligation I have, my dear, to your concern for preserving my property! It is all yours, and my heart too; you can do with them what you will.

DORIMENE: I shall take proper care of both of them . . . But here is our good man; he certainly looks extraordinary.

(Enter MONSIEUR JOURDAIN.)

DORANTE: Sir, madame and I have come to render homage to your new dignity, and to felicitate you on the proposed marriage of your daughter to the son of the Grand Turk.

M. JOURDAIN *(after making obeisances in the Turkish style):* Sir, I wish you the strength of serpents and the wisdom of lions.

DORIMENE: I am happy to be one of the first, Monsieur, to congratulate you upon the high degree of glory you have attained.

M. JOURDAIN: Madame, I wish your rosebush may be in bloom all year long. I am infinitely obliged to you for sympathetic interest in the honors which have come to me, and I take great joy in seeing you here again, so that I may make my very humble apologies for my wife's excesses.

DORIMENE: It was nothing at all; I can readily excuse her impulse. Your heart is no doubt precious to her; it is not strange that the possession of a man like you may expose her to some alarms.

M. JOURDAIN: The possession of my heart is entirely yours to dispose of.

DORANTE: You see, madame, that Monsieur Jourdain is not one of those people who are dazzled by prosperity. Even in his glory, he does not forget his old friends.

DORIMENE: That is the character of a really noble soul.

DORANTE: But where is His Turkish Highness? As your friends, we should like to pay him our respects.

M. JOURDAIN: There he is coming now. I have sent for my daughter, in order to give him her hand.

(Enter CLEONTE, in Turkish costume.)

DORANTE *(to CLEONTE):* Sir, as friends of your honorable father-in-law, we have come to make obeisance to Your Highness, and to respectfully assure Your Highness of our humble service.

M. JOURDAIN: Where is the interpreter, to tell him who you are, and make him understand what you are saying? You'll see that he'll answer you; he speaks Turkish wonderfully. Hello, hello! Where the deuce did he go to? *(to CLEONTE)* Strouf, strif, strof, straf. This gentleman is a grande segnore, grande segnore, grande segnore; and Madame is a granda dama granda dama. *(Recognizing that he fails to make himself understood)* Oh, dear! Sir, him French mamamouchi; Madame here, French female mamamouchi. I can't make it any clearer . . . Good! Here's the interpreter! *(Enter COVIELLE)* Where did you get off to? We can't say a thing without you. Just tell him that the gentleman and lady are persons of high rank, who have come to salute him, as my friends, and to assure him of their regards. *(To DORIMENE and DORANTE)* You see how he'll answer you.

COVIELLE: Alabala crociam acci borem alabamen.

CLEONTE: Catalequi tubal ourin soter amalouchen.

M. JOURDAIN: You see?

COVIELLE: He says: "May the rain of prosperity forever sprinkle the garden of your family."

M. JOURDAIN: Didn't I tell you he spoke Turkish?

DORANTE: It's certainly amazing.

(Enter LUCILE.)

M. JOURDAIN: Come here, daughter, come here. Come and give your hand to the gentleman, who does you the honor of asking to marry you.

LUCILE: Father! How you're gotten up! Are you acting in a play?

M. JOURDAIN: No, no; it isn't a play. It's a very serious matter, and one that does you the greatest honor you could conceive. Here is the husband I'm giving you.

LUCILE: Husband—to me, Father?

M. JOURDAIN: Yes, to you. Go on, shake hands with him, and thank heaven for your good fortune.

LUCILE: I don't want to get married.

M. JOURDAIN: Well, I want you to, and I'm your father.

LUCILE: Well, I won't.

M. JOURDAIN: Oh, talk, talk! Come on, I tell you. Here, give me your hand.

LUCILE: No, Father, I have told you, no power on earth can force me to take any other husband than Cléonte; and I'll go to any lengths, rather than—*(She recognizes CLEONTE)* It is true that you are my father, and I owe you entire obedience, and it is your right to dispose of me according to your decision.

M. JOURDAIN: Ah, I'm delighted to see you recognize your duty so quickly. It's always a pleasure to have an obedient daughter.

(Enter MADAME JOURDAIN.)

MME. JOURDAIN: What's this? What in the world is up? They say you're trying to marry your daughter to a circus clown!

M. JOURDAIN: Will you shut up, impertinence? You always come sticking your oar into everything, and there's no way to teach you to be reasonable.

MME. JOURDAIN: You're the one there's no getting any sense into; you go from one crazy fool trick to another. What's your idea? And what are you trying to do with this tomfool marriage?

M. JOURDAIN: I want to marry my daughter to the son of the Grand Turk.

MME. JOURDAIN: The son of the Grand Turk!

M. JOURDAIN: Yes. You can have the interpreter there pay him compliments for you.

MME. JOURDAIN: I don't care a hoot for any interpreter, and I'll tell him myself to his face that he won't have my daughter.

M. JOURDAIN: Once more, will you shut up?

DORANTE: What, Madame Jourdain, you are opposing such a happy opportunity as this? You refuse His Turkish Highness for a son-in-law?

MME. JOURDAIN: My good sir, mind your own business.

DORIMENE: It's a glorious honor, hardly to be turned down.

MME. JOURDAIN: Madame, I shall beg you also not to interfere in matters with which you have no concern.

DORANTE: It is our friendly feeling for you which makes us take an interest in your welfare.

MME. JOURDAIN: I don't need any of your friendly feelings.

DORANTE: But your daughter has yielded to her father's wishes.

MME. JOURDAIN: My daughter consents to marry a Turk?

438

DORANTE: Certainly.

MME. JOURDAIN: She can forget Cléonte?

DORANTE: Ah, well, what won't a girl do to be a great lady?

MME. JOURDAIN: I would strangle her with my own hands, if she ever did a trick like that.

M. JOURDAIN: Talk, talk, talk! I tell you that this marriage will take place.

MME. JOURDAIN: I tell you it won't.

M. JOURDAIN: Gabble, gabble, gabble!

LUCILE: Mother!

MME. JOURDAIN: You're a nasty girl!

M. JOURDAIN (*to* **MADAME JOURDAIN**)**:** You're scolding her because she obeys me?

MME. JOURDAIN: Yes; she belongs to me as well as to you.

COVIELLE (*to* **MADAME JOURDAIN**)**:** Madame!

MME. JOURDAIN: What are you trying to tell me, you?

COVIELLE: Just a word—

MME. JOURDAIN: I don't want to hear any "just a word" out of you.

COVIELLE (*to* **MONSIEUR JOURDAIN**)**:** Sir, if she will listen to me a moment in private, I promise you I'll make her consent to your desires.

MME. JOURDAIN: I won't consent.

COVIELLE: But just listen to me!

MME. JOURDAIN: I won't.

M. JOURDAIN: Listen to him!

MME. JOURDAIN: I don't want to listen to him.

M. JOURDAIN: He will tell you—

MME. JOURDAIN: I don't want him to tell me anything.

M. JOURDAIN: How obstinate women are! Will it do you any harm to hear what he says?

COVIELLE (*to* **MADAME JOURDAIN**)**:** Just listen to me; and afterwards you can do whatever you please.

MME. JOURDAIN: Well, all right. What?

COVIELLE (*to* **MADAME JOURDAIN**)**:** We have been trying to signal to you for the last half-hour. Don't you see that we're doing all this just to fall in with your husband's mania, and we're fooling him under this disguise, and it's Cléonte himself who is the son of the Grand Turk?

MME. JOURDAIN: Aha!

COVIELLE: And I'm Covielle!

MRS JOURDAIN *(aside to* COVIELLE*)*: Oh, well, in that case, I surrender.

COVIELLE: Don't give anything away.

MME. JOURDAIN *(to* MONSIEUR JOURDAIN*)*: Well, all right. I consent to the marriage.

M. JOURDAIN: Ah, now everybody's reasonable at last. You wouldn't listen to me. But I knew very well he would explain to you what it means to be the son of the Grand Turk.

MME. JOURDAIN: He's explained it to me very nicely, and I'm satisfied. Let's send out for a notary.

DORANTE: That's very well said. And Madame Jourdain, in order that you may have your mind entirely at ease, and dismiss any suspicion you may have conceived about your husband, Madame Dorimene and I shall make use of the same notary for our own marriage contract.

MME. JOURDAIN: I consent to that too.

M. JOURDAIN *(aside to* DORANTE*)*: That's just to throw dust in her eyes, I suppose?

DORANTE *(aside to* MONSIEUR JOURDAIN*)*: It's a good thing to play her along with this pretense.

M. JOURDAIN *(aside)*: Good, good. *(Aloud)* Have the notary sent for, right away.

DORANTE: While we're waiting for him to come and draft the contracts, let's have a look at our ballet. It will be a nice entertainment for His Turkish Highness.

M. JOURDAIN: A very good idea. Let's take our seats.

MME. JOURDAIN: How about Nicole?

M. JOURDAIN: I give her to the interpreter, and my wife to anyone that wants her.

COVIELLE: Sir, I thank you. *(Aside)* If anyone can find a madder madman, I'll go to Rome and tell it to the world.

(The play concludes with the Ballet of the Nations. As this has nothing to do with the previous action and characters, it is here omitted.)

Sor Juana Inés de la Cruz, Verses Against the Inconsequence of Men's Taste and Strictures

Juana de Asbaje (1648–1695), better known by her religious title, Sor Juana Inés de la Cruz—lived and died in Mexico. She has the honor of being one of the first poets of the New World. Though illegitimate by birth, she had the good fortune to be reared at the Viceroy's court, receiving an education more extensive than that given most women in her time. Her wide reading, her enormous library (over 4000 volumes), and her provocative poems brought her much the same kind of attention her European contemporary, St. Teresa of Ávila, attracted by her writings: a combination of respect and suspicion on the part of conservative male superiors who were both dazzled and alarmed by the unorthodox nature of her mind and talent. Predictably, Sor Juana's career as a nun was marked by controversy, and in an impassioned letter of self-vindication (*Respuesta a Sor Filotea*) she reflected on the conflict between art and religious devotion that she perceived in her own work.

As a counter-Reformation poet, Sor Juana exhibits many of the traits defining the imaginative and rhetorical style of the period: an analytical, at times confrontational wit, combining secular and sacred themes in a relentless probing of love, faith, and personal identity. Hers is more than a poetry of heightened self-consciousness; even the most obviously satiric poems reflect the rigor of a mind disciplined by spiritual self-examination.

VERSES AGAINST THE INCONSEQUENCE OF MEN'S TASTE AND STRICTURES

■

You stupid men, who do accuse
Women without good reason,
You are the cause of what you blame,
Yet this inference you refuse.

If you seek women's favor to win
With ardor beyond compare,
Why require them to be good,
When 'tis you who urge their sin?

You break down their resistance,
Then say quite seriously
That their lightness has achieved
What you won by your persistence.

You seek with stupid presumption
To find her whom you pursue
To be Thais when you woo her,
And Lucretia in your possession.

No woman can your favor win
Since even the most discreet
Is ungrateful if she keeps you out
And loose if she lets you in.

So how could she be born
Who would gain your love,
If an ungrateful woman displeases
And a complaisant one you scorn?

Your amorous labors give
Wings to their indiscretions,
When you have made women wicked
You wish them virtuously to live.

In a passion that is guilty
Who bears the greater blame:
She who falls on being entreated
Or he who falls to make entreaty?

When each is guilty of sin,
Which is the most to blame:
She who sins for payment,
Or he who pays for the sin?

Why are you so surprised
At the fault that is your own?
Either prize women as you make them,
Or make them to be prized.

To them no longer urge your suit,
And then with much more reason
Can you blame their affection
When they are in pursuit.

To assert this I have every right;
Your pride has many weapons,
Your persistence and your promises
Devil, world, and flesh unite.

translation by
—MURIEL KITTEL

442

The Enlightenment

Voltaire Francois-Marie Arouet, Candide

One of the world's wittiest and most influential writers, Voltaire (1694–1778) was a bold champion of freedom of thought and speech at a time when such ideas commonly landed their proponents in prison. Voltaire in fact was frequently arrested, imprisoned, and exiled for attacking the authoritarian religious and political institutions of his day. One of the leading creators of the Enlightenment, a movement that promoted reason over tradition and hereditary authority, Voltaire produced an endless stream of plays, poems, essays, novels, and philosophical tracts advocating social justice and personal liberty. Banished from France, he took refuge in Holland and then at the court of Frederick the Great, King of Prussia, with whom he later quarreled. After a turbulent public life, Voltaire retired to Ferney, a small village near Geneva, Switzerland, where he continued to aim stinging attacks on political tyranny and religious intolerance. His satirical wit and unorthodox opinions won him a wide audience; well before his death he was honored as one of Europe's leading thinkers.

Candide, or Optimism (1759), is a delightful travel–adventure novel that entertainingly mocks one of the popular philosophical notions of the time—that we live in the best of all possible worlds. In Voltaire's realistic worldview, neither human society nor physical nature justifies such optimism. The great Lisbon earthquake that killed 30,000 persons in 1755 amply demonstrated that natural events care nothing for human welfare. By taking his naive young hero, Candide, on a tour of different countries and cultures, Voltaire exposes the foibles, cruelties, and treacheries abounding in human nature, a further demonstration that things do not invariably work out "for the best." Dr. Pangloss, Candide's eternally optimistic tutor, maintains his positive outlook by resolutely ignoring the examples of social injustice and natural catastrophe he experiences. Candide begins his education in reality after being thrown out of the castle of Thunder-ten-tronckh for making love to the Baron's daughter, Cunegonde. After experiencing nearly every disaster conceivable, he is reunited with his love, whose lost beauty imparts yet another lesson in imperfection. Sobered and skeptical of false optimism, Candide at last concludes that it is safest and wisest to lead a quiet life, privately cultivating one's own garden.

CANDIDE
■

CHAPTER I

How Candide was Brought Up in a Noble Castle, and How He was Expelled from the Same

In the castle of Baron Thunder-ten-tronckh in Westphalia there lived a youth, endowed by Nature with the most gentle character. His face was the expression of his soul. His judgment was quite honest and he was extremely simple-minded; and this was the reason, I think, that he was named Candide. Old servants in the house suspected that he was the son of the

Baron's sister and a decent honest gentleman of the neighbourhood, whom this young lady would never marry because he could only prove seventy-one quarterings, and the rest of his genealogical tree was lost, owing to the injuries of time.

The Baron was one of the most powerful lords in Westphalia, for his castle possessed a door and windows. His Great Hall was even decorated with a piece of tapestry. The dogs in his stable-yards formed a pack of hounds when necessary; his grooms were his huntsmen; the village curate was his Grand Almoner. They all called him "My Lord," and laughed heartily at his stories.

The Baroness weighed about three hundred and fifty pounds, was therefore greatly respected, and did the honours of the house with a dignity which rendered her still more respectable. Her daughter Cunegonde, aged seventeen, was rosy-cheeked, fresh, plump and tempting. The Baron's son appeared in every respect worthy of his father. The tutor Pangloss was the oracle of the house, and little Candide followed his lessons with all the candour of his age and character.

Pangloss taught metaphysico-theologo-cosmologinology. He proved admirably that there is no effect without a cause and that in this best of all possible worlds, My Lord the Baron's castle was the best of castles and his wife the best of all possible Baronesses.

" 'Tis demonstrated," said he, "that things cannot be otherwise; for, since everything is made for an end, everything is necessarily for the best end. Observe that noses were made to wear spectacles; and so we have spectacles. Legs were visibly instituted to be breeched, and we have breeches. Stones were formed to be quarried and to build castles; and My Lord has a very noble castle; the greatest Baron in the province should have the best house; and as pigs were made to be eaten, we eat pork all the year round; consequently, those who have asserted that all is well talk nonsense; they ought to have said that all is for the best."

Candide listened attentively and believed innocently; for he thought Mademoiselle Cunegonde extremely beautiful, although he was never bold enough to tell her so. He decided that after the happiness of being born Baron of Thunder-ten-tronckh, the second degree of happiness was to be Mademoiselle Cunegonde; the third, to see her every day; and the fourth to listen to Doctor Pangloss, the greatest philosopher of the province and therefore of the whole world.

One day when Cunegonde was walking near the castle, in a little wood which was called The Park, she observed Doctor Pangloss in the bushes, giving a lesson in experimental physics to her mother's waiting-maid, a very pretty and docile brunette. Mademoiselle Cunegonde had a great inclination for science and watched breathlessly the reiterated experiments she witnessed; she observed clearly the Doctor's sufficient reason, the effects and the causes, and returned home very much excited, pensive, filled with the desire of learning, reflecting that she might be the sufficient reason of young Candide and that he might be hers.

On her way back to the castle she met Candide and blushed; Candide also blushed. She bade him good-morning in a hesitating voice; Candide replied without knowing what he was saying. Next day, when they left the table after dinner, Cunegonde and Candide found themselves behind a screen; Cunegonde dropped her handkerchief, Candide picked it up; she innocently held his hand; the young man innocently kissed the young lady's hand with remarkable vivacity, tenderness and grace; their lips met, their eyes sparkled, their knees trembled, their hands wandered. Baron Thunder-ten-tronckh passed near the screen, and, observing this cause and effect, expelled Candide from the castle by kicking him in the backside frequently and hard. Cunegonde swooned; when she recovered her senses, the Baroness slapped her in the face; and all was in consternation in the noblest and most agreeable of all possible castles.

CHAPTER II

What Happened to Candide among the Bulgarians

Candide, expelled from the earthly paradise, wandered for a long time without knowing where he was going, turning up his eyes to Heaven, gazing back frequently at the noblest of castles which held the most beautiful of young Baronesses; he lay down to sleep supperless between two furrows in the open fields; it snowed heavily in large flakes. The next morning the shivering Candide, penniless, dying of cold and exhaustion, dragged himself towards the neighbouring town, which was called Waldberghofftrarbkdikdorff. He halted sadly at the door of an inn. Two men dressed in blue noticed him.

"Comrade," said one, "there's a well-built young man of the right height."

They went up to Candide and very civilly invited him to dinner.

"Gentlemen," said Candide with charming modesty, "you do me a great honour, but I have no money to pay my share."

"Ah, sir," said one of the men in blue, "persons of your figure and merit never pay anything; are you not five feet five tall?"

"Yes, gentlemen," said he, bowing, "that is my height."

"Ah, sir, come to table; we will not only pay your expenses, we will never allow a man like you to be short of money; men were only made to help each other."

"You are in the right," said Candide, "that is what Doctor Pangloss was always telling me, and I see that everything is for the best."

They begged him to accept a few crowns, he took them and wished to give them an IOU; they refused to take it and all sat down to table.

"Do you not love tenderly . . ."

"Oh, yes," said he. "I love Mademoiselle Cunegonde tenderly."

"No," said one of the gentlemen. "We were asking if you do not tenderly love the King of the Bulgarians."

"Not a bit," said he, "for I have never seen him."

"What! He is the most charming of Kings, and you must drink his health."

"Oh, gladly, gentlemen." And he drank.

"That is sufficient," he was told. "You are now the support, the aid, the defender, the hero of the Bulgarians; your fortune is made and your glory assured."

They immediately put irons on his legs and took him to a regiment. He was made to turn to the right and left, to raise the ramrod and return the ramrod, to take aim, to fire, to double up, and he was given thirty strokes with a stick; the next day he drilled not quite so badly, and received only twenty strokes; the day after, he only had ten and was looked on as a prodigy by his comrades.

Candide was completely mystified and could not make out how he was a hero. One fine spring day he thought he would take a walk, going straight ahead, in the belief that to use his legs as he pleased was a privilege of the human species as well as of animals. He had not gone two leagues when four other heroes, each six feet tall, fell upon him, bound him and dragged him back to a cell. He was asked by his judges whether he would rather be thrashed thirty-six times by the whole regiment or receive a dozen lead bullets at once in his brain. Although he protested that men's wills are free and that he wanted neither one nor the other, he had to make a choice; by virtue of that gift of God which is called *liberty*, he determined to run the gauntlet thirty-six times and actually did so twice. There were two thousand men in the regiment. That made four thousand strokes which laid bare the muscles and nerves from his neck to his backside. As they were about to proceed to a third turn, Candide, utterly exhausted, begged as a favour that they would be so kind as to smash his head; he obtained this favour; they bound his eyes and he was made to kneel down. At that moment the King of the Bulgarians came by and inquired the victim's crime; and as this King was possessed of a vast genius, he perceived from what he learned about Candide that he was a young metaphysician very ignorant in worldly matters, and therefore pardoned him with a clemency which will be praised in all newspapers and all ages. An honest surgeon healed Candide in three weeks with the ointments recommended by Dioscorides. He had already regained a little skin and could walk when the King of the Bulgarians went to war with the King of the Abares.

CHAPTER III

How Candide Escaped from the Bulgarians and What Became of Him

Nothing could be smarter, more splendid, more brilliant, better drawn up than the two armies. Trumpets, fifes, hautboys, drums, cannons, formed a harmony such as has never been heard even in hell. The cannons first of all laid flat about six thousand men on each side; then the musketry removed from the best of worlds some nine or ten thousand blackguards who infested its surface. The bayonet also was the sufficient reason for the death of some thousands of men. The whole might amount to thirty thousand souls. Candide, who trembled like a philosopher, hid himself as well as he could during this heroic butchery.

At last, while the two Kings each commanded a Te Deum in his camp, Candide decided to go elsewhere to reason about effects and causes. He clambered over heaps of dead and dying men and reached a neighbouring village, which was in ashes; it was an Abare village which the Bulgarians had burned in accordance with international law. Here, old men dazed with blows watched the dying agonies of their murdered wives who clutched their children to their bleeding breasts; there, disembowelled girls who had been made to satisfy the natural appetites of heroes gasped their last sighs; others, half-burned, begged to be put to death. Brains were scattered on the ground among dismembered arms and legs.

Candide fled to another village as fast as he could; it belonged to the Bulgarians, and Abarian heroes had treated it in the same way. Candide, stumbling over quivering limbs or across ruins, at last escaped from the theatre of war, carrying a little food in his knapsack, and never forgetting Mademoiselle Cunegonde. His provisions were all gone when he reached Holland; but, having heard that everyone in that country was rich and a Christian, he had no doubt at all but that he would be as well treated as he had been in the Baron's castle before he had been expelled on account of Mademoiselle Cunegonde's pretty eyes.

He asked an alms of several grave persons, who all replied that if he continued in that way he would be shut up in a house of correction to teach him how to live.

He then addressed himself to a man who had been discoursing on charity in a large assembly for an hour on end. This orator, glancing at him askance, said: "What are you doing here? Are you for the good cause?"

"There is no effect without a cause," said Candide modestly. "Everything is necessarily linked up and arranged for the best. It was necessary that I should be expelled from the company of Mademoiselle Cunegonde, that I ran the gauntlet, and that I beg my bread until I can earn it; all this could not have happened differently."

"My friend," said the orator, "do you believe that the Pope is Anti-Christ?"

"I have never heard so before," said Candide, "but whether he is or isn't, I am starving."

"You don't deserve to eat," said the other. "Hence, rascal; hence, you wretch; and never come near me again."

The orator's wife thrust her head out of the window and seeing a man who did not believe that the Pope was Anti-Christ, she poured on his head a full . . . O Heavens! To what excess religious zeal is carried by ladies!

A man who had not been baptized, an honest Anabaptist named Jacques, saw the cruel and ignominious treatment of one of his brothers, a featherless two-legged creature with a soul; he took him home, cleaned him up, gave him bread and beer, presented him with two florins, and even offered to teach him to work at the manufacture of Persian stuffs which are made in Holland. Candide threw himself at the man's feet, exclaiming: "Doctor Pangloss was right in telling me that all is for the best in this world, for I am vastly more touched by your extreme generosity than by the harshness of the gentleman in the black cloak and his good lady."

The next day when he walked out he met a beggar covered with sores, dull-eyed, with the end of his nose fallen away, his mouth awry, his teeth black, who talked huskily, was tormented with a violent cough and spat out a tooth at every cough. [The beggar is Dr. Pangloss, a victim of the Bulgarian army, who joins Candide on an ill-fated voyage to Lisbon.]

CHAPTER V

Storm, Shipwreck, Earthquake, and What Happened to Dr. Pangloss, to Candide and the Anabaptist Jaques

Half the enfeebled passengers, suffering from that inconceivable anguish which the rolling of a ship causes in the nerves and in all the humours of bodies shaken in contrary directions, did not retain strength enough even to trouble about the danger. The other half screamed and prayed; the sails were torn, the masts broken, the vessel leaking. Those worked who could, no one co-operated, no one commanded. The Anabaptist tried to help the crew a little; he was on the main-deck; a furious sailor struck him violently and stretched him on the deck, but the blow he delivered gave him so violent a shock that he fell head-first out of the ship. He remained hanging and clinging to part of the broken mast. The good Jacques ran to his aid, helped him to climb back, and from the effort he made was flung into the sea in full view of the sailor, who allowed him to drown without condescending even to look at him. Candide came up, saw his benefactor reappear for a moment and then be engulfed for ever. He tried to throw himself after him into the sea; he was prevented by the philosopher Pangloss, who proved to him that the Lisbon roads had been expressly created for the Anabaptist to be drowned in them. While he was proving this *a priori*, the vessel sank, and every one perished except Pangloss, Candide and the brutal sailor who had drowned the virtuous Anabaptist; the blackguard swam successfully to the shore and Pangloss and Candide were carried there on a plank.

When they had recovered a little, they walked toward Lisbon; they had a little money by the help of which they hoped to be saved from hunger after having escaped the storm. Weeping the death of their benefactor, they had scarcely set foot in the town when they felt the earth tremble under their feet; the sea rose in foaming masses in the port and smashed the ships which rode at anchor. Whirlwinds of flame and ashes covered the streets and squares; the houses collapsed, the roofs were thrown upon the foundations, and the foundations were scattered; thirty thousand inhabitants of every age and both sexes were crushed under the ruins. Whistling and swearing, the sailor said: "There'll be something to pick up here."

"What can be the sufficient reason for this phenomenon?" said Pangloss.

"It is the last day!" cried Candide.

The sailor immediately ran among the debris, dared death to find money, found it, seized it, got drunk, and having slept off his wine, purchased the favours of the first woman of goodwill he met on the ruins of the houses and among the dead and dying. Pangloss, however, pulled him by the sleeve.

"My friend," said he, "this is not well, you are disregarding universal reason, you choose the wrong time."

"Blood and 'ounds!" he retorted, "I am a sailor and I was born in Batavia; four times have I stamped on the crucifix during four voyages to Japan; you have found the right man for your universal reason!"

Candide had been hurt by some falling stones; he lay in the street covered with debris. He said to Pangloss: "Alas! Get me a little wine and oil; I am dying."

"This earthquake is not a new thing," replied Pangloss. "The town of Lima felt the same shocks in America last year; similar causes produce similar effects; there must certainly be a train of sulphur underground from Lima to Lisbon."

"Nothing is more probable," replied Candide; "but, for God's sake, a little oil and wine."

"What do you mean, probable?" replied the philosopher; "I maintain that it is proved."

Candide lost consciousness, and Pangloss brought him a little water from a neighbouring fountain.

Next day they found a little food as they wandered among the ruins and regained a little strength. Afterwards they worked like others to help the inhabitants who had escaped death. Some citizens they had assisted gave them as good a dinner as could be expected in such a disaster; true, it was a dreary meal; the hosts watered their bread with their tears, but Pangloss consoled them by assuring them that things could not be otherwise.

"For," said he, "all this is for the best; for, if there is a volcano at Lisbon, it cannot be anywhere else; for it is impossible that things should not be where they are; for all is well."

A little, dark man, a familiar of the Inquisition, who sat beside him, politely took up the conversation, and said: "Apparently you do not believe in original sin; for, if everything is for the best, there was neither fall nor punishment."

"I most humbly beg your excellency's pardon," replied Pangloss still more politely, "for the fall of man and the curse necessarily entered into the best of all possible worlds."

"Then you do not believe in free-will?" said the familiar.

"Your excellency will pardon me," said Pangloss; "free-will can exist with absolute necessity; for it was necessary that we should be free; for in short, limited will . . ."

Pangloss was in the middle of his phrase when the familiar nodded to his armed attendant who was pouring out port or Oporto wine for him.

CHAPTER VI

How a Splendid Auto-da-fé was Held to Prevent Earthquakes, and How Candide was Flogged

After the earthquake which destroyed three-quarters of Lisbon, the wise men of that country could discover no more efficacious way of preventing a total ruin than by giving the people a splendid *auto-da-fé*. It was decided by the university of Coimbre that the sight of several persons being slowly burned in great ceremony is an infallible secret for preventing earthquakes.

Consequently they had arrested a Biscayan convicted of having married his fellow-godmother, and two Portuguese who, when eating a chicken, had thrown away the bacon; after dinner they came and bound Dr. Pangloss and his disciple Candide, one because he had spoken and the other because he had listened with an air of approbation; they were both carried separately to extremely cool apartments, where there was never any discomfort from the sun; a week afterwards each was dressed in a sanbenito and their heads were ornamented with paper mitres; Candide's mitre and sanbenito were painted with flames upside down and with devils who had neither tails nor claws; but Pangloss's devils had claws and tails, and his flames were upright.

Dressed in this manner they marched in procession and listened to a most pathetic sermon, followed by lovely plain-song music. Candide was flogged in time to the music, while the singing went on; the Biscayan and the two men who had not wanted to eat bacon were burned, and Pangloss was hanged, although this is not the custom. The very same day, the earth shook again with a terrible clamour.

Candide, terrified, dumbfounded, bewildered, covered with blood, quivering from head to foot, said to himself: "If this is the best of all possible worlds, what are the others? Let it pass that I was flogged, for I was flogged by the Bulgarians, but, O my dear Pangloss! The greatest of philosophers! Must I see you hanged without knowing why! O my dear Anabaptist! The best of men! Was it necessary that you should be drowned in port! O Mademoiselle Cunegonde! The pearl of women! Was it necessary that your belly should be slit!"

He was returning, scarcely able to support himself, preached at, flogged, absolved and blessed, when an old woman accosted him and said: "Courage, my son, follow me."

CHAPTER VII

How an Old Woman Took Care of Candide and How He Regained That Which He Loved

[The woman leads Candide to Cunegonde, who has miraculously survived the soldiers' attack and fled to Portugal.]

The old woman advised them to make less noise and left them alone.

"What! Is it you?" said Candide. "You are alive, and I find you here in Portugal! Then you were not raped? Your belly was not slit, as the philosopher Pangloss assured me?"

"Yes, indeed," said the fair Cunegonde; "but those two accidents are not always fatal."

"But your father and mother were killed?"

"'Tis only too true," said Cunegonde, weeping.

"And your brother?"

"My brother was killed too."

"And why are you in Portugal? And how did you know I was here? And by what strange adventure have you brought me to this house?"

"I will tell you everything," replied the lady, "but first of all you must tell me everything that has happened to you since the innocent kiss you gave me and the kicks you received."

Candide obeyed with profound respect; and, although he was bewildered, although his voice was weak and trembling, although his back was still a little painful, he related in the most natural manner all he had endured since the moment of their separation. Cunegonde raised her eyes to heaven; she shed tears at the death of the good Anabaptist and Pangloss, after which she spoke as follows to Candide, who did not miss a word and devoured her with his eyes.

CHAPTER VIII

Cunegonde's Story

"I was fast asleep in bed when it pleased Heaven to send the Bulgarians to our noble castle of Thunder-ten-tronckh; they murdered my father and brother and cut my mother to pieces. A large Bulgarian six feet tall, seeing that I had swooned at the spectacle, began to rape me; this brought me to, I recovered my senses, I screamed, I struggled, I bit, I scratched, I tried to tear out the big Bulgarian's eyes, not knowing that what was happening in my father's castle was a matter of custom; the brute stabbed me with a knife in the left side where I still have the scar."

"Alas! I hope I shall see it," said the naïf Candide.

"You shall see it," said Cunegonde, "but let me go on."

"Go on," said Candide.

She took up the thread of her story as follows: "A Bulgarian captain came in, saw me covered with blood, and the soldier did not disturb himself. The captain was angry at the brute's lack of respect to him, and killed him on my body. Afterwards, he had me bandaged and took me to his billet as a prisoner of war. I washed the few shirts he had and did the cooking; I must admit he thought me very pretty; and I will not deny that he was very well built and that his skin was white and soft; otherwise he had little wit and little philosophy; it was plain that he had not been brought up by Dr. Pangloss. At the end of three months he lost all his money and got tired of me; he sold me to a Jew named Don Issachar, who traded in Holland and Portugal and had a passion for women. This Jew devoted himself to my person but he could not triumph over it; I resisted him better than the Bulgarian soldier; a lady of honour may be raped once, but it strengthens her virtue. In order to subdue me, the Jew brought me to this country house. Up till then I believed that there was nothing on earth so splendid as the castle of Thunder-ten-tronckh; I was undeceived.

One day the Grand Inquisitor noticed me at Mass; he ogled me continually and sent a message that he wished to speak to me on secret affairs. I was taken to his palace; I informed him of my birth; he pointed out how much it was beneath my rank to belong to an Israelite. A proposition was made on his behalf to Don Issachar to give me up to His Lordship. Don Issachar, who is the court banker and a man of influence, would not agree. The Inquisitor threatened him with an *auto-da-fé*. At last the Jew was frightened and made a bargain whereby the house and I belong to both in common. The Jew has Mondays, Wednesdays and the Sabbath day, and the Inquisitor has the other days of the week. This arrangement has lasted for six months. It has not been without quarrels; for it has often been debated whether the night between Saturday and Sunday belonged to the old law or the new. For my part, I have hitherto resisted them both; and I think that is the reason why they still love me.

At last My Lord the Inquisitor was pleased to arrange an *auto-da-fé* to remove the scourge of earthquakes and to intimidate Don Issachar. He honoured me with an invitation. I had an excellent seat; and refreshments were served to the ladies between the Mass and the execution. I was indeed horror-stricken when I saw the burning of the two Jews and the honest Biscayan who had married his fellow-godmother; but what was my surprise, my terror, my anguish, when I saw in a sanbenito and under a mitre a face which resembled Pangloss's! I rubbed my eyes, I looked carefully, I saw him hanged; and I fainted. I had scarcely recovered my senses when I saw you stripped naked; that was the height of horror, of consternation, of grief and despair. I will frankly tell you that your skin is even whiter and of a more perfect tint than that of my Bulgarian captain. This spectacle redoubled all the feelings which crushed and devoured me. I exclaimed, I tried to say: 'Stop, Barbarians!' but my voice failed and my cries would have been useless. When you had been well flogged, I said to myself: 'How does it happen that the charming Candide and the wise Pangloss are in Lisbon, the one to receive a hundred lashes, and the other to be hanged, by order of My Lord the Inquisitor, whose darling I am? Pangloss deceived me cruelly when he said that all is for the best in the world.'

I was agitated, distracted, sometimes beside myself and sometimes ready to die of faintness, and my head was filled with the massacre of my father, of my mother, of my brother, the insolence of my horrid Bulgarian soldier, the gash he gave me, my slavery, my life as a kitchen-wench, my Bulgarian captain, my horrid Don Issachar, my abominable Inquisitor, the hanging of Dr. Pangloss, that long plain-song *miserere* during which you were flogged, and above all the kiss I gave you behind the screen that day when I saw you for the last time. I praised God for bringing you back to me through so many trials, I ordered my old woman to take care of you and to bring you here as soon as she could. She has carried out my commission very well; I have enjoyed the inexpressible pleasure of seeing you again, of listening to you, and of speaking to you. You must be very hungry; I have a good appetite; let us begin by having supper."

Both sat down to supper; and after supper they returned to the handsome sofa we have already mentioned; they were still there when Signor Don Issachar, one of the masters of the house, arrived. It was the day of the Sabbath. He came to enjoy his rights and to express his tender love.

CHAPTER XXVIII

What Happened to Candide, to Cunegonde, to Pangloss, to Martin, Etc.

[After many hilarious, grim, and highly improbable adventures, Pangloss and the Baron, Cunegonde's brother, turn up alive as convicts on a Turkish slave ship.]

"Pardon once more," said Candide to the Baron, "pardon me, reverend father, for having thrust my sword through your body."

"Let us say no more about it," said the Baron. "I admit I was a little too sharp; but since you wish to know how it was you saw me in a galley, I must tell you that after my wound was healed by the brother apothecary of the college, I was attacked and carried off by a Spanish raiding party; I was imprisoned in Buenos Ayres at the time when my sister had just left. I asked to return to the Vicar-General in Rome. I was ordered to Constantinople to act as almoner to the Ambassador of France. A week after I had taken up my office I met towards evening a very handsome young page of the Sultan. It was very hot; the young man wished to bathe; I took the opportunity to bathe also. I did not know that it was a most serious crime for a Christian to be found naked with a young Mahometan. A cadi sentenced me to a hundred strokes on the soles of my feet and condemned me to the galley. I do not think a more horrible injustice has ever been committed. But I should very much like to know why my sister is in the kitchen of a Transylvanian sovereign living in exile among the Turks."

"But, my dear Pangloss," said Candide, "how does it happen that I see you once more?"

"It is true," said Pangloss, "that you saw me hanged; and in the natural course of events I should have been burned. But you remember, it poured with rain when they were going to roast me; the storm was so violent that they despaired of lighting the fire; I was hanged because they could do nothing better; a surgeon bought my body, carried me home and dissected me. He first made a crucial incision in me from the navel to the collar-bone. Nobody could have been worse hanged than I was. The executioner of the holy Inquisition, who was a sub-deacon, was marvellously skilful in burning people, but he was not accustomed to hang them; the rope was wet and did not slide easily and it was knotted; in short, I still breathed. The crucial incision caused me to utter so loud a scream that the surgeon fell over backwards and, thinking he was dissecting the devil, fled away in terror and fell down the staircase in his flight. His wife ran in from another room at the noise; she saw me stretched out on the table with my crucial incision; she was still more frightened than her husband, fled, and fell on top of him. When they had recovered themselves a little, I heard the surgeon's wife, say to the surgeon: 'My dear, what were you thinking of, to dissect a heretic? Don't you know the devil always possesses them? I will go and get a priest at once to exorcise him.'

At this I shuddered and collected the little strength I had left to shout: 'Have pity on me!'

At last the Portuguese barber grew bolder; he sewed up my skin; his wife even took care of me, and at the end of a fortnight I was able to walk again. The barber found me a situation and made me lackey to a Knight of Malta who was going to Venice; but, as my master had no money to pay me wages, I entered the service of a Venetian merchant and followed him to Constantinople.

One day I took it into my head to enter a mosque; there was nobody there except an old

Imam and a very pretty young devotee who was reciting her prayers; her breasts were entirely uncovered; between them she wore a bunch of tulips, roses, anemones, ranunculus, hyacinths and auriculas; she dropped her bunch of flowers; I picked it up and returned it to her with a most respectful alacrity. I was so long putting them back that the Imam grew angry and, seeing I was a Christian, called for help. I was taken to the cadi, who sentenced me to receive a hundred strokes on the soles of my feet and sent me to the galleys. I was chained on the same seat and in the same galley as My Lord the Baron. In this galley there were four young men from Marseilles, five Neapolitan priests and two monks from Corfu, who assured us that similar accidents occurred every day. His Lordship the Baron claimed that he had suffered a greater injustice than I; and I claimed that it was much more permissible to replace a bunch of flowers between a woman's breasts than to be naked with one of the Sultan's pages. We argued continually, and every day received twenty strokes of the bull's pizzle, when the chain of events of this universe led you to our galley and you ransomed us."

"Well! my dear Pangloss," said Candide, "when you were hanged, dissected, stunned with blows and made to row in the galleys, did you always think that everything was for the best in this world?"

"I am still of my first opinion," replied Pangloss, "for after all I am a philosopher; and it would be unbecoming for me to recant, since Leibnitz could not be in the wrong and pre-established harmony is the finest thing imaginable like the plenum and subtle matter."

CHAPTER XXIX

How Candide Found Cunegonde and the Old Woman Again

While Candide, the Baron, Pangloss, Martin and Cacambo were relating their adventures, reasoning upon contingent or non-contingent events of the universe, arguing about effects and causes, moral and physical evil, free-will and necessity, and the consolations to be found in the Turkish galleys, they came to the house of the Transylvanian prince on the shores of Propontis.

The first objects which met their sight were Cunegonde and the old woman hanging out towels to dry on the line.

At this sight the Baron grew pale. Candide, that tender lover, seeing his fair Cunegonde sunburned, blear-eyed, flat-breasted, with wrinkles round her eyes and red, chapped arms, recoiled three paces in horror, and then advanced from mere politeness. She embraced Candide and her brother. They embraced the old woman; Candide bought them both.

In the neighbourhood was a little farm; the old woman suggested that Candide should buy it, until some better fate befell the group. Cunegonde did not know that she had become ugly, for nobody had told her so; she reminded Candide of his promises in so peremptory a tone that the good Candide dared not refuse her.

He therefore informed the Baron that he was about to marry his sister. "Never," said the Baron, "will I endure such baseness on her part and such insolence on yours; nobody shall ever reproach me with this infamy; my sister's children could never enter the chapters of Germany. No, my sister shall never marry anyone but a Baron of the Empire."

Cunegonde threw herself at his feet and bathed them in tears; but he was inflexible.

"Madman," said Candide, "I rescued you from the galleys, I paid your ransom and your sister's; she was washing dishes here, she is ugly, I am so kind as to make her my wife, and you pretend to oppose me! I should kill you again if I listened to my anger."

"You may kill me again," said the Baron, "but you shall never marry my sister while I am alive."

CHAPTER XXX

Conclusion

At the bottom of his heart Candide had not the least wish to marry Cunegonde. But the Baron's extreme impertinence determined him to complete the marriage, and Cunegonde urged it so warmly that he could not retract. He consulted Pangloss, Martin and the faithful Cacambo. Pangloss wrote an excellent memorandum by which he proved that the Baron had no rights over his sister and that by all the laws of the empire she could make a left-handed marriage with Candide. Martin advised that the Baron should be thrown into the sea; Cacambo decided that he should be returned to the Levantine captain and sent back to the galleys, after which he would be returned by the first ship to the Vicar-General at Rome. This was thought to be very good advice; the old woman approved it; they said nothing to the sister; the plan was carried out with the aid of a little money and they had the pleasure of duping a Jesuit and punishing the pride of a German Baron.

It would be natural to suppose that when, after so many disasters, Candide was married to his mistress, and living with the philosopher Pangloss, the philosopher Martin, the prudent Cacambo and the old woman, having brought back so many diamonds from the country of the ancient Incas, he would lead the most pleasant life imaginable. But he was so cheated by the Jews that he had nothing left but his little farm; his wife, growing uglier every day, became shrewish and unendurable; the old woman was ailing and even more bad-tempered than Cunegonde. Cacambo, who worked in the garden and then went to Constantinople to sell vegetables, was overworked and cursed his fate. Pangloss was in despair because he did not shine in some German university.

As for Martin, he was firmly convinced that people are equally uncomfortable everywhere; he accepted things patiently. Candide, Martin and Pangloss sometimes argued about metaphysics and morals. From the windows of the farm they often watched the ships going by, filled with effendis, pashas, and cadis, who were being exiled to Lemnos, to Mitylene and Erzerum. They saw other cadis, other pashas and other effendis coming back to take the place of the exiles and to be exiled in their turn. They saw the neatly impaled heads which were taken to the Sublime Porte. These sights redoubled their discussions; and when they were not arguing, the boredom was so excessive that one day the old woman dared to say to them: "I should like to know which is worse, to be raped a hundred times by negro pirates, to have a buttock cut off, to run the gauntlet among the Bulgarians, to be whipped and flogged in an *auto-da-fé*, to be dissected, to row in a galley, in short, to endure all the miseries through which we have passed, or to remain here doing nothing?"

"'Tis a great question," said Candide.

These remarks led to new reflections, and Martin especially concluded that man was born to live in the convulsions of distress or in the lethargy of boredom. Candide did not agree, but he asserted nothing. Pangloss confessed that he had always suffered horribly; but, having once maintained that everything was for the best, he had continued to maintain it without believing it.

One thing confirmed Martin in his detestable principles, made Candide hesitate more than ever, and embarrassed Pangloss. And it was this. One day there came to their farm Paquette and Friar Giroflée, who were in the most extreme misery; they had soon wasted their three thousand piastres, had left each other, made it up, quarrelled again, been put in prison, escaped, and finally Friar Giroflée had turned Turk. Paquette continued her occupation everywhere and now earned nothing by it.

"I foresaw," said Martin to Candide, "that your gifts would soon be wasted and would only make them the more miserable. You and Cacambo were once bloated with millions of piastres and you are no happier than Friar Giroflée and Paquette."

"Ah! Ha!" said Pangloss to Paquette, "so Heaven brings you back to us, my dear child? Do you know that you cost me the end of my nose, an eye and an ear! What a plight you are in! Ah! What a world this is!"

This new occurrence caused them to philosophise more than ever.

In the neighbourhood there lived a very famous Dervish, who was supposed to be the best philosopher in Turkey; they went to consult him; Pangloss was the spokesman and said: "Master, we have come to beg you to tell us why so strange an animal as man was ever created."

"What has it to do with you?" said the Dervish. "Is it your business?"

"But, reverend father," said Candide, "there is a horrible amount of evil in the world."

"What does it matter," said the Dervish, "whether there is evil or good? When his highness sends a ship to Egypt, does he worry about the comfort or discomfort of the rats in the ship?"

"Then what should we do?" said Pangloss.

"Hold your tongue," said the Dervish.

"I flattered myself," said Pangloss, "that I should discuss with you effects and causes, this best of all possible worlds, the origin of evil, the nature of the soul and pre-established harmony."

At these words the Dervish slammed the door in their faces.

During this conversation the news went round that at Constantinople two viziers and the mufti had been strangled and several of their friends impaled. This catastrophe made a prodigious noise everywhere for several hours. As Pangloss, Candide and Martin were returning to their little farm, they came upon an old man who was taking the air under a bower of orange-trees at his door. Pangloss, who was as curious as he was argumentative, asked him what was the name of the mufti who had just been strangled.

"I do not know," replied the old man. "I have never known the name of any mufti or of any vizier. I am entirely ignorant of the occurrence you mention; I presume that in general those who meddle with public affairs sometimes perish miserably and that they deserve it; but I never inquire what is going on in Constantinople; I content myself with sending there for sale the produce of the garden I cultivate."

Having spoken thus, he took the strangers into his house. His two daughters and his two sons presented them with several kinds of sherbet which they made themselves, caymac flavoured with candied citron peel, oranges, lemons, limes, pine-apples, dates, pistachios and Mocha coffee which had not been mixed with the bad coffee of Batavia and the Isles.

After which this good Mussulman's two daughters perfumed the beards of Candide, Pangloss and Martin.

"You must have a vast and magnificent estate?" said Candide to the Turk.

"I have only twenty acres," replied the Turk. "I cultivate them with my children; and work keeps at bay three great evils: boredom, vice and need."

As Candide returned to his farm he reflected deeply on the Turk's remarks. He said to Pangloss and Martin: "That good old man seems to me to have chosen an existence preferable by far to that of the six kings with whom we had the honour to sup."

"Exalted rank," said Pangloss, "is very dangerous, according to the testimony of all philosophers; for Eglon, King of the Moabites, was murdered by Ehud; Absalom was hanged by the hair and pierced by three darts; King Nadab, son of Jeroboam, was killed by Baasha; King Elah by Zimri; Ahaziah by Jehu; Athaliah by Jehoiada; the Kings Jehoiakim, Jeconiah and Zedekiah were made slaves. You know in what manner died Croesus, Astyages, Darius, Denys of Syracuse, Pyrrhus, Perseus, Hannibal, Jugurtha, Ariovistus, Caesar, Pompey, Nero, Otho, Vitellius, Domitian, Richard II of England, Edward II, Henry VI, Richard III, Mary Stuart, Charles I, the three Henrys of France, the Emperor Henry IV. You know . . ."
"I also know," said Candide, "that we should cultivate our gardens."

"You are right," said Pangloss, "for, when man was placed in the Garden of Eden, he was placed there *ut operaretur eum*, to dress it and to keep it; which proves that man was not born for idleness."

"Let us work without theorizing," said Martin; " 'tis the only way to make life endurable."

The whole small fraternity entered into this praiseworthy plan, and each started to make use of his talents. The little farm yielded well. Cunegonde was indeed very ugly, but she became an excellent pastry-cook; Paquette embroidered; the old woman took care of the linen. Even Friar Giroflée performed some service; he was a very good carpenter and even became a man of honour; and Pangloss sometimes said to Candide: "All events are linked up in this best of all possible worlds; for, if you had not been expelled from the noble castle, by hard kicks in your backside for love of Mademoiselle Cunegonde, if you had not been clapped into the Inquisition, if you had not wandered about America on foot, if you had not stuck your sword in the Baron, if you had not lost all your sheep from the land of Eldorado, you would not be eating candied citrons and pistachios here."

" 'Tis well said," replied Candide, "but we must cultivate our gardens."

Edmund Burke, A Philosophical Enquiry into the Origin of our Ideas of the Sublime and the Beautiful

Edmund Burke (1729–1797) is known today as a conservative political philosopher and vehement opponent of the French Revolution, but Burke first came before the eighteenth-century reading public as an estheticist, determined to redefine some of his generation's basic assumptions about art. In typical Enlightenment fashion, Burke set out to explain the *origin* of at least two current and fashionable terms—the "sublime" and the "beautiful"—and in a way that would both rationalize the use of those terms and explain the perceptual and mental processes each concept presupposed.

Burke's principal concern in this treatise is with the sublime, rather than the beautiful, and he establishes at the outset of his investigation that the experience of the sublime is "the strongest emotion which the mind is capable of feeling." He describes as sublime anything (in nature or in art) that produces feelings similar to terror, a state of mind Burke, and many of his contemporaries, found pleasurable as well as painful. What Burke leaves unclear is whether the sublime is simply a name given to a set of related sensory and emotive responses (that is, something *within* the perceiving subject) or a quality inherent in things themselves. A generation after the publication of the *Enquiry*, European philosophers were still debating this question.

Burke's influence on later Romantic esthetics was nearly as great as his influence on his own time. By emphasizing the crucial role played by intense feeling and imaginative association in the perceptual process, Burke was instrumental in shifting the focus of critical attention away from artforms reflective of the power of reason to artworks permeated by strong emotion.

A PHILOSOPHICAL ENQUIRY INTO THE ORIGIN OF OUR IDEAS OF THE SUBLIME AND BEAUTIFUL

PART I

SECTION VII

Of the SUBLIME

Whatever is fitted in any sort to excite the ideas of pain, and danger, that is to say, whatever is in any sort terrible, or is conversant about terrible objects, or operates in a manner analogous to terror, is a source of the *sublime;* that is, it is productive of the strongest emotion which the mind is capable of feeling. I say the strongest emotion, because I am satisfied the ideas of pain are much more powerful than those which enter on the part of pleasure. Without all doubt, the torments which we may be made to suffer, are much greater in their effect on the body and mind, than any pleasures which the most learned voluptuary could suggest, or than the liveliest imagination, and the most sound and exquisitely sensible body could enjoy. . . .

PART II

SECTION I

Of the passion caused by the SUBLIME

The passion caused by the great and sublime in *nature*, when those causes operate most powerfully, is Astonishment; and astonishment is that state of the soul, in which all its motions are suspended, with some degree of horror. In this case the mind is so entirely filled with its object, that it cannot entertain any other, nor by consequence reason on that object which employs it. Hence arises the great power of the sublime, that far from being produced by them, it anticipates our reasonings, and hurries us on by an irresistible force. Astonishment, as I have said, is the effect of the sublime in its highest degree; the inferior effects are admiration, reverence and respect.

SECTION II

Terror

No passion so effectually robs the mind of all its powers of acting and reasoning as fear. For fear being an apprehension of pain or death, it operates in a manner that resembles actual pain. Whatever therefore is terrible, with regard to sight, is sublime too, whether this cause of terror, be endued with greatness of dimensions or not; for it is impossible to look on any thing as trifling, or contemptible, that may be dangerous. There are many animals, who though far from being large, are yet capable of raising ideas of the sublime, because they are considered as objects of terror. As serpents and poisonous animals of almost all kinds. And to things of great dimensions, if we annex an adventitious idea of terror, they become without comparison greater. A level plain of a vast extent on land, is certainly no mean idea; the prospect of such a plain may be as extensive as a prospect of the ocean; but can it ever fill the mind with any thing so great as the ocean itself? This is owing to several causes, but it is owing to none more than this, that the ocean is an object of no small terror. Indeed terror is in all cases whatsoever, either more openly or latently the ruling principle of the sublime. . . .

SECTION III

Obscurity

To make any thing very terrible, obscurity seems in general to be necessary. When we know the full extent of any danger, when we can accustom our eyes to it, a great deal of the apprehension vanishes. Every one will be sensible of this, who considers how greatly night adds to our dread, in all cases of danger, and how much the notions of ghosts and goblins, of which none can form clear ideas, affect minds, which give credit to the popular tales concerning such sorts of beings. Those despotic governments, which are founded on the passions of men, and principally upon the passion of fear, keep their chief as much as may be from the public eye. The policy has been the same in many cases of religion. Almost all the heathen temples were dark. Even in the barbarous temples of the Americans at this day, they keep their idol in a dark part of the hut, which is consecrated to his worship. For this purpose too the druids performed all their ceremonies in the bosom of the darkest woods, and in the shade of the oldest and most spreading oaks. No person seems better to have understood the secret of heightening, or of setting terrible things, if I may use the expression, in their strongest light by the force of a judicious obscurity, than Milton. His description of Death in the second book is admirably studied; it is astonishing with what a gloomy pomp, with what a significant and expressive uncertainty of strokes and colouring he has finished the portrait of the king of terrors.

> *The other shape,*
> *If shape it might be called that shape had none*
> *Distinguishable, in member, joint, or limb;*
> *Or substance might be called that shadow seemed,*
> *For each seemed either; black he stood as night;*
> *Fierce as ten furies; terrible as hell;*
> *And shook a deadly dart. What seemed his head*
> *The likeness of a kingly crown had on.*

In this description all is dark, uncertain, confused, terrible, and sublime to the last degree. . . .

SECTION IV

Of the Difference Between CLEARNESS and OBSCURITY with Regard to the Passions. The Same Subject Continued.

. . . The ideas of eternity, and infinity, are among the most affecting we have, and yet perhaps there is nothing of which we really understand so little, as of infinity and eternity. We do not any where meet a more sublime description than this justly celebrated one of Milton, wherein he gives the portrait of Satan with a dignity so suitable to the subject.

> *He above the rest*
> *In shape and gesture proudly eminent*
> *Stood like a tower; his form had yet not lost*
> *All her original brightness, nor appeared*
> *Less than archangel ruin'd, and th' excess*
> *Of glory obscured: as when the sun new ris'n*
> *Looks through the horizontal misty air*
> *Shorn of his beams; or from behind the moon*
> *In dim eclipse disastrous twilight sheds*
> *On half the nations; and with fear of change*
> *Perplexes monarchs.*

Here is a very noble picture; and in what does this poetical picture consist? in images of a tower, an archangel, the sun rising through mists, or in an eclipse, the ruin of monarchs, and the revolutions of kingdoms. The mind is hurried out of itself, by a croud of great and confused images; which affect because they are crouded and confused. For separate them, and you lose much of the greatness, and join them, and you infallibly lose the clearness. The images raised by poetry are always of this obscure kind; though in general the effects of poetry, are by no means to be attributed to the images it raises; which point we shall examine more at large hereafter. But painting, when we have allowed for the pleasure of imitation, can only affect simply by the images it presents; and even in painting a judicious obscurity in some things contributes to the effect of the picture; because the images in painting are exactly similar to those in nature; and in nature dark, confused, uncertain images have a greater power on the fancy to form the grander passions than those have which are more clear and determinate. But where and when this observation may be applied to practice, and how far it shall be extended, will be better deduced from the nature of the subject, and from the occasion, than from any rules that can be given.

I am sensible that this idea has met with opposition, and is likely still to be rejected by several. But let it be considered that hardly any thing can strike the mind with its greatness, which does not make some sort of approach towards infinity; which nothing can do whilst we are able to perceive its bounds; but to see an object distinctly, and to perceive its bounds, is one and the same thing. A clear idea is therefore another name for a little idea. There is a passage in the book of Job amazingly sublime, and this sublimity is principally due to the terrible uncertainty of the thing described. *In thoughts from the visions of the night, when deep sleep falleth upon men, fear came upon me and trembling, which made all my bones to shake. Then a spirit passed before my face. The hair of my flesh stood up. It stood still,* but I could not discern the form thereof; *an image was before mine eyes; there was silence; and I heard a voice,—Shall mortal man be more just than God?* We are first prepared with the utmost solemnity for the vision; we are first terrified, before we are let even into the obscure cause of our emotion; but when this grand cause of terror makes its appearance, what is it? is it not, wrapt up in the shades of its own incomprehensible darkness, more aweful, more striking, more terrible, than the liveliest description, than the clearest painting could possibly represent it? . . .

SECTION V

Power

Besides these things which *directly* suggest the idea of danger, and those which produce a similar effect from a mechanical cause, I know of nothing sublime which is not some modification of power. And this branch rises as naturally as the other two branches, from terror, the common stock of every thing that is sublime. The idea of power at first view, seems of the class of these indifferent ones, which may equally belong to pain or to pleasure. But in reality, the affection arising from the idea of vast power, is extremely remote from that neutral character. For first, we must remember, that the idea of pain, in its highest degree, is much stronger than the highest degree of pleasure; and that it preserves the same superiority through all the subordinate gradations. From hence it is, that where the chances for equal degrees of suffering or enjoyment are in any sort equal, the idea of the suffering must always be prevalent. And indeed the ideas of pain, and above all of death, are so very affecting, that whilst we remain in the presence of whatever is supposed to have the power of inflicting either, it is impossible to be perfectly free from terror. Again, we know by experience, that for the enjoyment of pleasure, no great efforts of power are at all necessary; nay we know, that such efforts would go a great way towards destroying our satisfaction: for pleasure must be stolen, and not forced upon us; pleasure follows the will; and therefore we are generally affected with it by many things of a force greatly inferior to our own. But pain is always inflicted by a power in some way superior, because we never submit to pain willingly. So that strength, violence, pain and terror, are ideas that rush in upon the mind together. . . . I know some people are of opinion, that no awe, no degree of terror, accompanies the idea of power, and have hazarded to affirm, that we can contemplate the idea of God himself without any such emotion. I purposely avoided when I first considered this subject, to introduce the idea of that great and tremendous being, as an example in an argument so light as this; though it frequently occurred to me, not as an objection to, but as a strong confirmation of my notions in this matter. I hope, in what I am going to say, I shall avoid presumption, where it is almost impossible for any mortal to speak with strict propriety. I say then, that whilst we consider the Godhead merely as he is an object of the understanding, which forms a complex idea of power, wisdom, justice, goodness, all stretched to a degree far exceeding the bounds of our comprehension, whilst we consider the divinity in this refined and abstracted light, the imagination and passions are little or nothing affected. But because we are bound by the condition of our nature to ascend to these pure and intellectual ideas, through the medium of sensible images, and to judge of these divine qualities by their evident acts and exertions, it becomes extremely hard to disentangle our idea of the cause from the effect by which we are led to know it. Thus when we contemplate the Deity, his attributes and their operation coming united on the mind, form a sort of sensible image, and as such are capable of affecting the imagination. Now, though in a just idea of the Deity, perhaps none of his attributes are predominant, yet to our imagination, his power is by far the most striking. Some reflection, some comparing is necessary to satisfy us of his wisdom, his justice, and his goodness; to be struck with his power, it is only necessary that we should open our eyes. But whilst we contemplate so vast an object, under the arm, as it were, of almighty power, and invested upon every side with omnipresence, we shrink into the minuteness of our own nature, and are, in a manner, annihilated before him. And though a consideration of his other attributes may relieve in some measure our apprehensions; yet no conviction of the justice with which it is exercised, nor the mercy with which it is tempered, can wholly remove the terror that naturally arises from a force which nothing can withstand. . . .

Mary Wollstonecraft, A Vindication of the Rights of Women

Mary Wollstonecraft (1759–1797) has long been recognized as one of the earliest feminist critics of patriarchy and male domination of women through law and custom. Writing in the wake of the French Revolution and its advocacy of the universal "rights of man," Wollstonecraft insists that no revolutionary movement can possibly succeed in extending the privileges of the few to the many if one half of humankind is automatically excluded from the benefits of social change.

What Wollstonecraft pleads for, however, in her landmark essay, *A Vindication of the Rights of Women* (1792), is not simply women's right to vote or the right to an education, but that society redefine women's role to ensure social and intellectual equality with men. Without such equality, Wollstonecraft argues, the "progress of knowledge and virtue" and the rational pursuit of happiness—cornerstones of Enlightenment political theory—will be subverted in the very place where the moral development of the individual begins: in the home.

Wollstonecraft offers her readers, then, a vision of daughters, wives, and mothers as rational companions, informed and committed citizens, and independent moral agents capable of contributing their free talents to the evolution of human civilization—a vision that few of her male counterparts among the *philosophes* of the late eighteenth century (least of all Rousseau) were prepared to take seriously.

A VINDICATION OF THE RIGHTS OF WOMEN

■

[from Chapter IX]. . . let me return to the more specious slavery which chains the very soul of woman, keeping her for ever under the bondage of ignorance.

The preposterous distinctions of rank, which render civilization a curse, by dividing the world between voluptuous tyrants, and cunning envious dependents, corrupt, almost equally, every class of people, because respectability is not attached to the discharge of the relative duties of life, but to the station, and when the duties are not fulfilled the affections cannot gain sufficient strength to fortify the virtue of which they are the natural reward. Still there are some loop-holes out of which a man may creep, and dare to think and act for himself; but for a woman it is an Herculean task, because she has difficulties peculiar to her sex to overcome, which require almost superhuman powers.

A truly benevolent legislator always endeavours to make it the interest of each individual to be virtuous; and thus private virtue becoming the cement of public happiness, an orderly whole is consolidated by the tendency of all the parts towards a common centre. But, the private or public virtue of woman is very problematical; for Rousseau, and a numerous list of male writers, insist that she should all her life be subjected to a severe restraint, that of propriety. Why subject her to propriety—blind propriety, if she be capable of acting from

464

■

a nobler spring, if she be an heir of immortality? Is sugar always to be produced by vital blood? Is one half of the human species, like the poor African slaves, to be subject to prejudices that brutalize them, when principles would be a surer guard, only to sweeten the cup of man? Is not this indirectly to deny woman reason? For a gift is mockery, if it be unfit for use.

Women are, in common with men, rendered weak and luxurious by the relaxing pleasures which wealth procures; but added to this they are made slaves to their persons, and must render them alluring that man may lend them his reason to guide their tottering steps aright. Or should they be ambitious, they must govern their tyrants by sinister tricks, for without rights there cannot be any incumbent duties. The laws respecting woman, which I mean to discuss in a future part, make an absurd unit of a man and his wife, and then, by the easy transition of only considering him as responsible, she is reduced to a mere cypher.

The being who discharges the duties of its station is independent; and, speaking of women at large, their first duty is to themselves as rational creatures, and the next, in point of importance, as citizens, is that, which includes so many, of a mother. The rank in life which dispenses with their fulfilling this duty, necessarily degrades them by making them mere dolls. Or, should they turn to something more important than merely fitting drapery upon a smooth block, their minds are only occupied by some soft platonic attachment; or, the actual management of an intrigue may keep their thoughts in motion; for when they neglect domestic duties, they have it not in their power to take the field and march and counter-march like soldiers, or wrangle in the senate to keep their faculties from rusting.

I know that, as a proof of the inferiority of the sex, Rousseau has exultingly exclaimed, How can they leave the nursery for the camp!—And the camp has by some moralists been termed the school of the most heroic virtues; though, I think, it would puzzle a keen casuist to prove the reasonableness of the greater number of wars that have dubbed heroes. I do not mean to consider this question critically; because, having frequently viewed these freaks of ambition as the first natural mode of civilization, when the ground must be torn up, and the woods cleared by fire and sword, I do not choose to call them pests; but surely the present system of war has little connection with virtue of any denomination, being rather the school of *finesse* and effeminacy, than of fortitude.

Yet, if defensive war, the only justifiable war, in the present advanced state of society, where virtue can shew its face and ripen amidst the rigours which purify the air on the mountain's top, were alone to be adopted as just and glorious, the true heroism of antiquity might again animate female bosoms.—But fair and softly, gentle reader, male or female, do not alarm thyself, for though I have compared the character of a modern soldier with that of a civilized woman, I am not going to advise them to turn their distaff into a musket, though I sincerely wish to see the bayonet converted into a pruning-hook. I only recreated an imagination, fatigued by contemplating the vices and follies which all proceed from a feculent stream of wealth that has muddied the pure rills of natural affection, by supposing that society will some time or other be so constituted, that man must necessarily fulfil the duties of a citizen, or be despised, and that while he was employed in any of the department of civil life, his wife, also an active citizen, should be equally intent to manage her family, educate her children, and assist her neighbours.

But to render her really virtuous and useful, she must not, if she discharge her civil duties, want, individually, the protection of civil laws; she must not be dependent on her husband's bounty for her subsistence during his life, or support after his death—for how can a being be generous who has nothing of its own? or, virtuous, who is not free? The wife, in the present state of things, who is faithful to her husband, and neither suckles nor educates her children, scarcely deserves the name of a wife, and has no right to that of a citizen. But take away natural rights, and duties become null . . .

But what have women to do in society? I may be asked, but to loiter with easy grace; surely you would not condemn them all to suckle fools and chronicle small beer! No. Women might certainly study the art of healing, and be physicians as well as nurses. And midwifery, decency seems to allot to them, though I am afraid the word midwife, in our dictionaries, will soon give place to *accoucheur*, and one proof of the former delicacy of the sex be effaced from the language.

They might, also, study politics, and settle their benevolence on the broadest basis; for the reading of history will scarcely be more useful than the perusal of romances, if read as mere biography; if the character of the times, the political improvements, arts, &c. be not observed. In short, if it be not considered as the history of man; and not of particular men, who filled a niche in the temple of fame, and dropped into the black rolling stream of time, that silently sweeps all before it, into the shapeless void called—eternity.—For shape, can it be called, 'that shape hath none?'

Business of various kinds, they might likewise pursue, if they were educated in a more orderly manner, which might save many from common and legal prostitution. Women would not then marry for a support. as men accept of places under government, and neglect the implied duties; nor would an attempt to earn their own subsistence, a most laudable one! sink them almost to the level of those poor abandoned creatures who live by prostitution. For are not milliners and mantua-makers reckoned the next class? The few employments open to women, so far from being liberal, are menial; and when a superiour education enables them to take charge of the education of children as governesses, they are not treated like the tutors of sons, though even clerical tutors are not always treated in a manner calculated to render them respectable in the eyes of their pupils, to say nothing of the private comfort of the individual. But as women educated like gentlewomen, are never designed for the humiliating situation which necessity sometimes forces them to fill; these situations are considered in the light of a degradation; and they know little of the human heart, who need to be told, that nothing so painfully sharpens sensibility as such a fall in life.

Some of these women might be restrained from marrying by a proper spirit or delicacy, and others may not have had it in their power to escape in this pitiful way from servitude; is not that government then very defective, and very unmindful of the happiness of one half of its members, that does not provide for honest, independent women, by encouraging them to fill respectable stations? But in order to render their private virtue a public benefit, they must have a civil existence in the state, married or single; else we shall continually see some worthy woman, whose sensibility has been rendered painfully acute by undeserved contempt, droop like 'the lily broken down by a plow-share.' . . .

How much more respectable is the woman who earns her own bread by fulfilling any duty, than the most accomplished beauty!—beauty did I say?—so sensible am I of the beauty of moral loveliness, or the harmonious propriety that attunes the passions of a well-regulated mind, that I blush at making the comparison; yet I sigh to think how few women aim at attaining this respectability by withdrawing form the giddy whirl of pleasure, or the indolent calm that stupifies the good sort of women it sucks in.

Proud of their weakness, however, they must always be protected, guarded from care, and all the rough toils that dignify the mind.—If this be the fiat of fate, if they will make themselves insignificant and contemptible, sweetly to waste 'life away,' let them not expect to be valued when their beauty fades, for it is the fate of the fairest flowers to be admired and pulled to pieces by the careless hand that plucked them. In how many ways do I wish, from the purest benevolence, to impress this truth on my sex; yet I fear that they will not listen to a truth that dear bought experience has brought home to many an agitated bosom, nor willingly resign the privileges of rank and sex for the privileges of humanity, to which those have no claim who do not discharge its duties.

Those writers are particularly useful, in my opinion, who make man feel for man, independent of the station he fills, or the drapery of factitious sentiments. I then would fain convince reasonable men of the importance of some of my remarks, and prevail on them to weigh dispassionately the whole tenor of my observations.—I appeal to their understandings; and, as a fellow-creature, claim, in the name of my sex, some interest in their hearts. I entreat them to assist to emancipate their companion, to make her a *help meet* for them!

Would men but generously snap our chains, and be content with rational fellowship instead of slavish obedience, they would find us more observant daughters, more affectionate sisters, more faithful wives, more reasonable mothers—in a word, better citizens. We should then love them with true affection, because we should learn to respect ourselves; and the peace of mind of a worthy man would not be interrupted by the idle vanity of his wife, nor the babes sent to nestle in a strange bosom, having never found a home in their mother's.

The Romantic Revolution

Jean-Jacques Rousseau, The Reveries of the Solitary Walker

Along with Voltaire, Jean-Jacques Rousseau (1712–1778) was one of *the* preeminent literary and philosophical figures of the French Enlightenment, and one of the most unusual personalities of any age. Though a native of Geneva, Rousseau rose to fame in Paris. There he composed an opera (*The Village Soothsayer*, 1752), wrote a best-selling novel (*Julie*, 1761), and authored a number of philosophical essays whose provocative tone and often radical ideas so angered ecclesiastical authorities in France that he was finally forced into political exile to escape imprisonment. The most complete (if not the most truthful) account of Rousseau's life is to be found in his autobiography, the *Confessions* (1766–70), in which he reexamines the strange odyssey of his life, partly out of fascination with his own inner complexities, and partly out of a desire to vindicate himself from some of the wilder accusations leveled at him by his enemies—chief among them, Voltaire.

In *The Reveries of the Solitary Walker* (1792), which he began writing two years before his death, Rousseau continues the process of self-examination begun in the *Confessions* in a more meditative (and less defensive) frame of mind. Like St. Augustine, whose spiritual autobiography served as a possible precedent, Rousseau reviewed the events of his life in the hope of finding some meaningful pattern within the seemingly shapeless array of circumstance and recollection. To this task, Rousseau brought nearly all of the analytical skills of eighteenth-century science, as he attempted to take "barometer readings" of his state of mind. At the same time, and like the Romantics who would follow him, Rousseau's one great and enduring subject was *himself*, and those powers of the imagination through which the past could be brought back to life. Each of the essays incorporated in *The Reveries*—Rousseau refers to them as "walks"—constitutes a different stage or moment in the process of self-assessment and self-vindication. In the "Eighth Walk," Rousseau contemplates the many misfortunes of his life (nearly all of which he attributes to unnamed "enemies") and discovers in himself two very different forms of self-awareness and self-regard: self-esteem and self-love. Rousseau clearly approves of "self-esteem" since it represents an inward certainty of personal integrity. "Self-love," on the other hand, Rousseau sees as an unhealthy narcissism, a perverse preoccupation with one's own experience at the expense of all other realities. Rousseau was not alone in viewing *this* type of self-consciousness as a disease from which the future Romantic generation would suffer just as intensely as he had.

THE REVERIES OF THE SOLITARY WALKER
■

EIGHTH WALK

In meditating upon the dispositions of my soul during all the situations of my life, I am quite struck to see so little proportion between the different phases of my fate and the habitual feelings of well-being or uneasiness by which they affected me. My various, brief intervals of prosperity have left me almost no pleasant memory of the intimate and permanent manner in which they affected me. Conversely, during all the miserable moments of my life, I constantly felt myself filled with tender, touching, delightful sentiments which, pouring a salutary balm over the wounds of my broken heart, seemed to transform its suffering into pleasure. And separated from the memory of the evils I felt at the same time, only the gentle memory of those sentiments comes back to me. It seems to me that I have savored the sweetness of existence more, that I have really lived more, when my sentiments—drawn back around my heart, so to speak, by my fate—were not being wasted on all the objects of men's esteem which are of so little merit in themselves, but which are the sole concern of the people we believe to be happy.

When all was in order around me, when I was content with all that surrounded me and with the sphere in which I was to live, I filled it with my affectionate feelings. My expansive soul extended itself to other objects and, continually drawn outside myself by a thousand different kinds of fancies, by gentle attachments which continually busied my heart, I somehow forgot even myself. I was entirely devoted to what was alien to me; and in the continual agitation of my heart, I experienced all the vicissitudes of human things. This stormy life left me neither peace within nor rest without. Happy in appearance, I had not one sentiment which could withstand the test of reflection and truly please me. I was never perfectly satisfied with others or myself. The tumult of the world made my head swim; solitude bored me; I needed to move around constantly; and I was comfortable nowhere. I was, however, entertained, welcomed, well received, and treated with affection everywhere. I had not one enemy, no one ill-disposed toward me, no one envious of me. Since people sought only to do me favors, I often had the pleasure of doing favors for many people myself. And without wealth, without employment, without a protector, without great talents that were either well developed or well known, I enjoyed the advantages which went along with all that. And I saw nobody in any station whose lot appeared preferable to mine. What was I lacking, then, to be happy? I don't know, but I do know that I was not happy.

What am I lacking today to be the most unfortunate of mortals? Nothing of anything men have been able to do to make me so. And yet in this deplorable condition, I still would not change being or destiny with the most fortunate among them, and I still prefer to be myself in all my misery than to be any of those people in all their prosperity. Left only to myself, I feed, it is true, on my own substance; but it is not depleted. And I am sufficient unto myself, even though I ruminate on an empty stomach, so to speak, and though my withered imagination and my burned-out ideas furnish no more nourishment for my heart. My soul—clouded and obstructed by my organs—sinks down day by day and, [beneath the] weight of these heavy masses, no longer has enough vigor to thrust itself out of its old wrapping as it used to do.

Adversity forces us to this turning in on ourselves; and that is perhaps what renders it most unbearable for the greater part of men. As for me, who finds only faults for which to reproach myself, I blame them on my weakness and console myself, for premeditated evil never approached my heart . . .

In all the evils which befall us, we look more to the intention than to the effect. A shingle falling off a roof can injure us more but does not grieve us as much as a stone thrown on purpose by a malevolent hand. The blow sometimes goes astray, but the intention never misses its mark. Material suffering is what we feel least in the blows of fortune; and when the unfortunate do not know whom to blame for their misfortunes, they blame fate which they personify and to which they ascribe eyes and an intelligence to torment them intention- ally. Thus it is that a gambler, vexed by his losses, becomes furious at he knows not whom. He imagines a fate which relentlessly and intentionally torments him and, finding fuel for his anger, he becomes irritated and inflamed against the enemy he has created for himself. The wise man, who sees only the blows of blind necessity in all the misfortunes which befall him, does not have this insane agitation. He cries out in his suffering, but without being carried away, without anger. He feels only the material blow of the evil to which he is prey, and the beatings he receives injure his body in vain—not one reaches his heart.

It is a lot to have reached this point, but it is not all. If we stop here, we have indeed cut out the evil, but we have left the root. For this root is not in the beings who are alien to us, but in ourselves; and that is where we must exert ourselves to extract it completely. That is what I felt perfectly from the moment I began to turn back to myself. My reason showing me only absurdities in all the explanations I sought to give to what befalls me, I understood that the causes, the instruments, and the means of all that, unknown and inexplicable to me, ought not to matter to me. I understood that I ought to regard all the details of my fate as so many acts of pure fatality to which I ought not ascribe direction, intention, or moral cause. I understood that I had to submit to it without reasoning and without struggling, because that would be useless. I understood that since all I had yet to do on earth was to regard myself on it as a purely passive being, I ought not to use up, in futilely resisting my fate, the strength I had left to endure it. That is what I told myself; my reason and my heart acquiesced in it; and yet I still felt this heart of mine grumble. What gave rise to this grumbling? I sought for it and found it: it came from self-love which, after having become indignant about men, also rebelled against reason.

The discovery was not as easy to make as one might believe, for an innocent persecuted man considers his petty self-pride as pure love of justice for a long time. Still, once the true source is known, it can easily be dried up or at least diverted. Self-esteem is the greatest motive force of proud souls. Self-love, fertile in illusions, disguises itself and passes itself off as this esteem. But when the fraud is finally discovered and self-love can no longer hide itself, from then on it is no more to be feared; and even though we stifle it with difficulty, we at least easily overcome it.

I never had much of a bent for self-love, but this factitious passion had become magnified in me when I was in the world, especially when I was an author. I had perhaps even less of it than others, but I had it prodigiously. The terrible lessons I received soon confined it to its former limits. It began by revolting against injustice, but finished by disdaining it. By withdrawing into my soul and severing the external relations which make it demanding, by renouncing comparisons and preferences, it was satisfied with my being good in my own eyes. Then, again becoming love of myself, it returned to the natural order and delivered me from the yoke of opinion.

From that moment, I again found peace of soul and almost felicity. In whatever situation we find ourselves, it is only because of self-love that we are constantly unhappy. When self-love is quiet and reason speaks, reason eventually consoles us for all the bad things we have not been able to avoid. Reason annihilates them insofar as they do not immediately affect us; for by ceasing to be preoccupied with them, we are sure of avoiding their most poignant blows. They are nothing for the person who does not think about them. Offenses, acts of revenge, slights, insults, injustices are nothing for the person who, in the bad things he endures, sees only the bad itself and not any intention, for the person whose rank in his own esteem does not depend on the one others are willing to accord him. However men may wish to view me, they cannot change my being; and, regardless of their power and all their underhanded intrigues, I will continue to be what I am, whatever they might do and in spite of them. . . .

Everything brings me back to the happy and sweet life for which I was born. I pass three-fourths of my life occupied with instructive and even agreeable objects in which I indulge my mind and my senses with delight, or with the children of my fancy whom I have created according to my heart and whose company sustains its sentiments, or with myself alone, satisfied with myself and already full of the happiness I feel to be due me. In all this, love of myself does all the work; self-love has nothing to do with it. This is not the case during the sorrowful moments I still pass in the midst of men—a plaything of their treacherous flattery, bombastic and derisive compliments, and honeyed malignity. No matter what I might try to do, self-love then comes into play. The hatred and animosity I discern through the coarse wrapping of their hearts tear my own heart apart with sorrow; and the idea of being taken for a dupe in this foolish way adds a very childish spite to this sorrow—the result of a foolish self-love whose complete folly I sense, but which I cannot overcome. The efforts I have made to become inured to these rude and mocking looks are unbelievable. A hundred times I have passed along the public walks and through the most frequented spots with the sole intention of inuring myself to those cruel taunts. Not only have I not been able to succeed, I have not made any progress; and all my painful, but vain, efforts have left me as easy to disturb, to grieve, and to render indignant as before.

Dominated by my senses whatever I may do, I have never been able to resist their impulses; and as long as an object acts upon them, my heart does not fail to be affected. But these passing affections last only as long as the sensation which causes them. The presence of a hateful man violently affects me. But as soon as he disappears, the impression ceases. The instant I no longer see him, I no longer think about him. It matters little that I know he is going to pay attention to me; I cannot pay any attention to him. The evil I do not feel at this moment affects me in no way; the persecutor I do not see is nothing for me. I am aware of the advantage this position gives to those who dispense my fate. Let them dispense it, then, with no qualms whatever. I still prefer to have them torment me without resisting than to have to think about them so as to protect myself from their attacks.

The way my senses thus work upon my heart constitutes the sole torment of my life. The days I see no one I no longer think about my fate, I no longer feel it, I no longer suffer; I am happy and satisfied without distraction, without obstacle. But I can rarely escape any perceptible slight; and when I am least thinking about it, a gesture, a sinister look I perceive, a venomous word I hear, an ill-disposed person I meet, is enough to overwhelm me. All I am capable of in such a case is very quickly forgetting and fleeing. The disturbance in my heart disappears with the object which has caused it, and I return to calm as soon as I am alone. Or if something does worry me, it is the fear of encountering some new cause of sorrow along my way. That is my only torment, but it suffices to alter my happiness. I reside in the middle of Paris. When I leave my home, I long for the countryside and solitude. But it is necessary to go so far to seek it that before I can breathe easily, I find a thousand objects along my path which constrict my heart, and half the day is passed in anguish before I have reached the refuge I am seeking. At least I am happy when they let me reach my destination. The moment I slip away from the retinue of the wicked is delightful; and as soon as I find myself under the trees and in the midst of greenery, I believe I am in an earthly paradise and I savor an inner pleasure as intense as if I were the happiest of mortals.

Goethe, Faust (Part I)

One of the most versatile and productive thinkers in European history, Johann Wolfgang von Goethe (1749–1832) was a philosopher, scientist, poet, dramatist, and novelist. His early novel, *The Sorrows of Young Werther* (1774), triggered a German cult of feeling and emotion, *Sturm und Drang*, that stimulated the international Romantic Movement. Goethe spent most of his adult life in the small German state of Weimar, where he held a succession of administrative posts while producing a flood of books on science, criticism, and literature.

Goethe's finest achievement is *Faust*, a dramatic poem reinterpreting the medieval legend of the philosopher who sells his soul to obtain ultimate knowledge. A powerful work that explores the meaning of human experience, *Faust* dramatizes man's conflicting intellectual, emotional, and spiritual needs. With a deceptively simple style, the poem incorporates a wealth of philosophical and psychological concepts about God, human nature, and the purpose of life.

Part I, published in 1808, focuses on Faust's bargain with the Devil and the motives of the four principal characters. The "Prologue in Heaven" shows Mephistopheles, the cynical spirit of denial, eager to prove that God's human creation, represented by the world-weary and disillusioned Faust, is a failure. The Lord, embodying creative energy and eternal optimism, agrees to place Faust in the Devil's power because He believes that humanity's errors are the product of its restless striving toward perfection. Faust, yearning to escape his consciousness of futility, agrees that he can never be damned until he ceases to strive and lazily accepts the world as it is. Writing more than half a century before Darwin's *Origin of Species* (1859), Goethe anticipates evolutionary theory with his vision of humanity's endless struggle toward ethical and spiritual growth.

The following excerpts illustrate some of Goethe's views about man's attempts, despite his imperfections and follies, to discover the significance of human existence. God uses Mephistopheles, that part of the human mind which despairs of finding real meaning, to goad Faust on his quest for understanding. The power of evil, which values nothing, forces humankind to continue seeking the mysterious source of its discontent, a process for which Goethe's Lord created us.

FAUST   PART I

PROLOGUE   IN HEAVEN
(The Lord, the Heavenly Host, and later Mephistopheles. The three Archangels come forward and speak.)

RAPHAEL The sun sings in the ancient major,
in song-match with its brother-spheres,
and finishes its ordained journey
with thunder-crash about their ears.
Its face gives strength to all the angels

though none of them can fathom why;
the inconceivably great work shines,
new as on the founding day.

GABRIEL And swift, past understanding swift,
the splendor of the earth whirls past,
changing the paradisial brightness
for the night's deepness, shuddering, vast.
Broadly the ocean currents, foaming
out of the depths, are tossed and swirled,
and rocks and water hurtle onward
forever with the racing worlds.

MICHAEL And tempests bluster in a wager,
from sea to land, from land to sea,
raging, forging an encoiling
chain of deepest energy.
A dazzling desolation is flaming
with thundering strokes along the way.
But, Lord, your messengers must honor
the gentle power of your day.

ALL THREE This vision gives the angels power
though none of them can fathom you;
and all your wonderful creations
are splendid as on their first day.

MEPHISTOPHELES Since you, O Lord, once more approach and ask
how we are getting on, and since you used
to see me gladly, I have taken the risk
and come among your servants; but I can't
make pretty speeches, though the crowd here scoff
and scorn me, lest my pathos make you laugh—
if long ago you'd not dispensed with laughter.
I don't know how the suns and worlds are turned,
I only see how men will plague themselves.
The little earth-god's stamped in the old way
and is as odd as on creation day.
He'd be much better, Lord, if you'd not let
him have the merest glimpse of heavenly light
which he calls reason, using it at best
only to grow more bestial than the beasts.
He seems to me—I hope I'm not improper—
exactly like a spindly-legg'd grasshopper
that flits and flies and jumps,
then landing in the grass, will always sing
the same old worn-out song.

I wish that he were lost forever in the grass!
He digs his nose in every sort of trash.

THE LORD And is there nothing else you want to say?
Do you come here only to lodge complaints?
Is there nothing at all upon the earth that suits you?

MEPHISTOPHELES No, Lord! I find things there, as always, pretty bad.
Men grieve me so with the days of their lamenting,
I even hate to plague them with my torments.

THE LORD Do you know Faust?

MEPHISTOPHELES The Doctor?

THE LORD He's my servant!

MEPHISTOPHELES He serves you very strangely then, indeed.
For nothing earthly will he eat or drink, the fool.
A yeasty yearning has driven him so far,
he's only half-aware that he is mad.
He wants from the sky the fairest star,
and from earth the highest joy that's to be had;
yet everything near and everything far
can never satisfy his deeply stirred desire.

THE LORD Since, though confused, he serves me still,
I'll lead him soon toward a clearer view.
The gardener knows that when the branches green,
soon fruit and flowers will show what time can do.

MEPHISTOPHELES What will you bet? You'd lose him yet
if you let me lead him gently down my street!

THE LORD As long as he lives on earth,
I'll not forbid your trying.
Man is doomed to err as long as he is striving.

MEPHISTOPHELES Thank you. Because I always hate
to get involved with the dead and dying.
I'd rather have the fresh and rounded cheeks.
I'm never at home to a corpse.
I prefer, like a cat, to play with a mouse that squeaks.

THE LORD Very well then. It shall be as you wish.
Pervert this soul from its first source,
lead him—if you can get hold of him—
along your downward path; but when you lose
stand up and admit defeat.
A good man, struggling in his darkness,
will always be aware of the true course.

MEPHISTOPHELES Good, Lord, and it won't take me long!
I'll not be worried about this wager!
But when I win, please let me take
my triumph fully. He must gorge on dust,
and love it, like my aunt, the celebrated snake.

THE LORD Do as you will. I give you a free hand.
I have no hatred for the like of you.
Among destroyers, you must understand,
the rogue's the least offensive of the lot.
Man's active spirit easily falls asleep;
he's much too readily seduced by sloth.
Therefore, I gladly give him a companion
who prods and twists and must act as a devil.

(turning to the good angels)

But you, who are the real sons of the Lord,
rejoice in beauty's live dominions.
May the Becoming, which eternally moves and lives,
surround you with the friendly walls of love!
To all that wavers you must minister,
basing it firmly in enduring thoughts.

(The heavens close and the angels go out.)

MEPHISTOPHELES *(alone)* I like to see the Old Boy now and then,
and I take care not to cross him by a word.
It's very decent of so great a lord
to gossip with the Devil like a man.

THE TRAGEDY: FIRST PART

FAUST'S STUDY

FAUST What is your name?

MEPHISTOPHELES Now that seems to me rather petty
in one so scornful of the Word,
one who is sceptical of appearances,
and looks only for the depths of being.

FAUST We can usually recognize the identity
of such gentlemen as you by the name,
which shows itself all too plainly
when they call you the God of Flies, the Destroyer,
the Liar. So then, who are you?

MEPHISTOPHELES A part of that power
which always wills evil and always works good.

FAUST What does that riddle mean?

478

MEPHISTOPHELES I am the spirit that always denies! A good thing, too,
for all that exists deserves to be destroyed.
It would be much better if nothing were ever created.
So I'm everything that you call sin and destruction,
in short, evil—these are my proper element.

FAUST You call yourself a part, yet stand there whole.

MEPHISTOPHELES I speak the modest truth. Through man,
that silly little microcosm,
commonly thinks himself an entity.
I am part of the part that at first was all,
part of the darkness that gave birth to light,
that supercilious light which now disputes
with Mother Night her ancient rank and realm,
and yet can not succeed; however much it struggles,
it sticks to matter and can't get free.
Light flows from substance, makes it beautiful;
solids can check its path, so I hope it won't be long
till light and the world-stuff are destroyed together.

FAUST Now I understand your important duties!
You can't destroy things quite wholesale,
So you've started on a smaller scale.

MEPHISTOPHELES And really I haven't got far with it.
In spite of all I've undertaken
I can't get under the skin of this fat world,
this something that opposes the nothing.
Earth-quakes, tidal-waves, hurricanes, fires—no use,
the land and sea remain as calm as ever.
And that damned trash, the race of beasts and men—?
I can't get at them either, as I'd like.
How many of them I've buried!
Yet always there's fresh new blood
to go on circulating, on and on,
until I'm almost crazy! For out of the waters,
and out of the earth and the air,
thousands of seeds are unfolding everywhere,
in drouth and moisture, in heat and cold.
If I hadn't reserved fire for myself
I'd certainly have very little.

FAUST You dare to raise your cold devil's fist,
clenched vainly in malice,
against the ever-working, healing, creative power?
Try something else, you wayward son of Chaos!

479
■

MEPHISTOPHELES We'll take the matter under advisement
and consider it at our next meeting.
And now, may I go?

FAUST'S STUDY

(Faust and Mephistopheles strike a bargain.)

FAUST Who knocks? Come in! Who's bothering me again?

MEPHISTOPHELES Just me.

FAUST Come in!

MEPHISTOPHELES You must ask three times.

FAUST Come in, then!

MEPHISTOPHELES I like you this way.
I hope we'll hit it off together!
Here I am, come to chase away your wild moods,
gotten up as a nobleman in a red doublet trimmed with gold,
with a stiff silk cloak, a cock's feather
in my hat, and a long pointed sword.
I advise you to dress the same way.
Then we may travel easily,
while you discover what life can be.

FAUST Whatever the clothes, I still would feel the pain
of this earth's narrow life. I am too old
for play, too young to live without desire.
What more can the world allow me? Renounce!
You must renounce! That's the eternal song
every man hears ringing in his ear,
singing hoarsely every hour,
his whole life long.
I wake at dawn with horror; I could weep
bitterly, to see another day
which in its course will not fulfill one wish, not one:
a day that lessens with capricious disappointments
all my anticipated pleasures.
A day that checks my creative power
with a thousand grinning goblins of life.
Then when night sinks down, I must stretch out
on a bed of desperation that gives me no rest;
for even there wild dreams will frighten me.
The god who lives within can stir me deeply,
can sit like a king, throned on my own strength,
but has no power over external things;
and so, existence is a burden,
death wished-for, and life hated.

MEPHISTOPHELES And yet death's never a wholly welcome guest.

FAUST Happy that man whose brow death winds
with bloody laurels in the splendor of victory;
or he who is taken in a girl's arms
after the nimble maddening dance.
Oh, would that I had fallen dead,
overcome by the might of the great spirit!

MEPHISTOPHELES Yet, wasn't there someone on a certain night
who didn't drink the brown juice from the jug?

FAUST It seems, you like to spy.

MEPHISTOPHELES I'm not omniscient, but I do know many things.

FAUST Although a sweet familiar tone drew me
from dreadful frenzy and deceived the remnant
of childhood's feelings with echoes of happy times,
now I curse all that holds the soul with lures
and hocus-pocus, all that confines it with blinding flattery
to this cave of gloom. I curse above all
that false self-exaltation with which the mind
befuddles itself. Cursed be the blinding
of illusion that wraps our senses.
A curse on cheating dreams,
obsessions of glory and desire for an immortal name.
Cursed be all flattering possessions, like wife and child,
servant and plough. Damned be Mammon
when he incites us to rash acts
with hopes of wealth, or when he softens our beds
for futile pleasures. Cursed be the balsam-juice
of the grape, and the delights of love.
Accursed be hope and faith and, above all, patience!

CHORUS OF SPIRITS *(off-stage)*
Woe, woe!
You have destroyed
the splendid world
with a mighty fist.
It is shattered, and falls!
A demi-god broke it!
We carry the fragments
back to the nothingness.
We make lamentation
over lost beauty.
O mighty one
among earth's sons,
build it again, build it greater,

build it within yourself!
Begin the new way of life
brightly, more cheerfully,
and new songs will praise it!

MEPHISTOPHELES These little fellows
belong to my faction.
Hear how they shrewdly
advise you to act
and enjoy yourself.
Try the wide world;
abandon this solitude,
which dries up the brain
and stagnates the blood.

Stop playing with your grief
which, like a vulture, eats your life.
The worst society will let you feel
that you're a man among men.
And yet I don't mean that you should
be thrust among the stupid masses.
I'm not a high ranking devil, but if you'd like
to try your luck with me in a new life,
I'll gladly put myself at your disposal—
go where you will, do what you'd like to do,
be your companion—and if I suit you,
I'll be your servant and your slave.

FAUST What must I do for you in return?

MEPHISTOPHELES The debt can be handled on quite a long term.

FAUST No, no! The Devil is an egoist
and certainly not inclined to help
anyone for god's charity. State your conditions clearly;
a servant like you must be expensive.

MEPHISTOPHELES I'll bind myself to your service *here*
and do everything you ask of me;
Then when we meet over *yonder*, you shall do
as much for me as I've done for you.

FAUST What lies beyond doesn't worry me.
Suppose you break this world to bits, another may arise.
My joy springs from this earth,
this sun shines on my sorrows.
When I leave here, let come what must.
What do I care about it now, if hereafter

men hate or love, or if in those other spheres
there be an Above or a Below?

MEPHISTOPHELES In this mood you'll go far.
Commit yourself, and in the days to come
I'll use my arts for your pleasure.
I'll give you things that no man ever saw.

FAUST Poor devil, what have you to give?
Was ever the ambitious spirit of man
understood by one of your kind?
If you have food—it never satisfies;
you have red gold—that's fickle as mercury
and runs from the hands; a game—nobody wins;
a girl—right in my arms
she would make eyes at someone else;
suppose you give the godlike joy of honor—
it vanishes like a meteor!
Show me the fruit that rots before it's picked,
and trees that grow green again each day!

MEPHISTOPHELES I'm not afraid of such demands.
I can bring you such treasures without trouble.
But, my friend, the time will come
when we shall want to feast in peace.

FAUST If I ever rest on a lazy bed of ease,
then let me die at once. If you can beguile me
with blandishments, satisfy me with what I am,
or deceive me with pleasure,
let that be my last day. I'll bet on that!

MEPHISTOPHELES Taken!

FAUST Yes, taken and taken again!
If ever I say to any moment:
'Linger—you are so wonderful!'
Then you may throw me in chains.
I'll be ready for the earth.
Then let the death-bells toll, you'll be released.
The clock may stand still, the hands drop down,
and time come to an end, for all of me!

MEPHISTOPHELES Consider this carefully. We'll not forget it.

FAUST Stand on your legal rights.
My action is not rash. I'll not regret it.
As soon as I stagnate, I become a slave.
So what does it matter whose I am?

MEPHISTOPHELES I'll begin my service at once. Tonight
at the faculty dinner. But one thing more:
to provide for contingencies,
give me a couple of lines.

FAUST O you pedant, to want a written statement!
Did you never know a man who kept his word?
Isn't it enough that my spoken word
rules all my days until eternity?
Doesn't the world go raging in all its currents,
and would a promise bind me?

Yet, man has a fixation on this illusion;
and who would like to rid himself of it?
Happy is he who has the pure truth in him.
He will regret no sacrifice that keeps it.
But a parchment, signed and sealed, is a ghost
that everybody fears. The word dies on the pen,
and wax and leather remain our masters. Spirit of evil,
what do you want of me: bronze, marble, vellum, paper?
Shall I write with chisel, engraving tool, or goose-quill?
I let you have your choice.

MEPHISTOPHELES Come now! Don't get excited,
and oratorical!
A scrap of paper is enough for me,
and a little drop of blood to sign it.

FAUST If this will satisfy you fully,
then let's carry out the farce.

MEPHISTOPHELES Blood is a very special kind of juice.

FAUST Don't worry. I'll not break the bargain.
The goal of all my struggling's been just this
that I now promise. I aspired too high.
I'm merely on the level of the Devil.
The mighty spirit has scorned me;
nature has closed herself to me.
The thread of thought is broken;
and long ago all knowledge made me sick.
Let me put out my burning passion
in sloughs of lechery!
Let every wonder be made ready
that hides behind magic veils.
Let us throw ourselves into the rush of time,
into the swirls of chance, where pain and pleasure,
success and disappointment,

484

change and shift as luck goes:
restless activity's the only thing for man.

MEPHISTOPHELES Neither moderation nor goal is set for you.
You can sample and nibble at everything;
and snatch at things as you fly past.
And may you prosper in your pleasures,
but start at once and don't be timid!

FAUST Listen! It's not a question of joy.
I vow myself to excitement, intoxication,
the bitterest pleasures, amorous hatred,
and stirring remorse. My heart, now free
of the longing for learning, shall close itself
to no future pain. I mean to enjoy
in my innermost being all that is offered to mankind,
to seize the highest and the lowest,
to mix all kinds of good and evil,
and thus expand my Self till it includes
the spirit of all men—and, with them,
I shall be ruined and perish in the end.

MEPHISTOPHELES Listen to me, for I have chewed
this same tough food for many thousand years:
from cradle to coffin there's no man
who can digest this ancient sour dough.
You can believe me that this world was made
to suit a god who dwells in eternal light.
He has cast us devils into darkness;
for you it's enough to have only night and day.

FAUST But I will!

MEPHISTOPHELES A proper answer!
But I'm still troubled by one thing:
time is short and art is long.
I'd think you'd let yourself be instructed.
Associate yourself with a poet
and let him gallop through the fields of thought
and heap all noble qualities on your honored head:
the lion's courage, the stag's speed,
the fiery Italian blood,
the Northman's fortitude;
let him solve for you the secret that binds
cunning with magnanimity, and teaches you
how, with the instincts of youth's hot desires,
to fall in love according to a plan.

I'd like myself to meet with such man,
and I'd name him Sir Microcosm.

FAUST But what am I if I should fail to gain
the crown of mankind for which I struggle
with all my senses?

MEPHISTOPHELES In the end, you are exactly—what you are.
Put on a wig with a million curls,
put the highest heeled boots on your feet,
yet you remain in the end just what you are.

FAUST I feel how every effort has been in vain
to encompass human wisdom in my head,
and when I sit down finally
no new strength comes to me,
and I'm not taller by a hair or any nearer to infinity.

MEPHISTOPHELES My dear man, these things seem to you
just as they do to others.
We must manage more cleverly
before the joys of life escape us.
Damn it all! You must use hands and feet,
and head and sex to gain your ends!
And because I enjoy all these in play,
are they in any way less mine?
If I can hire six stallions,
is not all their power mine?
I dash away and act as big
as if I had two dozen legs.
Quick now, give up this idle pondering!
And let's be off into the great wide world!
I tell you: the fool who speculates on things
is like some animal on a dry heath,
led by an evil fiend in endless circles,
while fine green pastures lie on every side.

FAUST When do we start?

MEPHISTOPHELES As soon as we can.
This place is a torment.
What sort of life is it where a man
bores both himself and his students?
Leave that to your neighbor, Doctor Paunch!
Why should you slave to thresh out that old straw?
The best you know you can't show to the boys.
Right now I hear one at the door.

FAUST It's quite impossible for me to see him.

MEPHISTOPHELES The poor boy's waited so long already,
he mustn't go away uncomforted.
Come, give me your doctor's gown and hood.
This mask will suit me wonderfully.

(He changes his clothes.)

Go now and leave it to my wits!
A quarter-hour is all I'll need,
in which time go get ready for our trip!

(Faust goes out.)

MEPHISTOPHELES *(in the doctor's gown)* Scoff at all knowledge and despise
reason and science, those flowers of mankind.
Let the father of all lies
with dazzling necromancy make you blind,
then I'll have you unconditionally—
fate gave him a spirit that's ever pressing forward,
uncurbed; his rash impulses overleap
the joys of earth. I'll drag him through the wild life,
through the flat wasteland. I'll let him flounder,
stiffen, stick fast, and food and drink
shall bait his insatiate sense,
hovering before his greedy lips.
Vainly he'll beg me for refreshment,
and even if he hadn't given himself to the Devil,
he'd still be ruined in the end.

William Wordsworth, "Lines Composed a Few Miles Above Tintern Abbey"

In 1798, William Wordsworth (1770–1850) and his friend Samuel Taylor Coleridge (1772–1834) published *Lyrical Ballads*, a slim volume that revolutionized English poetry. Declaring their independence from older neo-Classic conventions, the two poets introduced themes that dominated the Romantic Movement—an intense love of nature, cultivation of strong emotion, interest in the feelings and language of the common man, and the individual's subjective response to his environment. Wordsworth focused on his psychological rapport with nature, whereas Coleridge explored the exotic and supernatural in such poems as "The Rime of the Ancient Mariner."

Wordsworth's meditative "Lines" composed near the ruins of Tintern Abbey contrasts the wild, exuberant joy he felt when experiencing nature while young with the more mature, reflective mood of later years. Although time has robbed him of boyish spontaneity and enthusiasm, it has given him a new role, to act as guide to his younger sister Dorothy, who represents the poet's earlier self, possessing the innocent freedom to interact heedlessly and intimately with the natural world.

LINES COMPOSED A FEW MILES ABOVE TINTERN ABBEY, ON REVISITING THE BANKS OF THE WYE DURING A TOUR. JULY 13, 1798

Five years have passed; five summers, with the length
Of five long winters! and again I hear
These waters, rolling from their mountain-springs
With a soft inland murmur.—Once again
Do I behold these steep and lofty cliffs,
That on a wild secluded scene impress
Thoughts of more deep seclusion; and connect
The landscape with the quiet of the sky.
The day is come when I again repose
Here, under this dark sycamore, and view
These plots of cottage-ground, these orchard-tufts,
Which at this season, with their unripe fruits,
Are clad in one green hue, and lose themselves
'Mid groves and copses. Once again I see
These hedge-rows, hardly hedge-rows, little lines
Of sportive wood run wild: these pastoral farms,
Green to the very door; and wreaths of smoke
Sent up, in silence, from among the trees!

With some uncertain notice, as might seem
Of vagrant dwellers in the houseless woods,
Or of some Hermit's cave, where by his fire
The Hermit sits alone.
                              These beauteous forms,
Through a long absence, have not been to me
As is a landscape to blind man's eye:
But oft, in lonely rooms, and 'mid the din
Of towns and cities, I have owed to them
In hours of weariness, sensations sweet,
Felt in the blood, and felt along the heart;
And passing even into my purer mind,
With tranquil restoration: —feelings too
Of unremembered pleasure: such, perhaps,
As have no slight or trivial influence
On that best portion of a good man's life,
His little, nameless, unremembered, acts
Of kindness and of love. Nor less, I trust,
To them I may have owed another gift,
Of aspect more sublime; that blessed mood,
In which the burthen of the mystery,
In which the heavy and the weary weight
Of all this unintelligible world,
Is lightened: —that serene and blessed mood,
In which the affections gently lead us on,—
Until, the breath of this corporeal frame
And even the motion of our human blood
Almost suspended, we are laid asleep
In body, and become a living soul:
While with an eye made quiet by the power
Of harmony, and the deep power of joy,
We see into the life of things.
                              If this
Be but a vain belief, yet, oh! how oft—
In darkness and amid the many shapes
Of joyless daylight; when the fretful stir
Unprofitable, and the fever of the world,
Have hung upon the beatings of my heart—
How oft, in spirit, have I turned to thee,
O sylvan Wye! thou wanderer thro' the woods,
How oft has my spirit turned to thee!

    And now, with gleams of half-extinguished thought,
With many recognitions dim and faint,
And somewhat of a sad perplexity,
The picture of the mind revives again:

While here I stand, not only with the sense
Of present pleasure, but with pleasing thoughts
That in this moment there is life and food
For future years. And so I dare to hope,
Though changed, no doubt, from what I was when first
I came among these hills; when like a roe
I bounded o'er the mountains, by the sides
Of the deep rivers, and the lonely streams,
Wherever nature led: more like a man
Flying from something that he dreads than one
Who sought the thing he loved. For nature then
(The coarser pleasures of my boyish days,
And their glad animal movements all gone by)
To me was all in all. —I cannot paint
What then I was. The sounding cataract
Haunted me like a passion: the tall rock,
The mountain, and the deep and gloomy wood,
Their colours and their forms, were then to me
An appetite; a feeling and a love,
That had no need of a remoter charm,
By thought supplied, nor any interest
Unborrowed from the eye.—That time is past,
And all its aching joys are now no more,
And all its dizzy raptures. Not for this
Faint I, nor mourn nor murmur; other gifts
Have followed; for such loss, I would believe,
Abundant recompense. For I have learned
To look on nature, not as in the hour
Of thoughtless youth; but hearing oftentimes
The still, sad music of humanity,
Nor harsh nor grating, though of ample power
To chasten and subdue. And I have felt
A presence that disturbs me with the joy
Of elevated thoughts; a sense sublime
Of something far more deeply interfused,
Whose dwelling is the light of setting suns,
And the round ocean and the living air,
And the blue sky, and in the mind of man:
A motion and a spirit, that impels
All thinking things, all objects of all thought,
And rolls through all things. Therefore am I still
A lover of the meadows and the woods,
And mountains; and of all that we behold
From this green earth; of all the mighty world
Of eye, and ear,—both what they half create,
And what perceive; well pleased to recognise

In nature and the language of the sense
The anchor of my purest thoughts, the nurse,
The guide, the guardian of my heart, and soul
Of all my moral being.
                         Nor perchance,
If I were not thus taught, should I the more
Suffer my genial spirits to decay:
For thou art with me here upon the banks
Of this fair river; thou my dearest Friend,
My dear, dear Friend; and in thy voice I catch
The language of my former heart, and read
My former pleasures in the shooting lights
Of thy wild eyes. Oh! yet a little while
May I behold in thee what I was once,
My dear, dear Sister! and this prayer I make,
Knowing that Nature never did betray
The heart that loved her; 'tis her privilege,
Through all the years of this our life, to lead
From joy to joy: for she can so inform
The mind that is within us, so impress
With quietness and beauty, and so feed
With lofty thoughts, that neither evil tongues,
Rash judgments, nor the sneers of selfish men,
Nor greetings where no kindness is, nor all
The dreary intercourse of daily life,
Shall e'er prevail against us, or disturb
Our cheerful faith, that all which we behold
Is full of blessings. Therefore let the moon
Shine on thee in thy solitary walk;
And let the misty mountain-winds be free
To blow against thee: and, in after years,
When these wild ecstasies shall be matured
Into a sober pleasure; when thy mind
Shall be a mansion for all lovely forms,
Thy memory be as a dwelling-place
For all sweet sounds and harmonies; oh! then,
If solitude, or fear, or pain, or grief,
Should be thy portion, with what healing thoughts
Of tender joy wilt thou remember me,
And these my exhortations! Nor, perchance—
If I should be where I no more can hear
Thy voice, nor catch from thy wild eyes these gleams
Of past existence—wilt thou then forget
That on the banks of this delightful stream
We stood together; and that I, so long
A worshipper of Nature, hither came

Unwearied in that service: rather say
With warmer love—oh! with far deeper zeal
Of holier love. Nor wilt thou then forget,
That after many wanderings, many years
Of absence, these steep woods and lofty cliffs,
And this green pastoral landscape, were to me
More dear, both for themselves and for thy sake!

George Gordon, Lord Byron, Prometheus

Of all the personalities who dominated the Romantic Movement in England, George Gordon, Lord Byron (1788–1824) was, for many of his contemporaries, the poet who epitomized many of the contradictions inherent in the Romantic style. Though he was born to aristocratic privilege, Byron identified with the downtrodden and the oppressed throughout his life, and his days were ended fighting for Greek independence from Ottoman rule. His finest poems and plays—works like *Childe Harold's Pilgrimage, Manfred,* and *Don Juan*—express a spirit of defiance and ironic resistance to fate, coupled with a sometimes melancholy, sometimes cynical recognition of human absurdity. For Byron, mankind was both "fire" and "clay," heroic in aspiration and abject in self-deception, and the tone of his works shifts, often unpredictably, from the tragic to the satiric with amazing ease.

The mythological yet thoroughly humanized figure of Prometheus in this poem embodies many of the ambivalent feelings Byron exhibited toward the revolutionary idealist who seeks to redeem the human race from its own weaknesses. Byron clearly admired the courage and terrible isolation of such a figure, and during his long, self-imposed exile from England, he came to identify with Prometheus, whose gift of fire might easily have been equated, in Byron's imagination, with the "gift" of poetry.

PROMETHEUS

TITAN! to whose immortal eyes
    The sufferings of mortality,
    Seen in their sad reality,
Were not as things that gods despise;
What was thy pity's recompense!
A silent suffering, and intense;
The rock, the vulture, and the chain,
All that the proud can feel of pain,
The agony they do not show,
The suffocating sense of woe,
    Which speaks but in its loneliness,
And then is jealous lest the sky
Should have a listener, nor will sigh
    Until its voice is echoless.
Titan! to thee the strife was given
    Between the suffering and the will
    Which torture where they cannot kill,
And the inexorable heaven,
And the deaf tyranny of fate,
The ruling principle of hate,

Which for its pleasure doth create
The things it may annihilate,
Refused thee even the boon to die:
The wretched gift eternity
      Was thine—and thou hast borne it well.
All that the Thunderer wrung from thee
Was but the menace which flung back
On him the torments of thy rack;
The fate thou didst so well foresee,
      But would not to appease him tell:
And in thy silence was his sentence,
And in his soul a vain repentance,
And evil dread so ill dissembled
That in his hand the lightnings trembled.

Thy godlike crime was to be kind.
      To render with thy precepts less
      The sum of human wretchedness,
And strengthen man with his own mind;
But baffled as thou wert from high,
Still in thy patient energy,
      In the endurance, and repulse
Of thine impenetrable spirit,
      Which earth and heaven could not convulse
A mighty lesson we inherit:
      Thou art a symbol and a sign
To mortals of their fate and force;
      Like thee, man is in part divine,
A troubled stream from a pure source;
And man in portions can foresee
His own funereal destiny;
His wretchedness, and his resistance,
And his sad unallied existence:
To which his spirit may oppose
Itself—an equal to all woes,
And a firm will, and a deep sense,
      Which even in torture can descry
Its own concentred recompense,
    Triumphant where it dares defy,
      And making death a victory.

John Keats, *Ode on a Grecian Urn*

Unlike his fellow Romantic poets, Byron and Shelley, John Keats (1795–1821) was humbly born and largely self-educated. Through reading the Greco-Roman classics and standard English authors such as Spenser and Milton, Keats rapidly developed a passion for beauty in art and literature. Plagued by poverty, ill-health, and a growing premonition of early death, Keats wrote poetry expressing the tension between his keen appetite for life's sensual and aesthetic pleasures and his terror of life's cruel brevity. Before dying at age 25, he composed some of the greatest odes in the English language, including the "Ode on a Grecian Urn" (1820). With its elegantly carved scenes depicting youthful lovers, shepherds, and musicians in ancient Greece, the urn represents the power of art to capture and preserve moments of exquisite beauty. Although art can symbolically rescue human experience from time's decay, it can do so only at the cost of living warmth and feeling. Keats' urn is a "*Cold Pastoral*," but it links generations of mortal humanity by picturing an unchanging and eternal ideal.

ODE ON A GRECIAN URN

I

Thou still unravish'd bride of quietness!
　　Thou foster-child of silence and slow time,
Sylvan historian, who canst thus express
　　A flowery tale more sweetly than our rhyme:
What leaf-fringed legend haunts about thy shape
　　Of deities or mortals, or of both,
　　　　In Tempe or the dales of Arcady?
　　What men or gods are these? What maidens loath?
What mad pursuit? What struggle to escape?
　　What pipes and timbrels? What wild ecstasy?

II

Heard melodies are sweet, but those unheard
　　Are sweeter; therefore, ye soft pipes, play on;
Not to the sensual ear, but, more endear'd,
　　Pipe to the spirit ditties of no tone:
Fair youth, beneath the trees, thou canst not leave
　　Thy song, nor ever can those trees be bare;
　　　　Bold Lover, never, never canst thou kiss,
　　Though winning near the goal—yet, do not grieve;
She cannot fade, though thou hast not thy bliss,
　　For ever wilt thou love, and she be fair!

III

Ah, happy, happy boughs! that cannot shed
   Your leaves, nor ever bid the Spring adieu;
And, happy melodist, unwearied,
   For ever piping songs for ever new;
More happy love! more happy, happy love!
    For ever warm and still to be enjoy'd,
      For ever panting and for ever young;
    All breathing human passion far above,
That leaves a heart high sorrowful and cloy'd,
   A burning forehead, and a parching tongue.

IV

Who are these coming to the sacrifice?
   To what green altar, O mysterious priest,
Lead'st thou that heifer lowing at the skies,
   And all her silken flanks with garlands dressed?
What little town by river or sea-shore,
   Or mountain-built with peaceful citadel,
    Is emptied of its folk, this pious morn?
   And, little town, thy streets for evermore
Will silent be; and not a soul to tell
   Why thou art desolate, can e'er return.

V

O Attic shape! Fair attitude! with brede
   Of marble men and maidens overwrought,
With forest branches and the trodden weed;
   Thou, silent form! dost tease us out of thought
As doth eternity: Cold Pastoral!
   When old age shall this generation waste,
    Thou shalt remain, in midst of other woe
   Than ours, a friend to man, to whom thou say'st,
"Beauty is truth, truth beauty," —that is all
   Ye know on earth, and all ye need to know.

Realism/Impressionism

Baudelaire, The Flowers of Evil

Ignored during his lifetime, after his death Charles Baudelaire (1821–1867) gradually became recognized as one of France's most original and creative poets. As a youth in Paris, Baudelaire led an eccentric, flamboyant life, cultivating aspects of human nature normally regarded as unfit for discussion in polite society. Baudelaire's poetry is intensely personal, exploring his sensuality, lust, perversity, and morbid passion for the dissolute and forbidden. When he discovered the writings of Edgar Allan Poe (1809–1845), he felt an immediate affinity with the American writer similarly fascinated by the occult, the paradoxical lure of beauty, death, and decay. Even without his own poetry, Baudelaire would have earned a place in French literature by introducing Poe's work to European audiences.

When *The Flowers of Evil*, a garland of profoundly introspective meditations on his own and the world's nature, was published in 1857, the book was condemned for blasphemy and obscenity. Refusing to delete the most offensive selections, Baudelaire worked four years to publish a second, enlarged edition in 1861. This version was also a failure and the poet, hoping to recoup his finances, made an unsuccessful lecture tour of Belgium. After a lingering illness and a stroke that left him paralyzed and speechless, he died in Paris in 1867.

Although many readers appreciate Baudelaire's daring sensuality, his spiritual aspirations are also important. Influenced by the Swedish mystic Swedenborg (1688–1772), Baudelaire came to believe that the material world corresponds to unseen realities in the spiritual world, a view he evoked in "Correspondences." Intrigued equally by satanism and Roman Catholic ritual, by sexual desire and spiritual longing, by eternal beauty and physical corruption, Baudelaire produced some of the most subtle and complex poems ever written.

CORRESPONDENCES

Nature is a temple where living columns rise,
Releasing at times a murmur of words half understood:
Within it man can wander as though within a wood
Of conscious symbols that watch him with familiar eyes.

Like prolonged echoes that distance mingles together
Into an obscure but endless unity,
Vast as light itself, or as the night sky,
Perfumes, colours and sounds all answer one another.

Some perfumes are cool as the flesh of young children,
Tender as oboes, or rainy prairies green
—And others overbearing, opulent, corrupt,

With the expansive power of things infinite,
Like amber and musk, benzoin and frankincense,
Singing the exaltation of the mind and senses.

INVITATION TO A VOYAGE
■

Sister, child,
Dream of being lulled
In the far joys of life there together,
Loving at will
Till we die, still
In that land of your own soul's weather,
Where the soft sky moistens
Fill my spirit with all the spells
And mysteries
Of your shining eyes
Through a traitorous tear as it spills.

　　　There, all is order, beauty,
　　　Ease, joy, tranquillity.

The years would gleam
In the aging sheen
Of the furniture in our room:
And flowers undreamt
Of, mingle their scent
With amber's cloudy perfume;
The ceiling's riches,
The mirror's dark reaches
Conspire an oriental glory
Where all might yet
Tell the soul's own secret
Lost and forgotten story.

　　　There, all is order, beauty,
　　　Ease, joy, tranquillity.

See the vessels that dream
On inlet and stream,
The sails of their wandering furled:
It was to take wing
With your lightest longing
They came up from the ends of the world.
The sun as it falls

Over fields and canals
Reveals a new city, entire
Chrysolite and rose;
The whole world's adrowse
By the warmth of its dying fire.

> There where all is order, beauty,
> Ease, joy, tranquillity.

THE CURSE
▪

Your courage, and yours alone,
Sisyphus, might lift this weight:
Whatever the will we dedicate,
Art is endless, and Time runs on.

Far from all celebrated tombs,
Towards the loneliest graveyard,
Like a muffled drum, my heart
Still beats out its funeral rhythms.

Many a jewel never to be known
Lies in depths of oblivion
Beyond reach of plummet or spade.

Many a flower exhales its secret
Perfume keener than regret
In depths of total solitude.

THE BLESSING
▪

When, by a decree of the sovereign power,
The poet makes his appearance in a bored world,
With fists clenched at the outrage, his horrified mother
Calls on a pitying God, at whom these curses are hurled:

"Why was I not made to litter a brood of vipers
Rather than conceive this human mockery?
My curses on that night whose ephemeral pleasures
Filled my womb with this avenging treachery!

Since I must be chosen among all women that are
To bear the lifetimes's grudge of a sullen husband,
And since I cannot get rid of this caricature,
—Fling it away like old letters to be burned,

On what you have devised for my punishment
I will let all your hate of me rebound,
I will torture this stunted growth until its bent
Branches let fall every blighted bud to the ground!"

And so she prepares for herself in Hell's pit
A place on the pyre made for a mother's crimes,
Blind, in the fury of her foaming hatred,
To the meaning and purpose of the eternal designs.

Meanwhile, under the care of an unseen angel,
The disinherited child revels in the sun's
Bright force; all that he eats and drinks can fill
Him with memories of the food that was heaven's.

The wind his plaything, any cloud a friend,
—The Spirit watching can only weep to see
How in childhood his way of the cross is lightened
By the wild bird-song of his innocent gaiety.

Those he would love look at him with suspicion
Or else, emboldened by his calm, experiment
With various possible methods of exciting derision
By trying out their cruelty on his complaint.

They mix ashes or unspeakable filth with the bread
And the wine of his daily communion, drop
Whatever he may have touched with affected dread,
And studiously avoid wherever he may step.

His mistress, parading her contempt in the street,
Cries: "Since he finds my beauty a thing to worship,
I'll be one of the ancient idols he talks about,
And make myself with gold out of the same workshop!

I will never have enough of his kneelings and offerings
Until I am sure that the choice foods, the wines
The 'nard', the 'incense', the 'myrrh' that he brings
He brings as other men would to the Virgin's shrines.

And when I am sick to death of trying not to laugh
At the farce of my black masses, I'll try the force
Of the hand he calls 'frail', my nails will dig a path
Like 'harpies', to the heart that beats for me, of course!

Like a nestling trembling and palpitating
I will pull that red heart out of his breast
And throw it down for my favourite dog's eating
—Let him do whatever he likes with the rest!"

A serene piety, lifting the poet's gaze,
Reveals heaven opening on a shining throne,
And the lower vision of the world's ravening rage
Is shut out by the sheet lightnings of his brain.

"Be blessed, oh my God, who givest suffering
As the only divine remedy for our folly,
As the highest and purest essence preparing
The strong in spirit for ecstasies most holy.

I know that among the uplifted legions
Of saints, a place awaits the Poet's arrival,
And that among the Powers, Virtues, Dominations,
He too is summoned to Heaven's festival.

I know that sorrow is the one human strength
On which neither earth nor hell can impose,
And that all the universe and all time's length
Must be wound into the mystic crown for his brows.

But all the treasury of buried Palmyra,
The earth's unknown metals, the sea's pearls,
Mounted by Thy hand, would be deemed an inferior
Glitter, to his diadem that shines without jewels.

For thou knowest it will be made of purest light
Drawn from the holy hearth of every primal ray,
To which all human eyes, if they were one bright
Eye, are only a tarnished mirror's fading day."

Dostoyevsky, The Brothers Karamazov

With Leo Tolstoy (1828–1910), Fyodor Mikhailovich Dostoyevsky (1821–1881) is one of the two greatest nineteenth century Russian novelists. An epileptic, compulsive gambler, and revolutionary, Dostoyevsky experienced many of the passions and obsessions that distinguish his fictional characters. Condemned to death in 1849 for political subversion, he faced a firing squad, only to have his sentence revoked at the last minute. Exiled to Siberia, he spent seven years at hard labor in the Czarist salt mines. His prison experiences provided the subject matter for the *House of the Dead* (1861).

Keenly sensitive to the disparity between the impoverished majority and affluent few in pre-Revolutionary Russia, Dostoyevsky created some of the most memorable scenes of human suffering in world literature. *Crime and Punishment* (1866) explores both abnormal psychology and the degradation of extreme poverty. His last and finest work, *The Brothers Karamazov* (1880) was completed only three months before his death. A triumph of psychological portraiture and social and cultural analysis, the novel dramatizes the moral and political conflicts between traditional attitudes of Russian society and new ideas from the West. The author's tension between intellectual rebellion and the desire for religious certainty animates many of Dostoyevsky's characters, including Ivan Karamazov, who narrates the tale of "The Grand Inquisitor" to his brother Alyosha, a gentle mystic. Ivan's parable imagines a confrontation between an aged cardinal, leader of the Inquisition in sixteenth century Spain, and Jesus of Nazareth, who reappears as a vulnerable human being. Ivan's Jesus, who wordlessly demands total freedom of choice for all people, represents a threat to church authority. Ironically, it is because the cynical Inquisitor feels compassion for a debased humanity, which is utterly dependent on the church to control its moral weaknesses, that he must execute Jesus in an *auto-da-fé*, the public burning of heretics.

THE GRAND INQUISITOR

■

And now the time came when [Jesus] wished to appear to the people, if only for a moment—to the tormented, suffering people, to the people sunk in filthy iniquity, but who loved him like innocent children. The action of my poem takes place in Spain, in Seville, during the most terrible time of the Inquisition, when fires were lighted every day throughout the land to the glory of God and

In the splendid *autos-da-fé*
Wicked heretics were burnt.

Oh, of course, this was not the second coming when, as he promised, he would appear at the end of time in all his heavenly glory, and which would be as sudden "as the lightning cometh out of the east, and shineth even unto the west". No, all he wanted was to visit his children only for a moment and just where the stakes of the heretics were crackling in the flames. In his infinite mercy he once more walked among men in the semblance of man as he had walked among men for thirty-three years fifteen centuries ago. He came down into the hot "streets and lanes" of the southern city just at the moment when, a day before, nearly a hundred heretics had been burnt all at once by the cardinal, the Grand Inquisitor, *ad majorem gloriam Dei* in "a magnificent auto da fé", in the presence of the king, the court, the knights, the cardinals, and the fairest ladies of the Court and the whole population of Seville. He appeared quietly, inconspicuously, but everyone—and that is why it is so strange—recognized him. That might have been one of the finest passages in my poem—I mean, why they recognized him. The people are drawn to him by an irresistible force, they surround him, they throng about him, they follow him. He walks among them in silence with a gentle smile of infinite compassion. The sun of love burns in his heart, rays of Light, of Enlightenment, and of Power stream from his eyes and, pouring over the people, stir their hearts with responsive love. He stretches forth his hands to them, blesses them, and a healing virtue comes from contact with him, even with his garments. An old man, blind from childhood, cries out to him from the midst of the crowd, "O Lord, heal me so that I may see thee", and it is as though scales fell from his eyes, and the blind man sees him. The people weep and kiss the ground upon which he walks. Children scatter flowers before him, sing and cry out to him: "Hosannah!" "It is he, it is he himself," they all repeat. "It must be he, it can be no one but he." He stops on the steps of the Cathedral of Seville at the moment when a child's little, open white coffin is brought in with weeping into the church: in it lies a girl of seven, the only daughter of a prominent citizen. The dead child is covered with flowers. "He will raise up your child", people shout from the crowd to the weeping mother. The canon, who has come out to meet the coffin, looks on perplexed and knits his brows. But presently a cry of the dead child's mother is heard. She throws herself at his feet. "If it is thou," she cries, holding out her hands to him, "then raise my child from the dead!" The funeral cortege halts. The coffin is lowered on to the steps at his feet. He gazes with compassion and his lips once again utter softly the words, "Talitha cumi"—"and the damsel arose". The little girl rises in the coffin, sits up, and looks around her with surprise in her smiling, wide-open eyes. In her hands she holds the nosegay of white roses with which she lay in her coffin. There are cries, sobs, and confusion among the people, and it is at that very moment that the Cardinal himself, the Grand Inquisitor, passes by the cathedral in the square. He is an old man of nearly ninety, tall and erect, with a shrivelled face and sunken eyes, from which, though, a light like a fiery spark still gleams. Oh, he is not wearing his splendid cardinal robes in which he appeared before the people the day before, when the enemies of the Roman faith were being burnt—no, at that moment he is wearing only his old, coarse, monk's cassock. He is followed at a distance by his sombre assistants and his slaves and his "sacred" guard. He stops in front of the crowd and watches from a distance. He sees everything. He sees the coffin set down at *his* feet, he sees the young girl raised from the dead, and his face darkens. He knits his grey, beetling brows and his eyes flash with an ominous fire. He stretches forth his finger and commands the guards to seize him. And so great is his power and so accustomed are the people to obey him, so humble and submissive are they to his will, that the crowd immediately makes way for the guards and, amid the death-like hush that descends upon the square, they lay hands upon him and lead *him* away. The crowd, like one man, at once bows down to the ground before the old Inquisitor, who blesses them in silence and passes on. The guards take their Prisoner to the dark, narrow, vaulted prison in the old building of the Sacred Court and lock him in there.

The day passes and night falls, the dark, hot and "breathless" Seville night. The air is "heavy with the scent of laurel and lemon". Amid the profound darkness, the iron door of the prison is suddenly opened and the old Grand Inquisitor himself slowly enters the prison with a light in his hand. He is alone and the door at once closes behind him. He stops in the doorway and gazes for a long time, for more than a minute, into his face. At last he approaches him slowly, puts the lamp on the table and says to him:

' "Is it you? You?"

'But, receiving no answer, he adds quickly: "Do not answer, be silent. And, indeed, what can you say? I know too well what you would say. Besides, you have no right to add anything to what you have said already in the days of old. Why, then, did you come to meddle with us? For you have come to meddle with us, and you know it. But do you know what is going to happen tomorrow? I know not who you are and I don't want to know: whether it is you or only someone who looks like him, I do not know, but tomorrow I shall condemn you and burn you at the stake as the vilest of heretics, and the same people who today kissed your feet, will at the first sign from me rush to rake up the coals at your stake tomorrow. Do you know that? Yes, perhaps you do know it," he added after a moment of deep reflection without taking his eyes off his prisoner for an instant.

'I'm afraid I don't quite understand it, Ivan,' said Alyosha, who had been listening in silence all the time, with a smile. 'Is it just a wild fantasy, or has the old man made some mistake, some impossible *qui pro quo?*

'You can assume it to be the latter,' laughed Ivan, 'if our modern realism has spoilt you so much that you can't bear anything fantastic. If you prefer a *qui pro quo*, then let it be so. It is true,' he laughed again, 'the old man was ninety and he might have long ago gone mad about his fixed idea. He might, too, have been struck by the Prisoner's appearance. It might, finally, have been simply delirium. A vision the ninety-year-old man had before his death, particularly as he had been greatly affected by the burning of a hundred heretics at the auto-da-fé the day before. What difference does it make to us whether it was a *qui pro quo* or a wild fantasy? The only thing that matters is that the old man should speak out, that at last he does speak out and says aloud what he has been thinking in silence for ninety years.'

'And is the Prisoner also silent? Does he look at him without uttering a word?'

'Yes,' Ivan laughed again, 'that's how it should be in all such cases. The old man himself tells him that *he* has no right to add anything to what had already been said before. If you like, this is the most fundamental feature of Roman Catholicism, in my opinion at any rate: "Everything," he tells him, "has been handed over by you to the Pope and, therefore, everything is now in the Pope's hands, and there's no need for you to come at all now—at any rate, do not interfere for the time being." They not only speak, but also write in that sense. The Jesuits do at any rate. I've read it myself in the works of their theologians. "Have you the right to reveal to us even one of the mysteries of the world you have come from?" my old man asks him and he replies for him himself. "No, you have not. So that you may not add anything to what has been said before and so as not to deprive men of the freedom which you upheld so strongly when you were on earth. All that you might reveal anew would encroach on men's freedom of faith, for it would come as a miracle, and their freedom of faith was dearer to you than anything even in those days, fifteen hundred years ago. Was it not you who said so often in those days, 'I shall make you free'? But now you have seen those 'free' men," the old man adds suddenly with a pensive smile. "Yes, this business has cost us a great deal," he goes on, looking sternly at him, "but we've completed it at last in your name. For fifteen centuries we've been troubled by this freedom, but now it's over and done with for good. You don't believe that it is all over? You look meekly at me and do not deign even to be indignant with me? I want you to know that now—yes, today—these men are more than ever convinced that they are absolutely free, and yet they themselves have brought their freedom to us and humbly laid it at our feet. But it was we who did it. And was that what you wanted? Was that the kind of freedom you wanted?"'

'I'm afraid I don't understand again,' Alyosha interrupted. 'Is he being ironical, is he laughing?'

'Not in the least. You see, he glories in the fact that he and his followers have at last vanquished freedom and have done so in order to make men happy. "For," he tells him, "it is only now (he is, of course, speaking of the Inquisition), that it has become possible for the first time to think of the happiness of men. Man is born a rebel and can rebels be happy? You were warned," he says to him. "There has been no lack of warnings and signs, but you did not heed the warnings. You rejected the only way by which men might be made happy, but, fortunately, in departing, you handed on the work to us. You have promised and you have confirmed it by your own word. You have given us the right to bind and unbind, and of course you can't possibly think of depriving us of that right now. Why, then, have you come to interfere with us?" '

'And what's the meaning of "there has been no lack of warnings and signs?" ' asked Alyosha.

'That, you see, is the chief thing about which the old man has to speak out.

' "The terrible and wise spirit, the spirit of self-destruction and non-existence," the old man went on, "the great spirit talked with you in the wilderness and we are told in the books that he apparently 'tempted' you. Is that so? And could anything truer have been said than what he revealed to you in his three questions and what you rejected, and what in the books are called 'temptations'? And yet if ever there has been on earth a real, prodigious miracle, it was on that day, on the day of the three temptations. Indeed, it was in the emergence of those three questions that the miracle lay. If it were possible to imagine, for the sake of argument, that those three questions of the terrible spirit had been lost without leaving a trace in the books and that we had to rediscover, restore, and invent them afresh and that to do so we had to gather together all the wise men of the earth—rulers, high priests, scholars, philosophers, poets—and set them the task of devising and inventing three questions which would not only correspond to the magnitude of the occasion, but, in addition, express in three words, in three short human sentences, the whole future history of the world and of mankind, do you think that the entire wisdom of the earth, gathered together, could have invented anything equal in depth and force to the three questions which were actually put to you at the time by the wise and mighty spirit in the wilderness? From those questions alone, from the miracle of their appearance, one can see that what one is dealing with here is not the human, transient mind, but the absolute and everlasting one. For in those three questions the whole future history of mankind is, as it were, anticipated and combined in one whole and three images are presented in which all the insoluble historical contradictions of human nature all over the world will meet. At the time it could not be so clearly seen, for the future was still unknown, but now, after fifteen centuries have gone by, we can see that everything in those three questions was so perfectly divined and foretold and has been so completely proved to be true that nothing can be added or taken from them.

' "Decide yourself who was right—you or he who questioned you then? Call to your mind the first question; its meaning, though not in these words, was this: 'You want to go into the world and you are going empty-handed, with some promise of freedom, which men in their simplicity and their innate lawlessness cannot even comprehend, which they fear and dread—for nothing has ever been more unendurable to man and to human society than freedom! And do you see the stones in this parched and barren desert? Turn them into loaves, and mankind will run after you like a flock of sheep, grateful and obedient, though for ever trembling with fear that you might withdraw your hand and they would no longer have your loaves.' But you did not want to deprive man of freedom and rejected the offer, for, you thought, what sort of freedom is it if obedience is bought with loaves of bread? You replied that man does not live by bread alone, but do you know that for the sake of that earthly bread the spirit of the earth will rise up against you and will join battle with you and conquer you, and all will follow him, crying 'Who is like this beast? He has given us fire from heaven!' Do you know that ages will pass and mankind will proclaim in its wisdom and science that there is no crime and, therefore, no sin, but that there are only hungry people. 'Feed them first and then demand virtue of them!'—that is what they will inscribe on their banner which they will raise against you and which will destroy your temple. A new building will rise where your temple stood, the dreadful Tower of Babel will rise up again, and though, like the first one, it will not be completed, yet you might have prevented the new tower and have shortened the sufferings of men by a thousand years for it is to us that they will come at last, after breaking their hearts for a thousand years with their tower! Then they will look for us again under the ground, hidden in the catacombs (for we shall again be persecuted and tortured), and they will find us and cry out to us 'Feed us, for those who have promised us fire from heaven have not given it to us!' And then we shall finish building their tower, for he who feeds them will complete it, and we alone shall feed them in your name, and we shall lie to them that it is in your name. Oh, without us they will never, never feed themselves. No science will give them bread so long as they remain free. But in the end they will lay their freedom at our feet and say to us, 'We don't mind being your slaves so long as you feed us!' They will, at last, realize themselves that there cannot be enough freedom and bread for everybody, for they will never, never be able to let everyone have his fair share! They will also be convinced that they can never be free because they are weak, vicious, worthless, and rebellious. You promised them bread from heaven, but, I repeat again, can it compare with earthly bread in the eyes of the weak, always vicious and always ignoble race of man? And if for the sake of the bread from heaven thousands and tens of thousands will follow you, what is to become of the millions and scores of thousands of millions of creatures who will not have the strength to give up the earthly bread for the bread of heaven? Or are only the scores of thousands of the great and strong dear to you, and are the remaining millions, numerous as the sand of the sea, who are weak but who love you, to serve only as the material for the great and the strong? No, to us the weak, too, are dear. They are vicious and rebellious, but in the end they will become obedient too. They will marvel at us and they will regard us as gods because, having become their masters, we consented to endure freedom and rule over them—so dreadful will freedom become to them in the end! But we shall tell them that we do your bidding and rule in your name. We shall deceive them again, for we shall not let you come near us again. That deception will be our suffering, for we shall be forced to lie. That was the meaning of the first question in the wilderness, and that was what you rejected in the name of freedom, which you put above everything else. And yet in that question lay hidden the great secret of this world. By accepting 'the loaves', you would have satisfied man's universal and everlasting craving, both as an individual and as mankind as a whole, which can be summed up in the words 'whom shall I worship?' Man, so long as he remains free, has no more constant and agonizing anxiety than to find as quickly as possible someone to worship. But man seeks to worship only what is incontestable, so incontestable, indeed, that all men at once agree to worship it all together. For the chief concern of those miserable creatures is not only to find something that I or someone else can worship, but to find something that all believe in and worship, and the absolutely essential thing is that they should do so all together. It is this need for universal worship that is the chief torment of every man individually and of mankind as a whole from the beginning of time. For the sake of that universal worship they have put each other to the sword. They have set up gods and called upon each other, 'Give up your gods and come and worship ours, or else death to you and to your gods!' And so it will be to the end of the world, even when the gods have vanished from the earth: they will prostrate themselves before idols just the same. You knew, you couldn't help knowing this fundamental mystery of human nature, but you rejected the only absolute banner, which was offered to you, to make all men worship you alone incontestably— the banner of earthly bread, which you rejected in the name of freedom and the bread from heaven. And look what you have done further—and all again in the name of freedom! I tell you man has no more agonizing anxiety than to find someone to whom he can hand over with all speed the gift of freedom with which the unhappy creature is born. But only he can gain possession of men's freedom who is able to set their conscience at ease. With the bread you were given an incontestable banner: give him bread and man will worship you, for there is nothing more incontestable than bread; but if at the same time someone besides yourself should gain possession of his conscience—oh, then he will even throw away your bread and follow him who has ensnared his conscience. You were right about that. For the mystery of human life is not only in living, but in knowing why one lives. Without a clear idea of what to live for man will not consent to live and will rather destroy himself than remain on the earth, though he were surrounded by loaves of bread. That is so, but what became of it? Instead of gaining possession of men's freedom, you gave them greater freedom than ever! Or did you forget that a tranquil mind and even death is dearer to man than the free choice in the knowledge of good and evil? There is nothing more alluring to man than this freedom of conscience, but there is nothing more tormenting, either. And instead of firm foundations for appeasing man's conscience once and for all, you chose everything that was exceptional, enigmatic, and vague, you chose everything that was beyond the strength of men, acting, consequently, as though you did not love them at all—you who came to give your life for them! Instead of taking possession of men's freedom you multiplied it and burdened the spiritual kingdom of man with its sufferings for ever. You wanted man's free love so that he should follow you freely, fascinated and captivated by you. Instead of the strict ancient law, man had in future to decide for himself with a free heart what is good and what is evil, having only your image before him for guidance. But did it never occur to you that he would at last reject and call in question even your image and your truth, if he were weighed down by so fearful a burden as freedom of choice? They will at last cry aloud that the truth is not in you, for it was impossible to leave them in greater confusion and suffering than you have done by leaving them with so many cares and insoluble problems. It was you yourself, therefore, who laid the foundation for the destruction of your kingdom and you ought not to blame anyone else for it. And yet, is that all that was offered to you? There are three forces, the only three forces that are able to conquer and hold captive for ever the conscience of these weak rebels for their own happiness—these forces are: miracle, mystery, and authority. You rejected all three and yourself set the example for doing so. When the wise and terrible spirit set you on a pinnacle of the temple and said to you: 'If thou be the Son of God, cast thyself down: for it is written, He shall give his angels charge concerning thee: and in their hands they shall bear thee up, lest at any time thou dash thy foot against a stone, and thou shalt prove then how great is thy faith in thy Father.' But, having heard him, you rejected his proposal and did not give way and did not cast yourself down. Oh, of course, you acted proudly and magnificently, like God. But men, the weak, rebellious race of men, are they gods? Oh, you understood perfectly then that in taking one step, in making a move to cast yourself down, you would at once have tempted God and have lost all your faith in him, and you would have been dashed to pieces against the earth which you came to save, and the wise spirit that tempted you would have rejoiced. But, I repeat, are there many like you? And could you really assume for a moment that men, too, could be equal to such a temptation? Is the nature of man such that he can reject a miracle and at the most fearful moments of life, the moments of his most fearful, fundamental, and agonizing spiritual problems, stick to the free decision of the heart? Oh, you knew that your great deed would be preserved in books, that it would go down to the end of time and the extreme ends of the earth, and you hoped that, following you, man would remain with God and ask for no miracle. But you did not know that as soon as man rejected miracle he would at once reject God as well, for what man seeks is not so much God as miracles. And since man is unable to carry on without a miracle, he will create new miracles for himself, miracles of his own, and will worship the miracle of the witch-doctor and the sorcery of the wise woman, rebel, heretic and infidel though he is a hundred times over. You did not come down from the cross when they shouted to you, mocking and deriding you: 'If thou be the Son of God, come down from the cross.' You did not come down because you hungered for a faith based on free will and not on miracles. You hungered for freely given love and not for the servile raptures of the slave before the might that has terrified him once and for all. But here, too, your judgement of men was too high, for they are slaves, though rebels by nature. Look round and judge: fifteen centuries have passed, go and have a look at them: whom have you raised up to yourself? I swear, man has been created a weaker and baser creature than you thought him to be! Can he, can he do what you did? In respecting him so greatly, you acted as though you ceased to feel any compassion for him, for you asked too much of him—you who have loved him more than yourself! Had you respected him less, you would have asked less of him, and that would have been more like love, for his burden would have been lighter. . . ." '

'They [the Jesuits] are not so clever and they have no such mysteries and secrets [states Alyosha]. Except perhaps only godlessness, that's all their secret. Your inquisitor doesn't believe in God—that's all his secret!'

'Well, suppose it is so! At last you've guessed it! And, in fact, it really is so. That really is his whole secret. But is that not suffering, particularly for a man like him who had sacrificed his whole life for a great cause in the wilderness and has not cured himself of his love of humanity? In his last remaining years he comes to the clear conviction that it is only the advice of the great and terrible spirit that could bring some sort of supportable order into the life of the feeble rebels, "the unfinished experimental creatures created as a mockery". And so, convinced of that, he sees that one has to follow the instructions of the wise spirit, the terrible spirit of death and destruction. He therefore accepts lies and deceptions and leads men consciously to death and destruction. Keeps deceiving them all the way, so that they should not notice where they are being led, for he is anxious that those miserable, blind creatures should at least on the way think themselves happy. And, mind you, the deception is in the name of him in whose ideal the old man believed so passionately all his life! Is not that a calamity? And even if there were only one such man at the head of the whole army of men "craving for power for the sake of filthy gains"—would not even one such man be sufficient to make a tragedy? Moreover, one man like that, standing at the head of the movement, is enough for the emergence of a real leading idea of the entire Roman Church with all its armies and Jesuits—the highest idea of this Church. I tell you frankly it's my firm belief that there was never any scarcity of such single individuals among those who stood at the head of the movement. Who knows, there may have been many such individuals among the Roman Pontiffs, too. Who knows, perhaps this accursed old man, who loves humanity so obstinately in his own particular way, still exists even now in the form of a whole multitude of such individual old men, and not by chance, either, but by agreement, as a secret society formed long ago to guard the mystery. To guard it from the weak and unhappy, so as to make them happy. I'm sure it exists and, indeed, it must be so. I can't help feeling that something of the same kind of mystery exists also among the freemasons at the basis of their organization. That is why the Catholics hate the freemasons so much, for they regard them as their competitors who are breaking up the unity of their idea, while there should be only one flock and one shepherd. However, I feel that in defending my theory I must appear to you as an author who resents your criticism. Let's drop it.'

'You're probably a freemason yourself!' Alyosha cried, unable to restrain himself. 'You don't believe in God,' he added, but this time in great sorrow. He imagined, besides, that his brother was looking mockingly at him. 'How does your poem end?' he asked suddenly, his eyes fixed on the ground. 'Or was that the end?'

'I intended to end it as follows: when the Inquisitor finished speaking, he waited for some time for the Prisoner's reply. His silence distressed him. He saw that the Prisoner had been listening intently to him all the time, looking gently into his face and evidently not wishing to say anything in reply. The old man would have liked him to say something, however bitter and terrible. But he suddenly approached the old man and kissed him gently on his bloodless, aged lips. That was all his answer. The old man gave a start. There was an imperceptible movement at the corners of his mouth; he went to the door, opened it and said to him: "Go, and come no more—don't come at all—never, never!" And he let him out into "the dark streets and lanes of the city". The Prisoner went away.'

'And the old man?'

'The kiss glows in his heart, but the old man sticks to his idea.'

Emily Dickinson, "The Soul Selects Her Own Society," "There's a Certain Slant of Light," and "It Was Not Death"

Today, Emily Dickinson is one of the most highly regarded poets of the nineteenth century, and certainly the most important woman of letters in America during that period. In her own time she was practically ignored, and remained practically unpublished. Her comparatively reclusive life and the disparaging comments of her principal literary mentor, Thomas Wentworth Higginson, conspired to discourage Dickinson from even attempting to publish the hundreds of poems she wrote during her lifetime. Only after her death, beginning with the first volume of her poems (edited by Higginson) in 1890, and continuing in successive volumes until 1945, were readers finally able to assess the scope of her talent.

Her poems are all miniatures of meditation and reflection on such subjects as love, death, God, friendship, time, and eternity. Her language and her poetic rhythms are idiosyncratic. She prefers to intimate rather than explain ideas or feelings, which results in economy of form coupled with an extraordinary range of suggestive, even provocative images and ideas.

THE SOUL SELECTS HER OWN SOCIETY

THE soul selects her own society,
Then shuts the door;
On her divine majority
Obtrude no more.
Unmoved, she notes the chariot's pausing
At her low gate;
Unmoved, an emperor is kneeling
Upon her mat.

I've known her from an ample nation
Choose one;
Then close the valves of her attention
Like stone.

THERE'S A CERTAIN SLANT OF LIGHT

THERE'S a certain slant of light,
On winter afternoons,
That oppresses, like the weight
Of cathedral tunes.

Heavenly hurt it gives us;
We can find no scar,
But internal difference
Where the meanings are.

None may teach it anything,
'Tis the seal, despair,—
An imperial affliction
Sent us of the air.

When it comes, the landscape listens,
Shadows hold their breath;
When it goes, 'tis like the distance
On the look of death.

IT WAS NOT DEATH
▪

IT was not death, for I stood up,
And all the dead lie down;
It was not night, for all the bells
Put out their tongues, for noon.

It was not frost, for on my flesh
I felt siroccos crawl,—
Nor fire, for just my marble feet
Could keep a chancel cool.

And yet it tasted like them all'
The figures I have seen
Set orderly, for burial,
Reminded me of mine,

As if my life were shaven
And fitted to a frame,
And could not breathe without a key;
And 't was like midnight, some,

When everything that tricked has stopped,
And space stares, all around,
Or grisly frosts, first autumn morns,
Repeal the beating ground.

But most like chaos,—stopless, cool,—
Without a chance or spar,
Or even a report of land
To justify despair.

Friedrich Nietzsche, The Gay Science, Twilight of the Idols

Friedrich Nietzsche (1844–1900) was one of the most radical exponents of a post-Christian view of moral values, and one of the most strident and complex philosophical personalities of the nineteenth century. Born into a family of Lutheran ministers, Nietzsche embraced and promoted atheism throughout his career, and he defiantly proclaimed the "death of God" as the accomplished fact of modern science. As a philosophical "naturalist," Nietzsche rejected the notion that either nature or history possessed any inherent meaning or goal. Within *human* nature, however, Nietzsche found a basic drive to achieve control over the natural and social environment, a form of psycho-physical energy he termed the "Will to Power." Evidence of this power drive could be found everywhere, Nietzsche believed, and any attempt to suppress it was futile and self-destructive for the individual as well as for an entire culture. Indeed, the fundamental error of Judeo-Christian culture, Nietzsche insisted, lay in its attempts to deny the nobility of aggression and in its determination to exalt a "slave morality" based on humility and submission.

For Nietzsche, the basic task of modern philosophy could be described as the "revaluation of all values," which entailed both a rejection of absolute values and an endorsement of the relativist position that value judgments are nothing more than functions of culture or rationalizations of the needs and fears of a particular group or class. Neither "goodness" nor "evil" can assume a fixed or universal meaning, and as the Will to Power makes its presence felt throughout history, values spontaneously undergo change, and thereby "revalue" (or devalue) themselves.

In presenting such arguments, Nietzsche emerged as an advocate of a post-Darwinian view of human behavior. No ethical theory, he believed, can possibly be sound or relevant to human experience if it ignores, or seeks to marginalize, the struggle for mastery and survival that characterizes all organic life on our planet. Prophetically, Nietzsche often attempted to imagine what an elite class of "overmen" ("supermen," in some translations of his works) would be like if they, like Nietzsche himself, elected a life of incessant struggle and danger, divorced from the moral and spiritual illusions that have sustained the Christianized West for centuries. The lurid, romantic appeal of such a figure was felt not only by Nietzsche's own generation, but even more powerfully by the emerging Fascist ideologues of the early twentieth century.

THE GAY SCIENCE
■

[4]

What preserves the species. The strongest and most evil spirits have so far advanced humanity the most: they have always rekindled the drowsing passions—all ordered society puts the passions to sleep; they have always reawakened the sense of comparison, of

515
■

contradiction, of joy in the new, the daring, and the untried; they force men to meet opinion with opinion, model with model. For the most part by arms, by the overthrow of boundary stones, and by offense to the pieties, but also by new religions and moralities. The same "malice" is to be found in every teacher and preacher of the new. . . . The new is always *the evil,* as that which wants to conquer, to overthrow the old boundary stones and the old pieties; and only the old is the good. The good men of every age are those who dig the old ideas deep down and bear fruit with them, the husbandmen of the spirit. But all land is finally exhausted, and the plow of evil must always return.

There is a fundamentally erroneous doctrine in contemporary morality, celebrated particularly in England: according to this, the judgments "good" and "evil" are condensations of the experiences concerning "expedient" and "inexpedient"; what is called good preserves the species, while what is called evil is harmful to the species. In truth, however, the evil urges are expedient and indispensable and preserve the species to as high a degree as the good ones—only their function is different.

[7]

Something for the industrious. . . . So far, everything that has given color to existence still lacks a history: or, where could one find a history of love, of avarice, of envy, of conscience, of piety, or of cruelty? Even a comparative history of law, or merely of punishment, is completely lacking so far. Has anyone yet conducted research into the different ways of dividing the day and the consequences of a regular arrangement of work, holiday, and rest? Does one know the moral effects of food? Is there a philosophy of nourishment? (The ever-renewed clamor for and against vegetarianism is sufficient proof that there is no such philosophy as yet.) Have the experiences of living together been assembled; for example, the experiences in the monasteries? Has the dialectic of marriage and friendship been presented as yet? . . .

[34]

Historia abscondita. Every great human being has a retroactive force: all history is again placed in the scales for his sake, and a thousand secrets of the past crawl out of their hideouts—into *his* sun. There is no way of telling what may yet become history some day. Perhaps the past is still essentially undiscovered! So many retroactive forces are still required!

[125]

The Madman. Have you not heard of that madman who lit a lantern in the bright morning hours, ran to the market place, and cried incessantly, "I seek God! I seek God!" As many of those who do not believe in God were standing around just then, he provoked much laughter. Why, did he get lost? said one. Did he lose his way like a child? said another. Or is he hiding? Is he afraid of us? Has he gone on a voyage? or emigrated? Thus they yelled and laughed. The madman jumped into their midst and pierced them with his glances.

"Whither is God" he cried. "I shall tell you. *We have killed him*—you and I. All of us are his murderers. But how have we done this? How were we able to drink up the sea? Who gave us the sponge to wipe away the entire horizon? What did we do when we unchained this earth from its sun? Whither is it moving now? Whither are we moving now? Away from all suns? Are we not plunging continually? Backward, sideward, forward, in all directions? Is there any up or down left? Are we not straying as through an infinite nothing? Do we not feel the breath of empty space? Has it not become colder? Is not night and more night coming on all the while? Must not lanterns be lit in the morning? Do we not hear anything yet of the noise of the gravediggers who are burying God? Do we not smell anything yet of God's decomposition? Gods too decompose. God is dead. God remains dead. And we have killed him. How shall we, the murderers of all murderers, comfort ourselves? What was holiest and most powerful of all that the world has yet owned has bled to death under our knives. Who will wipe this blood off us? What water is there for us to clean ourselves? What festivals of atonement, what sacred games shall we have to invent? Is not the greatness of this deed too great for us? Must not we ourselves become gods simply to seem worthy of it? There has never been a greater deed; and whoever will be born after us—for the sake of this deed he will be part of a higher history than all history hitherto."

Here the madman fell silent and looked again at his listeners; and they too were silent and stared at him in astonishment. At last he threw his lantern on the ground, and it broke and went out. "I come too early," he said then; "my time has not come yet. This tremendous event is still on its way, still wandering—it has not yet reached the ears of man. Lightning and thunder require time, the light of the stars requires time, deeds require time even after they are done, before they can be seen and heard. This deed is still more distant from them than the most distant stars—*and yet they have done it themselves*."

It has been related further that on that same day the madman entered divers churches and there sang his *requiem aeternam deo*. Led out and called to account, he is said to have replied each time, "What are these churches now if they are not the tombs and sepulchers of God?"

[250]

Guilt. Although the most acute judges of the witches, and even the witches themselves, were convinced of the guilt of witchery, the guilt nevertheless was non-existent. It is thus with all guilt.

[283]

Preparatory men. I welcome all signs that a more manly, a warlike, age is about to begin, an age which, above all, will give honor to valor once again. For this age shall prepare the way for one yet higher, and it shall gather the strength which this higher age will need one day—this age which is to carry heroism into the pursuit of knowledge and *wage wars* for the sake of thoughts and their consequences. To this end we now need many preparatory valorous men who cannot leap into being out of nothing—any more than out of the sand and slime of our present civilization and metropolitanism: men who are bent on seeking for that aspect in all things which must be *overcome*; men characterized by cheerfulness, patience, unpretentiousness, and contempt for all great vanities, as well as by magnanimity in victory and forbearance regarding the small vanities of the vanquished; men possessed of keen and free judgment concerning all victors and the share of chance in every victory and every fame; men who have their own festivals, their own weekdays, their own periods of mourning, who are accustomed to command with assurance and are no less ready to obey when necessary, in both cases equally proud and serving their own cause; men who are in greater danger, more fruitful, and happier! For, believe me, the secret of the greatest fruitfulness and the greatest enjoyment of existence is: to *live dangerously!* Build your cities under Vesuvius! Send your ships into uncharted seas! Live at war with your peers and yourselves! Be robbers and conquerors, as long as you cannot be rulers and owners, you lovers of knowledge! Soon the age will be past when you could be satisfied to live like shy deer, hidden in the woods! At long last the pursuit of knowledge will reach out for its due: it will want to *rule* and *own*, and you with it!

[285]

Excelsior! "You will never pray again, never adore again, never again rest in endless trust; you deny yourself any stopping before ultimate wisdom, ultimate goodness, ultimate power, while unharnessing your thoughts; you have no perpetual guardian and friend for your seven solitudes; you live without a view of mountains with snow on their peaks and fire in their hearts; there is no avenger for you, no eventual improver; there is no reason any more in what happens, no love in what will happen to you; no resting place is any longer open to your heart, where it has only to find and no longer to seek; you resist any ultimate peace, you want the eternal recurrence of war and peace. Man of renunciation, do you want to renounce all this? Who will give you the necessary strength? Nobody yet has had this strength." There is a lake which one day refused to flow off and erected a dam where it had hitherto flowed off: ever since, this lake has been rising higher and higher. Perhaps that very renunciation will also lend us the strength to bear the renunciation itself; perhaps man will rise ever higher when he once ceases to *flow out* into a god.

TWILIGHT OF THE IDOLS
■

THE FOUR GREAT ERRORS

8

What alone can be *our* doctrine? That no one *gives* man his qualities—neither God, nor society, nor his parents and ancestors, nor he himself. (The nonsense of the last idea was taught as "intelligible freedom" by Kant—perhaps by Plato already.) No one is responsible for man's being there at all, for his being such-and-such, or for his being in these circumstances or in this environment. The fatality of his essence is not to be disentangled from the fatality of all that has been and will be. Man is not the effect of some special purpose, of a will, and end; nor is he the object of an attempt to attain an "ideal of humanity" or an "ideal of happiness" or an "ideal of morality." It is absurd to wish to devolve one's essence on some end or other. We have invented the concept of "end": in reality there is no end.

One is necessary, one is a piece of fatefulness, one belongs to the whole, one is in the whole; there is nothing which could judge, measure, compare, or sentence our being, for that would mean judging, measuring, comparing, or sentencing the whole. But there is nothing besides the whole. That nobody is held responsible any longer, that the mode of being may not be traced back to a *causa prima*, that the world does not form a unity either as a sensorium or as "spirit"—that alone is the great liberation; with this alone is the innocence of becoming restored. The concept of "God" was until now the greatest objection to existence. We deny God, we deny the responsibility in God: only thereby do we redeem the world.

The Early Twentieth Century

Sigmund Freud, "The Relation of the Poet to Day-Dreaming"

The founder of psychoanalysis, Sigmund Freud (1856–1939) revolutionized Western civilization's concept of the self. The first to recognize fully that the unconscious mind influences waking behavior, Freud explored the content of dreams, infantile memories, obsessions, and anxieties to formulate a comprehensive theory of human psychology. Freudian theory assumes we are primarily sexual beings motivated by sexual energy. When repressed by social inhibitions, thwarted sexuality produces neuroses, such as the Oedipus complex in which the young male subconsciously wishes to eliminate his chief rival, the father, and possess the mother, source of nurturing and pleasure. Freud's argument that even young children experience strong sexual feelings, highly controversial at the time, is now widely accepted.

Freud's major works reveal a steady growth of his thought, beginning with *The Interpretation of Dreams* (1900) and including *Totem and Taboo* (1918), *Beyond the Pleasure Principle* (1922), and *Civilization and Its Discontents* (1930). Applying his theories of individual psychology to the behavior of societies and nations, Freud recognized that the desire to impose one's will on others, of which the sexual instinct is one manifestation, may drive states to war. Humanity must choose between the conflicting demands of Eros, the impulse to create, and Thanatos, the death wish that threatened to destroy Western civilization in two World Wars. Forced to flee his native Vienna after Nazi Germany occupied Austria in 1938, Freud, a Jew, died in exile in London.

Because repressed sexual energy also fuels the creative imagination, it serves to produce works of art, philosophy, and literature. In an early essay, "The Relation of the Poet to Day-Dreaming," Freud examines how the artist uses fantasies from unsatisfied wishes to create his work.

THE RELATION OF THE POET TO DAY-DREAMING[1]

We laymen have always wondered greatly—like the cardinal who put the question to Ariosto—how that strange being, the poet, comes by his material. What makes him able to carry us with him in such a way and to arouse emotions in us of which we thought ourselves perhaps not even capable? Our interest in the problem is only stimulated by the circumstance that if we ask poets themselves they give us no explanation of the matter, or at least no satisfactory explanation. The knowledge that not even the clearest insight into the factors conditioning the choice of imaginative material, or into the nature of the ability to fashion that material, will ever make writers of us does not in any way detract from our interest.

---

1. First published in *Neue Revue*, 1., 1908; reprinted in *Sammlung*, Zweite Folge. [Translated by I.F. Grant Duff.]

If we could only find some activity in ourselves, or in people like ourselves, which was in any way akin to the writing of imaginative works! If we could do so, then examination of it would give us a hope of obtaining some insight into the creative powers of imaginative writers. And indeed, there is some prospect of achieving this—writers themselves always try to lessen the distance between their kind and ordinary human beings; they so often assure us that every man is at heart a poet, and that the last poet will not die until the last human being does.

We ought surely to look in the child for the first traces of imaginative activity. The child's best loved and most absorbing occupation is play. Perhaps we may say that every child at play behaves like an imaginative writer, in that he creates a world of his own or, more truly, he rearranges the things of his world and orders it in a new way that pleases him better. It would be incorrect to think that he does not take this world seriously; on the contrary, he takes his play very seriously and expends a great deal of emotion on it. The opposite of play is not serious occupation but—reality. Notwithstanding the large affective cathexis of his play-world, the child distinguishes it perfectly from reality; only he likes to borrow the objects and circumstances that he imagines from the tangible and visible things of the real world. It is only this linking of it to reality that still distinguishes a child's 'play' from 'day-dreaming'.

Now the writer does the same as the child at play; he creates a world of phantasy which he takes very seriously; that is, he invests it with a great deal of affect, while separating it sharply from reality. Language has preserved this relationship between children's play and poetic creation. It designates certain kinds of imaginative creation, concerned with tangible objects and capable of representation, as 'plays', the people who present them are called 'players'. The unreality of this poetical world of imagination, however, has very important consequences for literary technique; for many things which if they happened in real life could produce no pleasure can nevertheless give enjoyment in a play—many emotions which are essentially painful may become a source of enjoyment to the spectators and hearers of a poet's work.

There is another consideration relating to the contrast between reality and play on which we will dwell for a moment. Long after a child has grown up and stopped playing, after he has for decades attempted to grasp the realities of life with all seriousness, he may one day come to a state of mind in which the contrast between play and reality is again abrogated. The adult can remember with what intense seriousness he carried on his childish play; then by comparing his would-be serious occupations with his childhood's play he manages to throw off the heavy burden of life and obtain the great pleasure of humour.

As they grow up, people cease to play, and appear to give up the pleasure they derived from play. But anyone who knows anything of the mental life of human beings is aware that hardly anything is more difficult to them than to give up a pleasure they have once tasted. Really we never can relinquish anything; we only exchange one thing for something else. When we appear to give something up, all we really do is to adopt a substitute. So when the human being grows up and ceases to play he only gives up the connection with real objects; instead of playing he then begins to create phantasy. He builds castles in the air and creates what are called day-dreams. I believe that the greater number of human beings create phantasies at times as long as they live. This is a fact which has been overlooked for a long time, and its importance has therefore not been properly appreciated.

The phantasies of human beings are less easy to observe than the play of children.

Children do, it is true, play alone, or form with other children a closed world in their minds for the purposes of play; but a child does not conceal his play from adults, even though his playing is quite unconcerned with them. The adult, on the other hand, is ashamed of his daydreams and conceals them from other people; he cherishes them as his most intimate possessions and as a rule he would rather confess all his misdeeds than tell his day-dreams. For this reason he may believe that he is the only person who makes up such phantasies, without having any idea that everybody else tells themselves stories of the same kind. Day-dreaming is a continuation of play, nevertheless, and the motives which lie behind these two activities contain a very good reason for this different behaviour in the child at play and in the day-dreaming adult.

The play of children is determined by their wishes—really by the child's *one* wish, which is to be grownup, the wish that helps to 'bring him up'. He always plays at being grown-up; in play he imitates what is known to him of the lives of adults. Now he has no reason to conceal this wish. With the adult it is otherwise; on the one hand, he knows that he is expected not to play any longer or to day-dream, but to be making his way in a real world. On the other hand, some of the wishes from which his phantasies spring are such as have to be entirely hidden; therefore he is ashamed of his phantasies as being childish and as something prohibited.

If they are concealed with so much secretiveness, you will ask, how do we know so much about the human propensity to create phantasies? Now there is a certain class of human beings upon whom not a god, indeed, but a stern goddess—Necessity—has laid the task of giving an account of what they suffer and what they enjoy. These people are the neurotics; among other things they have to confess their phantasies to the physician to whom they go in the hope of recovering through mental treatment. This is our best source of knowledge, and we have later found good reason to suppose that our patients tell us about themselves nothing that we could not also hear from healthy people.

Let us try to learn some of the characteristics of day-dreaming. We can begin by saying that happy people never make phantasies, only unsatisfied ones. Unsatisfied wishes are the driving power behind phantasies; every separate phantasy contains the fulfilment of a wish, and improves on unsatisfactory reality. The impelling wishes vary according to the sex, character and circumstances of the creator; they may be easily divided, however, into two principal groups. Either they are ambitious wishes, serving to exalt the person creating them, or they are erotic. In young women erotic wishes dominate the phantasies almost exclusively, for their ambition is generally comprised in their erotic longings; in young men egoistic and ambitious wishes assert themselves plainly enough alongside their erotic desires. But we will not lay stress on the distinction between these two trends; we prefer to emphasize the fact that they are often united. In many altar-pieces the portrait of the donor is to be found in one corner of the picture; and in the greater number of ambitious day-dreams, too, we can discover a woman in some corner, for whom the dreamer performs all his heroic deeds and at whose feet all his triumphs are to be laid. Here you see we have strong enough motives for concealment; a well-brought-up woman is, indeed, credited with only a minimum of erotic desire, while a young man has to learn to suppress the overweening self-regard he acquires in the indulgent atmosphere surrounding his childhood, so that he may find his proper place in a society that is full of other persons making similar claims.

We must not imagine that the various products of this impulse towards phantasy, castles in the air or day-dreams, are stereotyped or unchangeable. On the contrary, they fit themselves into the changing impressions of life, alter with the vicissitudes of life; every deep new impression gives them what might be called a 'date-stamp'. The relation of phantasies to time is altogether of great importance. One may say that a phantasy at one and the same moment hovers between three periods of time—the three periods of our ideation. The activity of phantasy in the mind is linked up with some current impression, occasioned by some event in the present, which had the power to rouse an intense desire. From there it wanders back to the memory of an early experience, generally belonging to infancy, in which this wish was fulfilled. Then it creates for itself a situation which is to emerge in the future, representing the fulfilment of the wish—this is the day-dream or phantasy, which now carries in it traces both of the occasion which engendered it and of some past memory. So past, present and future are threaded, as it were, on the string of the wish that runs through them all.

A very ordinary example may serve to make my statement clearer. Take the case of a poor orphan lad, to whom you have given the address of some employer where he may perhaps get work. On the way there he falls into a day-dream suitable to the situation from which it springs. The content of the phantasy will be somewhat as follows: He is taken on and pleases his new employer, makes himself indispensable in the business, is taken into the family of the employer, and marries the charming daughter of the house. Then he comes to conduct the business, first as a partner, and then as successor to his father-in-law. In this way the dreamer regains what he had in his happy childhood, the protecting house, his loving parents and the first objects of his affection. You will see from such an example how the wish employs some event in the present to plan a future on the pattern of the past.

Much more could be said about phantasies, but I will only allude as briefly as possible to certain points. If phantasies become over-luxuriant and over-powerful, the necessary conditions for an outbreak of neurosis or psychosis are constituted; phantasies are also the first preliminary stage in the mind of the symptoms of illness of which our patients complain. A broad bypath here branches off into pathology.

I cannot pass over the relation of phantasies to dreams. Our nocturnal dreams are nothing but such phantasies, as we can make clear by interpreting them.[2] Language, in its unrivalled wisdom, long ago decided the question of the essential nature of dreams by giving the name of 'day-dreams' to the airy creations of phantasy. If the meaning of our dreams usually remains obscure in spite of this clue, it is because of the circumstance that at night wishes of which we are ashamed also become active in us, wishes which we have to hide from ourselves, which were consequently repressed and pushed back into the unconscious. Such repressed wishes and their derivatives can therefore achieve expression only when almost completely disguised. When scientific work had succeeded in elucidating the distortion in dreams, it was no longer difficult to recognize that nocturnal dreams are fulfilments of desires in exactly the same way as day-dreams are—those phantasies with which we are all so familiar.

So much for day-dreaming; now for the poet! Shall we dare really to compare an imaginative writer with 'one who dreams in broad daylight', and his creations with day-dreams? Here, surely, a first distinction is forced upon us; we must distinguish between poets who, like the

---

2. Cf. Freud, *The Interpretation of Dreams*.

bygone creators of epics and tragedies, take over their material ready-made, and those who seem to create their material spontaneously. Let us keep to the latter, and let us also not choose for our comparison those writers who are most highly esteemed by critics. We will choose the less pretentious writers of romances, novels and stories, who are read all the same by the widest circles of men and women. There is one very marked characteristic in the productions of these writers which must strike us all: they all have a hero who is the centre of interest, for whom the author tries to win our sympathy by every possible means, and whom he places under the protection of a special providence. If at the end of one chapter the hero is left unconscious and bleeding from severe wounds, I am sure to find him at the beginning of the next being carefully tended and on the way to recovery; if the first volume ends in the hero being shipwrecked in a storm at sea, I am certain to hear at the beginning of the next of his hairbreadth escape—otherwise, indeed, the story could not continue. The feeling of security with which I follow the hero through his dangerous adventures is the same as that with which a real hero throws himself into the water to save a drowning man, or exposes himself to the fire of the enemy while storming a battery. It is this very feeling of being a hero which one of our best authors has well expressed in the famous phrase, '*Es kann dir nix g'schehen!*'[3] It seems to me, however, that this significant mark of invulnerability very clearly betrays—His Majesty the Ego, the hero of all day-dreams and all novels.

The same relationship is hinted at in yet other characteristics of these egocentric stories. When all the women in a novel invariably fall in love with the hero, this can hardly be looked upon as a description of reality, but it is easily understood as an essential constituent of a day-dream. The same thing holds good when the other people in the story are sharply divided into good and bad, with complete disregard of the manifold variety in the traits of real human beings; the 'good' ones are those who help the ego in its character of hero, while the 'bad' are his enemies and rivals.

We do not in any way fail to recognize that many imaginative productions have travelled far from the original naive day-dream, but I cannot suppress the surmise that even the most extreme variations could be brought into relationship with this model by an uninterrupted series of transitions. It has struck me in many so-called psychological novels, too, that only one person—once again the hero—is described from within; the author dwells in his soul and looks upon the other people from outside. The psychological novel in general probably owes its peculiarities to the tendency of modern writers to split up their ego by self-observation into many component-egos, and in this way to personify the conflicting trends in their own mental life in many heroes. There are certain novels, which might be called 'excentric', that seem to stand in marked contradiction to the typical day-dream; in these the person introduced as the hero plays the least active part of anyone, and seems instead to let the actions and sufferings of other people pass him by like a spectator. Many of the later novels of Zola belong to this class. But I must say that the psychological analysis of people who are not writers, and who deviate in many things from the so-called norm, has shown us analogous variations in their day-dreams in which the ego contents itself with the role of spectator.

If our comparison of the imaginative writer with the day-dreamer, and of poetic production with the day-dream, is to be of any value, it must show itself fruitful in some way or other.

---

3. Anzengruber. [The phrase means 'Nothing can happen to me!'—Trans.]

Let us try, for instance, to examine the works of writers in reference to the idea propounded above, the relation of the phantasy to the wish that runs through it and to the three periods of time; and with its help let us study the connection between the life of the writer and his productions. Hitherto it has not been known what preliminary ideas would constitute an approach to this problem; very often this relation has been regarded as much simpler than it is; but the insight gained from phantasies leads us to expect the following state of things. Some actual experience which made a strong impression on the writer had stirred up a memory of an earlier experience, generally belonging to childhood, which then arouses a wish that finds a fulfilment in the work in question, and in which elements of the recent event and the old memory should be discernible.

Do not be alarmed at the complexity of this formula; I myself expect that in reality it will prove itself to be too schematic, but that possibly it may contain a first means of approach to the true state of affairs. From some attempts I have made I think that this way of approaching works of the imagination might not be unfruitful. You will not forget that the stress laid on the writer's memories of his childhood, which perhaps seems so strange, is ultimately derived from the hypothesis that imaginative creation, like day-dreaming, is a continuation of and substitute for the play of childhood.

We will not neglect to refer also to that class of imaginative work which must be recognized not as spontaneous production, but as a re-fashioning of ready-made material. Here, too, the writer retains a certain amount of independence, which can express itself in the choice of material and in changes in the material chosen, which are often considerable. As far as it goes, this material is derived from the racial treasure-house of myths, legends and fairy-tales. The study of these creations of racial psychology is in no way complete, but it seems extremely probable that myths, for example, are distorted vestiges of the wish-phantasies of whole nations—the age-long dreams of young humanity.

You will say that, although writers came first in the title of this paper, I have told you far less about them than about phantasy. I am aware of that, and will try to excuse myself by pointing to the present state of our knowledge. I could only throw out suggestions and bring up interesting points which arise from the study of phantasies, and which pass beyond them to the problem of the choice of literary material. We have not touched on the other problem at all, i.e. what are the means which writers use to achieve those emotional reactions in us that are roused by their productions. But I would at least point out to you the path which leads from our discussion of day-dreams to the problems of the effect produced on us by imaginative works.

You will remember that we said the day-dreamer hid his phantasies carefully from other people because he had reason to be ashamed of them. I may now add that even if he were to communicate them to us, he would give us no pleasure by his disclosures. When we hear such phantasies they repel us, or at least leave us cold. But when a man of literary talent presents his plays, or relates what we take to be his personal day-dreams, we experience great pleasure arising probably from many sources. How the writer accomplishes this is his innermost secret, the essential *ars poetica* lies in the technique by which our feeling of repulsion is overcome, and this has certainly to do with those barriers erected between every individual being and all others. We can guess at two methods used in this technique. The writer softens the egotistical character of the day-dream by changes and disguises, and he bribes us by the offer of a purely formal, that is aesthetic, pleasure in the presentation of his phantasies. The increment of pleasure which is offered us in order to release yet greater pleasure arising from deeper sources in the mind is called an 'incitement premium' or technically, 'fore-pleasure'. I am of opinion that all the aesthetic pleasure we gain from the works of imaginative writers is of the same type as this 'fore-pleasure', and that the true enjoyment of literature proceeds from the release of tensions in our minds. Perhaps much that brings about this result consists in the writer's putting us into a position in which we can enjoy our own day-dreams without reproach or shame. Here we reach a path leading into novel, interesting and complicated researches, but we also, at least for the present, arrive at the end of the present discussion.

Franz Kafka, A Hunger Artist

Franz Kafka (1883–1924) belongs to a small but illustrious group of early twentieth-century writers—including Virginia Woolf, Marcel Proust, and James Joyce—whose experiments with literary form have profoundly altered the way we write and think about prose fiction. Kafka's dreamlike narratives, which literary historians have often likened to surrealist paintings in their deceptive transparency of style and effortless juxtaposition of the familiar and the absurd, thrust the reader into a fictive universe that is at once clearly defined and hopelessly irrational. In Kafka's world, a young man can awaken one morning to find himself transformed into a hideous insect or unjustly accused of some indescribable crime, or as in *A Hunger Artist* (1922), we can find ourselves in a society where "artists" are treated like caged animals and where suicidal fasting has become a spectator sport. In each of these tales, fantasy blends easily with realism. The deepest human fears suddenly intrude into an ostensibly waking existence, and nightmare experiences take on the coloration of everyday life.

Kafka's fiction draws on many of the same perceptions and cultural anxieties that lie at the center of the Freudian system of psychoanalysis: that is, a fundamental disbelief in the triumph of rationality, either at the personal or at the collective level, coupled with an almost obsessive awareness of the role guilt and repressed sexuality play in the development of the individual personality. Many of Kafka's protagonists express, or even act out, a need for self-punishment, which, in the most violent and fantastic stories, takes the form of imagined self-annihilation.

A HUNGER ARTIST

During these last decades the interest in professional fasting has markedly diminished. It used to pay very well to stage such great performances under one's own management, but today that is quite impossible. We live in a different world now. At one time the whole town took a lively interest in the hunger artist; from day to day of his fast the excitement mounted; everybody wanted to see him at least once a day; there were people who bought season tickets for the last few days and sat from morning till night in front of his small barred cage; even in the nighttime there were visiting hours, when the whole effect was heightened by torch flares; on fine days the cage was set out in the open air, and then it was the children's special treat to see the hunger artist; for their elders he was often just a joke that happened to be in fashion, but the children stood open-mouthed, holding each other's hands for greater security, marvelling at him as he sat there pallid in black tights, with his ribs sticking out so prominently, not even on a seat but down among straw on the ground, sometimes giving a courteous nod, answering questions with a constrained smile, or perhaps stretching an arm through the bars so that one might feel how thin it was, and then again withdrawing deep into himself, paying no attention to anyone or anything, not even to the all-important striking of the clock that was the only piece of furniture in his cage, but merely staring into vacancy with half-shut eyes, now and then taking a sip from a tiny glass of water to moisten his lips.

Besides casual onlookers there were also relays of permanent watchers selected by the public, usually butchers, strangely enough, and it was their task to watch the hunger artist day and night, three of them at a time, in case he should have some secret recourse to nourishment. This was nothing but a formality, instituted to reassure the masses, for the initiates knew well enough that during his fast the artist would never in any circumstances, not even under forcible compulsion, swallow the smallest morsel of food; the honor of his profession forbade it. Not every watcher, of course, was capable of understanding this, there were often groups of night watchers who were very lax in carrying out their duties and deliberately huddled together in a retired corner to play cards with great absorption, obviously intending to give the hunger artist the chance of a little refreshment, which they supposed he could draw from some private hoard. Nothing annoyed the artist more than such watchers; they made him miserable; they made his fast seem unendurable; sometimes he mastered his feebleness sufficiently to sing during their watch for as long as he could keep going, to show them how unjust their suspicions were. But that was of little use; they only wondered at his cleverness in being able to fill his mouth even while singing. Much more to his taste were the watchers who sat close up to the bars, who were not content with the dim night lighting of the hall but focused him in the full glare of the electric pocket torch given them by the impresario. The harsh light did not trouble him at all. In any case he could never sleep properly, and he could always drowse a little, whatever the light, at any hour, even when the hall was thronged with noisy onlookers. He was quite happy at the prospect of spending a sleepless night with such watchers; he was ready to exchange jokes with them, to tell them stories out of his nomadic life, anything at all to keep them awake and demonstrate to them again that he had no eatables in his cage and that he was fasting as not one of them could fast. But his happiest moment was when the morning came and an enormous breakfast was brought them, at his expense, on which they flung themselves with the keen appetite of healthy men after a weary night of wakefulness. Of course there were people who argued that this breakfast was an unfair attempt to bribe the watchers, but that was going rather too far, and when they were invited to take on a night's vigil without a breakfast, merely for the sake of the cause, they made themselves scarce, although they stuck stubbornly to their suspicions.

Such suspicions, anyhow, were a necessary accompaniment to the profession of fasting. No one could possibly watch the hunger artist continuously, day and night, and so no one could produce first-hand evidence that the fast had really been rigorous and continuous; only the artist himself could know that; he was therefore bound to be the sole completely satisfied spectator of his own fast. Yet for other reasons he was never satisfied; it was not perhaps mere fasting that had brought him to such skeleton thinness that many people had regretfully to keep away from his exhibitions, because the sight of him was too much for them, perhaps it was dissatisfaction with himself that had worn him down. For he alone knew, what no other initiate knew, how easy it was to fast. It was the easiest thing in the world. He made no secret of this, yet people did not believe him; at the best they set him down as modest, most of them, however, thought that he was out for publicity or else was some kind of cheat who found it easy to fast because he had discovered a way of making it easy, and then had the impudence to admit the fact, more or less. He had to put up with all that, and in the course of time had got used to it, but his inner dissatisfaction always rankled, and never yet, after any term of fasting—this must be granted to his credit—had he left the cage of his own free will. The longest period was fixed by his impresario at forty days, beyond that term he was not allowed to go, not even in great cities, and there was good reason for it, too. Experience had proved that for about forty days the interest of the public could be stimulated by a steadily increasing pressure of advertisement, but after that the town began to lose interest, sympathetic support began notably to fall off; there were of course local variations as between one town and another or one country and another, but as a general rule forty days marked the limit. So on the fortieth day the flower-bedecked cage was opened, enthusiastic spectators filled the hall, a military band played, two doctors entered the cage to measure the results of the fast, which were announced through a megaphone, and finally two young ladies appeared, blissful at having been selected for the honor, to help the hunger artist down the few steps leading to a small table on which was spread a carefully chosen invalid repast. And at this very moment the artist always turned stubborn. True, he would entrust his bony arms to the outstretched helping hands of the ladies bending over him, but stand up he would not. Why stop fasting at this particular moment, after forty days of it? He had held out for a long time, an illimitably long time; why stop now, when he was in his best fasting form? Why should he be cheated of the fame he would get for fasting longer, for being not only the record hunger artist of all time, which presumably he was already, but for beating his own record by a performance beyond human imagination, since he felt that there were no limits to his capacity for fasting? His public pretended to admire him so much, why should it have so little patience with him; if he could endure fasting longer, why shouldn't the public endure it? Besides, he was tired, he was comfortable sitting in the straw, and now he was supposed to lift himself to his full height and go down to a meal the very thought of which gave him nausea that only the presence of the ladies kept him from betraying, and even that with an effort. And he looked up into the eyes of the ladies who were apparently so friendly and in reality so cruel, and shook his head, which felt too heavy on its strengthless neck. But then there happened yet again what always happened. The impresario came forward, without a word—for the band made speech impossible—lifted his arms in the air above the artist, as if inviting Heaven to look down upon its creature here in the straw, this suffering martyr, which indeed he was, although in quite another sense; grasped him round the emaciated waist, with exaggerated caution, so that the frail condition he was in might be appreciated; and committed him to the care of the blenching ladies, not without secretly giving him a shaking so that his legs and body tottered and swayed. The artist now submitted completely; his head lolled on his breast as if it had landed there by chance; his body was hollowed out; his legs in a spasm of self-preservation clung close to each other at the knees, yet scrapped on the ground as if it were not really solid ground; and the whole weight of his body, a featherweight after all, relapsed onto one of the ladies who, looking round for help and panting a little—the post of honor was not at all what she had expected it to be—first stretched her neck as far as she could to keep her face at least free from contact with the artist, then finding this impossible, and her more fortunate companion not coming to her aid but merely holding extended on her own trembling hand the little bunch of knucklebones that was the artist's, to the great delight of the spectators burst into tears and had to be replaced by an attendant who had long been stationed in readiness. Then came the food, a little of which the impresario managed to get between the artist's lips, while he sat in a kind of half-fainting trance, to the accompaniment of cheerful patter designed to distract the public's attention from the artist's condition; after that, a toast was drunk to the public, supposedly prompted by a whisper from the artist in the impresario's ear; the band confirmed it with a mighty flourish, the spectators melted away, and no one had any cause to be dissatisfied with the proceedings, no one except the hunger artist himself, he only, as always.

So he lived for many years, with small regular intervals of recuperation, in visible glory, honored by the world, yet in spite of that troubled in spirit, and all the more troubled because no one would take his trouble seriously. What comfort could he possibly need? What more could he possibly wish for? And if some good-natured person, feeling sorry for him, tried to console him by pointing out that his melancholy was probably caused by fasting, it could happen, especially when he had been fasting for some time, that he reacted with an outburst of fury and to the general alarm began to shake the bars of his cage like a wild animal. Yet the impresario had a way of punishing these outbreaks which he rather enjoyed putting into operation. He would apologize publicly for the artist's behavior, which was only to be excused, he admitted, because of the irritability caused by fasting; a condition hardly to be understood by well-fed people; then by natural transition he went on to mention the artist's equally incomprehensible boast that he could fast for much longer than he was doing; he praised the high ambition, the good will, the great self-denial undoubtedly implicit in such a statement; and then quite simply countered it by bringing out photographs, which were also on sale to the public, showing the artist on the fortieth day of a fast lying in bed almost dead from exhaustion. This perversion of the truth, familiar to the artist though it was, always unnerved him afresh and proved too much for him. What was a consequence of the premature ending of his fast was here presented as the cause of it! To fight against this lack of understanding, against a whole world of nonunderstanding, was impossible. Time and again in good faith he stood by the bars listening to the impresario, but as soon as the photographs appeared he always let go and sank with a groan back on to his straw, and the reassured public could once more come close and gaze at him.

A few years later when the witnesses of such scenes called them to mind, they often failed to understand themselves at all. For meanwhile the aforementioned change in public interest had set in; it seemed to happen almost overnight; there may have been profound causes for it, but who was going to bother about that; at any rate the pampered hunger artist suddenly found himself deserted one fine day by the amusement seekers, who went streaming past him to other more favored attractions. For the last time the impresario hurried him over half Europe to discover whether the old interest might still survive here and there; all in vain; everywhere, as if by secret agreement, a positive revulsion from professional fasting was in evidence. Of course it could not really have sprung up so suddenly as all that, and many premonitory symptoms which had not been sufficiently remarked or suppressed during the rush and glitter of success now came retrospectively to mind, but it was now too late to take any countermeasures. Fasting would surely come into fashion again at some future date, yet that was no comfort for those living in the present. What, then, was the hunger artist to do? He had been applauded by thousands in his time and could hardly come down to showing himself in a street booth at village fairs, and as for adopting another profession, he was not only too old for that but too fanatically devoted to fasting. So he took leave of the impresario, his partner in an unparalleled career, and hired himself to a large circus; in order to spare his own feelings he avoided reading the conditions of his contract.

A large circus with its enormous traffic in replacing and recruiting men, animals and apparatus can always find a use for people at any time, even for a hunger artist, provided of course that he does not ask too much, and in this particular case anyhow it was not only the artist who was taken on but his famous and long-known name as well; indeed considering the peculiar nature of his performance, which was not impaired by advancing age, it could not be objected that here was an artist past his prime, no longer at the height of his professional skill, seeking a refuge in some quiet corner of a circus; on the contrary, the hunger artist averred that he could fast as well as ever, which was entirely credible; he even alleged that if he were allowed to fast as he liked, and this was at once promised him without more ado, he could astound the world by establishing a record never yet achieved, a statement which certainly provoked a smile among the other professionals, since it left out of account the change in public opinion, which the hunger artist in his zeal conveniently forgot.

He had not, however, actually lost his sense of the real situation and took it as a matter of course that he and his cage should be stationed, not in the middle of the ring as a main attraction, but outside, near the animal cages, on a site that was after all easily accessible. Large and gaily painted placards made a frame for the cage and announced what was to be seen inside it. When the public came thronging out in the intervals to see the animals, they could hardly avoid passing the hunger artist's cage and stopping there for a moment, perhaps they might even have stayed longer had not those pressing behind them in the narrow gangway, who did not understand why they should be held up on their way towards the excitements of the menagerie, made it impossible for anyone to stand gazing quietly for any length of time. And that was the reason why the hunger artist, who had of course been looking forward to these visiting hours as the main achievement of his life, began instead to shrink from them. At first he could hardly wait for the intervals; it was exhilarating to watch the crowds come streaming his way, until only too soon—not even the most obstinate self-deception, clung to almost consciously, could hold out against the fact—the conviction was borne in upon him that these people, most of them, to judge from their actions, again and again, without exception, were all on their way to the menagerie. And the first sight of them from the distance remained the best. For when they reached his cage he was at once deafened by the storm of shouting and abuse that arose from the two contending factions, which renewed themselves continuously, of those who wanted to stop and stare at him—he soon began to dislike them more than the others—not out of real interest but only out of obstinate self-assertiveness, and those who wanted to go straight on to the animals. When the first great rush was past, the stragglers came along, and these, whom nothing could have prevented from stopping to look at him as long as they had breath, raced past with long strides, hardly even glancing at him, in their haste to get to the menagerie in time. And all too rarely did it happen that he had a stroke of luck, when some father of a family fetched up before him with his children, pointed a finger at the hunger artist and explained at length what the phenomenon meant, telling stories of earlier years when he himself had watched similar but much more thrilling performances, and the children, still rather uncomprehending, since neither inside nor outside school had they been sufficiently prepared for this lesson—what did they care about fasting?—yet showed by the brightness of their intent eyes that new and better times might be coming. Perhaps said the hunger artist to himself many a time, things would be a little better if his cage were set not quite so near the menagerie. That made it too easy for people to make their choice, to say nothing of what he suffered from the stench of the menagerie, the animals' restlessness by night, the carrying past of raw lumps of flesh for the beasts of prey, the roaring at feeding times, which depressed him continually. But he did not dare to lodge a complaint with the management; after all, he had the animals to thank for the troops of people who passed his cage, among whom there might always be one here and there to take an interest in him, and who could tell where they might seclude him if he called attention to his existence and thereby to the fact that, strictly speaking, he was only an impediment on the way to the menagerie.

A small impediment, to be sure, one that grew steadily less. People grew familiar with the strange idea that they could be expected, in times like these, to take an interest in a hunger artist, and with this familiarity the verdict went out against him. He might fast as much as he could, and he did so; but nothing could save him now, people passed him by. Just try to explain to anyone the art of fasting! Anyone who has no feeling for it cannot be made to understand it. The fine placards grew dirty and illegible, they were torn down; the little notice board telling the number of fast days achieved, which at first was changed carefully every day, had long stayed at the same figure, for after the first few weeks even this small task seemed pointless to the staff; and so the artist simply fasted on and on, as he had once dreamed of doing, and it was no trouble to him, just as he had always foretold, but no one counted the days, no one, not even the artist himself, knew what records he was already breaking, and his heart grew heavy. And when once in a time some leisurely passer-by stopped, made merry over the old figure on the board and spoke of swindling, that was in its way the stupidest lie ever invented by indifference and inborn malice, since it was not the hunger artist who was cheating; he was working honestly, but the world was cheating him of his reward.

Many more days went by, however, and that too came to an end. An overseer's eye fell on the cage one day and he asked the attendants why this perfectly good stage should be left standing there unused with dirty straw inside it; nobody knew, until one man, helped out by the notice board, remembered about the hunger artist. They poked into the straw with sticks and found him in it. "Are you still fasting?" asked the overseer. "When on earth do you mean to stop?" "Forgive me, everybody," whispered the hunger artist; only the overseer, who had his ear to the bars, understood him. "Of course," said the overseer, and tapped his forehead with a finger to let the attendants know what state the man was in, "we forgive you." "I always wanted you to admire my fasting," said the hunger artist. "We do admire it," said the overseer, affably. "But you shouldn't admire it," said the hunger artist. "Well, then we don't admire it," said the overseer, "but why shouldn't we admire it?" "Because I have to fast, I can't help it," said the hunger artist. "What a fellow you are," said the overseer, "and why can't you help it?" "Because," said the hunger artist, lifting his head a little and speaking, with his lips pursed, as if for a kiss, right into the overseer's ear, so that no syllable might be lost, "because I couldn't find the food I liked. If I had found it, believe me, I should have made no fuss and stuffed myself like you or anyone else." These were his last words, but in his dimming eyes remained the firm though no longer proud persuasion that he was still continuing to fast.

"Well, clear this out now!" said the overseer, and they buried the hunger artist, straw and all. Into the cage they put a young panther. Even the most insensitive felt it refreshing to see this wild creature leaping around the cage that had so long been dreary. The panther was all right. The food he liked was brought him without hesitation by the attendants; he seemed not even to miss his freedom; his noble body, furnished almost to the bursting point with all that it needed, seemed to carry freedom around with it too; somewhere in his jaws it seemed to lurk; and the joy of life streamed with such ardent passion from his throat that for the onlookers it was not easy to stand the shock of it. But they braced themselves, crowded round the cage, and did not want ever to move away.

T. S. Eliot, "Sweeney Among the Nightingales," "The Hollow Men"

For many literary historians, the Modernist Movement in English poetry begins with T. S. Eliot (1888–1965). Eliot's poetic style—at least through 1935—with its pervasive and often bitter ironies, its intricate, allusive, and even elliptical metaphors, marks a decisive break with the lingering Romanticism of the late nineteenth century. But even more conspicuously Modernist is the philosophical perspective of his work, reflecting both personal anguish and intellectual disillusionment with Western civilization. In *The Waste Land* (1922), one of the longest and most ambitious poems of this era, Eliot constructs a quasi-allegory of spiritual exhaustion, loosely based on the myth of the Grail, through which he articulates his vision of the collapse of religious culture in the West and the desecration of its most sacred and potent symbols.

Sweeney of "Sweeney Among the Nightingales" (1918) (and two other poems bearing his name, "Sweeney Erect," and "Sweeney Agonistes") is Eliot's comic–grotesque image of everyman. Endowed with purely biological needs and drives, Sweeney's animality confirms the post-Darwinian thesis that mankind, divorced from God and deprived of any transcendent faith, is brutish and absurd. "The Hollow Men" (1925) carries Eliot's anatomy of the human condition one step further by projecting the reader into an underworld ("death's other kingdom") that is not unlike Dante's *Inferno:* a place of dead eyes, paralysis, and empty gestures. Yet, for all the nightmare horror this poem expresses, it retains a memory of the "multifoliate rose," a Dantean image of a divine splendor that has now become unattainable. For Eliot, who was on the threshold of religious conversion at this point in his life, the recovery of faith in the face of cultural breakdown and personal despair became part of the mystery of human experience which he labored to express in this poem. Despite the apocalyptic nihilism with which the poem ends, we can still hear echoes of a fragmented prayer Eliot's wasteland figures struggle to intone.

SWEENEY AMONG THE NIGHTINGALES

∎

Apeneck Sweeney spreads his knees
Letting his arms hang down to laugh,
The zebra stripes along his jaw
Swelling to maculate giraffe.

     The circles of the stormy moon
Slide westward toward the River Plate,
Death and the Raven drift above
And Sweeney guards the hornèd gate.

∎

Gloomy Orion and the Dog
Are veiled; and hushed the shrunken seas;
The person in the Spanish cape
Tries to sit on Sweeney's knees

Slips and pulls the table cloth
Overturns a coffee-cup,
Reorganized upon the floor
She yawns and draws a stocking up;

The silent man in mocha brown
Sprawls at the window-sill and gapes;
The waiter brings in oranges
Bananas figs and hothouse grapes;

The silent vertebrate in brown
Contracts and concentrates, withdraws;
Rachel *née* Rabinovitch
Tears at the grapes with murderous paws;

She and the lady in the cape
Are suspect, thought to be in league;
Therefore the man with heavy eyes
Declines the gambit, shows fatigue,

Leaves the room and reappears
Outside the window, leaning in,
Branches of wistaria
Circumscribe a golden grin;

The host with someone indistinct
Converses at the door apart,
The nightingales are singing near
The Convent of the Sacred Heart,

And sang within the bloody wood
When Agamemnon cried aloud,
And let their liquid siftings fall
To stain the stiff dishonoured shroud.

THE HOLLOW MEN

■

MISTAH KURTZ—HE DEAD.

A PENNY FOR THE OLD GUY.

I

We are the hollow men
We are the stuffed men
Leaning together
Headpiece filled with straw. Alas!
Our dried voices, when
We whisper together
Are quiet and meaningless
As wind in dry grass
Or rats' feet over broken glass
In our dry cellar

      Shape without form, shade without colour,
Paralysed force, gesture without motion;

      Those who have crossed
With direct eyes, to death's other Kingdom
Remember us—if at all—not as lost
Violent souls, but only
As the hollow men
The stuffed men.

II

Eyes I dare not meet in dreams
In death's dream kingdom
These do not appear:
There, the eyes are
Sunlight on a broken column
There, is a tree swinging
And voices are
In the wind's singing
More distant and more solemn
Than a fading star.

      Let me be no nearer
In death's dream kingdom
Let me also wear
Such deliberate disguises
Rat's coat, crowskin, crossed staves
In a field

Behaving as the wind behaves
No nearer—

    Not that final meeting
In the twilight kingdom

III

This is the dead land
This is cactus land
Here the stone images
Are raised, here they receive
The supplication of a dead man's hand
Under the twinkle of a fading star.

    Is it like this
In death's other kingdom
Waking alone
At the hour when we are
Trembling with tenderness
Lips that would kiss
Form prayers to broken stone.

IV

The eyes are not here
There are no eyes here
In this valley of dying stars
In this hollow valley
This broken jaw of our lost kingdoms

    In this last of meeting places
We grope together
And avoid speech
Gathered on this beach of the tumid river

    Sightless, unless
The eyes reappear
As the perpetual star
Multifoliate rose
Of death's twilight kingdom
The hope only
Of empty men.

V

Here we go round the prickly pear
Prickly pear prickly pear
Here we go round the prickly pear
At five o'clock in the morning.

       Between the idea
And the reality
Between the motion
And the act
Falls the Shadow

                                      For Thine is the Kingdom

       Between the conception
And the creation
Between the emotion
And the response
Falls the Shadow

                                      Life is very long

       Between the desire
And the spasm
Between the potency
And the existence
Between the essence
And the descent
Falls the Shadow

                                      For Thine is the Kingdom

       For Thine is
Life is
For Thine is the

       This is the way the world ends
This is the way the world ends
This is the way the world ends
Not with a bang but a whimper.

Jean-Paul Sartre, "Existentialism"

No literary figure of the post-war period has enjoyed greater prominence, or political notoriety, than Jean-Paul Sartre (1905–1980). Sartre's novels, plays, biographies, critical essays, and especially his philosophical writings, brought some of the more provocative concepts of existentialism before a wide audience. Like Voltaire, Sartre saw himself as much more than a man of letters; he saw his work as a vehicle for social advocacy, as a form of intellectual protest against what he called "bad faith"—that self-deceptive and complacent habit of judgment that sustains all systems of privilege and ideologies of oppression.

Sartrean existentialism begins where Nietzsche left off, with the "death" of God and the disappearance of all absolute and universal values. Sartre insisted that he was one of the few contemporary philosophers to recognize the critical importance of the decline of religious faith in the West. For Sartre, the absence of a Creator eliminated any general concept of "human nature," as well as the invalidation of any a priori value earlier philosophers presumed to be self-evidently true and common to all human cultures. "Existence," Sartre insisted, precedes "essence"—we exist in the world before, and independently of, any notion of moral goodness that we may choose to embrace or reject. Though we cannot help choosing one value or another—we are, Sartre reminds us, "condemned to be free"—the choices we make and the acts we commit are not the result of providence, or fate, or any determining force external to the individual will. We define ourselves, we create our "essence," in complete freedom, and we do so in a state of anxiety and forlornness as we confront both the absence of all moral certitude and the certainty of death.

However, neither anguish nor incertitude precludes the possibility of human solidarity or of social justice. Every act, Sartre argued, is an "exemplary" act, deriving its justification and meaning from a specific historical situation to which we are all responsible. Neither God (whose existence Sartre rejected) nor history can absolve the individual moral agent of the burden of choosing for oneself and for all humanity.

EXISTENTIALISM

■

When we conceive God as the Creator, He is generally thought of as a superior sort of artisan. Whatever doctrine we may be considering, whether one like that of Descartes or that of Leibnitz, we always grant that will more or less follows understanding or, at the very least, accompanies it, and that when God creates He knows exactly what He is creating. Thus, the concept of man in the mind of God is comparable to the concept of paper-cutter in the mind of the manufacturer, and, following certain techniques and a conception, God produces man, just as the artisan, following a definition and a technique, makes a paper-cutter. Thus, the individual man is the realization of a certain concept in the divine intelligence. . . .

Atheistic existentialism, which I represent, is more coherent. It states that if God does not exist, there is at least one being in whom existence precedes essence, a being who exists before he can be defined by any concept, and that this being is man, or, as Heidegger says human reality. What is meant here by saying that existence precedes essence? It means that first of all, man exists, turns up, appears on the scene, and, only afterwards defines himself. If man, as the existentialist conceives him, is indefinable, it is because at first he is nothing. Only afterward will he be something, and he himself will have made what he will be. Thus, there is no human nature, since there is no God to conceive it. Not only is man what he conceives himself to be, but he is also only what he wills himself to be after this thrust toward existence.

Man is nothing else but what he makes of himself. Such is the first principle of existentialism. It is also what is called subjectivity, the name we are labeled with when charges are brought against us. But what do we mean by this, if not that man has a greater dignity than a stone or table? For we mean that man first exists, that is, that man first of all is the being who hurls himself toward a future and who is conscious of imagining himself as being in the future. Man is at the start a plan which is aware of itself, rather than a patch of moss, a piece of garbage, or a cauliflower; nothing exists prior to this plan; there is nothing in heaven; man will be what he will have planned to be. Not what he will want to be. Because by the word "will" we generally mean a conscious decision, which is subsequent to what we have already made of ourselves. I may want to belong to a political party, write a book, get married; but all that is only a manifestation of an earlier, more spontaneous choice that is called "will." But if existence really does precede essence, man is responsible for what he is. Thus existentialism's first move is to make every man aware of what he is and to make the full responsibility of his existence rest on him. And when we say that a man is responsible for himself, we do not only mean that he is responsible for his own individuality, but that he is responsible for all men.

The word subjectivism has two meanings, and our opponents play on the two. Subjectivism means, on the one hand, that an individual chooses and makes himself; and, on the other, that it is impossible for man to transcend human subjectivity. The second of these is the essential meaning of existentialism. When we say that man chooses his own self, we mean that every one of us does likewise; but we also mean by that that in making this choice he also chooses all men. In fact, in creating the man that we want to be, there is not a single one of our acts which does not at the same time create an image of man as we think he ought to be. To choose to be this or that is to affirm at the same time the value of what we choose, because we can never choose evil. We always choose the good, and nothing can be good for us without being good for all.

If, on the other hand, existence precedes essence, and if we grant that we exist and fashion our image at one and the same time, the image is valid for everybody and for our whole age. Thus, our responsibility is much greater than we might have supposed, because it involves all mankind. If I am a workingman and choose to join a Christian trade-union rather than be a communist, and if by being a member I want to show that the best thing for man is resignation, that the kingdom of man is not of this world, I am not only involving my own case—I want to be resigned for everyone. As a result, my action has involved all humanity. To take a more individual matter, if I want to marry, to have children; even if this marriage depends solely on my own circumstances or passion or wish, I am involving all humanity in monogamy and not merely myself. Therefore, I am responsible for myself and for everyone else. I am creating a certain image of man of my own choosing. In choosing myself, I choose man.

This helps us understand what the actual content is of such rather grandiloquent words as anguish, forlornness, despair. As you will see, it's all quite simple.

First, what is meant by anguish? The existentialists say at once that man is anguish. What that means is this: the man who involves himself and who realizes that he is not only the person he chooses to be, but also a lawmaker who is, at the same time, choosing all mankind as well as himself, can not help escape the feeling of his total and deep responsibility. Of course, there are many people who are not anxious; but we claim that they are hiding their anxiety, that they are fleeing from it. Certainly, many people believe that when they do something, they themselves are the only ones involved, and when someone says to them, "What if everyone acted that way?" they shrug their shoulders and answer, "Everyone doesn't act that way." But really, one should always ask himself, "What would happen if everybody looked at things that way?" There is no escaping this disturbing thought except by a kind of double-dealing. A man who lies and makes excuses for himself by saying "not everybody does that," is someone with an uneasy conscience, because the act of lying implies that a universal value is conferred upon the lie.

Anguish is evident even when it conceals itself. This is the anguish that Kierkegaard called the anguish of Abraham. You know the story: an angel has ordered Abraham to sacrifice his son; if it really were an angel who has come and said, "You are Abraham, you shall sacrifice your son," everything would be all right. But everyone might first wonder, "Is it really an angel, and am I really Abraham? What proof do I have?"

There was a madwoman who had hallucinations; someone used to speak to her on the telephone and give her orders. Her doctor asked her, "Who is it who talks to you?" She answered, "He says it's God." What proof did she really have that it was God? If an angel comes to me, what proof is there that it's an angel? And if I hear voices, what proof is there that they come from heaven and not from hell, or from the subconscious, or a pathological condition? What proves that they are addressed to me? What proof is there that I have been appointed to impose my choice and my conception of man on humanity? I'll never find any proof or sign to convince me of that. If a voice addresses me, it is always for me to decide that this is the angel's voice; if I consider that such an act is a good one, it is I who will choose to say that it is good rather than bad.

Now, I'm not being singled out as an Abraham, and yet at every moment I'm obliged to perform exemplary acts. For every man, everything happens as if all mankind had its eyes fixed on him and were guiding itself by what he does. And every man ought to say to himself, "Am I really the kind of man who has the right to act in such a way that humanity might guide itself by my actions?" And if he does not say that to himself, he is masking his anguish.

There is no question here of the kind of anguish which would lead to quietism, to inaction. It is a matter of a simple sort of anguish that anybody who has had responsibilities is familiar with. For example, when a military officer takes the responsibility for an attack and sends a certain number of men to death, he chooses to do so, and in the main he alone makes the choice. Doubtless, orders come from above, but they are too broad; he interprets them, and on this interpretation depend the lives of ten or fourteen or twenty men. In making a decision he can not help having a certain anguish. All leaders know this anguish. That doesn't keep them from acting; on the contrary, it is the very condition of their action. For it implies that they envisage a number of possibilities, and when they choose one, they realize that it has value only because it is chosen. We shall see that this kind of anguish, which is the kind that existentialism describes, is explained, in addition, by a direct responsibility to the other men whom it involves. It is not a curtain separating us from action, but is part of action itself.

When we speak of forlornness, a term Heidegger was fond of, we mean only that God does not exist and that we have to face all the consequences of this. The existentialist is strongly opposed to a certain kind of secular ethics which would like to abolish God with the least possible expense. About 1880, some French teachers tried to set up a secular ethics which went something like this: God is a useless and costly hypothesis; we are discarding it; but, meanwhile, in order for there to be an ethics, a society, a civilization, it is essential that certain values be taken seriously and that they be considered as having an *a priori* existence. It must be obligatory, *a priori*, to be honest, not to lie, not to beat your wife, to have children, etc., etc. So we're going to try a little device which will make it possible to show that values exist all the same, inscribed in a heaven of ideas, though otherwise God does not exist. In other words—and this, I believe, is the tendency of everything called reformism in France—nothing will be changed if God does not exist. We shall find ourselves with the same norms of honesty, progress, and humanism, and we shall have made of God an outdated hypothesis which will peacefully die off by itself.

The existentialist, on the contrary, thinks it very distressing that God does not exist, because all possibility of finding values in a heaven of ideas disappears along with Him; there can no longer be an *a priori* Good, since there is no infinite and perfect consciousness to think it. Nowhere is it written that the Good exists, that we must be honest, that we must not lie; because the fact is we are on a plane where there are only men. Dostoievsky said, "If God didn't exist, everything would be possible." That is the very starting point of existentialism. Indeed, everything is permissible if God does not exist, and as a result man is forlorn, because neither within him nor without does he find anything to cling to. He can't start making excuses for himself.

If existence really does precede essence, there is no explaining things away by reference to a fixed and given human nature. In other words, there is no determinism, man is free, man is freedom. On the other hand, if God does not exist, we find no values or commands to turn to which legitimize our conduct. So, in the bright realm of values, we have no excuse behind us, nor justification before us. We are alone, with no excuses.

This is the idea I shall try to convey when I say that man is condemned to be free. Condemned, because he did not create himself, yet, in other respects is free; because, once thrown into the world, he is responsible for everything he does. The existentialist does not believe in the power of passion. He will never agree that a sweeping passion is a ravaging torrent which fatally leads a man to certain acts and is therefore an excuse. He thinks that man is responsible for his passion.

The existentialist does not think that man is going to help himself by finding in the world some omen by which to orient himself. Because he thinks that man will interpret the omen to suit himself. Therefore, he thinks that man, with no support and no aid, is condemned every moment to invent man. Ponge, in a very fine article, has said, "Man is the future of man." That's exactly it. But if it is taken to mean that this future is recorded in heaven, that God sees it, then it is false, because it would really no longer be a future. If it is taken to mean that, whatever a man may be, there is a future to be forged, a virgin future before him, then this remark is sound. But then we are forlorn.

The Later Twentieth Century

Wystan Hugh Auden, "The Unknown Citizen"

Although he enjoyed the benefits of an upper-middle class English upbringing and a classical education at Oxford University, Wystan Hugh Auden (1907–1973) championed the world's poor and powerless, especially against governmental and economic oppression. After serving as an ambulance driver for the liberal cause during the Spanish Civil War, Auden traveled widely in Iceland, China, and Europe, before settling in the United States, where he taught poetry at several American colleges. A prolific writer, Auden published numerous volumes of poetry and criticism notable for the precision and clarity with which they combined a love of personal freedom with an equally passionate commitment to self-discipline and the humane values of European civilization. Although Auden's concerns gradually shifted from left-wing politics to religious introspection, his poetry consistently expresses complex emotion with lucid control and wit.

"The Unknown Citizen" (1939) is a profoundly ironic epitaph to an ideal member of modern society, the productive worker who holds only government-approved opinions and dutifully consumes whatever corporations advertise. The poem's last two lines ask us to question the speaker's assumptions about good citizenship—the bureaucratic equation of conformity with a satisfying life.

THE UNKNOWN CITIZEN

■

(To JS/07/M/378
This Marble Monument
Is Erected by the State)

He was found by the Bureau of Statistics to be
One against whom there was no official complaint,
And all the reports on his conduct agree
That, in the modern sense of an old-fashioned word, he was a
    saint,
For in everything he did he served the Greater Community.
Except for the War till the day he retired
He worked in a factory and never got fired,
But satisfied his employers, Fudge Motors Inc.
Yet he wasn't a scab or odd in his views,
For his Union reports that he paid his dues,
(Our report on his Union shows it was sound)
And our Social Psychology workers found
That he was popular with his mates and liked a drink.

The Press are convinced that he bought a paper every day
And that his reactions to advertisements were normal in every
    way.
Policies taken out in his name prove that he was fully insured,
And his Health-card shows he was once in hospital but left it
    cured.
Both Producers Research and High-Grade Living declare
He was fully sensible to the advantages of the Instalment Plan
And had everything necessary to the Modern Man,
A phonograph, a radio, a car and a frigidaire.
Our researchers into Public Opinion are content
That he held the proper opinions for the time of year;
When there was peace, he was for peace; when there was war,
    he went.
He was married and added five children to the population,
Which our Eugenist says was the right number for a parent of
    his generation,
And our teachers report that he never interfered with their
    education.
Was he free? Was he happy? The question is absurd:
Had anything been wrong, we should certainly have heard.

Jorge Luis Borges, The Secret Miracle

A master of surrealist short fiction and poetry, Jorge Luis Borges (1899–   ) is probably the best-known Argentinian writer of this century. Although many of his stories and poems mirror the landscapes and the cultures of South America and, even more particularly, of his beloved Buenos Aires, Borges' imagined world is a world of dreams and of philosophical reveries, where the power of thought is often greater, and always more mysterious, than the force of matter. For Borges, time, space, and individual identity are all provisional realities, and he is repeatedly drawn to what he describes as the "tremendous conjecture" that the world is nothing but "an activity of mind/a dream of souls/without foundation or purpose or volume." Not surprisingly, the spectre of solipsism—that is, a total disbelief in any reality outside of or apart from the purely mental world of the individual consciousness—hovers over many of his tales, and the typical Borgesian protagonist finds himself wondering whether he is a figment of his own imagination or someone else's.

Borges' intense and scholarly interest in mysticism provides the backdrop for many of his more intricately structured dream-narratives, and in *The Secret Miracle* (1944), we find ourselves drawn into the inner world of a writer who, like Borges himself, has spent a lifetime searching for God (in works of literature) and denying the fixed reality of time. With characteristic literary tact, Borges preserves the "surreality" of his protagonist's interior universe—where miracles of self-and-world transcendence are entirely possible—while meticulously recording his passage through a murderous, nonmental world of time/space and without compromising either perspective. It is precisely this form of double vision, and the "magic realism" or surrealism it engenders, that links Borges to the European fabulist tradition of Franz Kafka (1883–1924) and Hermann Hesse (1877–1962).

THE SECRET MIRACLE

■

And God had him die for a hundred years and then revived him and said:
"How long have you been here?"
"A day or a part of a day," he answered.
Koran, II, 261

The night of March 14, 1943, in an apartment in the Zeltnergasse of Prague, Jaromir Hladik, the author of the unfinished drama entitled *The Enemies, of Vindication of Eternity*, and of a study of the indirect Jewish sources of Jakob Böhme, had a dream of a long game of chess. The players were not two persons, but two illustrious families; the game had been going on for centuries. Nobody could remember what the stakes were, but it was rumored that they were enormous, perhaps infinite; the chessmen and the board were in a secret tower. Jaromir (in his dream) was the first-born of one of the contending families. The clock struck the hour for the game, which could not be postponed. The dreamer raced over the sands of a rainy desert, and was unable to recall either the pieces or the rules of chess. At

547
■

that moment he awoke. The clangor of the rain and of the terrible clocks ceased. A rhythmic, unanimous noise, punctuated by shouts of command, arose from the Zeltnergasse. It was dawn, and the armored vanguard of the Third Reich was entering Prague.

On the nineteenth the authorities received a denunciation; that same nineteenth, toward evening, Jaromir Hladik was arrested. He was taken to an aseptic, white barracks on the opposite bank of the Moldau. He was unable to refute a single one of the Gestapo's charges; his mother's family name was Jaroslavski, he was of Jewish blood, his study on Böhme had a marked Jewish emphasis, his signature had been one more on the protest against the *Anschluss*. In 1928 he had translated the *Sepher Yezirah* for the publishing house of Hermann Barsdorf. The fulsome catalogue of the firm had exaggerated, for publicity purposes, the translator's reputation, and the catalogue had been examined by Julius Rothe, one of the officials who held Hladik's fate in his hands. There is not a person who, except in the field of his own specialization, is not credulous; two or three adjectives in Gothic type were enough to persuade Julius Rothe of Hladik's importance, and he ordered him sentenced to death *pour encourager les autres*. The execution was set for March 29th, at 9:00 A.M. This delay (whose importance the reader will grasp later) was owing to the desire on the authorities' part to proceed impersonally and slowly, after the manner of vegetables and plants.

Hladik's first reaction was mere terror. He felt he would not have shrunk from the gallows, the block, or the knife, but that death by a firing squad was unbearable. In vain he tried to convince himself that the plain, unvarnished fact of dying was the fearsome thing, not the attendant circumstances. He never wearied of conjuring up these circumstances, senselessly trying to exhaust all their possible variations. He infinitely anticipated the process of his dying, from the sleepless dawn to the mysterious volley. Before the day set by Julius Rothe he died hundreds of deaths in courtyards whose forms and angles strained geometrical probabilities, machine-gunned by variable soldiers in changing numbers, who at times killed him from a distance, at others from close by. He faced these imaginary executions with real terror (perhaps with real bravery); each simulacrum lasted a few seconds. When the circle was closed, Jaromir returned once more and interminably to the tremulous vespers of his death. Then he reflected that reality does not usually coincide with our anticipation of it; with a logic of his own he inferred that to foresee a circumstantial detail is to prevent its happening. Trusting in this weak magic, he invented, *so that they would not happen*, the most gruesome details. Finally, as was natural, he came to fear that they were prophetic. Miserable in the night, he endeavored to find some way to hold fast to the fleeting substance of time. He knew that it was rushing headlong toward the dawn of the twenty-ninth. He reasoned aloud: "I am now in the night of the twenty-second; while this night lasts (and for six nights more), I am invulnerable, immortal." The nights of sleep seemed to him deep, dark pools in which he could submerge himself. There were moments when he longed impatiently for the final burst of fire that would free him, for better or for worse, from the vain compulsion of his imaginings. On the twenty-eighth, as the last sunset was reverberating from the high barred windows, the thought of his drama, *The Enemies*, deflected him from these abject considerations.

Hladik had rounded forty. Aside from a few friendships and many habits, the problematic exercise of literature constituted his life. Like all writers, he measured the achievements of others by what they had accomplished, asking of them that they measure him by what he envisaged or planned. All the books he had published had left him with a complex feeling of repentance. His studies of the work of Böhme, of Ibn Ezra, and of Fludd had been characterized essentially by mere application; his translation of the *Sepher Yezirah*, by carelessness, fatigue, and conjecture. *Vindication of Eternity* perhaps had fewer shortcomings. The first volume gave a history of man's various concepts of eternity, from the immutable Being of Parmenides to the alterable past of Hinton. The second denied (with Francis Bradley) that all the events of the universe make up a temporal series, arguing that the number of man's possible experiences is not infinite, and that a single "repetition" suffices to prove that time is a fallacy . . . Unfortunately, the arguments that demonstrate this fallacy are equally fallacious. Hladik was in the habit of going over them with a kind of contemptuous perplexity. He had also composed a series of Expressionist poems; to the poet's chagrin they had been included in an anthology published in 1924, and no subsequent anthology but inherited them. From all this equivocal, uninspired past Hladik had hoped to redeem himself with his drama in verse, *The Enemies*. (Hladik felt the verse form to be essential because it makes it impossible for the spectators to lose sight of irreality, one of art's requisites.)

The drama observed the unities of time, place, and action. The scene was laid in Hradčany, in the library of Baron von Roemerstadt, on one of the last afternoons of the nineteenth century. In the first scene of the first act a strange man visits Roemerstadt. (A clock was striking seven, the vehemence of the setting sun's rays glorified the windows, a passionate, familiar Hungarian music floated in the air.) This visit is followed by others; Roemerstadt does not know the people who are importuning him, but he has the uncomfortable feeling that he has seen them somewhere, perhaps in a dream. They all fawn upon him, but it is apparent—first to the audience and then to the Baron—that they are secret enemies, in league to ruin him. Roemerstadt succeeds in checking or evading their involved schemings. In the dialogue mention is made of his sweetheart, Julia von Weidenau, and a certain Jaroslav Kubin, who at one time pressed his attentions on her. Kubin has now lost his mind, and believes himself to be Roemerstadt. The dangers increase; Roemerstadt, at the end of the second act, is forced to kill one of the conspirators. The third and final act opens. The incoherencies gradually increase; actors who had seemed out of the play reappear; the man Roemerstadt killed returns for a moment. Someone points out that evening has not fallen; the clock strikes seven, the high windows reverberate in the western sun, the air carries an impassioned Hungarian melody. The first actor comes on and repeats the lines he had spoken in the first scene of the first act. Roemerstadt speaks to him without surprise; the audience understands that Roemerstadt is the miserable Jaroslav Kubin. The drama has never taken place; it is the circular delirium that Kubin lives and relives endlessly.

Hladik had never asked himself whether this tragicomedy of errors was preposterous or admirable, well thought out or slipshod. He felt that the plot I have just sketched was best contrived to cover up his defects and point up his abilities and held the possibility of allowing him to redeem (symbolically) the meaning of his life. He had finished the first act and one or two scenes of the third; the metrical nature of the work made it possible for him to keep working it over, changing the hexameters, without the manuscript in front of him. He thought how he still had two acts to do, and that he was going to die very soon. He spoke with God in the darkness: "If in some fashion I exist, if I am not one of Your repetitions and mistakes, I exist as the author of *The Enemies*. To finish this drama, which can justify me and justify You, I need another year. Grant me these days, You to whom the centuries and time belong." This was the last night, the most dreadful of all, but ten minutes later sleep flooded over him like a dark water.

Toward dawn he dreamed that he had concealed himself in one of the naves of the

Clementine Library. A librarian wearing dark glasses asked him: "What are you looking for?" Hladik answered: "I am looking for God." The librarian said to him: "God is in one of the letters on one of the pages of one of the four hundred thousand volumes of the Clementine. My fathers and the fathers of my fathers have searched for this letter; I have grown blind seeking it." He removed his glasses, and Hladik saw his eyes, which were dead. A reader came in to return an atlas. "This atlas is worthless," he said, and handed it to Hladik, who opened it at random. He saw a map of India as in a daze. Suddenly sure of himself, he touched one of the tiniest letters. A ubiquitous voice said to him: "The time of your labor has been granted." At this point Hladik awoke.

He remembered that men's dreams belong to God, and that Maimonides had written that the words heard in a dream are divine when they are distinct and clear and the person uttering them cannot be seen. He dressed: two soldiers came into the cell and ordered him to follow them.

From behind the door, Hladik had envisaged a labyrinth of passageways, stairs, and separate buildings. The reality was less spectacular: they descended to an inner court by a narrow iron stairway. Several soldiers—some with uniform unbuttoned—were examining a motorcycle and discussing it. The sergeant looked at the clock; it was 8:44. They had to wait until it struck nine. Hladik, more insignificant than pitiable, sat down on a pile of wood. He noticed that the soldiers' eyes avoided his. To ease his wait, the sergeant handed him a cigarette. Hladik did not smoke; he accepted it out of politeness or humility. As he lighted it, he noticed that his hands were shaking. The day was clouding over; the soldiers spoke in a low voice as though he were already dead. Vainly he tried to recall the woman of whom Julia von Weidenau was the symbol.

The squad formed and stood at attention. Hladik, standing against the barracks wall, waited for the volley. Someone pointed out that the wall was going to be stained with blood; the victim was ordered to step forward a few paces. Incongruously, this reminded Hladik of the fumbling preparations of photographers. A big drop of rain struck one of Hladik's temples and rolled slowly down his cheek; the sergeant shouted the final order.

The physical universe came to a halt.

The guns converged on Hladik, but the men who were to kill him stood motionless. The sergeant's arm eternized an unfinished gesture. On a paving stone of the courtyard a bee cast an unchanging shadow. The wind had ceased, as in a picture. Hladik attempted a cry, a word, a movement of the hand. He realized that he was paralyzed. Not a sound reached him from the halted world. He thought: "I am in hell, I am dead." He thought: "I am mad." He thought: "Time has stopped." Then he reflected that if that was the case, his mind would have stopped too. He wanted to test this; he repeated (without moving his lips) Vergil's mysterious fourth Eclogue. He imagined that the now remote soldiers must be sharing his anxiety; he longed to be able to communicate with them. It astonished him not to feel the least fatigue, not even the numbness of his protracted immobility. After an indeterminate time he fell asleep. When he awoke the world continued motionless and mute. The drop of water still clung to his cheek, the shadow of the bee to the stone. The smoke from the cigarette he had thrown away had not dispersed. Another "day" went by before Hladik understood.

He had asked God for a whole year to finish his work; His omnipotence had granted it. God had worked a secret miracle for him; German lead would kill him at the set hour, but in his mind a year would go by between the order and its execution. From perplexity he passed to stupor, from stupor to resignation, from resignation to sudden gratitude.

He had no document but his memory; the training he had acquired with each added hexameter gave him a discipline unsuspected by those who set down and forget temporary, incomplete paragraphs. He was not working for posterity or even for God, whose literary tastes were unknown to him. Meticulously, motionlessly, secretly, he wrought in time his lofty, invisible labyrinth. He worked the third act over twice. He eliminated certain symbols as over-obvious, such as the repeated striking of the clock, the music. Nothing hurried him. He omitted, he condensed, he amplified. In certain instances he came back to the original version. He came to feel an affection for the courtyard, the barracks; one of the faces before him modified his conception of Roemerstadt's character. He discovered that the wearying cacophonies that bothered Flaubert so much are mere visual superstitions, weakness and limitation of the written word, not the spoken . . . He concluded his drama. He had only the problem of a single phrase. He found it. The drop of water slid down his cheek. He opened his mouth in a maddened cry, moved his face, dropped under the quadruple blast.

Jaromir Hladik died on March 29, at 9:02 A.M.

Translated by Harriet de Onís

Ernest Hemingway, "A Clean, Well-Lighted Place"

In his novels about the disillusionment and psychological dislocation that followed World War I, Ernest Hemingway (1898–1961) captured the spirit of his time. His first important short story collection, *In Our Time* (1924) expressed the post-War generation's spiritual exhaustion and its profound distrust of concepts such as honor and patriotism, with which world leaders had drawn the young into international slaughter. Rejecting traditional values, Hemingway's characters live detached, emotionally cool lives, committed only to intensely personal relationships, sensual pleasure, and acts of physical courage that demonstrate the individual's freedom to face death on his own terms. Pursuing a private ideal of manliness, the Hemingway hero typically acts alone, regarding life as a series of solo combats in which he proves his masculine competence.

A Farewell to Arms (1929), in which both love and ideals are lost in the horrors of war, explains the sense of futility and emotional numbness that distinguishes the characters in Hemingway's first novel, *The Sun Also Rises* (1926). The possibility of individual heroism in facing death is explored in *For Whom the Bell Tolls* (1940), based on the author's experience in the Spanish Civil War, and *The Old Man and the Sea* (1952). "A Clean, Well-Lighted Place" (1933) illustrates Hemingway's mastery of casual dialogue in which the speakers communicate almost monosyllabically. As his characters rarely espouse complex ideas or philosophical concepts, so Hemingway's prose is direct, simple, and terse. The narration is distant and clipped, befitting the characters' lack of commitment.

A CLEAN, WELL-LIGHTED PLACE

■

It was late and every one had left the café except an old man who sat in the shadow the leaves of the tree made against the electric light. In the daytime the street was dusty, but at night the dew settled the dust and the old man liked to sit late because he was deaf and now at night it was quiet and he felt the difference. The two waiters inside the café knew that the old man was a little drunk, and while he was a good client they knew that if he became too drunk he would leave without paying, so they kept watch on him.

"Last week he tried to commit suicide," one waiter said.

"Why?"

"He was in despair."

"What about?"

"Nothing."

"How do you know it was nothing?"

"He has plenty of money."

They sat together at a table that was close against the wall near the door of the café and looked at the terrace where the tables were all empty except where the old man sat in the shadow of the leaves of the tree that moved slightly in the wind. A girl and a soldier went by in the street. The street light shone on the brass number on his collar. The girl wore no head covering and hurried beside him.

"The guard will pick him up," one waiter said.

"What does it matter if he gets what he's after?"

"He had better get off the street now. The guard will get him. They went by five minutes ago."

The old man sitting in the shadow rapped on his saucer with his glass. The younger waiter went over to him.

"What do you want?"

The old man looked at him. "Another brandy," he said.

"You'll be drunk," the waiter said. The old man looked at him. The waiter went away.

"He'll stay all night," he said to his colleague. "I'm sleepy now. I never get into bed before three o'clock. He should have killed himself last week."

The waiter took the brandy bottle and another saucer from the counter inside the café and marched out to the old man's table. He put down the saucer and poured the glass full of brandy.

"You should have killed yourself last week," he said to the deaf man. The old man motioned with his finger. "A little more," he said. The waiter poured on into the glass so that the brandy slopped over and ran down the stem into the top saucer of the pile. "Thank you," the old man said. The waiter took the bottle back inside the café. He sat down at the table with his colleague again.

"He's drunk now," he said.

"He's drunk every night."

"What did he want to kill himself for?"

"How should I know."

"How did he do it?"

"He hung himself with a rope."

"Who cut him down?"

"His niece."

"Why did they do it?"

"Fear for his soul."

"How much money has he got?"

"He's got plenty."

"He must be eighty years old."

"Anyway I should say he was eighty."

"I wish he would go home. I never get to bed before three o'clock. What kind of hour is that to go to bed?"

"He stays up because he likes it."

"He's lonely. I'm not lonely. I have a wife waiting in bed for me."

"He had a wife once too."

"A wife would be no good to him now."

"You can't tell. He might be better with a wife."

"His niece looks after him."

"I know. You said she cut him down."

"I wouldn't want to be that old. An old man is a nasty thing."

"Not always. This old man is clean. He drinks without spilling. Even now, drunk. Look at him."

"I don't want to look at him. I wish he would go home. He has no regard for those who must work."

The old man looked from his glass across the square, then over at the waiters.

"Another brandy," he said, pointing to his glass. The waiter who was in a hurry came over.

"Finished," he said, speaking with that omission of syntax stupid people employ when talking to drunken people or foreigners. "No more tonight. Close now."

"Another," said the old man.

"No. Finished." The waiter wiped the edge of the table with a towel and shook his head.

The old man stood up, slowly counted the saucers, took a leather coin purse from his pocket and paid for the drinks, leaving half a peseta tip.

The waiter watched him go down the street, a very old man walking unsteadily but with dignity.

"Why didn't you let him stay and drink?" the unhurried waiter asked. They were putting up the shutters. "It is not half-past two."

"I want to go home to bed."

"What is an hour?"

"More to me than to him."

"An hour is the same."

"You talk like an old man yourself. He can buy a bottle and drink at home."

"It's not the same."

"No, it is not," agreed the waiter with a wife. He did not wish to be unjust. He was only in a hurry.

"And you? You have no fear of going home before your usual hour?"

"Are you trying to insult me?"

"No, hombre, only to make a joke."

"No," the waiter who was in a hurry said, rising from pulling down the metal shutters. "I have confidence. I am all confidence."

"You have youth, confidence and a job," the older waiter said. "You have everything."

"And what do you lack?"

"Everything but work."

"You have everything I have."

"No. I have never had confidence and I am not young."

"Come on. Stop talking nonsense and lock up."

"I am of those who like to stay late at the café," the older waiter said. "With all those who do not want to go to bed. With all those who need a light for the night."

"I want to go home and into bed."

"We are of two different kinds," the older waiter said. He was now dressed to go home. "It is not only a question of youth and confidence although those things are very beautiful. Each night I am reluctant to close up because there may be some one who needs the café."

"Hombre, there are bodegas open all night long."

"You do not understand. This is a clean and pleasant café. It is well lighted. The light is very good and also, now, there are shadows of the leaves."

"Good night," said the younger waiter.

"Good night," the other said. Turning off the electric light he continued the conversation with himself. It is the light of course but it is necessary that the place be clean and pleasant. You do not want music. Certainly you do not want music. Nor can you stand before a bar with dignity although that is all that is provided for these hours. What did he fear? It was not fear or dread. It was nothing that he knew too well. It was all a nothing and a man was nothing too. It was only that and light was all it needed and a certain cleanness and order. Some lived in it and never felt it but he knew it all was nada y pues nada y nada y pues nada. Our nada who art in nada, nada be thy name thy kingdom nada thy will be nada in nada as it is in nada. Give us this nada our daily nada and nada us our nada as we nada our nadas and nada us not into nada but deliver us from nada; pues nada. Hail nothing full of nothing, nothing is with thee. He smiled and stood before a bar with a shining steam pressure coffee machine.

"What's yours?" asked the barman.

"Nada."

"Otro loco más," said the barman and turned away.

"A little cup," said the waiter.

The barman poured it for him.

"The light is very bright and pleasant but the bar is unpolished," the waiter said.

The barman looked at him but did not answer. It was too late at night for conversation.

"You want another copita?" the barman asked.

"No, thank you," said the waiter and went out. He disliked bars and bodegas. A clean, well-lighted café was a very different thing. Now, without thinking further, he would go home to his room. He would lie in the bed and finally, with daylight, he would go to sleep. After all, he said to himself, it is probably only insomnia. Many must have it.

James Baldwin, "The Fire Next Time"

A leading American novelist and essayist, James Baldwin (1924–1987) vividly portrays the experience of black people in the United States. His autobiographical first novel, *Go Tell It On The Mountain* (1953), depicts the religious and intellectual awakening of the teenage son of a fundamentalist preacher in Harlem. In his subsequent fiction, such as *Another Country* (1962) and *Tell Me How Long the Train's Been Gone* (1968), Baldwin combines the passion of a populist minister with the emotional sensitivity of the artist to dramatize the ways in which American society dehumanizes and humiliates its minorities. *Giovanni's Room* (1956) explores the difficulties of homosexual love, whereas *Just Above My Head* (1979) traces the lives of several Harlem friends through three decades of war, poverty, and the civil rights movement.

At 24 years of age, Baldwin left the United States for France, where, in an atmosphere relatively free from racial discrimination, he produced most of his best work. His nonfiction includes *Notes of a Native Son* (1955), *Nobody Knows My Name* (1961), and *The Fire Next Time* (1963), powerful indictments of the moral blind spots that permit Americans to deny human dignity to ethnic and sexual minorities. Shortly before his death, Baldwin published *The Price of the Ticket: Collected Non-Fiction, 1948–1985* (1985) and *Evidence of Things Not Seen* (1986), an analysis of the serial murder of black youths in Atlanta.

THE FIRE NEXT TIME
∎

[MY DUNGEON SHOOK: A LETTER TO MY NEPHEW ON THE ONE HUNDREDTH ANNIVERSARY OF THE EMANCIPATION]

Now, my dear namesake, these innocent and well-meaning people, your countrymen, have caused you to be born under conditions not very far removed from those described for us by Charles Dickens in the London of more than a hundred years ago. (I hear the chorus of the innocents screaming, "No! This is not true! How *bitter* you are!" —but I am writing this letter to *you*, to try to tell you something about how to handle *them*, for most of them do not yet really know that you exist. I *know* the conditions under which you were born, for I was there. Your countrymen were *not* there, and haven't made it yet. Your grandmother was also there, and no one has ever accused her of being bitter. I suggest that the innocents check with her. She isn't hard to find. Your countrymen don't know that *she* exists, either, though she has been working for them all their lives.)

Well, you were born, here you came, something like fifteen years ago; and though your father and mother and grandmother, looking about the streets through which they were carrying you, staring at the walls into which they brought you, had every reason to be heavyhearted, yet they were not. For here you were, Big James, named for me—you were a big baby, I was not—here you were: to be loved. To be loved, baby, hard, at once, and forever, to strengthen you against the loveless world. Remember that: I know how black it looks today, for you. It looked bad that day, too, yes, we were trembling. We have not stopped trembling yet, but if we had not loved each other none of us would have survived. And now you must survive because we love you, and for the sake of your children and your children's children.

This innocent country set you down in a ghetto in which, in fact, it intended that you should perish. Let me spell out precisely what I mean by that, for the heart of the matter is here, and the root of my dispute with my country. You were born where you were born and faced the future that you faced because you were black and *for no other reason*. The limits of your ambition were, thus, expected to be set forever. You were born into a society which spelled out with brutal clarity, and in as many ways as possible, that you were a worthless human being. You were not expected to aspire to excellence: you were expected to make peace with mediocrity. Wherever you have turned, James, in your short time on this earth, you have been told where you could go and what you could do (and *how* you could do it) and where you could live and whom you could marry. I know your countrymen do not agree with me about this, and I hear them saying, "You exaggerate." They do not know Harlem, and I do. So do you. Take no one's word for anything, including mine—but trust your experience. Know whence you came. If you know whence you came, there is really no limit to where you can go. The details and symbols of your life have been deliberately constructed to make you believe what white people say about you. Please try to remember that what they believe, as well as what they do and cause you to endure, does not testify to your inferiority but to their inhumanity and fear. Please try to be clear, dear James, through the storm which rages about your youthful head today, about the reality which lies behind the words *acceptance* and *integration*. There is no reason for you to try to become like white people and there is no basis whatever for their impertinent assumption that *they* must accept *you*. The really terrible thing, old buddy, is that *you* must accept *them*. And I mean that very seriously. You must accept them and accept them with love. For these innocent people have no other hope. They are, in effect, still trapped in a history which they do not understand; and until they understand it, they cannot be released from it. They have had to believe for many years, and for innumerable reasons, that black men are inferior to white men. Many of them, indeed, know better, but, as you will discover, people find it very difficult to act on what they know. To act is to be committed, and to be committed is to be in danger. In this case, the danger, in the minds of most white Americans, is the loss of their identity. Try to imagine how you would feel if you woke up one morning to find the sun shining and all the stars aflame. You would be frightened because it is out of the order of nature. Any upheaval in the universe is terrifying because it so profoundly attacks one's sense of one's own reality. Well, the black man has functioned in the white man's world as a fixed star, as an immovable pillar: and as he moves out of his place, heaven and earth are shaken to their foundations. You, don't be afraid. I said that it was intended that you should perish in the ghetto, perish by never being allowed to go behind the white man's definitions, by never being allowed to spell your proper name. You have, and many of us have, defeated this intention; and by a terrible law, a terrible paradox, those innocents who believed that your imprisonment made them safe are losing their grasp of reality. But these men are your brothers—your lost, younger brothers. And if the word *integration* means anything, this is what it means: that we, with love, shall force our brothers to see themselves as they are, to cease fleeing from reality and begin to change it. For this is your home, my friend, do not be driven from it; great men have done great things here, and will again, and we can make America what

America must become. It will be hard, James, but you come from sturdy, peasant stock, men who picked cotton and dammed rivers and built railroads, and, in the teeth of the most terrifying odds, achieved an unassailable and monumental dignity. You come from a long line of great poets, some of the greatest poets since Homer. One of them said, *The very time I thought I was lost, My dungeon shook and my chains fell off.*

You know, and I know, that the country is celebrating one hundred years of freedom one hundred years too soon. We cannot be free until they are free. God bless you, James, and Godspeed.

Your uncle,
James

[DOWN AT THE CROSS: LETTER FROM A REGION OF MY MIND]

. . . I am very much concerned that American Negroes achieve their freedom here in the United States. But I am also concerned for their dignity, for the health of their souls, and must oppose any attempt that Negroes may make to do to others what has been done to them. I think I know—we see it around us every day—the spiritual wasteland to which that road leads. It is so simple a fact and one that is so hard, apparently, to grasp: *Whoever debases others is debasing himself.* That is not a mystical statement but a most realistic one, which is proved by the eyes of any Alabama sheriff—and I would not like to see Negroes ever arrive at so wretched a condition.

Now, it is extremely unlikely that Negroes will ever rise to power in the United States, because they are only approximately a ninth of this nation. They are not in the position of the Africans, who are attempting to reclaim their land and break the colonial yoke and recover from the colonial experience. The Negro situation is dangerous in a different way, both for the Negro qua Negro and for the country of which he forms so troubled and troubling a part. The American Negro is a unique creation; he has no counterpart anywhere, and no predecessors. The Muslims react to this fact by referring to the Negro as "the so-called American Negro" and substituting for the names inherited from slavery the letter "X." It is a fact that every American Negro bears a name that originally belonged to the white man whose chattel he was. I am called Baldwin because I was either sold by my African tribe or kidnapped out of it into the hands of a white Christian named Baldwin, who forced me to kneel at the foot of the cross. I am, then, both visibly and legally the descendant of slaves in a white, Protestant country and this is what it means to be an American Negro, this is who he is—a kidnapped pagan, who was sold like an animal and treated like one, who was once defined by the American Constitution as "three-fifths" of a man, and who, according to the Dred Scott decision, had no rights that a white man was bound to respect. And today, a hundred years after his technical emancipation, he remains—with the possible exception of the American Indian—the most despised creature in his country. Now, there is simply no possibility of a real change in the Negro's situation without the most radical and far-reaching changes in the American political and social structure. And it is clear that white Americans are not simply unwilling to effect these changes; they are, in the main, so slothful have they become, unable even to envision them. It must be added that the Negro himself no longer believes in the good faith of white Americans—if indeed, he ever could have. What the Negro *has* discovered, and on an international level, is that power to intimidate which he has always had privately but hitherto could manipulate only privately—for private ends often, for limited ends always. And therefore when the country speaks of a "new" Negro, which it has been doing every hour on the hour for decades, it is not really referring to a change in the Negro, which, in any case, it is quite incapable of assessing, but only to a new difficulty in keeping him in his place, to the fact that it encounters him (again! again!) barring yet another door to its spiritual and social ease. This is probably, hard and odd as it may sound, the most important thing that one human being can do for another—it is certainly *one* of the most important things; hence the torment and necessity of love—and this is the enormous contribution that the Negro has made to this otherwise shapeless and undiscovered country. Consequently, white Americans are in nothing more deluded than in supposing that Negroes could ever have imagined that white people would "give" them anything. It is rare indeed that people give. Most people guard and keep; they suppose that it is they themselves and what they identify with themselves that they are guarding and keeping, whereas what they are actually guarding and keeping is their system of reality and what they assume themselves to be. One can give nothing whatever without giving oneself— that is to say, risking oneself. If one cannot risk oneself, then one is simply incapable of giving. And, after all, one can give freedom only by setting someone free. This, in the case of the Negro, the American republic has never become sufficiently mature to do. White Americans have contented themselves with gestures that are now described as "tokenism." For hard example, white Americans congratulate themselves on the 1954 Supreme Court decision outlawing segregation in the schools; they suppose, in spite of the mountain of evidence that has since accumulated to the contrary, that this was proof of a change of heart—or, as they like to say, progress. Perhaps. It all depends on how one reads the word "progress." Most of the Negroes I know do not believe that this immense concession would ever have been made if it had not been for the competition of the Cold War, and the fact that Africa was clearly liberating herself and therefore had, for political reasons, to be wooed by the descendants of her former masters. Had it been a matter of love or justice, the 1954 decision would surely have occurred sooner; were it not for the realities of power in this difficult era, it might very well not have occurred yet. This seems an extremely harsh way of stating the case—ungrateful, as it were—but the evidence that supports this way of stating it is not easily refuted at all. In any event, the sloppy and fatuous nature of American good will can never be relied upon to deal with hard problems. These have been dealt with, when they have been dealt with at all, out of necessity—and in political terms, anyway, necessity means concessions made in order to stay on top. I think this is a fact, which it serves no purpose to deny, *but whether it is a fact or not, this is what the black population of the world, including black Americans, really believe.* The word "independence" in Africa and word "integration" here are almost equally meaningless; that is, Europe has not yet left Africa, and black men here are not yet free. And both of these last statements are undeniable facts, related facts, containing the gravest implications for us all. The Negroes of this country may never be able to rise to power, but they are very well placed indeed to precipitate chaos and ring down the curtain on the American dream.

This has everything to do, of course, with the nature of that dream and with the fact that we Americans, of whatever color, do not dare examine it and are far from having made it a reality. There are too many things we do not wish to know about ourselves. People are not, for example, terribly anxious to be equal (equal, after all, to what and to whom?) but they love the idea of being superior. And this human truth has an especially grinding force here, where identity is almost impossible to achieve and people are perpetually attempting to find their feet on the shifting sands of status. (Consider the history of labor in a country in which, spiritually speaking, there are no workers, only candidates for the hand of the boss's daughter.) Furthermore, I have met only a very few people—and most of these were not Americans—who had any real desire to be free. Freedom is hard to bear. . . .

Color is not a human or a personal reality: it is a political reality. But this is a distinction so extremely hard to make that the West has not been able to make it yet. And at the center of this dreadful storm, this vast confusion, stand the black people of this nation, who must now share the fate of a nation that has never accepted them, to which they were brought in chains. Well, if this is so, one has no choice but to do all in one's power to change that fate, and at no matter what risk—eviction, imprisonment, torture, death. For the sake of one's children, in order to minimize the bill that *they* must pay, one must be careful not to take refuge in any delusion—and the value placed on the color of the skin is always and everywhere and forever a delusion. I know that what I am asking is impossible. But in our time, as in every time, the impossible is the least that one can demand—and one is, after all, emboldened by the spectacle of human history in general, and American Negro history in particular, for it testifies to nothing less than the perpetual achievement of the impossible.

When I was very young, and was dealing with my buddies in those wine- and urine-stained hallways, something in me wondered, *What will happen to all that beauty?* For black people, though I am aware that some of us, black and white, do not know it yet, are very beautiful. And when I sat at Elijah's table and watched the baby, the women, and the men, and we talked about God's—or Allah's—vengeance, I wondered, when that vengeance was achieved, *What will happen to all that beauty then?* I could also see that the intransigence and ignorance of the white world might make that vengeance inevitable—a vengeance that does not really depend on, and cannot really be executed by, any person or organization, and that cannot be prevented by any police force or army: historical vengeance, a cosmic vengeance, based on the law that we recognize when we say, "Whatever goes up must come down." And here we are, at the center of the arc, trapped in the gaudiest, most valuable, and most improbable water wheel the world has ever seen. Everything now, we must assume, is in our hands; we have no right to assume otherwise. It we—and now I mean the relatively conscious whites and the relatively conscious blacks, who must, like lovers, insist on, or create, the consciousness of the others—do not falter in our duty now, we may be able, handful that we are, to end the racial nightmare, and achieve our country, and change the history of the world. If we do not now dare everything, the fulfillment of that prophecy, re-created from the Bible in song by a slave, is upon us: *God gave Noah the rainbow sign, No more water, the fire next time!*

Sylvia Plath, "Sheep in Fog," "Poppies in July"

Sylvia Plath (1932–1963) is a tragic figure on the American literary landscape of the 1960's. Her best-known volume of poems, *Ariel*, from which "Sheep in a Fog" and "Poppies in July" were selected, was published posthumously in 1965. It reflects, as directly as poetry can, the personal torment that drove her to suicide two years before. A fellow poet and former teacher, Robert Lowell (1917–1977), once described this volume as "the autobiography of a fever," and as confessional, self-exploratory statements of inadequacy and despair, these poems achieve a poignancy and eloquence that is almost unequalled in contemporary poetry.

Plath writes about the most intimate, at times terrifying, feelings with an economy of expression that imposes decorum upon near hysteria. In that respect, though perhaps in no other, she resembles Emily Dickinson (1830–1868), for whom poetic restraint also served as a necessary formal counterpoint to intense emotion. The subtext of many of these poems is the condition of woman in a world of irrational violence and betrayal, where no "father" (in heaven or on earth) exists who can redeem her hurt. This same dilemma appears as the focus of an earlier work as well, the autobiographical novel *The Bell Jar* (1963) in which Plath's protagonist struggles to resist an emotional environment defined by entrapment, loss of identity, and ultimately, despair.

SHEEP IN FOG

■

The hills step off into whiteness.
People or stars
Regard me sadly, I disappoint them.

The train leaves a line of breath.
O slow
Horse the colour of rust,

Hooves, dolorous bells—
All morning the
Morning has been blackening,

A flower left out.
My bones hold a stillness, the far
Fields melt my heart.

They threaten
To let me through to a heaven
Starless and fatherless, a dark water.

POPPIES IN JULY

■

Little poppies, little hell flames,
Do you do no harm?

You flicker, I cannot touch you.
I put my hands among the flames. Nothing burns.

And it exhausts me to watch you
 Flickering like that, wrinkly and clear red, like the skin of a mouth.

A mouth just bloodied.
Little bloody skirts!

There are fumes that I cannot touch.
Where are your opiates, your nauseous capsules?

If I could bleed, or sleep!—
If my mouth could marry a hurt like that!

Or your liquors seep to me, in this glass capsule,
Dulling and stilling.

But colourless. Colourless.

Acknowledgments

Selections from *The Epic of Gilgamesh*, translated, with an introduction and notes, by Maureen Gallery Kovacs, reprinted with the permission of the publishers, Stanford University Press. Copyright © 1985, 1989 by the Board of Trustees of the Leland Stanford Junior University.

"Utterance #217" from *Ancient Egyptian Literature*, three volumes, translated and edited by Miriam Lichtheim, reprinted with the permission of the University of California Press. Copyright © 1973, by the Regents of the University of California.

Excerpts from *The Jerusalem Bible*, copyright © 1966 by Darton, Longman & Todd, Ltd. and Doubleday, a division of Bantam, Doubleday, Dell Publishing Group, Inc. Used by permission of the publisher.

Selections from *The Iliad of Homer, The Wrath of Achilles*, translated by I.A. Richards, copyright © 1950. Reprinted with the permission of W.W. Norton & Company, Inc.

Oedipus Rex, translated by Dudley Fitts and Robert Fitzgerald, copyright © 1949 by Harcourt Brace Jovanovich, Inc. and renewed 1977 by Cornelia Fitts and Robert Fitzgerald. Reprinted by permission of the publisher.

The Bacchants, translated by Moses Hadas, in *Ten Plays by Euripides*. Reprinted by permission of the copyright holder, Mrs. Elizabeth C. Hadas.

Selections from *The Republic of Plato*, translated by F.M. Cornford, copyright © 1941. Reprinted by permission of Oxford University Press.

"To a Bride," "Parting," "Mother I Cannot Mind my Wheel" by Sappho, from *Greek Literature in Translation*, edited by Whitney Jennings Oates, Longman Publishing Group. Copyright © 1944, with permission of the publisher.

Excerpts from *History of the Peloponnesian War* by Thucydides, translated by Rex Warner (Penguin Classics, 1954), copyright © Rex Warner, 1954. Reproduced by permission of Penguin Books Ltd.

"Letter to Herodotus" by Epicurus, from *Greek Literature in Translation*, edited by Whitney Jennings Oates, Longman Publishing Group. Copyright © 1944, with permission of the publisher.

The Aeneid of Virgil, translated by Rolfe Humphries [Book I—lines 1–41; Book VI—lines 286–350, 580–840]. Reprinted with permission of Macmillan Publishing Company. Copyright ©1987 Macmillan Publishing Company.

Selections from *The Confessions of St. Augustine*, reprinted by permission of Sheed & Ward, Kansas City, Missouri.

From *The Rule of St. Benedict*. Copyright © by and reprinted by permission of Sheed and Ward, Ltd., England.

Reprinted from *The Song of Roland*, translated by Frederick Goldin, by permission of the translator and the publisher, W.W. Norton & Company, Inc. Copyright © 1978 by W.W. Norton & Company, Inc.

"Chaitivel" from *The Lais of Marie de France* translated by Glyn S. Burgess and Keith Busby (Penguin Classics, 1986), copyright Glyn S. Burgess and Keith Busby, 1986, pp. 105–108. Reproduced by permission of Penguin Books, Ltd.

Reprinted from the John Ciardi translation of *The Divine Comedy*, Dante Alighieri, with the permission of the publisher, W.W. Norton & Company, Inc. Copyright © 1954, 1957, 1959, 1960, 1961, 1965, 1967, 1970 by John Ciardi.

Selections from *The Canterbury Tales of Geoffrey Chaucer*, translated by R.M. Lumiansky. Copyright © 1948, 1975 by Simon & Schuster, Inc. Reprinted by permission of Simon & Schuster, Inc.

Excerpts from *The Renaissance Philosophy of Man*, edited by E. Cassirer [pp. 223–226] copyright © 1948. Reprinted by permission of The University of Chicago Press.

The Prince by Niccolo Machiavelli, translated by George Bull (Penguin Classics, Revised Edition, 1981), copyright © George Bull, 1961, 1975, 1981. Reproduced by permission of Penguin Books, Ltd.

The Book of the Courtier by Baldesar Castiglione, translated by George Bull (Penguin Classics, 1958), copyright © George Bull, 1967, pp. 325–340. Reproduced by permission of Peguin Books, Ltd.

Notes to accompany "The Tempest" from *The Complete Works of Shakespeare* by David Bevington. Copyright © 1980, 1973 by Scott, Foresman & Company. Reprinted by permission.

"The Would-Be Gentleman." From *Eight Plays by Moliere*, translated by Morris Bishop. Copyright © 1957 by Morris Bishop. Reprinted by permission of Random House, Inc.

"Sor Juana Ines de la Cruz." Credit to Angel Flores, editor of the *Anthology of Spanish Poetry*, originally published by Anchor Books (1961).

Selections from *A Philosophical Enquiry into the Origin of Our Ideas of the Sublime and the Beautiful* by Edmund Burke, copyright © 1958, Columbia University Press, New York. Used by permission.

From *A Vindication of the Rights of Woman*, A Norton Critical Edition, Edited by Carol H. Poston, copyright © 1975 by W.W. Norton & Company, Inc. Used by permission of W.W. Norton & Company, Inc.

Excerpt from Rousseau, *The Reveries of the Solitary Walker*, copyright © 1979 by New York University. Reprinted by permission of Harper & Row, Publishers, Inc.

Selections from Goethe: *Faust Part I*. Copyright © 1949 by New Directions Publishing Corporation. Translated by C.F. MacIntyre. Reprinted by permission of New Directions Publishing Corporation. U.S. and Canadian rights.

The Brothers Karamazov by Fyodor Dostoyevsky, translated by David Magarshack (Penguin Classics, 1958), copyright © David Magarshack, 1958, pp. 290–300 and 301–308. Reproduced by permission of Penguin Books, Ltd.

"Sweeney Among the Nightingales" and "The Hollow Men" by T.S. Eliot from *The Collected Poems 1909–1962*, copyright © 1936 by Harcourt Brace Jovanovich, Inc. Copyright © 1964, 1963 by T.S. Eliot, reprinted by permission of the publisher.

"A Hunger Artist" by Franz Kafka, translated by Willa and Edwin Muir from *Franz Kafka: the Complete Stories*, edited by Nahum N. Glatzer. Copyright © 1946, 1947, 1948, 1949, 1954, copyright © 1958, 1971 by Schocken Books, Inc. Reprinted by permission of Schocken Books, published by Pantheon Books, a division of Random House, Inc.

Selections from *On Creativity and the Unconscious*, by Sigmund Freud, copyright © 1958, Harper & Row, Publisher, Inc. Reprinted by permission of the publisher.

Excerpt from *Existentialism and Human Emotions* by Jean-Paul Sartre. Copyright © 1957 by Philosophical Library, Inc. Reprinted with permission of the publisher.

"The Unknown Citizen." Copyright © 1940 and renewed by 1968 by W.H. Auden. Reprinted from *W.H. Auden Collected Poems*, edited by Edward Mendelson, by permission of Random House, Inc.

"The Secret Miracle" by Jorge Luis Borges, from *Ficciones*, copyright © 1962 by Grove Press, Inc. Translated from the Spanish copyright © 1956 by Emece Editores, S.A. Buenos Aires. Reprinted with permission of the publisher.

"A Clean, Well-Lighted Place" by Ernest Hemingway from *Winner Take Nothing*, copyright © 1933 by Charles Scribner's Sons; renewal copyright © 1961 by Mary Hemingway. Reprinted with permission of Charles Scribner's Sons.

Excerpt from *The Fire Next Time* by James Baldwin, copyright © 1962, 1963 by James Baldwin. Used by permission of Doubleday, a division of Bantam, Doubleday, Dell Publshing Group, Inc.

"Sheep in Fog," "Poppies in July" by Sylvia Plath. Copyright © 1965 by Ted Hughes. From *The Collected Poems of Sylvia Plath*. Reprinted by permission of Harper & Row, Publishers, Inc.